Greenhill Bo

A HISTORY
OF THE
PENINSULAR
WAR

A HISTORY OF
THE PENINSULAR WAR

A HISTORY
OF THE
PENINSULAR
WAR

Marshal Soult, Duke of Dalmatia
from the portrait by Girardet

A HISTORY
OF THE
PENINSULAR WAR

Volume V:
October 1811 to August 31, 1812
Valencia, Ciudad Rodrigo, Badajoz,
Salamanca, Madrid

SIR CHARLES OMAN

Greenhill Books, London
Stackpole Books, Pennsylvania

Greenhill Books

This edition of *A History of the Peninsular War*, Volume V,
first published 2005 by Greenhill Books, Lionel Leventhal Limited,
Park House, 1 Russell Gardens, London NW11 9NN
and
Stackpole Books, 5067 Ritter Road, Mechanicsburg, PA 17055, USA

British Library Cataloguing-in Publication Data
Oman, Charles William Chadwick, Sir, 1860-1946
A history of the Peninsular War
Vol. 5: October 1811 to August 31, 1812 : Valencia,
Ciudad Rodrigo, Badajoz, Salamanca, Madrid
1. Peninsular War, 1807–1814
2. Peninsular War, 1807–1814 – Campaigns I. Title 940.2'7
ISBN 1-85367-634-9

Library of Congress Cataloging in Publication Data available

PUBLISHING HISTORY
A History of the Peninsular War, Volume V was first published in 1914
(Oxford) and is now reproduced exactly as the original edition, complete
and unabridged. The original maps have been re-presented by John
Richards, in the interests of clarity.

For more information on books published by Greenhill, please email
sales@greenhillbooks.com or visit www.greenhillbooks.com. You can also
write to us at Park House, 1 Russell Gardens, London NW11 9NN.

Printed and bound by CPD, Ebbw Vale

PREFACE

IN this volume Wellington's campaigning in 1812 is
followed no further than the day (August 31st) on
which he set out from Madrid to drive back Clausel
from the Douro. Reasons of space make it impossible to
include the siege of Burgos and the retreat which followed.
I had written the narrative of them, but found it impossible to add six long chapters to the 620 pages already
in print. The fact is that, from the point of view of
Wellington's army, the year 1812 was much more
tightly packed with military events than any which
had gone before. In 1809 there was nothing important
to chronicle after August : in 1810 the Anglo-Portuguese
did not come into the forefront of the war till July,
when Masséna had crossed the frontier and laid siege to
Almeida. In 1811 the year opened with a deadlock,
which was only ended by the commencement of Masséna's retreat on March 9th, and concluded with a
similar deadlock which endured from July to December
—interrupted only by the short campaign of El Bodon
and Aldea da Ponte, and this covered only a week
[Sept. 22–9]. In 1812 the great strategical operations
began on the first day of the year with the concentration
for the siege of Ciudad Rodrigo, and did not end till
the last week of November—which saw Wellington once
more encamped under the walls of that fortress. For
eleven months on end he had been on the move, with only

a brief rest in cantonments between April 24th, the day
when he gave up his pursuit of Marmont in Northern
Portugal, and the end of May, when his divisions began
to assemble again for the projected march on Salamanca.
But for this short break his operations were continuous,
and the narrative of them must of necessity be
lengthy.

The campaign of 1812 cannot be called the greatest
exhibition of military genius in Wellington's career :
that distinction must be given to the campaign of 1813.
But it included the battle of Salamanca, the most skilfully fought and the most decisive of all his victories,
' the beating of forty thousand men in forty minutes.'
And its earlier episodes, the two sudden strokes which
ended in the storming of Ciudad Rodrigo and of Badajoz,
deserve the closest attention, as showing a marvellous
power of utilizing opportunities, and solving time-
problems of the most complicated sort. We shall see
how Wellington, in face of an enemy whose whole force
was far superior to his own, so conducted his operations
that he had success in his hands before the French
armies could concentrate to overwhelm him. He would
have been victorious in 1812 even without the assistance
that was given him during the early months of the year
by Napoleon's misguided orders from Paris, and in the
summer by Soult's repeated and deliberate refusal to
co-operate with King Joseph and Marmont for the
general welfare of the French cause in Spain. The limits
of his success were largely extended by those adven-
titious circumstances, but even without them he must
have achieved great things by force of the combinations
which he had prepared.

The reader will find that I have devoted a good deal of space to the precise working out of the effect of Napoleon's successive dispatches to Marmont, with reference to the time at which each was received, and the influence which it had on the Marshal's movements. I am bound to say that careful study has convinced me that Marmont's justification of his own actions from January to May, written in the fourth volume of his *Mémoires*, is in the main fair and sensible, and that his criticism of his master's orders is as sound as it is lucid. Napier held the reverse opinion, but his arguments in support of it are unconvincing : he is set on proving his idol infallible at all costs, in this as in so many other cases.

I find myself equally at variance with Napier's estimate of the relative share of responsibility that falls on Soult upon the one side and King Joseph and Jourdan on the other, for the disasters of the summer of 1812. Jourdan's plan of campaign, set out in his 'May *Mémoire*' [see pp. 303–11], is a most clear-headed and practicable scheme ; the adoption of it would have reduced the effect of Wellington's strategy, and have set a limit to his successes. Soult wrecked the whole scheme by wilful disobedience, which sinned as much against military discipline as against common sense. The counter-projects which he kept sending to Jourdan and the King were founded on his own personal desires, not on a consideration of the general situation in the Peninsula. Soult had been kind and courteous to Napier while the historian was working at the French archives, and had placed his own private papers at his disposition. I think that the obligation was repaid by the mildness of the

censures passed on the Marshal's strange behaviour in
the summer of 1812.

A smaller proportion of the pages of this volume than
of its predecessors is occupied by the tale of those campaigns in the Peninsula in which the British took no
part. The year 1812 commences with the surrender of
Blake and the occupation of Valencia by the French.
When that great city and the army that had been driven
into it succumbed before Suchet's attack, there was no
longer any large Spanish force in the field, and the
operations of Lacy, Ballasteros, and the Galicians are
of only secondary importance and require no great
attention. Indeed the most effective service done
against the French in 1812 was that of the guerrilleros
of Aragon, Cantabria, and Navarre, whose obstinate
resistance immobilized such a large portion of the
230,000 imperial troops that lay in Spain. It will be
noted that I have had to devote a considerable number
of pages to a much-neglected episode of the summer of
1812—the campaigns against Caffarelli of the irregular
bands of the North, assisted by the fleet of Sir
Home Popham. It cannot be too often repeated
that by immobilizing the 35,000 men of the French
Army of the North, they co-operated in the most
effective way with Wellington, and had their share
in making the Salamanca campaign a success for the
allies.

I trust that I may have succeeded in making the
topographical details clear at Ciudad Rodrigo, Badajoz,
and more especially Salamanca, all of which I have
visited. I spent many hours going over the ground at
the Arapiles, and found that no mere map could have

enabled one to grasp the situation in a satisfactory fashion.

I have once more to express my indebtedness to the owners of two great files of Peninsular War documents, who were good enough to place them at my disposition and to allow me to bring them to Oxford. The D'Urban papers, lent to me by Mr. W. S. M. D'Urban, of Newport House, near Exeter, the grandson of Sir Benjamin D'Urban, Beresford's Chief-of-the-Staff, continue to be of immense value all through 1812. In the first half of the year Sir Benjamin was still at the Portuguese head-quarters, and his diary and correspondence give the views of those who had the best opportunity of knowing Wellington's plans from the inside. In June he was appointed to another post, that of commanding the detached Portuguese cavalry brigade which covered Wellington's left flank in the Salamanca campaign ; his notes as to his operations are of extreme interest throughout June, July, and August ; the narratives which he drew up concerning his own fortunes at the battle of Salamanca, and at the unfortunate combat of Majalahonda, have cleared up several obscure problems, which no published material could have enabled me to solve.

The papers of Sir George Scovell, lent me by his great-nephew, Mr. G. Scovell, of Hove, had already begun to be of use to me in the chronicle of 1811. But in 1812 they are of far greater importance, since it was early in that year that Scovell was placed by Wellington in charge of the toilsome duty of studying and decoding all French captured dispatches written in cipher. The originals were left in his hands, and only the interpre-

tations, written out in full, were made over to the
Commander-in-Chief. These originals, often scraps of
the smallest dimensions made to be concealed in
secret places about the person of the bearer, are
historical antiquities of the highest interest. Their
importance is so great that I have thought it necessary to give in Appendix XV a detailed account of
them, of the characteristics of the ' Great Paris Cipher '
—as Scovell called it—and of the contents of each
document.

I must mention, as in previous volumes, much kind
help given to me from abroad. The authorities of
the Paris War Office have continued to facilitate my
researches among their bulky *cartons*. I have to notice
with sincere regret the death of my old friend, M. Martinien, who did so much for me while I was compiling
volumes III and IV of this work. I much missed his
guidance while working over the material of 1812 during
the last two autumns. Colonel Juan Arzadun, of the
Madrid Artillery Museum, has continued to send me
occasional information, and I am specially obliged to
Don Rafael Farias for procuring for me, and making
me a present of, that very rare document the 1822
' Estados de los ejércitos españoles durante la guerra
contra Bonaparte,' a collection of morning-states and
tables of organization on which I had in vain tried to
lay hands during three successive visits to Madrid.
Another gift of the highest value was the complete set
of Beresford's *Ordens do Dia* for the Portuguese army,
ranging over the whole war. This most useful series
was presented to me by my friend Mr. Rafael
Reynolds, the companion of my last Portuguese tour,

who found a copy of this almost unprocurable file at
Lisbon.   I owe the two views of the field of Salamanca
to the camera of Mr. C. J. Armstrong, who sent them
to me along with many other interesting Peninsular
photographs.

Three friends in England have continued to give me
help of the most invaluable kind.   Mr. C. T. Atkinson,
Fellow of Exeter College, has looked through the whole
of my proofs, and furnished me with innumerable notes,
which enabled me to add to the accuracy of my narrative.   He has also written me an appendix, No. XIV,
concerning the English troops which in 1812 operated on
the East coast of Spain—and the others which formed the
garrisons of Gibraltar, Cadiz, and Tarifa.   The Hon. John
Fortescue, the historian of the British army, has not
only answered at length my queries on many obscure
problems, but has lent me the file of his transcripts of
French dispatches for 1812, a good many of which,
and those of high importance, were unknown to me.
They were especially valuable for Soult's operations.
Our narratives of the campaigns of 1812 will appear
almost simultaneously, and I think it will be found that
all our main opinions are in agreement.   Major J. H.
Leslie, R.A., has once more contributed to this volume
an 'Artillery Appendix' on the same lines as those for
1810 and 1811 in vols. III and IV.   His researches have
always proved exhaustive and invaluable for the history
of his old Corps.

Lastly, the compiler of the Index, a task executed
this summer under very trying conditions, must receive,
for the fifth time, my heartfelt thanks for her labour
of love.

As in previous volumes, the critic may find some slight discrepancies between the figures given with regard to strengths of regiments or losses in action in the text and in the Appendices. This results from the fact that many official documents contain incorrect arithmetic, which was only discovered by the indefatigable proof-readers of the Clarendon Press, who have tested all the figures, and found not infrequent (if minute) errors. The text was printed off before the Appendices were finally dealt with : where the numbers differ those in the Appendices are, of course, to be preferred. But the worst discrepancies do not get beyond units and tens.

C. OMAN.

Oxford :
  July 27, 1914.

Note.—When every page of the text, appendices, and index· of this volume has been printed off, and the final proofs of the preface are passing through my hands, comes the news that Great Britain is most unexpectedly involved in a war to which there can be no parallel named save the struggle that ended just a hundred years ago. May her strength be used as effectively against military despotism in the twentieth as it was in the nineteenth century.

Aug. 5, 1914.

CONTENTS

SECTION XXX

SUCHET'S CONQUEST OF VALENCIA, SEPTEMBER 1811–JANUARY 1812

SECTION XXXI

MINOR CAMPAIGNS OF THE WINTER OF 1811–12

SECTION XXXII

WELLINGTON'S FIRST CAMPAIGN OF 1812. JANUARY–APRIL

CONTENTS

SECTION XXXIII

THE SALAMANCA CAMPAIGN. MAY–AUGUST 1812

APPENDICES

CONTENTS

ILLUSTRATIONS

MAPS AND PLANS

SECTION XXX

SUCHET'S CONQUEST OF VALENCIA.
SEPTEMBER 1811—JANUARY 1812

CHAPTER I

THE INVASION OF VALENCIA. SIEGE OF SAGUNTUM.
SEPTEMBER—OCTOBER 1811

In the last volume of this work the chronicle of all the campaigns of 1811 was completed, save in one corner of Spain, where, on the eastern coast, the fortunes of the French armies have only been pursued down to the recall of Marshal Macdonald to Paris on October 28th. Already, before the Duke of Tarentum had been added to the list of the generals who had been withdrawn and superseded for failure in Catalonia, another series of operations had been begun in the East, which was destined to lead directly to one more Spanish disaster, but indirectly to the ruin of the French cause in Spain. For, as has already been pointed out in the last pages of the last volume [1], it was to be the diversion by Napoleon's orders of French divisions eastward, from the borders of Portugal to those of Valencia, that was to give Wellington his long-desired opportunity of opening a successful offensive campaign against his immediate opponents in the West. The fall of Valencia was to lead to the fall of Ciudad Rodrigo in January 1812.

It will be remembered that the Emperor's ambitious schemes for the conquest of the kingdom of Valencia, the last district of eastern Spain where he had as yet secured no solid foothold, had been deferred perforce till Figueras fell, on August 19, 1811. As long as that great fortress, which lies only a few miles from the French frontier, and blocks the main road from Perpignan to Barcelona, had been maintained against Macdonald by the

[1] vol. iv. pp. 587–91.

resolute Martinez, it was impossible to take up a new offensive campaign : all the disposable French troops in Catalonia were immobilized around the stubborn garrison. At length the remnant of the starving miqueletes had laid down their arms, and the troops which had been for so long blockading them became disposable for the assistance of Suchet, whose ' Army of Aragon ' was to deliver the main blow against Valencia.

Six days after the surrender of Figueras the news that the obstacle to advance had been at last removed reached Paris, on August 25, and on the same evening Berthier wrote, by his master's orders, to bid Suchet move forward : ' Everything leads us to believe that Valencia is in a state of panic, and that, when Murviedro has been taken and a battle in the open field has been won, that city will surrender. If you judge otherwise, and think that you must wait to bring up your siege artillery for the attack on the place, or that you must wait for a better season [i. e. early autumn] to commence the operation, I must inform you that, in every case, it is the imperative order of the Emperor that your head-quarters are to be on Valencian territory on or about September 15th, and as far forward towards the city as possible.'

The orders were feasible, and (as we shall see) were duly executed : but Napoleon had committed his usual mistake of undervaluing the tenacity of the Spanish enemy, whom he so deeply despised. Suchet set his troops in motion on September 15th ; he took Murviedro—but only after a desperate siege of two months—he beat the army of Valencia in a very decisive pitched battle, but the city by no means fulfilled the Emperor's prophecy by a prompt surrender. Fighting round its walls went on for five weeks after Murviedro fell : and it was not till troops had been brought to aid Suchet from very remote provinces, that he at last compelled the capitulation of Valencia after the New Year of 1812 had passed. Before the city yielded Wellington was on the move, far away on the Portuguese frontier, and it was not many days after Suchet's aide-de-camp brought the glorious news of the capitulation of Valencia, that Marmont's aide-de-camp followed, with the wholly unexpected and unwelcome tidings that the British had stormed Ciudad Rodrigo, and that the hold of the French army on Leon and

Castile had been shaken. The one piece of information was the complement and consequence of the other.

Suchet's invasion of Valencia, in short, was a much harder and more venturesome enterprise than his master had calculated. It was true that the Spanish forces in front of him seemed in September wholly incapable of holding him back. The Army of Catalonia had been reduced by a series of disasters, culminating in the falls of Tarragona and Figueras, to a mere remnant of 8,000 men, lurking in the high hills of the interior. The Army of Valencia had made a miserable exhibition of itself during the last year : it had brought no effective help to the Catalans, and whenever any of its detachments came into contact with the French, they had invariably suffered discreditable defeats, even when their numbers were far greater than those of the invaders. Of all the armies of Spain this was undoubtedly the one with the worst fighting reputation. It was to small profit that the Captain-General was raising yet newer and rawer battalions than those which already existed, to swell the numbers, but not the efficiency, of his command. In July the nominal total of the Valencian army, including the irregulars of the ' flying column ' of the Empecinado, had been just 30,000 men. By October there were 36,000 under arms, including the new ' Reserve Division [1],' whose six battalions of recruits had only 135 officers to 6,000 men—an allowance of one officer to 45 men, not much more than half of the proportion that is necessary even among good veteran troops. But in truth the only valuable fighting force that was present in the kingdom in September was the infantry of the two weak divisions of the old Albuera army, under Zayas and Lardizabal, whom Blake had brought round from Cadiz with him, when he assumed command of the Eastern provinces. They did not between them muster more than 6,000 bayonets, but were good old troops, who were to distinguish themselves in the oncoming campaign.

In addition, it was possible that Valencia might be able to

---

[1] ' The Reserve Division' consisted of a 3rd battalion from some of the old regiments of the Valencian army, viz. 1st of Savoya, Avila, Don Carlos, Volunteers of Castile, Cazadores de Valencia, Orihuela. They were each about 1,000 strong, but averaged only 22 officers per battalion.

draw a few thousand men to her aid from the depleted army of Murcia, which had suffered so severely at Soult's hands during the short campaign of the previous August [1]. But such assistance was purely problematical ; if Soult should stir again from the side of Andalusia, it would be impossible for General Mahy to bring a single Murcian battalion to the succour of Blake. If, by good fortune, he should not, only a fraction of Mahy's small army would be free, since the greater part of it would be required to watch the Andalusian frontier, and to protect the great naval arsenal and fortress of Cartagena.

If the regular troops only in eastern Spain had to be counted, it was certain that Suchet could dispose of numbers superior to his adversaries. The gross total of the French Army of Catalonia, where General Decaen had now taken Macdonald's place, was 30,000 men. That of Suchet's own ' Army of Aragon ' was nearly 50,000, if garrisons, sick, and drafts on the march are reckoned in it. With these deducted, it could still supply about 31,000 men of all arms for the field. But these were not the only resources available. On the upper Ebro, in Navarre and western Aragon, were the two newly arrived divisions of Reille and Severoli, which had entered Spain during the summer, and had hitherto had no occupation save a little hunting of Mina's guerrilleros. These two divisions counted 15,000 fresh troops of good quality, and Suchet reckoned on their assistance to cover his rear, when he should begin his march on Valencia. Technically they belonged to Dorsenne's ' Army of the North,' but Severoli's Italians had been promised as a reinforcement for Aragon already, and when Suchet asked for the grant of Reille's division also it was not denied him. There were 70,000 men in all to be taken into consideration when the attack on Valencia was planned out.

No such force, of course, could be set aside for the actual invasion. The reason why not half so many thousands could be utilized for the projected stroke was that the Spanish War, as we have already had to point out on many occasions, was not a normal struggle between regular armies. The French had not only to conquer but to occupy every province that they overrun. Wherever an adequate garrison was not left, the

---

[1] See vol. iv. pp. 475–83

guerrilleros and miqueletes inundated the country-side, cut all communications, and blockaded such small detachments as had been left far apart from the main army. Suchet's 70,000 men had to hold down Aragon and Catalonia, at the same time that they undertook the further extension of their master's power on the Valencian side.

Decaen in Catalonia had 23,000 men fit for service, not including sick and drafts on the march. Lacy's little army was not more than 8,000 strong in September : yet Suchet dared not take away a man from Catalonia. The large garrison of Barcelona, a whole division, and the smaller garrisons of Gerona, Rosas, and Mont Louis absorbed nearly half the effective total. The remainder were, as it turned out, not strong enough to keep the Catalans in check, much less to prosecute active offensive operations against them. It was in October, after Suchet had started against Valencia, that Lacy carried out the series of small successful raids against Igualada, Cervera, and Montserrat, which have been spoken of in an earlier chapter[1]. We need not wonder, then, that not a Frenchman was drawn from Catalonia : they were all wanted on the spot to keep a tight hold on the turbulent principality. The example of the surprise of Figueras in the last spring was sufficient to prove the necessity of keeping every point strongly garrisoned, on pain of possible disaster.

As to the Army of Aragon, it was far stronger than the Army of Catalonia, but on the other hand it had even more fortresses to garrison. Saragossa, Tortosa, Tarragona, Lerida, were large places, each absorbing several battalions. In addition there were the smaller strongholds of Jaca, Mequinenza, Monzon, Morella, requiring care. All these were regular fortresses, but they did not exhaust the list of points that must be firmly held, if the communications of Suchet's field-force with its distant base were to be kept free and unhampered. Southern Aragon and the mountain-ganglion where the borders of that kingdom and of Valencia and New Castile meet, in the roughest country of the whole Spanish peninsula, had to be guarded. For in this region lay the chosen hunting-ground of the guerrillero bands of the Empecinado, Duran, and many other lesser chiefs :

[1] See vol. iv. pp. 540–1.

and Mina himself, from his usual haunts in Navarre, not unfrequently led a raid far to the south of the Ebro. Suchet had therefore to place garrisons in Teruel, Daroca, Alcañiz, Calatayud, and Molina, none of which possessed modern fortifications. The detachments left to hold them had to utilize a large convent, a mediaeval castle, or some such post of defence, in case they were attacked by the roving hordes of the enemy. Able to protect themselves with ease against small parties, and to keep the roads open under ordinary circumstances, they were exposed to serious danger if the guerrilleros should mass themselves in force against any one garrison—more especially if the bands should have been lent a few cannon and gunners from the regular Spanish armies. For convents or old castles could not resist artillery fire.

To cover his rear Suchet was forced to set aside one whole division, that of Frère, thirteen battalions strong [1], and mustering over 7,000 men, and immense detachments of the three other French divisions of the Army of Aragon. The units told off for the field army left no less than 6,800 able-bodied men (besides sick and convalescents) behind them, while they took 22,000 to the front. Frère's division remained on the side of Western Catalonia, holding Lerida and Tortosa in force, and the intermediate places with small posts. The detachments from Musnier's, Harispe's, and Habert's French, and from Palombini's Italian divisions, took charge of Southern Aragon, leaving a company here and a battalion there. But the Marshal selected with great care the men who were to march on the Valencian expedition : each regiment drafted its most effective soldiers into the marching units, and left the recruits and the old or sickly men in the garrisons. Thus the battalions used in the oncoming campaign were rather weak, averaging not much over 450 men, but were composed entirely of selected veterans. The only doubtful element taken forward was the so-called 'Neapolitan Division' of General Compère, which was only 1,500 strong—in reality a weak brigade—and had no great reputation. But what was left of this corps was its best part—

[1] Composed at this time of the 14th and 42nd and 115th Line, and the 1st Léger, the first two and last each three battalions strong, the other (115th) with four.

the numerous men who wanted to desert had already done so, and its weaklings were dead by this time. Of his cavalry Suchet took forward almost the whole, leaving behind only two squadrons of the 4th Hussars for the service between the garrisons, and of the other regiments only the weakly men and horses [1]. Practically all his horse and field artillery also went forward with him.

Of his own Army of Aragon, Suchet, as we have thus seen, left nearly 14,000 men ' present under arms ' to cover his rear. But this was not enough to make matters wholly secure, so untameable were the Aragonese and Catalans with whom he had to deal. Indeed, if this force only had been left to discharge the appointed task, it is clear, from subsequent happenings, that he would have suffered a disaster during his absence in Valencia. He asked from the Emperor the loan of half Reille's division from Navarre, as well as the prompt sending to the front of Severoli's Italians, who had been promised him as a reinforcement when first they entered Spain. The petition was granted, and these troops entered northern Aragon, and took charge of the places along the Ebro, while the expeditionary army was on its way to Valencia. Most of them were ultimately brought forward to the siege of the great city, and without them neither could Aragon have been maintained nor Valencia captured. Practically we may say that Suchet, at his original start, took 26,000 men to beat the Valencians and capture their city, but that he left nearly 30,000 more behind him, to hold down the provinces already conquered and to deal with the guerrilleros.

Two main roads lead from the north to Valencia: the one, coming from Tortosa and Catalonia, hugs the coast of the Mediterranean, from which it is never more than a few miles distant. The other, far inland, and starting from Saragossa, follows the valley of the Xiloca among the hills of Southern Aragon, crosses the watershed beyond Teruel, and descends to the sea near Murviedro, where it joins the coast-road only a few miles north of Valencia. There is a third, and much inferior, route between these two, which starts from Mequinenza on the

---

[1] The 24th Dragoons left about 140 men behind, the 13th Cuirassiers 50 only, the Italian ' Dragoons of Napoleon ' 124, but the 4th Hussars about 500, much more than half their force.

Lower Ebro, crosses the mountainous Valencian frontier near Morella, and comes down to the coast at Castellon de la Plana, twenty miles north of Murviedro. Of these roads the first was as good as any in Spain, and was suitable for all manner of traffic : but it had the disadvantage of being flanked at a distance of only two miles by the small but impregnable fortress of Peniscola, which lies on a rocky headland thirty miles beyond Tortosa, and of being absolutely blocked by the little town of Oropesa, twenty miles further south. Oropesa was no more than a ruinous mediaeval place, with two castles hastily repaired, without any modern works : but since the road passed through it, no heavy guns or wagons starting from Tortosa could get further south till its forts had been captured.

The second road, that from Aragon by Teruel and Murviedro, is marked on contemporary maps as a post-route fit for all vehicles : but it passed through a very mountainous country, and was much inferior as a line of advance to the coast-road. It was not blocked by any fortress in the hands of the Spaniards, but between Teruel and Segorbe it was crossed by many ridges and ravines highly suitable for defence. The third track, that by Morella, was unsuitable for wheeled traffic, and could only be used by infantry and cavalry. Its one advantage was that Morella, its central point, had been already for some time in French hands, and contained a garrison and stores, which made it a good starting-point for a marching column.

Suchet determined to use all three of these roads, though such a plan would have been most hazardous against a wary and vigorous enemy : for though they all converge in the end on the same point, Murviedro, they are separated from each other by long stretches of mountain, and have no cross-communications. In especial, the road by Teruel was very distant from the other two, and any isolated column taking it might find itself opposed by immensely superior forces, during the last days of its march ; since Valencia, the enemy's base and headquarters, where he would naturally concentrate, lies quite close to the concluding stages of the route Teruel–Murviedro. It must have been in sheer contempt for his opponent—a contempt which turned out to be justified—that the Marshal sent a detachment of eleven battalions by this road, for such a force of

5,000 men might have been beset by the whole Valencian army, 30,000 strong, and the other columns could not have helped it. Suchet's arrangements were governed by a single fact—his siege artillery and heavy stores were parked at Tortosa, and from thence, therefore, along the coast road, must be his main line of advance, though it would be necessary to mask Peniscola and to capture Oropesa, before he could get forward to his objective—the city of Valencia. It might have seemed rational to move the whole field army by this route : but some of the troops destined for it were coming from distant points, and to march them down the Ebro bank to Tortosa would have taken much time. Moreover if the whole force concentrated there, it would all have to be fed from the magazines at Tortosa, and those lying in Aragon would be of no use. The Marshal started himself from this point, on September 15, with the division of Habert, and an infantry reserve formed of Robert's brigade of the division of Musnier, together with the whole of the cavalry and field artillery of the army. The siege-train guarded by the other brigade of Musnier's division—that of Ficatier—followed : but Musnier himself did not accompany the expedition, having been left in general charge of the detachments placed in garrison on the Ebro and in Upper Aragon. The whole column made up about 11,000 combatants.

The second column, consisting of the two auxiliary divisions— Palombini's eleven Italian battalions and Compère's 1,500 Neapolitans—took (without any artillery to hamper them) the mountain road by Alcañiz and Morella : they were slightly over 7,000 strong, and, if all went well, were destined to unite with the main body somewhere near Oropesa or Castellon de la Plana. It was not likely that this column would meet with much opposition.

But the third detachment, Harispe's 5,000 men from Upper Aragon, who were to take the inland and western road by Teruel, were essaying a very dangerous task, if the enemy should prove active and enterprising, more especially as they had no artillery and hardly any cavalry with them. Blake might have taken the offensive with 20,000 men against them, while still leaving something to contain—or at least to observe— Suchet's main column.

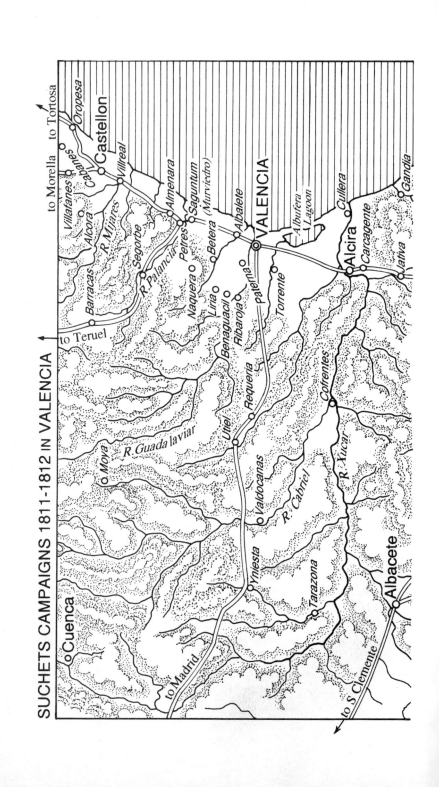

SUCHETS CAMPAIGNS 1811-1812 IN VALENCIA

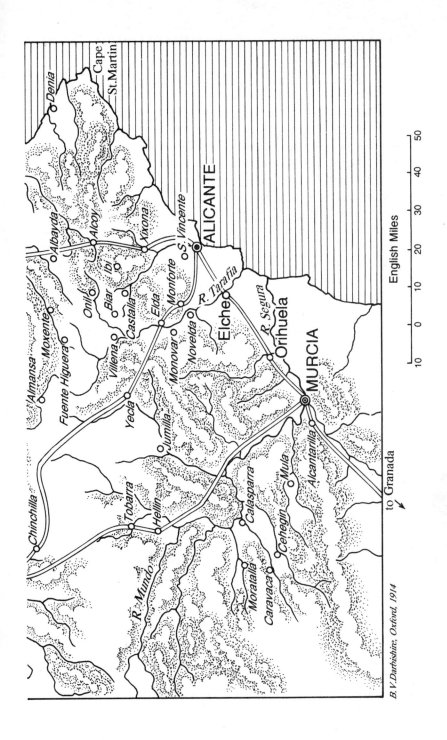

Denia

Cape
St.Martin

Abayda
Alcoy
Xixona
Onil
Ibi
Blar
Castalla
Monforte
S. Vincente
ALICANTE
Elda
R. Tarafia

Almansa
Moxente
Villena
Fuente Higuera
Yecla
Monovar
Novelda
Elche
Orihuela
R. Segura
MURCIA
Chinchilla
Tobarra
Jumilla
Hellin
R. Mundo
Calasparra
Mula
Alcantarilla
Caravaca
Moratalla
Cehegin

to Granada

| 10 | 0 | 10 | 20 | 30 | 40 | 50 |

English Miles

B.V.Darbishire, Oxford, 1914

The Spanish Commander-in-Chief, however, did nothing of the sort, and met the invasion with a tame and spiritless defensive on all its points. When Suchet's advance was reported, Blake had his forces in a very scattered situation. Of the 36,000 men of whom he could nominally dispose, the Empecinado's ' flying column ' was as usual detached in the mountains of Molina and Guadalajara, harassing small French garrisons. Zayas's division had been left far to the south at Villena, near Alicante, to work off the contagion of yellow fever which it had contracted while passing by Cartagena. For in that port the disease was raging terribly at the time. Obispo's division was in the high hills on the borders of Aragon. In the neighbourhood of Valencia were only the troops of Lardizabal and Miranda, with the main body of the cavalry. The Army of Murcia, which was destined to send succour if it should not find itself beset by Soult on the other side, was lying cantoned at various points in that province. As the French were at this time making no demonstration from the side of Granada, it now became clear that it would be able to send certain succours to Blake. But they were not yet designated for marching, much less assembled, and it was clear that they would come up very late.

This dispersion of the available troops did not, in the end, make much difference to the fate of the campaign, for Blake had from the first made up his mind to accept the defensive, to draw in his outlying detachments, and to stand at bay in the neighbourhood of Valencia, without attempting to make any serious resistance on the frontier. Since his arrival he had been urging on the construction of a line of earthworks, forming fortified camps, around the provincial capital. The ancient walls of Valencia itself were incapable of any serious resistance to modern artillery, but outside them, all along the banks of the Guadalaviar river, for some miles inland to the West, and as far as the sea on the East, batteries, *têtes-de-pont*, trenches, and even closed works of considerable size had been constructed. It was by holding them in force and with great numbers that Blake intended to check the invasion. In front of his chosen position, at a distance of twenty miles, there was a great advanced work—a newly restored fortress of crucial importance—the fastness of Saguntum, or ' San Fernando de Sagunto ' as it had

just been re-christened. This was the acropolis of one of the
most ancient towns of Spain, the Saguntum which had detained
Hannibal so long before its walls at the opening of the
Third Punic War. In the age of the Iberians, the Cartha-
ginians, and the Romans, and even down to the days of the
Ommeyad califs, there had been a large and flourishing city on
this site. But in the later middle ages Saguntum had declined
in prosperity and population, and the modern town—which
had changed its name to Murviedro (*muri veteres*) had shrunk
down to the foot of the hill. It was now a small open place of
6,000 souls, quite indefensible. But above it towered the steep
line of rock which had formed the citadel in ancient days : its
narrow summit was crowned with many ruins of various ages—
from cyclopean foundations of walls, going back to the time
of the ancient Iberians, to Moorish watch-towers and palaces.
The empty space of steep slope, from the acropolis down to the
modern town, was also sprinkled with decaying walls and
substructures of all sorts, among which were cisterns and
broken roadways, besides the remains of a large Roman
theatre, partly hewn out of the live rock.

There had been no fortifications by Murviedro when Suchet
last passed near Valencia, in his abortive raid of March 1810 [1].
On that occasion he had scaled the citadel to enjoy the view
and to take a casual survey of the picturesque ruins upon it [2].
But since then a great change had taken place. On the advice,
as it is said, of the English general, Charles Doyle [3], Blake had
determined to restore the citadel as a place of strength. This
was when he last held command in Valencia, and before he
joined the Cadiz Regency. But his idea had been carried out
after his departure by the Valencian Junta and the successive
Captains-General who had come after him. By means of more
than a year's work the citadel had been made a tenable fortress,
though one of an irregular and unscientific sort. The old
Iberian and Moorish walls had been repaired and run together
in a new *enceinte*, with material taken from the other ruins all
around. In especial the Roman theatre, hitherto one of the
most perfect in Southern Europe, had been completely gutted,

---

[1] See vol. iii. pp. 284–6.   [2] Suchet's *Mémoires*, ii. p. 156.
[3] See Arteche, xi. p. 123.

and its big blocks had proved most useful for building the foundations of weak points of the circuit of fortification. This was strong at some points, from the toughness and height of the old ramparts, but very sketchy at others. Where the slope was absolutely precipitous, a rough wall of dry stone without mortar alone had been carried along the edge of the cliff. The narrow summit of the rock formed a most irregular enclosure, varying much in height from one point to another. It was divided into four separate sections cut off from each other by cross-walls. The westernmost and lowest, facing the only point from which there is a comparatively gentle ascent to the summit, was crowned by a new battery called by the name of *Dos de Mayo*, to commemorate the Madrid Insurrection of 1808. Rising high in the centre of this work was an ancient bastion named the Tower of San Pedro. Much higher, on the extreme peak of the summit, was the citadel tower, called San Fernando, where the governor's flag flew, and from whence the whole fortress could be best surveyed. From this point the rock descended rapidly, and its long irregular eastern crest was surrounded by weakly-repaired walls, ending in two batteries called by the names of Menacho, the gallant governor of Badajoz [1], and Doyle, the English general who had suggested the fortification of the place. But the greater part of this eastern end of the works lay above slopes so precipitous that it seemed unlikely that they would ever be attacked. The western end, by the Dos Mayo battery, was the obvious point of assault by an enemy who intended to use regular methods.

The construction was by no means finished when Suchet's expedition began : many parts of the new walls were only carried up to half their intended height, and no regular shelter for the garrison had been contrived. Instead of proper barracks and casemates there were only rough 'leans-to,' contrived against old walls, or cover made by roofing in with beams old broken towers, and bastions. The hospital was the only spacious and regular building in the whole *enceinte* : the powder magazine was placed deep down in the cellars of the fort San Fernando. The armament of the place was by no means complete : the guns were being sent up just as Suchet started. Only seventeen

[1] See vol. iv. p. 56.

were ready, and of these no more than three were 12-pounders : the rest were only of the calibre of field artillery (4- and 8-pounders) or howitzers. A fortress which has only seventeen guns for an *enceinte* of 3,000 yards, and possesses no heavy guns to reply to the 18- or 24-pounders of a siege-train, is in a state of desperate danger.

Blake had thrown into the place a brigade under the command of Colonel Luis Andriani, consisting of five battalions, two each of the regiments of Savoya and Don Carlos, one of the Cazadores de Orihuela. Of these two were new ' third battalions [1] ' from the recently raised ' Division of Reserve,' incomplete in officers, only half drilled, and not yet fully provided with uniforms. The total force came to 2,663 officers and men, including about 150 artillerymen and sappers. It is probable that these troops would have made no better show in the open field than did the rest of the Valencian army, a few weeks later : but they showed behind walls the same capacity for unexpected resistance which had surprised the French on other occasions at Ciudad Rodrigo, Gerona, and Figueras. Andriani, the governor, seems to have made an honourable attempt to do his duty at the head of the doubtfully efficient garrison placed at his disposal.

In addition to Saguntum Blake held two outlying posts in his front, Peniscola on its lofty headland, garrisoned by about 1,000 men under General Garcia Navarro, and the half-ruined Oropesa, which he had resolved to hold, because it blocked the sea-coast road so effectively. But its only tenable points were two mediaeval towers, one in the town commanding the high-road, the other by the shore of the Mediterranean. Their joint garrisons did not amount to 500 men, and it was obvious that they could not hold out many days against modern artillery. But the gain of a day or two might conceivably be very valuable in the campaign that was about to begin. It is clear, however, that his main hope of resistance lay in the line of entrenched camps and batteries along the Guadalaviar, in front of Valencia : here he intended to make his real stand, and he

---

[1] The battalions were the 2nd and 3rd of Savoya (the last a new levy) the 1st and 2nd of Don Carlos, and the 3rd of Orihuela, this last raw and newly raised like the 3rd of Savoya.

hoped that Saguntum, so little distant from this line, would prove a serious hindrance to the enemy when he came up against it.

Suchet's three columns all started, as Napoleon had ordered, on September 15th. The Marshal's own main body, coming from Tortosa, reached Benicarlo, the first town across the Valencian frontier, next day, and on the 17th came level with Peniscola, whose garrison kept quiet within the limits of its isthmus. The Marshal left a battalion and a few hussars to observe it, and to see that it did not make sallies against his line of communication. On the 19th the head of the marching column reached Torreblanca, quite close to Oropesa. A reconnaissance found that the place was held, and came into contact with some Spanish horse, who were easily driven off. This was the first touch with Blake's field army that had been obtained. But the enemy was evidently not in force, and the garrison of Oropesa hastily retired into the two towers which ormed its only tenable positions. On a close inspection it was found that the tower in the town completely commanded the high-road, wherefore the Marshal took a slight circuit by suburban lanes round the place, with his main body and guns, and continued his advance, after leaving a few companies to blockade the towers. On the same evening he was joined by Palombini's column from Morella, consisting of the two Italian divisions. They had accomplished their march without meeting any resistance, though the road from Morella by San Matteo and Cabanes was rough and easily defensible. The united force, now 16,000 strong, proceeded on its march next day, and the Marshal was agreeably surprised when, on the morning of the 20th, the cavalry scouts on his right flank announced to him that they had come in touch with Harispe's column from Teruel, which had appeared at the village of Villafanes a few miles from the main road. Thus the whole army of invasion was happily united.

Harispe, as it turned out, had left Teruel on the 15th, in obedience to his orders, by the post-road to Segorbe and the coast. But hearing on the second day that a large Valencian force was holding the defile of Las Barracas, where the road crosses the watershed, he had turned off by a bad side-path to

Ruvielos in the upper valley of the Mijares, in the hope of
joining his chief without being forced to storm a difficult
position. Blake, as a matter of fact, much alarmed at the
approach of a flanking column on the Teruel side, and ignorant
of its strength, had sent the division of Obispo and some other
detachments to hold the pass. But no enemy came this way—
Harispe had diverged down the course of the Villahermosa
river, by a country road only practicable for a force without
guns or wheeled transport, and got down by rapid marches to
the coast-plain beyond Alcora, without having seen any enemy
save some scattered guerrillero bands. He had thoroughly
distracted Blake's attention and had run no danger, because he
took an unexpected and difficult route, in a direction quite
different from that by which the Spaniards expected him to
appear [1].

The whole army was now concentrated near Villafanes on
September 21, save the detachments left to block Peniscola and
Oropesa, and the brigade of Ficatier, which, escorting the siege ·
train, had been left at Tortosa, to await orders for starting when
there should be no enemy left in northern Valencia to molest it.
The heavy guns were to come forward down the coast-road,
first to breach the towers of Oropesa, and when the way past
them was clear, to play their part, if necessary, in the more
serious task of battering Saguntum.

On advancing from Castellon de la Plana on September 22
the French army found a very small Spanish rearguard—500 or
600 men—covering the bridge of Villareal over the Mijares.
They gave way before the first attack, which was a very
simple affair, since the river was nearly dry and everywhere fordable. No more was seen of the enemy next day,
and on the 23rd Suchet found himself on the banks of the
Palancia stream, which flows under the foot of the rock of
Saguntum. The Spaniards had retired still further towards
Valencia, leaving the fortress to its own resources. These were

[1] Vacani says that the Teruel column was intended by Suchet as a mere
demonstration, and was never intended to follow the high-road Teruel–
Segorbe, but to take a cross-route over the hills, such as was actually used
by it. But Suchet, in his *Mémoires*, makes no such statement (ii. p. 152), and
speaks as if Harispe had taken the Ruvielos route on his own responsibility.

unknown to Suchet, who was aware that the ruinous citadel had been rebuilt, but could not tell without further reconnaissance what was its strength. In order to invest the place, and to make closer investigation possible, Harispe's division crossed the Palancia to the right of Saguntum, Habert's to the left. The latter sent six companies into the town of Murviedro, and drove up some Spanish pickets from it into the fortress which towered above. The two divisions then joined hands to the south of Saguntum, completing its investment, while Palombini's Italians took post at Petres and Gillet on the road to Segorbe—to the north-west—in case Blake might have placed some of his troops on this side-route, with the object of troubling the siege by attacks from the rear. The cavalry went forward down the high-road to Valencia, and sent back news that they had explored as far as Albalete, only six miles from the capital, and had met no enemy. The division of Lardizabal and the cavalry of San Juan, which had been the observing force in front of Suchet, had retired beyond the Guadalaviar river, and had shut themselves up (along with the rest of Blake's army) in the entrenchments behind that stream. The Spanish general was evidently acting on the strictest principles of passive defence.

The French marshal determined not to seek his enemy on his chosen ground, till he should have taken Saguntum and brought up his siege-train to the front. The former condition he thought would not prove difficult to accomplish. A survey of the fortress revealed its extremely irregular and incomplete state of defence. Though the cliffs were in all parts steep and in some places inaccessible, many sections of the works above them were obviously unfinished and very weak. After a close reconnaissance by his engineer officers had been made, Suchet determined that it would be worth while to try an attempt at escalade on some of the most defective points, without waiting for the arrival of the siege-train. He set his sappers and carpenters to work to make sixty ladders, which were ready in full number on the third day. The front chosen for the assault was in the *enceinte* immediately overhanging the town of Murviedro, where two ancient gaps in the wall were clearly visible ; the new work was not half finished, and a low structure,

roughly completed with beams laid above the regular foundations, was all that blocked the openings. The masons of the
garrison were heard at night, working hard to raise the height
of the stone wall which was to replace the temporary wooden
parapets. There being no artillery available, they could not
be hindered in their building : but it did not seem to advance
very rapidly.

Suchet set apart for the actual escalade two columns, each
composed of 300 volunteers from Habert's division : they were
to be supported by a reserve of similar strength under Colonel
Gudin, which was formed up, completely under cover, within the
streets of Murviedro. At midnight on September 27th–28th the
stormers pushed forward under cover of the darkness, and in
small successive parties, into a large Roman cistern above the
ruined theatre, which was ' dead ground,' and not exposed to
fire from any part of the ramparts. Here they were only
120 yards from the two breaches. Meanwhile, as a diversion,
six Italian companies from Palombini's division were ordered
to make a noisy demonstration against the distant part of the
defences which lay under the tower of San Pedro[1]. General
Habert was to have 2,000 men more under arms, ready to
support the assailing column.

The stormers reached their appointed place apparently
undiscovered, and the attack would have been delivered—
according to Suchet's dispatch—without any preliminary firing,
but for an accident. The Marshal says that the Spaniards
had pushed an exploring patrol down the hillside, which fell in
with the French pickets and drew their fire. Thereupon the
assaulting columns in the cistern, thinking themselves discovered, let off a few shots and charged uphill, a little ahead
of the appointed time, and before the Italian demonstration
had begun[2]. The governor, Andriani, in his dispatch, makes no
mention of this, but merely says that about 2 a.m. his sentinels
thought that they detected movements on the slopes, and

[1] The complete orders for the attack may be read in the first *Pièce
justificative* in Belmas's history of the siege, pp. 115–17 of vol. iv of his
elaborate work.

[2] Vacani (v. p. 381) contradicts Suchet, saying that there was no Spanish
patrol, and that the French pickets fired from nervousness at an imaginary
foe.

that a short time afterwards a fierce attack was delivered. At any rate the garrison was not surprised as Suchet had hoped.

Owing to the lowness, however, of the walls blocking the two old breaches, the assailants had, in their first rush, a fair chance of breaking in. Many ladders were successfully planted, and repeatedly small parties of the French got a footing on the wooden parapets. If the garrison had flinched, the storm might have succeeded : but far from flinching, they offered a desperate resistance, overthrew the ladders, slew all who had gained the top of the *enceinte*, and kept up a furious musketry fire, which laid low many of the soldiers who kept pressing forward to the breaches. It was to no purpose that the demonstration by the Italians below San Pedro now began : the Spaniards fired hard and fast in this direction also, but did not withdraw any men from the real point of attack, where they maintained themselves very courageously. It was in vain that Colonel Gudin brought up his reserve : it could make no head, and the survivors threw themselves down among the rocks and ruins in front of the wall—unwilling to recede, but quite unable to advance. Seeing his attack a hopeless failure, Suchet ordered the stormers back just before daylight began to appear. They had lost 247 killed and wounded out of 900 men engaged : the garrison only 15 killed and less than 30 wounded [1].

The escalade having come to this disappointing conclusion, the Marshal saw that the siege of Saguntum would be anything but a quick business. It would be necessary to bring up the siege-train to the front : orders were sent back to Ficatier to start it at once from Tortosa ; but it had to batter and take Oropesa before it could even reach Murviedro. There were some weeks of delay before him, and meanwhile Blake might at last begin to show some signs of life. Suchet therefore disposed his army so as to provide both a blockading force and a covering force, to see that the blockade was not interfered with from without. It being evident that many days would elapse before

[1] Vacani makes the losses 360 instead of 247, and it is possible that Suchet has given only the casualties at the main assault, and not those in the distant demonstrations. Vacani says that the Italians lost 52 men in their false attack.

the siege artillery arrived, the French engineer officers got leave
to employ many detachments in preparing roads fit to bear
heavy guns up the western slopes of the hill of Saguntum,
from which alone the regular attack on the fortress could be
conducted. Several emplacements for batteries were also
chosen, and work upon them was begun.

From September 23rd, the day of Suchet's arrival before
Saguntum, down to October 16, when the heavy guns at last
arrived, the French army was practically ' marking time ' : the
idea which the Emperor had conceived, and which his lieutenant
had adopted, that Valencia could be conquered by a sudden
rush, had been proved false. Apparently Suchet had gained no
more by his rapid advance to the foot of the hill of Saguntum
than he would have obtained by marching in more leisurely
fashion, with his siege artillery in company, and taking Oropesa
on the way. The reduction of that place indeed was (as it
turned out) only a single day's task for heavy guns : and if the
Marshal had captured it on his march, he might have presented
himself before Saguntum with his siege-train, and have begun
an active attack on that fortress, some weeks before he was
actually able to get to serious work. In fact he might have
been battering Saguntum on October 1, instead of having to
wait till October 16th. But this is ' wisdom after the event ' :
Napoleon thought that Valencia could be ' rushed,' and
Suchet was bound to make the experiment that his master
ordered.

Blake meanwhile, finding, on September 23rd, that the enemy
was not about to advance against his lines, and learning soon
after that the French army had settled down before Saguntum,
had to revise his plans, since it was clear that he was not to be
attacked in his entrenchments as he had supposed. Three
courses were now open to him : either he might collect every
man for a decisive battle in the open, and try to raise the siege ;
or he might attempt to open up attacks on Suchet's line of
communications and on his base in Aragon, so as to force him
to retire by indirect operations ; or he might remain passive
behind the lines of the Guadalaviar. The last was an almost
unthinkable alternative—it would have ruined his reputation
for ever to sit quiet and do nothing, as Wellington had done

during the siege of Ciudad Rodrigo in 1810. Only a general
with an established reputation for courage and ability could
have dared to take such a course ; and Blake's record was a long
series of disasters, while he was detested by the Valencians one
and all—by the army, to whom he rightly preferred his own
excellent troops, no less than by the Captain-General Palacios,
and the Junta, whom he had sent out of the city to sit at
Alcira, when they showed a tendency to hamper his operations.
Practically he was forced by his situation to take some definite
offensive move against Suchet.

He chose that of indirect operations, having a well-rooted
distrust of the fighting powers of a great part of the troops that
were at his disposition. The record of the Valencian army he
knew : the state of the Murcian army, on which he could draw
for reinforcements, was represented to him in the most gloomy
colours by Mahy, who had recently replaced Freire in command.
On September 12th Mahy had written to him, to warn him that
the spirit of his troops was detestable : ' the Army of Murcia was
little better than a phantom : there were only four or five officers
for whom the rank and file had any respect or esteem, the rest
were regarded as timid or incapable : the men had no confidence
in themselves or their chiefs. The best thing to do would be to
break up the whole army, and incorporate it into the " Expeditionary Divisions," whose commanders were known as good
soldiers, and whose battalions were trustworthy [1].'

In view of these facts Blake resolved to threaten Suchet's
flanks with demonstrations, which he had no intention of
turning into attacks, but to endeavour to dislodge him from
his forward position by turning loose the guerrilleros of Aragon
on to his rear. With the former purpose he sent out two
detachments from the Valencian lines, Obispo's division to
Segorbe,—where it cut the French communication with Teruel
and southern Aragon,—Charles O'Donnell with Villacampa's
infantry and San Juan's horse to Benaguacil, a point in the
plains fifteen miles west of Saguntum, where his force formed a
link between Obispo and the main body of the Valencian army,

[1] See Mahy's letter to Blake on pp. 109–12 of vol. xi of Arteche. The
General is writing very carefully so as not to speak too ill of his army : but
his views are clear.

which still remained entrenched in the lines of the Guadalaviar [1]. These two detachments threatened Suchet's flank, and even his rear, but there was no intention of turning the threat into a reality.

The real movement on which Blake relied for the discomfiture of the invaders of Valencia was that of the guerrillero bands of Aragon and the neighbouring parts of Castile, to whom he had appealed for help the moment that Suchet commenced his march. He believed that the 6,000 or 7,000 men which Suchet had left scattered in small garrisons under General Musnier might be so beset and worried by the *partidas*, that the Marshal might be compelled to turn back to their aid. Even Mina from his distant haunts in Navarre had been asked to co-operate. This was an excellent move, and might have succeeded, if Musnier alone had remained to hold down Aragon. But Blake had forgotten in his calculations the 15,000 men of Reille and Severoli, cantoned in Navarre and along the Upper Ebro, who were available to strengthen the small force which lay in the garrisons under Musnier's charge.

The diversion of the guerrilleros, however, was effected with considerable energy. On September 26th the Empecinado and Duran appeared in front of Calatayud, the most important of the French garrisons in the mountains of western Aragon. They had with them 5,000 foot and 500 horse—not their full strength, for a large band of the Empecinado's men beset at the same time the remote castle of Molina, the most outlying and isolated of all Suchet's posts. Calatayud was held by a few companies of French, to which an Italian flying column of a battalion had just joined itself. The guerrilleros, coming in with a rush, drove the garrison out of the town into their fortified post, the large convent of La Merced, taking many prisoners in the streets. Duran then beleaguered the main body in the convent, while the Empecinado took post at the defile of El Frasno on the Saragossa road, to hold off any succour that Musnier might send up from the Aragonese capital. This precaution was justified—a column of 1,000 men came out of Saragossa, but was far too weak to force the pass and had to

---

[1] Blake kept under his own hand in the lines the divisions of Zayas, Lardizabal, Miranda, and the Reserve.

retire, with the loss of its commander, Colonel Gillot, and many men. Meanwhile Duran pressed the besieged in the convent with mines, having no artillery of sufficient calibre to batter its walls. After blowing down a corner of its chapel with one mine, and killing many of the defenders, the guerrillero chief exploded a second on October 3, which made such a vast breach that the garrison surrendered, still 560 strong, on the following day [1].

This success would have gone far to shake the hold of the French on Aragon, but for the intervention of Reille from Navarre. At the first news of the blockade of Calatayud, he had dispatched a column, consisting of the whole brigade of Bourke, 3,500 strong, which would have saved the garrison if it had had a less distance to march. But it arrived on the 5th to find the convent blown up, while the Spaniards had vanished with their prisoners. Bourke thereupon returned to Tudela, and the guerrilleros reoccupied Calatayud on his departure.

Meanwhile, however, the whole Italian division of Severoli, over 7,000 strong, marched down the Ebro to reinforce the small garrison of Saragossa. This large reinforcement restored the confidence of the French. Musnier himself took charge of it and marched at its head against Duran and the Empecinado. They wisely refused to fight, gave way, evacuated Calatayud, and took refuge in the hills (October 12). While the main field-force of the enemy was drawn off in this direction, Mina took up the game on the other side of the Ebro. Entering Aragon with 4,000 men he besieged the small garrison of Exea, which abandoned its post, and cut its way through the guerrilleros, till it met a column of 800 Italian infantry [2] sent out from Saragossa to bring it off. Colonel Ceccopieri, the leader of this small force, underrating the strength of his enemy, then marched to relieve the garrison of Ayerbe. He was surprised on the way by Mina's whole force, and in a long running fight between Ayerbe and Huesca was surrounded and slain. The column was exterminated, two hundred Italians were killed, six

[1] Vacani gives a long and interesting account of the siege (v. pp. 404–13) and attributes the weak defence to quarrels between the commander of the Italians and the French governor, Müller.

[2] Belonging to the 7th Line of Severoli's division.

hundred (including many wounded) were taken prisoners (October 16th).

Musnier returned in haste from Calatayud at the news of this disaster, but left the bulk of Severoli's division to occupy western Aragon. He then set himself, with the help of Reille, to hunt down Mina. But the latter, marching with ease between the columns that pursued him, for the peasantry kept him informed day by day of every movement of the enemy, retreated westward. Easily eluding the French, he made an extraordinary excursion, right across Navarre, Alava, and Biscay, down to the sea coast at Motrico, where he handed over his prisoners to the captain of the British frigate *Isis*, and then returned unharmed to his familiar haunts. Of such a delusive nature was the hold of the French on Northern Spain, that a column of 5,000 men could march for 200 miles across it without being intercepted or destroyed.

All these exploits of the guerrilleros were daring and well planned, but though they had given Musnier much trouble, and cost the French many a weary hour of march and countermarch, they had not cleared Aragon of the enemy, nor shaken Suchet's position. Indeed, on October 20, the general condition of affairs in Aragon was more favourable for the invaders than on September 20, for two fresh divisions had been drawn down into that province, and there were 20,000 French and Italian troops in it instead of 6,000. The petty disasters at Calatayud and Ayerbe were irritating rather than important. Suchet never for a moment felt inclined to relax his hold upon Valencia : that western Aragon was in an uproar affected him little, when his communication with his two main dépôts of stores at Tortosa and Morella was not interrupted.

Blake, it may be mentioned, did not content himself with setting the Empecinado and Duran in motion, he tried another division in another quarter with even less result. Rumours had reached him that King Joseph's Army of the Centre was about to co-operate with Suchet, by sending a column across the mountains to Cuenca and Requeña. The news was false, for though Napoleon had ordered the King to do what he could to help in the invasion of Valencia, Joseph had replied that he had not even one brigade to spare for a serious demonstration,

and had not moved—the guerrilleros gave sufficient occupation
to his much-scattered army, of which a large portion was composed of untrustworthy Spanish *Juramentados*. But, listening
to vain reports, Blake ordered Mahy to collect the best of his
Murcian troops and to march on Cuenca to meet the supposed
invaders. His subordinate, leaving Freire in command in
Murcia, took seven selected battalions of foot under Creagh and
the Marquis of Montijo, with 800 horse and one battery, and
moved from his camp at Mula by Hellin and Chinchilla northward. The distance to be covered was great, the roads after
Chinchilla very bad. Mahy arrived in front of Cuenca on
October 15th, to find that there was only one battalion and two
squadrons of Joseph's army there. This little force evacuated
the high-lying city in haste, and fled towards Madrid the
moment that the Murcians showed themselves. No other
French force could be heard of in any direction. At Cuenca
Mahy received a dispatch from Blake (who had apparently
discovered his mistake about the Army of the Centre), telling
him to descend from the mountains by Moya and Liria, and to
join the wing of the main army, which lay under Obispo at
Segorbe. It was only on the 23rd October that he came in : his
troops, the pick of the Murcian army, had been completely
wasted for some twenty days in a circular march against
a non-existent enemy. Meanwhile every man had been wanted
in Valencia.

Suchet, when once he had settled down to the siege of
Saguntum, had not failed to notice Blake's weak demonstration
against his flank by means of the divisions of Obispo and Charles
O'Donnell. He did not intend to tolerate it, and on September 30 had sent Palombini with his own Italian division and
Robert's French brigade to beat up Obispo's quarters at Segorbe.
The Spanish division made a poor attempt to defend itself on
a position in front of that town, but was easily beaten and
retired into the mountains. It was then the turn of Charles
O'Donnell ; when Palombini had come back to the camp,
Suchet took Harispe's division, with Robert's brigade, and two
regiments of cavalry, to evict the Spanish division from Benaguacil. O'Donnell made a slightly better fight than Obispo had
done, and deployed Villacampa's infantry behind an irrigation

canal, with San Juan's cavalry on his flanks. But the French were superior in numbers as well as in confidence : one fierce charge broke O'Donnell's line, and he had to retreat in haste to the hills behind him, losing 400 men, cut up in the pursuit by Suchet's cavalry, while the French casualties barely reached three officers and sixty men (October 2nd). Blake, who had been quite close enough to succour O'Donnell if he had chosen, made no attempt to aid him, and kept quiet behind his lines on the Guadalaviar. There the routed troops joined him next day.

Suchet, having thus cleared his flanks, settled down to the siege of Saguntum, where his heavy artillery was now much needed. The besieging army had to content itself for another fortnight with making preparations for the expected train— levelling roads and constructing approaches on the ground which was destined for the front of attack, at the west end of the hill of Saguntum.

Meanwhile the siege-train was lumbering down from Tortosa by the coast-road. On October 6th Suchet started to meet it, taking with him the 1,500 Neapolitans of Compère. On the 8th he reached Oropesa, where he found the small Spanish garrison still holding the two towers which have before been mentioned. The first guns that came up were turned against the tower by the high-road ; it was easily breached, and on the 10th surrendered : 215 men and four guns were captured. Next day came the turn of the other tower, that by the sea ; but before the siege-battery had opened on it, the British 74 *Magnificent* and a squadron of Spanish gunboats ran in-shore, and took off the garrison of 150 men in their boats, under the ineffective fire of the French.

The moment that the tower which blocked the high-road had fallen, and before that on the shore had been evacuated, Suchet began to push the head of his precious convoy of heavy artillery southward. It made such a good pace that the first guns arrived at the camp before Saguntum as early as the night of October 12th. Meanwhile the Marshal himself returned thither, escorted by Compère's Neapolitans : the brigade of Ficatier, which had escorted the train hitherto, was dispersed to cover the line of communications, placing its five battalions at Oropesa, Almenara, and Segorbe.

SECTION XXX : CHAPTER II

THE BATTLE OF SAGUNTUM. OCTOBER 1811

AFTER Charles O'Donnell and Obispo had been driven away from the threatening position upon Suchet's flank, Blake found himself during the early days of October in a very unpleasant dilemma. It was clear that his own feeble efforts to molest the French army were a complete failure. Presently the message reached him that Mahy's unlucky expedition to Cuenca had been absolutely useless. But the most disheartening news was that the attempt to overrun Aragon by means of the guerrilleros had failed ; its initial success, the capture of Calatayud on October 3, had only led to the inundation of the whole country-side in that direction by the numerous battalions of Reille and Severoli.

As the days wore on, Blake found himself obliged to confess that the idea of dislodging Suchet by operations in his rear was hopeless. The only remaining alternative for him was to endeavour to call together every available man, and to try to beat the French army in a great pitched battle. Considering the well-known disrepute of both the Murcian and the Valencian troops, the prospect was not one that the Spanish general could view with much confidence. But political reasons forced him to fight—his policy of passive resistance had made him so un-popular with the Valencians of all ranks, from the members of the exiled Junta down to the private soldiers, that if he had held back any longer it is probable that he might have been deposed or murdered by a conspiracy. Saguntum was holding out most gallantly, and the ignominy of leaving it to fall, without making any effort for its succour, was sufficiently evident. He made up his mind about the middle of October that he must advance and fight. But, being very properly determined to fight with all available resources, he had to await the descent of Mahy and the Murcians from Cuenca, and

by his own fault that important column could not be drawn
in to the main army before the 23rd. It was only on that
day that an advance in force became possible : for a week
and more Blake anxiously awaited the junction, and until it
took place he would not move.

Meanwhile Suchet, entirely unmolested, was pressing the
siege of Saguntum with all possible expedition. The first siege-
guns from Tortosa reached his camp, as has been already mentioned, on October 12th. But it was not till four days later that
the actual battering of the place began. Though paths had
been traced out, and the emplacements of batteries settled,
long ere the siege-train came up, the actual getting of the guns
into position proved a very tiresome business, on account of the
steep and rocky slopes over which they had to be dragged. And
the construction of approaches and parallels upon the hillside
progressed very slowly, because of the absence of earth—at
last it was found that soil to bind the loose stones of the ground
together would have, for the most part, to be carried up in
sandbags from the valley below, for hardly any could be scraped
together on the spot. The engineer officer who wrote the diary
of the siege confesses that if the Spanish garrison had only been
provided with heavy artillery, the approach-building would
have proved almost impossible [1]. But, as has been already
noted, there were but seventeen guns mounted in the whole
fortress, and of these only three were 12-pounders—the rest
being small field-pieces, too weak to batter down parapets of
even modest thickness. Moreover the very steepness of the
slope over which the siege-works were being advanced made
much of it ' dead ground,' which guns above could not properly
sweep or search out.

On the 11th of October the two generals, Vallée and Rogniat,
who had regularly commanded Suchet's artillery and engineers
during his previous sieges, arrived from the rear—both had been
in France on leave, and they had come forward with the train
from Tortosa to Oropesa. Their arrival added confidence to
the subordinates who had hitherto worked without them, for
the reputation of each for success was very great. Rogniat
immediately on his arrival made several important modifica-

[1] Belmas, iv. p. 97.

tions in the projected batteries, and showed how the approaches might be pushed forward to within seventy yards of the fortress, by taking advantage of favourable dips and rocky outcrops in the hillside.

On the 16th, five batteries were armed with the guns which had come up, and fire was opened upon the projecting western angle of the fortress, the tower of San Pedro. It proved to be made of ancient Moorish stone and mortar, almost as hard as iron, and crumbled very slowly. But the modern works below it, which were only a few months old, owned no such resisting power, and within two days showed signs of serious damage. The Spanish counter-fire was insignificant— there were very few guns available, and it was only when the approaches got within easy musket shot of the walls that the besiegers began to suffer appreciable casualties. For the Spanish infantry, disregarding the cannonade, kept up a furious fire against the heads of the saps all day and night.

On the afternoon of the 18th the engineer and artillery officers reported to Suchet that they had made a sufficient breach in the curtain of the work called the Dos Mayo battery, just where it joined on the tower of San Pedro, and that they regarded it as practicable for assault. The Marshal ordered that the storm should be fixed for the same evening, lest the Spaniards should succeed in repairing the breach during the hours of darkness. The column of assault consisted of 400 men, picked from Habert's division, supported by a reserve of Palombini's Italians. The fire of the siege artillery was kept up to the last moment, and did much harm to the garrison, who were very clearly seen piling gabions, sandbags, and stones on the ruinous lip of the breach, in disregard of the steady fire that kept pounding it down [1].

The assault was duly delivered at five o'clock, and proved a complete failure. The stormers found the breach most difficult to climb, as its face was entirely formed of big blocks of stone without earth or débris. The column won its way half up the ascent, and isolated officers and men got further, and were bayoneted or shot at close quarters by the defenders, who clustered very thickly at the top. But no general rush of men

[1] See narrative of Vacani, an eye-witness (vol. v. p. 399).

could reach the summit, where (it is said) the actual gap in the parapet was not more than six or seven feet broad. After several ineffective attempts to mount, the assailants came to a stand on the lower part of the slope, and opened a scattering fire on the Spaniards above them. Whereupon, seeing the opportunity lost, General Habert, who had been given charge of the operations, ordered the men to fall back to the trenches, and to abandon the assault.

This was a most creditable feat of arms for the garrison, who had hardly a cannon to help them, and held their own almost entirely by musketry fire, though they rolled some live shells, beams, and large stones down the breach at intervals. Their casualties were heavy, but those of the assailants, as was natural, much greater. Suchet lost at least 300 men, though in his dispatch to the Emperor[1] he gave an elaborate table of casualties showing a total of only 173. But his ' returns,' even the most specious looking of them, should never be trusted—as will be seen when we are dealing with the second battle of Castalla in a later volume. This excellent officer was as untrustworthy as Soult or Masséna in the figures which he sent to his master[2].

After this Suchet resolved to make no more attempts to storm Saguntum. ' When even the best of soldiers,' remarks Belmas, ' have made every effort to carry a place and have failed, they imagine that the place is impregnable. And if an attempt is made to lead them once more to an assault, they will not again act with the confidence which is needed to secure victory.' Wellington was to find this out at Burgos, a

---

[1] To be found in print in Belmas, iv. pp. 124–8.

[2] This indictment of Suchet must be supported by details. In his elaborate table of casualties by corps at the end of his dispatch of Oct. 20, he only allows for 3 officers killed and 8 wounded, 40 men killed and 122 wounded—total 173. But the lists of officers' casualties in Martinien show, on the other hand, *five* officers killed (Coutanceau, Saint Hilaire, Turno, Giardini, Cuny), and at least *ten* wounded (Mathis, Durand, Gauchet, D'Autane, Adhémar, Gattinara, Lamezan, D'Esclaibes, Maillard, Laplane), and probably three more.

Oddly enough, in his *Mémoires* (ii. p. 173) Suchet gives *by name* four officers killed at the breach (out of the five), while in his official report he had stated that there were only three killed altogether. We must trust rather Vacani, an eye-witness and a man much interested in statistics and casualties, when he gives the total of 300 for the losses, than Suchet's table.

year later. Indeed in their early stages the sieges of Saguntum
and Burgos show a rather notable parallelism, though their ends
were dissimilar. General Rogniat easily persuaded the Marshal
to drop the heroic method which had gained so little success,
and to fall back on the systematic work which is slow but certain [1].' Suchet gave permission to the engineers to establish
more batteries, and to defer all further attempts to storm till
the approaches should have been carried up to the very foot
of the walls, and the whole curtain of the Dos Mayo redoubt
should have been battered down.

The garrison, much encouraged by their successful effort
of the 18th, continued to make an obstinate resistance : as
the enemy sapped uphill towards them, they kept up such
a careful and deadly fire that the casualties in the trenches
amounted every day to 15 or 20 men. For the next six days
nothing decisive happened, though the works continued to
creep slowly forward : they had to be built with parapets
consisting entirely of earth brought from below, and made very
high, since the nearer they got to the works, the more did the
plunging fire from above search them out.

Meanwhile Blake was preparing, though with no great self-
confidence, to make an attack on Suchet's siege-lines, and was
only awaiting the arrival of Mahy and the Murcians before
striking. He began by trying a feeble diversion on the flank,
sending back Obispo's division once more to Segorbe, and
getting some of the Empecinado's bands to threaten Teruel, the
southernmost of the garrisons in Aragon. This so far annoyed the
French marshal that on the 20th of October he sent off Palombini, with one French and one Italian brigade and 400 horse,
to drive Obispo out of Segorbe, and to open the road to Teruel.
By so doing he placed himself in a dangerous position, for he
had detached 4,500 men on an excursion which could not take
less than four days, and if Blake had refused to wait for Mahy,
and had let Obispo amuse Palombini, he could have marched
against the siege-lines with 20,000 men, including all his best
troops, and would have found only 12,000, besides the gunners
of the siege artillery, left in the French camp. If Suchet had
left any detachments to maintain the blockade, as he probably

[1] Belmas, iv. p. 96.

would have done, he could only have fought with odds of less than one to two. If he had brought up all his battalions, the garrison would have sallied forth and destroyed his siege-works.

But Blake did not take his chance—whatever it may have been worth : he waited for Mahy, who was only due on the 23rd. Meanwhile Palombini made a rapid raid upon Segorbe : but Obispo, leaving two battalions only to make a show of resistance, crossed the hills by by-paths and drew in to Liria, on the flank of the main army, and in close touch with it. He could have been used for a battle, if Blake had chosen to deliver one upon the 22nd or 23rd. But the unlucky Spanish general did not so choose : and Palombini—finding nothing serious in front of him, and hearing that Teruel had been already relieved by Severoli—rightly returned by forced marches to Saguntum, which he reached on the afternoon of the 24th of October.

Meanwhile the long-expected Mahy arrived at Liria on the night of the 23rd, and found Obispo already lying there. The two forces united, and marched on the 24th to Betera, but there again divided, the Murcians going on to join Blake's main body, while the Valencian division received orders from the Commander-in-Chief to move as an independent flanking column, and from Naquera to fall upon the flank or right rear of Suchet's position in front of Saguntum.

On the same day Blake himself broke out of the lines behind the Guadalaviar, and after issuing a well-worded proclamation, in which he said that Andriani's gallant garrison must not perish unassisted, and declared a confidence which he must have been far from feeling in the resolution of his troops, advanced for some miles along the high-road, so as to place himself at nightfall within striking distance of the enemy.

His plan of operations, which was clearly set forth in his directions to Mahy [1], was ambitious in the highest degree, and aimed at the complete destruction of his enemy. Expecting to find Suchet drawn up to meet him in the plain south of Saguntum, it appears that he intended to fight a battle in which an immensely strong left wing was to turn and break down Suchet's right, while a weaker right wing (composed, however, of his

---

[1] Which may be read in full in Arteche, xi. pp. 157–9.

best troops) was to attack him frontally, and hold his main
body ' contained,' while the turning movement was delivered.
The left wing contained 26 battalions and nearly 20 squadrons,
making nearly 16,000 bayonets and 1,700 sabres [1]. The
detached division of Obispo, from Naquera, was to fall on the
extreme French right from the rear ; the two other Valencian
infantry divisions (Miranda and Villacampa), led by Charles
O'Donnell, were to tackle it in front. Mahy's Murcians were
to support O'Donnell, at the same time reaching out a hand
towards Obispo—in order to do this Mahy was directed to send
out two battalions (under a Colonel O'Ronan) to Cabezbort, a hillside intermediate between the point where Obispo was expected
and the left of the two other Valencian divisions. The left wing
had allotted to it the whole of the Murcian horse, 800 sabres,
and one of the two Valencian cavalry brigades, under General
San Juan, which was of about the same strength. It had also
18 guns.

So much for the left wing. The right wing, conducted by
Blake in person, which had advanced up the high-road from
Valencia towards Murviedro, consisted of the two ' Expeditionary Divisions ' of Zayas and Lardizabal, both very weak
because of the losses which they had suffered in the campaign
around Baza in August—each was eight battalions strong ;
but the former had only 2,500, the latter 3,000 men, so that the
units averaged well under 400 bayonets. But these were good
old troops, which had greatly distinguished themselves at
Albuera : they were the only part of Blake's army in which
any real confidence could be placed. In support of these
veterans the Commander-in-Chief brought up the Valencian
' Division of Reserve,' which consisted entirely of the newly
raised 3rd battalions of the regiments serving with Villacampa
and Miranda. They had only been under arms a few months,
were not fully equipped or clothed, and were dreadfully under-
officered ; for five strong battalions, of over 700 bayonets each,

---

[1] We are luckily in possession of the exact ' morning state ' of Blake's
army, which is printed in the rare Spanish government publication of
1822, *Estados de la Organizacion y Fuerza de los Ejercitos Españoles*,
pp. 184–7. Obispo had 3,400 men, Miranda 4,000, Villacampa 3,350,
Mahy 4,600 infantry, under Montijo and Creagh, and 830 horse. This wing
had 2 horse- and 2 field-batteries, 18 guns.

there were only 75 officers in all—fifteen per battalion, where
there should have been thirty, and these were the mere leavings
of the older units of each regiment, or else newly gazetted
ensigns. As a fighting force these 3,500 men were nearly
useless—and Blake put them where they were least likely to
get into trouble. They were divided into two brigades :
Brigadier-General Velasco seems to have been in command,
vice Acuña, who had the division during the autumn. The
right column was accompanied by the handful of horse belonging to the ' Expeditionary Force '—300 sabres under General
Loy—and by the second Valencian Cavalry Brigade under
General Caro, some 800 mounted men more. It was accompanied, like the other wing, by three batteries. Thus, counting
its gunners and sappers, the right wing had under 10,500 men,
while the immensely strong left had over 17,000. But it is
quality rather than mere numbers which counts in war—the
weak wing fought a good battle against equal strength, and
looked for a moment as if it might win. The strong wing
disgraced itself, and was routed by a fourth of its own numbers.

Suchet had been somewhat troubled by the first news of
Blake's sudden sally from Valencia, for though he desired a
battle, wherein success would probably win him the immediate
surrender of the hard-pressed garrison of Saguntum, yet he did
not wish that matters should be forced to a crisis in Palombini's
absence. It was only after the well-timed return of that
general to his camp, that he welcomed the approach of a decisive
action. But with Palombini at his disposition again, he was
eager to fight.

He had at this moment with him, in the lines before Saguntum, 35 battalions of foot (of which the three Neapolitan units
under Compère were mere skeletons, with little over a thousand
men between them), with 15 squadrons of horse and 36 field-
guns. He left behind him, to maintain the siege-works before
the fortress, two battalions of the 117th line from Habert's
division, and Balathier's Italian brigade, making four battalions
more. The weak Neapolitan brigade of Compère, only 1,400
men, even with its cavalry included, was placed in support of
the blockading force, at Gillet and Petres, to watch the road
from Segorbe, by which some outlying Spanish detachment

might possibly attempt to communicate with the garrison of Saguntum. This left for the line of battle 26 battalions—six of Habert's, eleven of Harispe's, four of Palombini's Italians, and five of Robert's reserve brigade. The total amounted to about 12,000 infantry, while the whole of the cavalry, except the two Neapolitan squadrons, was put in the field to the amount of some 1,800 sabres. Counting the gunners of the six batteries of artillery, Suchet's fighting force was not much over 14,000 men. He had left 4,000, besides the gunners of the siege-train and the sappers, to deal with the garrison of Saguntum. This was little more than half of Blake's numbers, for the Spanish general— as we have seen—was marching forward with 27,000 men in line. That Suchet gladly took the risk sufficiently shows his opinion of the quality of the greater part of the Valencian army. It seems, we must confess, rather hazardous to have left 4,000 men in the blockading corps, when forces were so unequal. In a similar case Beresford at Albuera took every man out of the trenches, and fought with his whole army. Andriani's garrison was not numerous enough to execute any really dangerous sally in the rear, and was so constricted, in its precipitous fastness, that it could not easily come down or deploy itself. Perhaps Suchet may have feared, however, that it would take the opportunity of absconding by some postern, if it were not shut in upon all sides. But there were to be moments during the battle when the Marshal would gladly have had the assistance of two or three more battalions of steady troops.

Suchet had chosen for his fighting-ground the narrow plain south of Saguntum, extending from the sea to the foot of the hills of the Sancti Espiritus range—a space of less than three miles in very flat ground. It was open for the most part, but sprinkled in certain sections with olives and carob-trees, and contained one or two slight eminences or mounds, which rose above the general surface, though only by a score or two of feet, so that they had a certain command over the adjoining flats. The left of the line, nearest to the sea, was formed of Habert's imperfect division, which, having detached two battalions for the blockade of Saguntum, had only six left— 2,500 bayonets—in line. The right consisted of Harispe's

division, which was stronger than Habert's, as it had nine
battalions in line, even after setting aside one regiment (the 44th)
for a flank-guard. Its force was about 3,600 bayonets. This
division lay to the right of the road from Murviedro to Valencia.
The reserve consisted of the Italian brigade (that of Saint Paul),
which had not been told off for the siege, and of the three French
cavalry regiments, in all 2,000 bayonets and 1,300 sabres. It
was drawn up half a mile in rear of Habert and Harispe, ready
to support either of them. The batteries, horse and foot,
accompanied their respective divisions.

We have thus accounted for 10,000 men. The remainder of
Suchet's fighting force constituted a flank-guard, to prevent
his line from being turned on its right, the side of the hills. It
originally consisted of Robert's ' reserve brigade,' five battalions,
or 2,500 bayonets, and of one cavalry regiment, Schiazzetti's
Italian dragoons—450 sabres—with one battery. These troops
were drawn up on the higher slopes of the Sancti Espiritus hills,
covering the pass of the same name and the country road which
goes over it. To these Suchet added, at the last moment, one
regiment from Harispe's division, the 44th, under the Brigadier
Chlopiski, who, being senior to Robert, took command of the
whole flank-guard. These two battalions—1,200 men—took
post on the hill-slopes to the left of Robert, half-way between
his position and that of Harispe's right. The whole force,
including the dragoons and the artillery, made about 4,300 men.
Compère's Neapolitans were too far to their left rear to be
reckoned an appreciable support, and had their own separate
task, though they were never called upon to discharge it. The
ground occupied by Chlopiski's 4,300 men was exceedingly
strong, and the Marshal hoped that they might be relied upon
to hold off the turning movement, which he was aware was
to be made against his inland flank. For he knew that Charles
O'Donnell was advancing from the direction of Betera, which
could only mean a projected attack on his own right. Had
he realized that not only O'Donnell, but also Obispo and
Mahy's Murcians, in all some 17,000 men, were about to operate
against Chlopiski, he must surely have strengthened his covering force, for the odds would have been impossible if the
Valencians had made any fight at all. But they did not !

On the morning of the 25th of October Suchet was ready to receive the attack which was impending. He could make out the general dispositions of the enemy, and the concentric advance of Obispo's, O'Donnell's, and Blake's own men was duly reported to him. It was on receiving notice of the heavy appearance of the second, or central, hostile column that he detached Chlopiski's two battalions to strengthen Robert's flank-guard. Presently, about 7 o'clock, the Spaniards came within touch ; the left, it would seem, somewhat before the right [1], the first shots being interchanged between the two battalions which Mahy had sent towards Cabezbort and Robert's troops. This was only a trifling skirmish, the Spaniards being completely checked. But soon after a serious attack was delivered.

The next advance was that of the two Valencian divisions under Charles O'Donnell, who were a long way ahead of the main body of Mahy's Murcians, their destined reserve. Blake's intention was apparently to strike with his left wing first, and to force in the French right before his own column delivered its blow. Everything depended on the successful action of the mass of Valencian and Murcian infantry against the small hostile force posted on the slopes of the Sancti Espiritus hills.

The divisions of Miranda and Villacampa duly descended from the lower opposite heights of the Germanels, crossed the bottom, and began to mount the opposing slope, Villacampa on the left, somewhat in advance, Miranda a little to his right

[1] There are terrible difficulties as to the timing of the battle of Saguntum. Suchet says that the first engagement was between Obispo's flanking division, coming over the hills on the west, and Robert. Schepeler says that Obispo arrived too late altogether, and was practically not in the fight (p. 472). I think that the explanation is that Suchet took O'Ronan's two battalions for Obispo, because they came from the direction where he was expected. I follow, in my timing of the battle, the very clear narrative of Vacani (v. pp. 440–1), who seems to make it clear that the main fighting on the French right was well over before that in the centre, and long before that on the left. Schepeler (who rode with Blake that day) also makes it certain that Lardizabal and Zayas were fighting long after Miranda, Villacampa, and Mahy had been disposed of. But difficulties remain, which could only be cleared up if we had a report by Obispo. General Arteche thinks that the action began fairly simultaneously all along the line, and follows Schepeler in saying that Obispo was late (xi. p. 174), the very reverse of Suchet's statement that he came, and was beaten, too early.

rear : behind them in support marched San Juan's Valencian cavalry. Beyond the latter there was a considerable gap to the nearest troops of Blake's own column, which had not yet come into action. Mahy, whose orders definitely said that he was to act as a reserve, and to protect O'Donnell's flank if the latter were checked, occupied the Germanels, when the Valencians had gone on, and was still at the top of his own slope, having to his left front the two detached battalions at Cabezbort under O'Ronan, when the clash came. Waiting till the two Valencian divisions and the cavalry in support were some little way up the hill, and had begun to drive in his skirmishers, Chlopiski moved down upon them with the whole of his modest force—Robert's five battalions in front, to the right of the pass and the road, his own two battalions of the 44th to its left and somewhat on the flank. Meanwhile Schiazzetti's regiment of Italian dragoons charged down the gap between the two bodies of infantry. As Villacampa was somewhat ahead of Miranda, the first crash fell upon him. Robert's infantry drove him without any difficulty right downhill, while the Italian dragoons rode at Miranda's battalions on his right. Villacampa's men fell into hopeless confusion, but what was worse was that Miranda's division, seeing their comrades break, gave way before the cavalry without making any resistance whatever, apparently before the French 44th had even got into touch with them on the flank. This was a disgraceful business : the 7,000 Valencian infantry, and the 1,700 cavalry in support, were routed in ten minutes by half their own numbers—one good cavalry regiment of 450 sabres sufficed to upset a whole division of seven battalions—if a single one of them had formed a steady square, the Italian horse ought to have been driven off with ease !

But this was not the end of the affair. San Juan's horse were close behind the routed divisions—O'Donnell ordered them up to save the wrecks of his infantry : at the same time Mahy hurried forward two battalions of his Murcians [1] to support San Juan, and began to advance with the rest of his division down the slope of the Germanels hill.

After making havoc of the Valencian foot, Chlopiski had

[1] Burgos and Tiradores de Cadiz.

halted his troops for a moment, wishing to be sure that matters were going well with the French main body before he committed himself to any further enterprise. But the temptation to go on was too great, for the routed Spanish troops and their supports were weltering together in confusion at the bottom of the hill. It is said that the dragoon colonel, Schiazzetti, settled the matter for his superior, by charging at San Juan's horse the moment that he had got his squadrons re-formed. The Valencian cavalry, though it outnumbered the Italians by two to one, turned tail at once and bolted, riding over the two battalions of Murcian infantry which were in its immediate rear, and carrying them away in its panic. Chlopiski then led on his seven battalions against the disordered mass in front of him, and swept the whole before him. It gave way and fled uphill, horse and foot, the Murcian cavalry brigade in reserve going off on the same panic-stricken way as the Valencian. It was some time before Mahy could get a single regiment to stand—but at last he found a sort of rearguard of two battalions (one of his own, one of Villacampa's [1]) which had kept together and were still capable of obeying orders. The French were now exhausted ; the infantry could not follow in regular formation so fast as their enemy fled ; the handful of cavalry was dispersed, driving in prisoners on every side. So Mahy and O'Donnell ultimately got off, with their men in a horde scattered over the country-side—the cavalry leading the stampede and the two rallied battalions bringing up the rear [2]. The Spanish left wing lost over 2,000 prisoners, mainly from Miranda's division, but only some 400 killed and wounded ; several guns from the divisional batteries were of course lost. All this was over so early in the day that the fighting on Blake's right wing was at its hottest just when the wrecks of his left were disappearing over the hills. Obispo, who came up too late to help,[3] and the two detached battalions under O'Ronan got off separately, more towards the north, retiring on Naquera.

The tale of this part of the battle of Saguntum is lamentable.

---

[1] Cuenca and Molina.

[2] O'Ronan's two battalions went off in a separate direction, unpursued, and joined Obispo, not being in the rout.

[3] See above, page 36.

There is no record so bad in the whole war : even the Gebora was a well-contested fight compared with this—and at Belchite the army that fled so easily gave way before numbers equal or superior to its own, not inferior in the proportion of one to three. The fact was that the Valencian troops had a long record of disasters behind them, were thoroughly demoralized, and could not be trusted for one moment, and that the Murcians (as Mahy confessed) were not much better. The defeat was rendered more shameful by the fact that the smaller half of Blake's Army, the ' Expeditionary Force,' was at the same moment making head in good style against numbers rather larger than its own, and seemed for a moment about to achieve a splendid success. If the Spanish left, 17,000 strong, could have ' contained ' half its own strength, if it could have kept 8,000 instead of 4,000 French employed for one hour, Blake might have relieved Saguntum and driven off Suchet. But the story is disgraceful. Mahy wrote next morning to Blake, ' I must tell you, with my usual bluntness, that you had better sell the horses of this cavalry, and draft the men into the infantry. I could not have believed in the possibility of such conduct, if I had not seen it with my own eyes take place and cost us so much [1].' Blake actually gave orders for one hussar regiment (a Murcian one) to be deprived of its horses and drafted out. But did the infantry behave much better ?

We may now turn to a less depressing narrative, the story of the operations of Blake's own wing. The Commander-in-Chief, as it will be remembered, had with him the ' Expeditionary Divisions,' the Valencian Reserve Division, and Loy's and Caro's 1,100 cavalry. He took post himself on the height called El Puig, with one brigade of the Valencians, to the south of the ravine of the Picador, which crosses the plain in a diagonal direction. The rest of the troops went forward in two columns : Zayas formed the right near the sea ; his flank was covered by a squadron of gunboats, which advanced parallel with him, as near the shore as their draught permitted. He was ordered to push on and get, if possible, round Suchet's flank, where Habert's line was ' refused,' because of the guns of the flotilla, whose fire the French wished to avoid. If successful

[1] Quoted in Arteche, xi. p. 178.

Zayas was to try to communicate with the garrison of Saguntum. Further inland Lardizabal's division, accompanied by
the 1,100 cavalry, and followed by the other brigade of the Valencian reserve, crossed the Picador at the bridge on the *chaussée*,
and deployed in the plain, directly opposite Harispe's division.
The whole force was about equal to the French opposed to it.

The two ' Expeditionary Divisions ' went forward in good
order and with great confidence : Suchet remarks in his
Mémoires that in all his previous campaigns he had never seen
Spanish troops advance with such resolution or in such good
order [1]. Zayas, on the sea-flank, became immediately engaged
with Habert, before the village of Puzzol, in a heavy fight, with
exactly equal numbers—each had about 2,500 men. Both
sides lost heavily, and neither had any advantage : Suchet had
ordered Habert not to take the offensive till matters were
settled in the centre, but the defensive proved costly, and the
Spaniards pushed on—these were the same battalions which
had behaved so well on the hill of Albuera—Irlanda, Patria, and
the Spanish and Walloon Guards.

Further to the left Lardizabal had deployed, after crossing
the ravine, with his two weak brigades in line ; the Valencian
reserve remained behind near the bridge, but Loy's and Caro's
cavalry came forward on the right in support. Opposite the front
brigade (Prieto's) was a long low mound, the last outlying spur
of the Sancti Espiritus range. This was soon seen by both sides to
be a point of vantage—the army that could occupy it would have
a good artillery position commanding the hostile line. Suchet
ordered up Harispe's right battalions to seize it, and galloped
thither in person at the head of his escort of fifty hussars.
But the Spaniards had also marked it, and the Marshal had
hardly reached its top when he found Prieto's skirmishers
swarming up the slope. He had to retire, and rode back to
bring up his infantry ; but, by the time that they had come
forward, the enemy had formed a hasty line of battle along the
mound, with a battery in its centre. Suchet had therefore to
attack—which he did in full force, the four battalions of the
7th Line forming a heavy column in the centre, while those of
the 116th and the 3rd of the Vistula deployed on each side

[1] *Mémoires*, ii. p. 182.

somewhat to the rear—a clear instance of the use of the *ordre mixte* which Napoleon loved. The left flank was covered by two squadrons of the 4th Hussars and one of the 13th Cuirassiers, brought out from the reserve.

This was bringing 3,600 bayonets to bear against 1,500, for Prieto's brigade counted no more upon the mound. The attack was successful, but not without severe loss : General Paris, leading on the 7th regiment, was wounded, as were both his aides-de-camp, and Harispe's horse was killed under him ; the Spanish artillery fire had been deadly. When the mound was stormed, the Spanish infantry were forced back, but by no means in disorder. They formed up again not far from its foot, and Lardizabal brought up his second brigade to support his first, placed two batteries in line, and stood to fight again. Suchet, having re-formed Harispe's men, found that he had before him a second combat on the flat ground. The infantry on both sides were heavily engaged, and six French guns had been brought forward to enfilade Lardizabal's right, when a new turn was given to the battle. The Spanish general ordered Loy's and Caro's 1,100 cavalry to charge in mass upon the three squadrons of hussars and cuirassiers which covered Harispe's left. The move was an unexpected one, and was concealed for some time by scattered carob-trees : the attack was well delivered, and the French horse, outnumbered by more than two to one, were completely routed and fled in disorder. Loy then wheeled in upon the French flank, captured three guns of the battery there placed, and nearly broke the 116th of the Line, which had only just time to fall back and form itself *en potence* to the rest of the division. The remainder of the Spanish cavalry pursued the retreating hussars.

The moment looked black for the Marshal : he himself confesses in his *Mémoires* that if Harispe's infantry had given way the battle might have been lost [1]. But he had still a reserve : he sent back orders to Palombini to bring up Saint Paul's four Italian battalions into the gap, and rode himself to the two squadrons of the 13th Cuirassiers which had not yet advanced into the fight. They were only 350 sabres, but the regiment was a fine one, and had won, at Margalef and other fields, a great

[1] *Mémoires*, ii. p. 185.

confidence in its ability to face long odds. They were launched straight at the victorious Spanish cavalry, whose main body was advancing in great disorder, and with its line broken by the groves of carob-trees, while the remainder had turned inward against the French infantry. The cuirassiers went straight through the squadrons opposed to them, and swept them away : whereupon even those units of the Spanish horse which had not been attacked wheeled round, and retreated hastily toward the Picador ravine and its bridge. The cuirassiers followed, up-setting everything in their front, and only halted on the edge of the ravine, where they were checked by the fire of the battery attached to the Valencian reserve, and the skirmishers of that body, who had lined the farther edge of the depression [1]. Both the Spanish brigadiers, Loy and Caro, had behaved very gallantly ; both were severely wounded, while trying to rally their men, and were left on the field as prisoners.

The defeat of the Spanish horse settled the day, which had for a moment looked doubtful. At the sight of the French hussars breaking, and the advance of their own line, the garrison of Saguntum, who had the whole field in view from their lofty perch, had lined their walls, cheering and waving their shakos in the air—despite of the shells from the siege-batteries which continued to play upon them. The cheers died down as the changed fortunes of the day became visible, and hearts sank in the fortress. But the fighting was not yet concluded.

The rout of Loy's and Caro's horse had not directly affected Lardizabal's infantry, for the victorious cuirassiers had galloped

---

[1] This account of the charge of the cuirassiers comes from the *Mémoires* of Colonel de Gonneville, who commanded their leading squadron. There is a curious point to be settled here. Marshal Suchet says (*Mémoires*, ii. p. 185) that he rode in person to the head of the regiment, and harangued it shortly on Margalef and other ancient glories, before bidding it charge. While speaking he was struck by a spent ball on the shoulder. But de Gonneville (who had read Suchet's book, as he quotes it in other places) says distinctly (p. 208 of his *Souvenirs militaires*) that he received no orders, and charged on his own responsibility. ' N'ayant là d'ordre à recevoir de personne, mais comprenant la nécessité d'arrêter cette masse de cavalerie qui arrivait à nous, &c. . . . je donnai le signal.' Was Suchet romancing about his little speech ? Or was de Gonneville, who wrote his *Mémoires* forty years later, oblivious ? Either hypothesis is difficult.

straight before them after the fugitives, though they had
also ridden over and captured a Spanish battery on the right
of the line of deployed battalions. The decisive blow in this
quarter was given by Saint Paul's Italians, who, issuing from
olive groves behind Harispe's left, came in upon the unprotected flank of Lardizabal's troops, which they rolled up,
driving away at the same time a few squadrons which had not
been affected by the charge of the cuirassiers. These last rode
in among their own infantry, which was already hotly engaged
with Harispe's battalions, and carried confusion down the line.
The division, which had hitherto fought most gallantly, gave
way, and retired in confusion towards the bridge over the
Picador, and the Cartuja where Lardizabal hoped to sustain
himself by means of the battery and the Valencian reserve
battalions which he left there.

Meanwhile Blake, from the summit of the knoll of El Puig,
had witnessed with impotent grief the rout of his right centre.
He had placed himself so far to the rear that no orders which
he sent reached Lardizabal in time, and the reserve which he had
kept under his own hand, three raw Valencian battalions and
a battery, would have been too weak to save the day, even if
it had not been so far—two miles—from the central focus of the
fight as to make its arrival in time quite impossible. The
General, from the moment that he had given the original order
to advance, exercised no influence whatever on the operations ;
one of his staff says that he sat on his horse in blank and stupid
amazement at the rout, and that some of those who watched
him thought him wanting in personal courage no less than in
decision [1]. But at last he roused himself to issue orders for the
retreat of his broken left and centre towards Valencia, and for
the instant withdrawal of his still intact right wing.

Here Zayas's division stood in a most difficult place, for
though it had been contending on equal terms with Habert's in
front of the village of Puzzol, it is one thing to keep up a standing fight, and another to withdraw from it with a victorious
enemy pushing in upon the flank. However, Zayas ordered his
battalions back, and though pressed by Habert, brought them
in good order across the ravine and back to the height of El Puig,

[1] Schepeler, p. 473.

SAGUNTUM

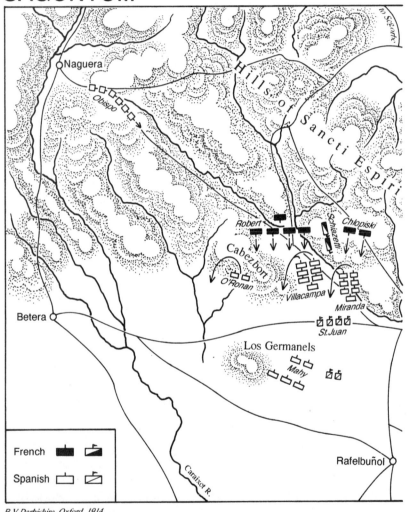

B.V.Darbishire, Oxford, 1914

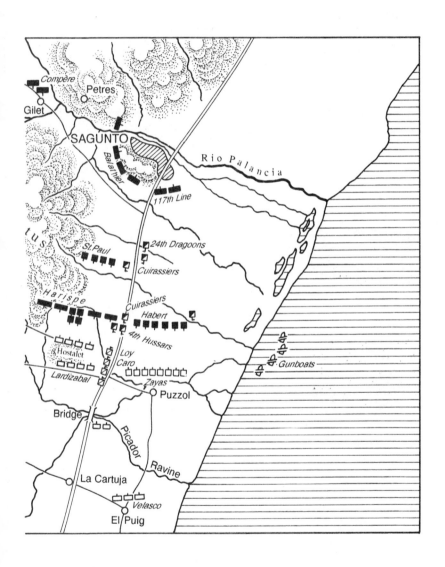

where Blake stood waiting him with his small reserve. Only one corps, the Walloon Guards, had thrown itself into the houses of Puzzol, could not be extracted from them in time, and was surrounded and captured. But this small disaster did much to save the rest of the division, for so many of the French closed in upon the village, where the Walloons made a good stand, that the pursuit was not so hotly pushed as it might have been. If Suchet could have pressed in upon Blake before Zayas joined him, the whole Spanish right column might have been completely cut off from its retreat. But the Marshal required some leisure to rearrange his line, after routing Lardizabal; and by the time that he had sent off the rallied 4th Hussars to help Chlopiski gather in prisoners, and had turned the Italians aside to march against Blake, with Harispe in support, nearly two hours had gone by, and the Spanish right, molested only by Habert, was drawing off towards safety. Following the road along the sea-shore, it reached the suburbs of Valencia without any further loss.

Not so the unfortunate remnant of Lardizabal's troops. They had halted at the Cartuja, behind the Picador, while their general strove to rally them on the reserve there left. This delay, though soldier-like and proper, enabled Suchet to catch them up : he charged them with his last fresh regiment, the 24th Dragoons, which had been kept in hand, apparently behind Habert's position, till the retreat of the Spanish right began. Then, attacking along the high-road, these squadrons broke in upon the half-rallied troops, swept them away, and captured two guns put in battery across the *chaussée*, and badly supported by the Valencian reserve battalions. Lardizabal's column went off in great disorder, and was hunted as far as the Caraixet stream, losing many prisoners to the dragoons, as well as four flags.

So ended the day ; the loss of the Spaniards was not very heavy in killed and wounded—about 1,000 it is said, mainly in Lardizabal's and Zayas's divisions—for the others did not stand to fight. But of prisoners they lost 4,641, including 230 officers and the two wounded cavalry brigadiers. Miranda's division contributed the largest proportion to the captives, though Zayas lost 400 men of the Walloon battalion, and

Lardizabal a still greater number out of his weak division of
3,000 bayonets [1]. Twelve guns were left behind, seven captured in the hard fighting in the right centre, five from O'Donnell's easily-routed divisions. The French casualties are given
by Suchet at about 130 killed and 590 wounded—probably an
understatement, as the regimental returns show 55 officers hit,
which at the ordinary rate of casualties should imply over
1,000 rank and file disabled. As a commentary on the fighting,
it may be remarked that Chlopiski and Robert, in dealing with
Obispo, O'Donnell, and Mahy, had only 7 officers *hors de
combat*, while Harispe and Habert lost 41 in the real fight with
Zayas and Lardizabal [2].

The actual losses in action were not the worst part of the
battle of Saguntum—the real disaster was the plain demonstration that the Valencian troops could not stand even against very
inferior numbers. It was to no purpose that the two gallant
'Expeditionary Divisions' had sacrificed themselves, and lost
one man in three out of their small force of 5,500 men in hard
fighting. They had been betrayed by their worthless associates
on the left. Blake's generalship had not been good—he dispersed his columns in the most reckless way, and kept no
sufficient reserves—but with the odds in his favour of 27,000
men to 14,000, he ought yet to have won, if the larger half of his
army had consented to fight. They did not : with such troops
no more could be hoped from further battles in the open field—
whatever the numerical odds might be. They could at most
be utilized behind walls and entrenchments, for purely passive
defence. And this, as we shall see, was the deduction that their
general made from the unhappy events of October 25.

Next morning Suchet sent in a summons to the garrison of
Saguntum, and the governor, Andriani, after short haggling
for terms, surrendered. He is not to be blamed : his garrison
had seen the rout of Blake's army with their own eyes, and
knew that there was no more hope for them. They were, as

---

[1] 2nd of Badajoz (two battalions) was almost exterminated, losing
17 officers, 21 sergeants, and 500 men, ' mostly prisoners,' out of 800 present.
See its history in the Conde de Clonard's great work on the Spanish army.

[2] The 16th Line (three battalions) alone, in fighting Zayas, lost just
double as many officers as the seven battalions of Chlopiski and Robert
in their engagement with Mahy, Miranda, and Villacampa !

we have seen, mainly raw troops, and their good bearing up to this moment, rather than their demoralization after the battle, should provoke notice. The French approaches were by this time within a few yards of the Dos Mayo redoubt and its hastily patched breaches. The artillery fire of the besiegers was rapidly levelling the whole work, and the next storm, made on a wide front of shattered curtain, must have succeeded. It is true that a governor of the type of Alvarez of Gerona would then have held out for some time in the castle of San Fernando. But Andriani's troops were not like those of Alvarez, and he himself was a good soldier, but not a fanatical genius. Two thousand three hundred prisoners marched out on the 26th, leaving not quite 200 men in hospital behind them. The 17 guns of the fortress were many of them damaged, and the store of shot and shell was very low, though there were plenty of infantry cartridges left [1].

[1] For details see Belmas, iv. pp. 140–3.

SECTION XXX: CHAPTER III

THE CAPTURE OF VALENCIA AND OF BLAKE'S ARMY. NOVEMBER 1811—JANUARY 1812

As the result of the disastrous battle of Saguntum Blake had lost the fortress which had served him so well as an outwork : while his field army was much decreased in numbers, and still more in self-confidence. It was obviously impossible that he should ever again attempt to take the offensive with it. But he was still in possession of Valencia and all its resources, and his carefully fortified lines along the Guadalaviar were so strong that even a defeated army could make some stand behind them. He had still, after all his losses, more than 22,000 men under arms [1]. Yet it is doubtful whether a resolute push on the part of the enemy would not have dislodged him, for more than half his army was in a state of complete demoralization.

Suchet, however, had made up his mind not to strike at once ; and when a few days had passed, and the Spaniards had been granted time to settle down into the lines, it would undoubtedly have been hazardous to attack them with the very modest numbers that the Army of Aragon had still in line. The chance would have been to press the pursuit hard, on the very day after the battle. But when the Marshal had counted up his losses in the trenches and the field, had deducted a small garrison for Saguntum, and had detached a brigade to escort to Tortosa his numerous prisoners, he thought himself too weak for a decisive blow. He would not have had 15,000 men in hand, unless he should call up Ficatier's brigade from Segorbe and Oropesa, and this he did not want to do, as he was entirely dependent for

[1] A battalion or two left in Valencia, when the rest of the army went out to deliver Saguntum, must be added to the 20,000 men who came back from the battle. These corps were 2nd of Leon of Lardizabal's division, and one battalion of Savoya belonging to Miranda.

food and stores on the line of communication which Ficatier was guarding. Accordingly he resolved to defer his next blow at Blake, till he should have summoned from Aragon Severoli's division, and Reille's too, if the Emperor would give him leave to requisition that force. He could not utilize Reille without that leave; but Severoli's troops belonged to his own army, and were at his disposition, if he should judge it possible to draw them southward without endangering the safety of Aragon. This he was prepared to do, if a sufficient garrison for that province could be provided from another source. And the only obvious source was the Army of the North : if the Emperor would consent to order Dorsenne to find troops to make Saragossa and the line of the Ebro secure, it would not be over rash to borrow both Severoli and Reille for operations against Valencia. But it was clear that it would take some weeks for the permission to be sent from Paris, and for the troops of the Army of the North to be moved, when and if the permission was granted. We shall see, as a matter of fact, that it was not till the end of December, two full months after the battle of Saguntum, that the two divisions were collected on the desired ground, and the final blow against Blake was delivered.

Meanwhile Suchet could do no more than place his divisions in the most favourable position for making the advance that would only be possible when Severoli, and perhaps Reille also, should arrive. With this object he pushed them forward on November 3 to the line of the Guadalaviar, close in front of Blake's long series of entrenchments. Harispe on the right advanced to Paterna, Habert on the left to the close neighbourhood of Valencia. He drove the Spanish outposts from the outlying suburb of Serranos, which lay beyond the lines and on the north side of the river, and also from the Grao, or port and mole which forms the outlet of Valencia to the sea. It was most unlucky for Blake, in the end, that his natural line of communication with the Mediterranean and the English fleet lay north of the Guadalaviar, and outside his line of fortifications. Indeed it looks as if there was a cardinal fault in the planning of the defences when the Grao was left outside them, for though rather remote from the city (two miles) it would be of inestimable importance, supposing that the French were to succeed in crossing the Guadalaviar and investing Valencia. With the port safe, the defenders could receive succour and supplies to any extent, and if finally reduced to extremity could retreat by sea. Some of the energy which had been expended in throwing up the immense fortified camp which embraced all the southern suburbs, and in lining the river westward with batteries, might well have been diverted to the fortification of the Grao and its connexion with the works of the city. But probably Blake, in his looking forward to the possible events of the future, did not contemplate among the contingencies to be faced that of his being shut up with the greater part of his army within the walls of Valencia. If he were forced from the lines of the Guadalaviar, he must have intended to fall back inland or southward, and not to allow himself to be surrounded in the capital. Otherwise it would have been absolutely insane for him to leave unfortified, and abandon without a struggle, Valencia's sole outlet to the sea.

Meanwhile finding himself for week after week unassailed in his lines, Blake had to take stock of his position, and see if there was anything that he could do to avert the attack which must come one day, and which would obviously be formidable. For it had become known to him, ere long, that Severoli's division, and probably other troops, were working in towards Valencia, and would certainly join Suchet before the winter was over. The only expedients of which Blake made use were to keep masses of men continuously at work strengthening his lines, and to renew the attempt, which he had made fruitlessly in September, for loosing Suchet's hold on Valencia by launching against his rear the irregulars of Aragon—the bands of the Empecinado, Duran, and the minor chiefs. To add some solidity to their hordes he detached from his army the Conde de Montijo, with one of the two brigades which Mahy had brought from Murcia. This turbulent nobleman, more noted for his intrigues than for his fighting power, was given a general command over all the bands, and marched to join them with three battalions [1] and a few guns—the latter provision

---

[1] One battalion each of Badajoz, Burgos, and Tiradores de Cuenca— under 2,000 men in all.

was intended to obviate the difficulty which the irregulars had experienced in October from their want of artillery. Blake intended to call up Freire from Murcia with another draft from the depleted 'Third Army,' whose best troops Mahy had already led to Valencia. But, as we shall see, this detachment was presently distracted to another quarter, and never joined the main force. The nominal strength of the mass of troops along the Guadalaviar was, however, increased by degrees, owing to the filling of the ranks of the divisions cut up at Saguntum by men from the half-trained reserve and dépôts. Miranda's division in particular, which had lost so many prisoners in the battle, was completed to more than its original strength by absorbing three raw 'third battalions' from the 'Reserve Division,' besides other drafts [1]. Blake also endeavoured to make use of 'urban guards' and other levies of irregular organization and more than doubtful value : the population in the north of the kingdom, behind Suchet's lines, were invited to form guerrillero bands : but the Valencians never showed the zeal or energy of the Catalans and Aragonese. The bands that appeared were few in numbers, and accomplished nothing of note. Indeed, it appears that the patriotic spirit of the province had run low. Mahy, in a letter to Blake of this month, complains bitterly that the peasantry refuse to convey letters for him, or even to give him information as to the position and movements of the French, while he knew that hundreds of them were visiting Suchet's camps daily in friendly fashion [2]. It appears that the people were sick of the war, and discontented with Blake, whose conduct to the local authorities was even more injurious to him than the uniform failure of all his military operations.

The diversion to be conducted by Montijo and the irregulars in Aragon constituted the only real hope of salvation for Blake and the city of Valencia. But it was, we may say, doomed from the first to failure, unless some favourable chance should intervene. A couple of thousand regulars, with the aid of guerrillero bands, hard to assemble, and not mustering at any

---

[1] Four thousand strong at Saguntum, it surrendered on January 8th, 5,513 strong. Of its quality, the less said the better.

[2] Mahy to Blake quoted at length in Arteche, xi. p. 196, footnote.

time more than 6,000 or 7,000 men collected on one spot, were sent to paralyse the movements of more than 20,000 French. For to that figure Reille's and Severoli's divisions, together with the original garrison left in Aragon under Musnier, most certainly amounted. It cannot be denied that the diversion gave much trouble to the enemy, but it never prevented him from executing any operation of primary importance. On October 27th the Italian general, Mazzuchelli, with one of Severoli's brigades, drove off the Empecinado, and relieved the long-besieged garrison of Molina, which he brought off, abandoning the castle. But as he was returning to his chief, who then lay at Daroca, the Empecinado fell on his marching column in the Pass of Cubillejo, and inflicted severe damage upon it [1]. Severoli then sent out a second column of 800 men, to relieve Almunia, on the road to Saragossa, another outlying garrison. But Duran surprised and scattered this party just as it reached its destination, and then captured the fort with its garrison of 140 men (October 31). This provoked the enemy to march against him in force, whereupon, after fighting an obstinate engagement with Mazzuchelli near Almunia, in which the Italians lost 220 men, he turned sideways, and descended upon Daroca, which his adversary had left weakly manned ; he stormed the town and laid siege to the fort. This brought down upon him Pannetier, with one of Reille's brigades : thereupon, wisely refusing to fight, Duran went up into the mountains of Molina (November 1811).

Here he was joined some weeks later by the regular brigade under the Conde de Montijo, which Blake had sent up from Valencia. This little detachment had threaded its way among Reille's columns, and had narrowly escaped destruction near Albarracin. The Conde, assuming chief command at the high-lying village of Mulmarcos, informed the Aragonese guerrilleros that something desperate must be done, to relieve the pressure on Valencia ; and after sending for the Empecinado, who was now beyond the mountains, in the province of Guadalajara, marched on Calatayud. Unfortunately the Partida chiefs, accustomed to conduct their expeditions on their own responsibility, viewed the advent of Montijo, a stranger of no great

[1] For details see Vacani, v. pp. 470–1.

military reputation, with jealousy and dislike. Duran and the Conde having reached Ateca near Calatayud, committed themselves to a serious combat with a column of 2,000 men from its garrison, having every expectation of being succoured by the Empecinado, who had reached their neighbourhood. He did not appear, however, and they were repulsed. Thereupon the Spaniards parted, the Conde and the regulars retiring to Torrehermosa, Duran to Deza, in the province of Soria. The Empecinado, when all was over, sent in a letter in which he explained that he had held off ' because his officers and soldiers had no confidence save in their own chief : ' but it was clear that he himself wrecked the expedition out of self-willed indiscipline.

The month of December was now far advanced, and nothing effective had been done to help Blake. The Aragonese bands had cost Reille and Severoli many toilsome marches, and had inflicted on them appreciable losses—Severoli's division was now 2,000 men weaker than it had been in September. But they had failed entirely to stop the larger movements of the enemy, who was able to move wherever he pleased with a column of 3,000 men, though any lesser force was always in danger of being harried or even destroyed. When Suchet determined that he would again risk trouble in his rear, and would bring both the divisions from the Ebro down to Valencia, no one could prevent him from doing so. It is true that Severoli and Reille were leaving behind them a country-side still infested by an active and obstinate enemy. But if their generalissimo judged that he was prepared to take this risk, and was determined to crush Blake before he completed the subjugation of Upper Aragon, there was nothing that could hinder him from carrying out his intention. By the middle of December Severoli was on his way to the Guadalaviar by way of Teruel, and Reille followed not far behind, though one of his brigades (Bourke's) had been distracted, by being ordered to conduct the prisoners from Saguntum to the French frontier, and the other (Pannetier's) had been drawn so far northward in hunting Montijo and Duran that it was several marches behind the leading columns.

It was not, however, Reille and Severoli alone who were set

in motion for the ruin of Blake and Valencia. Nor was Suchet's mind the final controlling force of the operations which were to spread all over eastern Spain in the months of December 1811 and January 1812. The Emperor, when he hurried the Army of Aragon forward in September, had explained that this was the crucial point of the war, and repeated in November that 'l'important, dans ce moment, est la prise de Valence.' Portugal could wait—Wellington, with 18,000 men sick, and forced to remain on the defensive,—was a negligible quantity during the winter : he should be dealt with in the spring by a general combination of all the French armies [1]. Acting on this comfortable but erroneous hypothesis, Napoleon determined to shift eastward and southward not only Reille and Severoli, but other troops from the armies which were directly or indirectly opposed to Wellington, so as to alter for a time the general balance of forces on the Portuguese side of the Peninsula. On October 18th, before the battle of Saguntum had been fought and won, Berthier had been directed to write to Marmont that, for the support of the invasion of Valencia, King Joseph and the Army of the Centre would be ordered to send troops to Cuenca, to take Blake in the rear. In consequence the Army of Portugal must 'facilitate the task of the King,' i.e. find detachments to occupy those parts of New Castile from which Joseph would have to withdraw the normal garrison for his expedition to Cuenca. But presently it became evident that the Army of the Centre would have great difficulty in providing a column strong enough to make this diversion, even if it were relieved in La Mancha, or the province of Toledo, by units belonging to Marmont. Napoleon then made the all-important determination to borrow troops from the Army of Portugal for the Valencian expedition. By this time he knew of the battle of Saguntum, and had received Suchet's appeals for reinforcements. His dispatch to Marmont of November 20th informs the Marshal that he must provide a division of 6,000 men of all arms, to join the disposable force which King Joseph can spare for the assistance of Suchet. The still more important dispatch of the next day varied the orders

---

[1] *Correspondance de Napoléon*, 18,267, and cf. pp. 590–2 of vol. iv of this work.

in an essential detail, by saying that the Marshal must send not ' a detachment of 6,000 men ' but *such a force as, united to the column supplied by King Joseph, would provide a total of* 12,000 *men for the diversion.*' And it was added that, in addition, the Army of Portugal would have to find 3,000 or 4,000 men more, to keep up the communications of the expeditionary force with its base in New Castile. The detachment might be made without any fear of adverse consequences, since Wellington had 20,000 men in hospital, and barely as many in a state to take the field, so no risk would be run in depleting the force opposed to him [1]. Napoleon, conveniently ignoring the exact wording of his own dispatch, reproached Marmont (when evil results had followed) for having detached ' an army corps and thirty guns ' for the diversion, instead of ' a light flying column [2].' But it will be seen that the Marshal was literally obeying the orders given him when he moved 12,000 men towards Valencia. For the Army of the Centre provided not much more than 3,000 men under General d'Armagnac for the Cuenca expedition [3], and Marmont had, therefore, to find 9,000 men to bring it up to the strength which the Emperor prescribed, as well as the 3,000–4,000 men to cover the line of communications.

All ·these dispatches reached Marmont's head-quarters at Plasencia with the tardiness that was normal in Spain, where officers bearing orders had to be escorted by detachments many hundreds strong, supposing that their certain arrival at their destination was desired. If they travelled rapidly and unescorted, they became the inevitable prey of the guerrilleros. The dispatch of October 18th, saying that Marmont must replace King Joseph's garrisons in La Mancha, came to hand on November 11, and the Marshal accordingly directed Foy's division, then at Toledo, to break itself up and occupy the

---

[1] See these dispatches printed in full in Marmont's *Mémoires*, iv. pp. 256–8. This wording is most important and should be studied with care. Note that Wellington's sick have gone up from 18,000 to 20,000 in twenty-four hours, to oblige the Emperor.

[2] Berthier to Marmont, January 23, 1812. Printed in the latter's *Mémoires*, iv. pp. 297–9.

[3] Though King Joseph had said that if Marmont took over the whole of La Mancha, he could then reinforce d'Armagnac up to 8,000 men. This he never really accomplished (Joseph to Berthier, Nov. 26).

various posts which the German division of the Army of the
Centre had been holding. Foy set out to fulfil these orders
on November 22.

The Emperor's second and third dispatches, those of November 20–21st, turned up on December 13th [1], and Marmont found
himself under orders to find 9,000 men for the Cuenca expedition,
—since d'Armagnac had only 3,000 men to contribute—and in
addition 3,000–4,000 more for the line of communications.
Now the Marshal was as fully convinced as his master that
Wellington was not in a condition to move, or to do any serious
harm, and under this impression, and being probably stirred
(as Napoleon afterwards remarked) [2] by the desire to increase
his own reputation by a dashing feat of arms, he resolved to
take charge of the expedition in person. He ordered that the
divisions of Foy and Sarrut—both weak units, the one of eight,
the other of nine battalions [3]—and Montbrun's light cavalry
should prepare to march under his own charge to join d'Armagnac, and move on Valencia. Another division should come
into La Mancha to take up the cantonments evacuated by Foy,
and keep over the line of communications. Clausel should be
left in charge of the remainder of the army, and observe
Wellington.

This scheme was never carried out, for on December 20
Marmont received another dispatch, ordering him to transfer
his head-quarters to Valladolid, and to move a large part of his
army into Old Castile. Of this more hereafter. But being thus
prevented (for his own good fortune as it turned out) from going
on the expedition, he gave over Foy's and Sarrut's divisions
to Montbrun, and bade him execute the diversion. He himself
went, as ordered, to Valladolid. If he had received the last
dispatch a little later, or had started a little earlier, he would
have been put in the ignominious position of being absent
from his own point of danger, when Wellington suddenly struck
at Ciudad Rodrigo in the early days of January.

---

[1] Date fixed by Marmont's letter to Berthier of Feb. 6.

[2] ' Sa Majesté (writes Berthier) pense que, dans cette circonstance, vous
avez plus calculé votre gloire personnelle que le bien de son service,'
Jan. 23, letter quoted above on the last page.

[3] Each division had about 4,000 or 4,500 men : the light cavalry about
1,700, so the whole would have made about 10,000 sabres and bayonets.

Montbrun, his substitute, had drawn together his forces in La Mancha by the 29th of December, but receiving from d'Armagnac, who was already on the move with 3,000 men, the assurance that the road from Cuenca to Valencia was practically impassable at midwinter, and that he could certainly get no guns along it, he resolved to take another route towards the scene of active operations. Accordingly he set out to march by the road San Clemente, Chinchilla, Almanza, which runs across the upland plain of La Mancha and Northern Murcia, and does not cross rough ground till it nears the descent to the sea-coast on the borders of Valencia. The column did not leave San Clemente and El Probencio till January 2, and (as we shall see) was too late to help Suchet, who had brought matters to a head long before it drew near him.

Meanwhile d'Armagnac, though his force was trifling [1], had been of far greater use. He had reoccupied Cuenca, but finding (as he had informed Montbrun) that the roads in that direction were impracticable, had swerved southward, avoiding the mountains, and getting to Tarazona in La Mancha, marched towards the passes of the Cabriel River, and the road on to Valencia by way of Requeña. His approach being reported to Blake, who had no troops in this direction save two battalions under Bassecourt, the Captain-General was seized with a natural disquietude as to his rear, for he had no accurate knowledge of the French strength. Wherefore he directed General Freire, with the succours which he had been intending to draw up from Murcia, to abandon the idea of reinforcing the main army, and to throw himself between d'Armagnac and Valencia [November 20]. The French general, beating the country on all sides, and thrusting before him Bassecourt's small force and the local guerrilleros, marched as far as Yniesta, and forced the passage of the Cabriel at Valdocañas, but finding that he had got far away from Montbrun, who did not march till many days after he himself had started, and being informed that Freire, with a very large force, was coming in upon his

[1] Apparently four or five battalions of the German division gathered from La Mancha, and a brigade of dragoons. Joseph calls it in his *Correspondance* 3,000 men, when describing this operation (Joseph to Berthier, Nov. 12, 1811).

rear, he stopped before reaching Requeña and turned back towards La Mancha [1]. He had succeeded, however, in preventing Freire from reinforcing Valencia, and the Murcian succours never got near to Blake. He even for a time distracted troops from the main Spanish army, for Zayas was sent for some days to Requeña, and only returned just in time for the operations that began on December 25th. The net outcome, therefore, of Montbrun's and d'Armagnac's operations was simply to distract Freire's division from Valencia at the critical moment— an appreciable but not a decisive result.

Meanwhile Suchet found himself able to deliver his decisive blow on the Guadalaviar. By his orders Severoli and Reille had drawn southward by way of Teruel, deliberately abandoning most of Aragon to the mercy of the insurgent bands ; for though Caffarelli had moved some battalions of the Army of the North to Saragossa and the posts along the Ebro, the rest of the province was left most inadequately guarded by the small force that had originally been committed to Musnier's charge, when first Suchet marched on Valencia. Musnier himself accompanied Severoli's division, leaving his detachments under Caffarelli's orders, for he had been directed to come to the front and assume the command of his old brigades, those of Ficatier and Robert, both now with the main army. When Reille and the Italians marched south, Aragon was exposed to the inroads of Montijo, Duran, the Empecinado, and Mina, all of whom had been harried, but by no means crushed, by the late marches and countermarches of the French. That trouble would ensue both Napoleon and Suchet were well aware. But the Emperor had made up his mind that all other considerations were to be postponed to the capture of Valencia and the destruction of Blake's army. When these ends were achieved, not only Reille and Severoli, but other troops as well, should be drawn northwards, to complete the pacification of Aragon, and to make an end of the lingering war in Catalonia.

Severoli had reached Teruel on November 30, but was ordered to await the junction of Reille's troops, and these were still

---

[1] D'Armagnac's obscure campaign will be found chronicled in detail in the narrative of the Baden officer, Riegel, iii. pp. 357–60, who shared in it along with the rest of the German division from La Mancha.

far off. Indeed Reille himself only started from Saragossa with Bourke's brigade on December 10th, and Pannetier's brigade (which had been hunting Duran in the mountains) was two long marches farther behind. Without waiting for its junction, Severoli and Reille marched from Teruel on December 20th, and reached Segorbe unopposed on the 24th. Here they were in close touch with Suchet, and received orders to make a forced march to join him, as he intended to attack the lines of the Guadalaviar on the 26th. To them was allotted the most important move in the game, for they were to cross the Guadalaviar high up, beyond the westernmost of Blake's long string of batteries and earthworks, and to turn his flank and get in his rear, while the Army of Aragon assailed his front, and held him nailed to his positions by a series of vigorous attacks. The point on which Reille and Severoli were to march was Ribaroja, fifteen miles up-stream from Valencia.

When the two divisions from Aragon should have arrived, Suchet could count on 33,000 men in line, but as Pannetier was still labouring up two marches in the rear, it was really with 30,000 only that he struck his blow—a force exceeding that which Blake possessed by not more than 6,000 or 7,000 bayonets. Considering the strength of the Spanish fortifications the task looked hazardous : but Suchet was convinced, and rightly, that the greater part of the Army of Valencia was still so much demoralized that much might be dared against it : and the event proved him wise.

On the night of December 25th all the divisions of the Army of Aragon had abandoned their cantonments, and advanced towards the Spanish lines—Habert on the left next the sea; Palombini to the west of Valencia, opposite the village of Mislata ; Harispe and Musnier farther up-stream, opposite Quarte. The cavalry accompanied this last column. Reille and Severoli, on their arrival, were to form the extreme right of the line, and would extend far beyond the last Spanish entrenchments. The weak Neapolitan division alone (now not much over 1,000 strong) was to keep quiet, occupying the entrenched position in the suburb of Serranos, which faced the city of Valencia. Its only duty was to hold on to its works, in case Blake should try a sortie at this spot, with the purpose of breaking the French line in two. That such a weak force was left to discharge such an important function, is a sufficient proof of Suchet's belief in Blake's incapacity to take the offensive.

The lines which the French were about to assail were rather long than strong, despite of the immense amount of labour that had been lavished on them during the last three months. Their extreme right, on the side of the sea, and by the mouth of the Guadalaviar was a redoubt (named after the Lazaretto hard by) commanding the estuary : from thence a long line of earthworks continued the defences as far as the slight hill of Monte Oliveto, which guarded the right flank of the great entrenched camp of which the city formed the nucleus. Here there was a fort outside the walls, and connected with them by a ditch and a bastioned line of earthworks, reaching as far as the citadel at the north-east corner of the town. From thence the line of resistance for some way was formed of the mediaeval wall of Valencia itself, thirty feet high and ten thick. It was destitute of a parapet broad enough to bear guns : but the Spaniards had built up against its back, at irregular distances, scaffolding of heavy beams, and terraces of earth, on which a certain amount of cannon were mounted. The gates were protected by small advanced works, mounting artillery. Blake had made Valencia and its three outlying southern and western suburbs of Ruzafa, San Vincente, and Quarte into a single place of defence, by building around those suburbs a great line of earthworks and batteries. It was an immense work consisting of bastioned entrenchments provided with a ditch eighteen feet deep, and filled in some sections with water. From the city the line of defence along the river continued as far as the village of Manises, with an unbroken series of earthworks and batteries. The Guadalaviar itself formed an outer obstacle, being a stream running through low and marshy ground, and diverted into many water-cuts for purposes of irrigation.

The continuous line of defences from the sea as far as Manises was about eight miles long. It possessed some outworks on the farther bank of the Guadalaviar, three of the five bridges which lead from Valencia northward having been left standing by Blake, with good *têtes-de-pont* to protect them from Suchet's attacks. Thus the Spaniards had the power to debouch on to the French side of the river at any time that they pleased. This fact added difficulties to the projected attack which the Marshal was planning.

The troops behind the lines of the Guadalaviar consisted of some 23,000 regulars, with a certain amount of local urban guards and armed peasantry whose number it is impossible to estimate with any precision—probably they gave some 3,000 muskets more, but their fighting value was almost negligible. The right of the line, near the sea, was entirely made over to these levies of doubtful value. Miranda's division manned the fort of Monte Oliveto and the whole north front of the city. Lardizabal garrisoned the earthworks from the end of the town wall as far as the village of Mislata. This last place and its works fell to the charge of Zayas. Creagh's Murcians were on Zayas's left at Quarte : finally the western wing of the army was formed by the Valencian divisions of Obispo and Villacampa; holding San Onofre and Manises, where the fortifications ended. The whole of the cavalry was placed so as to cover the left rear of the lines, at Aldaya and Torrente. A few battalions of the raw ' Reserve Division' were held in the city as a central reserve. The arrangements of Blake seem liable to grave criticism, since he placed his two good and solid divisions, those of Lardizabal and Zayas, in the strongest works in the centre of his line, but entrusted his left flank, where a turning movement by the French might most easily take place, to the demoralized battalions of Villacampa and Obispo, who had a consistent record of rout and disaster behind them. It is clear that lines, however long, can always be turned, unless their ends rest, as did those of Torres Vedras, on an impassable obstacle such as the sea. If the French should refuse to attack the works in front, and should march up the Guadalaviar to far beyond the last battery, it would be impossible to prevent them from crossing, all the more so because, after Manises, the network of canals and water-cuts, which makes the passage difficult in the lower course of the river, comes to an end, and the only obstacle exposed to the invader is a single stream of no great depth. Blake, therefore, should have seen that the critical point was the extreme west end of his lines, and should have placed there

his best troops instead of his worst. Moreover he appears to
have had no proper system of outposts of either cavalry or
infantry along the upper stream, for (as we shall see) the first
passage of the French was made not only without opposition,
but without any alarm being given. Yet there were 2,000
Spanish cavalry only a few miles away, at Torrente and Aldaya.

Suchet's plan of attack, which he carried out the moment
that Reille joined him, and even before the latter's rearmost
brigade had got up into line, was a very ambitious one, aiming
not merely at the forcing of the Guadalaviar or the investment
of Valencia, but at the trapping of the whole Spanish army. It
was conducted on such a broad front, and with such a dispersion
of the forces into isolated columns, that it argued a supreme
contempt for Blake and his generalship. Used against such
a general as Wellington it would have led to dreadful disaster.
But Suchet knew his adversary.

The gist of the plan was the circumventing of the Spanish
lines by two columns which, starting one above and the other
below Valencia, were to cross the river and join hands to the
south of the city. Meanwhile the main front of the works was
to be threatened (and if circumstances favoured, attacked) by
a very small fraction of the French army. Near the sea Habert's
division was to force the comparatively weak line of works at
the estuary, and then to cut the road which runs from Valencia
between the Mediterranean and the great lagoon of the Albufera. Far inland the main striking force of the army, composed of the divisions of Harispe and Musnier, with all the
cavalry, and with Reille's three brigades following close behind,
was to pass the Guadalaviar at Ribaroja, three or four miles
above Manises, and from thence to extend along the south
front of the Spanish lines, take them in the rear, and push on
so as to get into touch with Habert. Compère's weak Neapolitan
brigade was to block the bridge-heads out of which Blake might
make a sally northward. Palombini's Italians were to press
close up to Mislata, which Suchet judged to be the weakest
point in the Spanish lines, and to deliver against it an attack
which was to be pushed more or less home as circumstances
might dictate. The whole force employed (not counting Pannetier's brigade, which had not yet joined Reille) was just

30,000 men. Of these 25,000 were employed in the flanking movements ; less than 5,000 were left to demonstrate against Blake's front along the lines of the Guadalaviar.

The main and decisive blow was of course to be delivered by Harispe, Musnier, and Reille, who were to cross the river at a point where the Spaniards were unlikely to make any serious opposition, since it was outside their chosen ground of defence, and was clearly watched rather than held. If 20,000 men crossed here, and succeeded in establishing themselves south of Valencia by a rapid march, Blake would find his lines useless, and would be forced to fight in the open, in order to secure a retreat southward, or else to shut himself and his whole force up in the entrenched camp around the city. Suchet could accept either alternative with equanimity : a battle, as he judged, meant a victory, the breaking up of the Spanish army and the capture of Valencia. If, on the other hand, Blake refused to fight a general engagement, and retired within his camp, it would lead to his being surrounded, and the desired end would only be deferred for a few days. There were only two dangers—one was that the Spanish general might abscond southward with the bulk of his army, without fighting, the moment that he heard that his enemy was across the Guadalaviar. The second was that, waiting till the French main body was committed to its flank march, he might break out northward by the three bridges in his hands, overwhelm the Neapolitans, and escape towards Liria and Segorbe into the mountains. Suchet judged that his enemy would try neither of these courses ; he would not be timid enough to retreat on the instant that he learnt that his left wing was beginning to be turned ; nor would he be resourceful enough to strike away northward, as soon as he saw that the turning movement was formidable and certain of success. Herein Suchet judged aright.

At nightfall on the 25th–26th of December two hundred hussars, each carrying a voltigeur behind him, forded the Guadalaviar at Ribaroja, and threw out a chain of posts which brushed off a few Spanish cavalry vedettes. The moment that the farther bank was clear, the whole force of Suchet's engineers set to work to build two trestle-bridges for infantry, and to lay a solid pontoon bridge higher up for guns and

cavalry. A few hours later Harispe's division began to pass—
then Musnier's, lastly Boussard's cavalry. The defile took
a long time, and even by dawn Reille's three brigades had not
arrived or begun to pass. But by that time ten thousand
French were over the river. The Spanish vedettes had reported,
both to their cavalry generals at Aldaya and to Blake at
Valencia, that the enemy was busy at Ribaroja, but had not
been able to judge of his force, or to make out that he was
constructing bridges. Their commanders resolved that nothing
could be done in the dark, and that the morning light would
determine the character of the movement [1].

The late December sun soon showed the situation. Harispe's
division was marching on Torrente, to cut the high-road to
Murcia. The cavalry and one brigade of Musnier were preparing
to follow : the other brigade of the second division (Robert's)
was standing fast by the bridges, to cover them till Reille should
appear and cross. But while this was the most weighty news
brought to Blake, he was distracted by intelligence from two
other quarters. Habert was clearly seen coming down by the
seaside, to attack at the estuary; and Palombini was also
approaching in the centre, in front of Mislata. The daylight
was the signal for the commencement of skirmishing on each
of the three far-separated points. Blake, strange as it may
appear, made up his mind at first that the real danger lay on
the side next the sea, and that Habert's column was the main
striking force [2]. But when it became clear that this wing of the
French army was not very strong, and was coming on slowly,
he turned his attention to Palombini, whose attack on Mislata
was made early, and was conducted in a vigorous style. It was
to this point that he finally rode out from the city, and he took
up his position behind Zayas, entirely neglecting the turning
movement on his left—apparently because it was out of sight,
and he could not make the right deduction from the reports
which his cavalry had brought him.

---

[1] So Suchet's narrative (*Mémoires*, ii. pp. 214–15). Belmas says that only
one bridge was finished when Harispe and Musnier passed—the others after
dawn only.

[2] For Blake's opinions and actions see the record of his staff-officer,
Schepeler (pp. 502–3).

Meanwhile Harispe's column, pushing forward with the object of reaching the high-road from Valencia to Murcia, the natural route for Blake's army to take, if it should attempt to escape southward, ran into the main body of the Spanish horse, which was assembling in the neighbourhood of the village of Aldaya. The French infantry were preceded by a squadron of hussars, who were accompanied by General Boussard, the commander of Suchet's cavalry division. This small force was suddenly encompassed and cut up by several regiments of Martin Carrera's brigade. Boussard was overthrown and left for dead—his sword and decorations were stripped from his body. But more French squadrons began to come up, and Harispe's infantry opened fire on the Spaniards, who were soon forced to retire hurriedly—they rode off southward towards the Xucar river. They were soon completely out of touch with the rest of Blake's army.

Harispe's column then continued its way, sweeping eastward towards the Murcian *chaussée* in the manner that Suchet had designed ; but the rest of the operations of the French right wing were not so decisive as its commander had hoped. Mahy, learning of the movement of the encircling column, and seeing Robert's brigade massed opposite the extreme flank of his position at Manises, while some notice of Reille's near approach also came to hand, suddenly resolved that he would not be surrounded, and abandoned all his lines before they were seriously attacked. He had the choice of directing Villacampa and Obispo to retire towards Valencia and join Blake for a serious battle in the open, or of bidding them strike off southward and eastward, and escape towards the Xucar, abandoning the main body of the army. He chose the second alternative, and marched off parallel with Harispe's threatening column, directing each brigade to get away as best it could. His force at once broke up into several fractions, for the cross-roads were many and perplexing. Some regiments reached the Murcian *chaussée* before Harispe, and escaped in front of him, pursued by the French cavalry. Others, coming too late, were forced to forgo this obvious line of retreat, and to struggle still farther eastward, only turning south when they got to the marshy borders of the lagoon of Albufera. Obispo, with 2,000 of his men, was so closely hunted by the hostile cavalry that he barely found safety by striking along the narrow strip of soft ground between the lagoon and the sea. On the morning of the 27th he struggled through to Cullera near the mouth of the Xucar : Mahy, with the greater part of Villacampa's division and some of Obispo's and Creagh's, arrived somewhat earlier at Alcira, higher up the same stream, where he found the fugitive cavalry already established. The divisions were much disorganized, but they had lost very few killed or wounded, and not more than 500 prisoners. Mahy rallied some 4,000 or 5,000 men at Alcira, and Obispo a couple of thousand at Cullera, but they were a ' spent force,' not fit for action. Many of the raw troops had disbanded themselves and gone home.

Thus three-sevenths of Blake's army were separated from Valencia and their Commander-in-Chief without having made any appreciable resistance. But it seems doubtful whether Mahy should be blamed—if he had waited an hour longer in his positions his whole corps might have been captured. If he had retired towards Valencia he would have been, in all probability, forced to surrender with the rest of the army a few days later. And in separating himself from his chief he had the excuse that he knew that Blake's intention had been to retire towards the Xucar if beaten, not to shut himself up in Valencia. He may have expected that the rest of the army would follow him southward, and Blake (as we shall see) probably had the chance of executing that movement, though he did not seize it.

Meanwhile the progress of the engagement in other quarters must be detailed. Palombini made a serious attempt to break through the left centre of the Spanish lines at Mislata. His task was hard, not so much because of the entrenchments, or of the difficulty of crossing the Guadalaviar, which was fordable for infantry, but from the many muddy canals and water-cuts with which the ground in front of him abounded. These, though not impassable for infantry, prevented guns from getting to the front till bridges should have been made for them. The Italians waded through the first canal, and then through the river, but were brought to a stand by the second canal, that of Fabara, behind which the Spanish entrenchments lay. After

VALENCIA

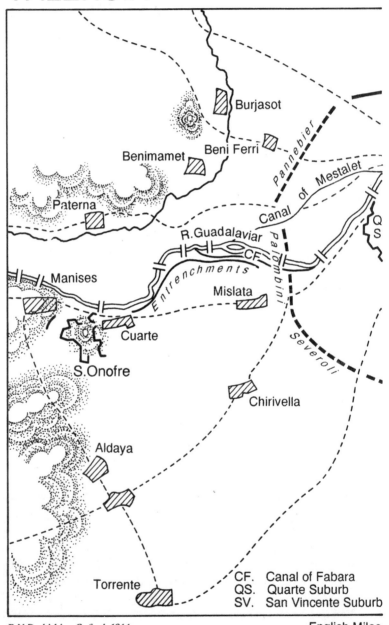

Burjasot

Beni Ferri

Benimamet

Pannebier

Canal of Mestalet

Paterna

R.Guadalaviar

Canal of Mestalet

Palombini

CF.

Entrenchments

Manises

Mislata

Q
S

Cuarte

Severoli

S.Onofre

Chirivella

Aldaya

Torrente

CF.	Canal of Fabara
QS.	Quarte Suburb
SV.	San Vincente Suburb

B.V.Darbishire, Oxford, 1914

English Miles

The Siege (Dec 1811 - Jan 1812)

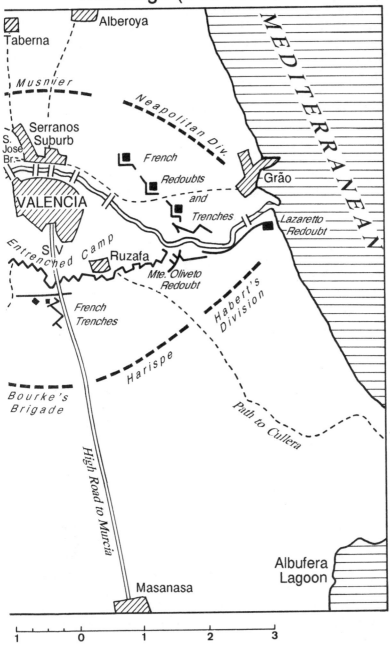

a furious fire-contest they had to retire as far as the river, under whose bank many sought refuge—some plunged in and waded back to the farther side. Palombini rallied them and delivered a second attack ; but at only one point, to the left of Mislata, did the assault break into the Spanish line. Zayas, aided by a battalion or two which Mahy had sent up from Quarte, vindicated his position, and repulsed the attack with heavy loss. But when the news came from the left that Harispe had turned the lines, and when Mahy's troops were seen evacuating all their positions and hurrying off, Zayas found himself with his left flank completely exposed.

Blake made some attempt to form a line *en potence* to Zayas's entrenchments, directing two or three of Creagh's battalions from Quarte and some of his reserve from the city to make a stand at the village of Chirivella. But the front was never formed—attacked by some of Musnier's troops these detachments broke up, Creagh's men flying to follow Mahy, and the others retiring to the entrenched camp.

Thereupon Blake ordered Zayas and Lardizabal, who lay to his right, to retreat into Valencia before they should be turned by the approaching French. The movement was accomplished in order and at leisure, and all the guns in and about the Mislata entrenchments were brought away. Palombini had been too hardly handled to attempt to pursue.

The General-in-Chief seemed stunned by the suddenness of the disaster. ' He looked like a man of stone,' says Schepeler, who rode at his side, ' when any observation was made to him he made no reply, and he could come to no decision. He would not allow Zayas to fight, and when a colonel (the author of this work) suggested at the commencement of the retreat that it would be well to burn certain houses which lay dangerously close to the entrenched camp, he kept silence. Whereupon Zayas observed in bitter rage to this officer : " Truly you are dull, my German friend ; do you not see that you cannot wake the man up ? " ' According to the narratives of several contemporaries there would still have been time at this moment to direct the retreating column southward and escape, as Obispo did, along the Albufera. For Habert (as we shall see) had been much slower than Harispe in his turning movement by the side of the

Mediterranean. Some, among them Schepeler, suggest that the whole garrison might have broken out by the northern bridges and got away. For Palombini was not in a condition to hinder them, and the Neapolitans in front of the bridge-heads were but a handful of 1,200 men. But the General, still apparently unconscious of what was going on about him, drew back into the entrenched camp, and did no more.

Habert, meanwhile, finally completed his movement, and joined hands with Harispe at last. His lateness was to be accounted for not by the strength of the opposition made by the irregular troops in front of him, but by the fact that his advance had been much hindered by the fire of the flotilla lying off the mouth of the Guadalaviar. Here there was a swarm of gunboats supported by a British 74 and a frigate. Habert would not commence his passage till he had driven them away, by placing a battery of sixteen siege-guns on the shore near the Grao. After much firing the squadron sheered off[1], and about midday the French division crossed the Guadalaviar, partly by fording, partly on a hastily constructed bridge, and attacked the line of scattered works defended by irregulars which lay behind. The Spaniards were successively evicted from all of them, as far as the fort of Monte Oliveto. Miranda's division kept within the entrenched camp, and gave no assistance to the bands without; but it was late afternoon before Habert had accomplished his task, and finally got into touch with Harispe.

Blake was thus shut up in Valencia with the divisions of Miranda, Zayas, and Lardizabal, and what was left of his raw reserve battalions : altogether some 17,000 fighting-men remained with him. The loss in actual fighting had been very small—about 500 killed and wounded and as many prisoners. The French captured a good many guns in the evacuated works and a single standard. Suchet returned his total casualties at 521 officers and men, of whom no less than 50 killed and 355 wounded were among Palombini's Italians—the only corps which can be said to have done any serious fighting[2]. The

---

[1] Napier says (iv. p. 30) that the gunboats fled without firing a shot. Suchet and Schepeler speak of much firing, as does Arteche.

[2] No less than three of the Italian colonels were hit, and thirty-four officers in all.

Marshal's strategical combination would have been successful almost without bloodshed, if only Palombini had not pressed his attack so hard, and with so little necessity. But the Spanish army, which was drawn out on a long front of nine miles, without any appreciable central reserve, and with no protection for its exposed flank, was doomed to ruin the moment that the enemy appeared in overwhelming force, beyond and behind its extreme left wing. Blake's only chance was to have watched every ford with great vigilance, and to have had a strong flying column of his best troops ready in some central position, from which it could be moved out to dispute Suchet's passage without a moment's delay. Far from doing this, he tied down his two veteran divisions to the defence of the strongest part of his lines, watched the fords with nothing but cavalry vedettes, and kept no central reserve at all, save 2,000 or 3,000 men of his untrustworthy 'Reserve Division.' In face of these dispositions the French were almost bound to be successful. A disaster was inevitable, but Blake might have made it somewhat less ruinous if he had recognized his real position promptly, and had ordered a general retreat, when Harispe's successful turning movement became evident. In this case he would have lost Valencia, but not his army.

As it was, a week more saw the miserable end of the campaign. Suchet's first precaution was to ascertain whether there was any danger from the fraction of the Spanish army which Mahy and Obispo had carried off. He was uncertain how strong they were, and whether they were prepared to attack him in the rear, supposing that he should sit down to the siege of Valencia. Accordingly he sent out at dawn on the 26th December two light columns of cavalry and voltigeurs against Alcira and Cullera, whither he knew that the refugees had retired. These two reconnaissances in force discovered the enemy in position, but the moment that they were descried Mahy retreated towards Alcoy, and Obispo towards Alicante—both in such haste and disorder that it was evident that they had no fighting spirit left in them.

Suchet, therefore, was soon relieved of any fear of danger from this side, and could make his arrangements for the siege. He sent back to the north bank of the Guadalaviar the whole

division of Musnier, which was there joined three days later by
Reille's belated brigade, that of Pannetier. Harispe, Habert,
Severoli, and Reille's other French brigade (that of Bourke)
formed the investment on the southern bank. Palombini lay
astride of the river near Mislata, with one brigade on each
bank. The whole force of 33,000 men was sufficient for the
task before it. The decisive blow would have to be given by
the siege artillery ; the whole train which had captured Saguntum had long been ready for its work. And it had before it not
regular fortifications of modern type, but, in part of the circumference of Blake's position, mediaeval walls not built to resist
artillery, in the rest the ditch and bank of the entrenched camp,
which, though strong as a field-work, could not be considered
capable of resisting a formal attack by a strong siege-train.

Blake was as well aware of this as Suchet, and he also knew
(what Suchet could not) that the population of 100,000 souls
under his charge had only 10 days' provision of flour and 19 or
20 of rice and salt fish. The city, like the army, had been
living on daily convoys from the south, and had no great
central reserves of food. If he should sit down, like Palafox
at Saragossa, to make an obstinate defence behind improvised
works, he would be on the edge of starvation in less than three
weeks. But such a defence was impossible in face of the spirit
of the people, who looked upon Blake as the author of all their
woes, regarded him as a tyrant as well as an imbecile, and were
as likely to rise against him as to turn their energies to resisting
the French. Palafox at Saragossa accomplished what he did
because the spirit of the citizens was with him : Blake was
despised as well as detested.

When he recovered his composure he called a council of war,
which voted almost unanimously[1] that the city was indefensible,
and that the army must try to cut its way out on the north
side of the Guadalaviar. If the sally had been made on the 27th
it might have succeeded, for it was not till late on that day
that Suchet's arrangements for the blockade of the north bank
were complete. But the investing line had been linked up

---

[1] Only Miranda voted against a sortie, and thought that nothing could
be done, except to hold out for a while in the walls and then surrender.
Arteche, xi. p. 241.

by the night of the 28th–29th, when Blake made his last stroke
for safety. At six in the evening the field army issued from
the gate of St. José and began to cross the bridge opposite it,
the westernmost of the three of which the Spaniards were in
possession. This led not to the great *chaussée* to Saguntum
and Tortosa, which was known to have been cut and entrenched
by the enemy, but to the by-road to Liria and the mountains.
Lardizabal headed the march, Zayas followed, escorting the
artillery and a considerable train, Miranda brought up the rear.
Charles O'Donnell was left to man the walls with the urban
guards and the ' Reserve Division,' and was given permission to
capitulate whenever he should be attacked.

Lardizabal's vanguard, under a Colonel Michelena, swerved
from the Liria road soon after passing the Guadalaviar, in order
to avoid French posts, and successfully got as far as the canal
of Mestalla before it was discovered or checked. The canal
was too broad to be passed by means of some beams and planks
which had been brought up. But Michelena got his men across,
partly by fording and partly over a mill-dam, and presently
got to the village of Burjasort, where the artillery of Palombini's
division were quartered. These troops, surprised in the dark,
could not stop him, and he pushed on through them and
escaped to the hills with his little force—one squadron, one
battalion, and some companies of Cazadores—some 500 or
600 men [1]. Lardizabal, who should have followed him without
delay, halted at the canal, trying to build a bridge, till the
French all along the line were alarmed by the firing at Burjasort
and began to press in upon him. He opened fire instead of
pushing on at all costs, and presently found himself opposed by
forces of growing strength. Blake thereupon made up his mind
that the sally had failed, and gave orders for the whole column
to turn back and re-enter Valencia. It seems probable that
at least a great part of the army might have got away, if an
attempt had been made to push on in Michelena's wake, for
the blockading line was thin here, and only one French regiment
seems to have been engaged in checking Lardizabal's exit.

---

[1] Not 5,000 as Napier (probably by a misprint) says on page 31 of his
4th vol. Apparently a misprint in the original edition has been copied in
all the later fourteen !

Be this as it may, the sortie had failed, and Blake was faced by complete ruin, being driven back with a disheartened army into a city incapable of defence against a regular siege, and short of provisions. Next morning the despair of the garrison was shown by the arrival of many deserters in the French camp. The inevitable end was delayed for only eleven days more. On January 1, most of the siege-guns having been brought across the Guadalaviar, Suchet opened trenches against two fronts of the entrenched camp, the fort of Monte Oliveto and the southern point of the suburb of San Vincente, both salient angles capable of being battered from both flanks. Seven batteries were built opposite them by January 4th, and the advanced works in front were pushed up to within fifty yards of the Spanish works. Thereupon Blake, before the siege-guns had actually opened, abandoned the whole of his entrenched camp on the next day, without any attempt at defence. The French discovering the evacuation, entered, and found eighty-one guns spiked in the batteries, and a considerable quantity of munitions.

Blake was now shut up in the narrow space of the city, whose walls were very unsuited for defence, and were easily approachable in many places under shelter of houses left undemolished, which gave cover only fifty yards from the ramparts. For no attempt had been made to clear a free space round the inner *enceinte*, in case the outer circuit of the camp should be lost. While fresh batteries were being built in the newly-captured ground, to breach the city wall, Suchet set all the mortars in his original works to throw bombs into Valencia. He gathered that the population was demoralized and probably the garrison also, and thought that a general bombardment of the place might bring about a surrender without further trouble. About a thousand shells were dropped into the city within twenty-four hours, and Suchet then (January 6th) sent a *parlementaire* to invite Blake to capitulate. The Captain-General replied magniloquently that ' although yesterday morning he might have consented to treat for terms allowing his army to quit Valencia, in order to spare the inhabitants the horrors of a bombardment, now, after a day's firing, he had learnt that he could rely on the magnanimity and resignation of the people.

The Marshal might continue his operations if he pleased, and would bear the responsibility for so maltreating the place.'

As a matter of fact the bombardment had been very effective, numerous non-combatants had perished, and the spirit of the population was broken. Many openly pressed for a surrender, and only a few fanatical monks went round the streets exhorting the citizens to resistance. The bombardment continued on the 7th and 8th, and at the same time Suchet pushed approaches close to the walls, and in several places set his miners to work to tunnel under them. Actual assault was never necessary, for on the 8th Blake held a council of war, which voted for entering into negotiation with the enemy. The report of this meeting sets forth that ' it had taken into consideration the sufferings of the people under these days of bombardment ; the cry of the populace was that an end must be put to its misery ; it was impossible to prolong the defence with any profit, without exposing the city to the horrors of an assault, in which the besiegers would probably succeed, considering the depressed condition of the garrison, and the feebleness of the walls. The citizens had not only failed to aid in the defence and to second the efforts of the regular troops, but were panic-stricken and demanded a surrender. The army itself did not seem disposed to do its duty, and after hearing the evidence of the commanders of different corps, the council decided in favour of negotiating to get honourable terms. If these were refused it might be necessary to continue a hopeless defence and die honourably among the ruins of Valencia [1].'

It is probable that Blake would really have accepted any terms offered him as ' honourable,' for he assented to all that Suchet dictated to him. A feeble attempt to stipulate for a free departure for the field army, on condition that the city and all its armaments and resources were handed over intact, met with the curt refusal that it deserved. A simple capitulation with the honours of war was granted : one clause, however, was looked upon by Blake as somewhat of a concession, though it really was entirely to Suchet's benefit. He offered to grant an exchange to so many of the garrison as should be equivalent

[1] See the long *procès verbal* of the Council's proceedings translated in Belmas, iv. pp. 203–6.

man for man, to French prisoners from the dépôts in Majorca and Cabrera, where the unfortunate remnants of Dupont's army were still in confinement. As this was not conceded by the Spanish government, the clause had no real effect in mitigating the fate of Blake's army[1]. Other clauses in the capitulation declared that private property should be respected, and that no inquiry should be made after the surrender into the past conduct of persons who had taken an active part in the revolution of 1808, or the subsequent defence of the kingdom of Valencia : also that such civilians as chose might have three months in which to transport themselves, their families, and their goods to such destination as they pleased. These clauses, as we shall see, were violated by Suchet with the most shocking callousness and shameless want of respect for his written word.

On January 9 the citadel and the gate adjacent were handed over to the French ; Blake (at his own request) was sent away straight to France, and did not remain to take part in the formal surrender of his troops and of the city. It would seem that he could not face the rage of the Valencians, and was only anxious to avoid even twenty-four hours of sojourn among them after the disaster. Napoleon affected to regard him as a traitor, though he had never done even a moment's homage to Joseph Bonaparte in 1808, and shut him up in close captivity in the donjon of Vincennes, where he remained very uncomfortably lodged till the events of April 1814 set him free[2].

The total number of prisoners yielded up by Valencia was 16,270 regular troops, of whom some 1,500 were sick or wounded in the hospitals. The urban guards and armed peasants, who

[1] The proposal of exchange came first to Mahy at Alicante ; he called a council of generals, which resolved that the release of so many French would profit Suchet overmuch, because many of them had been imprisoned at Alicante and Cartagena, and had worked on the fortifications there. They could give the Marshal valuable information, which he had better be denied. The proposal must therefore be sent on to the Regency at Cadiz. That government, after much debate, refused to ratify the proposal, considering it more profitable to the enemy than to themselves.

[2] Some notes about his captivity may be found in the *Mémoires* of Baron Kolli, the would-be deliverer of King Ferdinand, who was shut up in another tower of the castle.

were supposed to be civilians covered by the amnesty article in the capitulation, are not counted in the total. The regulars marched out of the Serranos gate on January 10, and after laying down their arms and colours were sent prisoners to France, marching in two columns, under the escort of Pannetier's brigade, to Saragossa. Twenty-one colours and no less than 374 cannon (mostly heavy guns in the defences) were given over, as also a very large store of ammunition and military effects, but very little food, which was already beginning to fail in the city when Blake surrendered.

To prevent unlicensed plunder Suchet did not allow his own troops to enter Valencia till January 14th, giving the civil authorities four days in which to make preparations for the coming in of the new régime. He was better received than might have been expected—apparently Blake's maladroit dictatorship had thoroughly disgusted the people. Many of the magistrates bowed to the conqueror and took the oath of homage to King Joseph, and the aged archbishop emerged from the village where he had hidden himself for some time, and ' showed himself animated by an excellent spirit' according to the Marshal's dispatch.

This prompt and tame submission did not save Valencia from dreadful treatment at the victor's hands. Not only did he levy on the city and district a vast fine of 53,000,000 francs (over £2,120,000), of which 3,000,000 were sent to Madrid and the rest devoted to the profit of the Army of Aragon, but he proceeded to carry out a series of atrocities, which have been so little spoken of by historians that it would be difficult to credit them, if they were not avowed with pride in his own dispatches to Berthier and Napoleon.

The second article of Blake's capitulation, already cited above, had granted a complete amnesty for past actions on the part of the Valencians—' Il ne sera fait aucune recherche pour le passé contre ceux qui auraient pris une part active à la guerre ou à la révolution,' to quote the exact term. In his dispatch of January 12 to Berthier, Suchet is shameless enough to write : ' I have disarmed the local militia : all guilty chiefs will be arrested, and all assassins punished ; *for in consenting to Article II of the Capitulation my only aim was to get the matter*

over quickly [1].' ' Guilty chiefs ' turned out to mean all civilians
who had taken a prominent part in the defence of Valencia :
' assassins ' was interpreted to cover guerrilleros of all sorts,
not (as might perhaps have been expected) merely those
persons who had taken part in the bloody riots against the
French commercial community in 1808 [2]. In his second
dispatch of January 17 Suchet proceeds to explain that he
has arrested 480 persons as ' suspects,' that a large number of
guerrillero leaders have been found among them, who have
been sent to the citadel and have been already shot, or will be
in a few days. He has also arrested every monk in Valencia ;
500 have been sent prisoners to France : five of the most guilty,
convicted of having carried round the streets a so-called ' banner
of the faith,' and of having preached against capitulation, and
excited the people to resistance, have been already executed.
Inquiries were still in progress. They resulted in the shooting
of two more friars [3]. But the most astonishing clause in the
dispatch is that ' all those who took part in the murders of the
French [in 1808] will be sought out and punished. Already
six hundred have been executed by the firmness of the Spanish
judge Marescot, whom I am expecting soon to meet [4].' It was
a trifling addition to the catalogue of Suchet's doings that
350 students of the university, who had volunteered to aid the
regular artillery during the late siege, had all been arrested and
sent off to France like the monks. Two hundred sick or footsore
prisoners who straggled from the marching column directed on
Teruel and Saragossa are said to have been shot by the wayside [5].
It is probable that innumerable prisoners were put to death in
cold blood after the capitulation of Valencia, in spite of Suchet's
guarantee that ' no research should be made as to the past.'
Of this Napier says no word [6], though he quotes other parts
of Suchet's dispatches, and praises him for his ' vigorous and
prudent ' conduct, and his ' care not to offend the citizens by
violating their customs or shocking their religious feelings.'

---

[1] See the dispatches printed in full in Belmas, Appendix, vol. iv, pp. 218–
20, and 226–7 of his great work.

[2] For which see vol. i. p. 68.

[3] The names of all seven friars are given by Toreno and Schepeler.

[4] Can the frightful figure of 600 be a mistake for 60 ?

[5] See Toreno, iii. p. 28.   [6] See his pages, iv. 33.

SECTION XXX : CHAPTER IV

SUCHET'S CONQUEST OF VALENCIA : SIDE-ISSUES AND CONSEQUENCES. JANUARY—MARCH 1812

WHEN once Suchet's long-deferred movements began, on December 26, 1812, his operations were so rapid and successful that the whole campaign was finished in fourteen days. The unexpected swiftness of his triumph had the result of rendering unnecessary the subsidiary operations which Napoleon had directed the Armies of Portugal, the Centre, and Andalusia, to carry out.

D'Armagnac, with his 3,000 men of the Army of the Centre, still lay at Cuenca when Suchet's advance began, hindered from further movement by the badness of the roads and the weather. Opposite him were lying Bassecourt's small force at Requeña—not 2,000 men—and the larger detachment of the Murcian army under Freire, which Blake had originally intended to draw down to join his main body. This seems to have consisted of some 4,000 foot and 1,000 horse [1] about the time of the New Year.

Far more important was the force under Montbrun, detached from the Army of Portugal, which had moved (all too tardily) from La Mancha and the banks of the Tagus, by Napoleon's orders. Assembled, as we have already shown [2], only on December 29th, it had started from San Clemente on January 2 to march against Blake's rear by the route of Almanza, the only one practicable for artillery at midwinter. Thus the expedition was only just getting under way when Suchet had already beaten Blake and thrust him into Valencia. It consisted of the infantry divisions of Foy and Sarrut, of the whole of the light cavalry of the Army of Portugal, and of five batteries

---

[1] On February 1st Freire's infantry division, though it had suffered much from desertion in the meanwhile, still numbered 3,300 men present, and his cavalry 850 sabres. See tables in *Los Ejércitos españoles*, pp. 149–50.

[2] See above, p. 56.

of artillery, in all about 10,000 men. Of the succour which had been promised from d'Armagnac's division, to raise the force to the figures of 12,000 men, few if any came to hand [1].

Montbrun marched with Sarrut and the cavalry by Albacete and Chinchilla, leaving Foy as a reserve échelon, to follow by slower stages and keep up the communication with La Mancha. Between Chinchilla and Almanza the advanced cavalry fell in with Freire's Spanish division, marching across its front. For on the news of Suchet's passage of the Guadalaviar on December 26, Freire had moved southward from his position on the Cabriel river, with the intention of joining Mahy, and so of building up a force strong enough to do something to succour Blake and the beleaguered garrison of Valencia. On January 6th Montbrun's horse came upon one of Freire's detachments, dispersed it, and took some prisoners. But the greater part of the Murcians succeeded in getting past, and in reaching Mahy at Alicante (January 9th).

So cowed was the country-side by the disasters about Valencia that Montbrun at Almanza succeeded in getting a letter carried by one of his staff to Valencia in two days [2]. It announced to Suchet his arrival on the rear of the Spanish army, and his intention of pressing on eastward so as to drive away Freire and Mahy and completely cut off the retreat of Blake towards Murcia. But when the dispatch was received Blake was already a prisoner, and his army had laid down its arms on the preceding day. Suchet, therefore, wrote a reply to Montbrun to thank him for his co-operation, to inform him that it was no longer necessary, and to advise him to return as quickly as possible toward the Army of Portugal and the Tagus, where his presence was now much more needed than on the coast of the Mediterranean. The Army of Aragon was strong enough to deal in due course with Mahy and Freire, and to take Alicante.

Montbrun, however, refused to accept this advice. He was

---

[1] According to Joseph's letter to Montbrun (*Correspondence of King Joseph*, viii. p. 294) a battalion or two may have joined Montbrun, as he tells that general that he is glad to know that the troops of his army have given satisfaction.

[2] Suchet, *Mémoires*, ii. p. 234, for dates.

probably, as his chief Marmont remarks, desirous of distinguishing himself by carrying out some brilliant enterprise as an independent commander [1]. Knowing that Mahy's and Freire's troops were in a very demoralized condition, and underrating the strength of the fortress of Alicante, he resolved to march against that place, which he thought would make little or no resistance. Accordingly he called forward Foy to Albacete and Chinchilla, left the main part of his guns in his charge, and marched on Alicante with the cavalry and Sarrut's division, having only one battery of horse artillery with him.

At the news of his approach Mahy, who had been at Alcoy since he abandoned the line of the Xucar on December 27th, retired into Alicante with Creagh's and Obispo's infantry. Bassecourt also joined him there, while Freire with his own column, Villacampa's division, and all the Murcian and Valencian cavalry, occupied Elche and other places in the neighbourhood. Over 6,000 regular infantry were within the walls of Alicante by January 15th. Montbrun on the following day drove Freire out of Elche westward, and presented himself in front of the new fortification of Alicante, which had been much improved during the last year, and included a new line of bastioned wall outside the old mediaeval *enceinte* and the rocky citadel. It is probable that Montbrun had no knowledge of the recent improvements to the fortress, and relied on old reports of its weakness. After advancing into the suburbs, and throwing a few useless shells into the place, whose artillery returned a heavy fire, he retreated by Elche and Hellin to Albacete [2]. As he went he laid waste the country-side in the most reckless fashion, and raised heavy requisitions of money in Elche, Hellin, and other places. This involved him in an angry correspondence with Suchet, who insisted that no commander but himself had a right to extort contributions in the region that fell into his sphere of operations.

[1] Marmont accuses Montbrun exactly as Napoleon accuses Marmont!

[2] On his first appearance he sent to summon Alicante, and received the proper negative answer. But Schepeler, who was in the place, says that the governor, General de la Cruz, showed signs of yielding. Fortunately the other generals did not. It would have been absurd to treat seriously a force of 4,000 infantry and 1,500 horse with only six light guns! (Schepeler, p. 520.)

Montbrun's raid was clearly a misguided operation. Alicante was far too strong to be taken by escalade, when it was properly garrisoned : the only chance was that the garrison might flinch. They refused to do so, and the French general was left in an absurd position, demonstrating without siege-guns against a regular fortress. His action had two ill-effects—the first was that it concluded the Valencian campaign with a fiasco —a definite repulse which put heart into the Spaniards. The second (and more important) was that it separated him from Marmont and the Army of Portugal for ten days longer than was necessary. His chief had given him orders to be back on the Tagus by the 15th–20th of January, as his absence left the main body too weak. Owing to his late start he would in any case have overpassed these dates, even if he had started back from Almanza on January 13th, after receiving the news of the fall of Valencia. But by devoting nine days to an advance from Almanza to Alicante and then a retreat from Alicante to Albacete, he deferred his return to Castile by that space of time. He only reached Toledo on January 31st with his main column. Foy's division, sent on ahead, arrived there on the 29th. Montbrun's last marches were executed with wild speed, for he had received on the way letters of the most alarming kind from Marmont, informing him that Wellington had crossed the Agueda with his whole army and laid siege to Ciudad Rodrigo. The Army of Portugal must concentrate without delay. But by the time that Montbrun reached Toledo, Rodrigo had already been twelve days in the hands of the British general, and further haste was useless. The troops were absolutely worn out, and received with relief the order to halt and wait further directions, since they were too late to save the fallen fortress. It is fair to Montbrun to remark that, even if he had never made his raid on Alicante, he would still have been unable to help his chief. If he had turned back from Almanza on January 13th, he would have been at Toledo only on the 22nd—and that city is nearly 200 miles by road from Ciudad Rodrigo, which had fallen on the 19th. The disaster on the Agueda was attributable not to Montbrun's presumptuous action, but to the Emperor's orders that the Army of Portugal should make a great detachment for the Valencian

campaign. Even if the raiding column had started earlier, as
Napoleon intended, it could not have turned back till it got
news of the capitulation of Blake, which only took place on
January 8th. And whatever might then have been its exact
position, it could not have been back in time to join Marmont
in checking the operations of Wellington, which (as we have
already stated) came to a successful end on January 19th.
Wherefore, though Montbrun must receive blame, the responsibility for the fall of Rodrigo lay neither with him nor with
Marmont, but with their great master.

Another diversion made by Napoleon's orders for the purpose
of aiding Suchet was quite as futile—though less from the fault
of the original direction, and more from an unforeseen set of
circumstances. Like Marmont and King Joseph, Soult had
also been ordered to lend Suchet assistance against Valencia,
by demonstrating from the side of Granada against Murcia and
its army. This order, issued apparently about November 19,
1811 [1], and repeated on December 6th, reached the Duke of
Dalmatia just when he had assembled all his disposable field-
forces for the siege of Tarifa, an operation where preparations
began on December 8th and which did not end till January 5th.
Having concentrated 13,000 men in the extreme southern point
of his viceroyalty, Soult had not a battalion to spare for a sally
from its extreme eastern point. He could not give up a great
enterprise already begun ; and it was only when it had failed,
and the troops from Tarifa were returning—in a sufficiently
melancholy plight—that Soult could do anything. But by this
time it was too late to help Suchet, who had finished his business
without requiring assistance from without.

Whether Soult was already aware of the surrender of Valencia
or not, when January 20th had arrived, he had before that day
issued orders to his brother, the cavalry general, Pierre Soult,
to take the light horse of the 4th Corps from Granada, and to
execute with them a raid against Murcia, with the object of
drawing off the attention of any Spanish troops left in that
direction from Suchet. The General, with about 800 sabres,

---

[1] It is alluded to in a dispatch of the Emperor to Berthier on that day.
' Le duc de Dalmatie a l'ordre d'envoyer une colonne en Murcie pour faire
une diversion.' St. Cloud, Nov. 19.

Marshal Suchet, Duke of Albufera
from the portrait by Charpentier

pushing on by Velez Rubio and Lorca, arrived before the gates of Murcia quite unopposed on January 25th. Freire had left no troops whatever to watch the borders of Granada, and had drawn off everything, save the garrison of Cartagena, toward the Valencian frontiers. Pierre Soult summoned the defenceless city, received its surrender, and imposed on it a ransom of 60,000 dollars. He entered next day, and established himself in the archbishop's palace ; having neither met nor heard of any enemy he was quite at his ease, and was sitting down to dine, when a wild rush of Spanish cavalry came sweeping down the street and cutting up his dispersed and dismounted troopers. This was General Martin La Carrera, whose brigade was the nearest force to Murcia when Soult arrived. Hearing that the French were guarding themselves ill, he had resolved to attempt a surprise, and, dividing his 800 men into three columns, assailed Murcia by three different gates. His own detachment cut its way in with success, did much damage, and nearly captured the French general. But neither of the other parties showed such resolution ; they got bickering with the French at the entries of the city, failed to push home, and finally retired with small loss. The gallant and unfortunate La Carrera, charging up and down the streets in vain search for his reinforcements, was finally surrounded by superior numbers, and died fighting gallantly.

His enterprise warned Soult that Spanish troops were collecting in front of him, and indeed Villacampa's infantry was not far off. Wherefore he evacuated Murcia next day, after raising so much of the contribution as he could, and plundering many private houses. The Spaniards reoccupied the place, and Joseph O'Donnell, now placed in command of the Murcian army in succession to Mahy, gave La Carrera's corpse a splendid funeral. Soult retreated hastily to the Granadan frontier, pillaging Alcantarilla and Lorca by the way. This was the only part taken by the French Army of Andalusia in the January campaign of 1812. The siege of Tarifa had absorbed all its energies.

Montbrun's and Pierre Soult's enterprises had little effect on the general course of events in eastern Spain. It was Suchet's own operations which, in the estimation of every observer from the Emperor downwards, were to be considered decisive.

When Valencia had fallen, every one on the French side supposed that the war was practically at an end in this region, and that the dispersion of the remnants of Mahy's and Freire's troops and the capture of Peniscola, Alicante, and Cartagena,—the three fortresses still in Spanish hands,—were mere matters of detail. No one could have foreseen that the region south of the Xucar was destined to remain permanently in the hands of the patriots, and that Suchet's occupation of Valencia was to last for no more than eighteen months. Two causes, neither of them depending on Suchet's own responsibility, were destined to save the kingdom of Murcia and the southern region of Valencia from conquest. The first was Napoleon's redistribution of his troops in eastern Spain, consequent on the approach of his war with Russia. The second was the sudden victorious onslaught of Wellington on the French in the western parts of the Peninsula. How the former of these causes worked must at once be shown—the effect of the latter cause did not become evident till a little later.

Of the 33,000 men with whom Suchet had conquered Valencia and captured Blake, no less than 13,000 under Reille had been lent him from the Army of the North, and were under orders to return to the Ebro as soon as possible. Indeed, till they should get back, Aragon, very insufficiently garrisoned by Caffarelli's division, was out of hand, and almost as much in the power of the Empecinado, Duran, and Montijo, as of the French. Moreover, so long as Caffarelli was at Saragossa, and his troops dispersed in the surrounding region, both Navarre and Old Castile were undermanned, and the Army of the North was reduced to little more than Dorsenne's two divisions of the Young Guard. To secure the troops for the great push against Valencia, so many divisions had shifted eastward, that Marmont and Dorsenne between them had, as the Emperor must have seen, barely troops enough in hand to maintain their position, if Wellington should make some unexpected move—though Napoleon had persuaded himself that such a move was improbable. In spite of this, he was anxious to draw back Reille's and Caffarelli's, no less than Montbrun's, men to more central positions.

But this was not all : in December the Emperor's dispatches

begin to show that he regarded war with Russia in the spring of
1812 as decidedly probable, and that for this reason he was
about to withdraw all the Imperial Guard from Spain. On
December 15th a note to Berthier ordered all the light and
heavy cavalry of the Guard—chasseurs, grenadiers à cheval,
dragoons, Polish lancers—to be brought home, as also its horse
artillery and the *gendarmes d'élite*. All these were serving in
the Army of the North, and formed the best part of its mounted
troops. This was but a trifling preliminary warning of his
intentions : on January 14, 1812—the results of the Valencian
campaign being still unknown—he directed Berthier to withdraw
from Spain the whole of the Infantry of the Guard and the
whole of the Polish regiments in Spain. This was an order
of wide-spreading importance, and created large gaps in the
muster-rolls of Suchet, Soult, and Dorsenne. Suchet's Poles
(three regiments of the Legion of the Vistula, nearly 6,000
men, including the detachments left in Aragon) formed a most
important part of the 3rd Corps. Soult had the 4th, 6th, and
9th Polish regiments and the Lancers, who had done such
good service at Albuera, a total of another 6,000 men. But
Dorsenne was to be the greatest sufferer—he had in the Army
of the North not only the 4th of the Vistula, some 1,500 bayonets,
but the whole of the infantry of the Young Guard, the two
divisions of Roguet and Dumoustier, twenty-two battalions
over 14,000 strong. The dispatch of January 14 directed that
Suchet should send off his battalions of the Legion 'immediately
after the fall of Valencia.' Soult was to draft away his Poles
'within twenty-four hours after the receipt of the order.'
Dorsenne, of course, could not begin to send off the Guard
Divisions of infantry till the troops lent from the Army of
the North (Reille and Caffarelli) were freed from the duties
imposed on them by the Valencian expedition. A supplementary order of January 27th told him that he might keep
them for some time longer if the English took the offensive—
news of Wellington's march on Rodrigo was just coming to
hand. ' Le désir,' says the Emperor, ' que j'ai d'avoir ma Garde
n'est pas tellement pressant qu'il faille la renvoyer avant que
les affaires aient pris une situation nouvelle dans le Nord [1].'

---

[1] Napoleon to Berthier, Paris, Jan. 27, 1812.

As a matter of fact some Guard-brigades did not get off till
March, though by dint of rapid transport, when they had once
passed the Pyrenees, they struggled to the front in time to take
part in the opening of the great Russian campaign in June.
The fourth brigade, eight battalions under Dumoustier, did not
get away till the autumn was over.

Thus the Emperor had marked off about 27,000 good veteran
troops for removal from the Peninsula, with the intention of
using them in the oncoming Russian war. The Army of the
North was to lose the best of its divisions—those of the South
and of Aragon very heavy detachments. Nothing was to come
in return, save a few drafts and *bataillons de marche* which
were lying at Bayonne. The Emperor in his dispatch makes
some curious self-justificatory remarks, to the effect that
he should leave the Army of Spain stronger than it had been
in the summer of 1811 ; for while he was withdrawing thirty-
six battalions, he had sent into the Peninsula, since June last,
forty-two battalions under Reille, Caffarelli, and Severoli. This
was true enough : but if the total strength of the troops now
dedicated to Spain was not less than it had been in June
1811, it was left weaker by 27,000 men than it had been in
December 1811.

Now Suchet, when deprived of Reille's aid, and at the same
time directed to send back to France his six Polish battalions,
was left with a very inadequate force in Valencia—not much
more than half what he had at his disposition on January 1.
It would seem that the Emperor overrated the effect of the
capture of Blake and the destruction of his army. At any
rate, in his dispatches to Suchet, he seemed to consider that
the whole business in the East was practically completed by
the triumph at the New Year. The Marshal was directed ' to
push an advanced guard towards Murcia, and put himself in
communication with the 4th Corps—the eastern wing of
Soult's army—which would be found at Lorca[1].' But the
operations of the troops of the Army of Andalusia in this
quarter were limited to the appearance for two days at Murcia
of Pierre Soult's small cavalry raid, of which Suchet got no
news till it was passed and gone. He was left entirely to his

[1] See Suchet's *Mémoires*, ii. pp. 237–8.

own resources, and these were too small for any further advance: the Emperor not only took away both Reille and the Poles, but sent, a few days later, orders that Palombini's Italian division, reduced by now to 3,000 men by its heavy casualties on December 26th, should be sent into southern Aragon against Duran and Montijo. The departure of Palombini (February 15th) left Suchet with less than 15,000 men in hand. It must be remembered that the conquest of a Spanish province always meant, for the French, the setting aside of a large immobilized garrison, to hold it down, unless it were to be permitted to drop back into insurrection. It was clear that with the bulk of the kingdom of Valencia to garrison, not to speak of the siege of the still intact fortress of Peniscola, Suchet would have an infinitesimal field-force left for the final move that would be needed, if Mahy and Freire were to be crushed, and Alicante and Cartagena—both strong places—to be beleaguered.

The Marshal had by the last week in January pushed Harispe's division to Xativa, beyond the Xucar, and Habert's to Gandia near the sea-coast. These 9,000 men were all his disposable force for a further advance: Valencia had to be garrisoned; Musnier's division had gone north, to cover the high-road as far as Tortosa and the Ebro; some of the Italians were sent to besiege Peniscola. Suchet might, no doubt, have pushed Habert and Harispe further forward towards Alicante, but he had many reasons for not doing so. That fortress had been proved—by Montbrun's raid—to be in a posture of defence: besides its garrison there were other Spanish troops in arms in the neighbourhood. To the forces of Freire, Obispo, Villacampa, and Bassecourt, there was added the newly-formed brigade of General Roche, an Irish officer lent by the British government to the Spaniards, who had been drilling and disciplining the cadres of the battalions handed over to him [1], till they were in a better condition than most of the other troops on this coast. The muster-rolls of the ' united 2nd and 3rd armies,' as these remnants were now officially styled, showed, on February 1, 1812, 14,000 men present, not including Villacampa's division,

---

[1] These were Chinchilla, 2nd of Murcia, and a new locally raised battalion called 2nd of Alicante. He was in March handed over also Canarias, Burgos, and Ligero de Aragon, which had belonged to Freire till that date.

which was moving off to its old haunts in Aragon. By March 1 this figure had risen to 18,000, many deserters who had gone home after the fall of Valencia having tardily rejoined the ranks of their battalions. Over 2,000 cavalry were included in the total—for nearly the whole of Blake's squadrons had escaped (not too gloriously) after the disastrous combats on December 26, 1812.

If Suchet, therefore, had moved forward with a few thousand men at the end of January, he would have risked something, despite of the depressed morale of his enemies. But in addition there was vexatious news from Catalonia, which presently caused the sending of part of Musnier's division beyond the Ebro, and it was reported (only too correctly) that the yellow fever had broken out with renewed violence at Murcia and Cartagena. An advance into the infected district might be hazardous. But most of all was any further initiative discouraged by the consideration that no help could be expected from Marmont or Soult. By the end of January Suchet was aware of Wellington's invasion of Leon, and of the siege of Ciudad Rodrigo. Not only did this move absorb all the attention of Marmont, Dorsenne, and King Joseph, but Soult was convinced that it boded evil for him also, and that a new attack on Badajoz was imminent. Hill's manœuvres in Estremadura (of which more elsewhere) attracted all his attention, and he let it be known that he had neither the wish nor the power to send expeditions eastward, to co-operate against Murcia. Last, but most conclusive, of all Suchet's hindrances was a grave attack of illness, which threw him on a bed of sickness early in February, and caused him to solicit permission to return to France for his convalescence. The Emperor (with many flattering words) refused this leave, and sent two of his body physicians to Valencia to treat the Marshal's ailment. But it was two months before Suchet was able to mount his horse, and put himself at the head of his army. From February to the beginning of April operations were necessarily suspended for the Army of Aragon, since its chief was not one of those who gladly hand over responsibility and the power of initiative to his subordinates.

Hence there was a long gap in the story of the war in south-eastern Spain from January to April 1812. The only events requiring notice during that period were the occupation by the French of Denia and Peniscola. The former, a little port on the projecting headland south of Valencia, was furnished with fortifications newly repaired during Blake's régime, and had been an important centre of distribution for stores and munitions of war, after the Spaniards lost the Grao of Valencia in November, since it was the nearest harbour to their positions along the Guadalaviar. In the general panic after Blake's surrender Mahy withdrew its garrison, but forgot to order the removal of its magazines. Harispe seized Denia on January 20, and found sixty guns mounted on its walls, and forty small merchant vessels, some of them laden with stores, in its port. He garrisoned the place, and fitted out some of the vessels as privateers. Mahy's carelessness in abandoning these resources was one of the reasons which contributed most to his removal from command by the Cadiz Regency. It was indeed a gross piece of neglect, for at least the guns might have been destroyed, and the ships brought round to Alicante.

The story of Peniscola, however, was far more disgraceful. This fortress sometimes called ' the little Gibraltar ' from its impregnable situation—it is a towering rock connected with the mainland by a narrow sand-spit 250 yards long—was one of the strongest places in all Spain. It had appeared so impregnable to Suchet, that, on his southward march from Tortosa to Valencia, he had merely masked it, and made no attempt to meddle with it [1]. Peniscola had suffered no molestation, and was regularly revictualled by Spanish and British coasting vessels from Alicante, Cartagena, and the Balearic Isles. The governor, Garcia Navarro, was an officer who had an excellent reputation for personal courage—taken prisoner at Falset in 1811 [2] he had succeeded in escaping from a French prison and had reported himself again for further service. The garrison of 1,000 men was adequate for such a small place, and was composed of veteran troops. In directing it to be formally beleaguered after the fall of Valencia, Suchet seems to have relied more on the general demoralization caused by the annihilation of Blake's army than on the strength of his means of attack.

[1] See above, p. 14. [2] See vol. iii. pp. 503–4.

On January 20th he ordered Severoli with two Italian and two French battalions to press the place as far as was possible, and assigned to him part of the siege-train that had been used at Saguntum. The trenches, on the high ground of the mainland nearest the place, were opened on the 28th, and on the 31st the besiegers began to sap downhill towards the isthmus, and to erect five batteries on the best available points. But it was clear that the fortress was most inaccessible, and that to reach its walls across the low-lying sand-spit would be a very costly business.

Nevertheless, when a summons was sent in to the governor on February 2nd, he surrendered at once, getting in return terms of an unusually favourable kind—the men and officers of the garrison were given leave either to depart to their homes with all their personal property, or to enlist in the service of King Joseph. This was a piece of mere treachery : Navarro had made up his mind that the cause of Spain was ruined by Blake's disaster, and had resolved to go over to the enemy, while there were still good terms to be got for deserters. As Suchet tells the story, the affair went as follows. A small vessel, sailing from Peniscola to Alicante, was taken by a privateer fitted out by Harispe at Denia. Among letters seized by the captors [1] was one from the governor, expressing his disgust with his situation, and in especial with the peremptory advice given him by the English naval officers who were in charge of the re-victualling service and the communications. He went on to say that he would rather surrender Peniscola to the French than let it be treated as a British dependency, whereupon the Marshal asked, and obtained, the surrender of the place. Napier expresses a suspicion—probably a well-founded one—that the letter may have been really intended for Suchet's own eye, and that the whole story was a piece of solemn deceit. ' Such is the Marshal's account of the affair—but the colour which he thought it necessary to give to a transaction so full of shame to Navarro, can only be considered as part of the price paid for Peniscola [2].' The mental attitude of the traitor is sufficiently expressed by

---

[1] Suchet says that the captain of the boat threw his letters overboard at the last moment, but that they floated and were picked up by the French. Was this a farce ?   Or is the whole story doubtful ?

[2] Napier, *Peninsular War*, iv. p. 38.

a letter which reached Suchet along with the capitulation.
' I followed with zeal, with fury I may say, the side which I considered the just one. To-day I see that to render Spain less
unhappy it is necessary for us all to unite under the King,
and I make my offer to serve him with the same enthusiasm.
Your excellency may be quite sure of me—I surrender a fortress
fully provisioned and capable of a long defence—which is the
best guarantee of the sincerity of my promise [1].'

The most astounding feature of the capitulation was that
Navarro got his officers to consent to such a piece of open
treachery. If they had done their duty, they would have
arrested him, and sent him a prisoner to Alicante. Demoralization
and despair must have gone very far in this miserable garrison.

The capture of Peniscola was Suchet's last success. He fell
sick not long after, and when he once more assumed the active
command of his troops in April, the whole situation of French
affairs in Spain was changed, and no further advance was
possible. The results of Wellington's offensive operations in
the West had begun to make themselves felt.

Meanwhile the remains of the Valencian and Murcian armies
were reorganizing themselves, with Alicante as their base and
central port of supply. Joseph O'Donnell, though not a great
general, was at least no worse than Blake and Mahy—of whom
the former was certainly the most maladroit as well as the
most unlucky of commanders, while the latter had shown
himself too timid and resourceless to play out the apparently
lost game that was left to his hand in January 1812. By March
there was once more an army in face of the French, and in
view of the sudden halt of the invaders and the cheerful news
from the West, hope was once more permissible. The main
body of O'Donnell's army remained concentrated in front of
Alicante, but Villacampa's division had gone off early to
Aragon, to aid in the diversion against Suchet's communications,
which was so constantly kept up by Duran and the Empecinado.
This was a good move : the weak point of the French occupation
was the impossibility of holding down broad mountain spaces,
in which small garrisons were useless and helpless, while heavy
columns could not live for more than a few days on any given spot.

[1] See letter printed in Belmas, iv. p. 248.

SECTION XXXI

MINOR CAMPAIGNS OF THE WINTER OF 1811–12

CHAPTER I

CATALONIA AND ARAGON

THE chronicle of the obstinate and heroic defence made by the Catalans, even after the falls of Tarragona and Figueras had seemed to make all further resistance hopeless, was carried in the last volume of this work down to October 28, 1811, when Marshal Macdonald, like St. Cyr and Augereau, was recalled to Paris, having added no more to his reputation than had his predecessors while in charge of this mountainous principality. We have seen how General Lacy, hoping against hope, rallied the last remnants of the old Catalan army, and recommenced (just as Macdonald was departing) a series of small enterprises against the scattered French garrisons. He had won several petty successes in evicting the enemy from Cervera, Igualada, and Belpuig—the small strongholds which covered the main line of communication east and west, through the centre of the land, between Lerida and Barcelona. The enemy had even been forced to evacuate the holy mountain of Montserrat, the strongest post on the whole line.

Hence when, in November, General Decaen arrived to take over Macdonald's task, he found before him a task not without serious difficulties, though the actual force of Spaniards in the field was far less than it had been before the disasters at Tarragona and Figueras. Lacy had a very small field army—he had reorganized 8,000 men by October, and all through his command the total did not grow very much greater. When he handed over his office to Copons fifteen months after, there were no more than 14,000 men under arms, including cadres and recruits. On the other hand he had a central position, a free range east and west, now that the line of French posts across Catalonia had been broken, and several points of more or less safe access to the sea. Munitions and stores, and occasionally very small reinforcements from the Balearic Isles, were still brought over by the British squadron which ranged along the coast. Some of the officers, especially the much tried and never-despairing Eroles, and the indefatigable Manso, were thoroughly to be relied upon, and commanded great local popularity. This Lacy himself did not possess—he was obeyed because of his stern resolve, but much disliked for his autocratic and dictatorial ways, which kept him in constant friction with the Junta that sat at Berga. Moreover he was a stranger, while the Catalans disliked all leaders who were not of their own blood : and he was strongly convinced that the brunt of the fighting must be borne by the regular troops, while the popular voice was all in favour of the *somatenes* and guerrilleros, and against the enforcement of conscription. Much was to be said on either side : the warfare of the irregulars was very harassing to the French, and had led to many petty successes, and one great one—the capture of Figueras. On the other hand these levies were irresponsible and untrustworthy when any definite operation was in hand : they might, or they might not, turn up in force when they were required : the frank disregard of their chiefs for punctuality or obedience drove to wild rage any officer who had served in the old army. With regular troops it was possible to calculate that a force would be where it was wanted to be at a given time, and would at least attempt to carry out its orders : with the *somatenes* it was always possible, nay probable, that some petty quarrel of rival chiefs, or some rival attraction of an unforeseen sort, would lead to non-appearance. To this there was the easy reply that ever since Blake first tried to make the Catalans work ' *militarmente* and not *paisanmente* ' the regular army for some two years had never gained a single battle, nor relieved a single fortress [1]. The best

---

[1] See notes on discussions of this sort in Sir Edward Codrington's *Memoirs*, i. pp. 264 and 277. He had seen much of the evils of both kinds of organization, and leaned on the whole to the irregulars, from a personal dislike for Lacy.

plan would probably have been to attempt to combine the
two systems : it was absolutely necessary to have a nucleus
of regular troops, but unwise to act like Blake and Lacy, who
tried to break up and discourage the *somatenes*, in order that
they might be forced into the battalions of the standing army.
The constant series of defeats on record had been caused rather
by the unskilful and over-ambitious operations of the generals
than by their insisting on keeping up the regular troops, who
had behaved well enough on many occasions. But too much
had been asked of them when, half-trained and badly led, they
were brought into collision with the veterans of France, without
the superiority of numbers which alone could make up for their
military faults.

Since the capture of Cervera, Belpuig, and Igualada in October,
the territories held by the French in Catalonia fell into two
separate and divided sections. On the western side, adjacent
to Aragon, Frère's division, left behind by Suchet, garrisoned
Lerida, Tarragona, and Tortosa : though it was a powerful
force of over 7,000 men, it could do little more than occupy these
three large places, each requiring several battalions. At the
best it could only furnish very small flying columns to keep
up the communication between them. It was hard to maintain
touch with the other group of French fortresses, along the sea-
coast road from Tarragona to Barcelona, which were often
obsessed by Spanish bands, and always liable to be molested
by Edward Codrington's British ships, which sailed up and
down the shore looking for detachments or convoys to shell.
The fort of the Col de Balaguer, twenty miles north of Tortosa,
was the look-out point towards Tarragona and the sole French
outpost in that direction.

In eastern Catalonia the newly-arrived commander, General
Decaen (a veteran whose last work had been the hopeless
defence of Bourbon and Mauritius, where he had capitulated
in 1810), had some 24,000 men in hand. But he was much
hampered by the necessity for holding and feeding the immense
Barcelona, a turbulent city which absorbed a whole division
for its garrison. It was constantly on the edge of starvation,
and was only revictualled with great trouble by vessels sailing
from the ports of Languedoc, of which more than half were

habitually captured by the British, or by heavy convoys labouring across the hills from Gerona, which were always harassed, and sometimes taken wholesale, by the Spanish detachments told off by Lacy for this end. Gerona and Figueras, both fortresses of considerable size, absorbed several battalions each. Smaller garrisons had also to be kept in Rosas, Hostalrich, Mataro, and Montlouis, and there were many other fortified posts which guarded roads or passes, and were worth holding. It was with difficulty that 6,000 or 8,000 men could be collected for a movable field-force, even by borrowing detachments from the garrisons. An additional nuisance cropped up just as Decaen took over the command : Lacy, seeing that the Pyrenean passes were thinly manned, sent Eroles with 3,000 men to raid the valleys of Cerdagne on the French side of the hills. The invaders beat two battalions of national guards near Puigcerda, and swept far down the valley (October 29–November 2), returning with thousands of sheep and cattle and a large money contribution levied from the villages. This raid (which enraged Napoleon [1]) made it necessary to guard the Pyrenees better, and to send up more national guards from the frontier departments.

Thus it came to pass that though Lacy had no more than 8,000 men available, and no fortress of any strength to serve as his base (Cardona and Seu d'Urgel, his sole strongholds, were mediaeval strongholds with no modern works), he paralysed the French force which, between Lerida and Figueras, could show more than three times that strength. Such was the value of the central position, and the resolute hatred of the countryside for its oppressors. Catalonia could only be held down by garrisoning every village—and if the army of occupation split itself up into garrisons it was helpless. Hence, during the winter of 1811–12 and the spring and summer of the following year, it may be said that the initiative lay with the Catalans, and that the enemy (despite of his immensely superior numbers) was on the defensive. The helplessness of the French was sufficiently shown by the fact that from June to December 1811 Barcelona was completely cut off from communication with

[1] Who called the raid an ' insult '—Napoleon to Berthier, Paris, Feb. 29, 1812, and compare letter of March 8.

Gerona and France. It was only in the latter month that Decaen, hearing that the place was on the edge of starvation, marched with the bulk of Lamarque's division from Upper Catalonia to introduce a convoy ; while Maurice Mathieu, the governor of Barcelona, came out with 3,000 men of the garrison to meet him, as far as Cardadeu. Lacy, determined that nothing short of a vigorous push by the enemy should make their junction possible, and relieve Barcelona, offered opposition in the defile of the Trentapassos, where Vives had tried to stop St. Cyr two years back, showing a front both to Decaen and to Mathieu. But on recognizing the very superior numbers of the enemy he wisely withdrew, or he would have been caught between the two French columns. Decaen therefore was able to enter Barcelona with his immense convoy. [December 3rd–4th, 1811.] The Spaniards retreated into the inland ; their head-quarters on the first day of the New Year were at Vich.

There being no further profit in pressing Barcelona for the time being, Lacy, in January, resolved to turn his attention to the much weaker garrison of Tarragona, which belonged to Frère's division and Suchet's army, and was not under Decaen's immediate charge. Its communications with Lerida and Tor-tosa were hazardous, and its stores were running low. The Spanish general therefore (about January 2) sent down Eroles's division to Reus, a few miles inland from Tarragona, with orders to cut all the roads leading into that fortress. The place was already in a parlous condition for want of food, and its governor had sent representations to Suchet that he was in need of instant succour. Therefore the moment that Valencia fell, the Marshal directed Musnier, whose division he had told off to hold the sea-coast between the Ebro and Guadalaviar, to march with the bulk of his men to Tortosa, to pick up what reinforce-ments he could from its garrison, and to open the road from thence to Tarragona.

Lafosse, the governor of Tortosa, was so impressed with the danger of his colleague in Tarragona, that he marched ahead along the coast-road before Musnier arrived, and reached the Col de Balaguer with a battalion of the 121st regiment and one troop of dragoons on January 18. Here he should have waited for the main column, but receiving false news that

Eroles had left Reus and returned to the north, he resolved to push on ahead and clear the way for Musnier, believing that nothing but local *somatenes* were in front of him. He had reached Villaseca, only seven miles from Tarragona, when he was suddenly surprised by Eroles descending on his flank with over 3,000 men. He himself galloped on with the dragoons towards Tarragona, and escaped, with only twenty-two men, into the fortress. But his battalion, after barricading itself in Villaseca village and making a good resistance for some hours, was forced to surrender. Eroles took nearly 600 prisoners, and over 200 French had fallen. Lafosse, sallying from Tarragona with all that could be spared from the garrison, arrived too late to help his men, and had to return in haste [January 19] [1].

Tarragona now seemed in imminent danger, and both Musnier at Tortosa and Maurice Mathieu at Barcelona saw that they must do their best to relieve the place, or it would be starved out. Musnier spent so much time in organizing a convoy that he was late, and the actual opening of the road was carried out by the governor of Barcelona. That great city chanced to be crammed with troops at the moment, since Lamarque's division, which had escorted the December convoy, was still lying within its walls. Maurice Mathieu, therefore, was able to collect 8,000 men for the march on Tarragona. Eroles, unfortunately for himself, was not aware of this, and believing that the enemy was a mere sally of the Barcelona garrison, offered them battle at Altafulla on January 24. The French had marched by night, and a fog chanced to prevent the Catalans from recognizing the strength of the two columns that were approaching them. Eroles found himself committed to a close fight with double his own numbers, and after a creditable resistance was routed, losing his only two guns and the rearguard with which he tried to detain the enemy. His troops only escaped by breaking up and flying over the hills, in what a French eye-witness described as *un sauve-qui-peut général*.

[1] There is an interesting account of the combat of Villaseca in Codrington's *Memoirs*, i. pp. 254–6 : he was present, having chanced to come on shore to confer with Eroles as to co-operation against Tarragona. An odd episode of the affair was that, when the French surrendered, they were found to have with them as prisoners Captains Flinn and Pringle, R.N., whom they had surprised landing at Cape Salou on the previous day.

About 600 of them in all were slain or taken : the rest assembled at Igualada three days later. Eroles blamed Lacy and Sarsfield for his disaster, asserting that the Captain-General had promised to send the division of the latter to his help. But his anger appears to have been misplaced, for at this very time Decaen, to make a division in favour of Maurice Mathieu's movement, had sent out two columns from Gerona and Figueras into Upper Catalonia. They occupied Vich, Lacy's recent head-quarters, on January 22, two days before the combat of Altafulla, and Sarsfield's troops were naturally sent to oppose them. After wasting the upper valleys, Decaen drew back to Gerona and Olot on the 29th, having sufficiently achieved his purpose. Tarragona, meanwhile, was thoroughly revictualled by Musnier, who brought up a large convoy from Tortosa. Reinforcements were also thrown into the place, and a new governor, General Bertoletti, who was to distinguish himself by a spirited defence in the following year.

In February the whole situation of affairs in Aragon and western Catalonia (eastern Catalonia was less affected), was much modified by the return from the south of the numerous troops which had been lent to Suchet for his Valencian expedition. It will be remembered that Napoleon had ordered that Reille should march back to the Ebro with his own and Severoli's divisions, and that shortly afterwards he directed that Palombini's division should follow the other two into Aragon. Thus a very large body of troops was once more available for the subjection of Aragon and western Catalonia, which, since Reille's departure in December, had been very inadequately garrisoned by Caffarelli's and Frère's battalions, and had been overrun in many districts by the bands of the Empecinado, Duran, Mina, and the Conde de Montijo. Napoleon's new plan was to rearrange the whole of the troops in eastern Spain.

Reille was to be the chief of a new ' Army of the Ebro,' composed of four field divisions—his own, Palombini's and Severoli's Italians, and a new composite one under General Ferino constructed from so many of Frère's troops as could be spared from garrison duty (seven battalions of the 14th and 115th of the line), and six more battalions (1st Léger and 5th of the line) taken half from Musnier's division of Suchet's army and half from

Maurice Mathieu's Barcelona garrison [1]. This last division never came into existence, as Suchet and Maurice Mathieu both found themselves too weak to give up the requisitioned regiments, which remained embodied respectively with the Valencian and Catalan armies. Nevertheless Reille had more than 20,000 men actually in hand, not including the fixed garrisons of Tarragona, Lerida, and the other fortresses on the borders of Aragon and Catalonia. This, when it is remembered that Caffarelli was still holding the Saragossa district, seemed an adequate force with which to make an end of the guerrilleros of Aragon, and then to complete, in conjunction with Decaen's Corps, the subjection of inland Catalonia. For this last operation was to be the final purpose of Reille : while Decaen was to attack Lacy from the eastern side, Reille (with Lerida as his base) was to fall on from the west, to occupy Urgel and Berga (the seat of the Catalan Junta and the centre of organized resistance), and to join hands with Decaen across the crushed remnants of the Spanish army [2]. So sure did the Emperor feel that the last elements of Catalan resistance were now to be destroyed, that he gave orders for the issue of the proclamation (drawn up long before [3]) by which the Principality was declared to be united to the French empire. It was to be divided into the four departments of the Ter [capital Gerona], Montserrat [capital Barcelona], Bouches-de-l'Ebre [capital Lerida], and Segre [capital Puigcerda]. Prefects and other officials were appointed for each department, and justice was to be administered in the name of the Emperor. The humour of the arrangement (which its creator most certainly failed to see) was that three-fourths of the territory of each department was in the hands of the patriots whom he styled rebels, and that none of his prefects could have gone ten miles from his *chef-lieu* without an escort of 200 men, under pain of captivity or death.

Reille's start was much delayed by the fact that one of his French brigades had been told off to serve as escort to the mass of Blake's prisoners from Valencia, and could not get quit of

---

[1] Napoleon to Berthier, Paris, Jan. 25, after the receipt of the news of the fall of Valencia.

[2] Details may be found in the dispatches of Feb. 29, and May 1st and 8th.

[3] See vol. iv. p. 215.

CATALONIA

B.V.Darbishire, Oxford, 1914

Scale of Miles

them till, marching by Teruel, it had handed them over for transference beyond the Pyrenees to the garrison of Saragossa. Of his two Italian divisions, Palombini's was instructed to devote itself to the clearing of southern Aragon, and the opening up of the communications between the French garrisons of Daroca, Teruel, and Calatayud. The other, Severoli's, called off from the siege of Peniscola, which had originally been entrusted to it [1], marched for Lerida in two columns, the one by the sea-coast and Tortosa, the other inland, by way of Morella and Mequinenza. When his troops had begun to concentrate on the borders of Aragon and Catalonia, in and about Lerida, Reille began operations by sending a column, one French brigade and one Italian regiment, to attack the ubiquitous Eroles, who, since his defeat at Altafulla a month before, had betaken himself to the inland, and the rough country along the valleys of the two Nogueras, with the object of covering Catalonia on its western front.

This expedition, entrusted to the French brigadier Bourke, ended in an unexpected check : Eroles offered battle with 3,000 men in a strong position at Roda, with a torrent bed covering his front (March 5). Bourke, having far superior numbers, and not aware of the tenacity of the Catalan troops, whom he had never before encountered, ordered a general frontal attack by battalions of the 60th French and 7th Italian line. It was handsomely repulsed, with such heavy loss— 600 casualties it is said—that the French retreated as far as Barbastro, pursued for some distance by the troops of Eroles, who thus showed that their late disaster had not impaired their morale [2]. This was a most glorious day for the Baron, one of the few leaders of real capacity whom the war in Catalonia revealed. He had been a civilian in 1808, and had to learn the elements of military art under chiefs as incapable as Blake and Campoverde. From a miquelete chief he rose to be a general in the regular army, purely by the force of his unconquerable

---

[1] See above, p. 88.

[2] The exact loss is uncertain, but Bourke himself was wounded, and Martinien's lists show 15 other casualties among French and Italian officers : Vacani (vi. p. 65) says that the 7th Italian line alone lost 15 killed and 57 wounded. A loss of 16 officers implies *at least* 300 men hit.

pertinacity and a courage which no disasters could break. As a local patriot he had an advantage in dealing with his Catalan countrymen, which strangers like Reding, Blake, Lacy, or Sarsfield never possessed, and their confidence was never betrayed. A little active man of great vivacity, generally with a cigar in the corner of his mouth, and never long still, he was not only a good leader of irregular bands, but quite capable of understanding a strategical move, and of handling a division in a serious action. His self-abnegation during his service under chiefs whose plans were often unwise, and whose authority was often exercised in a galling fashion, was beyond all praise [1].

The check at Roda forced Reille to turn aside more troops against Eroles—practically the whole of Severoli's division was added to the column which had just been defeated, and on March 13th such a force marched against him that he was compelled to retire, drawing his pursuers after him toward the upper course of the Noguera, and ultimately to seek refuge in the wilds of Talarn among the foot-hills of the higher Pyrenees. His operations with a trifling force paralysed nearly half Reille's army during two critical months of the spring of 1812. Meanwhile, covered by his demonstration, Sarsfield executed a destructive raid across the French border, overran the valleys beyond Andorra, and exacted a ransom of 70,000 dollars from Foix, the chief town of the department of the Arriège (February 19). This was the best possible reply to Napoleon's recent declaration that Catalonia had become French soil. The Emperor was naturally enraged ; he reiterated his orders to Reille to ' déloger les insurgents : il n'est que trop vrai qu'ils se nourrissent de France '—' il faut mettre un terme à ces insultes [2].' But though Reille pushed his marches far into the remote mountainous districts where the borders of Aragon and Catalonia meet, he never succeeded in destroying the bands which he was set to hunt down : a trail of burnt villages marked his course, but it had no permanent result. The inhabitants descended from the hills, to reoccupy their fields

---

[1] For numerous anecdotes of Eroles and lively pictures of his doings the reader may refer to the Memoirs of Edward Codrington, with whom he so often co-operated.

[2] Napoleon to Berthier, March 8th, 1812.

and rebuild their huts, when he had passed by, and the insurgents were soon prowling again near the forts of Lerida, Barbastro, and Monzon.

Palombini in southern Aragon had equally unsatisfactory experiences. Coming up from Valencia by the high-road, he had reached Teruel on February 19th, and, after relieving and strengthening the garrison there, set out on a circular sweep, with the intention of hunting down Gayan and Duran—the Conde de Montijo had just returned to the Murcian army at this moment [1], while the Empecinado was out of the game for some weeks, being, as we shall presently see, busy in New Castile. But the movements of the Italian general were soon complicated by the fact that Villacampa, with the remnants of his division, had started from the neighbourhood of Alicante and Murcia much at the same time as himself, to seek once more his old haunts in Aragon. This division had given a very poor account of itself while serving as regular troops under Blake, but when it returned to its native mountains assumed a very different efficiency in the character of a large guerrilla band. Appearing at first only 2,000 strong, it recruited itself up to a much greater strength from local levies, and became no mean hindrance to Palombini's operations.

On the 29th of February the Italian general relieved Daroca, and a few days later he occupied Calatayud, which had been left ungarrisoned since the disaster of the previous October [2]. After fortifying the convent of Nostra Señora de la Peña as a new citadel for this place, he split up his division into several small columns, which scoured the neighbourhood, partly to sweep in provisions for the post at Calatayud, partly to drive off the guerrilleros of the region. But to risk small detachments in Aragon was always a dangerous business ; Villacampa, who had now come up from the south, cut off one body of 200 men at Campillo on March 5, and destroyed six companies at Pozohondon on the 28th of the same month. Taught prudence by these petty disasters, and by some less successful attacks on others of his flying columns, Palombini once more drew his men

---

[1] Apparently about the same time that Villacampa and his division came up to replace him in Aragon.

[2] See above, page 21.

together, and concentrated them in the upland plain of Hused
near Daroca. From thence he made another blow at Villacampa,
who was at the same time attacked in the rear by a column sent
up by Suchet from Valencia to Teruel. The Spaniard, however,
easily avoided the attempt to surround him, and retired without much loss or difficulty into the wild Sierra de Albarracin
(April 18th). Meanwhile, seeing Palombini occupied in hunting
Villacampa, the guerrillero Gayan made a dash at the new
garrison of Calatayud, and entering the city unexpectedly
captured the governor and sixty men, but failed to reduce the
fortified convent in which the rest of the Italians took refuge
[April 29th]. He then sat down to besiege them, though he had
no guns, and could work by mines alone : but Palombini soon
sent a strong column under the brigadiers Saint Paul and
Schiazzetti, who drove off Gayan and relieved Calatayud
[May 9th].

Nevertheless three months had now gone by since the
attempt to reduce southern Aragon began, and it was now
obvious that it had been wholly unsuccessful. The hills and
great part of the upland plains were still in the possession of the
Spaniards, who had been often hunted but never caught nor
seriously mishandled. Palombini owned nothing more than
the towns which he had garrisoned, and the spot on which his
head-quarters chanced for the moment to be placed. His
strength was not sufficient to enable him to occupy every
village, and without such occupation no conquest could take
place. Moreover the time was at hand when Wellington's
operations in the West were to shake the fabric of French
power all over Spain—even in the remote recesses of the
Aragonese Sierras. Palombini was to be drawn off in July to
join the Army of the Centre and to oppose the English. And
with his departure such hold as the French possessed on the
rugged region between Calatayud, Saragossa, and Teruel was
to disappear.

It will be noted that during these operations of the spring no
mention has been made of the Empecinado, who had been so
prominent in this quarter during the preceding autumn and
winter. This chief was now at the bottom of his fortunes :
raiding in New Castile after his accustomed fashion, he had

been completely defeated by General Guy and a column of King Joseph's army near Siguenza (February 7). He lost 1,000 men, only saved his own person by throwing himself down an almost impracticable cliff, and saw his whole force dispersed. This affair is said to have been the result of treachery: one of the Empecinado's lieutenants, a certain guerrillero leader named Albuir (better known as El Manco from having lost a hand) being taken prisoner a few days before, saved his neck by betraying his chief's position and plans : hence the surprise. El Manco entered the King's service and raised a ' counter-guerrilla ' band, with which he did considerable harm for a space. The Empecinado had only collected 600 men even by April, when he joined Villacampa and aided him in a raid round Guadalajara [1].

Mina, on the other hand, the greatest of all the partisans, was doing some of his best service to the cause of liberty during the early months of 1812. This was the period when he was conducting his bloody campaign of reprisals against Abbé, the governor of Navarre, who had published in December 1811 the celebrated proclamation which not only prohibited any quarter for guerrilleros, but made their families and villages responsible for them, and authorized the execution of ' hostages ' levied on them, as well as the infliction of crushing fines. Mina replied by the formal declaration of a ' war of extermination against all French without distinction of rank,' and started the system of shooting four prisoners for every Spaniard, soldier or civilian, executed by the enemy. This he actually carried out for some months, till the French proclamation was withdrawn. The most horrid incident of this reign of terror was the shooting by the French, on March 21, of the four members of the ' insurrectional junta ' of the province of Burgos, all magistrates and civilians, whom they had captured in a raid, and the counter-execution of eighty French soldiers by the Curate Merino, one of Mina's colleagues, a few days later. This time of atrocities ended shortly after, when Abbé withdrew his proclamation and Mina followed his example.

On the departure of Reille's troops from Valencia it will be

---

[1] For all this see Schepeler, pp. 570–1 ; King Joseph's Letters (Ducasse), viii. pp. 291 and 305 ; and Toreno, iii. pp. 81–2.

remembered that one of his French brigades, that of Pannetier, had been sent as escort to the captive Spaniards of Blake's army. While the remainder of the new ' Army of the Ebro ' went off in the direction of Lerida, as has already been seen, this brigade was turned aside against Mina. Dorsenne at the same time directed the greater part of his available field-force to join in the hunt, and all such of Caffarelli's troops as were not shut up in garrisons were told off for the same purpose. These detachments, when added to the normal force of occupation in Navarre and Biscay, made up in all some 30,000 men. Divided into many columns, each of which was strong enough to face the 3,000 or 4,000 irregulars under Mina's command, they endeavoured to converge upon him, and to enclose him within the net of their operations. The chase was very hot in March : on the first of that month Caffarelli invaded the remote Pyrenean valley of Roncal, where it had been discovered that Mina kept his dépôts, his ammunition factory, and his hospitals. The valley was swept clean, but no appreciable number of the guerrilleros were captured. On the 24th, however, it looked as if disaster was impending, as three columns under Abbé, Dumoustier (who had a brigade of the Young Guard), and Laferrière had succeeded in disposing themselves around Mina's main body, between Sanguessa and Ochagavia. The guerrillero, however, saved himself by a night march of incredible difficulty across impracticable hills, and got away into Aragon. He was lost to sight, and was believed to have been too harassed to be formidable for many a day.

Such was not the true state of affairs. Mina at once came back to his old haunts, by a circuitous march through southern Navarre, and on April 9th performed one of his most notable exploits. On that day he surprised an immense convoy of convalescents, civilians, baggage, and food-stuffs, which was marching from Vittoria to Mondragon, in the Pass of Salinas (or Puerto de Arlaban). Though escorted by 2,000 men (including the whole of the 7th Polish regiment just drawn off from Soult for the Russian war), it was completely destroyed. Five hundred of the Poles were slain, 150 captured, and an enormous booty, including (it is said) several hundred thousand francs in cash, fell into Mina's hands. He also delivered 450 Spanish prisoners, who were being conducted to captivity beyond the Pyrenees.

Such an exploit naturally drew down once more upon Mina the attention of all the neighbouring French commanders : Dorsenne and Reille again sent columns to aid the governor of Navarre, and from the 23rd to the 28th of April Mina was being hunted by powerful detachments converging on him from all sides [1]. He himself was very nearly captured at Robres by General Pannetier—who surprised him at dawn, helped by treachery on the part of a subordinate guerrillero chief, and dispersed his followers for the moment [2]. But all who were not slain or captured rallied around their indomitable leader, and followed him in a hazardous retreat, in which he threaded his way between the converging columns of the French and ultimately escaped to the Rioja. He asserts in his Memoirs, and with truth, that he was at this time of the highest service to Wellington's main operations, since he attracted and detained beyond the Ebro such a large proportion of Dorsenne's Army of the North, that in April and May it had not a man to spare to help Marmont. Even Dumoustier's Guard division, under orders to return to France for the Russian war, was put into the pack of pursuers who tried in vain to hunt him down.

To sum up the results of all the operations in Catalonia, Aragon, and Navarre, which followed on the release of Reille's troops from the Valencian expedition, it may be said that Napoleon's scheme for the complete reduction of north-eastern Spain had completely failed by April. Large forces had been put in motion ; toilsome marches had been executed over many mountain roads in the worst season of the year ; all the bands of the insurgents had been more than once defeated and dispersed. But the country-side was not conquered : the

---

[1] There seems to be an error of dates in Napier, iv. p. 172, concerning Mina's operations, as the surprise of the convoy at Salinas is put *after* Mina's escape from Pannetier at Robres. But Mina's own Memoirs fix the date of the latter as April 23rd, 1812, while the former certainly happened on April 7th. Toreno (iii. p. 87) has got the sequence right.

[2] There is a curious and interesting account of this in Mina's own Memoirs, pp. 31–2, where he relates his narrow escape, and tells how he had the pleasure of hanging his treacherous lieutenant, and three local alcaldes, who had conspired to keep from him the news of Pannetier's approach.

isolated garrisons were still cut off from each other by the enemy, wherever the heavy marching columns had passed on. The communications were no more safe and free than they had been in December. The loss of men by sickness and in the innumerable petty combats and disasters had been immense. The game had yet to be finished, and the spare time in which it could be conducted was drawing to an end. For Wellington was on the march, and ere long not a man from the Armies of the North or the Centre was to be available to aid Reille, Suchet, and Decaen in their unending and ungrateful task. Gone, too, were the days in which reserves without end could be poured in from France : the Russian war was about to open, and when once it began reinforcements were to be drawn from Spain rather than sent into it. The invasion had reached its high-water mark in January 1812 before the walls of Valencia and Alicante.

SECTION XXXI: CHAPTER II

OPERATIONS OF SOULT IN ANDALUSIA: THE SIEGE OF TARIFA, DEC. 1811–JAN. 1812

In the south-west no less than in the south-east of Spain the month of January 1812 was to witness the last offensive movement of the French armies of invasion. But while Suchet's advance ended, as we have seen, in a splendid success, that of Soult was to meet with a disastrous check. Neither marshal was to have another chance of taking the initiative—thanks, directly or indirectly, to the working out of Wellington's great plan of campaign for the New Year.

In the previous volume the fortunes of Soult and the Army of Andalusia were narrated down to the first days of November 1811, when Hill's raid into Estremadura, after the surprise of Arroyo dos Molinos, ended with his retreat within the borders of Portugal. That raid had inflicted a severe blow on Drouet's corps of observation, which formed Soult's right wing, and covered his communications with Badajoz. But its net result was only to restrict the activities of the French on this side to that part of Estremadura which lies south of the Guadiana. Hill had made no attempt to drive away Drouet's main body, or to blockade Badajoz, and had betaken himself to winter quarters about Elvas, Portalegre, and Estremos. Consequently Drouet was able to settle down opposite him once more, in equally widespread cantonments, with his right wing at Merida, and his left at Zafra, and to devote his attention to sending successive convoys forward to Badajoz, whenever the stores in that fortress showed signs of running low. Drouet's force no longer bore the name of the ' 5th Corps '—all the old corps distinctions were abolished in the Southern Army this autumn, and no organization larger than that of the divisions was permitted to remain. The troops in Estremadura were simply for the future Drouet's and Daricau's divisions of the ' Armée du Midi.' The composition of this ' containing force,' whose whole purpose was now to observe Hill, was somewhat changed after midwinter : for the Emperor sent orders that the 34th and 40th regiments, the victims of Girard's carelessness at Arroyo dos Molinos, were to be sent home to France to recruit their much depleted ranks. They duly left Drouet, and marched off northward [1], but they never got further than Burgos, where Dorsenne detained them at a moment of need, so that they became attached to the ' Army of the North,' and (after receiving some drafts) were involved in the operations against Wellington in the valley of the Douro. Two regiments from Andalusia (the 12th Léger and 45th Line) came up to replace them in Drouet's division, but even then the French troops in Estremadura did not exceed 13,500 men, if the garrison of Badajoz (about 5,000 strong) be deducted. This constituted a field-force insufficient to hold back Hill when next he should take the offensive ; but all through November and far into December Hill remained quiescent, by Wellington's orders, and his adversary clung to his advanced positions as long as he could, though much disturbed as to what the future might bring forth.

Of the remainder of Soult's army, the troops in front of Cadiz, originally the 1st Corps, had been cut down to an irreducible minimum, by the necessity for keeping flank-guards to either side, to watch the Spanish forces in the Condado de Niebla on the west and the mountains of Ronda on the south. Even including the marines and sailors of the flotilla, there were seldom 20,000 men in the Lines, and the Spanish force in Cadiz and the Isle of Leon, stiffened by the Anglo-Portuguese detachment which Wellington always retained there, was often not inferior in numbers to the besiegers. The bombardment from the heavy Villoutreys mortars, placed in the works of the Matagorda peninsula, continued intermittently : but, though a shell occasionally fell in the city, no appreciable harm was done.

---

[1] Napoleon to Berthier, Dec. 30, 1811, speaks of the order to march having been *already* given. The two regiments were in Castile by March : when precisely they left Drouet I cannot say—perhaps as late as February.

The inhabitants killed or injured by many months of shelling could be counted on the fingers of two hands. The citizens had come to take the occasional descent of a missile in their streets with philosophic calm, and sang a derisive street ditty which told how

> ' De las bombas que tiran los Gavachos
> Se hacen las Gaditanas tirabuzones.'

' The splinters of the bombs that the French threw served the ladies of Cadiz as weights to curl their hair [1].'

The Fort of Puntales, on the easternmost point of the isthmus that links Cadiz to the Isle of Leon, felt the bombardment more severely, but was never seriously injured, and always succeeded in keeping up an effective return fire. With the artillery of those days—even when mortars of the largest calibre, specially cast in the arsenal of Seville, were used— Cadiz was safe from any real molestation.

Marshal Victor was still in command of the troops in the Lines at the end of 1811, but the Emperor gave orders for his return to France, when he ordered the Army of Andalusia to drop its organization into army-corps, and replaced them by divisions. He directed that the Marshal should set out at once, unless he was engaged in some serious enterprise at the moment that the summons arrived. This—as we shall see—chanced to be the case, and Victor was still hard at work in January, and did not leave Spain till early in April.

The third main section of Soult's troops consisted of the two infantry and one cavalry divisions which had lately formed the 4th Corps, and had, since their first arrival in the South, been told off for the occupation of the kingdom of Granada. The whole of the coast and the inland from Malaga as far as Baza fell to their charge. The corps had been a strong one— 16,000 foot and 4,000 horse—but was shortly to be reduced ; the order of December 30, recalling troops for the expected Russian war, took off the whole Polish infantry division of Dembouski, 5,000 bayonets : the regiment of Lancers of the Vistula, who had won such fame by their charge at Albuera,

---

[1] See Schepeler, p. 172.

was also requisitioned, but did not get off till the autumn. But in the last month of the old year the Poles were still present and available, and Soult was far from expecting their departure. Yet even before they were withdrawn the garrison of the kingdom of Granada was by no means too strong for the work allotted to it. The greater part of its available field-force had been drawn to the south-west, to curb the insurrection of the *Serranos* of the Ronda mountains, and the inroads of Ballasteros. The forces left in Granada itself and the other eastern towns were so modest that Soult protested, and apparently with truth, that he could not spare from them even a small flying column of all arms, to make the demonstration against Murcia in assistance of Suchet's operations which the Emperor ordered him to execute. Nothing, as it will be remembered, was done in this direction during December and January, save the sending out of Pierre Soult's raid [1], a mere affair of a single cavalry brigade.

The total force of the Andalusian army was still in December as high as 80,000 men on paper. But after deducting the sick, the garrison of Badajoz—5,000 men,—the troops of Drouet, entirely taken up with observing and containing Hill, the divisions in the Lines before Cadiz, and the obligatory garrisons of Granada, Malaga, Cordova, and other large towns, the surplus left over for active operations was very small. At the most ten or twelve thousand men, obtained by borrowing from all sides, could be formed to act as a central reserve, prepared to assist Drouet in Estremadura, Victor in the Cadiz region, or Leval in the East, as occasion might demand. During the two crises when Soult brought up his reserves to join Drouet, in the winter of 1811–12 and the spring of 1812, their joint force did not exceed 25,000 men. The Marshal was resolved to hold the complete circuit of Andalusia, the viceroyalty which brought him so much pride and profit; and so long as he persisted in this resolve he could make no offensive move, for want of a field army of competent strength.

Soult made some effort to supplement the strength of his garrisons by raising Spanish levies—both battalions and

[1] See above, p. 81.

squadrons of regulars, and units for local service in the style of urban guards. The former ' Juramentados ' never reached any great strength : they were composed of deserters, or prisoners who volunteered service in order to avoid being sent to France. Occasionally there were as many as 5,000 under arms—usually less. The men for the most part disappeared at the first opportunity, and rejoined the national army or the guerrilleros : the officers were less prone to abscond, because they were liable to be shot as traitors on returning to their countrymen. Two or three cases are recorded of such renegades who committed suicide, when they saw themselves about to fall into the hands of Spanish troops [1]. The urban guards or ' escopeteros ' were of a little more service, for the reason that, being interested in the preservation of their own families, goods, and houses, they would often prevent the entry into their towns of any roving Spanish force which showed itself for a moment. For if they admitted any small band, which went on its way immediately, and could make no attempt to defend them on the reappearance of the enemy, they were liable to be executed as traitors by the French, and their town would be fined or perhaps sacked. Hence it was to their interest, so long as Soult continued to dominate all Andalusia, to keep the guerrilleros outside their walls. But their service was, of course, unwilling ; and they were usually ready to yield on the appearance of any serious Spanish force, whose size was sufficient to excuse their submission in the eyes of Soult. Often a town was ostensibly held for King Joseph, but was privately supplying recruits, provisions, and money contributions to the national cause. Nevertheless there were real ' Afrancesados ' in Andalusia, people who had so far committed themselves to the cause of King Joseph that they could not contemplate the triumph of the Patriots without terror. When Soult evacuated Andalusia in September 1812 several thousand refugees followed him, rather than face the vengeance of their countrymen.

---

[1] One case is noted of a captain of the ' Juramentado ' detachment at Badajoz who blew himself from a gun when he saw the place taken (Lamare's *Défense de Badajoz*, p. 260). Carlos de España shot the other five Spanish officers captured on that occasion (Belmas, iv. p. 362).

During the midwinter of 1811–12 Soult's main attention was taken up by a serious enterprise in the extreme south of his viceroyalty, which absorbed all the spare battalions of his small central reserve, and rendered it impossible for him to take the offensive in any other direction. This was the attempt to crush Ballasteros, and to capture Tarifa, which rendered his co-operation in Suchet's Valencian campaign impossible.

General Ballasteros, as it will be remembered, had landed from Cadiz at Algeciras on September 4th, 1811, and had been much hunted during the autumn by detachments drawn both from the troops in the kingdom of Granada and those of Victor [1]. As many as 10,000 men were pressing him in October, when he had been forced to take refuge under the cannon of Gibraltar. But when want of food compelled the columns of Barrois, Sémelé, and Godinot to withdraw and to disperse, he had emerged from his refuge, had followed the retiring enemy, and had inflicted some damage on their rearguards [November 5, 1811]. His triumphant survival, after the first concentrated movement made against him, had much provoked Soult, who saw the insurrectionary movement in southern Andalusia spreading all along the mountains, and extending itself towards Malaga on the one side and Arcos on the other. The Marshal, therefore, determined to make a serious effort to crush Ballasteros, and at the same time to destroy one of the two bases from which he was wont to operate. Gibraltar was, of course, impregnable : but Tarifa, the other fortress at the southern end of the Peninsula, was not, and had proved from time to time very useful to the Spaniards. It was now their only secure foothold in southern Andalusia, and was most useful as a port of call for vessels going round from Cadiz to the Mediterranean, especially for the large flotilla of British and Spanish sloops, brigs, and gunboats, which obsessed the coast of Andalusia, and made the use of routes by the seaside almost impracticable for the enemy. Soult was at this time trying to open up communications with the Moors of Tangier, from whom he hoped to get horses for his cavalry, and oxen for the army before Cadiz. But he could not hope to accomplish anything in this way so long as Tarifa was the nest and victualling-place of

---

[1] See vol. iii. pp. 594–5.

privateers, who lay thick in the straits only a few miles from the coast of Morocco.

The main reason for attacking Tarifa, however, was that it had recently become the head-quarters of a small Anglo-Spanish field-force, which had been molesting the rear of the lines before Cadiz. The place had not been garrisoned in 1810, when Soult first broke into Andalusia : but a few months after General Colin Campbell, governor of Gibraltar, threw into it a small force, that same battalion of flank-companies of the 9th, 28th, 30th, and 47th Foot, which distinguished itself so much at Barrosa in the following year, when led by Colonel Brown of the 28th. This hard fighter had moved on with his regiment later in 1811, but his place had been taken by Major King of the 82nd—a one-legged officer of great energy and resolution [1]. The garrison was trifling down to October 1811, when General Campbell threw into Tarifa a brigade under Colonel Skerrett, consisting of the 2/47th and 2/87th, and some details [2], making (with the original garrison) 1,750 British troops. Three days later the Spaniards sent in from Cadiz another brigade [3] of about the same strength, under General Copons. After the French expedition against Ballasteros had failed, Copons and Skerrett went out and drove from Vejer the southernmost outposts of Victor's corps in the Lines (November 6th). A fortnight later they marched across the hills to Algeciras, and prepared to join Ballasteros in an attack on the French troops in the direction of Ronda, but returned to Tarifa on the news that Victor was showing a considerable force at Vejer, and threatening to cut them off from their base [4]. Ballasteros by himself was a sufficient nuisance to Soult, but when his operations began to be aided by another separate

[1] After the 28th went off, the flank-companies were those of the 2/11th, 2/47th, and 1/82nd, two from each battalion.

[2] 2/47th (8 companies) 570 men, 2/87th (560 men), 1 company 95th (75 men), 70 2nd Hussars K.G.L., 1 field-battery (Captain Hughes) 83 men, or in all 1,358 of all ranks.

[3] A battalion each of Irlanda and Cantabria, and some light companies of cazadores, with 120 gunners and 25 cavalry, amounting to about 1,650 men (sick included).

[4] For details of these operations see the anonymous *Defence of Tarifa* (London, 1812), and letters in Rait's *Life of Lord Gough*, i. pp. 69–70.

force, partly composed of British troops, the Duke of Dalmatia determined that a clean sweep must be made in southern Andalusia.

The idea of capturing Tarifa did not appear by any means impracticable. This little decayed place of 6,000 souls had never been fortified in the modern style, and was surrounded by nothing more than a mediaeval wall eight feet thick, with square towers set in it at intervals. There was a citadel, the castle of Guzman El Bueno [1], but this, too, was a thirteenth-century building, and the whole place, though tenable against an enemy unprovided with artillery, was reckoned helpless against siege-guns. It is described by one of its defenders as 'lying in a hole,' for it was completely commanded by a range of low heights, at no greater distance than 300 yards from its northern front. In the sea, half a mile beyond it, was a rocky island, connected with the mainland by a very narrow strip of sand, which was well suited to serve as a final place of refuge for the garrison, and which had been carefully fortified. It was furnished with batteries, of which one bore on the sand-spit and the town : a redoubt (Santa Catalina) had been erected at the point where the isthmus joined the mainland : several buildings had been erected to serve as a shelter for troops, and a great series of caves (Cueva de los Moros) had been converted into casemates and store-rooms : they were perfectly safe against bombardment. In the eyes of many officers the island was the real stronghold, and the city was but an outwork to it, which might be evacuated without any serious damage to the strength of the defence. Nevertheless something had been done to improve the weak fortifications of the place : the convent of San Francisco, seventy yards from its northern point, had been entrenched and loopholed, to serve as a redoubt, and some of the square towers in the *enceinte* had been strengthened and built up so as to bear artillery. The curtain, however, was in all parts far too narrow and weak to allow of guns being placed

---

[1] This was the famous knight who, holding the place for King Sancho IV in 1294, refused to surrender it when the Moors brought his son, captured in a skirmish, before the walls, and threatened to behead him if his father refused to capitulate. Guzman would not yield, saw his son slain, and successfully maintained the fortress.

upon it, and there was no glacis and practically no ditch, the whole wall to its foot being visible from the heights which overlook the city on its eastern side. There were only twenty-six guns available, and of these part belonged to the defences of the island. In the town itself there were only two heavy guns mounted on commanding towers, six field-pieces (9-pounders) distributed along the various fronts, and four mortars. When the siege actually began, the main defence was by musketry fire. It was clear from the topography of Tarifa that its northern front, that nearest to and most completely commanded by the hills outside, would be the probable point of attack by the enemy ; and long before the siege began preparations were made for an interior defence. The buildings looking on the back of the ramparts were barricaded and loopholed, the narrow streets were blocked with traverses, and some ' entanglements ' were contrived with the iron window-bars requisitioned from all the houses of the town, which served as a sort of *chevaux de frise.* The outer *enceinte* was so weak that it was intended that the main defence should be in the network of streets. Special preparations were thought out for the right-centre of the north front, where the walls are pierced by the ravine of a winter torrent of intermittent flow, called the Retiro. The point where it made its passage under the *enceinte* through a portcullis was the lowest place in the front, the walls sinking down as they followed the outline of the ravine. Wherefore palisades were planted outside the portcullis, entanglements behind it, and all the houses looking down on the torrent bed within the walls were prepared with loopholes commanding its course [1]. There was ample time for work, for while the first certain news that the French were coming arrived in November, the enemy did not actually appear before the walls till December 20. By that time much had been done, though the balance was only completed in haste after the siege had begun.

The long delay of the enemy was caused by the abominable condition of the roads of the district—the same that had given Graham and La Peña so much trouble in February 1811 [2] :

[1] For these precautions, the work of Captain Charles Smith, R.E., see the anonymous *Defence of Tarifa* (p. 62), and Napier, iv. pp. 59–60.

[2] See vol. iv. pp. 101–2.

moreover, any considerable concentration of troops in southern Andalusia raised a food problem for Soult. The region round Tarifa is very thinly inhabited, and it was clear that, if a large army were collected, it would have to carry its provisions with it, and secure its communication with its base, under pain of falling into starvation within a few days. Heavy guns abounded in the Cadiz lines, and Soult had no trouble in selecting a siege-train of sixteen pieces from them : but their transport and that of their ammunition was a serious problem. To complete the train no less than 500 horses had to be requisitioned from the field artillery and military wagons of the 1st Corps. While it was being collected, Victor moved forward to Vejer, near the coast, half-way between Cadiz and Tarifa, with 2,000 men, in order to clear the country-side from the guerrillero bands, who made survey of the roads difficult and dangerous. Under cover of escorts furnished by him, several intelligence officers inspected the possible routes : there were two, both passing through the mountainous tract between the sea and the lagoon of La Janda (which had given Graham so much trouble in the last spring). One came down to the waterside at the chapel of Virgen de la Luz, only three miles from Tarifa, but was reported to be a mere mule-track. The other, somewhat more resembling a road, descended to the shore several miles farther to the north, and ran parallel with it for some distance. But in expectation of the siege, the Spaniards, with help from English ships, had blown up many yards of this road, where it was narrowest between the water and the mountain. Moreover, ships of war were always stationed off Tarifa, and their guns would make passage along this defile dangerous. Nevertheless General Garbé, the chief French engineer, held that this was the only route practicable for artillery, and reported that the road could be remade, and that the flotilla might be kept at a distance by building batteries on the shore, which would prevent any vessel from coming close enough to deliver an effective fire. It was determined, therefore, that the siege-train should take this path, which for the first half of its way passes close along the marshy borders of the lagoon of La Janda, and then enters the hills in order to descend to the sea at Torre Peña.

On December 8th the siege-train was concentrated at Vejer, and in the hope that it would in four days (or not much more) reach its destination before Tarifa, Victor gave orders for the movement of the troops which were to conduct the siege. Of this force the smaller part, six battalions [1] and two cavalry regiments, was drawn from Leval's command, formerly the 4th Corps. These two divisions had also to provide other detachments to hold Malaga in strength, and watch Ballasteros. The troops from the blockade of Cadiz supplied eight battalions [2], and three more to keep up communications [3]; one additional regiment was borrowed from the brigade in the kingdom of Cordova, which was always drawn upon in times of special need [4]. The whole force put in motion was some 15,000 men, but only 10,000 actually came before Tarifa and took part in the siege.

The various columns, which were under orders to march, came from distant points, and had to concentrate. Barrois lay at Los Barrios, inland from Algeciras, with six battalions from the Cadiz lines, watching Ballasteros, who had once more fallen back under shelter of the guns of Gibraltar. To this point Leval came to join him, with the 3,000 men drawn from Malaga and Granada. The third column, under Victor himself, consisting of the siege-train and the battalions told off for its escort, came from the side of Vejer. All three were to meet before Tarifa : but from the first start difficulties began to arise owing to the bad weather.

The winter, which had hitherto been mild and equable, broke up into unending rain-storms on the day appointed for the start, and the sudden filling of the torrents in the mountains cut the communications between the columns. Leval, who had got as far as the pass of Ojen, in the range which separates the district about Algeciras and Los Barrios from the Tarifa region, was forced to halt there for some days : but his rear, a brigade under Cassagne, could not come forward to join him, nor did

[1] Two battalions each of 43rd Line and 7th and 9th Poles, and 16th and 21st Dragoons.

[2] Three of 16th Léger, two of 54th Line, one each of 27th Léger and 94th and 95th Line.

[3] Two of 63rd and one of 8th Line.

[4] 51st Line.

the convoy-column succeed in advancing far from Vejer. Victor sent three successive officers with escorts to try to get into touch with Cassagne, but each returned without having been able to push through. It was not till the 12th that a fourth succeeded in reaching the belated column, which only got under way that day and joined on the following afternoon. The siege-train was not less delayed, and was blocked for several days by the overflowing of the lagoon of La Janda, along whose shore its first stages lay. It only struggled through to the south end of the lagoon on the 14th, and took no less than four days more to cover the distance of sixteen miles across the hills to Torre Peña, where the road comes down to the sea. Forty horses, it is said, had to be harnessed to each heavy gun to pull it through [1]. Much of the ammunition was spoilt by the rain, which continued to fall intermittently, and more had to be requisitioned from the Cadiz lines, and to be brought forward by supplementary convoys.

These initial delays went far to wreck the whole scheme, because of the food problem. Each of the columns had to bring its own provisions with it, and, when stopped on the road, consumed stores that had been intended to serve it during the siege. The distance from Vejer to Tarifa is only thirty miles, and from Los Barrios to Tarifa even less : but the columns, which had been ordered to march on December 8th, did not reach their destination till December 20th, and the communications behind them were cut already, not by the enemy but by the vile weather, which had turned every mountain stream into a torrent, and every low-lying bottom into a marsh. The column with the siege artillery arrived two days later : it had got safely through the defile of Torre Peña : the sappers had repaired the road by the water, and had built a masked battery for four 12-pounders and two howitzers, whose fire kept off from the dangerous point several Spanish and English gunboats which came up to dispute the passage. The column from the pass of Ojen had been somewhat delayed in its march by a sally of Ballasteros, who came out from the Gibraltar lines on the 17th–18th and fell upon its rear with 2,000 men. He drove in the last battalion, but when Barrois turned back and attacked

---

[1] For details of this toilsome march see Belmas, iv. pp. 15–17.

him with a whole brigade, the Spaniard gave way and retreated
in haste to San Roque. Nevertheless, by issuing from his
refuge and appearing in the open, he had cut the communications
between the army destined for the siege and the troops at
Malaga. At the same time that Ballasteros made this diversion,
Skerrett, with his whole brigade and a few of Copons's Spaniards,
had issued from Tarifa to demonstrate against the head of the
approaching French column, and advanced some distance on
the road to Fascinas, where his handful of hussars bickered
with the leading cavalry in the enemy's front. Seeing infantry
behind, he took his main body no farther forward than the
convent of Nuestra Señora de la Luz, three miles from the
fortress. On the 19th the French showed 4,000 men on the
surrounding hills, and on the 20th advanced in force in two
columns, and pushed the English and Spanish pickets into
Tarifa, after a long skirmish in which the British had 31, the
Spaniards about 40 casualties, while the French, according
to Leval's report, lost only 1 officer and 3 men killed and
27 wounded. By four in the afternoon the place was invested—
the French pickets reaching from sea to sea, and their main
body being encamped behind the hills which command the
northern side of Tarifa. They could not place themselves near
the water, owing to the fire of two British frigates and a swarm
of gunboats, which lay in-shore, and shelled their flanks all day,
though without great effect.

Copons and Skerrett had divided the manning of the town and
island between their brigades on equal terms, each keeping two
battalions in the town and a third in the island and the minor
posts. Of the British the 47th and 87th had the former, King's
battalion of flank-companies (reinforced by 70 marines landed
from the ships) the latter charge. The convent of San Francisco
was held by a company of the 82nd, the redoubt of Santa
Catalina on the isthmus by one of the 11th. Seeing the French
inactive on the 21st—they were waiting for the siege-train
which was not yet arrived—Skerrett sent out three companies
to drive in their pickets, and shelled the heights behind which
they were encamped. On the following day the sortie was
repeated, by a somewhat larger force under Colonel Gough
of the 87th, covered by a flanking fire from the gunboats. The

right wing of the French pickets was driven in with some loss, and a house too near the Santa Catalina redoubt demolished. The besiegers lost 3 men killed and 4 officers and 19 men wounded, mainly from the 16th Léger. The sallying troops had only 1 man killed and 5 wounded (2 from the 11th, 4 from the 87th). That night the siege-train arrived, and was parked behind the right-hand hill of the three which face the northern side of Tarifa.

The engineer officers who had come up with the siege-train executed their survey of the fortress next morning, and reported (as might have been expected) that it would be best to attack the central portion of the north front, because the ground facing it was not exposed to any fire from the vessels in-shore, as was the west front, and could only be searched by the two or three guns which the besieged had mounted on the towers of Jesus and of Guzman, the one in the midst of the northern front, the other in a dominating position by the castle, at the southern corner. However, the 24-pounders on the island, shooting over the town, could throw shells on to the hillside where the French were about to work, though without being able to judge of their effect.

On the night of the 23rd the French began their first parallel, on their right flank of the central hill, at a distance of 300 yards from the walls : the approaches to it needed no spadework, being completely screened by a ravine and a thick aloe hedge. The besieged shelled it on the succeeding day, but with small effect—only 3 workers were killed and 4 wounded. On the 24th a minor front of attack was developed on the left-hand hill, where a first parallel was thrown up about 250 yards from the walls. The gunboats on the southern shore fired on this work when it was discovered, but as it was invisible to them, and as they could only shoot at haphazard, by directions signalled from the town, they generally failed to hit the mark, and did little to prevent the progress of the digging. The besiegers only lost 4 killed and 25 wounded this day, and on the original point of attack were able to commence a second parallel, in which there was marked out the place for the battery which was destined to breach the town wall at the lowest point of its circuit, just south of the bed of the Retiro torrent.

On the two following days the French continued to push forward with no great difficulty ; they completed the second parallel on the centre hill, parts of which were only 180 yards from the town. On the left or eastern hill the trenches were continued down the inner slope, as far as the bottom of the ravine, so as almost to join those of the right attack. On the 26th a violent south-east gale began to blow, which compelled the British and Spanish gunboats to quit their station to the right of Tarifa, lest they should be driven ashore, and to run round to the west side of the island which gave them shelter from wind coming from such a quarter. The French works were, therefore, only molested for the future by the little 6-pounders on the north-east (or Corchuela) tower, and the heavy guns firing at a high trajectory from the island and the tower of Guzman.

But the gale was accompanied by rain, and this, beginning with moderate showers on the 26th, developed into a steady downpour on the 27th and 28th, and commenced to make the spadework in the trenches more laborious, as the sappers were up to their ankles in mud, and the excavated earth did not bind easily into parapets owing to its semi-liquid condition. Nevertheless the plans of the engineers were carried out, and two batteries were finished and armed on the central hill, one lower down to batter the walls, the other higher up, to deal with the guns of the besieged and silence them if possible. The French lined all the advanced parallel with sharpshooters, who kept up a heavy fire on the ramparts, and would have made it difficult for the garrison to maintain a reply, if a large consignment of sandbags had not been received from Gibraltar, with which cover was contrived for the men on the curtain, and the artillery in the towers.

At eleven o'clock on the morning of the 29th the two French batteries opened [1], with twelve heavy guns. The weakness of the old town wall at once became evident : the first shot fired went completely through it, and lodged in a house to its rear. Before evening there was a definite breach produced, just south

---

[1] The breaching battery on the lower slope with four 16- and two 12-pounders : the upper battery with four howitzers for high-trajectory fire against the more distant guns of the besieged and the island, and two 12-pounders.

of the Retiro ravine, and it was clear that the enemy would be able to increase it to any extent that he pleased—the masonry fell to pieces the moment that it was well pounded. The two small field-guns on the tower of Jesus were silenced by 3 o'clock, and the heavy gun on Guzman's tower also ceased firing—of which more anon. By night only the distant guns on the island, and the ships in the south-western bay, were making an effective reply to the French.

This, from the psychological point of view, was the critical day of the siege, for on the clear demonstration of the weakness of the walls, Colonel Skerrett, who had never much confidence in his defences, proposed to evacuate the city of Tarifa. At a council of officers he argued in favour of withdrawing the garrison into the island, and making no attempt to hold the weak mediaeval walls which the French were so effectively battering. This would have been equivalent, in the end, to abandoning the entire foothold of the British on this point of the coast. For there was on the island no cover for troops, save two or three recently erected buildings, and the recesses of the ' Cueva de los Moros.' Some of the inhabitants had already taken refuge there, and were suffering great privations, from being exposed to the weather in tents and hastily contrived huts. It is clear that if 3,000 men, British and Spanish, had been lodged on the wind-swept rocks of the island, it would soon have been necessary to withdraw them ; however inaccessible the water-girt rock, with its low cliffs, might be, no large body of troops could have lived long upon it, exposed as they would have been not only to wind and wet, but to constant molestation by heavy guns placed in and about the city and the hills that dominate it. Meanwhile the French would have possessed the excellent cover of the houses of Tarifa, and would have effec- tively blocked the island by leaving a garrison to watch the causeway, the only possible exit from it. It is certain that the abandonment of the island would have followed that of the town within a few days : indeed Skerrett had already obtained leave from General Cooke, then commanding at Cadiz, to bring his brigade round to that port as soon as he should feel it necessary. He regarded the evacuation of the place as so certain, that he ordered the 18-pounder gun on Guzman's tower to be spiked this day, though it was the only piece of heavy calibre in the city [1]—the reason given was that one of its missiles (spherical case-shot) had fallen short within the streets, and killed or wounded an inhabitant. But the real cause was that he had fully decided on abandoning Tarifa that night or the following day, and thought the moving of such a big gun in a hurry impossible—it had been hoisted with great difficulty to its place by the sailors, with cranes and tackle [2].

Skerrett stated his decision in favour of the evacuation at the council of war, produced General Cooke's letter supporting his plan, and stated that Lord Proby, his second in command, concurred in the view of its necessity. Fortunately for the credit of the British arms, his opinion was boldly traversed by Captain C. F. Smith, the senior engineer officer, Major King commanding the Gibraltar battalion of flank-companies, and Colonel Gough of the 87th. The former urged that the town should be defended, as an outwork of the island, to thé last possible moment : though the breach was practicable, he had already made arrangements for cutting it off by retrenchments from the body of the town. The streets had been blocked and barricaded, and all the houses looking upon the back of the walls loopholed. Tarifa could be defended for some time in the style of Saragossa, lane by lane. He pointed out that such was the configuration of the ground that if the enemy entered the breach, he would find a fourteen-foot drop between its rear and the ground below, on to which he would have to descend under a concentric fire of musketry from all the neighbouring buildings. Even supposing that the worst came, the garrison had the castle to retire into, and this was tenable until breached by artillery, while a retreat from it to the island would always be possible, under cover of the guns of the flotilla. There was no profit or credit in giving up outworks before they were forced. Major King concurred, and said that his battalion, being

---

[1] According to some authorities he also spiked a 32-lb. carronade. See *Defence of Tarifa*, p. 63.

[2] The author of the *Defence of Tarifa* pretends not to know the real story (p. 63), saying that the spiking caused much ' indignation, apprehension, and discontent,' and that ' whence the order proceeded is unknown.' For the explanation see the letter from an officer of the garrison in Napier, iv, Appendix, p. 438.

Gibraltar troops, was under the direct orders of General Campbell, from whom he had received directions to hold Tarifa till
the last extremity. If Skerrett's brigade should embark, he and
the flank-companies would remain behind, to defend it, along
with Copons's Spaniards. Gough concurred in the decision, and
urged that the evacuation would be wholly premature and ' contrary to the spirit of General Campbell's instructions ' until it
was seen whether the French were able to effect a lodgement
inside the walls [1].

Skerrett's resolve was shaken—he still held to his opinion, but
dismissed the council of war without coming to a decision :
he tried to avoid responsibility by requesting the officers who
voted for further resistance to deliver him their opinions in
writing. This King, Smith, and Gough did, in the strongest
wording. The first named of these three resolute men sent that
same night a messenger by boat to Gibraltar, to inform General
Campbell of Skerrett's faint-hearted decision, and to observe
that, with a few companies more to aid his own flank-battalion
and the Spaniards, he would try to hold first Tarifa and then the
island, even if Skerrett withdrew his brigade. Campbell, angry
in no small degree, sent a very prompt answer to the effect
that the town should not be abandoned without the concurrence
of the commanding officers of artillery and engineers, while the
Gibraltar battalion should be concentrated in the island, in
order to ensure its defence even if Tarifa itself fell. Still more
drastic was an order to the officers commanding the transports
to bring their ships back at once to Gibraltar : this decisive
move made it impossible for Skerrett to carry out his plan [2].
A few days later Campbell sent two more flank-companies to
join the garrison—but they only arrived after the assault.

The idea of evacuating the town without attempting any
defence was all the more ignominious because Copons had
declared his intention of holding it to the last, had protested
against the spiking of the heavy gun in Guzman's tower, and

---

[1] Gough speaks of his reply that ' evacuation would be contrary to the
spirit of General Campbell's instructions,' as if given at an earlier date, but,
the 29th seems fixed by King's letter to Napier in appendix to the latter's
Peninsular War, iv. pp. 443–4, quoted above.

[2] See especially the notes from officers on the spot in Napier's appendix
to vol. iv. pp. 442–4.

next morning, when Leval summoned the place to surrender, sent in a most unhesitating, if somewhat bombastic [1], note of refusal. If Skerrett had withdrawn into the island, or taken to his ships, and Copons had been overwhelmed, fighting in the streets, the disgrace to the British flag would have been very great. As a sidelight on the whole matter, we may remember that this was the same officer who had refused to land his troops to defend the breach of Tarragona six months before. He was no coward, as he showed in many fights, and he died gallantly at Bergen-op-Zoom in 1814, but he was undoubtedly a shirker of responsibilities.

On the morning of the 30th the besiegers' batteries opened again, and enlarged the breach to a broad gap of thirty feet or more ; they also dismounted a field-piece which the besieged had hoisted on the Jesus tower, to replace those injured on the previous day. At midday Leval sent in the summons already recorded, and receiving Copons's uncompromising reply, directed the fire to continue. It was very effective, and by evening the breach was nearly sixty feet long, occupying almost the whole space between the tower at the portcullis over the ravine, and that next south of it. At dusk the garrison crept out to clear the foot of the breach, and began also to redouble the inner defences in the lanes and houses behind it. All work on both sides, however, was stopped, shortly after nightfall, by a most torrential downpour of rain, which drove the French from their batteries and the English and Spaniards from their repairing. The sky seemed to be falling—the hillsides became cataracts, and the Retiro ravine was soon filled with a broad river which came swirling against the walls, bearing with it fascines, planks, gabions, and even dead bodies washed out of the French lines. Presently the mass of débris, accumulating against the palisades erected in front of the portcullis, and urged on by the water, swept away these outer defences, and then, pressing against the portcullis itself, bent it inwards and twisted it, despite of its massive iron clamps, so as to make an opening

---

[1] ' Sin duda ignorará V.S. que me hallo yo en esta plaza, cuando se prononce á su gubernador que admite una capitulacion. Á la cabeza de mis tropas me encontrará V.S. y entonces hableremos.' See Arteche, appendix to vol. xi. p. 524.

into the town, down which everything went swimming through the ravine. The flood also swept away some of the defensive works on each side of the depression. When the hurricane was over, the rain still continued to fall heavily, but the garrison, emerging from shelter, commenced to repair their works, and had undone much of the damage by daylight [1].

If the besieged had been sorely incommoded by the tempest, the besiegers on the bare hillsides had been still worse tried. They had been forced to abandon their trenches and batteries, of which those high up the slope were water-logged, while those below had been largely swept away by the flood. The breach had been pronounced practicable by the engineers, and an assault had been fixed for dawn. But it was necessary to put it off for some hours, in order to allow the artillery to reoccupy their batteries, and recommence their fire, and the infantry to come up from the camps where they had vainly tried to shelter themselves during the downpour. Nevertheless the French commanders resolved to storm as soon as the men could be assembled, without waiting for further preparations. ' The troops,' says the French historian of the siege, ' unable to dry themselves, or to light fires to cook their rations, loudly cried out for an assault, as the only thing that could put an end to their misery.' A large force had been set apart for the storm, the grenadier and voltigeur companies of each of the battalions engaged in the sieges, making a total of over 2,200 men. They were divided into two columns—the grenadiers were to storm the breach ; the voltigeurs to try whether the gap at the Portcullis tower was practicable or not : they were to break in if possible, if not, to engage the defenders in a fusilade which should distract their attention from the main attack.

As soon as day dawned, the besieged could detect that the trenches were filling, and that the storm was about to break. They had time to complete their dispositions before the French moved : the actual breach was held by Copons with a battalion of his own troops [2] : the 87th, under Gough, occupied the walls

---

[1] For this, see Jones, *Sieges of the Peninsula*, ii. p. 477, from which Napier copies his narrative, iv. p. 55.

[2] Their part in the defence must not be denied to the Spaniards. Napier, with his usual prejudice, remarks (iv. p. 60) that Skerrett ' assigned the charge

both to right and left of the breach, including the Portcullis tower, with two companies in reserve. Captain Levesey with 100 of the 47th was posted in the south-eastern (Jesus) tower, which completely enfiladed the route which the enemy would have to take to the foot of the breach. The rest of the 47th was in charge of the south front of the town.

At nine o'clock the column of French grenadiers issued from the trenches near the advanced breaching battery, and dashed down the side of the Retiro ravine towards the breach, while the voltigeur companies, at the same time, running out from the approaches on the eastern hill, advanced by the opposite side of the ravine towards the Portcullis tower. Demonstrations to right and left were made by Cassagne's brigade on one flank and Pécheux's on the other. The progress of the storming column was not rapid—the slopes of the ravine were rain-sodden and slippery ; its bottom (where the flood had passed) was two feet deep in mud. The troops were forced to move slowly, and the moment that they were visible from the walls they became exposed to a very heavy fire of musketry, both from the curtain and the enfilading towers on each of their flanks. Of guns the besieged had only one available—a field-piece in the northern-most (or Corchuela) tower, which fired case-shot diagonally along the foot of the walls.

Nevertheless the French grenadiers pushed forward across the open space towards the breach, under a rain of bullets from the 87th which smote them on both flanks. The Fusiliers were firing fast and accurately, to the tune of *Garry Owen*, which the regimental band was playing by order of Gough just behind the breach, accompanied by bursts of shouts and cheering. On arriving at the foot of the walls, in great disorder, the French column hesitated for a moment ; many men began to fire instead of pressing on, but some bold spirits scaled the rough slope of the breach and reached its lip—only to get a momentary glimpse of the fourteen-foot drop behind it, and to fall dead.

of the breach entirely to the Spaniards, and if Smith had not insisted upon placing British troops alongside of them this would have ruined the defence, because hunger and neglect had so broken the spirit of these poor men that few appeared during the combat, and Copons alone displayed the qualities of a gallant soldier.'

The bulk of the column then swerved away to its right, and fell upon the palisades and other defences in front of the Portcullis tower, where the hasty repairs made after the flood of the preceding night did not look effective. Apparently many of the voltigeurs who had been already engaged in this quarter joined in their assault, which surged over the outer barricades and penetrated as far as the portcullis itself. It was found too well repaired to be broken down, and the stormers, crowded in front of it, and caught in an angle between the front wall defended by the 87th, and the flanking Jesus tower from which the 47th were firing, found the corner too hot for them, and suddenly recoiled and fled. The officer at the head of the forlorn hope gave up his sword to Gough through the bars of the portcullis, which alone separated them, and many other men at the front of the column also surrendered, rather than face the point-blank fire at close range which would have accompanied the first stage of their retreat.

This was a striking instance of an assault on a very broad breach, by a strong force, being beaten off by musketry fire alone. The French seem never to have had a chance in face of the steady resistance of the 87th and their comrades. Their loss is given by the official French historian at only 48 killed and 159 wounded, which seems an incredibly low figure when over 2,000 men were at close quarters with the besieged, in a very disadvantageous position, for some time [1]. The British lost 2 officers and 7 men killed, 3 officers, 2 sergeants, and 22 men wounded : the Spaniards had a lieutenant-colonel killed and about 20 men killed and wounded.

[1] Skerrett and Copons estimated the loss of the enemy at nearly 500, no doubt an exaggeration. But Leval's 207 seems far too few. The commanding officer of the 51st Ligne reports from his four flank-companies 7 officers and 81 men hit (Belmas, iv, Appendix, p. 58). Of the sapper detachment which led the column, from 50 men 43 were *hors de combat* (Belmas, iv. p. 31). It seems incredible that when 23 companies took part in the assault 5 of them should have suffered 131 casualties out of a total of 207. Martinien's tables show 18 officers killed and wounded on Dec. 31, a figure which proves nothing, for though at the usual casualty rate of 20 men per officer this would imply a total loss of 360, yet it is well known that in assaults the officers often suffer a loss out of all proportion to that of the rank and file. Eighteen officers hit might be compatible with a loss as low as 200 or as high as 400 in such a case.

The assault having failed so disastrously, the spirits of the besiegers sank to a very low pitch. The rain continued to fall during the whole day and the following night, and the already water-logged trenches became quite untenable. On New Year's Day, 1812, the dawn showed a miserable state of affairs—not only were the roads to the rear, towards Fascinas and Vejer, entirely blocked by the swelling of mountain torrents, but communications were cut even between the siege-camps. All the provision of powder in the siege-batteries was found to be spoilt by wet, and a great part of the cartridges of the infantry. Nearly a third of the horses of the train had perished from cold combined with low feeding. No rations were issued to the troops that day, and on the three preceding days only incomplete ones had been given, because of the impossibility of getting them up from the reserve dépôt, and many of the men wandered without leave for three miles to the rear in search of food or shelter. An exploring party of the 47th pushing out into the trenches found them quite unguarded[1] and full of water. Leval wrote a formal proposal for the abandonment of the siege to his chief, Victor, saying that the only choice was to save the army by retreat, or to see it perish in a few days if it remained stationary[2]. The Marshal, however, refused to turn back from an enterprise in which he considered his honour involved, and the tempest having abated on the night of Jan. 2nd–3rd, ordered the batteries and approaches to be remanned, and directed that an attempt should be made to sap forward toward the Jesus tower from the left advanced trenches. The work done was feeble—the batteries had fired only fifty shots by evening, and the repairs to the damaged works were very incomplete.

Even Victor's obstinacy yielded, however, when on the night of the 3rd–4th January another furious storm arose, and once more stopped all possibility of continuing operations. No food had now come up from the base for many days, and the stores at the front being exhausted, the Marshal saw that it was necessary to march at once. An attempt was made to withdraw the guns from the batteries, but only one 12-pounder and two howitzers were got off—the horses were so weak and the

[1] *Defence of Tarifa*, p. 47.
[2] See the letter in Belmas, iv. pp. 55–6.

ground so sodden that even when 200 infantry were set to help, most of the pieces could not be dragged more than a few yards. Wherefore the attempt was given over, the powder in the batteries was thrown open to the rain, the balls rolled into the Retiro ravine, the nine remaining heavy guns spiked.

On the night of the 4th–5th the army crawled off on the road to Vejer, abandoning nearly all its material in its camps. An attempt was made to fire a mass of abandoned vehicles, but the rain stopped it. Next morning the French were passing the defile of Torre Peña, under the not very effective fire of an English frigate, which kept as close to the shore as was possible on a very rough day. The four guns from the battery at this point were brought on, with much toil, and no wounded were abandoned. On the 6th the column reached Tayvilla, where it found a convoy and 100 horses, which were of inestimable value, for those with the field-force were completely spent. Nevertheless the one 12-pounder brought off from Tarifa was abandoned in the mud. On the 7th Vejer was reached, and the expedition was at an end. The troops of Victor's division, after a short rest, went back to the Cadiz Lines, those of Leval's division marched for Xeres.

Thus ended the leaguer of Tarifa, which cost the besiegers about 500 lives, more by sickness than by casualties in the trenches. There were also some deserters—fifteen Poles came over in a body and surrendered to Captain Carroll on the 3rd [1], and other individuals stole in from time to time. But the main loss to the French, beyond that of prestige, was that the battalions which had formed part of the expeditionary force were so tired out and war-worn, that for several weeks they continued to fill the hospitals in the Lines with sick, and were incapable of further active service. Wherefore Soult could not send any appreciable detachment to help Suchet on the side of Valencia : the cavalry brigade, which sacked Murcia on January 26 and killed La Carrera,[2] was his only contribution to the operations on the east side of Spain. The field-force which might otherwise have accompanied Pierre Soult's cavalry raid had been used up in the Tarifa expedition.

[1] *Defence of Tarifa*, p. 75.
[2] See page 8 above.

TARIFA

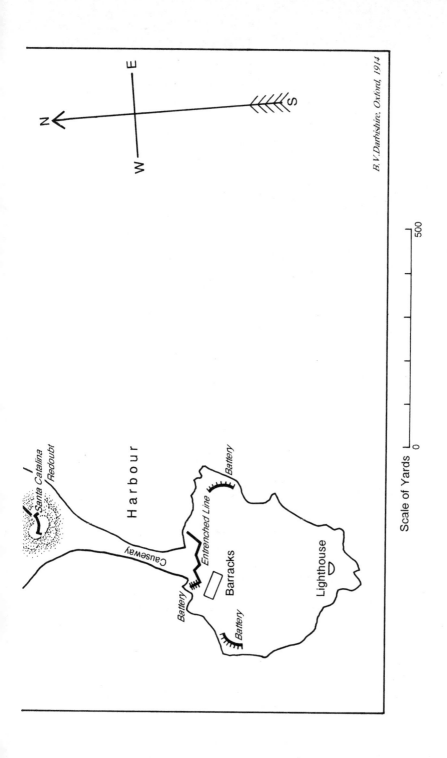

Santa Catalina
Redoubt

Harbour

Causeway

Battery

Entrenched Line

Battery

Barracks

Battery

Battery

Lighthouse

N
E
W
S

B.V.Darbishire, Oxford, 1914

Scale of Yards

0 500

Another distraction had come upon Soult while the Tarifa expedition was in progress. On December 27, six days after Victor and Leval commenced the siege, General Hill had once more begun to move on the Estremaduran side, after remaining quiescent for nearly two months since the surprise of Arroyo dos Molinos. His advance was a diversion made by Wellington's direct orders, with the purpose of drawing Soult's attention away from the pursuit of Ballasteros and the molesting of Tarifa [1]. It failed to achieve the latter purpose, since the operations of Victor had gone so far, before Hill moved, that the Marshal stood committed to the siege, and indeed only heard that Hill was on the move after the assault of December 31st had been made and beaten off. But it caused Soult to cut off all support from Victor, to turn his small remaining reserves in the direction of Estremadura, and to welcome as a relief, rather than to deplore as a disaster, the return of the defeated expeditionary force to the Lines of Cadiz on January 7th. For about that date Hill was pushing Drouet before him, and the reserves from Seville were moving northwards, so that Soult was pleased to learn that the 10,000 men from Tarifa had returned, and that, in consequence of their reappearance, he could draw off more men from the direction of Cadiz to replace the troops moved toward Estremadura.

Hill crossed the Portuguese frontier north of the Guadiana on December 27th, with his own division, Hamilton's Portuguese, two British cavalry brigades (those of Long and de Grey [2]) and one of Portuguese (4th and 10th regiments under J. Campbell of the former corps), or about 12,000 men. The small remainder of his force [3] was left about Elvas, to watch any possible movement of the French from the direction of Badajoz. His objective was Merida, where it was known that Dombrouski, with the greater part of the 5th French Division, was lying, in a position far advanced from the main body of Drouet's troops, who were cantoned about Zafra and Llerena. There was some hope of surprising this force, and a certainty of driving it in, and of throwing Drouet and Soult into a state of alarm.

---

[1] See Wellington to Hill, Dec. 18th, *Dispatches*, ix. pp. 465–6.

[2] But the last-named officer was absent.

[3] One Portuguese infantry and one Portuguese cavalry brigade.

Wellington directed Hill to keep to the desolate road north of
the Guadiana, because a winter raid from this direction would
be the last thing expected by the enemy. He bade his lieutenant
keep a wary eye in the direction of Truxillo and Almaraz, from
which the divisions of Marmont's army then in New Castile
might possibly descend upon his rear. But the warning turned
out to be superfluous, since, before Hill moved, Marmont had
been forced by the Emperor's orders to detach his troops on the
Tagus for the ruinous expedition under Montbrun to Alicante.

Marching very rapidly Hill reached Albuquerque on the 27th,
and La Rocca, only twenty miles from Merida, on the 28th.
On the next day [1] the prospect of surprising Dombrouski came
to an end by the merest of chances. The French general had
sent out that morning a small column to raise requisitions of
food in the villages on this road. A troop of hussars at its head
discovered Hill's advanced cavalry, near Navas de Membrillo,
and alarmed the infantry, three companies of the 88th regiment
under a Captain Neveux, who formed up and began to retreat
hastily towards Merida. Hill sent two squadrons each of the
13th Light Dragoons and 2nd Hussars of the King's German
Legion in pursuit, with orders to head off and capture, if possible,
these 400 men. The result was a combat of the same sort as
that of Barquilla in 1810, where it had already been shown that
steady infantry could not be ridden down by cavalry save
under very exceptional circumstances. Neveux, seeing the
dragoons hurrying forward, turned off the road, formed his
men in square, and made for a cork wood on a rising ground.
The cavalry overtook him, and delivered five determined
charges, which were all beaten off with heavy loss. We are
told that their order and impetus were both broken by scattered
trees outside the wood, but the main cause of their defeat was
the impossibility of breaking into a solidly-formed square of
determined men, well commanded [2]. After the final charge the

---

[1] Napier (iv. 49) wrongly puts the combat of Navas de Membrillo on
the 28th of December, not the 29th. The diaries of Stoltzenberg of the
2nd K.G.L. Hussars and Cadell of the 28th prove that the second date
is correct. No force could have marched from Albuquerque to Navas
in one day.

[2] Hill's dispatch has a handsome but ungrammatical testimony to the
enemy : ' the intrepid and admirable way in which the French retreated,

squadrons drew off, and Neveux hastened on through the wood, fell back again into the road, and reached Merida, though he lost a few men [1] by shells from Hawker's battery, which came up late in the day. The K.G.L. Hussars had 2 men killed and 1 officer and 17 men wounded : the 13th Light Dragoons 1 killed and 19 wounded.

Dombrouski, warned of the approach of the allies in force, immediately evacuated Merida, where Hill made prize of 160,000 lb. of wheat, unground, and a large magazine of biscuit. He found that the French had been fortifying the town, but the works were too unfinished to allow them to defend it. On January 1st Hill, continuing his advance, marched across the bridge of Merida on Almendralejo, thinking that Drouet might possibly have come up to help Dombrouski, and that he might force him to fight. This was not to be : the rearguard of the force from Merida was discovered drawn up in front of Almendralejo, but gave way at the first push : a small magazine of food was captured in the town.

It was now clear that Drouet did not intend to make a stand, but would fall back towards the Andalusian frontier, and wait for aid from Soult. Hill resolved to move his main body no further, but sent out a small flying column under Major-General Abercrombie, with orders to press the French rearguard as long as it would give way, but to halt and turn back on finding serious forces in front of him. This detachment (1/50th regiment, two squadrons 2nd Hussars K.G.L., two squadrons 10th Portuguese, three guns) passing Fuente del Maestre neared Los Santos on January 3rd, and found Dombrouski, with a rearguard of all arms, disposed to fight. This led to a sharp cavalry combat, between two squadrons of the 26th French Dragoons and the allied horse. One squadron of the hussars and one of the Portuguese, gallantly led by Colonel Campbell, charged the enemy in front, the other squadrons remaining in reserve. The dragoons, soon broken, lost 6 killed, many

the infantry formed in square, and favoured as he was by the nature of the country, of which he knew how to take the fullest advantage, prevented the cavalry alone from effecting anything against him.'

[1] Apparently two killed and nine wounded.

wounded, and 2 officers and 35 men prisoners. Thereupon the French infantry moved rapidly off southwards, making no attempt to stand. The victors lost 1 man killed and 14 wounded from the hussars, 1 officer and 5 men from the Portuguese.

Drouet was now concentrating at Llerena, and ready to give up all Estremadura north of that point. He was sending daily appeals for succour to Soult, who had little to give him, while Victor and the expeditionary force were away at Tarifa. On January 5th the Duke of Dalmatia wrote a dispatch which ordered that the siege should be abandoned—but long ere it came to hand Victor had been forced to depart, as we have seen, for reasons entirely unconnected with Hill's midwinter raid. Wellington's plan would have worked if the weather had not already driven Victor away, but had in actual fact no effect on his proceedings.

Hill, having accomplished all that could be done in the way of alarming Soult, held Merida and Almendralejo for a few days, with his advanced cavalry about Fuente del Maestre : but retired on January 13th to Albuquerque and Portalegre, to the intense relief of his enemy. The raising of the siege of Tarifa being known, there was no further reason for keeping Hill in an advanced position, which might have tempted Soult to make a great concentration and take the offensive. Wellington had no desire that he should do so, since the Army of Andalusia, while dispersed, was harmless, but might become dangerous if it should evacuate great regions, and so be able to collect in force. Soult did not wish to make such sacrifices unless he were obliged, and on hearing of Hill's retreat countermanded all orders for concentration, and contented himself with bringing back Drouet to Llerena and Zalamea, and with reopening his communication with Badajoz, which had been cut while the allies were at Fuente del Maestre. He did not at this time reoccupy Merida, partly because the position had been demonstrated to be dangerous by Hill's recent raid, partly because its main importance was that it covered the road to Truxillo and Almaraz and Marmont's army. But Marmont having, for the moment, no troops in this direction, owing to the Alicante expedition, it was useless to try to keep in touch with him.

Hill's expedition, by driving Drouet for some time from the

line of the Guadiana, made possible a sudden irruption of the Spaniards into La Mancha, where none of their regular troops had been since since the battle of Ocaña two years before. This raid was carried out by Morillo at the head of a brigade of the Estremaduran army of Castaños. That general had heard of the way in which the upper valley of the Guadiana had been denuded of troops, in order that the Army of the Centre might assist Suchet in the direction of Cuenca and Requeña [1]. Nothing was left in La Mancha save a few battalions of King Joseph's German Division, and a brigade of Treillard's dragoons, a force which could only provide garrisons for a few large towns and watch the high-road from Madrid to Andalusia. Morillo was directed to slip eastward through the gap made by Hill between the Armies of the South and Portugal, to endeavour to cut up the French posts, and to collect recruits and contributions in the country-side. With luck he might even break the line of communication between Soult and Madrid. His force of 3,000 men was insufficient for anything more than a raid.

Starting from Montanches near Caçeres on December 30th—three days after Hill's expedition had begun—Morillo crossed the Guadiana, and after making a fruitless dash at Belalcazar, the isolated French garrison which protected the northernmost corner of Andalusia, marched straight on by Agudo and Sarccruela into the heart of La Mancha, where he seized Ciudad Real, its capital [January 15]. The small French force quartered there fled at his approach, which was wholly unexpected—no Spanish army had ever marched up the valley of the Guadiana before. On the next day Morillo attacked Almagro, where there was a garrison of 500 men ; but before he had made any impression he was surprised by the arrival of General Treillard, with a column hastily gathered from the posts along the high-road. The Spanish general refused to fight, and, abandoning Ciudad Real, withdrew with little loss into the passes of the Sierra de Guadalupe, where his enemy declined to follow. Since Hill had by this time abandoned Merida and returned to Portugal, Morillo felt his position to be uncomfortably isolated, and feared that French troops from Estremadura or from the Tagus valley might intercept his way home-

[1] See page 56 above.

ward. The danger turned out to be imaginary, and on reaching Truxillo on January 30 the column was able to rest unmolested for a fortnight at that important strategical point, and then to retire at leisure to Montanches, its original starting-point.

Thus ended an extraordinary raid, which, though it had no positive results whatever, demonstrated two things clearly enough—one was the marching power of the Spanish infantry, which between December 28 and January 30 covered 250 miles of vile mountain roads in bitter weather, and came back intact with little loss [1], the other was the slightness of the French hold on La Mancha, where the appearance of a small brigade of 3,000 men upset the whole country-side. Morillo was only driven off by a concentration of many small garrisons, and, when they were withdrawn, the local guerrillero bands overran the land. Their chiefs, El Medico [Palarea], Chaleco, and others, did an immense amount of damage while the French were concentrated, and ravaged up to the very gates of Madrid. Chaos reigned in New Castile till Foy's and Sarrut's divisions came back from the Alicante expedition, and dispersed themselves along the valley of the Tagus at the beginning of February. For, as we have often had occasion to remark before, every province of Spain required not only to be conquered but to be held down by a permanent garrison. The moment that it was left too lightly held, the guerrilleros came down from the hills, occupied all the open country, and cut all communications.

[1] Napier (iv. p. 50) overrates the damage that Morillo suffered. He was not ' completely defeated ' by Treillard, because he absconded without fighting. In his elaborate dispatch he gives his whole loss as two killed and nine wounded. See his life by Rodriguez Villa, appendices to vol. ii, for an almost daily series of letters describing his march.

SECTION XXXI: CHAPTER III

POLITICS AT CADIZ AND ELSEWHERE

THE military operations in the South during the winter of
1811–12 were inconclusive, and only important in a negative
way, as showing that the initiative of the French armies was
spent in this direction. But it must not be forgotten that while
Soult had been brought to a standstill, Suchet's operations were
still progressing : January, indeed, saw the last great Spanish
disaster of the war, the fall of Valencia, so that the spirits of
government and people still ran very low. It was not till the
sudden irruption of Wellington into the kingdom of Leon had
ended in the capture of Ciudad Rodrigo (January 19), that
there was any great occasion for hopefulness. And for a long
time after that event its importance was not fully understood.
That the central turning-point of the war had come, that for the
future the allies were to be on the offensive, and the French on
the defensive, was not realized till Badajoz had fallen in April,
a blow which shook the whole fabric of King Joseph's power
throughout the regions where he seemed to reign. Nor was it
only the state of affairs in the Peninsula which, during the
winter of 1811–12, seemed sufficiently gloomy both for the
present and for the future. The news from the Spanish colonies
in America grew steadily worse : in most of the viceroyalties
of the Western world there was now a nucleus of trouble :
the name of Ferdinand VII was still used by the insurgents as
a rallying cry, except in Venezuela, where Miranda had proclaimed an independent republic in July 1811. But in La Plata
and Chili lip-loyalty to the sovereign was accompanied by
practical secession from the Spanish state : the *Cabildos* or
Juntas paid no attention to orders received from Cadiz. In
Mexico, though the capital and the greater part of the country
were still in the hands of the constituted authorities, there was
a lively insurrection on foot since September 1810, under the

priest Hidalgo—he was captured and executed in 1812, but his
death did not crush his faction. The Viceroyalty of Peru was
almost the only part of Spanish America which still remained
loyal. The Cortes at Cadiz made elaborate attempts to conciliate the Americans, but was unable to satisfy their expecta-
tions or to end their discontents. The deeply-rooted belief
of the Creoles that they and their country were still being
exploited for the benefit of Spain, could not be removed by any
declaration that they were now to be Spanish citizens with
full rights, or by giving them representation in the Cortes.
The idea of autonomy was already abroad in Spanish America,
and in every quarter ambitious men were quoting the precedent
of the revolt of the Thirteen United Colonies from Great Britain
in the previous generation. Truly Spain had committed an
unwise act when she joined France in wrecking the British
domination in North America. She revenged an old grudge
successfully, but she taught her own colonists a lesson impossible to forget and easy to copy.

The Peninsular War had hitherto been maintained in no small
degree by the money which kept flowing in from America :
what would happen if the treasure-ships with their regular
supply of silver dollars from the mines of Mexico and Peru
ceased altogether to come in ? Already affairs were looking so
threatening that, despite of all the needs of the campaign at
home, reinforcements were being sent out to the New World
from Cadiz and from Corunna : the Army of Galicia, as we
shall presently see, was nearly put out of action in the spring of
1812 by the dispatch of an over-great proportion of its trained
artillerymen to America [1]. Some French observers of the
situation formed the idea that the Spaniards, if pressed to
a decision between the possible loss of their colonies and the
chance of obtaining a free hand by peace with Napoleon, might
make the choice for empire rather than freedom. By acknowledging Joseph Bonaparte as king, and coming into the Napoleonic system, they might be able to turn their whole strength
against the discontented Americans. This idea had one fatal
error : any Spaniard could see that submission to France
meant war with Great Britain : and then the way across the

[1] See below, section xxxiii, page 337.

Atlantic would be closed. The British government would be forced into an alliance with the colonists ; it had already thought of this device in the old days before Napoleon's invasion of the Peninsula. Whitelock's unhappy Buenos Ayres expedition in 1807 had been sent out precisely to take advantage of the discontent of the Americans, and in the hope that they would rise against the mother country if promised assistance. The adventurer Miranda had spent much time in pressing this policy on the Portland cabinet. Whitelock's descent on the Rio de la Plata, it is true, had been as disappointing in the political as in the military line : he had got no help whatever from the disaffected colonists. But feeling in America had developed into much greater bitterness since 1807 : in 1812 actual insurrection had already broken out. British aid would not, this time, be rejected : the malcontents would buy it by the grant of liberal trading concessions, which the Cadiz government, even in its worst time of trouble, had steadily refused to grant. There was every chance, therefore, that a policy of submission to Napoleon would ensure the loss of America even more certainly and more rapidly than a persistence in the present war. It does not seem that any person of importance at Cadiz ever took into serious consideration the idea of throwing up the struggle for independence, in order to obtain the opportunity of dealing with the American question.

The idea, however, was in the air. This was the time at which King Joseph made his last attempt to open up secret negotiation with the patriots. His own condition was unhappy enough, as has been sufficiently shown in an earlier chapter : but he was well aware that the outlook of his enemies was no less gloomy. One of the numerous—and usually impracticable —pieces of advice which his brother had sent him was the suggestion that he should assemble some sort of a Cortes, and then, posing as a national king, try to open up communications with the Cadiz government, setting forth the somewhat unconvincing thesis that Great Britain, and not France, was the real enemy of Spanish greatness. The idea of calling a Cortes fell through : the individuals whom Joseph could have induced to sit in it would have been so few, so insignificant, and so unpopular, that such a body could only have provoked

contempt [1]. But an attempt was made to see if anything could
be done at Cadiz : the inducement which Joseph was authorized
to offer to the patriots was that immediately on his recognition
as a constitutional king by the Cortes—and a constitution was
to be drawn up in haste at Madrid—the French army should
retire from Spain, and the integrity of the realm should be
guaranteed. Napoleon even made a half-promise to give up
Catalonia, though he had practically annexed it to his empire in
the previous year [2].

Joseph and his ministers had no confidence either in the
Emperor's sincerity in making these offers, or in the likelihood
of their finding any acceptance among the patriots. He sent,
however, to Cadiz as his agent a certain Canon La Peña, a secret
Afrancesado, but a brother of Manuel La Peña, the incapable
general who had betrayed Graham at Barrosa. This officer was
on his trial at the moment for his misbehaviour on that occasion,
and the canon pretended to have come to assist him in his day
of trouble on grounds of family affection. It would seem that
he sounded certain persons but with small effect. Toreno, who
was present in Cadiz at the time, and well acquainted with
every intrigue that was in progress, says that the Regency never
heard of the matter, and that very few members of the Cortes
knew what La Peña was doing. It seems that he had conversa-
tions with certain freemasons, who were connected with lodges
in Madrid that were under French influence, and apparently
with one member of the ministry. ' I do not give his name,'
says the historian, ' because I have no documentary proof to
bear out the charge, but moral proof I have [3].' Be this as it
may, the labours of La Peña do not seem to have been very
fruitful, and the assertion made by certain French historians,
and by Napoleon himself in the *Mémorial de Ste-Hélène*, that the
Cortes would have proceeded to treat with Joseph, but for
Wellington's astonishing successes in the spring of 1812, has
little or no foundation. As Toreno truly observes, any open

---

[1] For all this scheme see the Memoirs of Miot de Melito, iii. pp. 215–16,
beside the Emperor's own dispatches. Note especially the instructions which
the French ambassador, Laforest, was to set before Joseph.

[2] See vol. iv. p. 215.

[3] Toreno, iii. p. 100.

proposal of the sort would have resulted in the tearing to pieces by the populace of the man hardy enough to make it. The intrigue had no more success than the earlier mission of Sotelo, which has been spoken of in another place [1]. But it lingered on, till the battle of Salamanca in July, and the flight of Joseph from Madrid in August, proved, to any doubters that there may have been, that the French cause was on the wane [2]. One of the most curious results of this secret negotiation was that Soult, hearing that the King's emissary was busy at Cadiz, and not knowing that it was at Napoleon's own suggestion that the experiment was being made, came to the conclusion that Joseph was plotting to abandon his brother, and to make a private peace with the Cortes, on condition that he should break with France and be recognized as king. He wrote, as we shall presently see, to denounce him to Napoleon as a traitor. Hence came no small friction in the following autumn.

These secret intrigues fell into a time of keen political strife at Cadiz—the famous Constitution, which was to cause so much bickering in later years, was being drafted, discussed, and passed through the Cortes in sections, all through the autumn of 1811 and the winter of 1811–12. The Liberals and the Serviles fought bitterly over almost every clause, and during their disputes the anti-national propaganda of the handful of *Afrancesados* passed almost unnoticed. It is impossible in a purely military history to relate the whole struggle, and a few words as to its political bearings must suffice.

The Constitution was a strange amalgam of ancient Spanish national tradition, of half-understood loans from Great Britain and America, and of political theory borrowed from France. Many of its framers had obviously studied the details of the abortive ' limited monarchy ' which had been imposed on Louis XVI in the early days of the French Revolution. From this source came the scheme which limited within narrow bounds the sovereign's power in the Constitution. The system evolved was that of a king whose main constitutional weapon

---

[1] See vol. ii. p. 168.

[2] Toreno says that the mistress of the Duke of Infantado was implicated in the negotiation, after he had become a regent, but that he himself had no treasonable intentions, being a staunch supporter of Ferdinand.

was that right of veto on legislation which had proved so
unpopular in France. He was to choose ministers who, like
those of the United States of America, were not to sit in parliament, nor to be necessarily dependent on a party majority in
the house, though they were to be responsible to it. There was
to be but one Chamber, elected not directly by the people—
though universal suffrage was introduced—but by notables
chosen by the parishes in local primary assemblies, who
again named district notables, these last nominating the actual
members for the Cortes.

The right of taxation was vested in the Chamber, and the
Ministry was placed at its mercy by the power of refusing
supply. The regular army was specially subjected to the
Chamber and not to the King, though the latter was left some
power with regard to calling out or disbanding the local militia
which was to form the second line in the national forces—at
present it was in fact non-existent, unless the guerrillero bands
might be considered to represent it.

The most cruel blows were struck not only at the King's
power but at his prestige. A clause stating that all treaties or
grants made by him while in captivity were null and void was
no doubt necessary—there was no knowing what documents
Napoleon might not dictate to Ferdinand. But it was unwise
to formulate in a trenchant epigram that ' the nation is free and
independent, not the patrimony of any family or person,' or
that ' the people's obligation of obedience ceases when the
King violates the laws.' And when, after granting their
sovereign a veto on legislation, the Constitution proceeded to
state that the veto became inoperative after the Cortes had
passed any act in three successive sessions, it became evident
that the King's sole weapon was to be made ineffective.
' Sovereignty,' it was stated, ' is vested essentially in the
nation, and for this reason the nation alone has the right to
establish its fundamental laws.' But the most extraordinary
attack on the principle of legitimate monarchy was a high-
handed resettlement of the succession to the throne, in which
the regular sequence of next heirs was absolutely ignored.
If King Ferdinand failed to leave issue, the crown was to go to
his brother Don Carlos : if that prince also died childless, the

Constitution declared that the infante Don Francisco and his sister the Queen of Etruria were both to be passed over. No definite reasons were given in the act of settlement for this astonishing departure from the natural line of descent. The real meaning of the clause concerning Don Francisco was that many suspected him of being the son of Godoy and not of Charles IV [1]. As to the Queen of Etruria, she had been in her younger days a docile tool of Napoleon, and had lent herself very tamely to his schemes. But it is said that the governing cause of her exclusion from the succession was not so much her own unpopularity, as the incessant intrigues of her sister Carlotta, the wife of the regent João of Portugal, who had for a long time been engaged in putting forward a claim to be elected as sole regent of Spain. She had many members of the Cortes in her pay, and their influence was directed to getting her name inserted in the list above that of her brother in the succession-roll, and to the disinheritance of her sister also. Her chance of ever reaching the throne was not a very good one, as both Ferdinand and Carlos were still young, and could hardly be kept prisoners at Valençay for ever. It is probable that the real object of the manœuvres was rather to place her nearer to the regency of Spain in the present crisis, than to seat her upon its throne at some remote date. For the regency was her desire, though the crown too would have been welcome, and sometimes not only the anti-Portuguese party in the Cortes, but Wellington and his brother Henry Wellesley, the Ambassador at Cadiz, were afraid that by patience and by long intrigue her partisans might achieve their object.

Wellington was strongly of opinion that a royal regent at Cadiz would be most undesirable. The personal influences of a *camarilla*, surrounding an ambitious but incapable female regent, would add another difficulty to the numerous problems of the relations between England and Spain, which were already sufficiently tiresome.

This deliberate humiliation of the monarchy, by clauses accentuated by phrases of insult, which angered, and were intended to anger, the *Serviles*, was only accomplished after long debate, in which protests of the most vigorous sort were

[1] See Villa Urrutia, i. p. 13 and ii. pp. 355-9.

made by many partisans of the old theory of Spanish absolutism. Some spoke in praise of the Salic Law, violated by the mention of Carlotta as heiress to the throne, others (ignoring rumours as to his paternity) defended Don Francisco, as having been by his youth exempted from the ignominies of Bayonne, and dwelt on the injustice of his fate. But the vote went against them by a most conclusive figure.

The majority in the Cortes, which made such parade of its political liberalism, did not pursue its theories into the realm of religion. After reading its fulsome declarations in favour of freedom, it is astounding to note the black intolerance of the clause which declares not only, as might naturally be expected, that ' the religion of the Spanish nation is, and ever shall be, the Catholic Apostolic Roman, the one true faith,' but that ' the nation defends it by wise laws, *forbidding the exercise of any other.*' Schism and unorthodoxy still remained political as well as ecclesiastical crimes, no less than in the time of Philip II. The Liberals, despite of murmurs by the *Serviles,* refused to recreate the Inquisition, but this was as far as their conception of religious freedom went.

Contemplating this exhibition of mediaeval intolerance, it is impossible to rate at any very high figure the ostentatious liberalism which pervades the greater part of the Constitution. We are bound to recognize in it merely the work of a party of ambitious politicians, who desired to secure control of the state-machine for themselves, and to exclude the monarchy from all share in its manipulation. No doubt any form of limited government was better than the old royal bureaucracy. But this particular scheme went much farther than the needs or the possibilities of the time, and was most unsuited for a country such as the Spain of 1812. When its meaning began to be understood in the provinces, it commanded no enthusiasm or respect. Indeed, outside the Cortes itself the only supporters that it possessed were the populace of Cadiz and a few other great maritime towns. Considered as a working scheme it had the gravest faults, especially the ill-arranged relations between the ministers (who did not form a real cabinet) and the Chamber, in which they were prohibited from sitting. In 1814 Lord Castlereagh observed, with great truth, that he could now say from certain experience, that in practice as well as in theory the Constitution of 1812 was one of the worst among the modern productions of its kind [1].

Among the many by-products of the Constitution was a change in the membership of the Regency. The old ' trinitarian ' body composed of Blake, Agar, and Cisgar, had long been discredited, and proposals for its dissolution had been debated, even before its further continuance was rendered impossible by Blake's surrender to the French at Valencia in the earliest days of 1812. A furious discussion in the Cortes had ended in a vote that no royal personage should be a member of any new regency, so that the pretensions of the Princess of Portugal were finally discomfited. The new board consisted of the Duke of Infantado, Joaquim Mosquera, a member of the Council of the Indies, Admiral Villavicencio, military governor of Cadiz, Ignacio Rodriguez de Rivas, and Henry O'Donnell, Conde de la Bispal, the energetic soldier whose exploits in Catalonia have been set forth in the last volume of this book. He was the only man of mark in the new regency : Infantado owed his promotion to his rank and wealth, and the fact that he had been the trusted friend of Ferdinand VII. He possessed a limited intelligence and little education, and was hardly more than a cipher, with a distinct preference for ' Serviles ' rather than for Liberals. Villavicencio had no military reputation, but had been an energetic organizer, and a fairly successful governor during the siege of Cadiz. Mosquera and Rivas were elected mainly because they were of American birth—their choice was intended to conciliate the discontented colonists. Neither of them was entitled by any great personal merit to the promotion which was thrust upon him. Henry O'Donnell, now at last recovered from the wound which had laid him on a sick bed for so many months in 1811 [2], was both capable and energetic, but quarrelsome and provocative : he belonged to that class of men who always irritate their colleagues

---

[1] The best and most recent account of all this, explaining many contradictions and some insincere suppression of fact in Toreno's great history, is to be found in chapter ix of vol. ii of Señor Villa Urrutia's *Relaciones entre España y Inglaterra 1808–14*.

[2] See vol. iv. p. 240.

into opposition, by their rapid decisions and imperious ways, especially when those colleagues are men of ability inferior to their own. The Duke of Infantado was absent for some time after his election—he had been serving as ambassador in London. Of the other four Regents two ranked as ' Serviles,' two as Liberals, a fact which told against their efficiency as a board. They had little strength to stand out against the Cortes, whose jealousy against any power in the State save its own was intense. On the whole it may be said that the substitution of the five new Regents for the three old ones had no great political consequences. The destiny of the patriot cause was not in the hands of the executive, but of the turbulent, faction-ridden, and ambitious legislative chamber, an ideally bad instrument for the conduct of a difficult and dangerous war. Fortunately it was neither the Regency nor the Cortes whose actions were to settle the fate of the campaign of 1812, but purely and solely Wellington and the Anglo-Portuguese army. The intrigues of Cadiz turned out to be a negligible quantity in the course of events.

In Lisbon at this time matters were much more quiet than they had been a little while back. The Portuguese government had abandoned any overt opposition to Wellington, such as had been seen in 1810, when the Patriarch and the President Souza had given him so much trouble. The expulsion of Mas-séna from Portugal had justified the policy of Wellington, and almost silenced his critics. He had not even found it necessary to press for the removal of the men whom he distrusted from the Council of Regency [1], in which the word of his loyal coadjutor, Charles Stuart, who combined the rather incompatible functions of British Ambassador and Regent, was now supreme. Open opposition had ceased, but Wellington complained that while compliance was always promised, ' every measure which I propose is frittered away to nothing, the form and the words remain, but the spirit of the measure is taken away in the execution [2].' This was, he remarked, the policy of the Portuguese government : they no longer refused him anything ; but

[1] Early in 1812, however, Wellington once more spoke of requiring Souza's retirement from office. *Dispatches*, ix. p. 88.
[2] Wellington to Charles Stuart, April 9, 1812. *Dispatches*, ix. p. 48.

if they thought that any of his demands might offend either
the Prince Regent at Rio Janeiro or the popular sentiment of
the Portuguese nation, they carried out his proposals in such
a dilatory fashion, and with so many exceptions and excuses,
that he failed to obtain what he had expected.

In this there was a good deal of injustice. Wellington does
not always seem to have realized the abject poverty which four
years of war had brought upon Portugal. The Regency calculated that, on account of falling revenue caused by the late
French invasion, for 1812 they could only count on 12,000,000
cruzados novos of receipts [1]—this silver coin was worth about
2*s*. 6*d*. sterling, so that the total amounted to about £1,500,000.
Of this three-fourths, or 9,000,000 cruzados, was set aside for
the army, the remainder having to sustain all the other expenses
of the State—justice, civil administration, roads, navy, &c. The
British subsidy had been raised to £2,000,000 a year, but it was
paid with the utmost irregularity : in one month of 1811 the
Portuguese treasury had received only £6,000, in another only
£20,000, instead of the £166,000 promised [2]. When such
arrears accumulated, it was no wonder that the soldiers starved
and the magazines ran low. It was calculated that to keep
the army up to its full numbers, and to supply all military needs
efficiently, 45,000,000 cruzados a year were required. Taking
the British subsidy as equalling 16,000,000, and the available
national contribution at 9,000,000 cruzados, there was little
more than half the required sum available. This Portuguese
calculation appears to be borne out by the note of Beresford's
chief of the staff, D'Urban, in February 1812. ' The Marshal
at Lisbon finds that, after a perfect investigation, it appears
that the expenditure must be nearly £6,000,000—the means at
present £3,500,000 ! *Nous verrons.*'

It is clear that the Portuguese government must have shrunk
from many of Wellington's suggestions on account of mere lack

---

[1] Napier (iv. p. 212) says that Portugal raised 25,000,000 cruzados this
year. I cannot understand this, comparing it with Soriano de Luz, iii.
p. 523, which quotes 12,000,000 cruzados as the total receipt of taxes for
1811. Does Napier include loans, and the inconvertible paper issued by the
government ?

[2] See complaints of the Conde de Redondo, the Portuguese finance
minister, in Soriano de Luz, iii. p. 520.

of resources. A third of the country had been at one time or another overrun by the French—the provinces north of the Douro in 1809, the Beira and northern Estremadura in 1810–11. It would take long years before they were in a position to make their former contributions to the expenses of the State. It was impossible to get over this hard fact : but Wellington thought that a rearrangement of taxes, and an honest administration of their levy, would produce a much larger annual revenue than was being raised in 1812. He pointed out, with some plausibility, that British money was being poured into Portugal by millions and stopped there : some one—the merchant and contractor for the most part—must be making enormous profits and accumulating untold wealth. Moreover he had discovered cases of the easy handling of the rich and influential in the matter of taxation, while the peasantry were being drained of their last farthing. Such little jobs were certain to occur in an administration of the *ancien régime* : fidalgos and capitalists knew how to square matters with officials at Lisbon. ' A reform in the abuses of the Customs of Lisbon and Oporto, a more equal and just collection of the Income Tax on commercial property, particularly in those large and rich towns [it is scandalous to hear of the fortunes made by the mercantile classes owing to the war, and to reflect that they contribute practically nothing to bear its burdens], a reform of the naval establishment and the arsenal, would make the income equal to the expenditure, and the government would get on without calling upon Great Britain at every moment to find that which, in the existing state of the world, cannot be procured, viz. money [1].' So wrote Wellington, who was always being irritated by discovering that the magazines of Elvas or Almeida were running low, or that recruits were not rejoining their battalions because there was no cash to arm or clothe them, or that troops in the field were getting half-rations, unless they were on the British subsidy list.

No doubt Wellington was right in saying that there was a certain amount of jobbery in the distribution of taxation, and that more could have been raised by a better system. But Portuguese figures of the time seem to make it clear that even

[1] See tables on pp. 324–5 of Halliday's *Present State of Portugal*, published in 1812.

if a supernatural genius had been administering the revenue instead of the Conde de Redondo, all could not have been obtained that was demanded. The burden of the war expenses was too heavy for an impoverished country, with no more than two and a half million inhabitants, which was compelled to import a great part of its provisions owing to the stress of war. The state of Portugal may be estimated by the fact that in the twelve months between February 1811 and January 1812 £2,672,000 worth of imported corn, besides 605,000 barrels of flour, valued at £2,051,780 more, was brought into the country and sold there [1]. On the other hand the export of wine, with which Portugal used to pay for its foreign purchases, had fallen off terribly : in 1811 only 18,000 pipes were sold as against an average of 40,000 for the eight years before the outbreak of the Peninsular War. An intelligent observer wrote in 1812 that the commercial distress of the country might mainly be traced to the fact that nearly all the money which came into the country from England, great as was the sum, found its way to the countries from which Portugal was drawing food, mainly to the United States, from which the largest share of the wheat and flour was brought. ' As we have no corresponding trade with America, the balance has been very great against this country : for the last three years this expenditure has been very considerable, without any return whatever, as the money carried to America has been completely withdrawn from circulation.'

The shrinkage in the amount of the gold and silver current in Portugal was as noticeable in these years as the same phenomenon in England, and (like the British) the Portuguese government tried to make up the deficiency by the issue of inconvertible paper money, which gradually fell in exchange value as compared with the metallic currency. The officers of the army, as well as all civil functionaries, were paid their salaries half in cash and half in notes—the latter suffered a depreciation of from 15 to 30 per cent. Among the cares which weighed on Wellington and Charles Stuart was that of endeavouring to keep the Regency from the easy expedient of issuing more and more of a paper currency which was already circulating at far less than its face value. This was avoided—fortunately for the

[1] Halliday's *Present State of Portugal*, p. 320.

Portuguese people and army, no less than for the Anglo-Portuguese alliance.

After all, the practical results of the efforts made by the Portuguese government were invaluable. Wellington could not have held his ground, much less have undertaken the offensive campaign of 1812, without the aid of the trusty auxiliaries that swelled his divisions to normal size. Without their Portuguese brigades most of them would have been mere skeletons of 3,000 or 4,000 men. Beresford's army was almost up to its full establishment in January 1812—there were 59,122 men on the rolls, when recruits, sick, men on detachment, and the regiment lent for the succour of Cadiz are all counted. Deducting, beyond these, the garrisons of Elvas, Abrantes, Almeida, and smaller places, as also the dismounted cavalry left in the rear [1], there were over 30,000 men for the fighting-line, in ten brigades of infantry, six regiments of cavalry, and eight field-batteries. Beresford, lately entrusted by orders from Rio Janeiro with still more stringent powers over the military establishment, was using them to the full. An iron hand kept down desertion and marauding, executions for each of those offences appear incessantly in the *Ordens do Dia*, which give the daily chronicle of the Portuguese head-quarters. In addition to the regular army it must be remembered that he had to manage the militia, of which as many as 52,000 men were under arms at one time or another in 1812. Counting the first and the second line together, there were 110,000 men enrolled—a fine total for a people of two and a half million souls.

Putting purely Portuguese difficulties aside, Wellington was much worried at this time by a trouble which concerned the British and not the local finances. This was the delay in the cashing of the ' *vales* ' or bills for payment issued by the Commissary-General for food and forage bought from the peasantry. As long as they were settled at short intervals, no difficulty arose about them—they were indeed treated as negotiable paper, and had passed from hand to hand at a lesser discount

---

[1] The deductions were—sick, 7,500 ; untrained recruits, 4,000 ; dismounted cavalry, 3,000 ; regiment at Cadiz, 1,500 ; garrisons (infantry and artillery) and men on detachment, 10,000 ; leaving some 33,000 for the field. By May the gross total had gone down to 56,674.

than the inconvertible Portuguese government papers. But all through the year 1811 the interval between the issue of the ' vale ' and its payment in cash at Lisbon had been growing longer, and an uncomfortable feeling was beginning to spread about the country-side. The peasantry were growing suspicious, and were commencing to sell the bills, for much less than their face value, to speculators who could afford to wait for payment. To recoup themselves for their loss they were showing signs of raising prices all round. Fortunately they were a simple race, and communication between districts was slow and uncertain, so that no general tendency of this sort was yet prevalent, though the symptoms were making themselves visible here and there. Hence came Wellington's constant applications for more cash from England at shorter notice. Late in the spring he devised a scheme by which interest at 5 per cent. was to be paid by the Commissary-General on bonds or certificates representing money or money's worth advanced to the British army, till the principal was repaid—two years being named as the period after which the whole sum must be refunded. This was a desperate measure, an endeavour to throw forward payment on to a remote future, ' when it is not probable that there will be the same difficulty in procuring specie in England to send abroad as there is at the present moment.' The plan [1] was never tried, and was not good : for how could small creditors of the English army be expected to stand out of their money—representing the price of their crops or their cattle— for so long a period as two years, even if they were, in the meantime, receiving interest on what was really their working capital ? Wellington himself remarked, when broaching the scheme to Lord Liverpool, that there remained the difficulty that no one could look forward, and say that the British army would still be in the Peninsula two years hence. If it had left Portugal—whether victorious and pushing towards the Pyrenees, or defeated and driven back on to Great Britain—how would the creditors communicate with the Commissary-General, their debtor ? They could only be referred to London, to which they would have no ready access : indeed many of them would

---

[1] Set forth in detail, and with a sample bond for 1,000 dollars added, in *Dispatches*, ix. pp. 104–5.

not know where, or what, London was. That such an idea should have been set forward only shows the desperate financial situation of the British army.

We shall have to be referring to this problem at several later points of the history of the campaign of 1812 [1] : at the opening of the invasion of Leon in June it reached its worst point, just before the great victory of Salamanca. But it was always present, and when Wellington's mind was not occupied with deductions as to the manœuvres of French marshals, it may undoubtedly be said that his main preoccupation was the normally depleted state of the military chest, into which dollars and guineas flowed, it is true, in enormous quantities, but only to be paid out at once, in settling arrears many months old. These were never fully liquidated, and began to accumulate again, with distressing rapidity, after every tardy settlement.

Whig historians have often tried to represent Wellington's financial difficulties as the fault of the home government, and it is easy to pick passages from his dispatches in which he seems to assert that he is not being supported according to his necessities. But a nearer investigation of the facts will not bear out this easy theory, the product of party spite. The Whigs of 1811–12 were occupied in decrying the Peninsular War as a failure, in minimizing the successes of Wellington, and in complaining that the vast sums of money lavished on his army were wasted. Napoleon was invincible, peace was the only way out of disaster, even if the peace must be somewhat humiliating. It was unseemly for their representatives, twenty years after, to taunt the Perceval and Liverpool ministries with having stinted Wellington in his hour of need. We have learnt to estimate at their proper value tirades against ' the administration which was characterized by all the corruption and tyranny of Mr. Pitt's system, without his redeeming genius.' We no longer think that the Napoleonic War was waged ' to repress the democratic principle,' nor that the cabinets which maintained it were ' the rapacious usurpers of the people's rights [2].'

---

[1] See especially below in chapter iii of section xxxiii. p. 349.

[2] For these phrases and much more abuse, see Napier, iv. p. 199, a most venomous and unjust passage.

Rather, in the spirit of Mr. Fortescue's admirable volume on *British Statesmen of the Great War*, shall we be prone to stand amazed at the courage and resolution of the group of British ministers who stood out, for long years and against tremendous odds, to defeat the tyrant of Europe and to preserve the British Empire. ' On the one side was Napoleon, an autocrat vested with such powers as great genius and good fortune have rarely placed in the hands of one man, with the resources of half Europe at his disposition, and an armed force unsurpassed in strength and devotion ready to march to the ends of the world to uphold his will. On the other were these plain English gentlemen, with not so much as a force of police at their back, with a population by nature five times as turbulent as it is now, and in the manufacturing districts inflamed alike by revolutionary teaching and by real distress, with an Ireland always perilously near revolt, with a House of Commons unreformed indeed, but not on that account containing a less factious, mischievous, and obstructive opposition than any other House of Commons during a great war. In face of all these difficulties they had to raise armies, maintain fleets, construct and pursue a military policy, and be unsuccessful at their peril. Napoleon might lose whole armies with impunity : five thousand British soldiers beaten and captured would have brought any British minister's head perilously near the block. Such were the difficulties that confronted Perceval, Liverpool, and Castlereagh : yet for their country's sake they encountered them without flinching [1].'

The winter of 1811–12 was not quite the darkest hour : the Russian war was looming in the near future, and Napoleon was already beginning to withdraw troops from Spain in preparation for it. No longer therefore, as in 1810 and the earlier half of 1811, was there a high probability that the main bulk of the French armies, under the Emperor himself, might be turned once more against the Peninsula. It was all but certain that England would soon have allies, and not stand practically alone in the struggle, as she had done ever since Wagram. Nevertheless, even with the political horizon somewhat brightened in the East, the time was a sufficiently anxious

[1] Fortescue's *British Statesmen*, pp. 277–8.

one. In Great Britain, as in the rest of Europe, the harvest of 1811 had been exceptionally bad, and the high price of bread, coinciding with much unemployment, was causing not only distress but wide-spread turbulence in the manufacturing districts. This was the year of the first outbreak of the ' Luddites,' and of their senseless exploits in the way of machine-smashing. The worst stringency of domestic troubles coincided with the gradual disappearance of the external danger from the ambition of Napoleon.

In addition it must be remembered that the Perceval cabinet, on which all the responsibilities fell, was by no means firmly established in power. When it first took office many politicians believed that it could not last for a single year. All through 1811 the Prince Regent had been in secret negotiation with the Whigs, and would gladly have replaced his ministers with some sort of a coalition government. And in January 1812 Lord Wellesley, by far the most distinguished man in the cabinet, resigned his post as Foreign Minister. He asserted that he did so because his colleagues had failed to accept all his plans for the support of his brother and the Peninsular army : and no doubt this was to a certain extent true. Yet it cannot be said that, either before or after his resignation, the Ministry had neglected Wellington ; in 1811 they had doubled his force of cavalry, and sent him about a dozen new battalions of infantry. It was these reinforcements which made the victories of 1812 possible, and in that year the stream of reinforcements did not cease—nine more infantry regiments came out, mostly in time for the great crisis in June [1]. In the autumn the dispatch of further succours had become difficult, because of the outbreak of the American war, which diverted of necessity to Canada many units that might otherwise have gone to Spain. It is impossible to maintain that Wellington was stinted of men : money was the difficulty. And even as regards money—which had to be gold or silver, since paper was useless in the Peninsula— the resources placed at his disposal were much larger than in previous years, though not so large as he demanded, nor as the growing scale of the war required.

It is difficult to acquit Wellesley of factiousness with regard

---

[1] *Per contra* five depleted second battalions went home.

to his resignation, and the most damaging document against him is the *apologia* drawn up by his devoted adherent Shawe [1], in the belief that it afforded a complete justification for his conduct : many of the words and phrases are the Marquess's own. From this paper no one can fail to deduce that it was not so much a quixotic devotion to his brother's interests, as an immoderate conception of his own dignity and importance that made Wellesley resign. He could not stand the free discussion and criticism of plans and policies which is essential in a cabinet. ' Lord Wellesley has always complained, with some justice, that his suggestions were received as those of a mere novice. . . . His opinions were overruled, and the opposition he met with could only proceed from jealousy, or from a real contempt for his judgement. It seemed to him that they were unwilling to adopt any plan of his, lest it might lead to his assuming a general ascendancy in the Cabinet. . . . He said that he took another view of the situation : the Government derived the most essential support from his joining it, because it was considered as a pledge that the war would be properly supported. . . . " The war is popular, and any government that will support Lord Wellington properly will stand. I do not think the war is properly supported, and I cannot, as an honest man, deceive the nation by remaining in office." . . . It is needless to particularize all the points of difference between Lord Wellesley and his colleagues : Spain was the main point, but he also disapproved of their obstinate adherence to the Orders in Council, and their policy towards America and in Sicily '—not to speak of Catholic Emancipation.

These are the words of injured pride, not of patriotism. The essential thing at the moment was that the war in Spain should be kept up efficiently. By resigning, Wellesley intended to break up the Ministry, and of this a probable result might have been the return to office of the Whigs, whose policy was to abandon the Peninsula and make peace with Napoleon. Wellesley's *apologia* acknowledges that his influence in the Cabinet had brought about, on more occasions than one, an increase of the support given to his brother, e.g. his colleagues had given in about additions to the Portuguese subsidy, and

[1] Printed in Wellington's *Supplementary Dispatches*, vii. pp. 257–88.

about extra reinforcements to the army. This being so, it was surely criminal in him to retire, when he found that some of his further suggestions were not followed. Would the wrecking of the Perceval cabinet, and the succession of the Whigs to power, have served Wellington or the general cause of the British Empire ?

Wellington himself saw the situation with clear eyes, and in a letter, in which a touch of his sardonic humour can be detected, wrote in reply to his brother's announcement of his resignation that ' In truth the republic of a cabinet is but little suited to any man of taste or of large views [1].' There lay the difficulty : the great viceroy loved to dictate, and hated to hear his opinions criticized. Lord Liverpool, in announcing the rupture to Wellington in a letter of a rather apologetic cast, explains the situation in a very few words : ' Lord Wellesley says generally that he has not the weight in the Government which he expected, when he accepted office. . . . The Government, though a cabinet, is necessarily *inter pares*, in which every member must expect to have his opinions and his dispatches canvassed, and this previous friendly canvass of opinions and measures appears necessary, under a constitution where all public acts of ministers will be hostilely debated in parliament.' The Marquess resented all criticism whatever.

The ministers assured Wellington that his brother's resignation would make no difference in their relations with himself, and invited him to write as freely to Lord Castlereagh, who succeeded Wellesley at the Foreign Office, as to his predecessor. The assurance of the Cabinet's good will and continued confidence was received—as it had been given—in all sincerity. Not the least change in Wellington's relations with the Ministry can be detected from his dispatches. Nor can it be said that the support which he received from home varied in the least, after his brother's secession from the Cabinet. Even the grudging Napier is forced to concede this much, though he endeavours to deprive the Perceval ministry of any credit, by asserting that their only chance of continuance in office depended on the continued prosperity of Wellington. Granting this, we must

---

[1] Wellington to Wellesley, camp before Badajoz, *Supplementary Dispatches*, vii. p. 307.

still conclude that Wellesley's resignation, even if it produced no disastrous results—as it well might have done—was yet an unhappy exhibition of pride and petulance. A patriotic statesman should have subordinated his own *amour propre* to the welfare of Great Britain, which demanded that a strong administration, pledged to the continuance of war with Napoleon, should direct the helm of the State. He did his best to wreck Perceval's cabinet, and to put the Whigs in power.

The crisis in the Ministry passed off with less friction and less results than most London observers had expected, and Lord Liverpool turned out to be right when he asserted that in his opinion [1] it would be of no material prejudice to the Perceval government. Castlereagh, despite of his halting speech and his involved phrases, was a tower of strength at the Foreign Office, and certainly replaced Wellesley with no disadvantage to the general policy of Great Britain.

Here the jealousies and bickerings in London may be left for a space. We shall only need to turn back for a moment to ministerial matters when, at midsummer, the whole situation had been transformed, for France and Russia were at last openly engaged in war, a great relief to British statesmen, although at the same time a new trouble was arising in the West to distract their attention. For the same month that started Napoleon on his way to Moscow saw President Madison's declaration of war on Great Britain, and raised problems, both on the high seas and on the frontiers of Canada, that would have seemed heart-breaking and insoluble if the strength of France had not been engaged elsewhere. But the ' stab in the back,' as angry British politicians called it, was delivered too late to be effective.

[1] Liverpool to Wellington, *Supplementary Dispatches*, vii. p. 257.

SECTION XXXII

WELLINGTON'S FIRST CAMPAIGN OF 1812

CHAPTER I

THE CAPTURE OF CIUDAD RODRIGO

It is with no small relief that we turn away from the annals of the petty warfare in the provinces and of the bickerings of politicians, to follow the doings of Wellington. All the ' alarms and excursions ' that we have been narrating were of small import, compared with the operations on the frontiers of Portugal and Leon which began at the New Year of 1812. Here we have arrived at the true backbone of the war, the central fact which governed all the rest. Here we follow the working out of a definite plan conceived by a master-mind, and are no longer dealing with spasmodic movements dictated by the necessities of the moment. For the initiative had at last fallen into Wellington's hands, and the schemes of Soult and Marmont were no longer to determine his movements. On the contrary, it was he who was to dictate theirs.

The governing factor in the situation in the end of December 1811 was, as we have already shown, the fact that Marmont's army had been so distracted by the Alicante expedition, undertaken by Napoleon's special orders, that it was no longer in a position to concentrate, in full force and within a reasonably short period of time. It was on December 13th [1] that the Duke of Ragusa received the definitive orders, written on November 20–1, that bade him to send towards Valencia, for Suchet's benefit, such a force as, when joined by a detachment from the Army of the Centre, should make up 12,000 men, and to find 3,000 or 4,000 more to cover the line of communications of the expedition. Accordingly orders were issued to Montbrun to take up the enterprise, with the divisions of Foy and Sarrut,

[1] For this date see Marmont to Berthier, from Valladolid, Feb. 6, 1812.

and his own cavalry; the concentration of the corps began on December 15th, and on December 29th it marched eastward from La Mancha [1] on its fruitless raid.

Wellington's policy at this moment depended on the exact distribution of the hostile armies in front of him. He lay with the bulk of his army wintering in cantonments along the frontier of Portugal and Leon, but with the Light Division pushed close up to Ciudad Rodrigo, and ready to invest it, the moment that the news should arrive that the French had so moved their forces as to make it possible for him to close in upon that fortress, without the danger of a very large army appearing to relieve it within a few days. On December 28th he summed up his scheme in a report to Lord Liverpool, in which he stated that, after the El Bodon–Aldea da Ponte fighting in September, he had ' determined to persevere in the same system till the enemy should make some alteration in the disposition of his forces [2].' In the meanwhile he judged that he was keeping Marmont and Dorsenne ' contained,' and preventing them from undertaking operations elsewhere, unless they were prepared to risk the chance of losing Rodrigo. ' It would not answer to remove the army to the frontiers of Estremadura (where a chance of effecting some important object might have offered), as in that case General Abadia [and the Spanish Army of Galicia] would have been left to himself, and would have fallen an easy sacrifice to the Army of the North [3].' Therefore Wellington refused to take the opportunity of descending upon Badajoz and driving Drouet out of Estremadura, though these operations were perfectly possible. He confined himself to ordering Hill to carry out the two raids in this direction, of which the first led to the destruction of Girard at Arroyo dos Molinos in October, and the second to the occupation of Merida and the expulsion of the French from central Estremadura at midwinter [December 27, 1811–January 13, 1812].

In October Wellington had hoped for some time that Rodrigo would be gravely incommoded for lack of provisions, for it was

[1] For details, see chapter iii of section xxx above.

[2] *Dispatches*, viii. p. 516.

[3] Wellington to Lord Liverpool, Dec. 28.

almost cut off from the army to which it belonged by the
guerrillero bands of Julian Sanchez, who dominated all the
country between the Agueda and Salamanca, while the Light
Division lay on the heights close above it, ready to pounce on
any convoy that might try to pass in. This expectation, however, had been disappointed, as a large amount of food had
been thrown into the place on November 2nd by General
Thiébault, the governor of Salamanca. This revictualling had
only been accomplished by a mixture of good management and
good luck. The governor saw that any convoy must have
a large escort, because of the guerrilleros, who would have cut
off a small one. But a large escort could not move very fast,
or escape notice. Wherefore, taking no mean risk, Thiébault
collected 3,400 men for a guard, stopped all exit of Spaniards
from Salamanca two days before the convoy started, gave out
a false destination for his movement, and sent out requisitions
for rations for 12,000 men in the villages between the starting-
place and Rodrigo. Wellington had been on the look-out for
some such attempt, and had intended that the Light Division,
from its lair at Martiago in the mountain-valleys above the city,
should descend upon any force of moderate size that might
approach. But receiving, rather late, the false news that at
least three whole divisions were to serve as escort, he forbade
Craufurd to risk anything till he should have received reinforcements. The same day the Agueda became unfordable owing
to sudden rains, and no troops could be sent across to join
Craufurd. Wherefore Thiébault got by, ere the smallness of
his force was realized, and retreated with such haste, after
throwing in the food, that the Light Division could not come
up with him [1]. Such luck could not be expected another
time !

Wellington had begun to hurry up the nearest divisions to
support Craufurd, and had supposed for two days that he
would have serious fighting, since he imagined that 15,000 or
18,000 men at least had been brought up to guard the convoy.
It was a grave disappointment to him to find that he had been
misled, for it was clear that Rodrigo would not be straitened

---

[1] For details of this operation see Thiébault's *Mémoires*, iv. pp. 538–43,
corroborated by Wellington's *Dispatches*, viii. pp. 373–5 and 385–6.

for food for many a day. He had now to fall back on his
original scheme of reducing the place by a regular siege, when
the propitious instant should come round.

Meanwhile, waiting for the moment when Marmont and
Dorsenne should disperse their troops into a less concentrated
position, he took preliminary measures to face that eventuality
when it should occur. The main thing was to get the battering-
train, with which Ciudad Rodrigo would have to be attacked,
close up to its objective. As we have already seen [1], it had
been collected far to the rear, at the obscure village of Villa da
Ponte near Trancoso. Between that spot and Rodrigo there
were eighty miles of bad mountain roads : if Wellington had
waited till he heard that Marmont had moved, before he began
to bring up his heavy guns, he would have lost many days.
Accordingly he commenced to push them forward as early as
November 12th : their temporary shelter was to be in the
fortress of Almeida, which was already so far restored that it
could be regarded as safe against anything short of a regular
siege. It was certain that Marmont would not come forward
at midwinter for any such operation, and against raids or
demonstrations the place was already secure. On December 4th
Wellington reported [2] to Lord Liverpool that it would be completely ' re-established as a military post ' within a few weeks ;
and on the 19th he announced that it was now ' a place of
security,' and could be trusted to resist any attack whatever.
But, long before even the first of these dates, it was beginning
to receive the siege-material which Alexander Dickson was
ordered to bring up from the rear. As early as November 22nd
the first division of heavy guns entered its gates : it was given
out—to deceive French spies—that the pieces were only
intended to arm the walls, and at the same time Dickson was
actively employed in mounting on them a number of guns of
heavy calibre, wrecked in the explosion when Brennier evacuated
Almeida in May 1811. Twenty-five of them were in position
before Christmas Day. The indefatigable artillery commandant
had also hunted out of the ruins no less than 8,000 round shot :

---

[1] See vol. iv. p. 549.

[2] *Dispatches*, viii, Report of Dec. 28 to Lord Liverpool on the late
campaign.

it was originally intended that they should go into the magazines of the garrison ; but, when the time for action came, Wellington sent the greater part of this stock of second-hand shot to the front, because they were immediately available, and ordered the Almeida stores to be replenished, as occasion served, by the later convoys that arrived from Villa da Ponte.

Nor was it in bringing forward guns and ammunition alone that Wellington was busy during December : he caused a great quantity of gabions and fascines to be constructed by the men of the four divisions nearest the front, giving two vintems ($2\frac{1}{2}d$.) for every fascine and four for every gabion. He had a very strong trestle-bridge cast across the Agueda at Marialva, seven miles north of Rodrigo and out of the reach of its garrison, and he began to collect carts from every direction. Not only were they requisitioned in Beira, but Carlos de España, who was lying in a somewhat venturesome position within the frontiers of Leon, ordered the Spanish peasantry, even as far as Tamames, to send every available ox-wain westward—and many came, though their owners were risking dire chastisement at the hands of the governor of the province of Salamanca.

Marmont, as we have seen, began to move troops eastward for Montbrun's Valencian expedition about December 15th. The first news of this displacement reached Wellington on the 24th, when he heard that Brennier's division had evacuated Plasencia and fallen back behind the Tietar, taking with it all its baggage, sick, and stores. This might be no more than a change of cantonments for a single division, or it might be a part of a general strategical move. Wellington wrote to Hill that evening, ' some say they are going to Valencia, some that they are to cross the Tagus. I will let you know if I should learn anything positive. I have not yet heard whether the movement has been general, or is confined to this particular division [1].' The right deduction was not drawn with certainty, because at the same time false intelligence was brought that Foy had started from Toledo and gone into La Mancha, but had returned again. This was a confused account of his movement ; but the rumour of his coming

[1] Wellington to Hill, *Dispatches*, viii. p. 482, compare Wellington to Liverpool, viii. pp. 485–6, of the next morning.

back discounted the certain news about Brennier's eastward move[1].

On the 29th came the very important additional information that on the 26th Clausel's Division, hitherto lying on the Upper Tormes, above Salamanca, had marched upon Avila, and that the division already at Avila was moving on some unknown eastward destination. At the same time Wellington received the perfectly correct information that all the cavalry of the Imperial Guard in Old Castile had already started for Bayonne, and that the two infantry divisions of the Young Guard, which formed the most effective part of Dorsenne's Army of the North, were under orders to march northward from Valladolid, and had already begun to move.[2] This was certain—less so a report sent in by Castaños to the effect that he had learnt that the whole Army of Portugal was about to concentrate at Toledo. On this Wellington writes to Graham that 'he imagines it is only a report from Alcaldes'—a class of correspondents on whose accuracy and perspicacity he was not accustomed to rely over-much[3].

But enough information had come to hand to make it clear that a general eastward movement of the French was taking place, and that the troops immediately available for the succour of Ciudad Rodrigo were both decreased in numbers and removed farther from the sphere of Wellington's future operations. He thought that the opportunity given justified him in striking at once, and had drawn at last the correct deduction : ' I conclude that all these movements have for their object to support Suchet's operations in Valencia, or even to co-operate with him[4].' If Marmont were extending his troops so far east as the Valencian border, and if Dorsenne were withdrawing divisions northward from Valladolid, it was clear that they could not concentrate in any short space of time for the deliverance of Rodrigo. It was possible that the siege might linger on long enough to enable the Armies of Portugal and the

---

[1] See *Dispatches*, viii. p. 520. See the Dickson MSS., edited by Major Leslie, for letter from Almeida in December.

[2] Wellington to Lord Liverpool, Jan. 1, *Dispatches*, viii. p. 524.

[3] See Wellington to Graham, Dec. 26, *Dispatches*, viii. p. 521.

[4] Wellington to Lord Liverpool, *Dispatches*, viii. p. 524.

North to unite ; Wellington calculated that it might take as much as twenty-four or even thirty days—an estimate which happily turned out to be exaggerated : in the end he stormed it only twelve days after investment. But even if Rodrigo should resist its besiegers sufficiently long to permit of a general concentration of the enemy, that concentration would disarrange all their schemes, and weaken their hold on many outlying parts of the Peninsula. ' If I do not succeed,' wrote Wellington, ' I shall at least bring back some of the troops of the Army of the North, and the Army of Portugal, and shall so far relieve the Guerrillas [Mina, Longa, Porlier] and the Spanish Army in Valencia [1].' The last-named force was, as a matter of fact, beyond saving, when Wellington wrote his letter to Lord Liverpool. But he could not know it, and if Blake had behaved with common prudence and foresight in the end of December, his game ought not to have been played out to a disastrous end early in January, just when the British were moving out to the leaguer of Rodrigo.

All the divisions cantoned upon or behind the Beira frontier received, on January 2nd–3rd, the orders which bade them prepare to push up to the line of the Agueda. Only the 6th Division, which lay farthest off, as far back as Mangualde and Penaverde near the Upper Mondego, was not brought up to the front within the next few days. The 1st Division had a long march from Guarda, Celorico, and Penamacor, the 4th and 5th Divisions very short ones from Aldea del Obispo and Alameda, Villa de Ciervo, and other villages near Almeida. The 3rd Division from Aldea da Ponte and Navas Frias had a journey greater than those of the two last-named units, but much less than that of the 1st Division. Finally the Light Division was, it may be said, already in position : its outlying pickets at Pastores and Zamorra were already within six miles of Rodrigo, and its head-quarters at Martiago only a short distance farther back.

By January 5th the divisions were all at the front, though their march had been carried out in very inclement weather— heavy snow fell on the night of the 1st–2nd of the month, and

---

[1] Another extract from the explanatory dispatch to Lord Liverpool, written on Jan. 1st, 1812.

continued to fall on the third ; while on the 4th the wind shifted, the snow turned to sleet, and the roads grew soft and slushy. The carts with stores and ammunition, pushing forward from Almeida, only reached Gallegos—ten miles away—in two days. The troops were well forward—the 1st Division at Espeja and Gallegos, the 3rd at Martiago and Zamorra, the 4th at San Felices, beyond the Agueda, the Light Division at Pastores, La Encina and El Bodon. But Wellington nevertheless had to put off the investment for three days, because the train was not to the front. On the 6th he crossed the Agueda with his staff and made a close reconnaissance of the place, unmolested by the garrison. But it was only on the 8th that the divisions, who were suffering severely from exposure to the wintry weather, received orders to close in and complete the investment.

Of the topography of Ciudad Rodrigo we have already spoken at some length, when dealing with its siege by Ney in 1810. The French occupation had made no essential change to its character. The only additions to its works made during the last eighteen months were the erection of a small fort on the summit of the Greater Teson, and the reinforcing by masonry of the three large convents in the suburb of San Francisco, which the Spaniards had already used as places of strength. The firstnamed work was a redoubt (named Redout Renaud, from the governor whom Julian Sanchez had kidnapped in October) : it mounted three guns, had a ditch and palisades, and was built for a garrison of seventy men. Its gorge contained a sally-port opening towards the town, and was closed with palisades only. Four guns on the stone roof of the fortified convent of San Francisco, and many more in the northern front of the *enceinte*, bore upon it, and were intended to make access to it dangerous and costly.

The breaches made during Ney's siege, in the walls facing the Tesons, had been well built up : but the new masonry, clearly distinguishable by its fresh colour from the older stone, had not set over well, and proved less hard when battered.

The garrison, supplied by the Army of the North, was not so numerous as it should have been, particularly when it was intended to hold not only the *enceinte* of the small circular town

but the straggling suburb outside. It consisted of a battalion
each of the 34th Léger and the 113th Line, from the division of
Thiébault (that long commanded in 1810–11 by Serras), making
about 1,600 men, with two companies of Artillery and a small
detachment of sappers—the whole at the commencement of
the siege did not amount to quite 2,000 of all ranks, even
including the sick in the hospital. The governor was General
Barrié, an officer who had been thrust into the post much
contrary to his will, because he was the only general of brigade
available at Salamanca when his predecessor Renaud was
taken by Julian Sanchez[1]. The strength of the garrison had
been deliberately kept low by Dorsenne, because of the immense
difficulty of supplying it with provisions. The first convoy for
its support had only been introduced by bringing up 60,000 men,
at the time of the fighting about El Bodon in September : the
second only by Thiébault's risky expedient on November 2nd.

The one thing that was abundant in the garrison of Ciudad
Rodrigo on January 8th, 1812, was artillery. Inside the place
was lying the whole siege-train of the Army of Portugal, which
Masséna had stored there when he started on his march into
Portugal in September 1811. No less than 153 heavy guns, with
the corresponding stores and ammunition, were parked there.
A small fortress was never so stocked with munitions of war,
and the besieged made a lavish and unsparing use of them
during the defence : but though the shot and shell were available
in unlimited quantities, the gunners were not—a fortunate thing
for the besiegers.

The details of the siege of Ciudad Rodrigo are interesting.
This was the only one of Wellington's sieges in which everything
went without a serious hitch from first to last—so much so that
he took the place in twelve days, when he had not dared to
make his calculation for less than twenty-four[2]. Even the
thing which seemed at first his greatest hindrance—the extreme

---

[1] For details of this see Thiébault's *Mémoires*, iv. p. 537, where Barrié's
frank dismay at his appointment, and the arguments used to overcome it,
are described at length.

[2] Wellington to Liverpool, *Dispatches*, viii. p. 536, Jan. 7th, 1812, ' I can
scarcely venture to calculate the time that this operation will take, but
I should think not less than twenty-four or twenty-five days.

inclemency of the weather—turned out in the end profitable. The sleet had stopped on the 6th, and a time of light frosts set in, without any rain or snow. This kept the ground hard, but was not bitter enough to freeze it for even half an inch below the surface ; the earth was not difficult to excavate, and it piled together well. A persistent north-east wind kept the trenches fairly dry, though it chilled the men who were not engaged in actual spade work to the very bones. The worst memory recorded in the diaries of many of the officers present in the siege is the constant necessity for fording the Agueda in this cold time, when its banks were fringed each morning with thin ice. For the camps of all the divisions, except the 3rd, which lay at Serradilla del Arroyo, some miles south-east of the city, were on the left bank of the river, and the only bridge was so far off to the north that it was little used, the short cut across the ford to the south of the town saving hours of time : ' and as we were obliged to cross the river with water up to our middles, every man carried a pair of iced breeches into the trenches with him [1].' There being very few villages in the immediate neighbourhood of Rodrigo, many of the brigades had to bivouac on the open ground—life being only made tolerable by the keeping up of immense fires, round which the men spent their time when off duty, and slept at night. But for the troops in the trenches there could be no such comfort : they shivered in their great coats and blankets, and envied those of their comrades who did the digging, which at any rate kept the blood circulating. It is said that several Portuguese sentries were found dead at their posts from cold and exhaustion each morning.

Wellington's general plan was to follow the same line which Ney had adopted in 1810, i.e. to seize the Greater Teson hill, establish a first parallel there, and then sap down to the lower Little Teson, on which the front parallel and the breaching batteries were to be established, at a distance of no more than 200 yards from the northern *enceinte* of the city. But he had to commence with an operation which Ney was spared—there was now on the crest of the Greater Teson the new Redout Renaud, which had to be got rid of before the preliminary preparation could be made.

[1] Kincaid, *Adventures in the Rifle Brigade*, p. 104.

This little work was dealt with in the most drastic and summary way. On the same evening on which the army crossed the Agueda and invested the fortress, the Light Division was ordered to take the redoubt by escalade, without any preliminary battering. In the dark it was calculated that the converging fires from the convent of San Francisco and the northern walls would be of little importance, since the French could hardly shell the work at random during an assault, for fear of hitting their own men ; and the attacking column would be covered by the night till the very moment when it reached its goal.

Colonel Colborne led the storming-party, which consisted of 450 men, two companies from each British battalion, and one each from the 1st and 3rd Caçadores [1]. His arrangements have received well-deserved praise from every narrator of the enterprise. The column was conducted to within fifty yards of the redoubt without being discovered ; then the two rifle companies and two of the 52nd doubled out to the crest of the glacis, encircled the work on all sides, and, throwing themselves on the ground, began a deliberate and accurate fire upon the heads of the garrison, as they ran to the rampart, roused at last by the near approach of the stormers. So close and deadly was the fire of this ring of trained marksmen, that after a few minutes the French shrank from the embrasures, and crouched behind their parapets, contenting themselves with throwing a quantity of grenades and live shells at haphazard into the ditch. Their three cannon were only fired once ! Such casual and ineffective opposition could not stop the veterans of the Light Division. For three companies of the 43rd and 52nd, forming the escalading detachment, came rushing up to the work, got into the ditch by descending the ladders which were provided for them, and then reared them a second time against the fraises of the rampart, up which they scrambled without much difficulty, finding the scarp not too steep and without a *revêtement*. The garrison

---

[1] I take Colborne's own account (see letter in his life by Moore Smith, p. 166). There were two companies each from the 1/43rd, 1/52nd, 2/52nd, and 95th, and one from each Caçador battalion. Jones wrongly says (p. 116) three companies of the 52nd only, Napier (as usual) omits all mention of the Portuguese. Cf. Harry Smith's *Autobiography*, i. p. 55.

flinched at once—most of them ran into their guard-house or crouched under the guns, and surrendered tamely. At the same time entrance was forced at another point, the gorge, where a company, guided by Gurwood of the 52nd, got in at the gate, which was either unlocked by some of the French trying to escape, or accidentally blown open by a live shell dropped against it [1]. Of the garrison two captains and forty-eight rank and file were unwounded prisoners, three were killed, and about a dozen more wounded. No more than four, it is said, succeeded in getting back into the town [2]. This sudden exploit only cost the stormers six men killed, and three officers [3] and sixteen men wounded. Colborne remarks in his report that all the losses were during the advance or in the ditch, not a man was hurt in the actual escalade, for the enemy took cover and gave way, instead of trying to meet the stormers with the bayonet.

The moment that the redoubt was stormed, the French gunners in the city and the convent of San Francisco opened a furious fire upon it, hoping to make it untenable. But this did little harm, for Colborne withdrew the stormers at once— and the important spot that night was no longer the work but the ground behind it, which was left unsearched. For here, by Wellington's orders, a first parallel 600 yards long was opened, and approaches to it along the top of the Teson were planned out. So little was the digging hindered, that by dawn the trenches were everywhere three feet deep and four broad, sites for three batteries had been marked out, and a communication had been run from the parallel up to the redoubt, whose rear wall was broken down into the ditch, so as to make it easily accessible.

It had been calculated that if the assault had failed, the

---

[1] In Moorsom's *History of the 52nd* it is stated that a sergeant of the French artillery, while in the act of throwing a live shell, was shot dead : the shell fell back within the parapet, and was kicked away by one of the garrison, on which it rolled down into the gorge, was stopped by the gate, and then exploded and blew it open (p. 152).

[2] So Belmas, iv. p. 266. Barrié's report says that there were 60 infantry and 13 gunners inside altogether. It is an accurate and very modest narrative, in which there is nothing to correct.

[3] Mein and Woodgate of the 52nd, and Hawkesley of the 95th. The last named died of his wounds.

redoubt could only have been reduced by regular battering for five days—that amount of time, therefore, was saved by the escalade. The operation contrasts singularly with the fruitless assaults on Fort San Cristobal at Badajoz during the summer months of the preceding year, to which it bore a considerable similarity. The difference of results may be attributed mainly to the superiority of the arrangements made by Colborne, more especially to the great care that he took to keep down the fire of the besieged by a very large body of marksmen pushed close up to the walls, and to the way in which he had instructed each officer in charge of a unit as to the exact task that was imposed on him. At San Cristobal there had been much courage displayed, but little management or intelligence in the command.

On the morning of January 9th, the first parallel, along the front of the Great Teson, was not so far advanced as to afford good cover, and the working parties were kept back till dark, and employed in perfecting the approaches from the rear : only fifty men were slipped forward into the dismantled Redout Renaud, to improve the lodgement there. The garrison fired fiercely all day on the parallel, but as there was little to shoot at, very small damage was done. At noon the 1st Division relieved the Light Division at the front : for the rest of the siege the arrangement was that each division took twenty-four hours at the front in turn, and then returned to its camp. The order of work was :

Light Division 8th–9th January, 12th–13th, 16th–17th, and for the storm on the 19th.

1st Division 9th–10th, 13th–14th, 17th–18th.

4th Division 10th–11th, 14th–15th, 18th–19th.

3rd Division 11th–12th, 15th–16th, and for the storm on the 19th.

The 1st Division had very responsible work on the second night of the siege, for when darkness had set in the first parallel had to be made tenable, and the three batteries in front of it developed. Owing to the very powerful artillery of the besieged, it was settled that the batteries were to be made of exceptional strength and thickness—with a parapet of no less than 18 feet breadth at the top. To procure the necessary earth it was determined that an exterior ditch should be dug in front of them, and that their floor (*terre-plain*) should be sunk 3 feet below the level of the hillside within. A row of large gabions was placed in front of the exterior ditch to give cover to the men digging it.

Great progress was made with the work under cover of the night, but when morning came the besieged, whose fire had been at haphazard during the night, could see the works and commenced to shoot more accurately. A curious *contretemps* was discovered at dawn. By some miscalculation the locality of the left-hand battery had been laid out a little too far to the east, so that half its front was blocked by the ruins of the Redout Renaud. This, of course, was the effect of working in pitch darkness, when the outline of that work was invisible even from a score or so of yards away. Possibly the error may have originated from the fact that, early in the night, the directing engineer officer, Captain Ross, was killed by a flanking shot from the convent of San Francisco. Thus the men constructing the battery had been deprived of all superior direction. In the morning Colonel Fletcher directed that the east end of the battery should have no guns ; the five which should have been placed there were to be transferred to the right-hand battery, which thus became designed for sixteen guns instead of eleven [1].

On the 10th–11th January, when the 4th Division had charge of the trenches the first parallel was nearly completed, the batteries continued to be built up, magazine emplacements were constructed in them, and a trench of communication between them was laid out. When daylight revealed to the French the exact situation of the three batteries, which were now showing quite clearly, a very fierce fire was opened on them, the rest of the works being neglected. The losses, which had hitherto been insignificant, began to grow heavy, and so many men were hit in the exterior trenches, which were being dug in front of each battery, that Wellington and Colonel Fletcher gave orders

---

[1] This mistake is acknowledged in Jones's *Sieges*, i. p. 120, and much commented on by Burgoyne [*Life and Correspondence*, i. p. 161], who complains that an immense amount of work was wasted, two nights' digging put in, the *terre-plain* levelled, and even some platforms laid, before the error was detected.

that they should be discontinued. Heavy damage was done
to the batteries themselves—the French adopted a system of
firing simultaneous flights of shells with long fuses at given
points, ' of which several falling together upon the parapets
blew away in an instant the work of whole hours.'

On the 11th–12th, with the 3rd Division in charge, the work
was continued ; the platforms were placed in the batteries, and
the splinter-proof timbers laid over the magazine emplacements.
But half the exertion of the men had to be expended in repairs :
as each section of the batteries was completed, part of it was
ruined by the besiegers' shells. ' The nights were long and bitter
cold, and the men could not decently be kept working for twelve
hours on end [1],' especially when it was considered that they
had to march four or five miles from their camps to the trenches
before commencing their task of digging, so that they did not
arrive fresh on the ground. Reliefs were therefore arranged to
exchange duty at one hour after midnight, so that no man was
at work for more than half of the cold hours of darkness.

On the 12th–13th, with the Light Division doing its second
turn at the front, the batteries were nearly completed, despite
of much heart-breaking toil at repairs. Wellington, before
starting the task of battering, put the problem to Colonel
Fletcher as to whether it would be possible to breach the walls
with the batteries in the first parallel, or whether these would
only be useful for subduing the fire of the besieged, and the
actual breaching would have to be accomplished by another
set of batteries, to be placed in a second parallel which was, as
yet, contemplated but not begun. Fletcher, after some cogita-
tion, replied that he thought it could be done, though Ney, in
the siege of 1810, had failed in such a project, and had breached
the walls with batteries in situations much farther forward.
Wellington's inquiry was dictated by his doubt as to whether
Marmont and Dorsenne might not be in a position to appear
with a heavy relieving force, before a second parallel could be
thrown up. There were, as yet, no signs of such a danger ; the
enemy having apparently been taken completely unawares by
the opening of the siege. But if the second parallel advanced
no faster in proportion than the first, and had to be built on

[1] Burgoyne, i. p. 162.

much more dangerous ground, it was clear that there was a risk of its taking an inordinate time to complete. On Fletcher's conclusion being made, Wellington decided that he would try to breach the walls with his original batteries, but would push forward a second parallel also : if Marmont and Dorsenne showed signs of rapid concentration, he would try to storm the place before the trenches were pressed forward to the neighbourhood of the walls. If they did not, he would proceed in more regular style, build a second and perhaps a third parallel, with batteries close to the *enceinte*, and end by blowing in the counterscarp, and assaulting from close quarters.

This resolution having been formed, Wellington ordered the second parallel to be commenced on the night of the 13th–14th, with the 1st Division in charge. Despite of a heavy fire from the French, who discovered (by throwing fire-balls) that men were at work in front of the first parallel, an approach by flying sap was pushed out, from the extreme right end of the original trenches, down the slope which separates the Great from the Lesser Teson, and a short length of excavation was made on the western end of the latter height, enough to allow of a small guard finding cover. This move brought the besiegers very close to the fortified convent of Santa Cruz, outside the north-western walls of the city, and lest it should give trouble during the succeeding operations Wellington ordered it to be stormed. The troops employed were 300 volunteers from the Line brigade of the German Legion and one company of the 5/60th. They broke down the palisades of the convent with axes, under a heavy fire, and as they entered the small garrison fled with some loss. That of the stormers was 6 killed and 1 officer and 33 men wounded [1]. Only by clearing the French out of this post could the zig-zags leading down from the first to the second parallel be completed without paying a heavy price in lives, for the musketry of the convent would have enfiladed them in several places. The same night the siege-guns, which had reached the camp on the 11th, were moved into the three batteries.

[1] See Schwertfeger's *History of the German Legion*, i. p. 353. Jones (*Sieges*, i. p. 125) is quite wrong in saying that the convent was carried 'with no loss.'

Next day (January 14–15) was a very lively one. General Barrié was convinced that the establishment of a second parallel on the Lesser Teson, only 200 yards from his walls, must not be allowed at any cost, and executed a sortie with 500 men, all that he could spare from the garrison. He (very cleverly) chose for his time the hour (11 a.m.) when the 4th Division was relieving the workmen of the First, for, as Jones remarks, ' a bad custom prevailed that as soon as the division to be relieved saw the relieving division advancing, the guards and workmen were withdrawn from the trenches, and the works were left untenanted for some time during the relief, which the French could observe from the steeple of the cathedral, where there was always an officer on the look-out.'

The sortie recaptured the convent of Santa Cruz, swept along the second parallel, where it upset the gabions and shovelled in some of the earth, and then made a dash at the first parallel, where it might have done much mischief in the batteries if General Graham and the engineer officer on duty had not collected a few belated workmen of the 24th and 42nd, who made a stand behind the parapet, and opened a fire which checked the advance till the relieving division came running up from the rear. The French then turned and retired with little loss into the place.

The advanced parallel and Santa Cruz were not reoccupied while daylight lasted, but at about 4.30 in the afternoon the three batteries opened with the 27 guns, which had been placed in them. Two 18-pounders in the left battery were directed against the convent of San Francisco, the rest against the northern part of the city, on the same point where Ney's breach had been made in 1810. Of the gunners, 430 in number, nearly 300 were Portuguese [1]. The fire opened so late in the day that by the time that it was growing steady and accurate dusk fell, and it was impossible to judge what its future effect would be.

Meanwhile, when the big guns were silent, the work of preparing for the nearer approach was resumed after dark. The most important move on the night of the 14th–15th was the storming of the convent of San Francisco by three companies

[1] See *Dickson Papers*, Jan. 1812.

of the 40th regiment. The garrison made little resistance, and retired, abandoning three guns and two wounded men. Immediately afterwards the posts in the neighbouring suburb were all withdrawn by Barrié, who considered that he could not afford to lose men from his small force in the defence of outlying works, when his full strength was needed for the holding of the town itself. Santa Cruz, on the other side, though recovered in the morning, was abandoned on this same night for identical reasons. The French general was probably wise, but it was a great profit to the besiegers to be relieved from the flanking fire of both these convents, which would have enfiladed the two ends of the second parallel. That work itself was re-occupied under the cover of the night : the gabions upset during the sortie of the morning were replaced, and much digging was done behind them. The zig-zags of the approach from the upper trenches on the Great Teson were deepened and improved. All this was accomplished under a heavy fire from the guns on the northern walls, which were so close to the second parallel that their shells, even in the dark, did considerable damage.

When day dawned on the 15th, the breaching batteries on the Great Teson opened again with excellent effect. Their fire was concentrated on the rebuilt wall of the *enceinte*, where the French breach of 1810 had been mended. It was necessary to batter both the town wall proper and the *fausse-braye* below it, so as to make, as it were, an upper and a lower breach, corresponding to each other, in the two stages of the *enceinte*. It will be remembered that, as was explained in our narrative of the French siege [1], the mediaeval ramparts of the old wall showed well above the eighteenth-century *fausse-braye* which ran around and below them, while the latter was equally visible above the glacis, which, owing to the downward slope from the Little Teson, gave much less protection than was desirable to the work behind it. The French breach had been carefully built up ; but, lime being scarce in the neighbourhood, the mortar used in its repairs had been of inferior quality, little better than clay in many places. The stones, therefore, had

[1] See vol. iii. p. 239. The illustration of Rodrigo on the morning after the storm, inserted to face page 176 of this volume, shows the facts excellently.

never set into a solid mass, even eighteen months after they had been laid, and began to fly freely under the continuous battering.

The breaching being so successful from the first, Wellington resolved to hurry on his operations, though there were still no signs that Marmont or Dorsenne was about to attempt any relief of the garrison. Yet it was certain that they must be on the move, and every day saved would render the prospect of their interference less imminent. Accordingly it was settled that the second parallel should be completed, and that, if possible, more batteries should be placed in it, but that it was to be looked upon rather as the base from which an assault should be delivered than as the ground from which the main part of the breaching work was to be done. That was to be accomplished from the original parallel on the Great Teson, and one more battery was marked out on this hill, close to the Redout Renaud, but a little lower down the slope, and slightly in advance of the three original batteries. From this new structure, whose erection would have been impossible so long as San Francisco was still held by the French, Wellington proposed to batter a second weak point in the *enceinte*, a mediaeval tower three hundred yards to the right of the original breach. All the attention of the French being concentrated on the work in the second parallel, this new battery (No. 4) was easily completed and armed in three days, and was ready to open on its objective on January 18th.

Meanwhile the completion of the second parallel proved a difficult and rather costly business. By Wellington's special orders all the energies of the British batteries were devoted to breaching, and no attempt was made to subdue the fire of those parts of the *enceinte* which bore upon the trenches, but were far from the points selected for assault. Hence the French, undisturbed by any return, were able to shoot fast and furiously at the advanced works, and searched the second parallel from end to end. It was completed on the 18th, and two guns were brought down into a battery built on the highest point of the Little Teson, only 180 yards from the walls. An attempt to sap forward from the western end of the second parallel, so as to get a lodgement a little nearer to the place, was completely

foiled by the incessant fire of grape kept up on the sap-head.
After many workmen had been killed, the endeavour to push
forward at this point was abandoned, such an advance forming
no essential part of Wellington's scheme. The enemy's fire on
the second parallel was made somewhat less effective on the
16th–18th by digging rifle-pits in front of the parallel, from
which picked marksmen kept up a carefully aimed fusillade on the
embrasures of the guns to left and right of the breach. Many
artillerymen were shot through the head while serving their
pieces, and the discharges became less incessant and much less
accurate. But the fire of the besieged was never subdued, and
the riflemen in the pits suffered very heavy casualties.

The 18th may be described as the crucial day of the siege.
The new battery (No. 4) on the Greater Teson opened that
morning against the tower which had been chosen as its objective.
By noon it was in a very ruinous condition, and at dusk all its
upper part fell forward 'like an avalanche,' as the governor
says in his report, and covered all the platform of the *fausse-braye*
below. Barrié remarks that this point was admirably chosen
by Wellington's engineers, ' it was unique in the *enceinte* for the
facilities which it offered for breaching and the difficulties for
defence. This is the spot where the walls are lowest, the
parapet thinnest, and the platforms both of the ramparts and
the *fausse-braye* narrowest. Moreover here had been situated
the gun which best flanked the original great breach[1].'

The garrison found it impossible either to repair the breaches
or to clear away the débris which had fallen from them. All
that could be done was to commence retrenchments and
inner defences behind them. This was done with some effect
at the great breach, where cuts were made in the ramparts on
each side of the demolished section, parapets thrown up behind
the cuts, and two 24-pounders dragged into position to fire
laterally into the lip of the easy slope of débris which trended
up to the ruined wall. At the second or smaller breach much
less was accomplished—the warning was short, for it had never
been guessed that this tower was to be battered, and the space
upon whic hwork could be done was very limited. It was hoped
that the narrowness of the gap might be its protection—it was

[1] See Barrié's report in appendix to Belmas, iv. p. 299.

but a seam in the wall compared with the gaping void at the first and greater breach.

On the morning of the 19th the fire was recommenced, with some little assistance from the two guns which had now begun to work from the advanced battery in the second parallel. The breaches continued to crumble: that at the tower looked as easy in slope (though not nearly so broad) as that at the original point of attack, and an incessant fire all day kept the enemy from making any repairs. No more could be done for the breaches, wherefore Wellington ordered that some of the siege-guns should turn their attention to silencing the French fire from the remoter points of the northern wall. Several of their guns were dismounted: but even by dusk there were many still making reply.

There was now nothing to prevent the assault from being delivered, since it had been settled that no attempt was to be made to sap up nearer the walls, or to blow in the counterscarp. Wellington wrote his elaborate directions for the storm sitting under cover in a trench of one of the advanced approaches, to which he had descended in order to get the closest possible view of the fortress [1].

The orders were as follows. The chosen time was seven o'clock, an hour sufficiently dark to allow the troops to get forward without being seen as they filled the trenches, yet soon enough after nightfall to prevent the French from doing any appreciable repairs to the breaches under cover of the dark.

The main assaults were to be delivered by the 3rd Division on the great breach, and by the Light Division on the lesser breach. There were also to be two false attacks delivered by small bodies of Portuguese troops, with the purpose of distracting the attention of the besieged to points remote from the main assault: either of them might be turned into serious attempts at escalade if the circumstances favoured.

The two brigades of the 3rd Division were given two separate ways of approaching the main breach. Campbell's brigade [2/5th, 77th, 2/83rd, 94th], after detaching the 2/83rd to line the second parallel, and to keep up a continual fire on the walls, was to assemble behind the ruined convent of Santa Cruz.

[1] Jones's *Sieges*, i. p. 137.

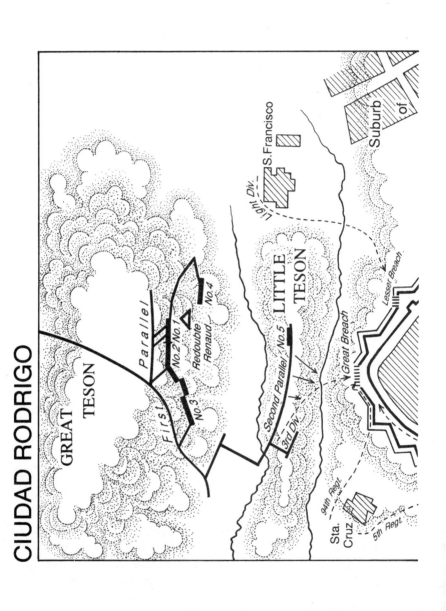

CIUDAD RODRIGO

GREAT TESON

LITTLE TESON

First Parallel

No.1 No.2

No.3

No.4

Redoubte Renaud

Second Parallel No.5

3rd Div.

Light Div.

S.Francisco

Suburb of

Great Breach

Lesser Breach

Sta. Cruz

94th Regt.

5th Regt.

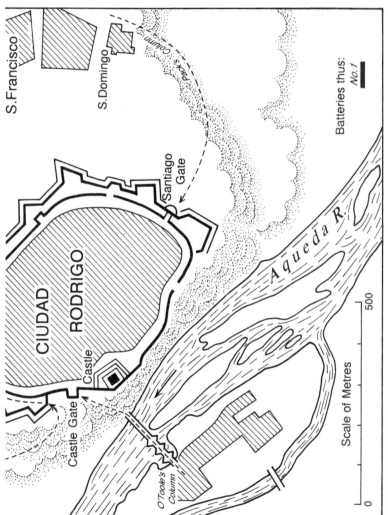

S.Francisco

S.Domingo

Pack's Column

Santiago Gate

CIUDAD RODRIGO

Castle

Castle Gate

O'Toole's Column

Aqueda R.

Batteries thus:
No.1 ▬

Scale of Metres

500

0

B.V.Darbishir; Oxford. 1914

Debouching from thence, the 2/5th, turning to the right, were to make for the place where the counterscarp (covering the whole north front) joined with the body of the place, under the castle and not far from the river. They were to hew down the gate by which the ditch was entered, jump down into it, and from thence scale the *fausse-braye* by ladders, of which a dozen, 25 feet long, were issued to them. It was probable that there would be few French found here, as the point was 500 yards west of the main breach. After establishing themselves upon the *fausse-braye*, they were to scour it eastward, clearing off any parties of the enemy that might be found upon it, and to push for the breach, where they would meet the main assaulting column. The 94th were to make a similar dash at the ditch, half-way between the point allotted to the 5th and the breach, but not to mount the *fausse-braye* : they were to move to their left along the bottom of the ditch, clearing away any palisades or other obstacles that might be found in it, and finally to join the main column. The 77th was to form the brigade-reserve, and support where necessary.

Mackinnon's brigade was to undertake the frontal storm of the great breach. Its three battalions (1/45th, 74th, 1/88th) were to be preceded by a detachment of 180 sappers carrying hay-bags, which were to be thrown into the ditch to make the leap down more easy. The head of the column was to be formed by 300 volunteers from all the battalions, then came the main body in their usual brigade order, the 1/45th leading. Power's Portuguese (9th and 21st Line) formed the divisional reserve, and were to be brought down to the second parallel when Mackinnon's column had ascended the breach.

A support on the left flank of the breach was to be provided by three companies of the 95th, detached from the Light Division, who, starting from beside the convent of San Francisco, were to carry out the same functions that were assigned to the 94th on the other side, viz. to descend into the ditch half-way between the two breaches, and proceed along its bottom, removing any obstacles found, till they joined Mackinnon's brigade at the foot of the wall.

Craufurd, with the rest of the Light Division, which was to move from the left of San Francisco, was to make the attack on the lesser breach. The storming-column was to be formed of Vandeleur's brigade (1/52nd and 2/52nd, four companies of the 1/95th, and the 3rd Caçadores). Barnard's brigade was to form the reserve, and to close in towards the place when the leading brigade should reach the ditch. The division was to detach marksmen (four companies of the 95th) who were to keep up a fire upon the enemy on the walls, just as the 2/83rd did for the 3rd Division. A provision of hay-bags carried by caçadores was made, in the same fashion as at the great breach.

The two subsidiary false attacks were to be made—one by Pack's Portuguese (1st and 16th regiments) on the outworks of the gate of Santiago on the south-east side of the town, the other by O'Toole's Portuguese battalion (2nd Caçadores), headed by the light company of the 2/83rd, on the outwork below the castle, close to the bank of the Agueda. This column would have to rush the bridge, which the French had left unbroken, because it was completely commanded by the castle and other works immediately above it. Both the Portuguese columns carried ladders, and were authorized to attempt an escalade, if they met little or no resistance at points so remote from the breaches, as was quite possible.

Both the Light and 3rd Divisions were fresh troops that night, as the 4th Division had been in charge of the trenches on the 19th. The stormers marched straight up from their distant camps to the starting-points assigned to them in the afternoon. The news that the Light Division had moved to the front out of its turn was the clearest indication to the whole army that the assault was fixed for that night.

A few minutes before seven o'clock the storm began, by the sudden rush of the 2/5th, under Major Ridge, from behind the convent of Santa Cruz, across the open ground towards the ditch on their left of the castle. The governor had expected no attack from this side, the troops on the walls were few, and it was only under a very scattering fire that the battalion hewed down the gate in the palisades, got down into the ditch, and then planted their ladders against the *fausse-braye*. They were established upon it within five minutes of their start, and then, turning to their left, drove along its platform, chasing before them a few small parties of the enemy. In this way they soon arrived at the heap of ruins representing the spot where *fausse-braye* and inner wall had been wellnigh battered into one common mass of débris. Here they found the 94th, who had entered the ditch at the same time as themselves, but a little to their left, and had met with equally feeble resistance, already beginning to mount the lower slopes of the breach. Thus by a curious chance these two subsidiary columns arrived at the crucial point a little before the forlorn hope of the main storming-column. Mackinnon's brigade, starting from the parallels, had to climb over the parapets of the trenches, and to cross rougher ground than the 5th and 94th : they were also hindered by the tremendous fire opened upon them : all the attention of the French had been concentrated on them from the first, as their route and their destination were obvious. Hence, unlike Campbell's battalions, they suffered heavily before they crossed the glacis, and they were delayed a little by waiting for the hay-bags which were to help their descent. When the storming-party, under Major Manners of the 74th, reached the breach, it was already covered by men of the 5th and 94th. The whole, mixed together, scrambled up the higher part of the débris under a deadly fire, and reached the lip of the breach, where they found before them a sixteen-foot drop into the level of the city, on to ground covered with entanglements, beams, *chevaux de frise*, and other obstacles accumulated there by the prescience of the governor. On each flank, for the whole breadth of the wall, was a cutting, surmounted by a parapet, on which was mounted a 24-pounder firing grape downwards on to them.

The head of the column had scarcely gained the lip of the breach when it was raked by the simultaneous discharge of these two guns, which absolutely exterminated the knot of men at its head. At the same time an explosion took place lower down, from some powder-bags which the enemy had left among the débris and fired by means of a train. The impetus of the column was checked, and it was some little time before more men fought their way up to the summit : a second discharge from the two flanking guns made havoc of these, and shut in by the cuts, upon a space of about 100 feet wide, with the impracticable descent into the town in front, the assailants came to a stand again. The only way out of the difficulty was to cross the cuts, and storm the parapets behind them. This was done at both ends : on the one side a small party of the 88th, throwing down their muskets, so as to have hands to climb with, scrambled over the gap and slew with their bayonets the gunners at the left-hand gun, before they could fire a third round : they were followed by many men of the 5th, and a footing was gained on the ramparts behind the obstacle [1]. On the right flank Major Wylde, the brigade-major of Mackinnon's brigade, found a few planks which the French had been using to bridge the cut before the storm, and which they had thrown down but neglected to remove. These were relaid in haste, and a mass of men of the 45th rushed across them under a dreadful fire, and forced the right-hand retrenchment. The garrison, giving way at both ends, fired a mine prepared under a postern of the upper wall as they retired [2]. This produced an explosion much more deadly than the one at the commencement of the storm ; it slew among others General Mackinnon, the senior brigadier of the 3rd Division, whose body was found thrown some distance away and much blackened with powder.

Meanwhile, even before the fighting at the great breach was over, the fate of Ciudad Rodrigo had been settled at another point. The storm of the lesser breach by the Light Division had been successful, after a shorter fight and with much less loss of blood. Vandeleur's brigade here conducted the assault, headed by 300 volunteers from the three British regiments of the division under Major George Napier of the 52nd : Lieutenant Gurwood of the same regiment had the forlorn hope of 25 men. The column did not come under fire for some time after leaving cover, but the assault had been expected, and a keen watch was being kept. Nevertheless the ditch was reached without any great loss, and the stormers leaped in, unaided for the most part by the hay-bags which 150 of Elder's caçadores were to

[1] For a lively account of this exploit see Grattan's *With the Connaught Rangers*, p. 154.

[2] Many narratives speak of General Mackinnon as being killed by the first explosion, and others (including Wellington's dispatch) call the second explosion that of an expense magazine fired by accident. Barrié's report, however, settles the fact that it was a regular mine : and for Mackinnon's death *after* the storming of the cuts I follow the narrative by an eye-witness appended at the end of the general's diary.

have cast down for them, for the greater part of the Portuguese were late in arriving [1]. They then began to plant their ladders, but the forlorn hope went wrong in an odd way, for moving too far to the left along the *fausse-braye* they scrambled up and over a traverse [2] which had been built across it, so finding themselves still on the same level. The head of the main storming party was better directed, and poured up the breach, which was very narrow but clean and clear : the only obstacle at its head was a disabled gun placed horizontally across the gap. Another piece, still in working order, had a diagonal view of the whole slope. The first discharge of this gun, crammed with grape, shattered the head of the column : Major Napier was dashed down with a mangled arm, Colonel Colborne, who was leading the 52nd, got a ball in the shoulder, and several other officers fell. At about the same moment General Craufurd, who was standing on the glacis above the ditch, directing the movements of the supports, received a bullet which passed through his arm, broke two ribs, and finally lodged in his spine. By his mortal hurt and the almost simultaneous wounding of his senior brigadier, Vandeleur, the command of the Light Division passed to Andrew Barnard of the 95th, who was leading the rear brigade.

But the division had been started on its way up the breach, and the gun on its flank got no second opportunity to fire. After its first discharge the survivors at the head of the column, now led by Uniacke and W. Johnston both of the 95th, dashed furiously up the remaining few feet of débris and reached the summit. The voltigeurs facing them broke before the onset, and since there were here no traverses or cuts to prevent the extension of the troops to right or left as they reached their goal, many hundreds were soon in possession of the ramparts

---

[1] Several narrators accuse them of shirking, but Geo. Napier writes (*Life*, p. 215), ' Neither Elder nor his excellent regiment were likely to neglect any duty, and I am sure the blame rested elsewhere, for George Elder was always ready for any service.' Compare George Simmons's autobiography—possibly he put things out by ordering the Portuguese company to carry the ladders, which he clearly was not authorized to do. [*A British Rifleman*, p. 221.]

[2] Some narrators say a low ravelin, but the best authority is in favour of its having been a traverse.

on each side of the breach. The men of the 52nd wheeled to the left and swept the ramparts as far as the Salamanca gate, which they found walled up : the 43rd and Rifles turned to the right, and came upon the French retreating from the great breach, where the 3rd Division were just bursting through. Some of them arrived just in time to suffer from the final explosion which killed Mackinnon and so many of his brigade [1].

With their line forced in two places simultaneously, the garrison could do no more : there was a little fighting in the streets, but not much. The majority of the garrison retired to the Plaza Mayor in front of the castle, and there laid down their arms in mass. At the same time the two Portuguese subsidiary attacks had succeeded. O'Toole's caçadores, headed by the light company of the 2/83rd, had not only captured by escalade the outwork against which they were directed, but found and hewed down its sally-port by which they got entrance into the town. Pack's brigade, on the other side of the place, stormed the redan in front of the Santiago gate, and lodged themselves therein, capturing its small garrison. The governor and his staff had taken refuge in the castle, a mediaeval building with a lofty square tower commanding the Agueda bridge. They had hardly any men with them, and wisely surrendered at the first summons [2].

Seven thousand excited and victorious soldiers, with all traces of regimental organization lost, were now scattered through the streets of Ciudad Rodrigo. This was the first time on which the Peninsular Army had taken a place by assault,

---

[1] The point has often been raised as to whether it was not the success of the Light Division at the lesser breach which enabled the 3rd Division to break through at the greater. Some Light Division diarists (e.g. Harry Smith) actually state that it was their attack on the rear of the defenders which made them flinch from a position which they had hitherto maintained. I think that the case is decided in favour of the 3rd Division by Belmas's statement that the French fired the mine at the great breach only when the 3rd Division had got through, combined with the fact that the leading men of the Light Division reached the back of the great breach just in time to suffer from the explosion, which killed Captain Uniacke of the 95th and a few others. Apparently, therefore, the breach was forced before the head of the Light Division stormers had come up, but only just before.

[2] There is considerable controversy as to what officer received Barrié's surrender. For the Gurwood-Mackie dispute see note in Appendix.

and the consequent confusion does not seem to have been foreseen by any one.   But while the officers and the steady men
were busy in collecting the French prisoners, throwing open
the gates, and seeing to the transport of the wounded into
houses, the baser spirits—and in every battalion, as Sir John
Colborne remarks [1], there were in those days from fifty to a
hundred incorrigibles—turned to plunder.   The first rush was
to the central brandy-store of the garrison, where hundreds got
drunk in a few minutes, and several killed themselves by
gorging raw spirits wholesale.   But while the mere drunkards
proceeded to swill, and then turned out into the streets firing
objectlessly in the air, the calculating rascals set themselves to
the plunder of private houses, which was a more profitable task
than rummaging the French magazines.   There was an immense
amount of unlicensed pillage and wanton destruction of
property—inexcusable in a place where only a small minority
of the people were *Afrancesados,* and the majority had been
getting ready to welcome their deliverers.   The officers did
their best to restore order, ‘ the voice of Sir Thomas Picton
was heard with the strength of twenty trumpets proclaiming
damnation to all and sundry, while Colonels Barnard and
Cameron with other active officers, seized the broken barrels of
muskets, which were lying about in great abundance, and
belaboured misdemeanants most unmercifully [2].’   But active
officers could not be everywhere—three houses, including the
spirit store in the great square, were set on fire by drunken
plunderers, and it was feared that a conflagration might arise,
which fortunately did not happen, for the solid stone structures
were not easily kindled.   The disorder, however, did not reach
the shameful pitch which was afterwards seen at Badajoz and
St. Sebastian.   A competent observer, present at all three
sacks, remarks that ‘ no town taken by assault suffered less than
Rodrigo.   It is true that soldiers of all regiments got drunk,
pillaged, and made great noise and confusion in streets and
houses, despite of every exertion of their officers to prevent it.
But bad and revolting as such scenes are, I never heard that
either the French garrison, after its surrender, or the inhabitants

[1] See his *Life and Letters,* p. 396.
[2] Kincaid, *Adventures in the Rifle Brigade,* p. 117.

suffered personal indignities or cruelty from the troops [1].' There
were apparently no lives lost, except those of a few men shot
accidentally by their drunken comrades, and of certain drunkards
who perished in the spirit store. The greater part of the men
were under control long before dawn, and were collected by their
officers on the ramparts : they marched out next morning,
when the 5th Division, newly arrived at the front from its
distant cantonments in Beira, came into the town. By an
unfortunate accident an explosion of an unsuspected magazine
took place, just as the French prisoners were being marched out,
and some of them and of their escort were killed [2]. The storming
regiments made a strange spectacle as they left the town. ' As
we marched over the bridge dressed in all varieties imaginable,
some with jack-boots on, others with white French trousers,
others in frock-coats with epaulettes, some even with monkeys
on their shoulders, we met the 5th Division on their way to
repair the breaches. They immediately formed upon the left
of the road, presented arms, and cheered us. I was afterwards
told that Lord Wellington, who saw us pass, inquired of his
staff, " Who the devil are *those* fellows [3] ? " '

The garrison, out of a little under 2,000 men present when
the siege began, showed 60 officers and 1,300 rank and file of
unwounded prisoners. Eight officers had been killed, 21
wounded, and about 500 rank and file, mostly on the day
of the assault. The artillery and engineers suffered most—of
8 artillery officers in the place 5 were killed or wounded, of
three engineer officers two fell.

---

[1] Leach's *Sketches in the Life of an Old Soldier*, p. 250. For an amusing
story about a plundering Connaught Ranger who came down a chimney, see
Grattan, p. 162. He tried to propitiate the officer who found him by
presenting him with a case of surgical instruments. Kincaid speaks of
worse than plunder—armed violence and some cases of rape.

[2] So Napier and most other authorities. John Jones, however, says that
the explosion was not accidental, but deliberate—some English deserters
had hidden themselves in a small magazine under the rampart. ' These
desperate men, on seeing an officer approach, deeming discovery and
capture inevitable, and assured that an ignominious death would follow,
blew themselves up in the magazine. The explosion first found vent
through the door, and shot the refugees up into the street, some alive, but
so mutilated, blackened, and distorted, as to be painful to behold.'

[3] Costello (a Light Division narrator), pp. 151-2.

The British and Portuguese loss during the whole siege was 9 officers killed and 70 wounded, and of other ranks 186 were killed and 846 wounded, with 10 missing—apparently deserters. Of these, 59 officers and 503 rank and file fell in the actual storm. The tables appended at the end of this volume demonstrate that the 3rd Division suffered far more heavily than the Light— the battalions with the greatest losses were the 2/5th and 94th, which were early on the great breach and got the benefit of the explosion. Of the 9 officers killed or mortally hurt two were generals, Craufurd and Mackinnon. The death of the former, who lingered in great agony for four days, though shot through to the spine, was no small event in the war : his talents were sadly missed in its latter years : an outpost officer of his capacity would have been invaluable to Wellington during the fighting in the Pyrenees in 1813, when the Light Division, though regimentally as good as ever, much lacked the skilful leading of its old chief. He was a man with many friends and many enemies : of his merits and defects I spoke at length in another place [1]. Here I feel compelled to quote nothing more than the words of his friend, Lord Londonderry—the Charles Stewart of the Peninsular War. ' He was an officer of whom the highest expectation had been formed, and who on every occasion found an opportunity to prove that, had his life been spared, the proudest hopes of his country would not have been disappointed, and he was a man to know whom in his profession without admiring him was impossible. To me his death occasioned that void which the removal of a sincere friend alone produces. While the memory of the brave and the skilful shall continue to be cherished by British soldiers, he will not be forgotten, and the hand which scrawls this humble tribute to his worth must be cold as his own, before the mind which dictates it shall cease to think of him with affection and regret [2].'

---

[1] See vol. iii. pp. 233–7.

[2] Londonderry's *Peninsular War*, ii. p. 268.

CIUDAD RODRIGO ON THE MORNING AFTER THE STORM
FROM THE ADVANCED BATTERY ON THE LESSER TESON

(A contemporary sketch.   To face p. 186)

SECTION XXXII: CHAPTER II

THE CONSEQUENCES OF THE FALL OF CIUDAD RODRIGO

THE extraordinary speed with which Wellington had in twelve days reduced Ciudad Rodrigo, a fortress that had held out for twenty-four days of open trenches when besieged by Ney in 1810, surprised the captor himself, who had reckoned on taking no shorter time in its leaguer than had the French. But it absolutely appalled his two adversaries, Marmont and Dorsenne, whose whole scheme of operations had rested on the idea that they could count on some three weeks or more for preparation, when the news that the place was invested got to their hands.

Thiébault, the governor of Salamanca, had been warning both the commander of the Army of the North and the commander of the Army of Portugal for some weeks that Wellington might move at any moment [1]. But his reports to the effect that the British were making gabions and fascines, preparing a bridge over the Agueda, and bringing up siege-guns to Almeida, made little or no impression on his superiors, because they had come to the conclusion that it was unlikely that Wellington would undertake a siege at midwinter. His preparations, they thought, were probably intended to force his enemies to concentrate, at a time when roads were bad and food unprocurable: 'ils n'ont d'autre but que de nous faire faire de faux mouvements,' said one of Marmont's aides-de-camp. It was only in the spring that the allied army would become really enterprising and dangerous.

Astonishing as it may appear, though Wellington's troops started on January 2nd, and though Rodrigo was invested and the Redout Renaud stormed on January 8th, the definitive

---

[1] See Thiébault's *Mémoires*, iv. pp. 551–2. Extracts from two of his letters are printed in Marmont's *Mémoires*, iv. pp. 280–1, and bear out all that he says in his own book.

news that the siege had actually begun only reached Salamanca on January 13th. No better proof could be given of the precarious nature of the French hold on the kingdom of Leon. The fact was that the guerrilleros of Julian Sanchez so obsessed all the roads from Salamanca to Rodrigo, that no messenger could pass without a very large escort. Barrié only got the news that he was attacked to Thiébault by entrusting it to a Spanish emissary, who carried his note in disguise, and by a long détour. Marmont and Dorsenne only received it on the 14th : King Joseph at Madrid only on the 25th. On the 13th Marmont was in such a state of blindness as to the actual situation that he was writing to Berthier that ' si l'armée anglaise passait l'Agueda j'attendrais sur la Tormès la division du Tage et les troupes que le Général Dorsenne pourrait m'amener, *mais sans doute ce cas n'arrivera pas.* Ciudad Rodrigo sera approvisionné jusqu'à la récolte, et à moins d'un siège il ne doit pas être l'objet d'aucune sollicitude [1].' Wellington, when this was written, had already passed troops over the Agueda some ten days back, and had been beleaguering Ciudad Rodrigo for five. Yet Marmont was dating from Valladolid, which was not much over 100 miles from the hard-pressed fortress. Truly, thanks to the guerrilleros, the ' fog of war ' was lying heavily round the Marshal.

Owing to a circumstance of which Wellington could have no knowledge, the moment which he chose for his advance was even more propitious than he guessed. He knew of the march of Montbrun towards Valencia, and had made it the determining factor in his operations. But he was not, and could not be, aware of another fact of high importance. On December 29th Marmont, then at Talavera, had received a dispatch from Paris, dated on the 13th of the same month, informing him that the Emperor had resolved on making a sweeping change with regard to the respective duties and stations of the Armies of the North and of Portugal. Hitherto Dorsenne had been in charge of the whole kingdom of Leon : the troops stationed in it belonged to his army, and on him depended the garrisons of Ciudad Rodrigo, Astorga, and its other fortresses. He was, therefore, responsible for the keeping back of Wellington from

[1] Marmont to Berthier, Valladolid, Jan. 13, 1812.

all the ground north of the Sierra de Gata. Marmont, with his
Army of Portugal, had to ' contain ' the Anglo-Portuguese army
south of that range, and had charge of the valley of the Tagus—
northern Estremadura and those parts of New Castile which
had been taken away from King Joseph's direct control. From
this central position the Duke of Ragusa had hitherto been
supposed to be able to stretch out a hand to Dorsenne, in case
of Wellington's making a move in the valley of the Douro, to
Soult in case of his showing himself opposite Badajoz. This
indeed Marmont had done : he had brought up his army
to Dorsenne's aid in September, at the time of El Bodon and
Aldea da Ponte : he had carried it down to the Guadiana and
assisted Soult to relieve Badajoz in June.

Berthier's dispatch [1], received on December 29th—it had
taken sixteen days to reach its destination—informed Marmont
that the Emperor had resolved to place the task of ' containing '
Wellington, when he should operate north of the Tagus, in the
hands of one instead of two commanders-in-chief. ' Considering
the importance of placing the command on the whole frontier
of Portugal under a single general, His Majesty has decided
that the provinces of Avila, Salamanca, Plasencia, Ciudad
Rodrigo, the kingdom of Leon, Palencia, and the Asturias,
shall belong to the Army of Portugal.' Along with them were
to be handed over to Marmont Souham's division, then lying
in the direction of Zamora, Benavente, and La Baneza, and
Bonnet's division, then in the Asturias—whose central parts
(as it will be remembered [2]) that general had reconquered in
November 1811. The district of the Army of the North was for
the future to be limited to the eastern parts of Old Castile,
Santander, Biscay, and Navarre. The real cause of this change,
though Berthier's dispatch lays no stress upon it, was the order
recently sent to Dorsenne, which bade him return to France
the two strong divisions of the Imperial Guard, which had
hitherto formed the most important and effective section of
the Army of the North. They were wanted for the probable
Russian war, and without them Napoleon rightly judged that
Dorsenne would be too weak to ' contain ' Wellington, hold

---

[1] Printed in full in Marmont's *Mémoires*, iv. pp. 271–6.
[2] See vol. iv. p. 586.

down all Leon, and observe the Galicians, in addition to hunting Mina and curbing the incursions of Longa and Porlier. Wherefore he resolved to confine the activity of the Army of the North to the lands east and north of Burgos, where its main task would be the crushing of Mina and his compatriots. Marmont should take upon his shoulders the entire responsibility for holding back the Anglo-Portuguese.

But, by the Emperor's orders, the Army of Portugal, though now charged with a much heavier task than before, was not to get any appreciable increase in numbers. It is true that Marmont was to take over the divisions of Souham and Bonnet, along with the regions that they were occupying. These were strong units, and would have increased his total strength by 16,000 men. But at the same time he was told that Thiébault's division [1], the other force in the kingdom of Leon, was not to be given him, but to be withdrawn eastward and to remain under Dorsenne. With it were to go other details belonging to the Army of the North, employed in garrison duty in the valley of the Douro, such as the Swiss battalions long garrisoning the city of Leon, Benavente, and Valladolid [2]. Now it was clear that if these garrisons were withdrawn, Marmont would have to find other troops from his own divisions to replace them. Moreover, he was in addition instructed that Bonnet's division, though now to be regarded as under his command, was not on any excuse to be moved out of the Asturias. ' It is indispensable that he should remain there, because in that position he menaces Galicia, and keeps down the people of the mountains. You would have to use more troops to guard all the edge of the plain from Leon to St. Sebastian than are required for the Asturias. It is demonstrable in theory, and clearly proved by experience, that of all operations the most important is the occupation of the Asturias, which makes the right of the army rest upon the sea, and continually threatens Galicia.'

If, therefore, Marmont was forbidden to use Bonnet, and had to replace all the existing garrisons of Leon (including that of Ciudad Rodrigo, as he was specially informed) by troops drawn from his own force, he was given a vast increase of territory to

[1] 34th Léger, 113th Line, 4th Vistula, Neuchâtel.
[2] Also two cavalry regiments, the 1st Hussars and 31st Chasseurs.

watch, but no appreciable increase of numbers to hold it—no more in fact than the difference between the strength of Souham's division (placed on the side of gain) and that of the new garrisons (placed on the side of loss). The net profit would be no more than 3,000 or 4,000 men at the most.

In addition the Marshal was restricted further as to the way in which he was to dispose of his army. He was told to leave one division (or, if he chose, two) in the valley of the Tagus, about Plasencia and Almaraz, for the purpose of keeping up his communication with Madrid and Andalusia. The rest of his army was to be moved across the Sierra de Gata into the valley of the Douro, and its head-quarters were to be placed at Valladolid, or if possible at Salamanca. Therefore, if Wellington advanced, only four and a half, or five and a half, divisions out of the eight now comprising the Army of Portugal, could be concentrated against him with promptitude : Bonnet and the troops left in the Tagus valley would be long in arriving. So would the nearest divisions of the Army of the North, of which the most westerly would be as far off as Burgos, the rest still farther towards the Pyrenees. Till he had received some of these outlying succours, Marmont would be too weak to resist Wellington. Five divisions (say 30,000 men) could not keep the Anglo-Portuguese contained—though eight might very possibly suffice.

But on December 29, 1811, Marmont had not eight divisions at his disposition. The Emperor's misguided order for the Valencian expedition was in progress of being executed, and it was precisely on that same day that Montbrun with two divisions of foot and one of horse was marching off eastward from La Mancha, in an excentric direction, which took him to the shore of the Mediterranean.

Marmont's available force, after this march began, was as follows :

(1) Souham's division at La Baneza, Benavente, and Zamora, watching Abadia's Army of Galicia. This unit had yet to be informed that it had become part of the Army of Portugal.

(2–3) Brennier's and Maucune's divisions at Almaraz and Talavera in the valley of the Tagus.

(4) Clausel's division at Avila.

(5) Ferey's division in La Mancha, keeping up communication with Montbrun's expeditionary column.

The other three divisions of the Army of Portugal, as now constituted, those of Bonnet in the Asturias, and of Foy and Sarrut in march for Valencia, were hopelessly out of reach.

Being directed, in very clear and decisive terms, to transfer himself in person to Valladolid or Salamanca, and to move the bulk of his troops thither from the valley of the Tagus, the Marshal had to obey. He directed Brennier's division alone to remain behind at Almaraz and Talavera. Maucune and Clausel, with Ferey presently to follow, began a toilsome march across the mountains to Leon. They had to abandon the magazines (such as they were) which had been collected for their subsistence in winter-quarters, and to march across bad roads, in the most inclement month of the year, through an unpeopled country, for cantonments where no stores were ready for them.

While Marmont was marching up in the early days of January to occupy his newly-designated positions, Dorsenne was employed in withdrawing his troops eastward, away from the neighbourhood of Wellington, towards the province of Burgos. He himself stopped behind at Valladolid, to see Marmont and hand over in person the charge of the districts which he was ordered to evacuate. His view of the situation at the moment may be judged by an extract from a letter which he directed to Marmont on January 5 [1].

' I have the honour to enclose herewith two letters dated on the 1st and 3rd instant from General Thiébault at Salamanca. I attach no credence to their contents, for during the last six months I have been receiving perpetually similar reports. . . . If, contrary to my opinion, the English have really made some tentative movements on Ciudad Rodrigo, and if Julian Sanchez has tried to cut our communication with that place, I can only attribute it to your recent movement on Valencia. In that case, the unforeseen reappearance of your Excellency here may make the enemy change his plan of operations, and may prove harmful to him.'

Thiébault had cried ' Wolf ! ' too often to please Dorsenne,

---

[1] Marmont, *Correspondance*, book xv *bis*, p. 287.

and the latter had no real apprehension that Wellington was already on the move. No more had Marmont. On arriving at Valladolid on January 13th he wrote to Berthier (five days after the trenches were opened at Rodrigo !), ' It is probable that the English may be on the move at the end of February, and then I shall have need of all my troops : I have, therefore, told Montbrun to start on his backward march towards me before the end of January [1].' By the end of January Rodrigo had already been for twelve days in the hands of the British army.

And if Dorsenne and Marmont were blind to the actual situation, so, most of all, was their master. The dispatch which gave over the charge of the kingdom of Leon to Marmont contains the following paragraph :

' If General Wellington (sic) after the rainy season is over (i.e. after February) should determine to take the offensive, you can then unite all your eight divisions for a battle : General Dorsenne from Burgos would support you, by marching up from Burgos to your assistance. But such a move is not to be expected (n'est pas présumable). The English, having suffered heavy losses, and experiencing great difficulties in recruiting their army, all considerations tend to make us suppose that they will simply confine themselves to the defence of Portugal. . . . Your various dispatches seem to prove that it is at present no longer possible for us to take the offensive against Portugal, Badajoz being barely provisioned, and Salamanca having no magazines. It is necessary, therefore, to wait till the crops of the present year are ripe [June !], and till the clouds which now darken the political situation to the North have disappeared. His Majesty has no doubt that you will profit by the delay, to organize and administer the provinces under your control with justice and integrity, and to form large magazines. . . . The conquest of Portugal and the immortal glory of defeating the English are reserved for you. Use therefore all possible means to get yourselves into good condition for commencing this campaign, when circumstances permit that the order for it should be given. . . . Suggestions have been made that Ciudad Rodrigo should be dismantled. The Emperor considers that

[1] Ibid., p. 291.

this would be a great mistake : the enemy, establishing himself
in that position, would be able to intercept the communications
between Salamanca and Plasencia, and that would be deplorable.
The English know quite well that if they press in upon Rodrigo,
or invest it, they expose themselves to be forced to deliver
a battle—that is the last thing they want : however, if they did
so expose themselves, it would be your duty to assemble your
whole army and march straight at them [1].'

Such being Napoleon's views at midwinter, it is strange to
find Napier asserting that the disasters of the French at this
time were caused partly by the jealousies of his lieutenants,
partly by their failing to understand his orders in their true
spirit, so that they neglected them, or executed them without
vigour [2]. Without denying that Marmont, Dorsenne, and
Soult were jealous of each other, we may assert that the real
fundamental origin of all their disasters was that their master
persisted in directing the details of the war from Paris, founding
his orders on data three weeks old, and sending those orders
to arrive another fortnight or three weeks after they had been
written. As a fair example of what was perpetually happening
we may cite the following dates. Wellington started to move
on January 1st, 1812, as Thiébault wrote to Dorsenne (on the
report of a Spanish spy) on January 3rd : on January 27 the
general information that the Anglo-Portuguese army had
crossed the Agueda, without any details, reached the Emperor,
and caused him to dictate a dispatch for Dorsenne, giving him
leave to detain the two divisions of the Imperial Guard under
orders for France, and to support Marmont with them : the
Emperor added that he hoped that by January 18th Montbrun
would be nearing Madrid, and that by the end of the month his
column would have joined the Army of Portugal. Eight days
before this dispatch was written Ciudad Rodrigo was already in
Wellington's hands : the news of its fall on January 19th seems
to have reached Paris on February 11th [3], whereupon, as we
shall presently see, the Emperor dictated another dispatch to
Marmont, giving elaborate instructions on the new condition

---

[1] Berthier to Marmont, Dec. 13, as above.
[2] *Peninsular War*, iv. p. 134.
[3] Correspondence in King Joseph's *Letters*, viii. pp. 306–7.

of affairs. This (travelling quicker than most correspondence)
reached Marmont at Valladolid on February 26[1] : but of what
use to the Marshal on that day were orders dictated upon the
basis of the state of affairs in Leon on January 19th ? ' On ne
dirige pas la guerre à trois ou quatre cents lieues de distance,'
as Thiébault very truly observed [2].

It was precisely Napoleon's determination to dictate such
operations as Montbrun's Alicante expedition, or the transference of Marmont's head-quarters from the valley of the
Tagus to Valladolid, without any possible knowledge of the
circumstances of his lieutenants at the moment when his orders
would come to hand, that was the fatal thing. With wireless
telegraphy in the modern style he might have received prompt
intelligence, and sent directions that suited the situation. But
under the conditions of Spain in 1812 such a system was pure
madness.

' The Emperor chose,' as Marmont very truly observes, ' to
cut down the numbers of his troops in Spain [by withdrawing
the Guards and Poles] and to order a grand movement which
dislocated them for a time, precisely at the instant when he
had increased the dispersion of the Army of Portugal, by
sending a detachment of 12,000 men against Valencia. He
was undoubtedly aware that the English army was cantoned
in a fairly concentrated position on the Agueda, the Coa, and
the Mondego. But he had made up his mind—I cannot make
out why—that the English were not in a condition to take
the field : in every dispatch he repeated this statement.' In
fairness to his master, Marmont should have added that he was
of the same opinion himself, that Dorsenne shared it, and that
both of them agreed to treat the Cassandra-like prophecies which
Thiébault kept sending from Salamanca as ' wild and whirling
words.'

Marmont reached Valladolid, marching ahead of the divisions
of Clausel and Maucune, on the 11th or 12th of January. He
found Dorsenne waiting for him, and they proceeded to concert
measures for the exchange of territory and troops which the
Emperor had imposed upon them. After dinner on the evening

---

[1] See Marmont's letter acknowledging its receipt in his *Correspondance*,
iv. pp. 342–3.   [2] *Mémoires*, iv. p. 554.

of the 14th arrived Thiébault's definite and startling news that
Wellington, with at least five divisions in hand, had invested
Rodrigo on the 8th, and was bringing up a heavy battering-
train. The siege had already been six days in progress.

This was very alarming intelligence. The only troops
actually in hand for the relief of Rodrigo were Thiébault's small
division at Salamanca, Souham's much larger division about
La Baneza and Benavente, and Clausel's and Maucune's
divisions, now approaching Valladolid from the side of Avila.
The whole did not make much more than 20,000 men, a force
obviously insufficient to attack Wellington, if he were in such
strength as Thiébault reported.   Dorsenne at once sent for
Roguet's division of the Imperial Guard from Burgos : Marmont ordered Bonnet to evacuate the Asturias and come down
by the route of Leon to join him : he also directed Brennier to
come up from the Tagus, and Ferey to hurry his march from
La Mancha.   Aides-de-camp were sent to hunt for Foy, who
was known to be on the borders of the Murcian regions, where
Montbrun had dropped him on his march to Alicante.   Montbrun himself, with the rest of his column, was also to turn back
as soon as the orders should reach him.

By this concentration Marmont calculated [1] that he would
have 32,000 men in line opposite Wellington by January 26
or 27th, as Bonnet, Brennier, and Dorsenne's Guards should
have arrived by then.   And by February 1 Ferey and Foy ought
also to be up, and more than 40,000 men would be collected.
Vain dates !   For Wellington captured Rodrigo on the 19th,
seven days before the Marshal and Dorsenne could collect even
32,000 men.

Meanwhile Marmont pushed on for Salamanca, where the
troops were to concentrate, having with him only the divisions
of Clausel and Maucune.   On January 21st he had reached
Fuente Sauco, one march north of Salamanca, when he received
the appalling news that Ciudad Rodrigo had been stormed by
Wellington two days before.   This was a thunderstroke—his
army was caught not half concentrated, and he was for the
moment helpless.   He advanced as far as Salamanca, and there
picked up Thiébault's division, but even so he had not more

[1] *Mémoires*, iv. p. 184.

that 15,000 men in hand, and dared not, with such a handful, march on Rodrigo, to endeavour to recover it before Wellington should have restored its fortifications. Bonnet had not yet even reached Leon : Ferey and Dorsenne's Guard division had not been heard of. As to where Foy and Montbrun might be at the moment, it was hardly possible to hazard a guess. The only troops that could be relied upon to appear within the next few days were the divisions of Souham and Brennier. Even with their help the army would not exceed 26,000 or 28,000 men.

Meanwhile Wellington, with seven divisions now in hand, for he had brought up both the 5th and the 7th to the front, was lying on the Agueda, covering the repairs of Ciudad Rodrigo. Marmont had at first thought that, elated by his recent success, the British general might push his advance towards Salamanca. He made no signs of doing so : all his troops remained concentrated on the Portuguese frontier, ready to protect the rebuilding of Rodrigo. Here, on the day after the storm, all the trenches were filled in, and the débris on the breaches removed. Twelve hundred men were then turned to the task of mending the breaches, which were at first built up with fascines and earth only, so as to make them ready within a few days to resist a *coup-de-main*. In a very short time they were more or less in a state of defence, and on February 15th Castaños produced a brigade of Spanish infantry to form the new garrison of the place. The work was much retarded by the weather. Throughout the time of the siege it had been bitterly cold but very dry : but on the 28th the wind shifted to the west, and for the nine days following there was incessant and torrential rain, which was very detrimental to the work. It had, however, the compensating advantage of preventing Marmont from making any advance from Salamanca. Every river in Leon was over its banks, every ford impassable, the roads became practically useless. When, therefore, on February 2nd[1] the Agueda rose to such a height that Wellington's trestle-bridge was swept away, and the stone town-bridge of Rodrigo was two feet under water, so that the divisions cantoned on the

---

[1] Napier says Jan. 29. But Jones, then employed in repairing Rodrigo, gives Feb. 2 in his diary of the work.

Portuguese frontier were cut off from the half-repaired fortress, there was no pressing danger from the French, who were quite unable to move forward.

Marmont, as we have seen, had reached Fuente Sauco on January 21st, and Salamanca on January 22nd. On the following day Souham, coming in from the direction of Zamora, appeared at Matilla, half way between Salamanca and Ciudad Rodrigo, so that he was in touch with his chief and ready to act as his advanced guard. But no other troops had come up, and on the 24th the Marshal received a hasty note from Dorsenne, saying that the division of the Young Guard from Burgos would not reach the Tormes till February 2[1]. With only four divisions at his disposition (Clausel, Maucune, Thiébault, Souham) Marmont dared not yet move forward, since he knew that Wellington had at least six in hand, and he shrank from committing himself to decisive action with little more than 20,000 men assembled. On the 28th Dorsenne sent in a still more disheartening dispatch than his last : he had now ordered Roguet's Guards, who had got as far forward as Medina del Campo, to return to Burgos[2]. The reasons given were that Mina had just inflicted a severe blow on General Abbé, the commanding officer in Navarre, by beating him near Pampeluna with a loss of 400 men, that the Conde de Montijo, from Aragon, had laid siege to Soria, and was pressing its garrison hard, and that another assembly of guerrillero bands had attacked Aranda del Duero, and would take it, if it were not succoured in a few days. ' I therefore trust that your excellency will approve of my having called back Roguet's division, its artillery, and Laferrière's horse, to use them for a *guerre à outrance* against the guerrillas.' Nothing serious—he added— would follow, as all reports agreed that Wellington was sitting tight near Ciudad Rodrigo, and would make no advance toward Salamanca.

No succours whatever, therefore, were to be expected from the Army of the North : Bonnet had only just recrossed the Cantabrian mountains, much incommoded by the bad weather in the passes, and Foy and Montbrun were only expected in the

---

[1] Dorsenne to Marmont, from Valladolid, Feb. 24.
[2] Same to same, from Valladolid, Feb. 27.

neighbourhood of Toledo early in February. Therefore Marmont abandoned all hope of attacking Wellington before Ciudad Rodrigo should be in a state of defence. The desperately rainy weather of January 28th to February 6th was no doubt the last decisive fact in making the Marshal give up the game. Before the rain had ceased falling, he concluded that all chance of a successful offensive move was gone, for he returned from Salamanca to Valladolid on February 5th.

On February 6th he wrote to Berthier[1] that he had ordered Montbrun and Foy, on their return from the Alicante expedition, to remain behind in the valley of the Tagus, and not to come on to Salamanca. His reason for abandoning all idea of a general concentration against Wellington in the kingdom of Leon, was that he was convinced that the next move of the British general would be to make a dash at Badajoz, and that he wished to have a considerable force ready in the direction of Almaraz and Talavera, with which he could succour the Army of the South, when it should be compelled to march, as in 1811, to relieve that fortress. His forecast of Wellington's probable scheme of operations was perfectly correct, and his idea that the best way to foil it would be to hold a large portion of his army in the valley of the Tagus was correct also. But he was not to be permitted to carry out his own plan : the orders from Paris, which he so much dreaded, once more intervened to prescribe for him a very different policy[2].

Wellington during the critical days from January 20th to

---

[1] Marmont to Berthier, Valladolid, Feb. 6. Not in Marmont's *Mémoires*, but printed in King Joseph's *Correspondance*, viii. p. 301.

[2] I must confess that all Napier's comment on Marmont's doings (vol. iv. pp. 94–5) seems to me to be vitiated by a wish to vindicate Napoleon at all costs, and to throw all possible blame on his lieutenant. His statements contain what I cannot but call a *suggestio falsi*, when he says that ' Bonnet quitted the Asturias, Montbrun hastened back from Valencia, Dorsenne sent a detachment in aid, and on Jan. 25 six divisions of infantry and one of cavalry, 45,000 men in all, were assembled at Salamanca, from whence to Ciudad is only four marches.' This misses the facts that (1) Marmont had only *four* divisions (Souham, Clausel, Maucune, and the weak division of Thiébault) ; (2) that Bonnet had not arrived, nor could for some days ; (3) that Dorsenne sent nothing, and on Jan. 27 announced that nothing would be forthcoming ; (4) that Montbrun (who was at Alicante on Jan. 16) was still far away on the borders of Murcia. With 22,000 men only in hand Marmont was naturally cautious.

February 6th was naturally anxious. He knew that Marmont would concentrate against him, but he hoped (as indeed he was justified in doing) that the concentration would be slow and imperfect, and that the Marshal would find himself too weak to advance from Salamanca. His anxiety was made somewhat greater than it need have been, by a false report that Foy and Montbrun were already returned from the Alicante expedition— he was told that both had got back to Toledo by the beginning of January [1]—a most mischievous piece of false news. An equally groundless rumour informed him that Bonnet had left the Asturias, many days before his departure actually took place. On January 21 he wrote to Lord Liverpool that Bonnet had passed Benavente on his way to Salamanca, and that ' the whole of what had gone eastward ' [i. e. Foy and Montbrun] was reported to be coming up from the Tagus to Valladolid, so that in a few days Marmont might possibly have 50,000 men in hand [2]. To make himself strong against such a concentration he ordered Hill, on January 22, to bring up three brigades of the 2nd Division to Castello Branco, with which he might join the main army at a few days' notice [3]. At the same time he directed General Abadia to send a force to occupy the Asturias, which must be empty since Bonnet had evacuated it. It was not till some days later that he got the reassuring, and correct, news that Foy and Montbrun, instead of being already at the front in Castile, were not even expected at Toledo till January 29th, and that Bonnet had started late, and was only at La Baneza when February had already begun. But, by the time that he had received this information, it had already become evident that Marmont was not about to take the offensive, and Ciudad Rodrigo was already in a condition to resist a *coup-de-main*; while, since the whole siege-train of the Army of Portugal had

---

[1] See *Dispatches*, viii. p. 547.

[2] I fancy that Wellington's erroneous statement that Marmont had six divisions collected at Salamanca on the 23rd–24th [misprinted by Gurwood, *Dispatches*, viii. p. 577, as ' the 6th Division ! '] was Napier's source for stating that such a force was assembled, which it certainly was not, Wellington reckoned that Marmont had Souham, Clausel, Maucune, Thiébault, and two divisions from the East, which last had not really come up—and never were to do so.

[3] Wellington to Hill, Jan. 22, *Dispatches*, viii. p. 566.

been captured therein, it was certain that the Marshal could
not come up provided with the artillery required for a regular
siege.

By February 12th the real state of affairs became clear, ' the
enemy has few troops left at Salamanca and in the towns on the
Tormes, and it appears that Marshal Marmont has cantoned
the right of his army on the Douro, at Zamora and Toro, the
centre in the province of Avila, while one division (the 6th) has
returned to Talavera and the valley of the Tagus.' This was
nearly correct : Marmont, on February 6th, had defined his
position as follows—two divisions (those just returned from
the Alicante expedition) in the valley of the Tagus ; one, the
6th (Brennier), at Monbeltran, in one of the passes leading from
the Tagus to the Douro valley ; one (Clausel) at Avila; three
on the Douro and the Esla (Zamora, Toro, Benavente) with
a strong advanced guard at Salamanca. The heavy detachment towards the Tagus, as he explained, was to provide for
the probable necessity of succouring Badajoz, to which Wellington was certain to turn his attention ere long.

Marmont was perfectly right in his surmise. Ciudad Rodrigo
had hardly been in his hands for five days, when Wellington
began to issue orders presupposing an attack on Badajoz. On
January 25th Alexander Dickson was directed to send the 24-lb.
shot and reserve powder remaining at the artillery base at
Villa da Ponte to be embarked on the Douro for Oporto, where
they were to be placed on ship-board [1]. Next day it was
ordered that sixteen howitzers of the siege-train should start
from Almeida overland for the Alemtejo, each drawn by eight
bullocks, while twenty 24-pounders were to be shipped down
the Douro from Barca de Alva to Oporto, and sent round from
thence to Setubal, the seaport nearest to Elvas [2]. On the 28th
Dickson himself was ordered to start at once for Setubal, in
order that he might be ready to receive each consignment on its
arrival, and to make arrangements for its transport to Elvas [3],
while a dispatch was sent to Hill [4] definitely stating that, if all

[1] *Dickson Papers*, ii. p. 571.
[2] Wellington, *Dispatches*, viii. pp. 568–9.
[3] *Dickson Papers*, ii. p. 576.
[4] Wellington to Hill, *Dispatches*, viii. p. 571.

went well, the siege of Badajoz was to begin in the second week
of March.

These plans were drawn up long before it was clear that the
army might not have to fight Marmont on the Agueda, for the
defence of Ciudad Rodrigo. ' If they should move this way,
I hope to give a good account of them,' Wellington wrote to
Douglas (the British officer attached to the Army of Galicia) [1] :
but he judged it more likely that no such advance would be
made. ' I think it probable that when Marmont shall have
heard of our success, he will not move at all [2].' Meanwhile
there was no need to march the army southward for some time,
since the artillery and stores would take many weeks on their
land or water voyage, when roads were bad and the sea vexed
with winter storms. So long as seven divisions were cantoned
behind the Agueda and Coa, Marmont could have no certain
knowledge that the attack on Badajoz was contemplated,
whatever he might suspect. Therefore no transference southward of the divisions behind the Agueda was begun till
February 19th. But Wellington, with an eye on Marmont's
future movements, contemplated a raid by Hill on the bridge
of Almaraz, the nearest and best passage which the French
possessed on the Tagus. If it could be broken by a flying
column, any succours from the Army of Portugal to the Army
of the South would have to take a much longer route and waste
much time [3]. The project was abandoned, on Hill's report that
he doubted of its practicability, since a successful *coup-de-main*
on one of the bridge-head forts might not secure the actual
destruction of the boats, which the French might withdraw to
the farther side of the river, and relay at their leisure [4]. But,
as we shall see, the scheme was postponed and not entirely
rejected : in May it was carried out with complete success.

While Wellington was awaiting the news that his siege
artillery was well forward on the way to Elvas, Marmont had
been undergoing one of his periodical lectures from Paris.
A dispatch sent to him by Berthier on January 23, and received

---

[1] Wellington to Sir Howard Douglas, Jan. 22, *Dispatches*, viii. p. 568.
[2] Wellington to Hill, *Dispatches*, viii. p. 567, same day as last.
[3] Wellington to Hill, Jan. 28, *Dispatches*, viii. pp. 571-2 and 586-7.
[4] Wellington to Hill, Feb. 12, *Dispatches*, viii. p. 603.

at Valladolid on February 6th—fourteen days only having been occupied by its travels—had of course no reference to Wellington or Ciudad Rodrigo, the news of the investment of that fortress having only reached Paris on January 27th. It was mainly composed of censures on Montbrun's Alicante expedition, which Napoleon considered to have been undertaken with too large a force—'he had ordered a flying column to be sent against Valencia, a whole army corps had marched.' But the paragraph in it which filled Marmont with dismay was one ordering him to make over at once 6,000 men to the Army of the North, whose numbers the Emperor considered to be running too low, now that the two Guard divisions had been directed to return to France.

'Twenty-four hours after the receipt of this dispatch you will start off on the march one of your divisions, with its divisional artillery, and its exact composition as it stands at the moment of the arrival of this order, and will send it to Burgos, to form part of the Army of the North. His Majesty forbids you to change any general belonging to this division, or to make any alterations in it. In return you will receive three provisional regiments of detachments, about 5,000 men, whom you may draft into your battalions. They are to start from Burgos the day that the division which you are ordered to send arrives there. All the Guards are under orders for France, and can only start when your division has reached that place. . . . The Army of the North will then consist of three divisions : (1) that which you are sending off ; (2) Caffarelli's division (due at Pampeluna from Aragon) ; (3) a third division which General Dorsenne will organize from the 34th Léger, the 113th and 130th of the line and the Swiss battalions. . . . By this arrangement the Army of the North will be in a position to aid you with two divisions if the English should march against you [1].'

<hr>

[1] The ' third division ' practically represented Thiébault's old division of the Army of the North, which had long held the Salamanca district. This division was to be deprived of its Polish regiment (recalled to France with all other Poles) and to be given instead the 130th, then at Santander. But the 130th really belonged to the Army of Portugal (Sarrut's division), though separated from it at the moment. So Marmont was being deprived of one regiment more.

Along with this dispatch arrived another from Dorsenne [1], clamouring for the division which was to be given him—he had already got the notice that he was to receive it, as he lay nearer to France than Marmont. He promised that the three provisional regiments should be sent off, as the Emperor directed, the moment that the ceded division should reach him. The Duke of Ragusa could not refuse to obey such peremptory orders from his master, and ordered Bonnet's division, from Benavente and Leon, to march on Burgos. His letter acknowledging the receipt of the Emperor's dispatch was plaintive. 'I am informed that, according to the new arrangement, the Army of the North will be in a position to help me with two divisions if I am attacked. I doubt whether His Majesty's intentions on this point will be carried out, and in no wise expect it. I believe that I am justified in fearing that any troops sent me will have to be long waited for, and will be an insignificant force when they do appear. Not to speak of the slowness inevitable in all joint operations, it takes so long in Spain to get dispatches through, and to collect troops, that I doubt whether I shall obtain any help at the critical moment. . . . The net result of all is that I am left much weaker in numbers.'

Marmont might have added that the three provisional regiments, which he was to receive in return for Bonnet's division and the 130th Line, were no real reinforcement, but his own drafts, long due to arrive at the front, but detained by Dorsenne in Biscay and Old Castile to garrison small posts and keep open communications. And he was not destined to receive them as had been promised : Dorsenne wrote on February 24 apologizing for not forwarding them at once : they were guarding the roads between Irun and Vittoria, and could not be spared till other troops had been moved into their scattered garrisons to relieve them.

On January 27th the news of the advance of Wellington against Ciudad Rodrigo had at last reached Paris—eight days after the fortress had fallen. It caused the issue of new orders by the Emperor, all exquisitely inappropriate when they reached Marmont's hands on February 10th. The Marshal had been

[1] Dorsenne to Marmont, from Uñas, Feb. 5.

contemplating the tiresome results of the storm of the fortress for nearly three weeks, but Napoleon's orders presupposed much spare time before Rodrigo would be in any danger : Dorsenne is to stop the march of the Guards towards France, and to bring up all the forces he can to help the Army of Portugal : Montbrun will be back at Madrid by January 18 [on which day he was really in the middle of the kingdom of Murcia], and at the front in Leon before February 1st. After his arrival the Army of Portugal will be able to take up its definitive line of action. Finally, there is a stab at Marmont, ' the English apparently have advanced in order to make a diversion to hamper the siege of Valencia ; they only did so because they had got information of the great strength of the detachment which the Army of Portugal made in that direction [1].'

The Marshal could only reply by saying that the orders were all out of date, that he had (as directed) given up Bonnet's division to the Army of the North, and that, Ciudad Rodrigo having fallen far earlier than any one had expected, and long before any sufficient relieving force could be collected, he had been unable to save it, and had now cantoned his army (minus Bonnet) with four divisions in the valley of the Douro and three in the valley of the Tagus, in expectation of an approaching move on the part of Wellington towards Badajoz.

These dispositions had not long been completed when another dispatch arrived from Paris, dated February 11th, in which the Emperor censured once more all his lieutenant's actions, and laid down for him a new strategical policy from which he was forbidden to swerve.

' The Emperor regrets that when you had the division of Souham and three others united [i. e. on January 23] you did not move on Salamanca, to make out what was going on. That would have given the English much to think about, and might have been useful to Ciudad Rodrigo. The way to help the army under the present circumstances is to place its head-quarters at Salamanca, and concentrate your force there, detaching one division to the Tagus valley and also reoccupying the Asturias. [This concentration] will oblige the enemy to

[1] Napoleon to Berthier, Jan. 27.

remain about Almeida and in the North, for fear of an invasion
of Portugal. You might even march on Rodrigo, and, if you
have the necessary siege artillery, capture the place—your
honour is bound up with it. If want of the artillery or of food
renders it necessary to put off such an operation, you could at
least make an incursion into Portugal, and advance towards the
Douro and Almeida. This menace would keep the enemy
" contained ".... Your posture should be offensive, with Salamanca as base and Almeida as objective : as long as the
English know that you are in strength at Salamanca they will
not budge : but if you retire to Valladolid yourself, and scatter
divisions to the rear, and above all if you have not got your
cavalry effective by the time that the rainy season ends, you
will expose all the north of Spain to misfortunes.

' It is indispensable to reoccupy the Asturias, because more
troops are needed to hold the edge of the plain as far as Biscay
than to keep down that province. Since the English ' are
divided into two corps, one in the South and the other opposite
you, they cannot be in heavy strength : you ought to outnumber
them greatly. . . . I suppose that you consider the English mad,
for you believe them capable of marching against Badajoz when
you are at Salamanca, i. e. of allowing you to march to Lisbon
before they can get back. They will only go southward if you,
by your ill-devised schemes, keep two or three divisions detached on the Tagus : that reassures them, and tells them that
you have no offensive projects against them.

' To recapitulate, the Emperor's intentions are that you
should stop at Salamanca, that you should reoccupy the
Asturias, that your army should base itself on Salamanca, and
that from thence you should threaten the English.'

It may seem profane to the worshippers of the Emperor to
say that this dispatch was purely wrong-headed, and argued
a complete misconception of the situation. But it is impossible
to pass any other verdict on it. Marmont, since Bonnet's
division had been stolen from him, had seven divisions left, or
about 44,000 men effective, including cavalry and artillery.
The Emperor tells him to keep one division on the Tagus, to
send a second to occupy the Asturias. This leaves him about
34,000 net to concentrate at Salamanca. With this force he is

to attempt to besiege Rodrigo, or at least to execute a raid as far as Almeida and the Douro. ' The English are divided and so must be much numerically inferior to you.' But, as a matter of fact, the only British detachment that was not under Wellington's hand at the moment was Hill's 2nd Division, and he had just brought that up to Castello Branco, and would have had it with him in five days, if Marmont had advanced from Salamanca. The Marshal would have seen 55,000 men falling upon his 34,000 if he had moved on any day before the 20th of February, and Wellington was ' spoiling for a fight,' or, in his own quiet phraseology, ' if the French move this way, I hope to give a good account of them [1].' Supposing Marmont had, by some evil inspiration, done what the Emperor had wished him to do before the orders came, he would have been crushed by almost double numbers somewhere in the neighbourhood of Rodrigo or Almeida. The battle of Salamanca would have been fought six months too soon.

This is the crucial objection to Napoleon's main thesis : he underrated Wellington's numbers and his readiness to give battle. As to details we may observe (1) that there was no siege-train to batter Rodrigo, because the whole of the heavy guns of the Army of Portugal had been captured in that fortress. (2) That Wellington was ' mad ' enough to march upon Badajoz with his whole army, precisely because he knew that, even if Marmont should invade Portugal, he could never get to Lisbon. He realized, as the Emperor did not, that an army of five or six divisions could not march on Lisbon in the casual fashion recommended in this dispatch, because it would starve by the way. Central Portugal, still suffering from the blight of Masséna's invasion, could not have sustained 30,000 men marching in a mass and trying to live upon the country in the usual French style. And Marmont, as his adversary well knew, had neither great magazines at his base, nor the immense transport train which would have permitted them to be utilized. The best proof of the impracticability of Napoleon's scheme was that Marmont endeavoured to carry it out in April, when nothing lay in front of him but Portuguese militia, and failed to penetrate more than a few marches into the land, because he

[1] Wellington to Douglas, *Dispatches*, viii. p. 568.

could not feed his army, and therefore could not keep it concentrated.

The Marshal knew long beforehand that this plan was hopeless. He wrote to Berthier from Valladolid on February 26th as follows :

' Your Highness informs me that if my army is united at Salamanca the English would be " mad " to move into Estremadura, leaving me behind them, and free to advance on Lisbon. But they tried this precise combination in May 1811, though all my army was then quite close to Salamanca, and though the Army of the North was then twice as strong as it is to-day, and though the season was then later and allowed us to find provender for our horses, and though we were then in possession of Ciudad Rodrigo. They considered at that time that we could not undertake such an operation [as a march on Lisbon], and were perfectly right. Will they think that it is practicable to-day, when all the conditions which I have just cited are changed to our disadvantage, and when they know that a great body of troops has returned to France ? . . . Consequently no movement on this side can help Badajoz. The only possible course is to take measures directly bearing on that place, if we are to bring pressure upon the enemy and hope to attain our end. The Emperor seems to ignore the food question. This is the important problem ; and if it could be ended by the formation of base-magazines, his orders could be executed with punctuality and precision. But we are far from such a position —by no fault of mine. . . . When transferred to the North in January, I found not a grain of wheat in the magazines, not a sou in the treasury, unpaid debts everywhere. As the necessary result of the absurd system of administration adopted here, there was in existence a famine—real or artificial—whose severity was difficult to realize. We could only get food for daily consumption in our cantonments by using armed force : there is a long distance between this state of affairs and the formation of magazines which would allow us to move the army freely. . . . The English army is always concentrated and can always be moved, because it has an adequate supply of money and transport. Seven or eight thousand pack-mules bring up its daily food—hay for its cavalry on the banks of the Coa and

Marshal Marmont. Duke of Ragusa

Agueda has actually been sent out from England [1]. His Majesty may judge from this fact the comparison between their means and ours—we have not four days' food in any of our magazines, we have no transport, we cannot draw requisitions from the most wretched village without sending thither a foraging party 200 strong : to live from day to day we have to scatter detachments to vast distances, and always to be on the move. . . . It is possible that His Majesty may be dissatisfied with my arguments, but I am bound to say that I cannot carry out the orders sent me without bringing about a disaster ere long. If His Majesty thinks otherwise, I must request to be superseded—a request not made for the first time : if I am given a successor the command will of course be placed in better hands [2].'

This was an admirable summary of the whole situation in Spain, and might have caused the Emperor to change his policy, if he had not by this time so hardened himself in his false conceptions as to be past conviction. As Marmont complains, his master had now built up for himself an imaginary picture of the state of affairs in the Peninsula, and argued as if the situation was what he wished it to be, not what it actually was. ' Il suppose vrai tout ce qu'il voudrait trouver existant [3].'

A subsequent letter from Paris, dated February 21st and received about March 2nd, contained one small amelioration of Marmont's lot—he was told that he might take back Bonnet's division, and not cede it to Dorsenne, on condition that he sent it at once to occupy the Asturias. But it then proceeded to lay down in the harshest terms the condemnation of the Marshal's strategy :

' The Emperor charges me to repeat to you that you worry too much about matters with which you have no concern. Your mission was to protect Almeida and Rodrigo—and you have let them fall. You are told to maintain and administer

---

[1] An exaggeration, but hay was actually brought to Lisbon and Coimbra, and used for the English cavalry brigades, which had been sent to the rear and cantoned on the Lower Mondego.

[2] Marmont to Berthier, Valladolid, Feb. 26. Marmont's *Mémoires*, iv. pp. 344–5.

[3] Marmont's ' Observations on the Imperial Correspondence of Feb. 1812,' *Mémoires*, iv. p. 512.

the North, and you abandon the Asturias—the only point from which it can be dominated and contained. You are getting into a state of alarm because Lord Wellington sends a division or two towards Badajoz. Now Badajoz is a very strong fortress, and the Duke of Dalmatia has 80,000 men, and can draw help from Marshal Suchet. If Wellington were to march on Badajoz [he had done so the day before this letter was written] you have a sure, prompt, and triumphant means of bringing him back— that of marching on Rodrigo and Almeida.'

Marmont replied, with a suppressed rage that can be read between the lines even more clearly than in his earlier letters, ' Since the Emperor attributes to me the fall of Almeida, which was given up before I had actually taken over the command of this army [1], I cannot see what I can do to shelter myself from censures at large : . . . I am accused of being the cause of the capture of Ciudad Rodrigo : it fell because it had an insufficient garrison of inferior quality and a bad commandant. Dorsenne was neither watchful nor prescient. Was it for me to take care of a place not in my command, and separated from me by a chain of mountains, and by the desert that had been made by the six months' sojourn of the Army of Portugal in the valley of the Tagus ? . . . I am blamed for having cantoned myself in the valley of the Tagus after repulsing Lord Welling- ton beyond the Coa [at the time of El Bodon], but this was the result of the imperative orders of the Emperor, who assigned me no other territory than the Tagus valley. Rodrigo was occupied by troops of the Army of the North. . . . I have ordered General Bonnet to reoccupy the Asturias at once, and quite see the importance of the occupying of that province. . . . I am told that the Emperor thinks that I busy myself too much about the interests of others, and not enough about my own. I had considered that one of my duties (and one of the most difficult of them) was to assist the Army of the South, and that duty was formally imposed on me in some twenty dispatches, and specially indicated by the order which bade me leave three divisions in the valley of the Tagus. To-day I am informed that I am relieved of that duty, and my position becomes simpler

---

[1] To be exact, it was on May 10 that Marmont took over the command from Masséna, and Almeida was evacuated by Brennier that same night.

and better ! But if the Emperor relies with confidence on the
effect which demonstrations in the North will produce on the
mind of Wellington, I must dare to express my contrary
opinion. Lord Wellington is quite aware that I have no
magazines, and is acquainted with the immensely difficult
physical character of the country, and its complete lack of food
resources at this season. He knows that my army is not in
a position to cross the Coa, even if no one opposes me, and that
if we did so we should have to turn back at the end of four days,
unable to carry on the campaign, and with our horses all starved
to death [1].'

This and much more to the same effect had apparently some
effect on the mind of the Emperor. But the result was confusing
when formulated on paper. Berthier replied on March 12 :

' Your letters of February 27 and 28 and March 2 have been
laid before the Emperor. His Majesty thinks that not only
must you concentrate at Salamanca, but that you must throw
a bridge across the Agueda, so that, if the enemy leaves less
than five divisions north of the Tagus, you may be able to
advance to the Coa, against Almeida, and ravage all northern
Portugal. If Badajoz is captured by two divisions of the enemy
its loss will not be imputed to you, the entire responsibility will
fall on the Army of the South. If the enemy leaves only two,
three, or even four divisions north of the Tagus, the Army of
Portugal will be to blame if it does not at once march against
the hostile force before it, invest Almeida, ravage all northern
Portugal, and push detachments as far as the Mondego. Its
rôle is simply to " contain " six British divisions, or at least five :
it must take the offensive in the North, or, if the enemy has
taken the initiative, or other circumstances necessitate it, must
dispatch to the Tagus, by Almaraz, the same number of
divisions that Lord Wellington shall have dispatched to conduct
the siege of Badajoz.'

This double-edged document reached Salamanca on March 27,
eleven days after Wellington had invested Badajoz. The whole
allied field army had marched for Estremadura in the last days
of February, and not a single British division remained north

---

[1] I extract these various paragraphs from Marmont's vast dispatch of
March 2, omitting much more that is interesting and apposite.

of the Tagus. In accordance with the Emperor's dispatches of
February 11th and of February 18th, Marmont had already
concentrated the bulk of his resources at Salamanca, drawing
in everything except Bonnet (destined for the Asturias), Souham,
who was left on the Esla to face the Army of Galicia, and the
equivalent of another division distributed as garrisons in
Astorga, Leon, Palencia, Zamora, and Valladolid. With five
divisions in hand, or just coming up, he was on the move, as
the Emperor had directed, to threaten Rodrigo and Almeida
and invade northern Portugal.

The Paris letter of March 12, quoted above, suddenly imposed
on Marmont the choice between continuing the attack on
Portugal, to which he was committed, or of leading his whole
army by Almaraz to Badajoz—it must be the whole army,
since he was told to send just as many divisions southward
as Wellington should have moved in that direction, and every
one of the seven units of the allied army had gone off.

Since Badajoz was stormed on April 6th, only ten days after
Marmont received on March 27 the Emperor's dispatch of
March 12, it is clear that he never could have arrived in time
to help the fortress. In June 1811 he had accomplished a
similar movement at a better season of the year, and when
some time had been allowed for preparation, in fifteen days, but
only by making forced marches of the most exhausting sort. It
could not have been done in so short a time in March or April,
when the crops were not ripe, the rivers were full, and the roads
were far worse than at midsummer. Moreover (as we shall
presently see) Wellington had placed a large containing force
at Merida, half-way between Almaraz and Badajoz, which
Marmont would have had to drive in—at much expense of
time.

The Marshal's perplexity on receiving the dispatch that came
in upon March 27 was extreme. 'The instructions just received,'
he wrote to Berthier, ' are wholly contradictory to those of
February 18 and February 21, imperative orders which forced
me, against my personal conviction, to abandon my own plan,
and to make it impossible to do what I regarded as suitable to
the interests of the Emperor. The letters of February 18 and
February 21 told me that his Majesty thought me a meddler in

matters which did not concern me : he told me that it was
unnecessary for me to worry about Badajoz, " a very strong
fortress supported by an army of 80,000 men." . . . He gave me
formal orders to abandon any idea of marching to succour it,
and added that if Lord Wellington went thither, he was to be
left alone, because by advancing to the Agueda I could bring
him back at once. The letters of the 18th and 21st made it
quite clear that His Majesty freed me from all responsibility
for Badajoz, provided I made a demonstration on the Agueda.
. . . To-day your Highness writes that I *am* responsible for
Badajoz, if Lord Wellington undertakes its siege with more than
two divisions. The concluding paragraph of your letter seems
to give me permission to succour the place, by bringing up
troops to the Tagus. So, after imperative orders have wrecked
my original arrangement, which had prepared and assured an
effective help for Badajoz, and after all choice of methods has
been forbidden to me, I am suddenly given an option when it is
no longer possible to use it. . . . To-day, when my troops from the
Tagus valley have repassed the mountains, and used up the
magazines collected there at their departure, when it is impossible to get from Madrid the means to establish a new magazine
at Almaraz, my army, if it started from this point [Salamanca],
would consume every scrap of food that could be procured
before it could possibly reach Badajoz. . . . The movement was
practicable when I was in my original position : it is almost
impracticable now, considering the season of the year, and the
probable time-limit of the enemy's operations. . . . After ripe
reflection on the complicated situation, considering that my
main task is to hold down the North, and that this task is much
greater than that of holding the South, taking into consideration
the news that an English force is said to be landing at Corunna
(an improbable story, but one that is being repeatedly brought
me), considering that the Portuguese and Galician troops
threaten to take the offensive from Braganza, remembering that
your letters of February 18 and 21 state that Suchet's Army of
Aragon is reckoned able to reinforce the Army of the South,
and considering that my dispositions have been made (in spite
of immense preliminary difficulties) for a fifteen days' march
on the Agueda, which is already begun, I decide in favour of

continuing that operation, though I have (as I said before) no great confidence in its producing any effective result.

' Accordingly I am putting the division that came up from the Tagus in motion for Plasencia, with orders to spread the rumour that it is to rejoin the army by the pass of Perales and enter Portugal ; I start from here with three more divisions for the Agueda ; . . . if I fought on the Tormes I could put one more division in line, five in all : the number of seven divisions of which the Emperor speaks could only be concentrated if the Army of the North [1] could send two divisions to replace my own two now on the lines of communications and the Esla.'

The recapitulation of all this correspondence may seem tedious, but it is necessary. When it is followed with care I think that one definite fact emerges. Napoleon was directly and personally responsible for the fall of Badajoz. Down to March 27th Marmont was strictly forbidden to take any precautions for the safety of that fortress, and was censured as a meddler and an alarmist, for wishing to keep a strong force in the valley of the Tagus, ready to march thither. On March 27 he was suddenly given an option of marching to Estremadura with his whole army. It appears to be an option, not a definite order, for Berthier's sentence introducing the new scheme is alternative—the Army of Portugal is ' to take the offensive in the North *or*, under certain circumstances, to march for Almaraz.' But this point need not be pressed, for if taken as a definite order it was impracticable : Marmont received it so late that, if he had marched for Badajoz with the greatest possible speed, he would have reached it some days after the place was stormed. The fact that he believed that he would never have got there at all, because lack of food would have stopped him on the way, is indifferent. The essential point of Napoleon's responsibility is that he authorized the march too late, after having most stringently forbidden it, in successive letters extending over several weeks.

---

[1] Marmont writes the Army of the Centre, evidently in confusion for the Army of the North. The nearest posts of the Army of the Centre were 150 miles away from the Esla, while the Army of the North at Burgos was much closer. Moreover, the Army of the Centre had not two infantry divisions, but only one—d'Armagnac's—and some *Juramentado* regiments.

That a march on Badajoz by the whole Army of Portugal (or so much of it as was not required to contain the Galicians and to occupy Asturias), if it had begun—as Marmont wished—in February or early March, would have prevented Wellington from taking the fortress, is not certain. A similar march in June 1811 had that effect, at the time of the operations on the Caya. But Wellington's position was much better in February 1812 than it had been eight months earlier. This much, however, is clear, that such an operation had a possible chance of success, while Napoleon's counter-scheme for a demonstration on the Agueda and an invasion of the northern Beira had no such prospect. The Emperor, for lack of comprehension of the local conditions, misconceived its efficacy, as Marmont very cogently demonstrated in his letters. Northern Portugal was a waste, where the Marshal's army might wander for a few days, but was certain to be starved before it was many marches from the frontier. Napier, in an elaborate vindication of the Emperor, tries to argue that the Marshal might have taken Rodrigo by escalade without a battering-train, have assailed Almeida in similar fashion, have menaced Oporto and occupied Coimbra [1]. He deliberately ignores one essential condition of the war, viz. that because of the French system of ' living on the country,' Marmont had no magazines, and no transport sufficient to enable his army to conduct a long offensive campaign in a devastated and hostile land. His paragraphs are mere rhetoric of the most unfair kind. For example, he says, ' Wellington with 18,000 men [2] escaladed Badajoz, a powerful fortress defended by an excellent governor and 5,000 French veterans : Marmont with 28,000 men would not attempt to escalade Rodrigo, although its breaches were scarcely healed and its garrison disaffected.' This statement omits the essential details that Wellington had a large siege-train, had opened three broad breaches in the walls of Badajoz, and, while the enemy was fully occupied in defending them, escaladed distant points of the *enceinte* with success. Marmont had no siege-train, and therefore could have made no breaches ; he would have had to cope with an undistracted garrison, holding ramparts everywhere

---

[1] See chapter vii of book iv, *Peninsular War*, iv. pp. 138–40.

[2] Why omit the 30,000 men of Graham and Hill ?

intact.   Moreover, Ciudad Rodrigo and its outworks form
a compact fortress, of not half the circumference of Badajoz
and its dependencies.   If Ney and Masséna, with an adequate
siege apparatus, treated Rodrigo with respect in 1810, and
proceeded against it by regular operations, Marmont would
have been entirely unjustified in trying the desperate method
of escalade in 1812.   The fortifications, as Napier grudgingly
admits, were ' healed ' : an escalade against Carlos de España's
garrison would certainly have met the same fate as Suchet's
assault on Saguntum, a much weaker and unfinished stronghold.
But it is unnecessary to follow into detail Napier's controversial
statements, which are all part of a wrong-headed scheme to
prove Napoleon infallible on all occasions and at all costs.

The governing facts cannot be disputed : Marmont in
February placed three divisions on the Tagus, which were to
form the advanced guard of an army that was to march to the
relief of Badajoz, whose siege he foresaw.   Napoleon told him
not to concern himself about Badajoz, and compelled him to
concentrate his army about Salamanca.   He instructed him
that the proper reply to an attack on Badajoz by Wellington
was an invasion of northern Portugal, and gave him elaborate
instructions concerning it.   Marmont reluctantly obeyed, and
was starting on such an expedition when he was suddenly told
that he might move on Badajoz.   But he only received this
permission ten days before that fortress was stormed : it was
therefore useless.   The Emperor must take the responsibility.

SECTION XXXII : CHAPTER III

THE SIEGE OF BADAJOZ. MARCH–APRIL 1812

IN narrating the troubles of the unlucky Duke of Ragusa, engaged in fruitless strategical controversy with his master, we have been carried far into the month of March 1812. It is necessary to return to February 20th in order to take up the story of Wellington's march to Estremadura. We have seen that he commenced his artillery preparations in January, by sending Alexander Dickson to Setubal, and dispatching a large part of his siege-train southward, partly by sea, partly across the difficult mountain roads of the Beira.

The Anglo-Portuguese infantry and cavalry, however, were not moved till the guns were far on their way. It was Wellington's intention to show a large army on the frontier of Leon till the last possible moment. He himself kept his old head-quarters at Freneda, near Fuentes de Oñoro, till March 5th, in order that Marmont might be led to persist in the belief that his attention was still concentrated on the North. But, starting from February 19th, his divisions, one by one, had made their unostentatious departure for the South : on the day when he himself followed them only one division (the 5th) and one cavalry brigade (V. Alten's) still remained behind the Agueda. The rest were at various stages on their way to Elvas. Most of the divisions marched by the route Sabugal, Castello Branco, Villa Velha, Niza. But the 1st Division went by Abrantes, in order to pick up there its clothing for the new year, which had been brought up the Tagus in boats from Lisbon to that point. Some of the cavalry and the two independent Portuguese brigades of Pack and Bradford, whose winter cantonments had been rather to the rear, had separate routes of their own, through places so far west as Thomar[1] and Coimbra. The three

---

[1] This was the case with G. Anson's brigade and Bradford's Portuguese infantry. Pack went by Coimbra, Slade's cavalry brigade by Covilhão, and the horse artillery of Bull and McDonald with it.

brigades of the 2nd Division, under Hill, which had been brought up to Castello Branco at the beginning of January, were at the head of the marching army, and reached Portalegre, via Villa Velha, long before the rest of the troops were across the Tagus. Indeed, the first of them (Ashworth's Portuguese) started as early as February 2nd, and was at Castello de Vide, near Elvas, by February 8th, before the troops behind the Agueda had begun to move [1].

The lengthy column of infantry which had marched by Castello Branco and the bridge of Villa Velha was cantoned in various places behind Elvas, from Villa Viçosa to Portalegre, by March 8th : the 1st Division, coming in from the Abrantes direction, joined them on March 10th, and halted at Monforte and Azumar. Only the 5th Division and the two Portuguese independent brigades were lacking, and of these the two former were expected by the 16th, the latter by the 20th. With the exception of the 5th Division the whole of Wellington's field army was concentrated near Elvas by the 16th. Only the 1st Hussars of the King's German Legion, under Victor Alten, had been left to keep the outpost line in front of Ciudad Rodrigo, in order that the French vedettes in Leon should not detect

---

[1] Nothing is rarer, as all students of the Peninsular War know to their cost, than a table of the exact movements of Wellington's army on any march. For this particular movement the whole of the detailed orders happen to have been preserved in the D'Urban Papers. The starting-places of the units were :—

1st Division—Gallegos, Carpio, Fuentes de Oñoro.
3rd Division—Zamorra (by the Upper Agueda).
4th Division—San Felices and Sesmiro.
5th Division—Ciudad Rodrigo.
6th Division—Albergaria (near Fuente Guinaldo).
7th Division—Payo (in the Sierra de Gata).
Light Division—Fuente Guinaldo.
Bradford's Portuguese—Barba del Puerco.
Pack's Portuguese—Campillo and Ituero.

The marches were so arranged that the 7th Division passed through Castello Branco on Feb. 26, the 6th Division on Feb. 29, the Light Division on March 3, the 4th Division on March 5. All these were up to Portalegre, Villa Viçosa, or Castello de Vide, in touch with Elvas, by March 8. The 1st Division, coming by way of Abrantes, joined on March 10. Pack and Bradford, who had very circuitous routes, the one by Coimbra, the other by Thomar, were not up till several days later (16th). The 5th Division did not leave Rodrigo till March 9.

that all the army of Wellington had disappeared, as they were
bound to do if only Portuguese or Spanish cavalry showed at
the front [1]. Counting Hill's corps, now long returned to its old
post in front of Badajoz, there were now nearly 60,000 troops
nearing Elvas, viz. of infantry, all the eight old Anglo-Portuguese
divisions, plus Hamilton's Portuguese division [2], and Pack's and
Bradford's independent Portuguese brigades. Of cavalry not
only were all the old brigades assembled (save Alten's single
regiment), but two powerful units now showed at the front for
the first time. These were the newly-landed brigade of German
heavy dragoons under Bock [3], which had arrived at Lisbon on
January 1st, and Le Marchant's brigade of English heavy
dragoons [4], which had disembarked in the autumn, but had not
hitherto been brought up to join the field army. Of Portuguese horse J. Campbell's brigade was also at the front : the
other Portuguese cavalry brigade, which had served on the
Leon frontier during the preceding autumn, had been made
over to General Silveira, and sent north of the Douro. But
even after deducting this small brigade of 900 sabres, Wellington's mounted arm was immensely stronger than it had ever
been before. He had concentrated it on the Alemtejo front, in
order that he might cope on equal terms with the very powerful
cavalry of Soult's Army of Andalusia.

The Commander-in-Chief himself, travelling with his wonted
speed, left his old head-quarters at Freneda on March 5th, was
at Castello Branco on the 8th, at Portalegre on the 10th, and
had reached Elvas, his new head-quarters, on the 12th. Before
leaving the North he had made elaborate arrangements for the
conduct of affairs in that quarter. They are contained in two
memoranda, given the one to Castaños, who was still in command both of the Galician and the Estremaduran armies of
Spain, and the other to Generals Baccelar and Silveira, of whom
the former was in charge of the Portuguese department of the

---

[1] The other regiment of V. Alten's brigade (11th Light Dragoons) was on
March 12 at Ponte de Sor, on its way to the South.

[2] Which lay at Arronches and Santa Ollaya.

[3] 1st and 2nd Heavy Dragoons K.G.L.

[4] 3rd Dragoons, 4th and 5th Dragoon Guards. They had been lying
during the winter in the direction of Castello Branco.

North, with head-quarters at Oporto, and the other of the Tras-os-Montes, with head-quarters at Villa Real [1].

It was a delicate matter to leave Marmont with nothing save the Spaniards and Portuguese in his front. Of the former the available troops were (1) the Army of Galicia, four weak field divisions, making about 15,000 men, of whom only 550 were cavalry, while the artillery counted only five batteries. There were 8,000 garrison and reserve troops in Corunna, Vigo, Ferrol, and other fortified posts to the rear, but these were unavailable for service [2]. Abadia still commanded the whole army, under the nominal supervision of Castaños. He had one division (3,000 men under Cabrera) at Puebla Senabria on the Portuguese frontier, two (9,000 men under Losada and the Conde de Belveder) at Villafranca, observing the French garrison of Astorga and Souham's division on the Esla, which supported that advanced post, and one (2,500 men under Castañon) on the Asturian frontier watching Bonnet. (2) The second Spanish force available consisted of that section of the Army of Estremadura, which lay north of the Sierra de Gata, viz. Carlos de España's division of 5,000 men, of whom 3,000 had been thrown into Ciudad Rodrigo, so that the surplus for the field was small, and of Julian Sanchez's very efficient guerrillero cavalry, who were about 1,200 strong and were now counted as part of the regular army and formally styled ' 1st and 2nd Lancers of Castille.'

The Portuguese troops left to defend the northern frontier were all militia, with the exception of a couple of batteries of artillery and the cavalry brigade of regulars which had been with Wellington in Leon during the autumn, under Madden, but was now transferred to Silveira's charge, and set to watch the frontier of the Tras-os-Montes, with the front regiment at Braganza. Silveira in that province had the four local regiments of militia, of which each had only one of its two battalions actually embodied. Baccelar had a much more important force, but of the same quality, the twelve regiments

---

[1] Dated Feb. 24 and 27, *Dispatches*, viii. pp. 629 and 638.

[2] These figures are those of January, taken from the ' morning state ' in *Los Ejércitos españoles*, the invaluable book of 1822 published by the Spanish Staff.

forming the divisions of Trant and J. Wilson, and comprising all the militia of the Entre Douro e Minho province and of northern Beira. Three of these regiments were immobilized by having been told off to serve as the garrison of Almeida. Farther south Lecor had under arms the two militia regiments of the Castello Branco country, watching their own district. The total force of militia available on the whole frontier must have been about 20,000 men of very second-rate quality : each battalion had only been under arms intermittently, for periods of six months, and the officers were for the most part the inefficient leavings of the regular army. Of the generals Silveira was enterprising, but over bold, as the record of his earlier campaigns sufficiently demonstrated—Trant and Wilson had hitherto displayed equal energy and more prudence : but in the oncoming campaign they were convicted of Silveira's fault, over-confidence. Baccelar passed as a slow but fairly safe commander, rather lacking in self-confidence.

Wellington's very interesting memoranda divide the possibilities of March–April into three heads, of which the last contains three sub-sections :—

(1) Marmont may, on learning that Badajoz is in danger, march with practically the whole of his army to succour it, as he did in May–June 1811. If this should occur, Abadia and Carlos de España will advance and boldly take the offensive, laying siege to Astorga, Toro, Zamora, Salamanca, and other fortified posts. Silveira will co-operate with his cavalry and infantry, within the bounds of prudence, taking care that his cavalry, which may support Abadia, does not lose communication with, and a secure retreat upon, his infantry, which will not risk itself.

(2) Marmont may leave a considerable force, perhaps the two divisions of Souham and Bonnet, in Leon, while departing southward with the greater part of his army : ' this is the operation which it is probable that the enemy will follow.' What the Army of Galicia can then accomplish will depend on the exact relative force of itself and of the French left in front of it, and on the state of the fortified places on the Douro and Tormes [Toro, Zamora, Salamanca] and the degree of equipment with which General Abadia can provide himself for siege-

work. But España and Julian Sanchez must make all the play that they can, and even Porlier and Longa, from distant Cantabria, must be asked to co-operate in making mischief. Silveira and Baccelar will support, but risk nothing.

(3) Marmont may send to Estremadura only the smaller half of his army, and keep four or five divisions in the north, a force strong enough to enable him to take the offensive. He may attack either (*a*) Galicia, (*b*) Tras-os-Montes, or (*c*) the Beira, including Almeida and Ciudad Rodrigo.

(*a*) If Marmont should invade Galicia, Abadia had better retreat, but in the direction that will bring him near the frontiers of Portugal (i. e. by Puebla Senabria) rather than on Lugo and Corunna. In that case Silveira and Baccelar will be on the enemy's flank and rear, and will do as much mischief as they can on his communications, always taking care that they do not, by pushing too far into Leon, lose their communication with the Galicians or with Portugal. In proportion as the French may advance farther into Galicia, Baccelar will take measures to collect the whole of the militia of the Douro provinces northward. Carlos de España and Julian Sanchez ought to have good opportunities of making trouble for the enemy in the Salamanca district, if he pushes far from his base.

(*b*) If Marmont should invade Tras-os-Montes [not a likely operation, owing to the roughness of the country], Baccelar and Silveira should oppose him in front, while Abadia would come down on his flank and rear, and annoy him as much as possible. ' Don Carlos and the guerrillas might do a great deal of mischief in Castille.'

(*c*) If Marmont should attack Beira, advancing by Ciudad Rodrigo and Almeida, both these fortresses are in such a state of defence as to ensure them against capture by a *coup-de-main*, and are supplied with provisions to suffice during any time that the enemy could possibly remain in the country. Baccelar and Silveira will assemble all the militia of the northern provinces in Upper Beira, and place themselves in communication with Carlos de España. They will endeavour to protect the magazines on the Douro and Mondego [at Celorico, Guarda, Lamego, St. João de Pesqueira], and may live on the last in case of urgent necessity, but not otherwise, as these stores could not easily be replaced. An attempt should be made, if possible, to draw the enemy into the Beira Baixa (i. e. the Castello Branco country) rather than towards the Douro. Abadia will invade northern Leon ; what he can do depends on the force that Marmont leaves on the Esla, and the strength of his garrisons at Astorga, Zamora, Toro, &c. Supposing Marmont takes this direction, Carlos de España will destroy before him all the bridges on the Yeltes and Huebra, and that of Barba del Puerco, and the three bridges at Castillejo, all on the Lower Agueda.

It will be seen that the alternative (2) was Marmont's own choice, and that he would have carried it out but for Napoleon's orders, which definitively imposed upon him (3 c) the raid into northern Beira. With the inconclusive operations resulting from that movement we shall deal in their proper place. It began on March 27th, and the Marshal was over the Agueda on March 30th. The last British division had left Ciudad Rodrigo three weeks before Marmont advanced, so difficult was it for him to get full and correct information, and to collect a sufficiently large army for invasion. On the 26th February he was under the impression that two British divisions only had yet marched for Badajoz, though five had really started. On March 6th, when only the 5th Division remained in the North, he still believed that Wellington and a large fraction of his army were in their old positions. This was the result of his adversary's wisdom in stopping at Freneda till March 5th; as long as he was there in person, it was still thought probable by the French that only a detachment had marched southward. Hence came the lateness of Marmont's final advance : for a long time he might consider that he was, as his master ordered, ' containing ' several British divisions and the Commander-in-Chief himself.

Meanwhile, on taking stock of his situation at Elvas on March 12th, Wellington was reasonably satisfied. Not only was the greater part of his army in hand, and the rest rapidly coming up, but the siege material had escaped all the perils of storms by sea and rocky defiles by land, and was much where he had expected it to be. The material which moved by road, the sixteen 24-lb. howitzers which had marched on January 30th, and a convoy ·of 24-pounder and 18-pounder travelling-

carriages and stores, which went off on February 2, had both
come to hand at Elvas, the first on February 25th, the second
on March 3, and were ready parked on the glacis. This was
a wonderful journey over mountain roads in the most rainy
season of the year. The sea-borne guns had also enjoyed
a surprising immunity from winter storms ; Dickson, when
he arrived at Setubal on February 10th, found that the 24-
pounders from Oporto had arrived thirty-six hours before him,
and on the 14th was beginning to forward them by river-boat
to Alcacer do Sal, from where they were drawn by oxen to
Elvas, along with their ammunition [1]. The only difficulty
which arose was that Wellington had asked Admiral Berkeley,
commanding the squadron at Lisbon, to lend him, as a supplementary train, twenty 18-pound ship guns. The admiral sent
twenty Russian guns (leavings of Siniavins's squadron captured
in the Tagus at the time of the Convention of Cintra). Dickson
protested, as these pieces were of a different calibre from the
British 18-pounder, and would not take its shot. The admiral
refused to disgarnish his own flagship, which happened to be
the only vessel at Lisbon with home-made 18-pounders on
board. Dickson had to take the Russian guns perforce, and to
cull for their ammunition all the Portuguese stores at Lisbon,
where a certain supply of round shot that fitted was discovered,
though many thousands had to be rejected as ' far too low.'
On March 8th the whole fifty-two guns of the siege-train were
reported ready, and the officer commanding the Portuguese
artillery at Elvas announced that he could even find a small
supplement, six old heavy English iron guns of the time of
George II, which had been in store there since General Burgoyne's expedition of 1761, besides some Portuguese guns of
similar calibre. The old brass guns which had made such bad
practice in 1811 were not this time requisitioned—fortunately
they were not needed. The garrison of Elvas had for some
weeks been at work making gabions and fascines, which were all
ready, as was also a large consignment of cutting-tools from the
Lisbon arsenal, and a train of twenty-two pontoons. Altogether
the material was in a wonderful state of completeness.

[1] For details see Jones, *Sieges of the Peninsula*, Appendix in vol. i.
pp. 421–5, and the *Dickson Papers*, ed. Leslie, for Feb. 1812.

For the service of the siege Wellington could dispose of about 300 British and 560 Portuguese artillerymen, a much larger force than had been available at the two unlucky leaguers of 1811. Colonel Framingham was the senior officer in this arm present, but Wellington had directed that Alexander Dickson should take charge of the whole service of the siege, just as he had been entrusted with all the preparations for it. There were fifteen British, five German Legion, and seventeen Portuguese artillery officers under his command. The Portuguese gunners mostly came from the 3rd or Elvas regiment, the British were drawn from the companies of Holcumbe, Gardiner, Glubb, and Rettberg.[1] Under Colonel Fletcher, senior engineer officer, there were 115 men of the Royal Military Artificers present at the commencement of the siege, and an additional party came up from Cadiz during its last days. But though this was an improvement over the state of things in 1811, the numbers were still far too small ; there were no trained miners whatever, and the volunteers from the line acting as sappers, who were instructed by the Artificers, were for the most part unskilful— only 120 men of the 3rd Division who had been at work during the leaguer of Ciudad Rodrigo were comparatively efficient. The engineer arm was the weak point in the siege, as Wellington complained in a letter which will have to be dealt with in its proper place. He had already been urging on Lord Liverpool the absolute necessity for the creation of permanent units of men trained in the technicalities of siege-work. Soon after Rodrigo fell he wrote, ' I would beg to suggest to your lordship the expediency of adding to the Engineer establishment a corps of sappers and miners. It is inconceivable with what disadvantage we undertake a siege, for want of assistance of this description. There is no French *corps d'armée* which has not a battalion of sappers and a company of miners. We are obliged to depend for assistance of this sort upon the regiments of the line ; and, although the men are brave and willing, they want the knowledge and training which are necessary. Many casualties occur, and much valuable time is lost at the most critical period of the siege [2].'

---

[1] For details see Duncan's *History of the Royal Artillery*, ii. pp. 318–19.
[2] Wellington, *Dispatches*, viii. p. 601.

The situation on March 12th, save in this single respect, seemed favourable. It was only fourteen miles from Elvas, where thè siege-train lay parked and the material was ready, to Badajoz. Sufficient troops were already arrived not only to invest the place, but to form a large covering army against any attempt of Soult to raise the siege. There was every reason to believe that the advance would take the French unawares. Only Drouet's two divisions were in Estremadura, and before they could be reinforced up to a strength which would enable them to act with effect some weeks must elapse. Soult, as in 1811, would have to borrow troops from Granada and the Cadiz Lines before he could venture to take the offensive. Unless he should raise the siege of Cadiz or evacuate Granada, he could not gather more than 25,000 or 30,000 men at the very most : and it would take him three weeks to collect so many. If he approached with some such force, he could be fought, with very little risk : for it was not now as at the time of Albuera : not three Anglo-Portuguese infantry divisions, but eight were concentrated at Elvas : there would be nine when the 5th Division arrived. Not three British cavalry regiments (the weak point at Albuera), but fourteen were with the army. If Soult should push forward for a battle, 40,000 men could be opposed to him, all Anglo-Portuguese units of old formation, while 15,000 men were left to invest Badajoz. Or if Wellington should choose to abandon the investment for three days (as Beresford had done in May 1811) he could bring 55,000 men to the contest, a force which must crush Soult by the force of double numbers, unless he should raise the siege of Cadiz and abandon Granada, so as to bring his whole army to the Guadiana. Even if he took that desperate, but perhaps necessary, measure, and came with 45,000 men, leaving only Seville garrisoned behind him, there was no reason to suppose that he could not be dealt with.

The only dangerous possibility was the intervention of Marmont with five or six divisions of the Army of Portugal, as had happened at the time of the operations on the Caya in June 1811. Wellington, as we have seen in his directions to Baccelar and Castaños, thought this intervention probable. But from the disposition of Marmont's troops at the moment of his own

departure from Freneda, he thought that he could count on
three weeks, or a little more, of freedom from any interference
from this side. Two at least of Marmont's divisions (Souham
and Bonnet) would almost certainly be left in the North, to
contain the Galicians and Asturians. Of the other six only one
(Foy) was in the valley of the Tagus : the rest were scattered
about, at Salamanca, Avila, Valladolid, &c., and would take
time to collect [1]. Wellington was quite aware of Marmont's
difficulties with regard to magazines ; he also counted on the
roughness of the roads, the fact that the rivers were high in
March, and (most of all) on the slowness with which information
would reach the French marshal [2]. Still, here lay the risk, so
far as Wellington could know. What he could not guess was
that the movement which he feared had been expressly forbidden to Marmont by his master, and that only on March 27th
was permission granted to the Marshal to execute the march to
Almaraz. By that time, as we have already seen, it was too
late for him to profit by the tardily-granted leave.

But it was the possibility of Marmont's appearance on the
scene, rather than anything which might be feared from Soult,
which made the siege of Badajoz a time-problem, just as that
of Ciudad Rodrigo had been. The place must, if possible, be
taken somewhere about the first week in April, the earliest date
at which a serious attempt at relief was likely to be made [3].

On March 14th, every preparation being complete, the pontoon train, with a good escort, moved out of Elvas, and was
brought up to a point on the Guadiana four miles west of

[1] For Wellington's speculations (fairly correct) as to Marmont's distribution of his troops, see *Dispatches*, viii. p. 618, Feb. 19, to Graham.

[2] Wellington to Victor Alten, March 5, *Dispatches*, viii. p. 649, makes
a special point of ' the difficulties which the enemy experiences in getting
intelligence ' as a means of gaining time for himself.

[3] Napier (iv. p. 98) tries to make out that Wellington's siege began ten days
later than he wished and hoped, by the fault of the Portuguese Regency.
I cannot see how Badajoz could have been invested on the 6th of March,
when (as the route-directions show) the head of the marching column from
the Agueda only reached Portalegre on the 8th. The movement of the
army was not delayed, so far as I can see, by the slackness of Portuguese
management at Lisbon or Elvas. But Wellington certainly grumbled.
Did he intend that Hill alone should invest Badajoz, before the rest of
the army arrived ?

Badajoz, where it was laid without molestation. On the next day Le Marchant's heavy dragoons crossed, but (owing to an accident to one of the boats) no more troops. On the 16th, however, the 3rd, 4th, and Light Divisions passed, and invested Badajoz without meeting any opposition : the garrison kept within the walls, and did not even prevent Colonel Fletcher, the commanding engineer, from approaching for purposes of reconnaissance to the crest of the Cerro de San Miguel, only 200 yards from the *enceinte*. The investing corps of 12,000 bayonets was under Beresford, who had just returned from a short and stormy visit to Lisbon, where he had been harrying the regency, at Wellington's request, upon financial matters, and had been dealing sternly with the Junta de Viveres, or Commissariat Department [1]. The situation had not been found a happy one. ' After a perfect investigation it appears that the expenditure must be nearly £6,000,000—the means at present are £3,500,000 ! A radical reform grounded upon a bold and fearless inquiry into every branch of the revenue, expenditure, and subsidy, and an addition to the latter from England, can alone put a period to these evils. To this Lord Wellington, though late, is now turning his eyes. And when the Marshal, in conjunction with our ambassador, shall have made his report, it must be *immediately* acted upon—for there is no time to lose [2].'

The investment was only part of the general movements of the army on the 16th. The covering-force was proceeding to take up its position in two sections. Graham with the 1st, 6th, and 7th Divisions, and Slade's and Le Marchant's horse, crossed the Guadiana, and began to advance down the high road to Seville, making for Santa Marta and Villafranca. Hill with the other section, consisting of his own old troops of the Estremaduran army, the 2nd Division and Hamilton's Portuguese, Long's British and Campbell's Portuguese cavalry, marched by the north bank of the Guadiana, via Montijo, towards

---

[1] D'Urban's diary, Feb. 7–16 : he accompanied Beresford, being his Chief-of-the-Staff.

[2] I spare the reader the question of Portuguese paper money and English exchequer bills, which will be found treated at great length in Napier, iv. pp. 97–9. Napier always appears to think that cash could be had by asking for it at London, in despite of the dreadful disappearance of the metallic currency and spread of irredeemable bank-notes which prevailed in 1812.

Merida, which had not been occupied by either party since January 17th. These two columns, the one 19,000, the other 14,000 strong, were to drive in the two French divisions which were at this moment cantoned in Estremadura—Drouet was known to be lying about Zafra and Llerena, covering the Seville *chaussée*, Daricau to have his troops at Zalamea and Los Hornachos, watching the great passage of the Guadiana at Merida. As each division with its attendant cavalry was not much over 6,000 strong, there was no danger of their combining so as to endanger either of the British columns. Each was strong enough to give a good account of itself. Hill and Graham were to push forward boldly, and drive their respective enemies before them as far as the Sierra Morena, so that Soult, when he should come up from Seville (as he undoubtedly would in the course of a few weeks), should have no foothold in the Estremaduran plain to start from, and would have to manœuvre back the containing force in his front all the way from the summit of the passes to Albuera.

In addition to these two columns and the investing corps at Badajoz, Wellington had a reserve of which some units had not yet come up, though all were due in a few days, viz. the 5th Division, Pack's and Bradford's independent Portuguese brigades, and the cavalry of Bock and Anson—about 12,000 men—: the last of them would be up by the 21st at latest.

There was still one more corps from which Wellington intended to get useful assistance. This was the main body of the Spanish Army of Estremadura, the troops of Penne Villemur and Morillo, about 1,000 horse and 4,000 foot [1], which he destined to play the same part in this campaign that Blake had played during the last siege of Badajoz. By Castaños's leave this little force had been moved from its usual haunts by Caçeres and Valencia de Alcantara, behind the Portuguese frontier, to the Lower Guadiana, from whence it was to enter the Condado de Niebla. It passed Redondo on March 17th on its way towards San Lucar de Guadiana, feeding on magazines provided by its allies ; Penne Villemur's orders were that he

---

[1] The Conde had 1,114 horse and 3,638 foot on Jan. 1, not including two of Morillo's battalions then absent. The total force used for the raid was probably as above.

should establish himself in the Condado (where there was still a small Spanish garrison at Ayamonte), and strike at Seville, the moment that he heard that Soult had gone north towards Estremadura. The city would be found ill-garrisoned by convalescents, and *Juramentados* of doubtful loyalty : if it were not captured, its danger would at any rate cause Soult to turn back, just as he had in June 1811, for he dared not lose his base and arsenal. It was hoped that Ballasteros with his roving corps from the mountain of Ronda would co-operate, when he found that the troops usually employed to ' contain ' him had marched off. But Ballasteros was always a ' law unto himself,' and it was impossible to count upon him : he particularly disliked suggestions from a British quarter, while Castaños was always sensible and obliging [1].

Before dealing with the operations of the actual siege of Badajoz, which require to be studied in continuous sequence, it may be well to deal with those of the covering corps.

Graham marched in two columns, one division by Albuera, two by Almendral. He ran against the outposts of Drouet at Santa Marta, from which a battalion and a few cavalry hastily retired to Villafranca, where it was reported that Drouet himself was lying. Graham judged that the French general would probably retire towards Llerena by the main road, and hoped to harass, if not to surprise him, by a forced night march on that place. This was executed in the night of the 18th–19th, but proved a disappointment : the vanguard of the British column entered Llerena only to find it empty—Drouet had retired not southward but eastward, so as to get into touch with Daricau's division at Zalamea—he had gone off by Ribera to Los Horna-chos. Graham thereupon halted his main body at Zafra, with the cavalry out as far as Usagre and Fuente Cantos. A dispatch from Drouet to his brigadier Reymond was intercepted on the 21st, and showed that the latter, with four battalions at Fregenal, had been cut off from his chief by the irruption of the British down the high-road, and was ordered to rejoin him by way of Llerena. Graham thought that he might catch this little force, so withdrew his cavalry from Llerena, in order that Reymond

---

[1] Details in a dispatch to Colonel Austin of March 15, *Dispatches*, viii. p. 666. General scheme in a letter to Castaños of Feb. 16. Ibid., p. 614.

might make his way thither unmolested, and be caught in a trap by several British brigades converging upon him by a night march. This operation, executed on the night of the 25th, unfortunately miscarried. The French actually entered Llerena, but as the columns were closing in upon them an unlucky accident occurred. Graham and his staff, riding ahead of the 7th Division, ran into a cavalry picket, which charged them. They came back helter-skelter on to the leading battalion of the infantry, which fired promiscuously into the mass, killed two staff officers, and nearly shot their general [1]. The noise of this outburst of fire, and the return of their own dragoons, warned the 1,800 French in Llerena, who escaped by a mountain path towards Guadalcanal, and did not lose a man.

Improbable as it would have been judged, Drouet had abandoned the Seville road altogether, and gone off eastward. His only communication with Soult would have to be by Cordova: clearly he had refused to be cut off from Daricau: possibly he may have hoped to await in the direction of Zalamea and Castuera the arrival of troops from the Army of Portugal, coming down by Truxillo and Medellin from Almaraz. For Soult and his generals appear to have had no notice of the Emperor's prohibition to Marmont to send troops to Estremadura. On the other hand the Duke of Ragusa had written, in perfect good faith, before he received the imperial rescript, that he should come to the aid of Badajoz with four or five divisions, as in June 1811, if the place were threatened.

On the 27th Graham resolved to pursue Drouet eastward, even hoping that he might slip in to the south of him, and drive him northward in the direction of Merida and Medellin, where he would have fallen into the arms of Hill's column. He had reached Llera and La Higuera when he intercepted another letter—this time from General Reymond to Drouet; that officer, after escaping from Llerena on the night of the 25th–26th, had marched to Azuaga, where he had picked up another

---

[1] ' Something too like a panic was occasioned at the head of the 7th by the appearance of the few French dragoons and the galloping back of the staff and orderlies. A confused firing broke out down the column without object ! Mem.—Even British troops should not be allowed to load before a night attack.' D'Urban's diary, March 26.

detachment under General Quiot. He announced that he was making the best of his way towards Fuente Ovejuna, behind the main crest of the Sierra Morena, by which circuitous route he hoped to join his chief.

Graham thought that he had now another opportunity of surprising Reymond, while he was marching across his front, and swerving southward again made a second forced night march on Azuaga. It failed, like that on Llerena three days before—the French, warned by *Afrancesados*, left in haste, and Graham's exhausted troops only arrived in time to see them disappear.

Reymond's column was joined next day at Fuente Ovejuna by Drouet and Daricau, so that the whole of the French force in Estremadura was now concentrated—but in an unfavourable position, since they were completely cut off from Seville, and could only retire on Cordova if further pressed. Should Soult wish to join them with his reserves, he would have to march up the Guadalquivir, losing four or five days.

Graham and his staff were flattering themselves that they had won a considerable strategical advantage in this matter, when they were disappointed, by receiving, on March 30, a dispatch from Wellington prohibiting any further pursuit of Drouet, or any longer stay on the slopes of the Sierra Morena. The column was ordered to come back and canton itself about Fuente del Maestre, Almendralejo, and Villafranca. By April 2nd the three divisions were established in these places. Their recall would seem to have been caused by Wellington's knowledge that Soult had by now concentrated a heavy force at Seville, and that if he advanced suddenly by the great *chaussée*, past Monasterio and Fuente Cantos, Graham might be caught in a very advanced position between him and Drouet, and find a difficulty in retreating to join the main body of the army for a defensive battle on the Albuera position [1].

Meanwhile Hill, with the other half of the covering army, had been spending a less eventful fortnight. He reached Merida

---

[1] For details of this forgotten campaign I rely mainly on D'Urban's unpublished diary. As he knew Estremadura well, from having served there with Beresford in 1811, he was lent to Graham, and rode with his staff to advise about roads and the resources of the country.

on March 17 and found it unoccupied. Drouet was reported to be at Villafranca, Daricau to be lying with his troops spread wide between Medellin, Los Hornachos, and Zalamea. Hill crossed the Guadiana and marched to look for them : his first march was on Villafranca, but Drouet had already slipped away from that point, avoiding Graham's column. Hill then turned in search of Daricau, and drove one of his brigades out of Don Benito near Medellin. The bulk of the French division then went off to the south-east, and ultimately joined Drouet at Fuente Ovejuna, though it kept a rearguard at Castuera. Hill did not pursue, but remained in the neighbourhood of Merida and Medellin, to guard these two great passages of the Guadiana against any possible appearance of Marmont's troops from the direction of Almaraz and Truxillo. Wellington (it will be remembered) had believed that Marmont would certainly come down with a considerable force by this route, and (being ignorant of Napoleon's order to the Marshal) was expecting him to be heard of from day to day. As a matter of fact only Foy's single division was in the Tagus valley at Talavera : that officer kept receiving dispatches for his chief from Drouet and Soult, imploring that Marmont should move south without delay. This was impossible, as Foy knew ; but he became so troubled by the repeated requests that he thought of marching, on his own responsibility, to try to join Drouet. This became almost impracticable when Drouet and Daricau withdrew southward to the borders of Andalusia : but Foy then thought of executing a demonstration on Truxillo, on his own account, hoping that it might at least distract Wellington. On April 4 he wrote to Drouet that he was about to give out that he was Marmont's advanced guard, and to march, with 3,000 men only, on that point, leaving the rest of his division in garrison at Talavera and Almaraz ; he would be at Truxillo on the 9th [1]. If he had started a week earlier, he would have fallen into the hands of Hill, who was waiting for him at Merida with four times his force. But the news of the fall of Badajoz on the 6th reached him in time to prevent him from running into the lion's mouth. Otherwise, considering Hill's enterprise and

[1] The letter may be found in King Joseph's *Correspondance*, viii. pp. 345–6. See also Girod de l'Ain's *Vie militaire du Général Foy*, pp. 368–9.

Foy's complete lack of cavalry, there might probably have been something like a repetition of the surprise of Arroyo dos Molinos.

So much for the covering armies—it now remains to be seen how Wellington dealt with Badajoz, in the three weeks during which Graham and Hill were keeping the peace for him in southern and eastern Estremadura.

On surveying the fortress upon March 16th the British engineers found that it had been considerably strengthened since the last siege in June 1811. Fort San Cristobal had been vastly improved—its glacis and counterscarp had been raised, and a strong redoubt (called by the French the Lunette Werlé, after the general killed at Albuera) had been thrown up on the rising slope where Beresford's breaching batteries had stood, so that this ground would have to be won before it could be again utilized. On the southern side of the Guadiana the Castle had been provided with many more guns, and some parts of the precipitous mound on which it stood had been scarped. The breach of 1811 had been most solidly built up. No danger was feared in this quarter—it was regarded as the strongest part of the defences. The approach toward the much more accessible bastions just below the Castle had been made difficult, by damming the Rivillas stream : its bridge near the San Roque gate had been built up, and the accumulated water made a broad pool which lay under the bastions of San Pedro and La Trinidad ; its overflow had been turned into the ditch in front of San Pedro, and, by cutting a *cunette* or channel, a deep but narrow water obstruction had been formed in front of the Trinidad also—the broad dry ditch having a narrow wet ditch sunk in its bottom just below the counterscarp. This inundation was destined to give great trouble to the besiegers. The Pardaleras fort had been connected with the city by a well-protected trench between high earthen banks. Finally the three bastions on the south side next the river, San Vincente, San José, and Santiago, had been strengthened by demi-lunes, which they had hitherto lacked, and also by driving a system of mines from their counterscarps under the glacis : these were to be exploded if the besiegers should push up their trenches and breaching batteries close to the walls on this side, which was one of the weakest in the city, since it was not covered, as were the other fronts, by outlying works like the **Pardaleras** and **Picurina** forts or the San Roque lunette. The existence of this series of mines was revealed to the besiegers by a French sergeant-major of sappers, a skilful draughtsman, who had been employed in mapping out the works. Having been insulted, as he conceived, by his captain, and refused redress by the governor, he fled to the British camp in a rage, and placed his map (where the mines are very clearly shown) and his services at the disposition of Wellington [1]. The identical map, a very neat piece of work, lies before me as I write these lines, having passed into the possession of General D'Urban, the chief of the Portuguese staff. It was in consequence of their knowledge of these defences that the British engineers left the San Vincente front alone [2].

The garrison on March 15th consisted of five battalions of French regulars, one each from certain regiments belonging to Conroux, Leval, Drouet, and Daricau (2,767 men), of two battalions of the Hesse-Darmstadt regiment of the Rheinbund division of the Army of the Centre (910 men), three companies of artillery (261 men), two and a half companies of sappers (260 men), a handful of cavalry (42 men), a company of Spanish Juramentados, and (by casual chance) the escort of a convoy which had entered the city two days before the siege began. The whole (excluding non-combatants, medical and commissariat staff, &c.) made up 4,700 men, not more than an adequate provision for such a large place. The governor, Phillipon, the commandants of artillery and engineers (the last-named, Lamare, was the historian of the three sieges of Badajoz), and nearly all the staff had been in the fortress for more than a year. The battalions of the garrison (though not

---

[1] This man is mentioned in Wellington's *Dispatches*, viii. p. 609 : ' The *Sergent-major des Sapeurs* and *Adjudant des travaux* and the French miner may be sent in charge of a steady non-commissioned officer to Estremoz, there to wait till I send for them.'

[2] This renegade's name must have been Bonin, or Bossin : I cannot read with certainty his extraordinary signature, with a *paraphe*, at the bottom of his map. The English engineers used it, and have roughly sketched in their own works of the third siege on top of the original coloured drawing.

the same as those who had sustained the assaults of 1811) had been many months settled in the place, and knew it almost as well as did the staff. They were all picked troops, including the German regiment, which had an excellent record. But undoubtedly the greatest factor in the defence was the ingenuity and resource of the governor, which surpassed all praise : oddly enough Phillipon did not show himself a very skilful mover of troops in the field, when commanding a division in the Army of Germany in 1813, after his capture and exchange : but behind the walls of Badajoz he was unsurpassable [1].

The scheme of attack which Wellington, under the advice of his engineers, employed against Badajoz in March 1812 differed entirely from that of May–June 1811. The fact that the whole was a time-problem remained the same : the danger that several of the French armies might, if leisure were granted them, unite for its relief, was as clear as ever. But the idea that the best method of procedure was to assail the most commanding points of the fortress, whose capture would make the rest untenable, was completely abandoned. Fort San Cristobal and the lofty Castle were on this occasion to be left alone altogether. The former was only observed by a single Portuguese brigade (first Da Costa's and later Power's). The second was not breached, or even battered with any serious intent. This time the front of attack was to be the bastions of Santa Maria and La Trinidad, on the south-eastern side of the town. The reason for leaving those of San Vincente and San José, on the south-western side, unassailed—though they were more accessible, and defended by no outer forts—was apparently the report of the renegade French sergeant-major spoken of above ; ' they were countermined, and therefore three or four successive lodgements would have to be formed against them [2].' To attack Santa Maria and the Trinidad a preliminary operation was necessary—they were covered by the Picurina fort, and only from the knoll on which that work stands could they be battered with effect. The Picurina was far weaker

---

[1] When he commanded the 1st Division of the 1st Corps under Vandamme, and was present when that corps was nearly all destroyed on Aug. 30, 1813, at Culm.

[2] Jones, *Sieges of the Peninsula*, i. p. 163.

than the Pardaleras fort, from whose site a similar advantage could be got against the bastions of San Roque and San Juan. It must therefore be stormed, and on its emplacement would be fixed the batteries of the second parallel, which were to do the main work of breaching. The exceptional advantage to be secured in this way was that the counterguard (inner protective bank) within the *glacis* of the Trinidad bastion was reputed to be so low, that from the Picurina knoll the scarp of the bastion could be seen almost to its foot, and could be much more effectively battered than any part of the defences whose upper section alone was visible to the besieger.

Despite, therefore, of the need for wasting no time, and of the fact that the preliminary operations against the Picurina must cost a day or two, this was the general plan of attack adopted. The investment had been completed on the evening of the 16th : on the same day 120 carts with stores of all kinds marched from Elvas, and on the 17th these were already being deposited in the Engineers' Park, behind the Cerro de San Miguel, whose rounded top completely screened the preparations from the sight of the garrison.

The besieged had no notion whatever as to the front which would, on this third attempt, be selected for the attack of the British. The elaborate fortifications and improvements made in the Castle and San Cristobal tend to show that these old points of attack were expected to be once more assailed. Hence the besiegers got the inestimable advantage of an unmolested start on the night of March 17th. Colonel Fletcher had risked the dangers of drawing the first parallel at a very short distance from the Picurina fort. On a night of tempestuous rain and high wind, a parallel 600 yards long was picketed out, on a line ranging only from 160 to 200 yards from the covered-way of the work, and 1,800 workmen in the course of the night threw up the parallel, and 4,000 feet of a communication-trench, leading backward to the head of a ravine in the hill of San Miguel, which gave good cover for bringing men and material up from the rear. Not a shot was fired by the French all through the night, and at dawn the parallel and approach were already 3 feet deep and 3 feet 6 inches wide—a good start.

With daylight the enemy discovered what had been done,

and opened a furious fire both of cannon and musketry upon
the trenches. The three nearest bastions of the fortress joined
in with their heavy guns, but the 18th was a day of such
constant rain that even at a distance of only 500 or 600 yards
it was impossible to see much, or take accurate aim at the
trenches. The working parties went on deepening and im-
proving the parallel and the communication behind it, without
suffering any great loss.

During the night of the 18th–19th they were able to trace
out and begin two batteries, destined to breach the Picurina,
in the line of the parallel, and to extend it at both ends, from
the Rivillas on one side to the foot of the hill of San Miguel
on the other.

This was visible on the following morning, and Phillipon
thought the prospects of the fort so bad that he resolved to
risk a sortie, to destroy at all costs the trenches which were so
dangerously near to their objective. At midday two battalions
—1,000 men—starting from the lunette of San Roque, dashed
up the hill, got into the north end of the parallel, and drove out
the working parties for a distance of some 500 yards: they carried
off many entrenching tools, for which the governor had offered
the *bonus* of one dollar a piece. But they had no time to do
any serious damage to the parallel, for the guard of the trenches
and the working parties, rallying fifty yards up the hill, came
down on them in force, within a quarter of an hour, and evicted
them again after a sharp tussle. The loss on the two sides was
very different—the British lost 150 men, the besieged 304, of
whom many were drowned in the inundation, while trying to
take short cuts through it to the gates. The effect of the sortie
had been practically *nil*, as far as destroying the works went.
During this skirmish Colonel Fletcher was wounded in the
groin by a ball, which hit his purse, and while failing to penetrate
further, forced a dollar-piece an inch into his thigh. He was
confined to his tent for some fourteen days, and his subordinates,
Majors Squire and Burgoyne, had to take up his duty, though
Wellington ordered that he should still retain nominal charge
of the work, and consulted him daily upon it.

On the next night (March 20th) the parallel and approach
against the Picurina being practically complete, and only the

battery emplacements in it requiring to be finished, the engineers
of the besieging army resolved to continue the line of trenches
into the flat ground in front of the Bastion of San Pedro and
the Castle, it being intended that batteries should be constructed
here to play on the Trinidad and the neighbouring parts of the
fortress, when the Picurina should have fallen. It would save
time to have everything ready on this side, when the fort should
have been mastered. Trouble at once began—not only from
the enemy's fire, which swept all this low ground, but
still more from the continuous bad weather. The rain which
had easily run away from the sloping trenches on the Cerro de
San Miguel, lodged in the new works, could not be drained off,
and melted away the earth as fast as it was thrown up. Mud
cast into the gabions ran off in the form of slimy water, and
the parapets could only be kept upright by building them of
sandbags. The men were actually flooded out of the trenches
by the accumulated water, which was almost knee deep. In
the rear the Guadiana rose, and washed away the two bridges
which connected the army with its base at Elvas. The deluge
lasted four days and was a terrible hindrance, it being impossible
to finish the parallel in the low ground, or to begin moving the
battering-guns, even those destined for the long-completed
batteries on the Cerro de San Miguel.

It was not till the afternoon of the 24th that fine weather at
last set in ; this permitted the guns to be brought at once into
the two batteries facing the Picurina, and, after herculean
efforts, into other batteries (nos. 4 and 5) in the low ground
also. Three days at least had been lost from the vile weather.

On the morning of the 25th all the batteries opened simultaneously, ten guns against the Picurina, eighteen against the
parts of the fortress behind it. The fort was completely
silenced, as was the little lunette of San Roque. Not much
damage appeared to have been inflicted on the Picurina beyond
the breaking of many of its palisades, and the degradation of
its salient angle. But Wellington ordered that it should be
stormed that night, in order that he might make up for the lost
time of the 20th–24th.

The storm was duly carried out by General Kempt and 500
men of the Light and the 3rd Divisions, at ten o'clock that

night. It was a desperate affair, for the ditch was deep, and not
in the least filled with rubbish, and the scarp was intact save
at the extreme salient angle. Though the garrison's guns had
been silenced, they kept up a furious fire of musketry, which
disabled 100 men before the stormers reached the ditch. The
main hope of the assault had been that two turning columns
might break in at the gorge : but it was found so strongly closed,
with a double row of palisades and a cutting, that all efforts to
force an entrance were repelled with loss. Baffled here, one
party tried the desperate expedient of casting three long
ladders, not into, but *across* the ditch on the right flank of the
fort, which though deep was not so broad but that a 30-foot
ladder would reach from its lip to the row of fraises, or projecting beams, ranged horizontally at the top of the scarp some
feet below the brim of the parapet. The ladders sagged down
but did not break, and some fifty men headed by Captain Oates
of the 88th ran across on the rungs and got a lodgement inside
the fort. At the same moment General Kempt launched the
reserve of the storming party—100 men, mostly from the
2/83rd and headed by Captain Powys of that regiment—at the
exact salient of the fort, the only place where it was seriously
damaged, and succeeded in breaking in. The garrison, who
made a stubborn resistance, were overpowered—83 were killed
or wounded, the governor, Colonel Gaspard-Thierry, and
145 taken prisoners, only 1 officer and 40 men escaped into the
town. The losses of the stormers had been over 50 per cent.
of the men engaged ! Four officers and 50 rank and file were
killed, 15 officers and 250 men wounded, out of a little over 500
who joined in the assault. Phillipon tried a sortie from the
lunette of San Roque, just as the fort fell, in hopes to recover it :
but the battalion which came out was easily beaten off by the
fire of the men in the trenches to the right, and lost 50 killed
and wounded.

The last stage of the siege had now been reached. By
capturing the Picurina on its commanding knoll, the British had
established themselves within 400 yards of the Trinidad and
450 yards of the Santa Maria bastions, which they could batter
with every advantage of slope and ground. But it was a very
costly business to make the necessary lodgement in the ruined

fort, to demolish it, and throw its earth in the reverse direction, and to build in its gorge the two batteries (nos. 8, 9), which were to breach the body of the place. The fire of three bastions bore directly on the spot where the batteries were to be placed, and there was also a most deadly enfilading fire from the high-lying Castle, and even from the distant San Cristobal. Though the three batteries in the flat ground (to which a fourth was presently added) endeavoured to silence this fire, they only succeeded in doing so very imperfectly, for the French kept replacing one gun by another, from their ample store, when any were disabled. From the 26th to the 30th four days were employed in building the Picurina batteries, with great loss of life all the time, which fell mainly on the engineer officers who were directing the work and on the sappers under their orders. The French covered the whole of the Picurina knoll with such a hail of projectiles that no amount of cover seemed to guarantee those labouring in it from sudden death. When the batteries had been completed, the bringing forward of the guns and the ammunition cost many lives more. Twice there were considerable explosions of powder, while the magazines in the batteries were being filled.

At last, however, on March 30, one of the two new batteries in the gorge of the Picurina was able to open, and on the 31st the other followed suit, supported by a third supplementary battery (no. 7), planned under the left flank of the fort. The practice was excellent, but at first the effect was not all that had been hoped : the Trinidad and the Santa Maria bastions were solidly built and resisted well. On April 2, however, both began to show considerable and obvious injury, and it was clear that a few days more would ruin them. But there was one serious *contretemps* : the inundation between the Picurina and the fortress showed no signs of going down—it had been swollen by the rains of the 20th–24th, and could not flow away so long as the dam at the lunette of San Roque kept it back. While the water was held up, the breaches, soon about to develop, could only be got at by a narrow and curved route, between the inundation and the steep slope on which stands the Pardaleras. It had been intended that the assault should be delivered from the trenches, but this was impossible till the

Rivillas should have fallen to its usual insignificant breadth and depth. Hence efforts were made to burst the dam at all costs, but neither did artillery fire suffice, nor a venturesome expedition on the night of the 2nd of April by the engineer Lieutenant Stanway and 20 sappers, who slipped down the ravine and laid powder-bags against the dam, despite of the French fire. The powder exploded, but did not do its work. For several days an attempt was made to sap down to the dam from the second parallel. But it cost so many lives at the head of the sap, and the zig-zags advanced so slowly, that on the 3rd of April the attempt was given up, and it was determined that the breaches must be assaulted from the west bank of the Rivillas only.

Meanwhile the two breaches, the larger one in the front of the Trinidad bastion, the smaller in the flank of the Santa Maria, began to be very apparent, and gave good hope to the besiegers. The French, however, delayed their progress by the most gallant efforts : 200 men worked in the ditch after dark, to clear away the débris that was falling into it. This they did under constant artillery fire from the batteries, which played on the ditch with grape at intervals in the night, and killed scores of the workmen. They also deepened the ditch at the foot of the counterscarp, till it was 18 feet from the covered-way to the bottom of its level. The ruined parapets were built up every night with earth and wool-packs, only to be destroyed again every morning. The garrison began to feel uncomfortable, for not only was the loss of life great, but the furious fire, by which they strove to keep down the efficiency of the siege-batteries, had begun to tell so much on their reserves of ammunition that, by April 3, there was no common shell left, and very little grape—of the round-shot much more than half had been expended. Phillipon was obliged to order the artillerymen to be sparing, or a few days more would leave him helpless. As the French fire slackened, that of the besiegers grew more intense, and Wellington put forward the last twelve guns of his siege-park, hitherto reserved, to form some new supplementary batteries on the right of his line [nos. 10, 11, 12].

On April 4th the breaches were both growing practicable, and

news from the South warned Wellington that he must hurry ;
Soult was at last over the Sierra Morena with all the troops
that he could scrape together from Andalusia.   It was lucky
indeed that Marmont was not marching to join Soult, but
was executing a raid into central Portugal, not by his own
wish but by the special orders of the Emperor, as has already
been explained elsewhere.   His irruption into the Beira was
absolutely disregarded by Wellington : for as long as the two
French armies were not united, the British commander did
not much fear either of them.   Still, if Soult came close up to
Badajoz, it would be necessary to send part of the siege-troops
to join the covering force—and this would be inconvenient.
Wherefore Wellington resolved to strike at once, while Soult
was still four or five marches away.

On the 4th the breaches, both in the Trinidad and in Santa
Maria, looked practicable—on the morning of the 5th they were
certainly so.   But the question was raised as to whether the
mere practicability of the breaches was enough to ensure success
—it was clearly made out that the garrisons were building
a semicircular inner retrenchment among the houses of the
town, which would cut off the breaches, and give a second line
of resistance.   Moreover Colonel Fletcher, who was just out of
bed, his wound of the 19th March being on the mend, reported
from personal observation that it was clear that all manner of
obstacles were being accumulated behind both breaches, and
every preparation made for a desperate defence of them.
Wherefore Wellington ordered the storm to be put off for a day,
and turned two batteries on to a new spot, where Spanish
informants reported that the wall of the curtain was badly
built, between Santa Maria and the Trinidad.   So true was this
report, that a very few hours battering on the morning of the
6th made a third breach at this point, as practicable as either
of the others.

To prevent the enemy from getting time to retrench this
third opening into the town, the storm was ordered for 7.30
o'clock on the same evening—it would have been well if the
hour had been kept as first settled.

SECTION XXXII: CHAPTER IV

THE STORM OF BADAJOZ. APRIL 6, 1812

THE arrangements which Wellington made for the assault—a business which he knew would be costly, and not absolutely certain of success—were as follows.

The Light and 4th Divisions were told off for the main attack at the three breaches. They were forced to make it on the narrow front west of the Rivillas, because the inundation cramped their approach on the right. The 4th Division, under Colville, was to keep nearest to that water, and to assail the breach in the Trinidad bastion and also the new breach in the curtain to its left. The Light Division was to devote itself to the breach in the flank of Santa Maria. Each division was to provide an advance of 500 men, with which went twelve ladders and a party carrying hay-bags to cast into the ditch. For the counterscarp not being ruined, it was clear that there would be a very deep jump into the depths. The two divisions followed in columns of brigades, each with a British brigade leading, the Portuguese in the centre, and the other British brigade in the rear. Neither division was quite complete—the 4th having to provide the guard of the trenches that night, while the Light Division detached some of its rifles, to distract the attention of the enemy in the bastions to the left, by lying down on the glacis and firing into the embrasures when their cannon should open. Hence the Light Division put only 3,000, the 4th 3,500 men into the assault. When the breaches were carried, the Light Division was to wheel to the left, the 4th to the right, and to sweep along the neighbouring bastions on each side. A reserve was to be left at the quarries below the Pardaleras height, and called up when it was needed.

In addition to the main assault two subsidiary attacks were to be made—a third (as we shall see) was added at the last moment. The guards of the trenches, furnished by the 4th

Division, were to try to rush the lunette of San Roque, which was in a dilapidated condition, and were to cut away the dam if successful. A much more serious matter was that, on the express petition of General Picton, he was allowed to make an attempt to take the Castle by *escalade*. This daring officer argued that all the attention of the enemy would be concentrated on the breaches, and that the Castle was in itself so strong that it was probable the governor would only leave a minimum garrison in it. He had marked spots in its front where the walls were comparatively low, owing to the way in which the rocky and grassy slope at its foot ran up and down. The escalade was to be a surprise—the division was to cross the Rivillas at a point far below the inundation, where the ruins of a mill spanned the stream, and was to drag ladders up the steep mound to the foot of the wall.

Two demonstrations, or false attacks, were to be made with the intention of distracting the enemy—one by Power's Portuguese brigade beyond the Guadiana, who were to threaten an escalade on the fort at the bridge-head : the other by the Portuguese of the 5th Division against the Pardaleras. At the last moment—the order does not appear in the full draft of the directions for the storm—Leith, commanding the 5th Division, was told that he might try an escalade, similar to that allotted to Picton, against the river-bastion of San Vincente, the extreme north-west point of the defences, and one that had hitherto been left entirely untouched by the besiegers. For this he was to employ one of his two British brigades, leaving the other in reserve.

Every student of the Peninsular War knows the unexpected result of the storm : the regular assault on the breaches failed with awful loss, but all the three subsidiary attacks, on San Roque, the Castle, and San Vincente, succeeded in the most brilliant style, so that Badajoz was duly taken, but not in the way that Wellington intended.

The reason why the main assault failed was purely and simply that Phillipon and his garrison put into the defence of the breaches not only the most devoted courage, but such an accumulation of ingenious devices as had never before been seen in a siege of that generation—apparently Phillipon must share the credit with his commanding engineer, Lamare, the historian of the siege. The normal precaution of cutting off the breaches by retrenchments on both sides, and of throwing up parapets of earth, sandbags, and wool-packs behind them, was the least part of the work done. What turned out more effective was a series of mines and explosive barrels planted at the foot of the counterscarp, and connected with the ramparts by covered trains. This was on the near side of the ditch, where there was dead ground unsearched by the besiegers' artillery. In the bottom of it, and at the foot of the breaches, had been placed or thrown all manner of large cumbrous obstacles, carts and barrows turned upside down, several large damaged boats, some rope entanglements, and piles of broken gabions and fascines. The slopes of the breaches had been strewn with crowsfeet, and were covered with beams studded with nails, not fixed, but hung by ropes from the lip of the breach ; in some places harrows, and doors studded with long spikes, were set upon the slope. At the top of each breach was a device never forgotten by any observer, the *chevaux de frise*, formed of cavalry sword-blades[1] set in foot-square beams, and chained down at their ends. For the defence of the three breaches Phillipon had told off 700 men, composed of the light and grenadier companies of each of his battalions, plus the four fusilier companies of the 103rd Line—about 1,200 men in all. A battalion of the 88th was in the cathedral square behind, as general reserve. The two Hessian battalions were on the left, holding the Castle, the lunette of San Roque, and the San Pedro bastion. The three other French battalions occupied the long range of bastions from San Juan to San Vincente. As there had been many casualties, the total of the available men had sunk to about 4,000, and since nearly half of them were concentrated at or behind the breaches, the guard was rather thin at other points— especially (as Picton had calculated) at the Castle, which, though its front was long, was held by only 250 men, mostly Hessians.

It was a most unfortunate thing that the time of the assault, originally fixed for 7.30, was put off till 10—and that the siege-batteries slacked down after dark. For the two hours thus

[1] These swords were those of the large body of Spanish dismounted cavalry which had surrendered at the capitulation in March 1811.

granted to the besieged were well spent in repairing and strengthening all their devices for defence. An earlier assault would have found the preparations incomplete, especially in the matter of the combustibles placed in the ditch.

It would be useless, in the narrative of the doings of this bloody night, to make any attempt to vie with those paragraphs of lurid description which make Napier's account of the storm of Badajoz perhaps the most striking section of one of the most eloquent books in the English language. All that will be here attempted is to give a clear and concise note of what happened between ten and one o'clock on the night of April 6, 1812, so far as it is possible to secure a coherent tale from the diaries and memoirs of a number of eye-witnesses. Burgoyne and Jones of the Royal Engineers, Dickson the commander of the Artillery, Grattan and McCarthy from the 3rd Division, Leith Hay of the 5th, and Kincaid, Simmons, and Harry Smith of the Light Division, along with many more less well-known authorities, must serve as our instructors, each for the part of the storm in which he was himself concerned.

It had been intended, as was said above, that all the columns should converge simultaneously on their points of attack, and for that reason the distances between the starting-point of each division and its objective had been calculated with care. But, as a matter of fact, the hour of 10 p.m. was not quite accurately kept. On the right Picton's division was descried by the French in the Castle as it was lining the first parallel, and was heavily fired upon at 9.45, whereupon the general, seeing that his men were discovered, ordered the advance to begin at once—the 3rd Division was fording the Rivillas under a blaze of fire from the Castle and the San Pedro bastion before 10 struck on the cathedral clock. On the other hand, at the western flank, the officer in charge of the ladder and hay-bag party which was to lead the 5th Division, lost his way along the bank of the Guadiana, while coming up from the Park to take his place at the head of Leith's men. The column had to wait for the ladders, and was more than an hour late in starting. Only the central attack, on the three breaches, was delivered with exact punctuality.

It is perhaps best to deal with this unhappy assault first—it

was a horrible affair, and fully two-thirds of the losses that
night were incurred in it. The two divisions, as ordered, came
down the ravine to the left of the Pardaleras hill without being
discovered : the line of vision from the town was in their
favour till they were actually on the glacis, and heavy firing
against Picton's column was heard as they came forward. The
4th Division was turning to the right, the Light Division to the
left, just as they drew near the ditch, when suddenly they were
descried, and the French, who were well prepared and had
long been waiting for the expected assault, opened on them
with musketry from all the breaches, and with artillery from
the unruined flanking bastions. The storm began as unhappily
as it was to end. The advance of the 4th Division bearing to
the right, came on a part of the ditch into which the inundation
had been admitted—not knowing its depth, nor that the
French had made a six-foot cutting at the foot of the counterscarp. Many men, not waiting for the ladders, sprang down
into the water, thinking it to be a mere puddle. The leading
files nearly all perished—the regimental record of the Welsh
Fusiliers shows twenty men drowned—that of the Portuguese
regiment which was behind the Fusiliers as many as thirty.
Finding the ditch impassable here, the rest of the 4th Division
storming-party swerved to the left, and, getting beyond the
inundation, planted their ladders there : some came down in
this way, more by simply taking a fourteen-foot leap on to the
hay-bags, which they duly cast down. At the same moment
the advance of the Light Division descended in a similar fashion
into the ditch farther to the left, towards Santa Maria. Many
men were already at the bottom, the rest crowded on the edge,
where the French engineers fired the series of fougasses, mines,
and powder-barrels which had been laid in the ditch. They
worked perfectly, and the result was appalling—the 500 volunteers who formed the advance of each division were almost all
slain, scorched, or disabled. Every one of the engineer officers
set to guide the column was killed or wounded, and the want
of direction, caused by the absence of any one who knew the
topography of the breaches, had the most serious effect during
the rest of the storm. Of the Light Division officers with the
advance only two escaped unhurt.

There was a horrible check for a minute or two, and then the heads of the main column of each division reached the edge of the ditch, and began to leap down, or to make use of those of the ladders which had not been broken. The gulf below was all ablaze, for the explosions had set fire to the carts, boats, broken gabions, &c., which the French had set in the ditch, and they were burning furiously—every man as he descended was clearly visible to the enemy entrenched on the top of the breaches. The troops suffered severely as they dribbled over the edge of the counterscarp, and began to accumulate in the ditch. From the first there was great confusion—the two divisions got mixed, because the 4th had been forced to swerve to its left to avoid the inundation, and so was on ground originally intended for the Light. Many men mistook an unfinished ravelin in the bottom of the ditch for the foot of the central breach, and climbed it, only to find themselves on a mass of earth divided by a wide sunken space from the point they were aiming at. To get to the foot of the largest breach, that in the Trinidad bastion, it was necessary to push some way along the blazing bottom of the ditch, so as to turn and get round the end of the inundation. The main thrust of the attack, however, went this way, only part of the Light Division making for the Santa Maria breach, on which it had been intended that all should concentrate. As to the central breach in the curtain, it seems that few or none made their way[1] thither : the disappointment on reaching the top of the ravelin in front of it, made all who got alive to that point turn right or left, instead of descending and pushing straight on. Jones records that next morning there was hardly a single body of an English soldier on the central breach, while the slopes and foot of each of the two flank breaches were heaped with hundreds of corpses. This was a misfortune, as the curtain breach was the easiest of the three, and having been made only that afternoon was not retrenched like the others.

From ten to twelve the surviving men in the ditch, fed by the coming up of the rear battalions of each division, and finally by the reserve, delivered a series of desperate but disorderly attacks

---

[1] This fact, much insisted on by Jones, is disputed by certain Light Division witnesses, but does not seem to be disproved by them.

on the Trinidad and Santa Maria breaches. It is said that on no occasion did more than the equivalent of a company storm at once—each officer as he struggled to the front with those of his men who stuck to him, tried the breach opposite him, and was shot down nearer or farther from its foot. Very few ever arrived at the top, with its *chevaux de frise* of sword-blades. The footing among the beams and spikes was uncertain, and the French fire absolutely deadly—every man was armed with three muskets. Next morning observers say that they noted only one corpse impaled on the *chevaux de frise* of the Trinidad breach, and a few more under it, as if men had tried to crawl below, and had had their heads beaten in or blown to pieces. But the lower parts of the ascent were absolutely carpeted with the dead, lying one on another.

More than two hours were spent in these desperate but vain attempts to carry the breaches : it is said that as many as forty separate assaults were made, but all to no effect—the fire concentrated on the attacked front was too heavy for any man to face. At last the assaults ceased : the survivors stood—unable to get forward, unwilling to retreat—vainly answering the volleys of the French on the walls above them by an ineffective fire of musketry. Just after twelve, Wellington, who had been waiting on the hill above, receiving from time to time reports of the progress of the assault, sent down orders for the recall of the two divisions. They retired, most unwillingly, and formed up again, in sadly diminished numbers, not far from the glacis. The only benefit obtained from their dreadful exertions was that the attention of the French had been concentrated on the breaches for two hours—and meanwhile (without their knowledge) the game had been settled elsewhere.

The losses had been frightful—over one man in four of those engaged : the Light Division had 68 officers and 861 men killed and wounded out of about 3,000 present : the 4th Division 84 officers and 841 men out of 3,500. The Portuguese battalions which served with them had lost 400 men more—altogether 2,200 of the best troops in Wellington's army had fallen—and all to no result.

But while the main stroke failed, each of the subsidiary attacks, under Picton and Leith, had met with complete success,

and despite of the disaster on the breaches, Badajoz was at
Wellington's mercy by midnight. The success of either escalade
by itself would have been enough to settle the game.

Picton's division, as already mentioned, had been detected by
the French as it was filing into the parallel below the Castle : and
since a heavy fire was at once opened on it, there was no use
in halting, and the general gave the order to advance without
delay. The men went forward on a narrow front, having to
cross the Rivillas at the ruined mill where alone it was fordable.
This was done under fire, but with no great loss. The palisade
on the other bank of the stream was broken down by a general
rush, and the storming-party found itself at the foot of the
lofty Castle hill. To get the ladders up it was a most difficult
business—the slope was very steep, almost precipitous in
parts, and the ladders were thirty feet long and terribly heavy.
Though no assault had been expected here, and the preparations
were not so elaborate as at the breaches, yet the besieged were
not caught unprepared, and the column, as it climbed the hill,
was torn by cannon shot and thinned by musketry. The French
threw fire-balls over the wall, and other incandescent stuff
(*carcasses*), so there was fair light by which to see the stormers.
Picton was hit in the groin down by the Rivillas, and the charge
of the assault fell to his senior brigadier, Kempt, and Major
Burgoyne of the Engineers. The narrow space at the foot of
the walls being reached, the ladders were reared, one after the
other, toward the south end of the Castle wall. Six being at last
ready in spots close to each other, an attempt was made to
mount, with an officer at the head of each. But the fire was so
heavy, that no man reached the last rungs alive, and the
enemy overthrew all the ladders and broke several of them.
One is said to have been pulled up by main force into the
Castle ! Meanwhile the besieged cast heavy stones and broken
beams into the mass of men clustering along the foot of the
wall, and slew many. But the 3rd Division was not spent—
Kempt's brigade had delivered the first rush—Champlemond's
Portuguese headed the second, when they had climbed the
slope—but also to no effect. Lastly the rear brigade—Campbell's—came up, and gave a new impetus to the attack. There
was now a very large force, 4,000 men, striving all along the base

of the wall, on a front of some 200 yards. Wherever footing could be found ladders were reared, now at considerable distances from each other. The garrison of the Castle was not large—two Hessian and one French company and the gunners, under 300 men, and when simultaneous attacks were delivered at many points, some of them were scantily opposed. Hence it came that in more places than one men at last scrambled to the crest of the wall. A private of the 45th is said to have been the first man whose body fell inside, not outside, the battlements—the second, we are told, was an ensign (McAlpin) of the 88th, who defended himself for a moment on the crest before he was shot. The third man to gain the summit was Colonel Ridge of the 5th Fusiliers, who found a point where an empty embrasure made the wall a little lower, entered it with two or three of his men, and held out long enough to allow more ladders to be planted behind him, and a nucleus to gather in his rear. He pushed on the moment that fifteen or twenty men had mounted, and the thin line of defenders being once pierced the resistance suddenly broke down—all the remaining ladders were planted, and the 3rd Division began to stream into the Castle. Picton was by this time again in command ; he had recovered his strength, and had hobbled up the slope, relieving Kempt, who was by now also wounded. The time was about eleven o'clock, and the din at the breaches down below showed that they were still being defended.

It took some time to dislodge the remainder of the garrison from the Castle precinct ; many took refuge in the keep, and defended it from stair to stair, till they were exterminated. But by 12 midnight all was over, and Picton would have debouched from the Castle, to sweep the ramparts, but for the fact that all its gates, save one postern, were found to have been bricked up—the French having intended to make it their last point of resistance if the town should fall. The one free postern being at last found, the division was preparing to break out, when the head of its column was attacked by the French general reserve, a battalion of the 88th, which Phillipon had sent up from the cathedral square, when he heard that the Castle had been forced. There was a sharp fight before the French were driven off, in which (most unhappily) Ridge, the hero of the escalade, was shot dead. By the time that this was over, Badajoz had been entered at another point, and Picton's success was only part of the decisive stroke. But as he had captured in the Castle all the French ammunition reserve, and nearly all their food, the town must anyhow have fallen, because of his daring exploit. The loss of the division was not excessive considering the difficulties they had overcome, about 500 British and 200 Portuguese out of 4,000 men engaged.

Meanwhile, in the valley below the Castle, the guards of the trenches had stormed the lunette of San Roque, and were hard at work cutting the dam, so that in an hour or two the inundation was beginning to drain off rapidly. This also would have been a decisive success, if nothing else had been accomplished elsewhere.

The blow, however, which actually finished the business, and caused the French to fail at the breaches, was delivered by quite another force. It will be remembered that a brigade—Walker's—of the 5th Division, had been directed to escalade the remote river-bastion of San Vincente. It was nearly an hour late, because of the tiresome mistake made by the officer charged with the bringing up of the ladders from the Park. And only at a few minutes past eleven did Leith, heading the column, arrive before the palisades of the covered way, near the Guadiana. Walker's men were detected on the glacis, and a heavy artillery fire was opened on them from San Vincente and San José, but they threw down many of the palisades and began to descend into the ditch—a drop of 12 feet. There was a cut in the bottom, to which water from the Guadiana had been let in, and the wall in front was 30 feet high. Hence the first attempts to plant the ladders were unavailing, and many men fell. But coasting around the extreme north end of the bastion, close to the river, some officers found that the flank sloped down to a height of only 20 feet, where the bastion joined the water-side wall. Three or four ladders were successfully planted here, while the main attention of the garrison was distracted to the frontal attack, and a stream of men of the 4th, 30th, and 44th began to pour up them. The French broke before the flank attack : they were not numerous, for several companies had been drawn off to help at the breaches, and the bastion was

won. As soon as a few hundred men were formed, General
Walker led them along the ramparts, and carried the second
bastion, that of San José. But the two French battalions
holding the succeeding western bastions now massed together,
and made a firm resistance in that of Santiago. The stormers
were stopped, and an unhappy incident broke their impetus—
some lighted port-fires thrown down by the French artillerymen were lying about—some one called out that they were the
matches of mines. Thereupon the advancing column instinc-
tively fell back some paces—the French charged and drove
them in, and the whole retired fighting confusedly as far as
San Vincente. Here General Leith had fortunately left a reserve
battalion, the 2/38th, which, though only 230 strong, stopped
the panic and broke the French advance. Walker's brigade
rallied and advanced again—though its commander was
desperately wounded—and once more the enemy were swept
all along the western bastions, which they lost one by one.

Some of the 5th Division descended into the streets of the
town, and pushing for the rear of the great breaches, by a long
détour through the silent streets, at last came in upon them,
and opened a lively fire upon the backs of the enemy who were
manning the retrenchments. The main body, however, driving
before them the garrison of the southern bastions, hurtled in
upon the flank of the Santa Maria. At this moment the 4th and
Light Divisions, by Wellington's orders, advanced again towards
the ditch, where their dead or disabled comrades were lying
so thick. They thought that they were going to certain death,
not being aware of what had happened inside the city. But as
they descended into the ditch only a few scattering shots
greeted them. The French main body—for 2,000 men had been
driven in together behind the breaches—had just thrown down
their arms and surrendered to the 5th Division. Even when
there was no resistance, the breaches proved hard to mount, and
the obstructions at the top were by no means easy to remove.

The governor, Phillipon, had escaped into San Cristobal
with a few hundred men, and surrendered there at dawn, having
no food and little ammunition. But he first sent out the few
horsemen of the garrison to run the gauntlet of the Portuguese
pickets, and bear the evil news to Soult.

Thus fell Badajoz : the best summary of its fall is perhaps
that of Leith Hay, who followed his relative, the commander
of the 5th Division, in the assault on San Vincente :—

' Had Lord Wellington relied on the storming of the breaches
alone, the town would not have been taken. Had General Leith
received his ladders punctually and escaladed at 10, as intended,
he would have been equally successful, and the unfortunate
divisions at the breaches would have been saved an hour of
dreadful loss. If Leith had failed, Badajoz would still have
fallen, in consequence of the 3rd Division carrying the Castle—
but not till the following morning ; and the enemy might have
given further trouble. Had Picton failed, still the success of
the 5th Division ensured the fall of the place.' The moral would
seem to be that precautions cannot be too numerous—it was
the afterthoughts in this case, and not the main design, that
were successful and saved the game.

Wellington himself, in a document—a letter to Lord Liverpool—that long escaped notice, and did not get printed in its
right place in the ninth volume of his *Dispatches*[1], made
a commentary on the perilous nature of the struggle and the
greatness of the losses which must not be suppressed. He
ascribed them to deficiencies in the engineering department.
' The capture of Badajoz affords as strong an instance of
the gallantry of our troops as has ever been displayed. But
I greatly hope that I shall never again be the instrument of
putting them to such a test as they were put to last night.
I assure your lordship that it is quite impossible to carry
fortified places by *vive force* without incurring grave loss and
being exposed to the chance of failure, unless the army should
be provided with a sufficient trained corps of sappers and
miners. . . . The consequences of being so unprovided with the
people necessary to approach a regularly fortified place are,
first, that our engineers, though well-educated and brave, have
never turned their minds to the mode of conducting a regular
siege, as it is useless to think of that which, in our service, it is
impossible to perform. They think that they have done their
duty when they have constructed a battery, with a secure

---

[1] My attention was called to this letter, found among Lord Liverpool's
papers in 1869, by Mr. F. Turner, of Frome.

communication to it, which can breach the place. Secondly, these breaches have to be carried by *vive force* at an infinite sacrifice of officers and soldiers. . . . These great losses could be avoided, and, in my opinion, time gained in every siege, if we had properly trained people to carry it on. I declare that I have never seen breaches more practicable in themselves than the three in the walls of Badajoz, and the fortress must have surrendered with these breaches open, if I had been able to " approach " the place. But when I had made the third breach, on the evening of the 6th, I could do no more. I was then obliged either to storm or to give the business up ; and when I ordered the assault I was certain that I should lose our best officers and men. It is a cruel situation for any person to be placed in, and I earnestly request your lordship to have a corps of sappers and miners formed without loss of time.'

The extraordinary fact that no trained corps of sappers and miners existed at this time was the fault neither of Wellington nor of the Liverpool ministry, but of the professional advisers of the cabinets that had borne office ever since the great French War broke out. The need had been as obvious during the sieges of 1793–4 in Flanders as in 1812. That the Liverpool ministry could see the point, and wished to do their duty, was shown by the fact that they at once proceeded to turn six companies of the existing corps of ' Royal Military Artificers ' into sappers. On April 23, less than three weeks after Badajoz fell, a warrant was issued for instructing the whole corps in military field-works. On August 4 their name was changed from ' Royal Military Artificers ' to ' Royal Sappers and Miners.' The transformation was much too late for the siege of Burgos, but by 1813 the companies were beginning to join the Peninsular Army, and at San Sebastian they were well to the front. An end was at last made to the system hitherto prevailing, by which the troops which should have formed the rank and file of the Royal Engineers were treated as skilled mechanics, mainly valuable for building and carpentering work at home stations.

One more section, a most shameful one, must be added to the narrative of the fall of Badajoz. We have already had to tell of the grave disorders which two months before had followed the storm of Ciudad Rodrigo. These were but trifling and venial compared with the offences which were committed by the men who had just gone through the terrible experiences of the night of April 6th. At Rodrigo there was much drunkenness, a good deal of plunder, and some wanton fire-raising : many houses had been sacked, a few inhabitants were maltreated, but none, it is believed, were mortally hurt. At Badajoz the outrages of all kinds passed belief ; the looting was general and systematic, and rape and bloodshed were deplorably common. Explanatory excuses have been made, to the effect that the army had an old grudge against the inhabitants of the city, dating back to the time when several divisions were quartered in and about it, after Talavera. It was also said that all the patriotic inhabitants had fled long ago, and that those who had remained behind were mainly *Afrancesados*, traitors to the general cause. There was some measure of truth in both allegations : it was no doubt true that there had been quarrels in 1809, and that many loyalist families had evacuated the city after the French occupation, and had transferred themselves to other parts of Estremadura. The population at the time of the British storm was not two-thirds of the normal figure. But these excuses will not serve. There can be no doubt that the outrages were in no sense reasoned acts of retribution, but were a simple outburst of ruffianism.

Old military tradition in all the armies of Europe held that a garrison which refused to surrender when the breaches had become practicable was at the mercy of the conqueror for life and limb, and that a town resisting to extremity was the natural booty of the stormers. In the eighteenth century there were countless instances of a fortress, defended with courage up to the moment when an assault was possible, surrendering on the express plea that the lives of the garrison were forfeit if it held out, when resistance could no longer be successful. The attacking party held that all the lives which it lost after the place had become untenable were lost unnecessarily, because of the unreasonable obstinacy of the besieged : the latter therefore could expect no quarter. This was not an unnatural view when the circumstances are considered. The defender of a wall or a breach has an immense advantage over the stormer, till the moment when the latter has succeeded in closing, and

BADAJOZ

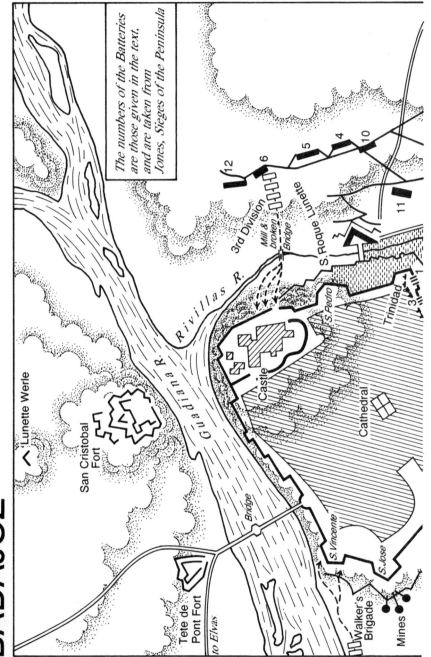

The numbers of the Batteries are those given in the text, and are taken from Jones, Sieges of the Peninsula

Lunette Werle

San Cristobal Fort

Tete de Pont Fort

to Elvas

Bridge

Guadiana R.

Rivillas R.

3rd Division

Mill & broken Bridge

S. Roque Lunette

Castle

S. Pedro

Trinidad

Cathedral

S. Vincente

S. Jose

Walker's Brigade

Mines

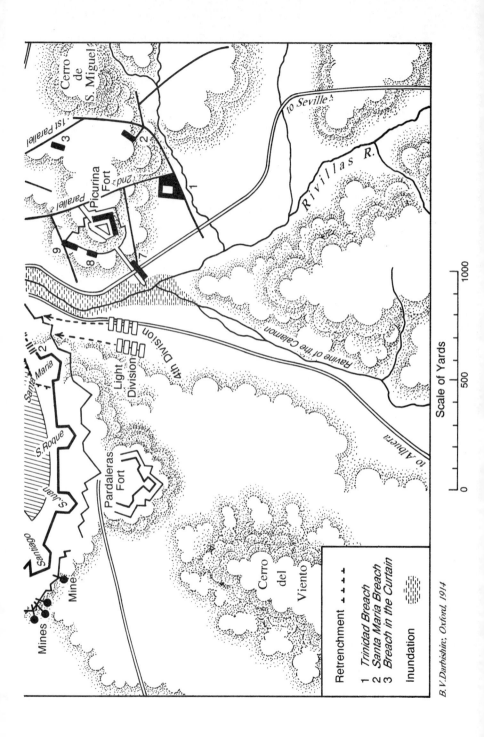

Cerro de S. Miguel

to Seville

Rivillas R.

1st Parallel

2nd Parallel

Picurina Fort

3

2

1

9

8

7

Ravine of the Calamon

to Albuera

Cerro de S. Miguel

4th Division

Light Division

Santa Maria

S. Roque

S. Juan

Santiago

Pardaleras Fort

Mines

Mine

Cerro del Viento

Retrenchment

1 Trinidad Breach
2 Santa Maria Breach
3 Breach in the Curtain

Inundation

Scale of Yards

0   500   1000

B.V.Darbishire, Oxford, 1914

in bringing his superior numbers to bear. In a curious hortatory address which Phillipon published to his garrison [1], the passage occurs, ' realize thoroughly that a man mounting up a ladder cannot use his weapon unless he is left unmolested : the head comes up above the parapet unprotected, and a wary soldier can destroy in succession as many enemies as appear at the ladder-top.' This is perfectly true : but Phillipon naturally avoided stating the logical conclusion, viz. that when the stormers finally succeed in crowning the ramparts, they will be particularly ill-disposed towards the garrison who have, till the last moment, been braining their comrades or shooting them through the head at small risk to themselves. When the assailant, after seeing several of his predecessors on the ladder deliberately butchered by a man under cover, gets by some special piece of luck on a level with his adversary, it will be useless for the latter to demand quarter. If it is a question of showing mercy, why did not the other side begin ? *Que messieurs les assassins commencent*, as the French humorist remarked to the humanitarian, who protested against capital punishment for murderers. There is a grim story of a party of Tuscan soldiers of the 113th Line, who were pinned into a ravelin on the flank of the lesser breach at Rodrigo, and after firing to the last minute upon the flank of the Light Division, threw down their arms, when they saw themselves cut off, calling out that they were ' *poveros Italianos* '—' So you're not French but *Italians* are you—then here 's a shot for you,' was the natural answer [2] :—reflections as to the absence of any national enmity towards the victors should have occurred to the vanquished before, and not after, the breach was carried. The same thing happened at the Castle of Badajoz to the companies, mainly Hessians, who so long held down the stormers of the 3rd Division. If the defenders of the breaches escaped summary massacre, it was because the breaches were not carried by force, and the main body of the French surrendered some time after the assault had ceased, and to troops of the 5th Division, who had not been personally engaged with them.

[1] Printed in Belmas, iv, Appendix, p. 369, and dated March 26.
[2] The story may be found in Kincaid, p. 114, and in several other sources.

It was universally held in all armies during the wars of the early nineteenth century that the garrison which resisted to the last moment, after success had become impossible, had no rights. Ney wrote to the governor of Ciudad Rodrigo in 1810, ' further resistance will force the Prince of Essling to treat you with all the rigour of the laws of war. You have to choose between honourable capitulation and the terrible vengeance of a victorious army [1].' Suchet, in more brutal words, told the governor of Tortosa that he should put to the sword a garrison which resisted instead of capitulating ' when the laws of war make it his duty to do so, large breaches being opened and the walls ruined [2].' A very clear statement of this sanguinary theory is found in a passage in the Memoirs of Contreras, the unlucky governor of Tarragona in 1811 [3]. ' The day after the storm General Suchet had me brought before him on a stretcher [he was severely wounded] and in presence of his chief officers and of my own, told me in a loud voice that I was the cause of all the horrors which his troops had committed in Tarragona, because I had held out beyond the limit prescribed in the laws of war, and that those laws directed him to have me executed, for not capitulating when the breach was opened ; that having taken the place by assault he had the right to slay and burn *ad infinitum*.' I replied that ' if it is true that the laws of war state that, if the besieger gets in, he may deliver to the sword and the flames town and garrison, and if they therefore suggest as a proper moment for capitulation that when an assault has become practicable, it is nevertheless true that they do not prohibit the besieged from resisting the assault, if he considers that he can beat it off : I had sufficient forces to hold my own, and should have done so if my orders had been properly carried out. Therefore I should have been called a coward if I had not tried to resist, and no law prohibited me from repulsing an assault if I could.'

But, as has been pointed out recently [4], Wellington himself may be quoted in favour of this theory. In a letter written to

---

[1] Document in Belmas, iii. p. 287. [2] Ibid., p. 442.

[3] Published in the collection of *Mémoires sur la guerre d'Espagne* in 1821.

[4] By Colonel Callwell, in an article in *Blackwood's Magazine* for September 1913.

Canning in 1820 concerning quite another matter, he remarked,
' I believe that it has always been understood that the defenders
of a fortress stormed have no claim to quarter, and the practice
which prevailed during the last century of surrendering fortresses
when a breach was opened, and the counterscarp blown in, was
founded on this understanding. Of late years the French
availed themselves of the humanity of modern warfare, and
made a new regulation that a breach should stand one assault
at least. The consequence of this regulation of Bonaparte's
was the loss to me of the flower of my army, in the assaults on
Ciudad Rodrigo and Badajoz. I should have thought myself
justified in putting both garrisons to the sword, and if I had
done so at the first, it is probable that I should have saved
5,000 men at the second. I mention this to show you that the
practice which refuses quarter to a garrison that stands an
assault is not a *useless* effusion of blood.'

Comparatively few of the garrisons of Rodrigo and Badajoz
were shot down, and those all in hot blood in the moment after
the walls were carried. Suchet's army was much more pitiless
at Tarragona, where a great part of the Spanish garrison was
deliberately hunted down and slaughtered. But there was,
of course, a much more bitter feeling between French and
Spaniards than between English and French.

The only reason for enlarging on this deplorable theme is
that there was a close connexion in the minds of all soldiers of
the early nineteenth century, from the highest to the lowest
ranks, between the idea that an over-obstinate garrison had
forfeited quarter, and the idea that the town they had defended
was liable to sack. This may be found plainly stated in Lannes's
summons to Palafox at Saragossa in January 1809 [1], in the
capitulation-debate before the surrender of Badajoz in 1811, in
Augereau's address to the inhabitants of Gerona [2], in Leval's
summons to the governor of Tarifa [3], and with special emphasis
in Suchet's threatening epistle to Blake on the day before the
fall of Valencia : ' in a few hours a general assault will precipitate into your city the French columns : if you delay till this
terrible moment, it will not be in my power to restrain the fury

[1] See Belmas, ii. p. 381.   [2] Ibid., ii. pp. 844–5.
[3] Text in the *Defence of Tarifa*, p. 64, and in Arteche.

of the soldiery, and you alone will be responsible before God and man for the evils which will overwhelm Valencia. It is the desire to avert the complete destruction of a great town that determines me to offer you honourable terms of capitulation[1].' It was hardly necessary in the Napoleonic era to enlarge on the connexion between storm and sack—it was presupposed. Every governor who capitulated used to put in his report to his own government a mention of his ' desire to spare the unfortunate inhabitants the horrors of a storm.'

This idea, sad to say, was as deeply rooted in the minds of British as of French soldiers. It is frankly confessed in many a Peninsular diary. ' The men were permitted to enjoy themselves (!) for the remainder of the day,' says Kincaid in his narrative of the fall of Badajoz, ' and the usual frightful scene of plunder commenced, which officers thought it prudent to avoid for the moment by retiring to the camp[2].' ' The troops were, of course, admitted to the immemorial privilege of tearing the town to pieces,' says another writer on another occasion[3]. The man in the ranks regarded the connexion of storm and sack as so close that he could write, ' the prisoners being secured and the gates opened, we were allowed to enter the town *for the purpose of plundering it*[4].' But perhaps the most eye-opening sentence on the subject is Wellington's official order of April 7, 1812, issued late in the day, and when the sack had already been going on for fifteen or eighteen hours, ' It is now full time that the plunder of Badajoz should cease ; an officer and six steady non-commissioned officers will be sent from each regiment, British and Portuguese, of the 3rd, 4th, 5th, and Light Divisions into the town, at 5 a.m. to-morrow morning, to bring away any men still straggling there[5].'

It was unfortunately the fact that Badajoz was a Spanish and not a French town, and this adds a special shame to the lamentable outrages which were perpetrated in its streets for many hours after the storm. It is comparatively seldom in war that an army takes by assault a town which does not belong to the hostile power. The only parallel of recent years

---

[1] Belmas, iv. p. 202.   [2] Kincaid, p. 39.   [3] Leith Hay, ii. pp. 256–7.
[4] Memoirs of Donaldson of the 94th, p. 158.
[5] Wellington, *Supplementary Dispatches*, vii. p. 311.

to the sack of Badajoz had been that of Lübeck in November 1806. Blücher's Prussian corps, retiring before the pursuing French, trespassed on neutral territory by seizing on the old Hanseatic city, which lay in its way, and endeavouring to defend it. The magistrates protested, but were powerless, as they had no armed force at their disposition. Then the French came upon the scene, and, after a fierce fight, won their way over wall and ditch and took the place. They sacked it from end to end with every circumstance of atrocity [1] : Marshal Bernadotte, when importuned by the Burgomaster to stay the horrors, said that he was sorry, but that his troops only recognized the fact that they were in a stormed town—he and his officers could only succeed in calling them off after the city had been half destroyed. This was sufficiently horrible ; but to sack a town belonging to a friendly nation is a shade worse than to sack a neutral place—and this the British troops did.

Two short quotations from eye-witnesses may serve to show the kind of scenes that prevailed in Badajoz from the early hours of the morning on April 7th down to the following night.

' Unfortunate Badajoz,' writes one narrator [2], ' met with the usual fate of places taken at the point of the bayonet. In less than an hour after it fell into our possession it looked as if centuries had gradually completed its destruction. The surviving soldier, after storming a town, considers it as his indisputable property, and thinks himself at liberty to commit any enormity by way of indemnifying himself for the risking of his life. The bloody strife has made him insensible to every better feeling : his lips are parched by the extraordinary exertions that he has made, and from necessity, as well as inclination, his first search is for liquor. This once obtained, every trace of human nature vanishes, and no brutal outrage can be named which he does not commit. The town was not only plundered of every article that could be carried off, but whatever was useless or too heavy to move was wantonly

---

[1] It is said on good first-hand authority that all the inmates of an asylum for female lunatics were raped. See Lettow-Vorbeck, *Geschichte des Krieges von 1806–7*, ii. p. 384.

[2] Hodenberg of the K.G.L. See his letters published in *Blackwood's Magazine* for March 1913, by myself.

destroyed. Whenever an officer appeared in the streets the
wretched inhabitants flocked round him with terror and
despair, embraced his knees and supplicated his protection.
But it was vain to oppose the soldiers : there were 10,000 of
them crowding the streets, the greater part drunk and dis-
charging their pieces in all directions—it was difficult to escape
them unhurt. A couple of hundred of their women from the
camp poured also into the place, when it was barely taken,
to have their share of the plunder. They were, if possible,
worse than the men. Gracious God ! such tigresses in the
shape of women ! I sickened when I saw them coolly step over
the dying, indifferent to their cries for a drop of water, and
deliberately search the pockets of the dead for money, or even
divest them of their bloody coats. But no more of these scenes
of horror. I went deliberately into the town to harden myself
to the sight of human misery—and I have had enough of it : my
blood has been frozen with the outrages I witnessed.'

Another eye-witness gives a passing glimpse of horrors.
' Duty being over, I chanced to meet my servant, who seemed
to have his haversack already well filled with plunder. I asked
him where the regiment was : he answered that he did not
know, but that he had better conduct me to the camp, as
I appeared to be wounded. I certainly was hit in the head, but
in the excitement of the escalade had not minded it, nor had
I felt a slight wound in my leg : but, as I began to be rather
weak, I took his advice, and he assisted me on. In passing what
appeared to be a religious house I saw two soldiers dragging
out an unfortunate nun, her clothes all torn : in her agony she
knelt and held up a cross. Remorse seized one of the men, who
appeared more sober than the other, and he swore she should
not be outraged. The other soldier drew back a step and shot
his comrade dead. At this moment we found ourselves surrounded by several Portuguese : they ordered us to halt, and
presented their muskets at us. I said to my servant, "throw
them some of your plunder : " he instantly took off his haversack and threw it among them : some dollars and other silver
coin rolled out. They then let us pass—had he not done so they
would have shot us—as they did several others. We got safe
to the bastion, and my servant carried me on his back to the

camp, where I got a draught of water, fell asleep instantly, and
did not waken till after midday [1].'

' In justice to the army '—we quote from another authority [2]
—' I must say that the outrages were not general : in many
cases they were perpetrated by cold-blooded villains who had
been backward enough in the attack. Many risked their lives
in defending helpless women, and, though it was rather a
dangerous moment for an officer to interfere, I saw many of
them running as much risk to prevent inhumanity as they did
in the preceding night while storming the town.' The best-
known incident of the kind is the story of Harry Smith of the
95th, who saved a young Spanish lady in the tumult, and
married her two days later, in the presence of the Commander-
in-Chief himself, who gave away the bride. This hastily-wedded
spouse, Juana de Leon, was the Lady Smith who was the
faithful companion of her husband through so many campaigns
in Spain, Belgium, and South Africa, and gave her name to the
town in Natal which, nearly ninety years after the siege of
Badajoz, was to be the scene of the sternest leaguer that British
troops have endured in our own generation. Harry Smith's
narrative of the Odyssey of himself and his young wife in
1812–14, as told in his autobiography, is one of the most
romantic tales of love and war that have ever been set down on
paper.

It was not till late in the afternoon of the 7th that Wellington,
as has been already mentioned, came to the rather tardy conclusion that ' it was now full time that the plunder of Badajoz
should cease.' He sent in Power's Portuguese brigade to clear
out those of the plunderers who had not already gone back
exhausted to their camps, and erected a gallows in the cathedral
square, for the hanging of any criminals who might be detected
lingering on for further outrages. Authorities differ as to
whether the Provost Marshal did, or did not, put his power in
action : the balance of evidence seems to show that the mere
threat sufficed to bring the sack to an end. The men were
completely exhausted : Napier remarks that ' the tumult
rather subsided than was quelled.'

[1] *Recollections of Col. P. P. Nevill, late Major 63rd* [but with the 30th at
Badajoz], pp. 15–16.   [2] Donaldson of the 94th, p. 159.

SECTION XXXII: CHAPTER V

OPERATIONS OF THE FRENCH DURING THE SIEGE OF BADAJOZ

BEFORE proceeding to demonstrate the wide-spreading results of the fall of the great Estremaduran fortress, it is necessary to follow the movements of the French armies which had been responsible for its safety.

Soult had been before Cadiz when, on March 11, he received news from Drouet that troops were arriving at Elvas from the North, and on March 20 the more definite information that Wellington had moved out in force on the 14th, and invested Badajoz on the 16th. The Marshal's long absence from his head-quarters at Seville at this moment, when he had every reason to suspect that the enemy's next stroke would be in his own direction, is curious. Apparently his comparative freedom from anxiety had two causes. The first was his confidence that Badajoz, with its excellent governor and its picked garrison, could be relied upon to make a very long defence. The second was that he was fully persuaded that when the time of danger arrived he could count on Marmont's help—as he had in June 1811. On February 7 he wrote to his colleague [1] that he had just heard of the fall of Rodrigo, that Wellington's next movement would naturally be against Badajoz, and that he was glad to learn that Montbrun's divisions, on their return from Alicante, were being placed in the valley of the Tagus. ' I see with pleasure that your excellency has given him orders to get in touch with the Army of the South. As long as this communication shall exist, the enemy will not dare to make a push against Badajoz, because at his first movement we can join our forces and march against him for a battle. I hope that it may enter into your plans to leave a corps between the Tagus and the Guadiana, the Truxillo road, and the Sierra de Guadalupe, where it can feed, and keep in touch with the troops which I keep in the Serena [the district about Medellin, Don

---

[1] The letter is printed in Marmont's *Correspondance*, iv. pp. 304–5.

Benito, and Zalamea, where Daricau was cantoned].   I am
persuaded that, when the campaigning season begins, the enemy
will do all he can to seize Badajoz, because he dare attempt
nothing in Castille so long as that place offers us a base from
which to invade Portugal and fall upon his line of communications. . . . I am bound, therefore, to make a pressing demand
that your left wing may be kept in a position which makes the
communication between our armies sure, so that we may be
able, by uniting our disposable forces, to go out against the
enemy with the assurance of success.'

This was precisely what Marmont had intended to do. He
was convinced, like Soult, that Wellington's next move would
be against Badajoz, and he placed Montbrun and the divisions
of Foy, Brennier, and Sarrut about Talavera, Monbeltran, and
Almaraz, precisely in order that they might be in easy touch
with Drouet. On February 22 he wrote to his colleague explaining his purpose in so doing, and his complete acquiescence in
the plan for a joint movement against Wellington, whenever
the latter should appear on the Guadiana [1]. His pledge was
quite honest and genuine, and in reliance on it Soult made
all his arrangements. These, however, appear to have been
rather loose and careless : the Marshal seems to have felt such
complete confidence in the combination that he made insufficient
preparations on his own side. No reinforcements were sent
either to Badajoz or to Drouet, whose 12,000 men were dispersed in a very long front in Estremadura, reaching from
Medellin and Don Benito on the right to Fregenal on the left.
This is why Graham, when he moved forward briskly on
March 17th, found no solid body of the enemy in front of him,
but only scattered brigades and regiments, which made off in
haste, and which only succeeded at last in concentrating so
far to the rear as Fuente Ovejuna, which is actually in Andalusia, and behind the crest of the Sierra Morena. We may add
that having been advised by Drouet as early as March 11th [2]

---

[1] This Soult quotes in his recriminatory letter to Marmont of April 8,
and in his angry dispatch to Berthier of the same date (printed in King
Joseph's *Correspondance*, viii. p. 355).

[2] The date is proved by the letter from Soult to Marmont of March 11,
printed in Marmont's *Mémoires*, iv. p. 359.

that British troops were accumulating behind Elvas, Soult
ought to have taken the alarm at once, to have moved back to
Seville from Santa Maria by Cadiz, where he lay on that date,
and to have issued orders for the concentration of his reserves.
He did none of these things, was still in front of Cadiz on
March 20 [1], and did not prescribe any movement of troops till,
on that day, he received Drouet's more definite and alarming
news that Wellington was in person at Elvas, and had moved
out toward Badajoz on the 16th. Clearly he lost nine days by
want of sufficient promptness, and had but himself to blame
if he could only start from Seville with a considerable field-force
on March 30. All that he appears to have done on March 11
was to write to Marmont that the long-foreseen hypothesis of
a move of Wellington on Badajoz was being verified, and that
they must prepare to unite their forces. Jourdan has, therefore,
some justification for his remark that he does not see why
Soult should have been before Cadiz, amusing himself by
throwing shells into that place [2] as late as March 20th.

From the 20th to the 30th of that month Soult was busily
engaged in organizing the relief-column which, after picking
up Drouet on the way, was to march to the succour of Badajoz.
He could not venture to touch the divisions of Conroux and
Cassagne, which together were none too strong to provide for
the manning of the Cadiz Lines and the fending off of Ballasteros
from their rear. But he called off the whole division of Barrois,
nearly 8,000 strong [3], Vichery's brigade of infantry from
Leval's division in the province of Granada [4], and six regiments
of Digeon's and Pierre Soult's dragoons. This, with the corresponding artillery, made a column of some 13,000 men, with

[1] The date is proved by Soult's letter to the Emperor of that date
from Santa Maria, in which he announces his intention to start, and
says that he is writing to Marmont, to get him to unite the armies as
soon as possible.   [2] See his *Mémoires*, p. 377.

[3] To be exact, 7,776 officers and men on March 1. He also brought with
him some 'bataillons d'élite' of grenadier companies from Villatte's division.

[4] The 55th, three battalions about 1,500 strong, the fourth being left at
Jaen. Soult says in his dispatch of April 8 that he took a whole *brigade*
from Leval, but the states of April 14 show the 32nd and 58th regiments
of Leval's division, and three of the four battalions of the 43rd, all left
in the kingdom of Granada. Apparently three battalions of the 55th and
one of the 43rd marched, about 2,200 strong.

which the Marshal started from Seville on the 30th March, crossed the Guadalquivir at Lora del Rio next day, and moved on Constantina and Guadalcanal. An interesting complication would have been caused if Graham had been allowed to stop with his 19,000 men at Azuaga and Llerena, where he was directly between Soult and Drouet's position at Fuente Ovejuna, and if Hill from Merida had moved against Drouet's corps. But as Wellington had withdrawn Graham's column to Villafranca on March 31, there was nothing left to prevent Drouet from coming in from his excentric position, and joining his chief at Llerena on April 4th, with the 12,000 men of his own and Daricau's divisions. This gave the Marshal some 25,000 men[1] in hand, a force which would be manifestly incapable of raising the siege of Badajoz, for he knew that Wellington had at least 45,000 men in hand, and, as a matter of fact, the arrival of the 5th Division and other late detachments had raised the Anglo-Portuguese army to something more like 55,000 sabres and bayonets.

Wellington's orders, when he heard that Soult was in the passes, and that Drouet was moving to join him, directed Graham to fall back on the Albuera position, and Hill to join him there by the route of Lobon and Talavera Real, if it should appear that all the French columns were moving directly to the relief of Badajoz, and none of them spreading out eastward towards the Upper Guadiana[2]. These conditions were realized,

---

[1] Though he calls them only 21,000 in his dispatches. But the figures [see Appendix no. VIII] show 23,500. The total in the monthly reports indicate 25,000 as more likely.

[2] The orders to Hill issued by Wellington on April 4 and 5 (*Dispatches*, ix. p. 30) contemplate two possibilities: (1) Soult is marching with his whole force on Villafranca, and Foy is remaining far away : in this case Hill is to move *en masse* on Albuera. This is the case that actually occurred ; (2) if Foy is moving toward the Upper Guadiana, and Soult is showing signs of extending to join him, Howard's British and Ashworth's Portuguese brigades and Campbell's Portuguese horse will stay at Merida as long as is prudent, in order to prevent the junction, and will break the bridge at the last moment and then follow Hill.

Wellington, when he wrote his first orders of the 4th to Hill, was intending to storm Badajoz on the 5th, and knew, by calculating distances, that Soult could not be in front of Albuera till the 7th. He ultimately chanced another day of bombardment, running the time limit rather fine. But there was no real risk with Graham and Hill at Albuera : Soult could not have forced them.

as Soult moved in one solid body towards Villafranca and
Fuente del Maestre : so Hill evacuated Merida, after destroying
its bridge, and joined Graham on the old Albuera ground on
April 6th. They had 31,000 men, including four British
divisions and four British cavalry brigades, and Wellington
could have reinforced them from the lines before Badajoz with
two divisions more, if it had been necessary, while still leaving
the fortress adequately blockaded by 10,000 or 12,000 men.
But as Soult did not appear at Fuente del Maestre and Villafranca till the afternoon of April 7th, a day after Badajoz had
fallen, this need did not arise. The Marshal, learning of the
disaster, hastily turned back and retired towards Andalusia,
wisely observing that he ' could not fight the whole English
army.' It is interesting to speculate what would have happened
if he had lingered five days less before Cadiz, had issued
his concentration orders on the 14th or 15th instead of the
20th March, and had appeared at Villafranca on the 2nd instead
of the 7th of the next month. His dispatch of April 17 states
that he had intended to fight, despite of odds, to save Badajoz :
if he had done so, and had attacked 40,000 Anglo-Portuguese
with his 25,000 men, he must inevitably have suffered a dreadful
disaster. He must have fought a second battle of Albuera
with much the same strength that he had at the first, while his
enemy would have had six British divisions instead of two, and
an equal instead of a wholly inferior cavalry. The result of
such a battle could hardly have failed to be not only a crushing
defeat for the French, but the prompt loss of all Andalusia ; for
thrown back on that kingdom with a routed army, and unable
to gather in promptly reserves scattered over the whole land,
from the Cadiz Lines to Granada and Malaga, he must have
evacuated his viceroyalty, and have retreated in haste either
on La Mancha or on Valencia.

It is most improbable, however, that Soult would really have
ventured to attack the Albuera position [1], in spite of the

---

[1] He says in his letter to Berthier of April 8 that he had intended (but
for the fall of Badajoz) to move by his right that morning, to the lower
course of the Guadajira river—which would have brought on an action near
Talavera Real, lower down the stream of the Albuera than the battle-spot
of May 1811.

confident language of his ex-post-facto dispatches. His whole
plan of operations depended on his being joined by the
Army of Portugal, in accordance with Marmont's promise of
February 22nd. And he was well aware, by a letter sent by
Foy to Drouet on March 31st, and received on April 6th, that
he could expect no help from the North for many weeks, if any
came at all. That Badajoz was never relieved was due, not to
Soult's delay in concentrating (though this was no doubt
unwise), nor to his over-confidence in Phillipon's power of
resistance, which was (as it turned out) misplaced. He wrote
to Berthier that ' the garrison wanted for nothing—it had still
food for two months, and was abundantly provided with
munitions : its total strength was 5,000 men : it had victoriously
repulsed three assaults : the men were convinced that, however
great a hostile force presented itself before the breaches, it
would never carry them : Phillipon had been informed on
March 28th that I was marching to his help : the troops were
in enthusiastic spirits, though they had already lost 500 men
in successful sorties : my advanced guard was at only one long
day's march from the place, when it succumbs ! ' It was
indeed an *évènement funeste* !

But Soult's late arrival and miscalculation of the time that
the siege would take, were neither of them the causes of the
fall of Badajoz. It would have fallen none the less if he had
arrived on the Albuera upon April 2nd. The fate of the place
was really settled by Napoleon's dispatches to Marmont, with
which we dealt at great length in an earlier chapter [1]. The
orders of February 11 and February 21 (received by the Duke
of Ragusa on February 26 and March 2 respectively) forbade
him to worry about Badajoz, ' a very strong fortress supported
by an army of 80,000 men,' and told him to withdraw to
Salamanca two of the three divisions which he was keeping in
the valley of the Tagus, and to reply to any movement of
Wellington into Estremadura by invading Northern Portugal.
The plan which Soult and Marmont had concerted for a joint
relief of Badajoz was expressly forbidden by their master, on
his erroneous hypothesis that a thrust at Ciudad Rodrigo and
Almeida must bring Wellington home again. Marmont's

[1] See chapter ii above, pp. 54, 55.

promise of co-operation, sent off on February 22nd to Seville, was rendered impossible—through no fault of his—by the imperial dispatch received four days later, which expressly forbade him to stand by it. ' The English will only go south-ward if you, by your ill-devised scheme, keep two or three divisions detached on the Tagus : that reassures them, and tells them that you have no offensive projects against them.' So Marmont, protesting and prophesying future disaster, was compelled to withdraw two divisions from the central position on the Tagus, and to leave there only Foy's 5,000 men— a negligible quantity in the problem. Nor was this all—he was not even allowed to send them back, since the whole Army of Portugal was ordered to march into the Beira.

Soult, therefore, was justified in his wrath when he wrote to Marmont that he had been given a promise and that it had been broken, ' if there had been the least attempt to concert operations between the armies of Portugal and the South, the English army would have been destroyed, and Badajoz would still be in the power of the Emperor. I deplore bitterly the fact that you have not been able to come to an arrangement with me on the subject.' But the wrath should have been directed against the Emperor, not against his lieutenant, who had so unwillingly been forced to break his promise. The only censure, perhaps, that can be laid upon Marmont is that he should have made it more clear to Soult that, by the new directions from Paris, he was rendered unable to redeem his pledge. Soult was not, however, without warnings that some-thing of the kind might happen : Berthier had written to him on February 11th, and the letter must have arrived by the middle of March, that the Emperor was displeased to find him appealing for troops of the Army of Portugal to be moved to Truxillo, and that he ought to be more dependent on his own strength[1]. It would have been better if the Emperor's trusty scribe had explained to Soult that Marmont was expressly forbidden, in a dispatch written that same day, to keep more than one division on the Tagus, or to worry himself about the danger of Badajoz.

---

[1] Berthier to Soult, Feb. 11. The same date as the fatal dispatch sent to Marmont, who was given a copy of that to Soult as an enclosure.

Marmont's original plan for joining Soult via Almaraz might have failed—he himself confesses it in one of his replies to Berthier. But it was the only scheme which presented any prospect of success. By making it impossible Napoleon rendered the fall of Badajoz certain. For it is no defence whatever to point out that his dispatch of March 12th, which reached Salamanca on March 27, finally gave Marmont the option of going southward. By that time it was too late to try the move : —if the Duke of Ragusa had marched for Almaraz and Truxillo next morning, he would still have been many days too late to join Soult before April 6th, the date on which Badajoz fell.

Summing up the whole operation, we must conclude that Wellington's plan, which depended for its efficacy on the slowness with which the French always received information, and the difficulty which they always experienced in concentrating and feeding large bodies of troops in winter or early spring, was bound to be successful, unless an improbable conjunction of chances had occurred. If Marmont and Soult had both taken the alarm at the earliest possible moment, and had each marched with the strongest possible field army, Soult with the 25,000 men that he actually collected, Marmont with the three divisions that lay on the Tagus on March 1st, and three more from Castile [1], they might have met east of Merida somewhere about the last days of March. In that case their united strength would have been from 50,000 to 55,000 men : Wellington had as many, so that he would not have been bound down to the mere defensive policy that he took up on the Caya in June–July 1811, when his numbers were decidedly less than now. But the chance that both Marmont and Soult would do the right thing in the shortest possible time was unlikely. They would have had terrible difficulties from the torrential rains that prevailed in the last ten days of March, and the consequent badness of the roads. Marmont's (if not Soult's) food-problem would have been a hard one, as he himself shows in several of his letters. Soult got his first definite alarm on

---

[1] More probably he would have brought only *two* divisions from north of the mountains, as he had to leave Bonnet to look after the Asturians, and Souham's single division would hardly have sufficed to contain the Galicians, the Portuguese, and the Guerrilleros.

March 11th : Marmont could hardly move till he had learnt
that Wellington had started for Estremadura in person : till
this was certain, he could not be sure that the main body of the
Anglo-Portuguese army was not still behind the Agueda.
Wellington only left Freneda on March 5th, and Marmont did
not know of his departure till some days later. If the two
marshals had each issued prompt concentration orders on
March 11, it still remains very doubtful if they would have met
in time to foil Wellington's object. As a matter of fact Soult
(as we have seen) delayed for nine days before he determined
to concentrate his field-force and march on Badajoz, and this
lateness would have wrecked the combination, even if Marmont
had been more ready than his colleague.

Still there was some chance that the armies might have joined,
if Napoleon had not intervened with his misguided refusal to
allow Marmont to keep three divisions in the valley of the
Tagus or to ' worry about affairs that did not concern him.'
Wellington could not know of these orders : hence came his
anxieties, and his determination to hurry the siege of Badajoz
to a conclusion at the earliest possible date. He was never—as
it turned out—in serious danger, but he could not possibly be
aware of the fact that Marmont was fettered by his instructions.
It was only the gradual accumulation of reports proving that
the Army of Portugal was moving against Ciudad Rodrigo,
and not on Almaraz, that finally gave him comparative ease of
mind with regard to the situation. As to Soult, he somewhat
over-estimated his force, taking it at 30,000 or even 35,000 men
rather than the real 25,000 : this was, no doubt, the reason
why he resolved to fight with his ' covering army ' ranged on
the Albuera position, and not farther forward. If he had known
that on April 1 Soult had only 13,000 men at Monasterio, and
was still separated from Drouet, he might possibly have been
more enterprising.

No signs of Marmont's arrival being visible, Wellington could
afford to contemplate with great equanimity Soult's position
at Villafranca on April 7th. If the Marshal moved forward he
would be beaten—but it was almost certain that he would
move back at once, for, as it will be remembered, precautions
had been taken to give him an alarming distraction in his

rear, by means of the operations of Penne Villemur and Ballasteros [1]. This combination worked with perfect success, far more accurately than Blake's similar raid on Seville had done in June 1811. Ballasteros, it is true, did much less than was in his power. He started from his refuge under the guns of Gibraltar, passed down from the Ronda mountains, and reached Utrera, in the plain of the Guadalquivir less than twenty miles from Seville, on April 4. But he then swerved away, having done more to alarm than to hurt the French, though he had a force of 10,000 infantry and 800 horse [2], sufficient to have put Seville in serious peril. But Penne Villemur and Morillo, though they had not half the numbers of Ballasteros, accomplished all that Wellington required : having slipped into the Condado de Niebla almost unobserved, they pushed rapidly eastward, and occupied San Lucar la Mayor, only twelve miles from Seville, on April 4, the same day that Ballasteros appeared at Utrera. Their cavalry pushed up so boldly toward the suburbs that they had to be driven off by cannon-shot from the *tête-de-pont* at the bridge of Triana. General Rignoux, governor of Seville, had a very motley and insufficient garrison, as Wellington had calculated when he sent Penne Villemur forth. The only organized units were a battalion of ' Swiss ' Juramentados—really adventurers of all nations—and a regiment of Spanish horse, making 1,500 men altogether : the rest consisted of convalescents and weakly men belonging to the regiments in the Cadiz Lines, and of 600 dismounted dragoons. These made up some 2,000 men more, but many were not fit to bear arms. In addition there were some companies of the recently raised ' National Guards.' The enormous size of Seville, and the weakness of its old wall, compelled Rignoux to concentrate his force in the fortified Cartuja convent, leaving only small posts at the gates and the bridge. He sent at once, as Wellington had hoped, pressing appeals to Soult, saying that he was beset by 14,000 men, and that the citizens would probably rise and let in the enemy.

On the 6th Ballasteros received false news that Conroux was

---

[1] See above, p. 229.

[2] Infantry divisions of Cruz Murgeon (5,400 men) and the Prince of Anglona (4,300 men) and five squadrons of horse, besides irregulars.

marching against him with the troops from the Cadiz Lines, and drew back into the mountains. It is said that he was wilfully deceived by persons in the French interest ; at any rate he must have been badly served by his cavalry and intelligence officers, who ought to have been able to tell him that there was no foundation for the report. Penne and Morillo, however, though disappointed at failing to meet their colleague's army, made a great parade of their small force under the walls of Seville, and skirmished with the French at the bridge-head of Triana, and under the walls of the Cartuja, so boldly that Rignoux expected a serious attack. They could only have accomplished something more profitable if the people of Seville had risen, but no disturbance took place. After remaining in front of the place all the 7th and 8th of April, they disappeared on the 9th, having received news of the fall of Badajoz, and drawn the correct deduction that Soult would turn back to hunt them when freed from his other task. Wellington, indeed, had written to give them warning to that effect on the very morning that they retired [1]: but they anticipated the danger, and were safely behind the Rio Tinto when Soult turned up in hot haste at Seville on the 11th, after four days of exhausting forced marches.

The Marshal had left the two divisions of Drouet and Daricau with Perreymond's cavalry in Estremadura, to act as an observing force, and had marched with his remaining 13,000 men to save Seville, which owing to Ballasteros's timidity had never been in any real danger. But the Spanish diversion had nevertheless had precisely the effect that Wellington had expected and desired. During Soult's short absence of twelve days great part of the open country of Andalusia had fallen out of his control, the communications with La Mancha and King Joseph had been cut off, and the guerrilleros had blockaded all the smaller French posts. The hold of the invaders upon the kingdom was never so secure as it had been before the fall of Badajoz.

Ballasteros, after his fiasco in front of Seville, made two fruitless attempts against isolated French garrisons. He failed at the Castle of Zahara on April 11th. One of his columns in an assault on Osuna two days later got into the town and

---

[1] Wellington to Col. Austin from Badajoz, April 9.

killed or captured 60 of the defenders, but failed to take the citadel, where the remainder defended themselves till Pierre Soult was reported to be at hand, and the Spaniards withdrew [1]. He ended his campaign of raids, however, with a more successful stroke. Hearing that the brigadier Rey, with three battalions and some dragoons, was marching from Malaga to relieve the garrison of Ronda, he fell upon him at Alhaurin on the 14th with his main body, encompassed him with fourfold strength, and drove him in rout back to Malaga, capturing his two guns and inflicting more than 200 casualties upon him [2]. Ballasteros then hoped to seize on Malaga, where the French were much alarmed, and prepared to shut themselves up in the citadel of Gibalfaro. But the news that Pierre Soult and Conroux were approaching with a strong column caused the Spaniards to retire to the mountains above Gibraltar [April 19th]. Thus the operations in Andalusia, which had opened with Soult's march to Badajoz, came to an end, with no ruinous disaster to the French, but with a diminution of their prestige, and a distinct weakening of their hold on the kingdom. In the Condado de Niebla Soult made no attempt to reoccupy lost ground, and east of Granada his line of posts had recoiled considerably on the Murcian side : Baza and Ubeda had been abandoned for good. It was but a vain boast when the Marshal wrote to Berthier that, after he had set all things to rights in the central parts of Andalusia, he intended to organize a general concentration to crush Ballasteros, and that his next task would be to lay siege for a second time to Tarifa, ' the loss of which place would be more injurious to the English and the Insurgents than that of Alicante, or even that of Badajoz— against which last-named fortress I ought to make no attack

---

[1] Napier, I know not on what authority, says that Osuna was only defended by ' Juramentados ' who made a gallant resistance against their own countrymen. But Soult, in a letter to Berthier dated April 21 from Seville, says that Osuna was held by some companies of the 43rd Line and a detachment of the 21st Dragoons. He cannot be wrong. Moreover, the 43rd shows losses at Osuna, April 13, in Martinien's tables.

[2] Martinien's tables show three officers killed and nine wounded at ' Alora near Malaga ' on this date, in the 43rd, 58th Line, and 21st Dragoons. Soult's dispatch makes out that only Rey's advanced guard under Maransin was cut up, and that the main body defeated the Spaniards . If so, why did they retreat on Malaga ?

till I shall have finished matters on the Tarifa side, and so have nothing to fear on my left flank [1].'

To complete the survey of the fortunes of the Army of the South in April, it only remains that we should mention the doings of Drouet, now left once more with his two old divisions to form the ' corps of observation ' opposite the Anglo-Portuguese. Soult during his retreat had dropped his lieutenant at Llerena, with orders to give back on Seville without fighting any serious action, if the enemy should pursue him in force, but if he were left alone to hold his ground, push his cavalry forward, and keep a strong detachment as near the Upper Guadiana as possible. For only by placing troops at Campanario, Medellin, and (if possible) Merida, could communication be kept up via Truxillo and Almaraz with the Army of Portugal.

As it turned out, Drouet was not to be permitted to occupy such a forward position as Soult would have liked. He was closely followed by Stapleton Cotton, with Le Marchant's and Slade's heavy and Ponsonby's [2] light cavalry brigades, who brought his rearguard to action at Villagarcia outside Llerena on April 11th. This was a considerable fight. Drouet's horse was in position to cover the retirement of his infantry, with Lallemand's dragoons in first line, and Perreymond's hussars and chasseurs in support. Lallemand evidently thought that he had only Ponsonby's brigade in front of him, as Le Marchant's was coming up by a side-road covered by hills, and Slade's was far out of sight to the rear. Accordingly he accepted battle on an equal front, each side having three regiments in line. But, just as the charge was delivered, the 5th Dragoon Guards, Le Marchant's leading regiment, came on the ground from the right, and, rapidly deploying, took the French line in flank and completely rolled it up [3]. The enemy went to the rear in

---

[1] Soult to Berthier from Seville, April 17, 1812.

[2] This officer was in command of the brigade of Anson, then absent on leave, which at this time consisted of the 12th, 14th, and 16th Light Dragoons.

[3] There is a good account of all this in the admirable diary of Tomlinson of the 16th, which I so often have had to cite. He has an interesting note that the 16th in their charge found a stone wall in their way, and that the whole regiment took it in their stride, and continued their advance in perfect order (p. 150).

confusion, and the pursuit was continued till, half-way between
Villagarcia and Llerena, the French rallied on their reserve
(2nd Hussars) behind a broad ditch. Cotton, who had not let
his men get out of hand, re-formed Anson's brigade and delivered
a second successful charge, which drove the French in upon
Drouet's infantry, which was in order of battle to the left of
Llerena town. It was impossible to do more, as three cavalry
brigades could not attack 12,000 men of all arms in a good
position. But a few hours later the whole French corps was
seen in retreat eastward : it retired to Berlanga and Azuaga on
the watershed of the Sierra Morena, completely abandoning
Estremadura.

The French (outnumbered, if Slade's brigade be counted, but
it was far to the rear and never put in line) lost 53 killed and
wounded and 4 officers and 132 rank and file taken prisoners.
Cotton's casualties were 14 killed and 2 officers and 35 men
wounded : he insisted that his success would have been much
greater if Ponsonby had held back a little longer, till the whole of
Le Marchant's squadrons came on the field—Lallemand would
then have been cut off from Llerena and his line of retreat, and
the greater part of his brigade ought to have been captured,
though the light cavalry in the second line might have got off[1].
However, the affair was very creditable to all concerned.

Hill's infantry did not follow the retreating French, and had
halted about Almendralejo and Villafranca, only the cavalry
having gone on in pursuit to Llerena. The rest of the Anglo-
Portuguese army was already in movement for the North, as
Wellington had given up the idea, which had somewhat tempted
him at first, of pursuing Soult to Seville and trying to upset the
whole fabric of French power in Andalusia. Of this more in its
due place. Suffice it to say here that he fell back on his old
partition of forces, leaving Hill in Estremadura as his ' corps
of observation ', with precisely the same force that he had been

---

[1] Soult only acknowledges a loss of three officers and about 110 men in his
dispatch of April 21 to Berthier, adding the ridiculous statement that the
British had 100 killed and many more wounded, and that the 5th Dragoon
Guards had been practically destroyed. Martinien's tables show four
French officers wounded and one killed, but (of course) take no account
of unwounded prisoners. The British lost two missing, men who had
ridden ahead in the pursuit into the French infantry.

given in 1811, save that one British cavalry brigade (that of Slade) was added. The rest of the corps consisted of the 2nd Division, Hamilton's two Portuguese brigades, Long's British and John Campbell's Portuguese horse [1]. The whole amounted to about 14,000 men, sufficient not only to hold Drouet in check, but also to keep an eye upon the French troops in the valley of the Tagus, against whom Wellington was now meditating a raid of the sort that he had already sketched out in his correspondence with Hill in February.

So much for the Army of Andalusia and its fortunes in April 1812. We must now turn to those of Marmont and the Army of Portugal during the same critical weeks.

The Duke of Ragusa, as it will be remembered, had been caught at Salamanca, on March 27th, by Napoleon's dispatch giving him an over-late option of detaching troops to the relief of Badajoz. But being already committed to the invasion of Portugal prescribed by the Emperor's earlier letters, and having his field-force and his magazines disposed for that project, he had resolved to proceed with it, though he had no great belief in the results that would follow from his taking the offensive [2]. As he informed his master, there was nothing at which he could strike effectively. ' It would seem that His Majesty thinks that Lord Wellington has magazines close behind the frontier of northern Portugal. Not so. These magazines are at Abrantes, or in Estremadura. His hospitals are at Lisbon, Castello Branco, and Abrantes. There is nothing of any importance to him on the Coa.' And how was Almeida or Ciudad Rodrigo to be assailed in such a way as to cause Wellington any disquietude, when the Army of Portugal had not a single heavy gun left ? ' General Dorsenne had the happy idea of leaving in Rodrigo, a fortress of inferior character on the front of our line, the whole siege-train prepared for this army at great expense, so that new guns of large calibre must actually be brought up from France.'

---

[1] This was the brigade formerly under Barbaçena, 4th and 10th regiments.

[2] Mes dispositions étant faites pour une marche de quinze jours sur l'Agueda, déjà commencée, je continue ce mouvement, sans cependant (je le répète) avoir une très grande confiance dans les résultats qu'il doit donner.' Marmont to Berthier, March 27.

Marmont's striking force was not so large as he would have wished. Bonnet was, by the Emperor's orders, beginning his advance for the reoccupation of the Asturias. Foy was in the valley of the Tagus. Souham had to be left on the Esla, to observe the Army of Galicia. This left five divisions for active operations : but the Marshal came to the conclusion that he must split up one more (Ferey's) to hold Valladolid, Salamanca, Zamora, Toro, Avila, Benavente, and other places, which in an elaborate calculation sent to Berthier he showed to require 4,910 men for their garrisons. He therefore marched with four infantry divisions only [Clausel, Maucune, Sarrut, Brennier] and 1,500 light cavalry, about 25,000 men in all : his division of dragoons was left behind in Leon, to keep open communication between his various garrisons. A rather illusory help was sought by sending to Foy, who then lay at Almaraz, orders to the effect that he might push a detachment to Plasencia, and give out that he was about to join the main army by the pass of Perales. But Foy's real concern, as he was told, was to keep up communication with the Army of the South, and to give any help that was possible on the side of Truxillo, if (by some improbable chance) the Army of the Centre should be able to lend him the aid of any appreciable number of battalions.

On the 30th the French army appeared in front of Rodrigo, and Carlos de España, leaving 3,000 men as garrison there, under General Vives, retired with the small remainder of his division towards the Portuguese frontier. He was pursued and molested by the enemy's cavalry, not having been covered or assisted, as Wellington had directed, by Victor Alten's regiment of German Hussars. That officer, neglecting his orders in the most flagrant fashion, did not retire slowly and in a fighting posture, when the French drove in his line of vedettes in front of Rodrigo, but collected his regiment and rode hard for Castello Branco, without concerning himself in the least as to the safety of the Spanish and Portuguese forces in his neighbourhood, or the procuring of intelligence as to the strength and the purpose of the French army. His carelessness or shirking of responsibility, which was to be displayed in still worse form as the campaign went on, drew on him such a sharp and bitter rebuke from Wellington that it is a wonder that he was not sent home forthwith [1].

Marmont looked at Rodrigo, but refused to attempt anything against it, though he was informed that the garrison was undisciplined and dispirited. Without siege artillery he held that it was useless to attack the place. After sending in a formal summons to Vives (who gave the proper negative answer in round terms), and throwing into the streets a few shells from the howitzers attached to his field-batteries, he told off Brennier's division to blockade Rodrigo, as also to guard a flying bridge which he cast across the Agueda at La Caridad, a few miles up-stream.

His next move was to send forward Clausel with two divisions to investigate the state of Almeida. He had heard that its walls were unfinished, and thought that there might be some chance of executing a *coup-de-main* against it. The general, however, came back next day, reporting that he thought the scheme impossible. He had apparently been deterred from pressing in upon the place both by the defiant attitude of the governor, Le Mesurier, whose outposts skirmished outside the walls for some time before allowing themselves to be driven in, and still more by the sight of a considerable force of Portuguese troops encamped close to the town on the other side of the Coa. This was Trant's militia, the first detachment that had got to the front of the various bodies of troops which Wellington had told off for the defence of the Beira. They had taken up the strong position behind the bridge of the Coa, which Craufurd had so obstinately defended against Ney in July 1810.

[1] Wellington to V. Alten, April 18, ' You were desired " not to be in a hurry," to give them (España and General Baccelar) your countenance so far as might be in your power, and to tell them that you were left in the front for a particular object. . . . I beg you to observe that if you had assembled the 1st Hussars at Pastores on March 30 and April 1, the Agueda being then scarcely fordable for cavalry, you could have kept open the communications between Almeida and Ciudad Rodrigo. . . . You wrote on the seventh from Castello Branco that you knew nothing about the enemy ! and instead of receiving from you (as I had expected) a daily account of their operations, you knew nothing, and, from the way in which you made your march, all those were driven off the road who might have given me intelligence, and were destined to keep up the communication between me and Carlos de España.'

On the alarm being given on March 29th that Marmont was marching against that province, and not against Galicia or the Tras-os-Montes, Wellington's orders suiting that contingency were carried out with more or less accuracy. Silveira, with the Tras-os-Montes militia and his small body of regular cavalry, began to move on Lamego, where Baccelar, the chief commander in the North, had concentrated the regiments from the Oporto region and the Beira Alta, even before Marmont had left Salamanca. General Abadia had been requested to press forward against the French on the Esla, so as to threaten the flank and rear of the invading army. He did not accomplish much, being convinced that the forces left opposite him were too strong to be lightly meddled with. But he directed a raid to be made from the Western Asturias towards the city of Leon, and the division at Puebla de Senabria threatened Benavente. Both movements were executed too late to be of any importance in affecting the course of the campaign.

Baccelar had been ordered to avoid committing himself to a general action with any large body of the enemy, but to show such a mass of troops concentrated that Marmont would have to keep his main body together, and to act cautiously on the offensive. His primary duty was to cover, if possible, the large magazines at São João de Pesqueira and Lamego on the Douro, and the smaller ones at Villa da Ponte, Pinhel, and Celorico. To these Wellington attached much importance, as they were the intermediate dépôts from which his army drew its sustenance when it was on the northern frontier, and he knew that he would be requiring them again ere many weeks had passed. As long as Marmont remained near Almeida, it was necessary to keep a force as far forward as possible, behind the very defensible line of the Coa, and Trant was advanced for this purpose, though he was directed not to commit himself. His presence so close to Almeida was very valuable, as he would have to be driven off before the Marshal formally invested the place. Le Mesurier, the governor, was not at all comfortable as to his position : though he had a proportion of British artillery left with him, the whole of the infantry of the garrison consisted of Beira militia, who had no experience under arms. On taking over charge of the place, on March 18, the governor

had complained that though the walls were in a sufficient state
of repair, and there were plenty of guns forthcoming, yet few
or none of them were mounted ready for service, the powder
magazines were insufficiently sheltered, and many details of
fortification (palisades, platforms, &c.) had to be completed in
a hurry[1]. However, the place looked so sound for defence
when Clausel reconnoitred it, that—as we have seen—he
made no attempt to invest it, and promptly withdrew, reporting to his chief that Almeida was not to be taken by a *coup-
de-main.*

Marmont then made the move which Wellington had most
desired, and which in his dispatch to Baccelar he had specified
as the happiest thing that could come about. Instead of
sitting down before Almeida or Ciudad Rodrigo, or making
a push against the dépôts on the Douro, he turned southward
towards the Lower Beira, and (leaving Brennier behind to
guard communications) marched with three divisions to
Sabugal via Fuente Guinaldo. This policy could have no
great results—the Marshal might ravage the country-side, but
such a movement with such a force could not possibly alarm
Wellington overmuch, or draw him away from the siege of
Badajoz if he were determined to persevere in it. There was
nothing of importance to him in central Beira—only minor
dépôts at Celorico and Castello Branco, much less valuable than
the larger ones at Lamego and São João de Pesqueira on the
Douro. ' He can do no more,' as an acute observer on the
Portuguese staff remarked, ' than drive off some cattle, burn
some cottages, and ruin a few wretched peasants[2].' For the
country about the sources of the Zezere and round Castello
Branco is one of the most thinly peopled districts of
Portugal.

To meet Marmont's southern move Baccelar brought up
Trant's and Wilson's militia by a parallel march to Guarda,
while Le Cor, with the two regiments of the Beira Baixa, held
on at Castello Branco till he should be evicted from it. To

---

[1] For complaints by Le Mesurier as to the defects of the place when he
took over charge of it on March 18, see his letter of the 28th of the same
month, to Wellington, in the Appendix to Napier, iv. pp. 450–1.

[2] The observation comes from D'Urban's unpublished Journal.

Wellington's intense disgust [1], Victor Alten, whose orders directed him to fall back no farther than that town, continued his precipitate retreat with the German Hussars to the bridge of Villa Velha on the Tagus, and began to take measures to destroy that all-important link of communications between north and south. Fortunately he was stopped before he had done the damage. The bridge was only taken over to the south bank, not committed to the flames.

Halting at Sabugal, on April 8th, Marmont sent out flying columns, which ravaged the country-side as far as Penamacor, Fundão, and Covilhão, and dispatched Clausel with a whole division against Castello Branco, the one important place in the whole region. Le Cor evacuated it on April 12th, after burning such of the magazines as could not be removed in haste : and Clausel—who occupied it for two days—did not therefore get possession of the stores of food which his chief had hoped to find there. In revenge the town and the small proportion of its inhabitants who did not take to the hills were badly maltreated : many buildings, including the bishop's palace, were burnt.

Hearing that Marmont had dispersed the larger portion of his army with flying columns, and was lying at Sabugal, on the 12th, with only a few thousand men, Trant conceived the rash idea that it would be possible to surprise him, at his head-quarters, by a night march of his own and Wilson's combined divisions from Guarda. The distance was about twenty miles over mountain roads, and the scheme must have led to disaster, for—contrary to the information which the militia generals had gathered—the Marshal's concentrated main body was still stronger than their own, despite of all his detachments [2].

---

[1] Wellington to Alten, *Dispatches*, ix. p. 69. 'You were positively ordered by your instructions to go to Castello Branco and no farther. The reason for this instruction was obvious. First the militia of Lower Beira would be there in the case supposed [that of Marmont's making an invasion south of the Douro], and they *were* there. Secondly, as soon as I should be informed of the enemy's approach to the Coa, it would be necessary for me to assemble a force at Castello Branco—of which the foundation would be the 1st Hussars K.G.L. Yet notwithstanding my orders you marched from Castello Branco on the 8th, and crossed the Tagus on the 9th. Till I received your letter I did not conceive it possible that you could so far disregard your instructions.'

[2] I cannot resist quoting here, as an example of Trant's over-daring and

' You could not have succeeded in your attempt, and you would
have lost your division and that of General Wilson [1],' wrote
Wellington to Trant, when the scheme and its failure were
reported to him a week later.   It was fortunately never tried,
owing to Baccelar's having made objections to his subordinate's hare-brained plan.

But the best comment on the enterprise is that on the very
night (April 13–14) which Trant had fixed for his march, he
was himself surprised by Marmont, so bad had been his arrangements for watching the country-side.   The Marshal had learnt
that there was an accumulation of militia at Guarda threatening
his flank, and resolved to give it a lesson.   He started with
a brigade each from Sarrut's and Maucune's divisions and five
squadrons of light cavalry—about 7,000 men—and was, at
dawn, on the 14th, at the foot of the hill of Guarda, where he
had the good luck to cut off all Trant's outposts without their
firing a shot—so badly did the militia keep their look-out.
' Had he only dashed headlong into the town he might have
captured Wilson's and my divisions without losing probably
a single man,' wrote Trant.   But the ascent into Guarda was
long and steep, and Marmont, who had only cavalry up, did
not guess how careless were his adversaries.   He took proper
military precautions and waited for his infantry : meanwhile
the Portuguese were roused, almost by chance as it seems.
' My distrust of the militia with regard to the execution of
precautions,' continues Trant, ' had induced me at all times to
have a drummer at my bedroom door, in readiness to beat to

reckless temperament, his letter to Wilson, urging him to co-operate in
the raid, which was lent me by Wilson's representative of to-day :—

GUARDA, 11th April, 1812.

MY DEAR WILSON,—I arrived last night.   Hasten up your division :
there never was a finer opportunity of destroying a French corps, in other
words and in my opinion, their 2nd Division : but I have no certainty of
what force is the enemy.   At any rate send me your squadron of cavalry, or
even *twenty* dragoons.   I am very ill-treated by Baccelar in regard to cavalry.
Push on yourself personally.   You know how happy I shall be in having
you once more as the partner of my operations.   Order up everything you
can from Celorico to eat : here there is *nothing*.—Yrs. N. T.

The French 2nd Division was Clausel's, as it chanced, the one that was
precisely *not* at Sabugal, but executing the raid on Castello Branco.

[1] Wellington to Trant, *Dispatches*, ix. p. 73.

arms. This was most fortunately the case on the night of
April 13, 1812, for the first intimation that I had of the enemy
being near at hand was given me by my servant, on bringing
me my coffee at daybreak on the 14th. He said that there was
such a report in the street, and that the soldiers were assembling
at the alarm rendezvous. I instantly beat to arms, and the
beat being as instantly taken up by every drummer in the
place, Marmont, who was at that very moment with his
cavalry at the entrance of the town, held back. I was myself
the first man out of the town, and he was not then 400 yards
away [1].'

The Marshal, in his account of the affair, says that the
Portuguese formed up on the heights by the town, apparently
ready to fight, but drew off rapidly so soon as he had prepared
for a regular attack on the position. Wise not quite in time,
the two militia generals sent their men at a trot down the steep
road at the back of the place, with the single troop of regular
dragoons that they possessed bringing up the rear. It had now
begun to rain in torrents, and Trant and Wilson having obtained
two or three miles start, and being able to see no distance
owing to the downpour, thought that they had got off safe.
This was not the case : Marmont realized that his infantry
could not catch them, but seeing their hurry and disorder
ordered his cavalry—his own escort-squadron and the 13th
Chasseurs—to pursue and charge the rearguard of the retreating
column. They overtook it by the bridge of Faya, three miles
outside Guarda, where the road to Celorico descends on a steep
slope to cross the river. The leading French squadron scattered
the forty dragoons at the tail of Trant's division, and rode on,
mixed with them, against the rearguard battalion (that of
Oporto). The militiamen, startled and caught utterly by
surprise, tried to form across the road and to open fire : but
the rain had damped their cartridges, and hardly a musket
gave fire. Thereupon the battalion went to pieces, the men
nearest the French throwing down their guns and asking for
quarter, while those behind scattered uphill or downhill from
the road, seeking safety on the steep slopes. The charge swept
downhill on to the battalion of Aveiro, and the other successive

1 Narrative of Trant in Napier's Appendix to vol. iv. p. 451.

units of the Oporto brigade, which broke up in confusion. Five
of their six colours were taken, and 1,500 prisoners were cut off,
while some tumbled into the Mondego and were drowned, by
losing their footing on the steep hillside. Hardly a Frenchman
fell, and not very many Portuguese, for the *chasseurs*, finding
that they had to deal with helpless militiamen who made no
resistance, were sparing with the sabre [1]. The greater part of
the prisoners were allowed, in contempt, to make off, and only
a few hundred and the five flags were brought back to Marmont
at Guarda. The pursuit did not penetrate so far as Wilson's
division, which got across the Mondego while Trant's was being
routed, and formed up behind the narrow bridge, where the
chasseurs, being a trifling force of 400 men, did not think fit
to attack them. The French infantry had marched over twenty
miles already that day, and were dead beat : Marmont did not
send them down from Guarda to pursue, in spite of the brilliant
success of his cavalry.

The day after the ' Rout of Guarda ' Marmont pushed an
advanced guard to Lagiosa, half-way to Celorico, where Trant
and Wilson had taken refuge, with their ranks short of some
2,000 men scattered in the hills. Thereupon the militia
generals set fire to the stores, and evacuated Celorico, falling
back into the hills towards Trancoso. But finding that the
French were not coming on, they halted ; and when they
ascertained that the enemy was actually returning to Guarda,
they came back, extinguished the fires, and rescued great part
of the magazines. Marmont's unexpected forbearance was
caused by the fact that the news of the fall of Badajoz reached
him on the 15th, along with a report from Clausel (who had
just evacuated Castello Branco) that Wellington's army had

---

[1] There is an account of this rout from the French side in the *Mémoires*
of Parquin, of the 13th Chasseurs, an officer mentioned in Marmont's
dispatch as having taken one of the flags. Parquin calls it that of the
regiment of *Eurillas*. There was no such corps : those which lost
standards were Aveiro, Oliveira, and Penafiel. A lengthy account may
be found also in Beresford's *Ordens do Dia* for May 7, where blame and
praise are carefully distributed, and the curious order is made that the
disgraced regiments are to leave their surviving flags at home, till they
have washed out the stain on their honour by good service in the
field.

already started northward, and that its advanced guard was across the Tagus at Villa Velha.

This was startling, nay appalling, intelligence. Badajoz had been reckoned good for a much longer resistance, and the news had come so slowly—it had taken nine days to reach Marmont—that it was possible that the British army was already in a position to cut off his expeditionary force from its base on the Agueda. Wherefore Marmont hastily evacuated Guarda, and was back at Sabugal by the 16th, where Clausel and the other dispersed fractions of his army joined him. Here he regarded himself as reasonably safe, but determined to retire behind the Spanish frontier ere long, raising the blockade of Ciudad Rodrigo. ' My troops,' he wrote to Berthier on that day, ' have used up the little food to be gathered between the Tagus and the Zezere ; and now that the enemy is on the Tagus I cannot possibly remain on the Mondego, as I should be leaving him on my line of communications. I shall fall back to the right bank of the Agueda. If the enemy resolves to pursue me thither I shall fight him. If not I shall fall back on Salamanca, because of the absolute impossibility of feeding an army between the Agueda and the Tormes.'

Marmont remained at Sabugal and its neighbourhood for nearly a week—by the 22nd he had drawn back a few miles to Fuente Guinaldo—with about 20,000 men. His position was more dangerous than he knew ; for on the 18th the heavy rains, which began on the day of the combat of Guarda, broke his bridge over the Agueda at La Caridad, so that he was cut off from Brennier and from Salamanca. He was under the impression that Wellington had only brought up a couple of divisions against him, and that these were still south of Castello Branco [1],

[1] Marmont to Berthier : Fuente Guinaldo, April 22. ' Les rapports des prisonniers sont que trois divisions de l'armée anglaise reviennent sur le Coa. Mais cette nouvelle ayant été donnée avec affectation par les parlementaires, et n'ayant vu jamais autre chose que le seul 1er de Hussards Allemands, qui était précédemment sur cette rive, et point d'infanterie, ni rien qui annonce la présence d'un corps de troupes, je suis autorisé à croire que c'est un bruit qu'on a fait courir à dessein, et qu'il n'y a pas d'Anglais en présence. Je suis à peu près certain qu'il a parti de Portalègre deux divisions, qui se sont portées à Villa Velha : mais il me paraît évident qu'elles ne se sont beaucoup éloignées du Tage.' The actual situation was 1st Hussars K.G.L. Quadraseyes in front of Sabugal : Light Division,

whereas as a matter of fact seven had marched ; and on the day that he wrote this incautious estimate Wellington's head-quarters were at Penamacor, the Light and 3rd Divisions were closing in on Sabugal, the 4th and 5th were a full march north of Castello Branco, and the 1st, 6th, and 7th were at Losa, quite close to that city. Thirty-six hours more of delay would have placed Marmont in the terrible position of finding himself with a broken bridge behind him, and 40,000 enemies closing in upon his front and flank.

To explain the situation, Wellington's movements after the capture of Badajoz must now be detailed. It had been his hope, though not his expectation, that Soult might have remained at Villafranca after hearing of the disaster of the 6th April ; in this case he had intended to fall upon him with every available man, crush him by force of numbers, and then follow up his routed army into Andalusia, where the whole fabric of French occupation must have crumpled up. But Soult wisely retreated at a sharp pace ; and the idea of following him as far as Seville, there to find him reinforced for a general action by all the troops from the Cadiz Lines and Granada, was not so tempting as that of bringing him to battle in Estremadura. On the day after the fall of Badajoz Wellington formulated his intentions in a letter to Lord Liverpool. ' It would be very desirable that I should have it in my power to strike a blow against Marshal Soult, before he could be reinforced. . . . But it is not very probable that he will risk an action in the province of Estremadura, which it would not be difficult for him to avoid ; and it is necessary for him that he should return to Andalusia owing to the movements of General Ballasteros and the Conde de Penne Villemur . . . if he should retire into Andalusia I must return to Castille [1].'

The reason given by Wellington for his resolve to turn north again was that Carlos de España had informed him that Ciudad Rodrigo, though otherwise tenable enough, had only provisions

---

Sabugal : 3rd Division, Sortelha : 4th Division, Pedrogão, 5th Division, Alpedrinha ; 1st, 6th, 7th Divisions, Losa : Pack's Portuguese, Memoa. The map will show what a fearful situation Marmont would have been in had he halted for another day.

[1] Wellington to Liverpool, April 7, *Dispatches*, ix. p. 43.

for twenty-three days, partly from what Wellington called the general policy of ' Mañana ' [1]—of shiftless procrastination—partly from the definite single fact that a very large convoy provided from the British magazines on the Douro had been stopped at Almeida on March 30th. This, in Wellington's estimation, was the fault of Victor Alten, who, if he had held the outposts beyond the Agueda for a day longer, might have covered the entry of the convoy into Ciudad Rodrigo [2]. Marmont's operations on the Coa and the Agueda would have been quite negligible from the strategic point of view but for this one fact. He might ravage as far as Guarda or Castello Branco without doing any practical harm, but it could not be permitted that he should starve Rodrigo into surrender : even allowing for a firm resistance by the garrison, and a judicious resort to lessened rations, the place would be in danger from the third week of April onward. Wherefore, unless Marmont withdrew into Spain by the middle of the month, he must be forced to do so, by the transference of the main body of the Anglo-Portuguese Army to the North.

The Marshal, during the critical days following the fall of Badajoz, showed no such intention. Indeed he advanced to Sabugal on the 8th, seized Castello Branco on the 12th, and executed his raid on Guarda upon the 13th–14th. Ignorant of the fall of Badajoz, he was naturally extending the sphere of his operations, under the belief that no serious force was in his front. While he was overrunning Beira Baixa, Ciudad Rodrigo continued to be blockaded by Brennier, and its stores were now running very low.

On April 11th [3] Wellington made up his mind that this state of things must be brought to an end, and he determined that no mere detachment should march, but a force sufficient to

---

[1] Wellington to Henry Wellesley, April 4, *Dispatches*, ix. p. 29.

[2] Wellington to Alten, April 18, *Dispatches*, ix. p. 68, ' I beg to observe that if you had assembled the 1st Hussars at Pastores on the 30th March and 1st April . . . you would have kept open the communication between Almeida and Ciudad Rodrigo, and the convoy would probably have got into the latter place.'

[3] The date can be fixed from D'Urban's Journal : ' Marmont has blockaded Rodrigo, reconnoitred Almeida, and has now made an inroad as far as Fundão : all this obliges a movement toward him. April 11.'

overwhelm Marmont if he could be brought to action. The movement began with the march of the 11th Light Dragoons and Pack's and Bradford's Portuguese to Elvas on the afternoon of the 11th April, all being ordered to move on Arronches and Portalegre. On the 12th a larger force started off from the camps around Badajoz and on the Albuera position : the 3rd and Light Divisions moved (following Pack and Bradford) on Portalegre via Arronches, the 4th and 5th, making a shorter move, to Campo Mayor on the same road, the 7th from Valverde to Elvas. The 1st and 6th under Graham, bringing up the rear, went off on the 13th from Valverde and Elvas northward. Orders were sent to Stapleton Cotton, then in pursuit of Drouet in southern Estremadura, to come with Anson's and Le Marchant's cavalry brigades to join the main army, leaving only Slade's and Long's to Hill. Bock's Heavy Dragoon brigade of the King's German Legion was also directed to take part in the general movement.

Only Hill, with the troops that had served under him since the summer of 1811, plus one new cavalry brigade, was left behind in Estremadura to ' contain ' Drouet. It was highly unlikely that Soult would be heard of in that province, as he had his own troubles in Andalusia to keep him employed. Indeed Wellington in his parting message to this trusty lieutenant told him that it was ' impossible ' that the enemy could assemble enough troops to incommode him at present, and explained that his chief duty would be to cover the repairing of Badajoz, into which three Portuguese line regiments [1] under Power, hitherto forming the garrisons of Elvas and Abrantes, were thrown, to hold it till Castaños should provide 3,000 Spaniards for the purpose.

The movement of the army marching against Marmont was rapid and continuous, though it might have been even more swift but for the fact that the whole long column had to pass the bridge of Villa Velha, the only passage of the Tagus that lay straight on the way to the Lower Beira : to send troops by Abrantes would have cost too much time. On the 16th the Light and 3rd Divisions crossed the bridge, on the 17th some cavalry and Pack's and Bradford's Portuguese, while the 4th,

------

[1] 5th and 17th from Elvas, 22nd from Abrantes.

5th, and 6th Divisions were now close to the river at Castello de Vide and Alpahão, and only the 1st was rather to the rear at Portalegre [1]. Alten's German Hussars, picked up at Castello Branco on the 18th by the head of the column, were the only cavalry which Wellington showed in his front. This was done on principle : Marmont knew that this regiment was in his neighbourhood, and if it pressed in upon his outposts, it told him nothing as to the arrival of new troops opposite him. As we have already seen, when quoting one of his dispatches [2], he drew the inference that Wellington intended, and so late as the 22nd believed that his adversary's main army was still behind the Tagus, and that at most two divisions had come up to Villa Velha—but probably no further.

Steadily advancing, the column, with the 3rd and Light Divisions leading, reached Castello Branco on the 17th. They found that it had been reoccupied on the 15th by Alten's Hussars and Le Cor's militia ; but it was in a dreadful state of dilapidation owing to the ravages of Clausel's troops during the two days of their flying visit. Clear information was received that Marmont was still at Sabugal, and his vedettes lay as far south as Pedrogão. The British staff were in hopes that he might be caught. ' His ignorance (as we hope) of the real force in march against him may end in his destruction,' wrote D'Urban to Charles Stewart on the 18th, ' for he has put the Agueda in his rear, which the late rains have made impassable : his situation is very critical. If he discovers his error at once, he may get off by his left down the Perales road, and so reach Plasencia : but if he does not, and waits to be *driven* out of the ground he holds, I don't see how he is to get away. Lord Wellington will be all closed up by the 21st ; meanwhile he shows little to his front, and avoids giving serious alarm : the fairest hopes may be entertained of a decisive blow [3].'

It looked indeed as if Marmont was waiting over-long : on the 17th–18th his exploring parties came as far south as Idanha Nova, where by an ill chance they captured Wellington's most famous intelligence-officer, Major Colquhoun Grant, who there

---

[1] All these movements are taken from the elaborate tables in D'Urban's Journal for these days.
[2] See above, p. 288.   [3] Letter in the D'Urban Papers.

commenced that extraordinary series of adventures which are
told in detail in the life of his brother-in-law, Dr. McGrigor,
Wellington's chief medical officer. He escaped at Bayonne,
and returned to England via Paris and the boat of a Breton
fisherman [1].

The rear of the column had dropped behind somewhat, owing
to the incessant rains which had set in from April 14th, and
which had broken Marmont's bridge four days later. Wellington had given the 4th Division leave to halt for a day, because
of the state of the roads and the entire want of cover for the
night in the desolate tract between Villa Velha and Abrantes [2].
It reached Castello Branco, however, on the 20th, on which day
only (by some extraordinary mismanagement) Wellington got
the tardy news of Trant's disaster at Guarda on the morning
of the 14th. And this news was brought not by any official
messenger, but by a fugitive ensign of militia, who garnished
it with all manner of untrue additions—whereupon Beresford
had him tried and shot, for deserting his troops and spreading
false intelligence. Clearly Trant, Wilson, and Baccelar between
them should have got the true narrative to head-quarters before
six days had elapsed.

The 21st April was the critical day of this campaign. Marmont was still at Fuente Guinaldo, on the wrong side of the
Agueda, and his bridge at La Caridad was still broken and
not relaid. Though unaware that Wellington was close upon him
with an overwhelming force, whose existence he denied (as we
have seen) in a letter sent off so late as the 22nd, he was yet
feeling uncomfortable, both because of his broken communications, and because he had used up his food. Wherefore he gave
orders that his artillery, using very bad side-roads, should pass
the Agueda by the bridge of Villarubia, a small mountain

---

[1] See the *Life of Surgeon-General Sir Jas. McGrigor*, pp. 284–96. I have
before me, among the Scovell papers, Grant's original signed parole as far
as Bayonne, witnessed by General Lamartinière, the chief of Marmont's
staff. It was captured by *Guerrilleros* in Castile, and sent to Wellington.
Accompanying it is the General's private letter, commending Grant to the
attention of the French police, with the explanation that he was only
not treated as a spy because he was captured in British uniform, though
far in the rear of the French outpost line.

[2] Wellington to Graham, Castello Branco, April 18, *Dispatches*, ix. p. 70.

crossing quite near its source, which would take it, not by
the ordinary route past Ciudad Rodrigo, but by Robledo to
Tamames, through a very difficult country.[1] He himself with
the infantry stood fast on the 21st and 22nd, unaware of his
dangerous position.

For the allies were closing in upon him—the head-quarters
of Wellington were on the 21st at Pedrogão, the 1st German
Hussars, covering the advance, had reached Sabugal, and the
Light and 3rd Divisions were close behind, as were Pack's and
Bradford's Portuguese, while the 4th and 5th were both
beyond Castello Branco. On the morning of the 22nd the head
of the infantry column had passed Sabugal, and the Hussars
were in front of them, pushing in Marmont's vedettes. A delay
of twenty-four hours more on the part of the French would
have brought the armies into collision, when Marmont gave
orders for his infantry to retreat across the Agueda by the fords
near Ciudad Rodrigo, where the water on that day had at last
fallen enough to render the passage possible, though difficult
and dangerous. The leading division marched on the 22nd, the
rest on the 23rd : by the night of the latter day all were across
the river, and retiring rapidly on Salamanca ; for, as Marmont
truly observed, there was not a ration of food to be got out of
the devastated country between Rodrigo and the Tormes.

The odd part of this sudden, if long-deferred, retreat was that
it was made without the slightest knowledge that it was
imperative, owing to Wellington's near approach ; in the letter
announcing it to Berthier the Marshal reiterates his statement
that he does not believe that Wellington has a man north of
Castello Branco save the 1st Hussars K.G.L. The retreat
is only ordered because it is clear that, with 20,000 men only in
hand, it is useless to continue the tour of devastation in the

---

[1] Marmont to Berthier, Fuente Guinaldo, April 22 [original intercepted
dispatch in Scovell Papers] : ' J'ai eu la plus grande peine à faire arriver
mon artillerie sur la rive droite de cette rivière. Les ponts que j'avais fait
construire sur l'Agueda ayant été détruits par les grandes crues d'eau, et
n'ayant pas la faculté de les rétablir, je n'ai su d'autre moyen que de la
diriger par les sources de cette rivière, et les contreforts des montagnes.'
The wording of Wellington's intercepted copy differs slightly from that of
the duplicate printed in Ducasse's *Correspondence of King Joseph*, viii.
pp. 404–10.

Beira. ' Your highness may judge that the result of the
diversion which I have sought to make in favour of the Army
of the South has been practically nil. Such a movement could
only be effective if carried out with a force great enough to
enable me to march against the enemy with confidence, and to
offer him battle, even if he had every available man collected.
With 18,000 or 19,000 men (reduced to 15,000 or 16,000 because
I have to leave detachments to keep up communications) I could
not move far into Portugal without risk, even if I have no one
in front of me, and the whole hostile army is on the farther bank
of the Tagus. For if I passed the Zezere and marched on
Santarem, the enemy—master of Badajoz and covered by the
Guadiana—could pass the Tagus behind me, and seize the
defiles of Zarza Major, Perales, and Payo, by which alone I could
return. . . . There are several places at which he could cross the
Tagus, above and below Alcantara, and so place himself by
a rapid and secret movement that my first news of him would
be by the sound of cannon on my line of communications—and
my position would then be desperate [1].'

The real danger that was threatening him, on the day that he
wrote this dispatch, Marmont did not suspect in the least,
indeed he denied its existence. But he moved just in time, and
was across the Agueda when, on the 24th, Wellington had his
head-quarters at Alfayates, and three divisions at Fuente
Guinaldo, which the French had only evacuated on the preceding
day, with three more close behind. Only the 1st and 6th, under
Graham, were still at Castello Branco and Losa. Evidently
if the fords of the Agueda had remained impassable for another
twenty-four hours, Marmont's four divisions would have been
overwhelmed by superior numbers and driven against the
bridgeless river, over which there would have been no escape.
As it was, he avoided an unsuspected danger, and returned to
Salamanca with his army little reduced in numbers, but with
his cavalry and artillery almost ruined : his dispatch of the
22nd says that he has lost 1,500 horses, and that as many more
needed a long rest if they were ever again to be fit for service.

On the 24th Wellington bade all his army halt, the forced

---

[1] Intercepted dispatch in the Scovell Papers, Fuente Guinaldo, April 22,
quoted above.

marches which they had been carrying out for the last ten days having failed to achieve the end of surprising and overwhelming Marmont, who had obtained an undeserved escape. On the 26th he paid a flying visit to Ciudad Rodrigo, whose safety he had at least secured, and commended General Vives for his correct attitude during the three weeks of the late blockade. The next movements of the allied army belong to a different series of operations, and must be dealt with in a new section.

SECTION XXXIII

THE SALAMANCA CAMPAIGN

CHAPTER I

KING JOSEPH AS COMMANDER-IN-CHIEF

On March 16, 1812, the day on which Wellington opened his trenches before Badajoz, the Emperor Napoleon took a step of no small importance with regard to the control of his armies in Spain. He had now made up his mind that the long-threatened war with Russia must begin within a few months, and that he must leave Paris ere long, and move forward to some central point in Germany, from which he could superintend the preparations for a campaign, the greatest in scale of any which he had hitherto undertaken. He was persuaded that war was inevitable : the Czar Alexander had dared to dispute his will; and in the state of megalomania, to which his mind had now accustomed itself, he could tolerate no opposition. Yet he was aware, in his more lucid moments, that he was taking a great risk. On March 7th Colonel Jardet, Marmont's confidential aide-de-camp, was granted an interview, in which he set forth all the difficulties of the Army of Portugal. The Emperor heard him out, and began, ' Marmont complains that he is short of many resources—food, money, means, &c. . . . Well, here am I, about to plunge with an immense army into the heart of a great country which produces *absolutely nothing.*' And then he stopped, and after a long silence seemed suddenly to rouse himself from a sombre reverie, and looking the colonel in the face asked, ' How will it all end ? ' Jardet, thrown off his balance by such a searching query, stammered that it would of course end in the best possible fashion. But he went out filled with gloomy forebodings, inspired by his master's evident lack of confidence in the future [1].

Some weeks were yet to elapse before the Emperor's actual

[1] See Marmont's *Mémoires,*-iv. p. 202. Jardet's long report to Marmont was captured on its journey out to Salamanca from Paris, and lies among the Scovell Papers.

departure from France; but, ere he went, he had to set in good working order the conduct of his policy during his absence, and of all its complicated machinery the Spanish section was one of the most puzzling and the most apt to get out of order. It was clearly impossible that he should continue to send from Dresden or Wilna elaborate orders every five or ten days, as he had been wont to do from Paris. If it took three weeks to get an order to Seville in February, it might take five or six in July, when the imperial head-quarters might be in some obscure Lithuanian hamlet. Something must be done to solve the problem of continuous policy, and of co-operation between the five armies of Spain, and after much consideration the Emperor dictated to Berthier the solution which he thought least bad—

'Send by special messenger a dispatch to the King of Spain, informing him that I confide to him the command of all my Spanish armies, and that Marshal Jourdan will serve as his Chief-of-the-Staff. You will send, at the same time, a similar intimation to that marshal. You will inform the King that I shall keep him advised of my political intentions through my ambassador at Madrid. You will write to Marshal Suchet, to the Duke of Dalmatia, and the Duke of Ragusa that I have entrusted the King with the charge of all my armies in his realm, and that they will have to conform to all the orders which they may receive from the King, to secure the co-operation of their armies. You will write, in particular, to the Duke of Ragusa that the necessity for obtaining common action between the Armies of the South, of Valencia, and of Portugal, has determined me to give the King of Spain control over all of them, and that he will have to regulate his operations by the instructions which he will receive. To-morrow you will write in greater detail to the King, but the special messenger must start this very night for Bayonne [1].'

Of the bundle of dispatches that for the King was delivered at Madrid on March 28th, after twelve days of travel. Marmont

---

[1] King Joseph had been prepared for the formal proposal by a tentative letter sent off to him about three weeks earlier, on February 19, inquiring whether it would suit him to have Jourdan as his Chief-of-the-Staff, supposing that the Emperor went off to Russia and turned over the command in Spain to him. See Ducasse's *Correspondence*, ix. p. 322.

got his a little later, as he had started on his Portuguese expedition when it reached Salamanca. Communication between his field-force and his base being difficult, owing to the activity of Julian Sanchez, it appears to have been on March 30, when before Ciudad Rodrigo, that he became aware that he had a new commander-in-chief [1]. Soult was apprised of the situation much later, because, when preparing for his expedition to relieve Badajoz, he had ordered his posts in the Sierra Morena to be evacuated, and the communication with La Mancha to be broken off for the moment. It seems that he must have got Berthier's dispatch quite late in April, as on the 17th of that month he was only acknowledging Paris letters of February 23rd [2], and the first courier from Madrid got through only some time later. Suchet would appear also to have been advised of the change of command very late—he published the imperial decree in his official gazette at Valencia only on May 10, giving as its date the 29th instead of the 16th of March [3], which looks as if the first copy sent to him had miscarried, and the repetition made thirteen days later had alone reached him. These dates are only worth giving as illustrations of the extreme difficulty of getting orders from point to point in Spain during the French occupation, even when Andalusia and Valencia were supposed to be thoroughly subdued.

It will be noted that in Napoleon's instructions to Berthier no mention is made of either the Army of Catalonia or the Army of the North [4]; and it might have been thought that, clinging

[1] This is proved by Berthier's letter to King Joseph of April 16 (Ducasse's *Correspondence of King Joseph*, viii. p. 382), which says that he has just received Marmont's dispatch of March 30 acknowledging his own of March 16, and that the Marshal now knows that he must obey orders from Madrid.   [2] Soult to Berthier from Seville, April 17.

[3] A copy of this print is among the Scovell Papers : it does credit to the Valencian press by its neat appearance.

[4] The question about the Army of the North is a very curious one. The authorized copy of the dispatch of May 16, printed in Napoleon's correspondence and in Ducasse's *Correspondence of King Joseph*, certainly omits its name. But the King declared that in his original copy of it Dorsenne and his army were mentioned as put under his charge. In one of the intercepted dispatches in the Scovell Papers, Joseph writes angrily to Berthier, giving what purports to be a verbatim duplicate of the document, and in this duplicate, which lies before my eyes as I write this, the Army of the North *is* cited with the rest.

to the theory of his paper annexation of Spain north of the Ebro, he was deliberately exempting from the King's control the troops in the districts on which he had resolved to lay hands for his own benefit. But a supplementary dispatch of April 23rd placed Decaen and the garrison of Catalonia under the general charge of Suchet, and as that marshal had been directed to obey King Joseph's military instructions, the four new 'French' departments on the Ebro were now theoretically under the same general command as the rest of Spain. As to the Army of the North, Dorsenne wrote (April 19th), with evident glee, to say that he was exempted from obedience to the King, by not being included in the list of recipients of the dispatch of March 16, and that he regretted his inability to carry out a series of orders which Jourdan had sent him. But he had not many more days to serve in his present capacity, and his successor, Caffarelli, though equally recalcitrant in spirit, presently received a formal notice that he was under King Joseph's command.

Napoleon's general policy in placing the supreme control of all the Spanish armies in the hands of one chief, and bringing to an end (in theory at least) the system of separate viceroyalties was undoubtedly the right one.   And it cannot be disputed that one second-rate commander-in-chief is more effective than four good ones, working each for his own private and local profit and glory. But in this particular case the new arrangement was not likely to bring about any great change for the better, owing to the personal equation.   During the last three years Napoleon had been inflicting affronts at short intervals upon his brother, had annexed integral portions of his realm, had disregarded most of his complaints and suggestions, and had allowed him to become the butt of the viceroys, whose insults and injuries he had never been allowed to resent. They had raided the districts assigned to his personal governance[1], had plundered his magazines, imprisoned his officials, and set up courts of justice of their own to supersede the regular magistracy of the land. The Emperor had never punished such

---

[1] One of Marmont's colonels in the province of Segovia was at this moment threatening to use armed force against the King's troops for resisting his requisitions. See Miot, iii. p. 222.

proceedings ; at the most he had ordered that they should
cease, when they were injurious to the progress of the French
arms in Spain. It was useless to issue a sudden order that for
the future the marshals were under Joseph's control, and that
' he must make them obey him,' as the phrase ran in one letter
to Madrid. As the King's minister, Miot de Melito, wrote,
' What chance was there of success when all the individuals
concerned were at variance with each other ? The marshals
had been accustomed for three years to absolute independence.
The new Chief-of-the-Staff, in spite of his acknowledged capacity,
was known to be out of favour with the Emperor, and in
consequence could exercise no moral authority over the masters
of the armies. The apparent testimonial of confidence which
was given to the King, by making him Commander-in-Chief, was
a matter to cause disquietude rather than satisfaction[1].' The
plain fact was that Napoleon was over-busy, worried with other
problems, and he merely took the easiest and simplest method
of throwing the burden of the Spanish war on to the shoulders
of another. The consequences, be they what they might be,
were now of little importance, compared with the success or
failure of the impending Russian campaign.

Jourdan sums up the situation in much the same terms.
' The King for two years had been allowed to have no direct
relations with the generals-in-chief : he had no exact knowledge
of the military situation in each of their spheres of command,
nor was he better informed as to the strength, organization,
and distribution of the troops under their orders. Unable to
use his new authority till he had got together detailed statements as to these data, he directed his chief-of-the-staff to ask
for reports. Dorsenne replied that he should not send any at
present, because Berthier, when announcing to him that the
Armies of the South, of Portugal, and of Aragon had been put
under the King's orders, had informed him that the Emperor
would let him know in due course what was to be done with
the Army of the North. Marshal Suchet demonstrated that
he had received special instructions from the Emperor, which
presently were seen to make the King's authority over the
Army of Aragon quite illusory. Soult had removed all the

---

[1] See Miot de Melito's *Mémoires*, iii. p. 215.

posts on the lines of communication when he marched to relieve
Badajoz, and showed so little zeal in reopening them, that even
in May it was not known at Madrid whether he was yet aware
that he was under the King's orders. Marmont was the only
one who sent without delay the report which had been asked
for—but he announced at the same time that, in obedience to
the Emperor's earlier orders, he was already operating beyond
the Agueda, to make a diversion for the relief of Badajoz [1].'

Of what use was it to send orders to the marshals, when they
could plead that the execution of them was rendered impossible
by instructions received directly from the Emperor, which
prescribed a different policy ? Unfortunately for King Joseph
each commander-in-chief still preserved his direct communication with the Minister of War at Paris : even after the Emperor
had started for Poland in May, each continued to send in his
own plans, and to demonstrate how far superior they were to
those prescribed by King Joseph. Soult, in particular, generally
commenced a dispatch by demonstrating that the directions
received from Madrid could not possibly be executed, and then
produced an elaborate scheme of his own, which would be
beneficial for the Army of Andalusia, but impracticable for those
of Portugal, Valencia, and the Centre. When his suggestions
were rejected, he wrote privately to Paris, declaring that Joseph
and Jourdan were absolutely incapable, and sometimes adding
that the King was trying to serve his private interests rather
than those of his brother and suzerain. It was the accidental
receipt by Joseph of an intercepted letter of Soult's to the
Minister of War, in which he was accused of absolute treason
to the Emperor, that brought about the final rupture between
the King and the Marshal, and led to the recall of the latter to
France [2].

King Joseph, though liable to fits of depression and despair,
was, on the whole, of a mercurial and self-sufficient temperament.
A few weeks before the receipt of the Emperor's dispatch

---

[1] Jourdan's *Mémoires*, p. 384.

[2] Oddly enough this letter was in duplicate, and while one copy fell into
Joseph's hands, the other was captured by guerrilleros and sent to Welling-
ton. The cipher was worked out by Scovell, and the contents gave
Wellington useful information as to the relations between Soult and the
King. See below, pages 530–39.

granting him the command of the Spanish armies, all his letters had been full of complaints and threats of abdication. But the decree of March 16th filled him with a sudden confidence—at last his military talents should be displayed and recognized ; he would, as his brother desired, ' make the marshals obey him ; ' for the future the armies should all act together for a single end, and not be guided by the selfish interests of their leaders. He accepted the position of Commander-in-Chief with undisguised pleasure, and proceeded to draw out schemes of his own, with Jourdan as his adviser in technical matters of military logistics.

It cannot be denied that the ' *Mémoire* of May 1812 [1],' in which Jourdan set forth the situation after the fall of Badajoz, and the policy which he considered that it demanded, is a document of much greater merit than might have been expected. It is by far the best summary of the position of the French power in Spain that was ever drawn up, and it recognizes with great clearness the two main limitations of that power, which were (1) that the imperial troops were an army of occupation rather than a genuine field army, and (2) that the Napoleonic system, by which hosts were supposed to ' live on the country-side,' might be applicable for a short campaign in Lombardy or Bavaria, but was impossible for protracted manœuvres in an exhausted and thinly-peopled land like central Spain. Jourdan's note on the *Mémoire* sums up the situation in a few lines—' Two measures were indispensable : one wás to render the army mobile, by giving it ample transport, and by establishing large magazines on all lines of communication : without these all permanent concentration of heavy forces, and all continuous operations were impossible. The second was to abandon the deplorable system of occupying as much territory as possible—of which the real object was double : firstly, to enable the armies to live on the country-side ; secondly, to appear in the eyes of Europe to be dominant over the whole of Spain.'

The *Mémoire* itself is worth analysing. Its gist runs as follows :—

    ' (1) The recent departure of the Imperial Guards, the Poles,

[1] Printed whole in Jourdan's *Mémoires*, pp. 386–94.

and other troops, and the lack of any adequate system of transport or magazines, renders the Imperial Army—though still 230,000 men strong—incapable of undertaking any offensive operations. The present situation is exceptionally trying, because of the successes of Wellington, and the deplorable effect on Spanish public opinion of the recent annexation [Catalonia], the arbitrary government of the generals, and the famine which has lately prevailed. The discontent thereby engendered has led to the enormous increase in the number of the guerrillero bands. It has also encouraged the government at Cadiz to multiply its levies and its military energy.

(2) It is not yet certain whether the Emperor intends the Army of the North to be at the King's disposal. General Dorsenne refuses to send in reports or to accept orders. But since its recent reduction in numbers [by the departure of the Imperial Guard, and the transfer of Souham's and Bonnet's divisions to the Army of Portugal] it is believed that it has not more than 48,000 men under arms, and it appears to be a fact that it can do no more than hold down the wide regions committed to its charge, and guard the line of communications with France. Even if placed at the King's disposition, it can furnish no important reinforcements to other armies. Nevertheless it should be put under his control, as it might under certain circumstances be called upon to lend a moderate force for a short time.

(3) As to the Army of Aragon [60,000 men, including the divisions in Catalonia] : the King was informed that Marshal Suchet was placed under his command, and that if he needed reinforcements he might draw on the troops in Valencia. He therefore [during the siege of Badajoz] ordered the Marshal to send a division to join the Army of the Centre for an indispensable operation [1]. The Marshal sent a formal declaration in reply, to the effect that he could not execute this order, and that he was even about to withdraw from Cuenca the regiment that he had placed there, as its absence imperilled the safety of Valencia. He says that the Emperor has placed Catalonia under his charge, and that he is authorized to employ his

---

[1] i.e. for the collection of troops in the valley of the Tagus, to join Foy and operate for the relief of Badajoz.

whole force for the protection of the provinces entrusted to him. Apparently, then, the Army of Aragon cannot co-operate in operations outside its own sphere, and the Marshal's special instructions place him in an exceptional position. His relations with the King consist in a polite exchange of views, not in the giving and taking of orders—his Majesty's control over this army is purely illusory.

(4) As to the Army of the South, Marshal Soult has about 54,000 men effective [not including *Juramentados*, &c.]. The Cadiz Lines and the garrisons pin down a large force to fixed stations. The Marshal has also to keep a considerable flying column in hand, to hunt Ballasteros and other partisans. For operations outside the bounds of Andalusia he can only collect a field-force of 24,000 men ; this is the total figure of the corps that tried to relieve Badajoz, and in its absence Seville was nearly lost. The posts in the Sierra Morena were called in at that time, and have never come back : correspondence with the Army of the South is therefore precarious and slow.

(5) The Army of Portugal has 52,000 men effective. It holds the front line against Wellington ; its divisions are much scattered, because it has to live on the country, and has also to furnish several important garrisons. One division of 6,000 men is fixed down in the Asturias by the Emperor's special orders. The garrisons of Astorga, Valladolid, Salamanca, Leon, Palencia, &c., absorb 6,000 or 7,000 men more. Only 29,000 infantry [or a total of 35,000 of all arms] are available as a field-force to use against the English, if they attack on the front of the Tormes. If Marshal Marmont has to march out of his own sphere, to join in a combined operation against Wellington [e. g. in Estremadura], he can bring a still smaller force— say 25,000 men. The Army of Portugal is many months in arrear of its pay, and has hardly any transport or magazines : the troops have become terrible marauders—largely from necessity.

(6) Lastly we come to the Army of the Centre. It consists of 9,500 men borne on the Imperial muster-rolls, and 5,800 troops belonging to the King [his Guards and Hugo's *Juramentados*, horse and foot]. There are also at present in Madrid 3,200 drafts for the Army of the South, temporarily retained—so that the

whole makes up 18,500 men. But only 15,000 are effective, the remainder consisting of dépôts, dismounted cavalry, train, &c. Having to hold down the extensive provinces of Madrid, Segovia, Guadalajara, Toledo, La Mancha, and Cuenca, this force is a mere " army of occupation." It can provide no troops for expeditions outside its own territory, and is spread so thin that even Madrid would be in danger without the Royal Guards. The pay is eight months in arrear.

(7) Civil administration is still localized : the commanders of the armies levy their own taxes, and nothing comes to Madrid. The King has to feed the Army of the Centre, and to maintain his civil service, from the revenues of New Castile alone. None of the marshals will help another with money or stores. The claim of the King to rule all Spain seems absurd to the people, so long as he cannot exercise any civil control outside the *arrondissement* of the Army of the Centre.

(8) Conclusion. All offensive operations are impossible, as long as the imperial armies have to hold down the entirety of the occupied provinces. If Lord Wellington concentrates all his forces, he can march with 60,000 men [not including Spaniards] against either the Army of Portugal or the Army of the South. Neither of them can assemble a sufficient force to resist him, unless they abandon whole provinces. The King has ordered Soult and Marmont to march to each other's aid if either is attacked. But they have to unite, coming from remote bases, while the enemy can place himself between them and strike at one or the other. The lines of communication between them are long and circuitous. It is easily conceivable that one of them may be attacked and beaten before the other is even aware of the danger. A catastrophe is quite possible if Lord Wellington should throw himself suddenly, with his whole force, upon either the Army of Portugal or that of the South.

The only possible way of dealing with this danger is to collect a central reserve of 20,000 men at Madrid, which can be promptly transferred to right or left, to join either Soult or Marmont as the conditions of the moment dictate. The Army of the Centre cannot serve this purpose—it is not a field-force, but an immovable army of occupation. If the Emperor could send a new corps of this size from France, Marmont could be reinforced up to a strength sufficient to enable him to face Wellington, and to besiege Ciudad Rodrigo.

But the present posture of European affairs [the Russian war] probably makes it impossible to draw such a corps from France. This being so, the central reserve must be obtained from troops already existing in the Peninsula. The only way to find them is for the Emperor to consent to the evacuation of Andalusia. Thirty thousand men of the Army of the South can then be placed to cover Madrid, in La Mancha : this force would be ample against any Spanish levies that might come up to the Sierra Morena from Cadiz and elsewhere. The remainder of the Army of the South must form the central reserve, and prepare to reinforce Marmont. The Army of Portugal would then be so strong that Wellington could not dare to take the offensive—he would be hopelessly outnumbered. If this scheme is approved by the Emperor, he may be certain that, when he comes back from Poland, his Spanish armies will be in the same secure defensive position in which he leaves them now. The right wing rests on the Bay of Biscay in the Asturias : the left on the Mediterranean in Valencia.

When Andalusia is evacuated, the remaining provinces in French occupation will not be able to pay or feed the 54,000 men of the Army of the South, in addition to the armies already stationed in them ; a liberal subsidy from Paris will be necessary. In addition the King must, for the sake of his prestige, be given real civil authority over all the provinces.

It will only be when all authority, civil, military, and administrative, is concentrated in one hand, that of the King, and when His Majesty shall have received from the Emperor instructions suiting the present posture of affairs, that he can be fully responsible for Spain.'

On the whole this is a very well-reasoned document. It was perfectly true that the offensive power of the French in the Peninsula had shrunk to nothing, because no province could be held down without a large garrison. If left unoccupied, it would burst into revolt and raise an army. This was the inevitable nemesis for a war of annexation directed against a proud and patriotic people. There were 230,000 French troops in Spain ; but so many of them were tied down to occupation duty, that only about 50,000 or 60,000 could be collected to curb Wellington, unless some large province were evacuated. Either Andalusia or else Valencia must be abandoned. The former was the larger and the more wealthy; but it was more remote from the strategical centre of operations in Madrid, much more infested by the bands of the patriots, and it lay close to the sphere of operations of Wellington—the great disturbing element in French calculations. Moreover its evacuation would set free a much larger field army. Against this was to be set the adverse balance in loss of prestige : as long as Cadiz appeared to be beleaguered, the national government of Spain looked like a handful of refugees in a forlorn island. To abandon the immense lines in front of it, with their dependent flotilla (which must be burnt, since it could not be removed), would be a conclusive proof to all Europe that the main frontal offensive against the Spanish patriots had failed. Seville and Granada, great towns of world-wide fame, would also have to be abandoned. Andalusia was full of *Afrancesados*, who must either be shepherded to Madrid, or left to the vengeance of their countrymen.

But to weigh prestige against solid military advantage, though it might appeal to Napoleon—whose reputation as universal conqueror was part of his political stock-in-trade— did not occur to the common-sense intellect of Jourdan. He voted for the evacuation of Andalusia : so did his friend and master, King Joseph. Possibly their decision was not rendered more unwelcome by the fact that it would certainly be most distasteful to Soult, whom they both cordially detested. The Viceroy should pay at last for the selfish policy of the General: his realm, for the last two years, had been administered with much profit and glory to himself, but with little advantage to the King at Madrid, or the general prosperity of the French cause in Spain. Whether personal motives entered into the decision of Joseph and Jourdan we need not trouble to consider : it was certainly the correct one to take.

Permission to evacuate Andalusia was therefore demanded from the Emperor : King Joseph did not dare to authorize it on his own responsibility. Meanwhile, long before the *Mémoire* of May 1812 had been completed or sent off, to Napoleon, he issued the orders which he thought himself justified in giving in the interim, to act as a stop-gap till the permission should be granted. Marmont was told to fall back on his own old policy of keeping a large detachment in the Tagus valley, in order that he might get into touch with Drouet and Soult's Estremaduran corps of observation. He was directed to send two divisions of infantry and a brigade of light cavalry to join Foy, who was still in the direction of Almaraz and Talavera. They were to be ready to act as the advance of the Army of Portugal for a march on Truxillo and Merida, if Wellington's next move should turn out to be an attack on Soult in Andalusia. In a corresponding fashion, Soult was ordered to reinforce Drouet up to a force of 20,000 men, and to push him forward to his old position about Almendralejo, Zalamea, Merida, and Medellin, in order that he might march via Truxillo to join the Army of Portugal, in case the Anglo-Portuguese army should choose Salamanca, not Seville, as its next objective. The small part of the Army of the Centre that could be formed into a field-force—three battalions and two cavalry regiments, under General d'Armagnac—was directed to move to Talavera, to relieve Foy there if he should be called to move either north to join Marmont on the Tormes, or south to join Soult on the Guadiana [1]. To replace these troops, drawn from the provinces of Cuenca and La Mancha, Joseph—as we have already seen [2]—requested Suchet to send ' a good division ' from Valencia by Cuenca, on to Ocaña in La Mancha [3]. In this way the King and Jourdan thought they would provide for active co-operation between the Armies of Portugal and Andalusia, whether Wellington should make his next move to the South or the North.

It is curious, but perhaps not surprising, to find that these orders, the first-fruits of Joseph's new commission as Commander-in-Chief, were obeyed neither by Suchet, by Soult, nor by Marmont.

The former, as we have already seen, when analysing Jourdan's *Mémoire* of May 1812, not only refused to send a division

---

[1] See Jourdan to Berthier of April 3, 1812.
[2] See Jourdan's *Mémoire*, quoted above, p. 304.
[3] Jourdan to Suchet, April 9, 1812.

to Ocaña, but stated that he should be obliged to withdraw the regiment that he was keeping at Cuenca, because he was authorized by the Emperor to reserve all his own troops for the defence of his own sphere of action, in Valencia, Aragon, and Catalonia. Soult declared that it was impossible for him to reinforce Drouet—'he could not keep 20,000 men on the Guadiana unless he received large reinforcements : all that he could promise was that the force in Estremadura should move up again to Medellin and Villafranca, possibly even to Merida, if Wellington had really gone northward with his main army. Drouet, with his 10,000 or 12,000 men, might serve to " contain " Hill and the British detachment in Estremadura, and his position would prevent the enemy from making any important movement in the valley of the Tagus. Meanwhile he himself must, as an absolute necessity, lay siege to Tarifa for the second time, and make an end of Ballasteros: no more troops, therefore, could be sent to Drouet : but when Tarifa and Ballasteros had been finished off, the siege of Cadiz should be pressed with vigour.' This reply is not only a blank refusal to obey the King's orders, but amounts to a definite statement that the local affairs of Andalusia are more important than the general co-operation of the French armies in Spain. As we shall presently see, Soult was ready to formulate this startling thesis in the plainest terms—he was, ere long, to propose that the King and the Army of the Centre should evacuate Madrid and retire upon Andalusia, when things went wrong with the Army of Portugal.

As to Marmont, his reply to King Joseph's dispatch was couched in terms of less open disobedience, but it was by no means satisfactory. He wrote from Salamanca, on April 29th, after his return from the raid to Sabugal and Guarda, that he had now learnt (what he did not know ten days before), that Wellington had been pursuing him with five divisions. This force was still in the Beira, and the British general himself had been at Ciudad Rodrigo on the 26th. It was, therefore, quite clear that Soult had not ' the whole English army on his shoulders.' This being so, it was not necessary to send into the valley of the Tagus such a large force as was asked. But one division should move to Avila at once, and could drop down on to Talavera in two days, if it turned out to be necessary. Two more should be cantoned about Arevalo and the Pass of Piedrahita [20 miles north-west of Avila] respectively, points from which they could be transferred to the valley of the Tagus in a few days. Marmont then proceeded to warn Jourdan against any scheme for concentrating any considerable force in the direction of La Mancha, urging that he must be able to collect as many of his divisions opposite Wellington as possible, in case of an advance by the Anglo-Portuguese army towards the Tormes. All that was necessary on the Tagus was to have the forts at Almaraz well garrisoned and provided with stores, so that troops dropping down from Avila on a southward march should find a base and magazines ready for them. Summing up, he ends with a dictum that ' if we defend Andalusia by sacrificing the Army of Portugal, we may save that province for the moment, but the North will be in danger : if a disaster occurs there, Andalusia will soon be lost also. If, on the contrary, we make its defence in the North, the South may be lost, but the North still remains secure.' By these somewhat cryptic words, Marmont seems to mean that, looking at the affairs of Spain at large, Andalusia may be lost without any shock to the imperial domination in Leon and Old Castile. But a disaster in Leon or Old Castile entails inevitably the loss of Andalusia also. This was true enough, though Soult refused to see it.

But the result of Marmont's very partial fulfilment of Joseph's orders, and of Soult's and Suchet's entire neglect of them, was that Jourdan's main design of providing for close and speedy co-operation between the Armies of Portugal and Andalusia was completely foiled. When, on May 17th–19th, Hill made his celebrated irruption into the valley of the Tagus, with the object of destroying the bridge and forts of Almaraz, the point where the interests of Soult and Marmont were linked together, he found no French troops within fifty miles of his objective, save the single division of Foy and D'Armagnac's 3,000 men from the Army of the Centre. Marmont's nearest division in support was at Avila, Soult's in the Sierra Morena ; both lay so far off from Almaraz that Hill could not only deliver his blow, but could depart at leisure when it was struck, without any risk of being beset by superior forces. If King Joseph's orders of April had been carried out, Wellington's stroke in May would have been impossible—or risky to the verge of rashness. Indeed we may be certain, on Wellington's record, that he would not have made it, if three French divisions, instead of one, had been about Talavera and Almaraz. We may add that his self-reliance during the Salamanca campaign rested largely on the fact that Soult could not succour Marmont, within any reasonable space of time, even if he wished to do so, because the bridge of Almaraz was broken. Wherefore Jourdan and King Joseph must be pronounced to have been wise in their foresight, and the Dukes of Ragusa and Dalmatia highly blameworthy for their disregard of the orders given them. They looked each to their own local interests, not to the general strategic necessities of the French position in Spain, which the King and his Chief-of-the-Staff were keeping in mind.

So far their precautions were wise : to blame them for not taking the tremendous step of evacuating Andalusia without the Emperor's leave, and concentrating such a force in central Spain as would have paralysed Wellington's offensive, would be unjust. They dared not have given such an order—and if they had, Soult would have disobeyed it.

Napoleon himself, indeed, would have agreed with Soult at this time. For not long after Jourdan's *Mémoire* of May 1812, with its request for leave to abandon Andalusia, had started on its journey for Dresden, there arrived at Madrid a dispatch from Berthier, setting forth the final instructions left by the Emperor before he started from Paris on May 9th. It was of a nature to strike dismay into the heart of the level-headed and rather despondent Jourdan ; for it ignored all the difficulties which his recently dispatched appeal set forth with such clearness. The King was directed to keep a grip on all the conquered provinces of Spain, and to extend their limits till the enemy should be extirpated. The conquest of Portugal might be postponed till ' les événements détermineraient absolument cette mesure.' The region to which the Emperor devoted most attention was the sphere of the Army of the North. ' This is the part on which it is indispensable to keep a firm hold, never to allow the enemy to establish himself there, or to threaten the line of communications. Wherefore a most active war must be waged upon the "Brigands" [Mina, Porlier, Longa, &c.]: it is of no use to hunt and scatter them, leaving them power to reunite and to renew their incursions. As to the English, the present situation seems rather to require a defensive posture : but it is necessary to maintain an imposing attitude in face of them, so that they may not take any advantage of our position. The strength of the forces at the King's disposition enables him to do, in this respect, all that circumstances may demand. Such are the principal ideas which the Emperor, before departing, has expressed on the Spanish problem.'

This was a heart-breaking document. Just when the King and Jourdan had demonstrated that they had no available field army left to hold back Wellington, they were informed that their forces were ample for the purpose. When they had asked leave to evacuate Andalusia they are told to 'conserver les conquêtes et les étendre successivement.' They had been wishing to concentrate at all costs a central reserve—now they were directed to spread the already scattered army of occupation over a still greater surface—presumably the Emperor's phrase meant that he wished to see Murcia, the Catalonian inland, the whole of the Asturias, and the Condado de Niebla garrisoned, in addition to all that was held already. The one central problem to Joseph and Jourdan was how to face Wellington's expected onslaught by making the armies co-operate—the Emperor forbids concentration, and recommends ' the assumption of an imposing attitude ! ' As if Wellington, whose knowledge of the movements and plans of his adversaries was beginning to appear almost uncanny to them, was to be contained by ' attitudes,' imposing or otherwise.

The unhappy Commander-in-Chief and Chief-of-the-Staff of the united armies of Spain were reduced to a sort of apathetic despair by the Emperor's memorandum. Jourdan, in his *Mémoires*, appears to shrug the shoulders of resignation in commenting on its effect. ' If only instead of " hold all you have, and conquer the rest bit by bit," we had been told that we might evacuate some provinces and concentrate the troops, there would have been much good in the instructions. The King might have dared to abandon the South in order to keep down the North, if he had not received this dispatch. But he could not take that portentous step without the imperial permission. All that he could now do, was to reiterate his directions to Soult and Marmont that they must so place their troops as to be able to succour each other. We shall see how they obeyed those orders [1].'

So, by the special and deliberate directions of the Emperor, the 230,000 effective men ' present under arms,' forming the five imperial armies of Spain, were placed at the mercy of Lord Wellington and his modest force of eight divisions of Anglo-Portuguese. In a flight of angry rhetoric, Berthier, writing under Napoleon's dictation, had once asked whether it was reasonable ' *que quarante mille Anglais gâtent toutes les affaires d'Espagne.*' The reply of the fates was to be that such a contingency was perfectly possible, under the system which the Emperor had instituted, and with the directions which he persisted in giving.

[1] Jourdan's *Mémoires*, pp. 395–6.

SECTION XXXIII: CHAPTER II

THE BRIDGE OF ALMARAZ. MAY 1812

On April 24th Wellington halted his pursuing army at Fuente Guinaldo and Sabugal, on hearing that Marmont had escaped him by a margin of twenty-four hours. The French were in full march for Salamanca, and it was impossible to pursue them any further, firstly because the allied army needed a few days of rest after the forced march from Badajoz, and secondly because its train had dropped behind, food was nearly out, and convoys had to be brought up from Lamego and São João de Pesqueira. There was, of course, nothing to be got out of the unhappy region in which Marmont's locusts had just been spread abroad. The only fortunate thing was that the Duke of Ragusa had turned his raid against the Beira Baixa, and left the great dépôts on the Douro unmolested. From them ample sustenance could be got up, in a week, to the positions behind the Agueda and Coa where the army had halted.

Wellington, as it will be remembered, had contemplated an attack on Andalusia after Badajoz fell. But the necessity for seeing to the relief and revictualling of Almeida and Ciudad Rodrigo had brought him up to the frontiers of Leon with the main body of his host. In the position where he now lay, he was well placed for an advance on Salamanca, and an attack on the Army of Portugal. To return to Estremadura would involve a long and weary countermarch. Moreover there was no doubt that operations in Leon would be more decisive than operations in Andalusia. As Marmont was to write to Berthier a few days later, a victory of the allies in the North would involve the evacuation of the South by Soult, while a victory in Andalusia would leave the French power in the valleys of the Douro and Tagus unshaken [1]. Advancing from the line of the

---

[1] See above, p. 311.

Agueda against Salamanca and Valladolid, Wellington would have his base and his main line of communications in his direct rear, safe against any flank attack. A raid against Andalusia, even if successful, would separate him from Lisbon, and compel him to take up a new base at Cadiz—a doubtful expedient. But what seems, in the end, to have been the main cause for Wellington's choosing Leon rather than Andalusia as his next sphere of operations, was that Marmont (as he judged) had the larger available army for field movements outside his own ground. Soult was more pinned down to his viceroyalty by local needs : he would not raise the siege of Cadiz or evacuate Granada and Cordova. Therefore he could not collect (as his movement at the time of the fall of Badajoz had shown) more than 24,000 men for an offensive operation. This was the absolute limit of his power to aid Marmont. But the latter, if he chose to evacuate Asturias and other outlying regions, could bring a much larger force to help Soult. Therefore an attack on Andalusia would enable the enemy to concentrate a more numerous defensive force than an attack on Leon. ' Of the two armies opposed to us that of Portugal can produce the larger number of men for a distant operation. Marmont has nothing to attend to but the British army, as he has been repeatedly told in [intercepted] letters from Berthier. By abandoning Castille and Leon for a short time he may lose some plunder and contributions, but he loses nothing that can permanently affect his situation, or which he could not regain as soon as he has a superiority, particularly of cavalry, in the open plains of Castille. Marmont's, then, being what may be called of the two the *operating* army, the movement which I might make into Andalusia would enable the enemy to bring the largest body of men to act together on one point. It would be a false movement, and this must by all means be avoided [1].'

This decision was not made immediately on Marmont's retreat of April 24th : for some days after the British head-quarters settled down at Fuente Guinaldo, Wellington had not quite made up his mind between the two operations : his letters to Lord Liverpool, to Hill, and Graham, are full of the needs of the moment, and do not lay down any general strategical

[1] *Dispatches*, ix. p. 173.

plan. The staff, in their discussions with each other, canvassed the situation. ' While Marmont remains in Old Castile
he [Wellington] must leave a certain force near the frontier
of the Beira. But leaving the 3rd, 4th, 5th Divisions, and
Pack's and Bradford's Portuguese (perhaps 18,000 men) for
that purpose, he can move upon Andalusia, if he wishes, with
the 1st, 6th, 7th, and Light Divisions, afterwards picking up
Power's Portuguese brigade and all General Hill's *corps d'armée*
—perhaps 36,000 infantry. This would do.' So wrote D'Urban
the chief of the Portuguese staff in his private diary, on May 5,
evidently after discussion with Beresford, and others of those
who were nearest the centre of decision. Wellington, however,
was pondering over alternatives : he could not move for a week
or two at the best, for he had to replenish his stores at the front,
and to see that the repairs and revictualling of Almeida and
Rodrigo were completed, before he could start on any offensive
movement. In that time, too, he would be able to learn how
Marmont was disposing of his army, and whether Soult was
showing any tendency to reinforce Drouet's force in Estremadura.

It seems that an insight into his enemies' purposes was
made specially easy for Wellington at this moment by the
successive capture of a great deal of French correspondence.
When Marmont was in Portugal, between the 1st and 23rd of
April, three of the duplicates of his dispatches were captured,
one by Portuguese Ordenança, the others by Julian Sanchez
between Rodrigo and Salamanca [1]. They were all in cipher,
but the ingenuity of Captain Scovell, the cipher-secretary at
head-quarters, was capable of dealing with them, and from
them could be made out a great deal about the strength of the
Marshal's army, and his general views on the campaign. If
they had been taken and sent in a little earlier, they might have
enabled Wellington to complete that surprise and dispersion of
the French expeditionary force which had been in his mind.

[1] The cipher-originals are all in the Scovell papers, worked out into
their interpretation by that ingenious officer : Wellington only kept the
fair copies for himself. The dispatches are dated Sabugal, 11 April (to
Brennier about the Agueda bridge); Sabugal, April 16 (to Berthier); Fuente
Guinaldo, April 22 (to Berthier). The last two are full of the most acri-
monious criticism of Napoleon's orders for the invasion of Beira. Scovell
made out much, but not all, of the contents of these letters.

But though they arrived too late for this purpose, they were valuable, as showing Marmont's dislike of the imperial orders that he had been sent to carry out, and his preference for his own schemes. They were also full of bitter complaints of the neglect in which the Army of Portugal was left as to pay, stores, and transport. Wellington might reasonably deduce from them that any reconcentration of that army would be slow, and that if it had to march to reinforce Soult in the South, the effort would be a severe one.

But shortly after Marmont's return to Salamanca, his adversary got an even more valuable insight into his plans. The guerrilleros carried off, between Salamanca and Valladolid, an officer bearing five dispatches, dated April 28 and April 30th. One was directed to Dorsenne, two to Berthier, one to Jourdan, the fifth contained the parole to Bayonne of the great scout, Colquhoun Grant [1]. The first, couched in very peremptory terms, asked for food—the Army of Portugal must absolutely receive 8,000 quintals of wheat, once promised, without delay— it was in a state of danger and penury, and could not keep concentrated to face the British. Of the letters to Berthier one announced that Bonnet's division was duly in march for the Asturias, and that without it the Marshal thought his own strength dangerously low. The other asked for 4,000,000 francs owing to the Army of Portugal for pay and sustenance, and declared that, unless money came to hand at once, it was impossible to see how the troops were to be kept alive in the two months still remaining before harvest. A postscript asked for a siege-train to be sent on at all costs—the Marshal had heard that one was on the way from Bayonne : but nothing was known about it at Burgos. The letter to Jourdan was the most important of all [2] : it was the document, already quoted in the previous chapter, in which the Marshal detailed his intentions as to the dispersion of his army, protested against being obliged to send too many men into the valley of the Tagus, and explained the importance of the bridge-forts and magazines at Almaraz, by which his troops at Avila, &c., would

---

[1] All the originals are in the Scovell Papers.

[2] It is the one printed in Ducasse's *Correspondence of King Joseph*, viii. pp. 413–17.

debouch southward whenever they were ordered to concentrate for a junction with Soult. ' On ne peut agir que par Lugar Nuevo [the name by which Marmont always designates the Almaraz forts] . . . il faut bien se garder de jeter trop de troupes sur le Tage, et se contenter de bien assurer une défense de huit jours pour les forts de Lugar Nuevo et Mirabete, temps suffisant pour que les troupes rassemblées à Avila débouchent. . . . Un dépôt de 400 à 500 mille fanegas (qui n'est pas au delà de ce que Madrid et La Manche peuvent fournir) donnerait les moyens d'agir sans compromettre la subsistance des troupes.'

Undoubtedly it was the deciphering of the greater part of this letter, which set forth so clearly the importance of the Almaraz bridge, and showed at the same time that only one French division [Foy's at Talavera] was anywhere near it, that determined Wellington to make the sudden stroke at that central strategical point which he had thought of in February [1]. At that time he had refused to try it, because there were three French divisions on the Tagus. Now there was only one at Talavera, two marches from Almaraz, and the nearest reinforcements at Avila were two very long marches from Talavera. The possibility presented itself that a column might strike at Almaraz from somewhere on the Portuguese frontier, and take the place by a *coup-de-main*, with or without first beating Foy, whose strength of 5,000 men was perfectly known to Wellington.

Hill could count on two or three days of undisturbed operations before the nearest reinforcing division, that of Foy, could reach Almaraz: on four or five more, before troops from Avila could come up. It must be noted that everything would depend on the absolute secrecy that could be preserved as to the start of the expedition: but on this Wellington thought that he could count. The Spanish peasantry seldom or never betrayed him: the French had no outlying posts beyond Almaraz which might give them warning. The garrison was in a normal state of blockade by guerrillero bands haunting the Sierra de Guadalupe.

It may be added that a blow at Almaraz was just as useful as a means for keeping Soult from joining Marmont as Marmont from joining Soult. It would be profitable

[1] See above, p. 202.

if Wellington's final decision should be given in favour
of an Andalusian expedition.   But his mind was by now
leaning towards an attack on Leon rather than on the South.
The final inclination may have been given by the receipt of
another intercepted dispatch—Soult's to Jourdan of April 17[1],
sent in by guerrilleros who had probably captured the bearer
in the Sierra Morena about April 20th.   This document, which
we have already had occasion to quote for another purpose[2],
was full of angry denunciations of Marmont for letting Badajoz
fall unaided, and served to show that, if Soult had to help the
Army of Portugal, he would do so with no good will to its
commander.   Moreover it was largely occupied by proposals
for the circumventing of Ballasteros and the siege of Tarifa—
movements which would disperse the Army of the South even
more than it was already dispersed, and would clearly prevent it
from succouring Marmont within any reasonable space of time.

The decision that Hill should make his long-deferred *coup-
de-main* upon Almaraz first appears in Wellington's dispatches
on May 4th[3], but Hill had been warned that the operation was
likely to be sanctioned some days earlier, on April 24, and again
more definitely on April 30th[4].   That the final judgement of
Wellington was now leaning in favour of the advance on
Salamanca rather than the Andalusian raid appears to emerge
from a note of D'Urban dated May 6th—' The retirement of
Marmont within a given distance—the slow progress of the
Spaniards at Rodrigo, which renders it unsafe to leave that
place and this frontier—the retiring altogether of Soult, and
the state of his army not making him dangerous now—these
and other combining reasons determine Lord Wellington to
make his offensive operation *north* of the Tagus, and to
move upon Marmont. All necessary preparations making, but
secretly : it will be very feasible to keep the movement unforeseen till it begins.   Meanwhile General Hill is to move upon
and destroy everything at Almaraz[5].'

---

[1] Original in the Scovell Papers. Place of capture uncertain, but clearly
taken by guerrilleros between Seville and Madrid.

[2] See above, pp. 269–70.

[3] Wellington to Graham, Fuente Guinaldo, May 4, *Dispatches*, ix. p. 114.

[4] Ibid., p. 101.   [5] D'Urban's unpublished diary, under May 6.

The orders for Hill's move were given out on May 7th. He was to march from his head-quarters at Almendralejo with two British brigades (Howard's and Wilson's) of the 2nd Division, and the Portuguese brigade attached to the division (Ashworth's), one British cavalry regiment (13th Light Dragoons), and to cross the Guadiana at Merida. Beyond the Guadiana he would pick up Campbell's Portuguese cavalry brigade, which was lying at Arroyo dos Molinos. The march was then to be as rapid as possible, via Jaraicejo and Miravete. The expeditionary force made up 7,000 men in all.

There were left in Estremadura to 'contain' Drouet the two English cavalry brigades of Hill's force (Slade's and Long's)[1], one British infantry brigade (Byng's) of the 2nd Division, Hamilton's Portuguese division, and Power's unattached Portuguese brigade (late the garrison of Elvas, and more recently acting as that of Badajoz). The whole would make up 11,000 men. Power, or at least some of his regiments, was now disposable, because the Spaniards destined to hold Badajoz had begun to arrive, and more were daily expected [2].

But this was not the only precaution taken against Drouet, who had recently been reported as a little inclined to move northward from Fuente Ovejuna—detachments of his cavalry had been seen as far north as Zalamea [3]. Wellington determined to move down towards the Guadiana the southern or right wing of his main army—the 1st and 6th Divisions under Graham. First one and then the other were filed across the bridge of Villa Velha and sent to Portalegre. Here they would be in a position to support the force left in front of Drouet, if Soult should unexpectedly reinforce his Estremaduran corps. Wellington acknowledged that he disliked this wide extension of his army, but justified himself by observing that, if he had now his left wing almost touching the Douro, and his right wing almost touching the Sierra Morena, he might risk the situation, because he was fully informed as to Marmont's similar dispersion. The Army of Portugal was scattered from the Asturias to

[1] Minus, of course, the 13th Light Dragoons.
[2] Erskine was the senior officer left with the corps—a dangerous experiment. One marvels that Wellington risked it after previous experience.
[3] Wellington to Graham, May 7, *Dispatches*, ix. p. 128.

Talavera, and from its want of magazines and transport, which Marmont's intercepted dispatches made evident, would be unable to concentrate as quickly as he himself could.

The movement of Graham's two divisions from the Castello Branco region to south of the Tagus had an additional advantage. If reported to the French it would tend to make them believe that the next offensive operation of the allied army would be in the direction of Andalusia, not towards the Tormes. If Soult heard of it, he would begin to prepare to defend his own borders, and would not dream that Marmont was really the enemy at whom Wellington was about to strike; while Marmont, on the other hand, thinking that Soult was to be the object of Wellington's attentions, might be less careful of his own front. The expedition to Almaraz would not undeceive either of them, since it was well suited for a preliminary move in an attack on Andalusia, no less than for one directed against Leon.

Hill's column reached Merida on May 12th, but was delayed there for some hours, because the bridge, broken in April, had not yet been repaired, as had been expected, the officers sent there having contented themselves with organizing a service of boats for the passage. The bridge was hastily finished, but the troops only passed late in the day; they picked up in the town the artillery and engineers told off for the expedition, Glubb's British and Arriaga's Portuguese companies of artillery, who brought with them six 24-pounder howitzers, a pontoon train, and wagons carrying some 30-foot ladders for escalading work. The importance attached to the raid by Wellington is shown by the fact that he placed Alexander Dickson, his most trusted artillery officer, in charge of this trifling detachment, which came up by the road north of the Guadiana by Badajoz and Montijo to join the main column.

Once over the Guadiana, Hill reached Truxillo in three rapid marches [May 15], and there left all his baggage-train, save one mule for each company with the camp-kettles. The most difficult part of the route had now been reached, three successive mountain ranges separating Truxillo from the Tagus. On the 16th, having crossed the first of them, the column reached Jaraicejo : at dawn on the 17th, having made a night march, it was nearing the Pass of Miravete, the last defile above the river. Here, as Hill was aware, the French had outlying works, an old castle and two small forts, on very commanding ground, overlooking the whole defile in such a way that guns and wagons could not possibly pass them. The British general's original intention was to storm the Miravete works at dawn, on the 17th, and at the same time to attack with a separate column the forts at the bridge. With this purpose he divided his troops into three detachments. Ashworth's Portuguese and the artillery were to keep to the *chaussée*, and make a demonstration of frontal attack on the Castle: General Tilson-Chowne [interim commander of the 2nd Division at the moment [1]] was, with Wilson's brigade and the 6th Caçadores, to make a détour in the hills to the left and to endeavour to storm the Castle from its rear side. General Howard, with the other British brigade, was to follow a similar bridle path to the right, and to descend on to the river and attack the forts by the bridge.

A miscalculation had been made—the by-paths which the flanking columns were to take proved so far more steep and difficult than had been expected, that by dawn neither of them had got anywhere near its destination. Hill ordered them to halt, and put off the assault. This was fortunate, for by a long and close reconnaissance in daylight it was recognized that the Castle of Miravete and its dependent outworks, Forts Colbert and Senarmont, were so placed on a precipitous conical hill that they appeared impregnable save by regular siege operations, for which the expeditionary force had no time to spare. The most vexatious thing was that the garrison had discovered the main column on the *chaussée*, and it could not be doubted that intelligence must have been sent down to the lower forts, and most certainly to Foy at Talavera also. After a thorough inspection of the ground, Hill concluded that he could not hope to master Miravete, and, while it was held against him, his guns could not get through the pass which it so effectively commanded. It remained to be seen what could be done with the forts at the bridge.

The Almaraz forts crowned two hills on each side of the

---

[1] This was the Tilson of 1809 : he had lengthened his name.

Tagus. The stronger, Fort Napoleon, occupied the end of a long
rising ground, about 100 yards from the water's edge; below
it, and connecting with it, was a masonry *tête-de-pont* covering
the end of the pontoon-bridge. The weaker work, Fort Ragusa,
was on an isolated knoll on the north bank, supporting the
other end of the bridge. Fort Napoleon mounted nine guns,
had a good but unpalisaded ditch around its bastioned front,
and a second retrenchment, well palisaded, with a loopholed
stone tower within. Fort Ragusa was an oblong earthwork.
mounting six guns, and also provided with a central tower.
It had as outwork a *flèche* or lunette, commanding the north
end of the bridge. The small *tête-de-pont* mounted three guns
more. Half a mile up-stream was the ruined masonry bridge
which had formed the old crossing, with the village of Almaraz
on the north bank behind it. Between the *éte-de-pont* and
the old bridge were the magazines and storehouses in the
village of Lugar Nuevo.

The garrison of the works consisted of a depleted foreign
corps, the *régiment de Prusse* or 4th Étranger, mustering under
400 bayonets, of a battalion of the French 39th of the Line,
and of two companies of the 6th Léger, from Foy's division,
with a company of artillery and another of sappers. The
whole may have amounted to 1,000 men, of whom 300 were
isolated in the high-lying Castle of Miravete, five miles from
the bridge-head. The governor, a Piedmontese officer named
Aubert, had manned Fort Napoleon with two companies of
the 6th and 39th. The foreign corps and one company of the
6th were in Fort Ragusa and the bridge-head; Miravete was
held by the centre companies of the 39th.

Though delay after the French had got the alarm was
dangerous, Hill spent the whole of the 17th in making fruitless
explorations for vantage-ground, from which Miravete might
be attacked. None was found, and on the 18th he made up his
mind to adopt a scheme hazardous beyond his original intention. It would be possible to mask the Castle by a false attack,
in which all his artillery should join, and to lead part of his
infantry over the hills to the right, by a gorge called the Pass
of La Cueva, for a direct attack by escalade, without the help
of guns, upon the Almaraz forts.

The detachment selected for this purpose was Howard's brigade (1/50th, 1/71st, 1/92nd), strengthened by the 6th Portuguese Line from Ashworth's brigade, and accompanied by 20 artillerymen in charge of the ladders. So rough was the ground to be covered, that the long 30-foot ladders had to be sawn in two, being unwieldy on slopes and angles, as was soon discovered when they were taken off the carts for carriage by hand. The route that had to be followed was very circuitous, and though the forts were only five miles, as the crow flies, from the place where the column left the road, it took the whole night to reach them. An eye-witness [1] describes it as a mazy sheep-walk among high brushwood, which could not have been used without the help of the experienced peasant-guide who led the march. The men had to pass in Indian file over many of its stretches, and it resulted from long walking in the darkness that the rear dropped far behind the van, and nearly lost touch with it. Just before dawn the column reached the hamlet of Romangordo, a mile from the forts, and rested there for some time before resuming its march.

The sun was well up when, at 6 o'clock, the leading company, coming to the edge of a thicket, suddenly saw Fort Napoleon only 300 yards in their front. The French had been warned that a column had crossed the hills, and had caught some glimpse of it, but had lost sight of its latest move : many of the garrison could be seen standing on the ramparts, and watching the puffs of smoke round the Castle of Miravete, which showed that the false attack on that high-lying stronghold had begun. General Tilson-Chowne was making a noisy demonstration before it, using his artillery with much ostentation, and pushing up skirmishers among the boulders on the sides of the castle-hill [2].

Hill was anxious to assault at once, before the sun should rise higher, or the garrison of the forts catch sight of him. But some time had to be spent to allow a sufficient force to accumulate in the cover where the head of the column was hiding. So

---

[1] Captain MacCarthy of the 50th.

[2] The statement in Jones's *Sieges*, i. p. 259, that the enemy were unaware of the turning column is disproved by the official reports of the surviving French officers Sève and Teppe.

slowly did the companies straggle in, that the General at last resolved to escalade at once with the 50th and the right wing of the 71st, all that had yet come up. Orders were left behind that the left wing of the 71st and the 92nd should attack the bridge-head entrenchment when they arrived, and the 6th Portuguese support where they were needed.

At a little after 6 o'clock the 900 men available, in three columns of a half-battalion each, headed by ladder parties, started up out of the brake on the crest of the hillside nearest Fort Napoleon, and raced for three separate points of its *enceinte*. The French, though taken by surprise, had all their preparations ready, and a furious fire broke out upon the stormers both from cannon and musketry. Nevertheless all three parties reached the goal without any very overwhelming losses, jumped into the ditch, and began to apply their ladders to such points of the rampart as lay nearest to them. The assault was a very daring one—the work was intact, the garrison adequate in numbers, the assailants had no advantage from darkness, for the sun was well up and every man was visible. All that was in their favour was the suddenness of their onslaught, the number of separate points at which it was launched, and their own splendid dash and decision. Many men fell in the first few minutes, and there was a check when it was discovered that the ladders were over-short, owing to their having been sawn up before the start. But the rampart had a rather broad berm [1], a fault of construction, and the stormers, discovering this, climbed up on it, and dragging some of the ladders with them, relaid them against the upper section of the defences, which they easily overtopped. By this unexpected device a footing was established on the ramparts at several points simultaneously—Captain Candler of the 50th is said to have been the first man over the parapet : he was pierced by several balls as he sprang down, and fell dead inside. The garrison had kept up a furious fire till the moment when they saw the

[1] The berm is the line where the scarp of the ditch meets the slope of the rampart : the scarp should be perpendicular, the rampart-slope tends backward, hence there is a change on this line from the vertical to the obtuse in the profile of the work. The berm should have been only a foot or so wide and was three.

assailants swarm over the parapet—then, however, there can
be no doubt that most of them flinched [1] : the governor tried
to lead a counter-charge, but found few to follow him ; he was
surrounded, and, refusing to surrender and striking at those
who bade him yield, was piked by a sergeant of the 50th and
mortally wounded. So closely were the British and French
mixed that the latter got no chance of manning the inner work, or
the loopholed tower which should have served as their rallying-
point. Many of the garrison threw down their arms, but the
majority rushed out of the rear gate of the fort towards the
neighbouring redoubt at the bridge-head. They were so closely
followed that pursuers and pursued went in a mixed mass into
that work, whose gunners were unable to fire because their
balls would have gone straight into their own flying friends.
The foreign garrison of the *tête-de-pont* made little attempt to
resist, and fled over the bridge [2]. It is probable that the British
would have reached the other side along with them if the
centre pontoons had not been sunk : some say that they were
struck by a round-shot from Fort Ragusa, which had opened
a fire upon the lost works ; others declare that some of the
fugitives broke them, whether by design or by mischance of
overcrowding [3].

This ought to have been the end of Hill's sudden success,
since passage across the Tagus was now denied him. But the
enemy were panic-stricken ; and when the guns of Fort
Napoleon were trained upon Fort Ragusa by Lieutenant Love
and the twenty gunners who had accompanied Hill's column,
the garrison evacuated it, and went off with the rest of the
fugitives in a disorderly flight towards Naval Moral. The
formidable works of Almaraz had fallen before the assault of

---

[1] The official report of the French captain, Sêve of the 6th Léger, accuses
the grenadiers of the 39th of giving way and bolting at the critical moment,
and this is confirmed by the report of the *chef de bataillon* Teppe of the
39th, an unwilling witness.

[2] According to Teppe's narrative they left the walls, and many hid in
the bakehouses, while most of the officers headed the rush for the bridge.

[3] Foy says that the centre link of the bridge was not a regular pontoon
but a river boat, which could be drawn out when the garrison wanted to
open the bridge for any purpose, and being light it collapsed under the
feet of the flying crowd (p. 163).

900 men—for the tail of Hill's column arrived on the scene to find all over [1]. Four grenadiers of the 92nd, wishing to do something if they had been disappointed of the expected day's work, stripped, swam the river, and brought back several boats which had been left moored under Fort Ragusa. By means of these communication between the two banks was re-established, and the fort beyond the river was occupied [2].

The loss of the victors was very moderate—it fell mostly on the 50th and 71st, for Chowne's demonstration against Miravete had been almost bloodless—only one ensign and one private of the 6th Caçadores were wounded. But the 50th lost one captain and 26 men killed, and seven officers and 93 men wounded, while the half-battalion of the 71st had five killed and five officers and 47 men wounded [3]. The 92nd had two wounded. Thus the total of casualties was 189.

Of the garrison the 4th Étranger was pretty well destroyed— those who were neither killed nor taken mostly deserted, and its numbers had gone down from 366 in the return of May 15 to 88 in that of July 1. The companies of the 39th and 6th Léger also suffered heavily, since they had furnished the whole of the unlucky garrison of Fort Napoleon. Hill reports 17 officers and 262 men taken prisoners, including the mortally wounded governor and a *chef de bataillon* of the 39th [4]. It is probable that the whole loss of the French was at least 400.

The trophies taken consisted of a colour of the 4th Étranger, 18 guns mounted in the works, an immense store of powder and round-shot, 120,000 musket cartridges, the 20 large pontoons forming the bridge, with a store of rope, timbers, anchors, carriages, &c., kept for its repair, some well-furnished workshops,

[1] The 92nd and the right wing of the 71st reached the *tête-de-pont* just as the fugitives from Fort Napoleon entered it, and swept away the garrison. They only lost two wounded.

[2] Gardyne's history of the 92nd gives the names of two of these gallant men, Gauld and Somerville.

[3] Hill's total of casualties is 2 officers and 31 men killed: 13 officers and 143 wounded. The second officer killed was Lieutenant Thiele of the Artillery of the K.G.L., accidentally blown up by a mine on the day of the evacuation. But two of the wounded officers died.

[4] Teppe by name, whose narrative, written in captivity, is our best source for the French side. It is a frank confession of misbehaviour by the troops—particularly the 4th Étranger.

and a large miscellaneous magazine of food and other stores. All this was destroyed, the pontoons, &c., being burnt, while the powder was used to lay many mines in the forts and bridge-head, which were blown up very successfully on the morning of the 20th, so that hardly a trace of them remained. Thiele of the German artillery, the officer charged with carrying out the explosions, was unfortunately killed by accident : a mine had apparently failed ; he went back to see to its match, but it blew up just as he was inspecting it.

Having accomplished his purpose with complete success, Hill moved off without delay, and by two forced marches reached Truxillo and his baggage on the 21st. Here he was quite safe : Foy, being too weak to pursue him to any effect, followed cautiously, and only reached Miravete (whose garrison he relieved) on the 23rd and Truxillo on the 25th, from whence he turned back, being altogether too late. He had received news of Hill's movement rather late on the 17th, had been misin-formed as to his strength, which report made 15,000 men instead of the real 7,000, and so had been disposed to act cautiously. He had ordered a battalion of the 6th Léger from Naval Moral to join the garrison of Almaraz, but it arrived on the afternoon of the 19th, only in time to hear from fugitives of the disaster [1]. He himself was confident that the forts could hold out eight days even against artillery, which was also Marmont's calculation. Hence their fall within 48 hours of Hill's appearance was a distressing surprise : Foy had calcu-lated on being helped not only by D'Armagnac from Talavera but by the division of Clausel from Avila, before moving to fight Hill and relieve them.

Wellington appears to have been under the impression that this expedition, which Hill had executed with such admirable celerity and dispatch, might have been made even more decisive, by the capture of the castle of Miravete, if untoward circumstances had not intervened. In a letter to Lord Liver-pool, written on May 28 [2], he expresses the opinion that Tilson-Chowne might have taken it on the night of the 16th—which

---

[1] D'Armagnac also sent the battalion of Frankfort for the same purpose, which arrived late with less excuse. See Foy, p. 375.

[2] *Dispatches*, ix. p. 189.

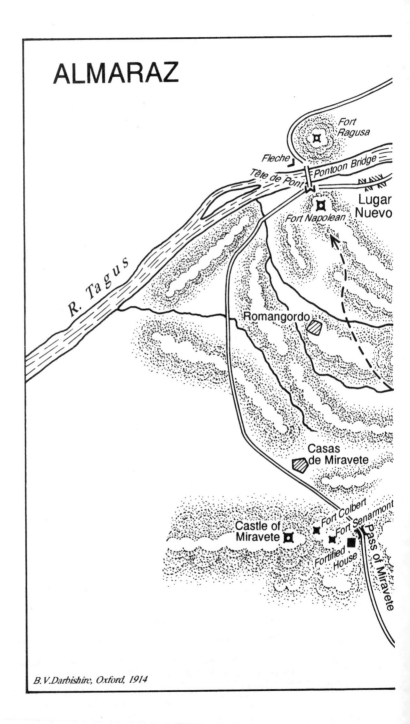

ALMARAZ

Fort Ragusa

Fleche

Tête de Pont

Pontoon Bridge

Fort Napolean

Lugar Nuevo

R. Tagus

Romangordo

Casas de Miravete

Fort Colbert

Fort Senarmont

Castle of Miravete

Fortified House

Pass of Miravete

B.V.Darbishire, Oxford, 1914

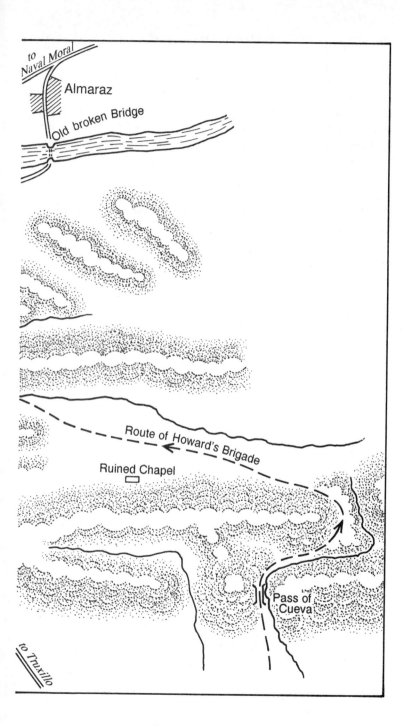

to Naval Moral

Almaraz

Old broken Bridge

Route of Howard's Brigade

Ruined Chapel

Pass of Cueva

to Truxillo

must appear a hazardous decision to those who look at the precipitous position of the place and the strength of its defences. He also says that Hill might have stopped at Almaraz for a few days more, and have bombarded Miravete with Dickson's heavy howitzers, if he had not received false news from Sir William Erskine as to Drouet's movements in Estremadura. There can be no doubt, as we shall see, about the false intelligence : but whether the bombardment would have been successful is another thing. Probably Wellington considered that the garrison would have been demoralized after what had happened at Almaraz.

As to Drouet's movements, having received rather tardy notice of Hill's northward march from Merida, he had resolved to make a push to ascertain what was left in his front. Lallemand's dragoons, therefore, pressed out in the direction of Zafra, where they came into contact with Slade's outposts and drove them in. At the same time Drouet himself, with an infantry division and some light cavalry, advanced as far as Don Benito, near Medellin, on the 17th May, from whence he pushed patrols across the Guadiana as far as Miajadas. This movement, made to ascertain whether Hill had departed with his whole corps, or whether a large force had been left in Estremadura, was reported to Sir William Erskine, the commander of the 2nd cavalry division, along with rumours that Soult was across the Sierra Morena and closely supporting Drouet. Erskine sent on the news to Graham at Portalegre, and to Hill, who was then before Miravete, with assertions that Soult was certainly approaching. This, as Wellington knew, was unlikely, for the Marshal had been before Cadiz on the 11th, and could not possibly have crossed the Sierra Morena by the 17th. As a matter of fact he only learnt on the 19th, at Chiclana, that Hill had started, and Drouet's move was made purely to gain information and on his own responsibility. But Graham, naturally unaware of this, brought up his two divisions to Badajoz, as he had been directed to do if Estremadura were attacked during Hill's absence. And Hill himself was certainly induced to return promptly from Almaraz by Erskine's letter, though it is doubtful whether he would have lingered to besiege Miravete even if he had not received it. For Foy might have been reinforced by D'Armagnac and the Avila division up to a strength which would have made Hill's longer stay on the Tagus undesirable.

Drouet did no more ; indeed, with his own force he was quite helpless against Hill, since when he discovered that there was a large body of allied troops left in Estremadura, and that more were coming up, it would have been mad for him to move on Merida, or take any other method of molesting the return of the expedition from Almaraz. Though Soult spoke of coming with a division to his aid, the succours must be many days on the way, while he himself could only act effectively by marching northward at once. But if he had taken his own division he would have been helpless against Hill, who could have beaten such a force ; while if he had crossed the Guadiana with his whole 12,000 men, he would have been cut off from Soult by the ' uncontained ' allied force left in Estremadura, which he knew to be considerable.

But to move upon Almaraz on his own responsibility, and without Soult's orders, would have been beyond Drouet's power: he was a man under authority, who dared not take such a step. And when Soult's dispatches reached him, they directed him not to lose touch with Andalusia, but to demonstrate enough to bring Hill back. The Marshal did not intend to let Drouet get out of touch with him, by bidding him march toward the Tagus.

Hill's column, then, was never in any danger. But Wellington, who had for a moment some anxiety in his behalf, was deeply vexed by Erskine's false intelligence, which had given rise to that feeling, and wrote in wrath to Henry Wellesley and Graham [1] concerning the mischief that this very incapable officer had done. He was particularly chagrined that Graham had been drawn down to Badajoz by the needless alarm, as he was intending to bring him back to join the main army within a short time, and the movement to Badajoz had removed him three marches from Portalegre, so that six days in all would be wasted in bringing him back to his original starting-point. It is curious that Wellington did not harden his heart to get rid of Erskine

---

[1] To both on June 1. *Dispatches*, ix. p. 197. Erskine's name is the blank to be filled up.

after this mishap : but though he wrote bitterly about his subordinate's incapacity, he did not remove him. ' Influence ' at home was apparently the key to his long endurance : it will be remembered that this was by no means the first of Erskine's mistakes [1].

The fall of the Almaraz forts, as might have been expected, was interpreted by Marmont and Soult each from his own point of view. The former, rightly as it turned out, wrote to Foy that he must be prepared to return to Leon at short notice, and that the Army of the Centre and Drouet must guard the valley of the Tagus on his departure [2]. Soult, on the other hand, having heard of Graham's arrival at Badajoz and Hill's return to Merida, argued that the allies were massing on the Guadiana for an advance into Andalusia. He made bitter complaints to Jourdan that he had violated the rules of military subordination by sending a letter to Drouet warning him that he might be called up to the Tagus. It was unheard of, he said, to communicate directly with a subordinate, who ought to be written to only through the channel of his immediate superior. He even threatened to resign the command of the Army of the South [3]—but when Joseph showed no signs of being terrified by this menace, no more was heard of it. The viceroyalty of Andalusia was not a thing to be lightly given up.

It soon became evident to Wellington that the surprise of Almaraz was not to be resented by the enemy in any practical form. Foy was not reinforced, nor was Drouet brought up to the Tagus : it was clear that the French were too weak to take the offensive either in the North or the South, even under such provocation. They could not even rebuild the lost bridge : the transport from Madrid of a new pontoon train as a substitute for the lost boats was beyond King Joseph's power. One or two boats were finally got to Almaraz—but nothing that could serve as a bridge. Nor were the lost magazines ever replaced.

It was at this same time that Wellington took in hand a scheme for facilitating his communications north and south, which was to have a high strategical importance. As long as Ciudad Rodrigo and Badajoz were in the enemy's hands, the

[1] See vol. iv. pp. 133 and 191.   [2] Marmont to Foy, June 1.
[3] See Jourdan's *Mémoires*, pp. 399–400.

most eastern crossing of the Tagus practicable for the Anglo-
Portuguese army was the boat-bridge of Villa Velha. But when
these two fortresses were regained, it was possible to open up
a line farther east, which had not been available for two years.
Since Mayne blew up the ancient Roman bridge of Alcantara in
June 1809[1], the Middle Tagus had been impassable for both sides.
The allies had usually been in possession of both banks of the
Tagus in this direction, but so intermittently that it had never
been worth their while to restore the passage, which would
have been lost to them whenever the French (as not unfrequently happened) extended their operations into the Coria–
Zarza Mayor country on the north bank, or the Caçeres–Albuquerque country on the other. But when the enemy had lost
both Badajoz and Rodrigo, and had no posts nearer to Alcantara
than the Upper Tormes, the forts of Miravete, and Zalamea,
when, moreover, he had adopted a distinctly defensive attitude
for many months, Wellington thought it worth while to recover
possession of a passage which would shorten the route from
Estremadura to the frontiers of Leon by a hundred miles, and
would therefore give him an advantage of six marches over
the enemy in transferring troops from north to south. Whether
Almaraz were again seized and reoccupied by the French
mattered little : the restoration of Alcantara would be safe and
profitable.

Accordingly, on May 24th, Colonel Sturgeon[2] and Major
Todd of the Royal Staff Corps were sent to Alcantara to report
on the practicability of restoring the broken arch, which,
owing to the immense depth of the cañon of the Tagus, overhung
the river by no less than 140 feet. It was intended that if the
engineering problem should prove too hard, a flying bridge of
rafts, boats, or pontoons should be established at the water
level[3]. But Sturgeon and Todd did more than Wellington
had expected, and succeeded in a very few days in establishing
a sort of suspension-bridge of ropes between the two shattered

[1] See vol. ii. p. 444.

[2] An officer probably better remembered by the general reader as the
husband of Sarah Curran, Robert Emmet's sometime fiancée, than as the
executor of some of Wellington's most important engineering works. He
fell before Bayonne in 1814.

[3] See Wellington to Graham, 23rd and 24th May. *Dispatches*, ix. pp. 163–5.

piers of Trajan's great structure. The system adopted was that of placing at each end of the broken roadway a very large and solid beam, clamped to the Roman stones, by being sunk in channels cut in them. These beams being made absolutely adhesive to the original work, served as solid bases from which a series of eighteen cables were stretched over the gap. Eight more beams, with notches cut in them to receive the cables, were laid at right angles across the parallel ropes, and lashed tight to them. The long cables were strained taut with winches : a network of rope yarn for a flooring was laid between the eight beams, and on this planks were placed, while a screen of tarpaulins supported on guide-ropes acted as parapets. The structure was sound enough to carry not only infantry and horses, but heavy artillery, yet could always be broken up in a short time if an enemy had ever appeared in the neighbourhood [1]. Several times it was rolled up, and then replaced.

When the completion of the repairs of Alcantara and the destruction of the French bridge of Almaraz are taken together, it must be concluded that Wellington's work in May gave him an advantage over the French of at least ten or twelve marches in moving troops from north to south or vice versa. For the route from Ciudad Rodrigo to Merida, now open to him, had at least that superiority over the only itinerary of the enemy, which would be that by Avila, Talavera, Toledo, and the eastern passes of the Sierra Morena. Though the narrow bridge of Arzobispo on the Middle Tagus still remained in French hands, it did not lead on to any good road to Estremadura or Andalusia, but on to the defiles of the Mesa d'Ibor and the ravines of the Sierra de Guadalupe. No large force could march or feed in those solitudes.

All was now ready for the advance upon the Tormes, which Wellington had made up his mind to execute.

[1] The best and most elaborate account of this is in Leith Hay, i. pp. 300–1.

SECTION XXXIII: CHAPTER III

WELLINGTON'S ADVANCE INTO LEON

It was not till June 13th that Wellington crossed the Agueda and began his march upon Salamanca, the first great offensive movement against the main fighting army of the French since the advance to Talavera in 1809. But for many days beforehand his troops were converging on Fuente Guinaldo and Ciudad Rodrigo from their widely-spread cantonments. Graham's divisions quitted Portalegre on May 30th, and some of the other troops, which had been left on the western side of the Beira, had also to make an early start. Every available infantry unit of the Anglo-Portuguese army had been drawn in, save the 2nd Division and Hamilton's Portuguese—left as usual with Hill in Estremadura—and Power's new Portuguese brigade—once the garrisons of Elvas and Abrantes—which had become available for the field since the fall of Badajoz made it possible to place those fortresses in charge of militia. Its arrival made Hill stronger by 2,000 in infantry than he had ever been before, and he was also left the three brigades (Long's and Slade's British and John Campbell's Portuguese) of Erskine's cavalry division. The total was 18,000 men. Wellington's own main army, consisting of the seven other infantry divisions, Pack's and Bradford's Portuguese brigades, and the cavalry of Anson, Bock, Le Marchant, and Victor Alten, made up a force of 48,000 men, of which 3,500 were cavalry : there were only eight British and one Portuguese batteries with the army—a short allowance of 54 guns.

But though these 48,000 men constituted the striking force, which was to deal the great blow, their action was to be supported by a very elaborate and complicated system of diversions, which were intended to prevent the French armies of the South, North, Centre, and Aragon from sending any help to

Marmont, the foe whom Wellington was set on demolishing. It is necessary to explain the concentric scheme by which it was intended that pressure should be brought to bear on all the outlying French armies, at the same moment at which the Anglo-Portuguese main body crossed the Agueda.

Soult had the largest force—over 50,000 men, as a recently captured morning-state revealed to his adversary[1]. But he could not assemble more than some 24,000 men, unless he abandoned the siege of Cadiz and the kingdom of Granada— half his army was pinned down to occupation-work. Wherefore Wellington judged that his field-force could be ' contained ' by Hill, if only means were found of preventing him from reinforcing Drouet's divisions in Estremadura by any appreciable succours. This means lay to hand in the roving army of Ballasteros, whose random schemes of campaign were often irrational, but had the solitary advantage of being quite inscrutable. He might do anything—and so was a most tiresome adversary for Soult to deal with, since his actions could not be foreseen. At this moment Wellington had urged the Cadiz Regency to stir up Ballasteros to activity, and had promised that, if Soult concentrated against him, Hill should press in upon Drouet, and so call off the Marshal's attention. Similarly if Soult concentrated against Hill, Ballasteros was to demonstrate against Seville, or the rear of the Cadiz Lines. There was always the possibility that the Spanish general might refuse to obey the orders of his Government, or that he might commit himself to some rash enterprise and get badly beaten. Both these chances had to be risked. The one that occurred was that Ballasteros took up the idea desired, but acted too early and too incautiously, and sustained a severe check at the battle of Bornos (June 1). Fortunately he was ' scotched but not slain,' and kept together a force large enough to give Soult much further trouble, though he did not prevent the Marshal from sending reinforcements to Drouet and putting Hill upon the defensive. Of this more in its due place.

So much for the diversion against Soult. On the other flank Wellington had prepared a similar plan for molesting the

[1] See Wellington to Henry Wellesley at Cadiz, June 7. *Dispatches*, ix. p. 219.

French in the Asturias, and threatening Marmont's flank and rear, at the same moment that his front was to be assailed. The force here available was Abadia's Army of Galicia, which nominally counted over 24,000 men, but had 6,000 of them shut up in the garrisons of Corunna, Ferrol, and Vigo. About 16,000 could be put into the field by an effort, if only Abadia were stirred up to activity. But there were many hindrances : this general was (like most of his predecessors) at strife with the Galician Junta. He was also very jealous of Sir Howard Douglas, the British Commissioner at Corunna, who was in favour with the Junta and people, and was inclined to resent any advice offered by him [1]. His army was not only (as in 1810–11) very short of cavalry—there were only about 400 effective sabres—but also of artillery. For the Cadiz government, searching for troops to send against the rebels of South America, had recently drafted off several batteries, as well as several foot regiments, to the New World. The most effective units had been taken, to the wild indignation of the Galicians, who wanted to keep the troops that they had raised for their own protection. There were only about 500 trained artillery-men left in Galicia, and when deduction was made for the garrisons of Ferrol, Vigo, and Corunna, very few remained for the active army. Abadia had, therefore, many excuses to offer for taking the field late, and with insufficient equipment [2]. It was fortunate that his superior, Castaños, who commanded (as Captain-General both of Estremadura and Galicia) all the troops in western Spain, fell in completely with Wellington's plan, and brought pressure to bear upon his subordinate, coming up to Santiago in person to expedite matters.

The part which the Army of Galicia was to play in the general scheme was that of marching upon Astorga, and laying siege to the considerable French garrison which was isolated in that rather advanced position. If Marmont should attempt to succour it, he would be left weak in front of the oncoming

---

[1] An extraordinary case of Abadia's ill will occurred in this spring : a damaged transport, carrying British troops to Lisbon, having put in to Corunna to repair, permission was refused for the men to land : apparently it was suspected that they were trying to garrison Corunna.

[2] For all this Galician business see the *Life of Sir Howard Douglas*, pp. 120–60.

British invasion. If he did not, its fall would turn and expose his right flank, and throw all the plains of northern Leon into the power of the allies. A move in force upon Astorga would also have some effect on the position of General Bonnet in the Asturias, and ought certainly to keep him uneasy, if not to draw him away from his conquests.

It will be remembered that Bonnet had been directed to reoccupy the Asturias by Napoleon's special command, and by no means to Marmont's liking[1]. He marched from Leon on May 15, by the road across the pass of Pajares, which he had so often taken before on similar expeditions. The Asturians made no serious resistance, and on May 17–18 Bonnet seized Oviedo and its port of Gijon. But, as in 1811, when he had accomplished this much, and planted some detachments in the coast towns, his division of 6,000 men was mainly immobilized, and became a string of garrisons rather than a field-force. It was observed by Porlier's Cantabrian bands on its right hand, and by Castañon's division of the Army of Galicia on its left, and was not strong enough to hunt them down, though it could prevent them from showing themselves anywhere in the neighbourhood of Oviedo.

But if the Galicians should lay siege to Astorga, and push advanced guards beyond it, in the direction of the city of Leon, it was clear that Bonnet's position would be threatened, and his communications with his chief, Marmont, imperilled. Wellington, who knew from intercepted dispatches the importance attached by the Emperor to the retention of the Asturias, judged that Bonnet would not evacuate it, but would spend his energy in an attempt to hold back the Galicians and keep open his connexion with Leon. He thus hoped that the French division at Oviedo would never appear near Salamanca—an expectation in which he was to be deceived, for Marmont (disregarding his master's instructions) ordered the evacuation of the Asturias the moment that he discovered the strength of the attack that was being directed against his front on the Tormes. Hence Wellington's advance cleared the Asturias of the enemy, and enabled the Galicians to besiege Astorga unmolested for two months—good results in themselves, but

[1] See above, p. 210.

not the precise benefits that he had hoped to secure by putting the Galician army in motion.

No item of assistance being too small to be taken into consideration, Wellington also directed Silveira to advance from the Tras-os-Montes, with the four militia regiments of that province [1], to cross the Spanish frontier and blockade Zamora, the outlying French garrison on the Douro, which covered Marmont's flank, as Astorga did his rear. To enable this not too trustworthy irregular force to guard itself from sudden attacks, Wellington lent it a full brigade of regular cavalry [2], which was entrusted to General D'Urban, who dropped the post of Chief-of-the-Staff to Beresford to take up this small but responsible charge. His duty was to watch the country on each side of the Douro in Silveira's front, so as to prevent him from being surprised, and generally to keep Wellington informed about Marmont's right wing, when he should begin to concentrate. Toro, only 20 miles farther up the Douro than Zamora, was another French garrison, and a likely place for the Marshal to use as one of his minor bases. Silveira being as rash as he was enterprising, it was D'Urban's task to see that he should be warned betimes, and not allowed to get into trouble. He was to retreat on Carvajales and the mountains beyond the Esla if he were attacked by a superior force.

A much more serious diversion was prepared to distract the free movement of the French Army of the North, from which Caffarelli might naturally be expected to send heavy detachments for Marmont's assistance, when the British striking-force should advance on Salamanca. Caffarelli's old enemies were the patriot bands of Cantabria and Navarre, who had given his predecessor, Dorsenne, so much trouble earlier in the year. Mina, on the borders of Navarre, Aragon, and Old Castile, was very far away, and not easy to communicate with or to bring into the general plan, though his spirit was excellent. But the so-called 'Seventh Army,' under Mendizabal, was near enough to be treated as a serious factor in the general scheme. This force consisted of the two large bands under Porlier in

[1] Chaves, Braganza, Miranda, Villa Real.
[2] Silveira already had Nos. 11 and 12, D'Urban brought up Nò. 1, which had not hitherto operated on this frontier.

Cantabria, and Longa in the mountains above Santander, each of which was several thousands strong : these were supposed to be regular divisions, though their training left much to be desired : in addition there were several considerable guerrilla ' partidas ' under Merino, Salazar, Saornil, and other chiefs, who lived a hunted life in the provinces of Burgos, Palencia, and Avila, and were in theory more or less dependent on Mendizabal. The chief of the Seventh Army was requested to do all that he could to keep Caffarelli employed during the month of June—a task that quite fell in with his ideas—he executed several very daring raids into Old Castile, one of which put the garrison of Burgos in great terror, as it was surprised at a moment when all its better items chanced to be absent, and nothing was left in the place but dépôts and convalescents [1].

But the main distraction contrived to occupy the French Army of the North was one for which Wellington was not primarily responsible, though he approved of it when the scheme was laid before him. This was a naval expedition to attack the coast-forts of Cantabria and Biscay, and open up direct communication with Mendizabal's bands from the side of the sea. The idea was apparently started by Sir Howard Douglas and Sir Home Popham, the former of whom was a great believer in the *guerrilleros,* and the latter a strong advocate of the striking power of the navy. Nothing serious had been done on the Biscay coast since the two expeditions of 1810, of which the former had been very successful, but the latter had ended in the disastrous tempest which wrecked Renovales's flotilla on that rocky shore [2]. Lord Liverpool consented to give Popham two battalions of marines and a company of artillery, to add to the force provided by the crews of the *Venerable,* his flagship, five frigates (*Surveillante, Rhin, Isis, Diadem, Medusa*), and several smaller vessels. The plan was to proceed eastward along the coast from Gijon, to call down Longa and Porlier to blockade each isolated French garrison from the land side, and to batter it with heavy ship guns from the water. The opportunity was to be taken at the same time of making over to the Cantabrian bands a large store of muskets and munitions which had been prepared for them. The arrange-

---

[1] See Thiébault, *Mémoires,* v. p. 561.   [2] See vol. iii. pp. 486–7.

ments were made in May, and Popham's squadron was ready
to move precisely at the same moment that Wellington crossed
the Agueda. Its first descent was made on June 17th, a day
exactly suitable for alarming the Army of the North at the
same time that Marmont's first appeals for help were likely to
reach Caffarelli. The plan, as we shall see, worked exceedingly
well, and the fact that the Army of Portugal got no reinforcements from Burgos or Biscay was due entirely to the dismay
caused to Caffarelli by this unexpected descent on his rear.
He conceived that the squadron carried a large landing force,
and that he was about to see Biscay slip out of his hands. The
tale of this useful diversion will be told in its due place.

There was yet one more item in the long list of outlying
distractions on which Wellington relied for the vexing of the
French. He was strongly of opinion that Suchet would spare
troops to reinforce King Joseph at Madrid, if his own invasion
of Leon had a prosperous start. Indeed, he somewhat over-
valued the Duke of Albufera's will and power to interfere in
central Spain, his idea being that King Joseph had a much
more direct control over the Valencian and Aragonese armies
than was really the case. One of the king's intercepted dispatches, directing Suchet to send troops into La Mancha, had
fallen into his hands, and he was unaware that the Marshal
had refused to obey it, and had found plausible reasons to
cloak his disobedience [1].

The opportunity of finding means to harass Suchet depended
on the general posture of affairs in the Mediterranean caused
by the outbreak of the Russian war. As long as Napoleon
kept a large army in Italy, there was always a possibility that
he might some day try a descent on Sicily, where the authority
of King Ferdinand rested on the bayonets of a strong British
garrison. There were a dozen red-coated battalions always
ready in Sicily, beside the rather inefficient forces of King
Ferdinand. In September 1810 Murat had massed a Franco-
Neapolitan army at Reggio, and tried an actual invasion, which
ended ignominiously in the capture of the only two battalions
that succeeded in landing. But by the early spring of 1812 it
was known that nearly all the French troops in Italy had been

[1] See above, p. 304. The intercepted cipher is in the Scovell Papers.

moved northward, and a great part of Murat's Neapolitan army with them. By April, indeed, there was only one French division left in the whole Peninsula, nearly all the old ' Army of Italy ' having marched across the Alps. Lord William Bentinck, the commander of the British forces in Sicily, had early notice of these movements, and being a man of action and enterprising mind, though too much given to wavering councils and rapid changes of purpose, was anxious to turn the new situation to account. He was divided between two ideas— the one which appealed to him most was to make a bold descent on the under-garrisoned Italian peninsula, either to stir up trouble in Calabria—where the ruthless government of Murat's military satraps had barely succeeded in keeping down rebellion, but had not crushed its spirit—or, farther away, in the former dominions of the Pope and the small dukes of the Austrian connexion. But the memory of the fruitless attempt against the Italian mainland in 1809 under Sir John Stuart survived as a warning : it was doubtful whether the occasional adventurers who came to Palermo to promise insurrection in northern Italy had any backing [1], and though Calabria was a more promising field, it was to be remembered that such troops as the enemy still retained were mainly concentrated there. Thus it came to pass that Lord William Bentinck at times despaired of all Italian expeditions, and thought of sending a force to Catalonia or Valencia to harass Suchet. ' I cannot but imagine,' he wrote, ' that the occasional disembarkation at different points of a large regular force must considerably annoy the enemy, and create an important diversion for other Spanish operations [2].' But when he wrote this, early in the year, he was hankering after descents on Elba and Corsica— the latter a most wild inspiration ! These schemes the ministry very wisely condemned : Lord Liverpool wrote in reply that ' though there might be a considerable degree of dissatisfaction, and even of ferment, pervading the greater part of Italy,' there was no evidence of any systematic conspiracy to shake off the yoke of France. Corsica and Elba, even if conquered, would

[1] See Lord Wellesley to Lord W. Bentinck, December 27, 1811, in Wellington's *Supplementary Dispatches*, vii. p. 249.
[2] Bentinck to Lord Liverpool, January 25, 1812, ibid., pp. 290–1.

only be of secondary importance. A diversion to be made upon
the east coast of Spain would be far the best way in which the
disposable force in Sicily could be employed. Wellington had
been informed of the proposal, and might probably be able
to lend part of the garrison of Cadiz, to make the expedition
more formidable. Sir Edward Pellew, the admiral commanding
on the Mediterranean station, would be able to give advice, and
arrange for the co-operation of the fleet [1]. Lord Liverpool
wrote on the next day (March 4) to inform Wellington of the
answer that had been made to Bentinck, but pointed out that
probably the aid could only be given from May to October, as
the expedition would depend on the fleet, and naval men
thought that it would be impossible to keep a large squadron
in attendance on the Sicilian force during the winter months.
The troops would probably have to return to their old quarters
at the close of autumn [2].

Wellington, as it chanced, was already in communication
with Bentinck, for the latter had sent his brother, Lord
Frederick, to Lisbon, with a dispatch for the Commander-in-
Chief in Portugal, in which he stated that he leaned himself
to the Corsican scheme, but that if the home government
disliked it, he would be prepared to send in April or May an
expedition of 10,000 men to operate against Suchet [3]. The
letter from London reached Wellington first, about March 20th [4],
and was a source of great joy to him, as he saw that the Cabinet
intended to prohibit the Italian diversion, and wished to direct
Bentinck's men towards Spain. He wrote to London and to
Palermo, to state that a descent upon the coast of Catalonia
seemed to him ' the most essential object.' It should be aimed
at Barcelona or Tarragona : it might not succeed so far as its
immediate object was concerned, but it would have the infallible
result of forcing Suchet to come up with all his available forces
from Valencia, and would prevent him from interfering in the

---

[1] Liverpool to Bentinck, March 4.   Wellington's *Supplementary Dispatches*, vii. p. 300.

[2] Liverpool to Wellington, March 5, ibid., p. 301.

[3] Bentinck to Wellington, February 23, ibid., p. 296.

[4] The answer to Lord Liverpool went off on March 20, that to Bentinck
on March 24th.

affairs of western and central Spain during the next campaign.
Ten thousand men, even with such aid as Lacy and the Catalan
army might give, were probably insufficient to deal with a place
of such strength as Barcelona ; but Tarragona, which was
weakly garrisoned, might well be taken.   Even if it were not,
a great point would be gained in opening up communication
with the Catalans, and throwing all the affairs of the French
in eastern Spain into confusion.   Bentinck was advised in the
strongest terms to land north of the Ebro, and not in Valencia :
an attack on Catalonia would draw Suchet out of Valencia,
which would then fall of its own accord.   Wellington added,
writing to Lord Liverpool only, not to Bentinck, that he did
not see how any appreciable aid could be got from the Cadiz
garrison, or those of Tarifa or Cartagena [1] : the British regiments there had been cut down to a necessary minimum, but
there were 1,400 Portuguese and two foreign regiments, of
whom some might possibly be spared.   The government must
give him a definite order to detach such and such battalions,
and it should be done—the responsibility being their own.   Lord
Frederick Bentinck arrived from Palermo at Badajoz just after
that place fell : Wellington charged him with additional advices
for his brother, to the effect that he would send him a siege-
train and officers and gunners to work it, which might serve
to batter Tarragona, if that proved possible.   Though he could
himself spare no British troops, the Spanish Regency should
be urged to lend, for an expedition to Catalonia, two divisions,
one under Roche at Alicante, the other under Whittingham in
Majorca, which consisted each of 3,000 men recently entrusted
for training to those British officers.   Their aid was hardly likely
to be refused, and they had been better trained, fed, and clothed
of late than other Spanish troops.   Wellington was not deceived
in this expectation, the Regency very handsomely offered to
place both divisions at Bentinck's disposition [2], and they

---

[1] Whither the 2/67th, a company of artillery, and five companies of
De Watteville's Swiss regiment had been sent, on the news of Blake's
disasters before Valencia. *Dispatches*, viii. p. 448.

[2] The best source of information about these subsidized corps is the life
of Sir Samford Whittingham, who raised and disciplined one of them in
Majorca, on the skeletons of the old regiments of Cordova, Burgos, and
5th Granaderos Provinciales. He had only 1,500 men on January 1, 1812,

turned out to have swelled in numbers of late, owing to vigorous
recruiting of dispersed men from Blake's defunct army. The
available figure was far over the 6,000 of which Wellington
had spoken.

There seemed, therefore, in May to be every probability that
a force of some 17,000 men might be available for the descent
on Catalonia which Wellington advised: and both Admiral
Pellew and Roche and Whittingham made active preparations
to be found in perfect readiness when Lord William Bentinck
should start off the nucleus of the expeditionary force from
Palermo [1]. Wellington had fixed the third week in June as the
date at which the appearance of the diversion would be most
effective [2]. On June 5th he was able to state that two separate
divisions of transports had already been sent off from Lisbon,
one to Alicante and one to Majorca, to pick up the two Spanish
divisions.

Now, however, came a deplorable check to the plan, which
only became known to Wellington when he had already committed himself to his campaign against Marmont. Bentinck
could never get out of his head the original idea of Italian
conquest which he had laid before the Cabinet in January.
There was no doubt that it had been discouraged by the home
government, and that he had received very distinct instructions
that Spain was to be the sphere of his activity, and that he was
to take Wellington into his councils. But Lord Liverpool's
dispatch had contained the unfortunate phrase that ' unless
the project of resistance to the French power in Italy should
appear to rest upon much better grounds than those of which
we are at present apprised,' the diversion to Catalonia was the

and 2,200 on February 21, but had worked them up to over 3,000 by April.
Roche, who had to work on the cadres of Canarias, Alicante, Chinchilla,
Voluntarios de Aragon, 2nd of Murcia, and Corona, had 5,500 men ready
on March 1, and more by May. Whittingham maintains that his battalions
always did their duty far better than other divisions, commanded by
officers with unhappy traditions of defeat, and attributes the previous
miserable history of the Murcian army to incapacity and poor spirit in
high places.

[1] Henry Wellesley to Wellington. *Supplementary Dispatches*, vii. p. 320.

[2] See as evidence of eagerness Whittingham's letter to Pellew of May 28
in the former's *Memoirs*, p. 161.

obvious course [1].' This gave a discretionary power to Bentinck, if he should judge that evidence of discontent in Italy had cropped up in unexpected quantity and quality since March. It does not appear, to the unprejudiced observer, that such evidence was forthcoming in May. But Bentinck, with his original prejudice in favour of a descent on Italy running in his brain, chose to take certain secret correspondence received from the Austrian general Nugent, and other sources, as justification for holding back from the immediate action in eastern Spain, on which Wellington had been led to rely. No troops sailed from Palermo or Messina till the very end of June, and then the numbers sent were much less than had been promised, and the directions given to Maitland, the general entrusted with the command, were by no means satisfactory [2]. The underlying fact would appear to be that, since March, Bentinck had begun to be alarmed at the intrigues of the Queen of Sicily, and feared to send away British troops so far afield as Spain. That notorious princess and her incapable spouse had been deprived in the preceding autumn of their ancient status as absolute sovereigns, and a Sicilian constitution and parliament, somewhat on the British model, had been called into being. For some time it had been supposed that Caroline, though incensed, was powerless to do harm, and the native Sicilians were undoubtedly gratified by the change. But Bentinck presently detected traces of a conspiracy fostered by the Queen among the Italian and mercenary troops employed by the Sicilian government : and, what was more surprising, it was suspected (and proved later on) that the court had actually opened up negotiations with Napoleon and even with Murat, in order to get rid of the English from Sicily at all costs [3]. In view of the

---

[1] Liverpool to Bentinck, 4th March, quoted above.

[2] See Wellington to Lord W. Bentinck in *Dispatches*, ix. pp. 60–1.

[3] That veritable 'stormy petrel of politics,' Sir Robert Wilson, was passing through Sicily in May, and seems to have acted a mischievous part in visiting the Queen, and allowing her to set before him all her grievances against Bentinck, and the 'Jacobin Parliament' that he was setting up. She told Wilson that Bentinck 'went to jails and took evidence of miserable wretches, actual malefactors or suspects, inducing them to say what he wished for his plans, and acting without any substantiating facts.' As to the army Wilson gathered that 'the Neapolitan soldiery hate us to a man, the Germans would adhere to us, the native Sicilians at least not

fact that there were 8,000 Italian and foreign troops of doubtful disposition quartered in Sicily, Bentinck was seized with qualms at the idea of sending away a large expedition, mainly composed of British regiments. In the end he compromised, by detaching only three British and two German Legion battalions, along with a miscellaneous collection of fractions of several foreign corps, making 7,000 men in all[1]. They only arrived off the coast of Catalonia on July 31st, and Maitland's freedom of operations was hampered by instructions to the effect that ' the division of the Sicilian army detached has for its first object the safety of Sicily ; its employment on the Spanish coast is temporary.' He was told that he was liable to be withdrawn at any moment, if complications arose in Sicily or Italy, and was not to consider himself a permanent part of the British army in Spain. Yet at the same time that Bentinck had given these orders, the home government had told Wellington to regard the expeditionary force as placed at his disposal, and authorized him to send directions to it.

All this worked out less unhappily than might have been expected ; for though Wellington got little practical military help from the Sicilian corps, and though Maitland's operations were most disappointing and started far too late, yet the knowledge that great transport squadrons were at Alicante and Majorca, and the rumour that a large force was coming from Sicily, most certainly kept Suchet in a state of alarm, and prevented him from helping Soult or King Joseph. It is interesting to find from his correspondence [2] that in the earliest days of July he was anxiously watching the ships at Alicante, and expecting a descent either on Valencia or on Catalonia, though Maitland was yet far away, and did not appear off

act against us.' But there were only 2,000 Sicilians and 1,900 Germans, and 8,000 Neapolitans and other Italians, eminently untrustworthy. [So untrustworthy were they, indeed, that the Italian corps sent to Spain in the autumn deserted by hundreds to the French.] See Wilson's *Private Diary*, 1812–15, pp. 35–62.

[1] For details, see table in Appendix no. XIII.

[2] Suchet's correspondence (in the Archives of the French War Ministry) begins to be anxious from July 6 onward. On that date he hears that ships are at Alicante to take Roche on board, who is to join a very large English force, and 15,000 (!) men from Majorca. On July 13th he hears that Maitland is to have 17,000 men, though only 3,000 British regulars.

Palamos till July 31. The fear of the descent was an admirable
help to Wellington—perhaps more useful than its actual
appearance at an early date might have been, since the expeditionary troops were decidedly less in numbers than Wellington
had hoped or Suchet had feared. At the same time the
news that the Sicilian force had not sailed, and perhaps might
never appear, reached Salamanca at one of the most critical
moments of the campaign, and filled Wellington with fears
that the Army of Valencia might already be detaching troops
against him, while he had calculated upon its being entirely
distracted by the projected demonstration [1]. The news that
Maitland had sailed at last, only came to hand some time
after the battle of Salamanca had been won, when the whole
position in Spain had assumed a new and more satisfactory
aspect.

Such were the subsidiary schemes with which Wellington
supported his main design of a direct advance against Marmont's army. Some of them worked well—Hill, Home
Popham, and Mendizabal did all, and more than all, that had
been expected of them, in the way of containing large French
forces. Others accomplished all that could in reason have
been hoped—such was the case with Silveira and Ballasteros.
Others fell far below the amount of usefulness that had been
reckoned upon—both the Galician army and the Sicilian army
proved most disappointing in the timing of their movements
and the sum of their achievements. But on the whole the
plan worked—the French generals in all parts of Spain were
distracted, and Marmont got little help from without.

It is certain that, at the moment of Wellington's starting on
his offensive campaign, the thing that gave him most trouble
and anxiety was not the timing or efficacy of the various diver-

---

[1] Wellington to Lord Bathurst, July 14: ‘I have this day received
a letter from Lord W. Bentinck of the 9th of June, from which I am
concerned to observe that his Lordship does not intend to carry into
execution the operation on the east coast of the Peninsula, until he shall
have tried the success of another plan on the coast of Italy. I am apprehensive that this determination may bring upon us additional forces of the
Army of Aragon: but I still hope that I shall be able to retain at the close
of this campaign the acquisitions made at its commencement.’ *Dispatches*,
ix. p. 285.

sions that he had planned, but a purely financial problem. It was now a matter of years since the money due for the pay and maintenance of the army had been coming in with terrible unpunctuality. Officers and men had grown to regard it as normal that their pay should be four or six months in arrears : the muleteers and camp followers were in even worse case. And the orders for payment (*vales* as they were called) issued by the commissariat to the peasantry, were so tardily settled in cash, that the recipients would often sell them for half or two-thirds of their face value to speculators in Lisbon, who could afford to wait many months for the money.

This state of things was deplorable : but it did not proceed, as Napier usually hints, and as Wellington himself seems some-times to have felt, from perversity on the part of the home government. It was not the case that there was gold or silver in London, and that the ministers did not send it with sufficient promptness. No one can be so simple as to suppose that Lord Liverpool, Mr. Perceval, the Marquess of Wellesley, or Lord Castlereagh, did not understand that the Army of Portugal must have cash, or it would lose that mobility which was its great strength. Still less would they wittingly starve it, when the fortunes of the ministry were bound up with the successful conduct of the war.

But the years 1811–12, as has been already pointed out in the last volume of this work, were those of the greatest stringency in the cash-market of Great Britain. The country was abso-lutely drained dry of metallic currency in the precious metals : no silver had been coined at the Mint since the Revolutionary war began : no guineas since 1798. England was transacting all her internal business on bank-notes, and gold was a rare commodity, only to be got by high prices and much searching. This was the time when the Jews of Portsmouth used to board every home-coming transport, to offer convalescents or sailors 27*s.*, or even more, in paper for every guinea that they had on them. The Spanish dollar, though weighing much less than an English five-shilling piece (when that valuable antiquity could be found [1]), readily passed for six shillings in paper. And even

---

[1] No silver crowns had been coined since 1760 at the Mint. They weighed 463 grains : the Spanish dollar only 415 grains.

this coin could not now be got so easily as in 1809 or 1810, for the growing state of disturbance in the Spanish-American colonies was beginning to affect the annual import of silver from the mines of Mexico and Peru, which had for a long time been the main source from which bullion for Europe was procured. To buy dollars at Cadiz with bills on London was becoming a much more difficult business. In May 1812 a special complication was introduced—Lord William Bentinck wishing to provide Spanish coin for the expedition which was about to sail for Catalonia, sent agents to Gibraltar, who bought with Sicilian gold all the dollars that they could procure, giving a reckless price for them, equivalent to over six shillings a dollar, and competing with Wellington's regular correspondents who were at the same moment offering only 5s. 4d. or 5s. 6d. for the coin. Of course the higher offer secured the cash, and Wellington made bitter complaints that the market had been spoilt, and that he suddenly found himself shut out from a supply on which he had hitherto reckoned with security [1]. But the competition was only transient, though very tiresome at a moment when silver coin was specially wanted for payments in Leon. For, as Wellington remarked, the people about Salamanca had never seen the British army before, and would be wanting to do business on a prompt cash basis, not being accustomed to credit, as were the Portuguese.

The army started upon the campaign with a military chest in the most deplorable state of depletion. ' We are absolutely bankrupt,' wrote Wellington, ' the troops are now five months in arrears instead of one month in advance. The staff have not been paid since February ; the muleteers not since June 1811 ! and we are in debt in all parts of the country. I am obliged to take money sent me by my brother [Henry Wellesley, British Minister at Cadiz] for the Spaniards, in order to give my own troops a fortnight's pay, who are really suffering for want of money [2].' Some weeks before this last complaint Wellington had sounded an even louder note of alarm. ' We owe not less than 5,000,000 dollars. The Portuguese troops and establishments are likewise in the greatest distress, and

---

[1] See Wellington to Lord Bathurst. *Dispatches*, vii. p. 370.
[2] Ibid., vii. p. 319.

it is my opinion, as well as that of Marshal Beresford, that we must disband part of that army, unless I can increase the monthly payments of the subsidy. The Commissary-General has this day informed me that he is very apprehensive that he will not be able to make good his engagements for the payment for the meat for the troops. If we are obliged to stop that payment, your Lordship may as well prepare to recall the army, for it will be impossible to carry up salt meat (as well as bread) to the troops from the sea-coast. . . . It is not improbable that we may not be able to take advantage of the enemy's comparative weakness in this campaign *for sheer want of money* [1].' One almost feels that Wellington is here painting the position of the army in the blackest possible colours, in order to bring pressure on his correspondent at home. But this dismal picture was certainly reflected in the language of his staff at the time : a letter from his aide-de-camp, Colin Campbell, speaks (on May 30) of the depleted state of the military chest being a possible curb to the campaign : ' Lord W. cannot take supplies with him to enable him to do more than demonstrate towards Valladolid, when so good an opportunity offers, and an inconsiderable addition would suffice. The harvest is ripening, the country round Salamanca is full of all requisite supplies, but they are not procurable without cash [2].'

Yet it is hard to be over-censorious of the home government. They were in the most bitter straits for money. Gold and silver were simply not to be got in the quantities that Wellington required. The amount actually sent was very large : it would have been larger if economic conditions had not been desperate. The rupture with the United States of America which took place in June (fortunately too late to serve Napoleon's purpose), had just added a new source of anxiety to the troubles of the Cabinet : both money and men were now wanted for Canada. There can be no doubt that when Lord Bathurst wrote, in the middle of the Salamanca campaign, that ' £100,000 in cash, chiefly gold, had been sent off,' and that

---

[1] Wellington to Lord Liverpool, April 22. *Supplementary Dispatches*, vii. p. 318.

[2] Campbell to Shawe. *Supplementary Dispatches*, vii. p. 362.

'I wish to God we could assist you more in money,' he was writing quite honestly, and amid most adverse financial circumstances. Great Britain was at the most exhausting point of her long struggle with Napoleon. The Russian war had begun— but there was no sign as yet that it was to be the ruin of the Emperor : his armies seemed to be penetrating towards Moscow in the old triumphant style : many politicians spoke of a humiliating peace dictated to Czar Alexander in the autumn as the probable end of the campaign, and speculated on Napoleon's appearance at Madrid in 1813 as a possible event. Wheat had risen in this spring to 130s. the quarter. The outbreak of the long-threatened but long-averted American war looked like the last blow that was to break down the British Empire. It was no wonder that the national credit was low in June 1812. There was nothing to revive it till Wellington's Salamanca triumph in July : nor did any one understand that Napoleon's star had passed its zenith, till the news of the disasters of the Moscow retreat began to drift westward in November and December.

Meanwhile, if the financial outlook was gloomy, the actual military situation was more promising than it had ever been before. Well aware, from intercepted dispatches, of the quarrels of his adversaries, and perfectly informed as to their numbers and their cantonments, Wellington considered with justice that he had such a game in his hands as he had never before had set before him. On June 13th he crossed the Agueda with his army in three parallel columns. The left was under charge of Picton, and consisted of the 3rd Division, Pack's and Bradford's Portuguese, and Le Marchant's brigade of heavy dragoons. The centre, which Beresford conducted, was composed of the Light, 4th, and 5th Divisions. It was preceded by Alten's German hussars, and accompanied by Bock's dragoons. The right column, under Graham, had the 1st, 6th, and 7th Divisions, with a regiment of Anson's horse for purposes of exploration. It is to be noted that both Picton and Graham were destined to remain only a few weeks with the army : the former had taken the field ere his Badajoz wound was properly healed : it broke open again, he fell into a high fever, and had to be sent to the rear. Wellington's brother-in-law, Pakenham, took over charge of the 3rd Division on June 28th. Graham had been suffering for some months from an affection of the eyes, which the physicians told him might at any time grow worse and threaten his sight. He persisted on staying with the army till the last possible moment, but became more blind each day, and was compelled to throw up his command on July 6th and to return to England for skilled medical advice. Thus, during the greater part of the Salamanca campaign, Wellington was working without his best-trusted lieutenants—Craufurd was dead, both Picton and Graham invalided. In consequence of Graham's departure a very difficult point was raised. If some illness or wound should disable the Commander-in-Chief, to whom would the charge of operations fall [1]? Wellington considered that Beresford was entitled to expect the succession, and deprecated the sending out of some senior officer from England with a commission to act as second in command. He observed that no one coming fresh from home would have a real grasp of the conditions of the war : that he would probably start with *a priori* views, and have to unlearn them in a time of imminent danger. Moreover, a second-in-command was, when his superior was in good health, either an unnecessary person or else a tiresome one, if he presumed on his position to offer advice or remonstrances. Fortunately the question remained a wholly academic one, since Wellington's iron physique, and unbroken luck when bullets were flying, never failed him. An understudy turned out to be superfluous.

The three columns of the allied army advanced on a very narrow front of not more than ten miles, though the cavalry spread out considerably to the flanks. On the 13th the columns bivouacked on the Guadapero river, in front of Ciudad Rodrigo, between Santi Espiritus and Tenebron. On the 14th they advanced four leagues to the Huebra, and camped on each side of San Muñoz, with head-quarters at Cabrillas. On the 15th a rather longer march took them to Matilla and Cayos. Nothing had yet been seen of any enemy. It was only on the 16th, in the morning, that the advanced cavalry of the centre column, after crossing the Valmusa river, came into contact with two squadrons of French *chasseurs,* not more than two leagues

---

[1] Wellington to Bathurst. *Dispatches*, ix. p. 277.

CENTRAL SPAIN

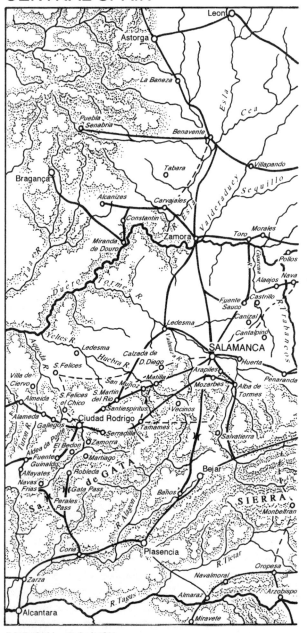

B.V.Darbishire, Oxford, 1914

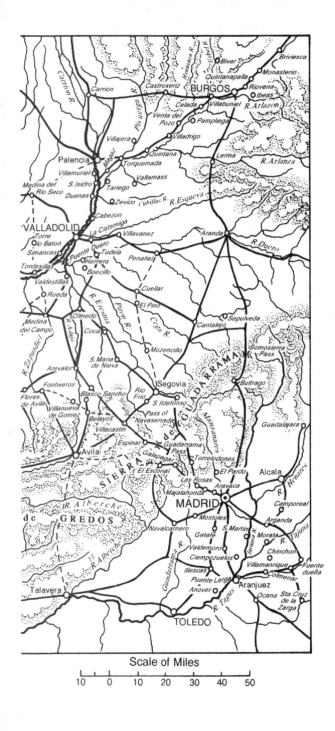

Scale of Miles

10   0   10   20   30   40   50

outside of Salamanca. These outposts gave way when pushed, and retired across the Tormes. The British army bivouacked in sight of Salamanca that night, and received the information that Marmont had already evacuated the city, save for a garrison left in its three new forts [1].

The Army of Portugal had been caught, just as Wellington had hoped, in a condition of wide dispersion. It was not that Marmont did not expect the attack, but that, till the day when it should be actually delivered, he dared not concentrate, because of his want of magazines and the paucity of transport. He had resolved that he must be content to abandon all the land west of Salamanca, in order that his point of concentration should be out of reach of his enemy's first stroke. It was fixed at Bleines and Fuente Sauco, twenty miles north of Salamanca on the road to Toro. On the morning of the 14th, when the news that Wellington was over the Agueda first reached him, the Marshal issued orders to all his divisions to march on this point, not even excepting that of Bonnet in the Asturias. For, despite of the Emperor's wish to keep a hold upon that province, Marmont held, and rightly, that it was more important to place in front of the Anglo-Portuguese every possible bayonet, and he could not spare a solid division of 6,500 men. Unfortunately for him, however, it was clear that Bonnet could not arrive for fifteen or twenty days. The other seven divisions were concentrated by the fifth night from the giving of the alarm [2]. They formed a mass of 36,000 infantry, with 80 guns, but only 2,800 horse. This total does not include either Bonnet, nor three battalions of Thomières's division left to hold Astorga, nor small garrisons placed in Toro, Zamora, the Salamanca forts,

[1] The itinerary of this march in detail may be found in the excellent Diary of Tomkinson of the 16th Light Dragoons.

[2] Foy, who had been drawn away from the Tagus after the affair at Almaraz, had to march from Avila, Clausel from Peñaranda, Ferey from Valladolid, Sarrut from Toro, Maucune and Brennier had been at Salamanca, Thomières came from Zamora. Boyer's dragoons were at Toro and Benavente, Curto's light cavalry division had been with Maucune and Brennier at Salamanca. Valladolid, Avila, and Benavente were the most distant points : but the troops from them were all up by the 19th. Nor was it possible for Wellington to interfere with the concentration, though possibly he might have forced Foy from Avila to make a détour, if he had followed Marmont very close.

and certain other posts farther east [1]. Nor does it take account of a dépôt of 3,000 men, including many dismounted dragoons, at Valladolid. The total of the field army, including artillery, sappers, &c., was about 40,000 of all arms.

This force was distinctly inferior in number to that of the Anglo-Portuguese, who, without counting three infantry battalions on their way to the front from Lisbon, or D'Urban's Portuguese horse on the side of Zamora, had some 40,000 infantry in line, and 3,500 excellent cavalry, in which arm Wellington, for the first time in his life, had a slight advantage over the enemy. Carlos de España was also approaching, with the 3,000 Spanish infantry that were available after the garrison of Ciudad Rodrigo had been completed, and in all the allied army must have had 48,000 men at the front [2]. The balance of numbers, of which each general was pretty well informed, was such as to make both sides careful—Marmont was 8,000 men short of his adversary's power, and was particularly depressed by the knowledge of his inferiority in cavalry, an arm on which the French had hitherto relied with confidence. But the horse of the Army of Portugal had never recovered from the consequences of Masséna's retreat in the last spring, and all the regiments were very weak : while Wellington was at last profiting from the liberal way in which the home government had reinforced his mounted arm during the autumn of 1811. He had ten British regiments with him, whereas at Fuentes de Oñoro he had owned but four.

On the other hand Wellington, among his 48,000 men, had only 28,000 British ; there were 17,000 Portuguese and 3,000 Spaniards with him, and excellent though the conduct of the former had been during the late campaign, it would be hypocrisy to pretend that their commander could rely upon them under all circumstances, as he would have done upon a corresponding number of British infantry. He was ready to give battle, but it must be a battle under favourable conditions. Marmont felt much the same : it was necessary to beat Wellington if the French domination in Spain was to be preserved. But it would

---

[1] Nor do we reckon the regiment of Sarrut's division (130th) permanently detached at Santander.

[2] See tables of the armies of both sides in the Appendix no. IX.

be rash to attack him in one of his favourite defensive positions :
there must be no more Bussacos. And every available man
must be gathered in, before a general action was risked. The
only justification for instant battle would be the unlikely chance
of catching the Anglo-Portuguese army in a state of dispersion
or some other unlucky posture—and Wellington's known
caution did not make such a chance very probable.

Marmont's main purpose, indeed, was to hold Wellington
' contained ' till he should have succeeded in bringing up
Bonnet, and also reinforcements from the Armies of the North
and Centre—if not even from some distant forces. On Bonnet's
eventual arrival he could rely—but not on any fixed date for
his appearance, for it was difficult to get orders promptly to
the Asturias, and there might be many unforeseen delays in
their execution. But Marmont was also counting on aid from
Caffarelli, which would presumably reach him even before
Bonnet appeared. In expectation of Wellington's advance, he
had written to the Commander of the Army of the North on
May 24th and 30th, and again on June 5th, asking for assurances
of help, and reminding his colleague of the Emperor's directions.
The answers received were, on the whole, satisfactory : the last
of them, dated at Vittoria on June 14th, said that the disposable
field-force was 8,000 men, including a brigade of light cavalry
and 22 guns. They should march from Vittoria as soon as some
troops of Abbé's division arrived from Pampeluna to replace
them, and they should be écheloned along the high-road from
Burgos to Valladolid ready to move up when called upon[1]. It
must be remembered that on this date Caffarelli was answering
a hypothetical inquiry as to his exact power to help, not
a definite demand for men, since Wellington had only crossed
the Agueda on the previous day, and nothing was known at
Vittoria of his actual start. But the dispatch was encouraging,
as it seemed to show a good spirit, and named the exact force
available, and the route that it would take. Marmont received
it upon the 19th, just as he had completed his own concentration
at Fuente Sauco. It seemed to justify him in believing that
before July 1 he would have 8,000 men from Caffarelli at

[1] See Caffarelli to Marmont of June 10 and June 14th in Marmont's
Mémoires, iv. pp. 408–10.

his disposition, including, what was specially valuable, 1,000 horse.

The dispatches from King Joseph and Jourdan were less satisfactory. At this moment they were in a state of hesitation caused by contradictory intelligence. ' Your letter of June 6th,' wrote Jourdan to Marmont, 'says that Wellington will soon fall upon you. But we have similar letters from Soult, declaring that the blow is to be delivered against him : he encloses two notes of June 2nd and 5th from General Daricau in Estremadura, declaring that 60,000 of the allies are just about to begin an invasion of Andalusia. We are too far off from the scene of operations to determine whether it is you or the Duke of Dalmatia who is deceived. We can only tell you, meanwhile, not to be misled by demonstrations, and to be ready to start off three divisions to Soult's help without a moment's delay, if Lord Wellington's real objective is Andalusia. Similarly we have sent Soult express orders that he shall move Drouet to the north bank of the Tagus, if Wellington has called up Hill to join him, and is making the true attack on you. Caffarelli has stringent orders to support you with what troops he can collect, when you are able to tell him definitely that you are the person threatened, not Soult [1].'

It is clear that the hallucinations of the Duke of Dalmatia were most valuable to Wellington, who had foreseen them long ago by a study of intercepted dispatches. Whatever happened, Soult could not refrain from believing that he had the great rôle to play, and that his Andalusian viceroyalty was the centre of all things. At this moment his picture of Wellington about to move on Cordova with 60,000 men seems to have been a belated conception caused by Graham's march to Elvas on May 20. He had not yet realized that ten days later Graham's corps had gone northward again, and had joined Wellington on the Agueda about the time that he was writing his alarmist letters. There was nothing in front of him save Hill's 18,000 men : but he refused to see the facts, and deceived Joseph and Jourdan for some days by the definite and authoritative restatement of absolutely erroneous intelligence. Hence it was not till Marmont was able to say, without any

[1] Jourdan to Marmont, June 14th, in *Mémoires*, iv. pp. 411–12.

possible chance of error, that Wellington was across the Agueda, and had advanced to Salamanca at the head of at least 40,000 men, that the King and his Chief-of-the-Staff at last recognized the true seat of danger. Long after they had detected it, they continued (as we shall see) to receive preposterous dispatches from Soult, still maintaining that they were mistaken, and still discovering excuses for not obeying the peremptory orders that they sent him.

SECTION XXXIII: CHAPTER IV

THE SALAMANCA FORTS. TEN DAYS OF MANŒUVRES, JUNE 20TH–30TH, 1812

WELLINGTON'S conduct on reaching Salamanca was not that which might have been expected. When a general has, by a careful and well-arranged concentration, collected all his own troops into one solid mass, and then by a rapid advance has thrown himself into the midst of the scattered cantonments of an enemy who has no superiority to him in numbers, it is natural for him to press his pursuit vigorously. Far the most effective way of opening the campaign would have been to cut up the two divisions which Marmont had just led out of Salamanca, or at least to follow them so closely that they could be brought to action before all the outlying divisions had come in. This would certainly have been Napoleon's method.

Wellington, however, wanted to fight a battle in one of his favourite defensive positions, and he thought that he had a means of compelling Marmont to attack him, by laying siege to the Salamanca forts. After Ciudad Rodrigo and Badajoz, no French marshal would like to see a third important post captured ' under his nose.' The British general judged that Marmont would fight him, in order to save his prestige and his garrison. And since he believed that Bonnet would not evacuate the Asturias, and that Caffarelli would send help late, if at all, he thought that he could count upon a superiority of numbers which rendered victory certain.

This seems to be the only rational way of explaining Wellington's conduct on June 17th. On arriving in front of Salamanca his army made a majestic encircling movement, Picton's column crossing the Tormes by the fords of El Canto below the city, Beresford's and Graham's by those of Santa Marta above it. The use of the unbroken town-bridge was made impossible by Marmont's forts. The heads of the two columns met on the

north side, and they then moved three miles on, and took up
a long position below the heights of San Cristobal, which lie
outside Salamanca on its northern and eastern front. These
formed the chosen defensive fighting-ground which Wellington
had already in his mind.

Only the 14th Light Dragoons and Clinton's infantry of the
6th Division turned into Salamanca by the Toro gate, and
acted as Wellington's escort, while he was received by the
municipality and made his arrangements for the attack on the
forts, which, though they commanded the bridge, had no
outlook on the spacious arcaded Plaza Mayor, where the
reception took place. It was a lively scene. ' We were received
with shouts and *vivas*,' writes an eye-witness. ' The inhabitants
were out of their senses at having got rid of the French, and
nearly pulled Lord Wellington off his horse. The ladies were
the most violent, many coming up to him and embracing him.
He kept writing orders upon his sabretash, and was interrupted
three or four times by them. What with the joy of the people,
and the feeling accompanying troops about to attack a fortress,
it was a half-hour of suspense and anxiety, and a scene of such
interest as I never before witnessed [1].'

Head-quarters were established that night in the city, and
Clinton's division invested the forts, which looked formidable
enough to require close study before they were attacked. The
rest of the army took up its bivouacs, with the cavalry out
in front, and remained practically without movement on the
ground now selected, for the next two days, till Marmont
came to pay his expected visit.

The three Salamanca forts were built on high ground in the
south-west corner of the city, which overlooks the long Roman
bridge. To make them Marmont had destroyed a great part of
the old University quarter of the place, levelling the majority
of the colleges—for Salamanca, till 1808, had been a university
of the English rather than the usual continental type, and had
owned a score of such institutions. Nearly all the buildings on
the slopes had been pulled down, leaving a wide open glacis
round three massive convents, which had been transformed into
places of strength. San Vincente occupied the crest of the knoll

[1] Tomkinson's *Diary*, p. 162.

overlooking the river, and lay in the extreme angle of the old
city wall, which enclosed it on two sides. The smaller strongholds, San Cayetano and La Merced, were separated from San
Vincente by a narrow but steep ravine, and lay close together
on another rising-ground of about the same height. The three
formed a triangle with crossing fires, each to a large extent
commanding the ground over which the others would have to
be approached. The south and west sides of San Vincente and
La Merced overhung precipitous slopes above the river, and
were almost inaccessible. The north sides of San Cayetano and
San Vincente were the only fronts that looked promising for
attack, and in each elaborate preparations had been made in
view of that fact. Marmont had originally intended to enclose
all three forts and many buildings more—such as the Town
Hospital, the convent of San Francisco, and the colleges of
Ireland and Cuenca, in an outer *enceinte*, to serve as a large
citadel which would contain several thousand men and all his
magazines. But money and time had failed, and on the slopes
below the forts, several convents and colleges, half pulled to
pieces, were still standing, and offered cover for besiegers at
a distance of some 250 yards from the works. The garrison
consisted of six flank-companies from the 15th, 65th, 82nd, and
86th of the line and the 17th Léger, and of a company of
artillery, under the *chef de bataillon* Duchemin of the 65th. They
made up a total of 800 men, and had thirty-six guns in position,
of which, however, the greater part were only light field-pieces :
two guns (commanding the bridge) were in La Merced, four in
San Cayetano, the remaining thirty in San Vincente, the most
formidable of the three.

Wellington had come prepared to besiege ' three fortified
convents,' and had been sent a confused sketch of them drawn
by an amateur's hand [1]. They turned out much stronger than
he had been led to expect, owing to the immense amount of
hewn stone from the demolished colleges and other buildings
that was available to build them up. The walls had been
doubled in thickness, the windows stopped, and scarps and
counterscarps with solid masonry had been thrown around them.
The roofs of the two minor forts had been taken off, and the

[1] Jones, *Sieges*, i. p. 269.

upper stories casemated, by massive oak beams with a thick coating of earth laid upon them. This surface was so strong that guns, protected by sandbag embrasures, had been mounted on it at some points. There was also an ample provision of palisades, made from strong oak and chestnut beams. Altogether it was clear that the works would require a systematic battering, and were not mere patched-up mediaeval monasteries, as had been expected.

It was, therefore, most vexatious to find that the very small battering-train which Wellington had brought with him from Ciudad Rodrigo was obviously insufficient for the task before it ; there were no more than four iron 18-pounder guns, with only 100 rounds of shot each, at the front ; though six 24-pound howitzers, from the train that had taken Badajoz, were on their way from Elvas to join, and were due on the 20th. It was not, however, howitzers so much as more heavy 18- or 24-pounders that were required for battering, and the lack of them at the moment was made all the more irksome by the known fact that there were plenty of both sorts at Rodrigo and Almeida, five or six marches away. The mistake was precisely the same that was to be made again at Burgos in the autumn—undervaluation of the means required to deal with works of third-class importance. Whether Wellington himself or his artillery and engineer advisers were primarily responsible is not clear [1].

The responsibility for the working out of the little siege with inadequate means fell on Lieut.-Colonel Burgoyne, as senior engineer (he had with him only two other officers of that corps and nine military artificers !), and Lieut.-Colonel May, R.A., who was in charge of the four 18-pounders. The latter borrowed three howitzers from field-batteries to supplement his miserable means, and afterwards two 6-pounder field-guns, which, of course, were only for annoying the garrison, not for battering.

It looked at first as if the only practicable scheme was to build a battery for the 18-pounders on the nearest available ground, 250 yards from San Vincente to the north, and lower down the knoll on which that fort stood. There was good cover from ruined buildings up to this distance from the French

---

[1] At any rate Dickson was not, as he was with the howitzers that were coming up from Elvas, and had not started from Rodrigo with the army.

works. On the night of the occupation of Salamanca 400 workmen of the 6th Division commenced a battery on the selected
spot and approaches leading to it from the cover in the ruins.
The work done was not satisfactory : it was nearly full moon,
the night was short, and the enemy (who knew well enough
where the attack must begin), kept up a lively fire of artillery
and musketry all night. Unfortunately the 6th Division
workmen had no experience of sieges—they had never used
pick or shovel before, and there were only two engineer officers
and nine artificers to instruct them. ' Great difficulty was
found in keeping the men to work under the fire : the Portuguese
in particular absolutely went on hands and knees, dragging
their baskets along the ground [1].' By daylight the projected
line of the battery was only knee-high, and gave no cover, so
that the men had to be withdrawn till dusk. An attempt had
been made during the night to ascertain whether it were
possible to creep forward to the ditch, and lay mines there, to
blow in the counterscarp. But the party who tried to reach
the ditch were detected by the barking of a dog, who alarmed
the French out-picket, and the explorers had to retire with
several men wounded.

Seeing that the fire of the garrison was so effective, the
officers in charge of the siege asked for, and obtained from
Wellington, three hundred marksmen to keep down the *tiraillade*.
They were taken from the Light Brigade of the King's German
Legion, and spread among the ruins to fire at the embrasures
and loopholes of the French. They also hoisted, with some
difficulty, two field-guns on to the first floor of the convent of
San Bernardo, which lies north-west of San Vincente, and kept
up a lively discharge ' out of the drawing-room window, so to
speak. We fired for some hours at each other, during which
time an unlucky shot went as completely through my captain's
(Eligé's) heart as possible. But considering how near we were,
I am much surprised that our loss was so slight—one killed and
one wounded at my own gun [2].' But the fire of the San Vincente
artillery was by no means silenced.

[1] Burgoyne's diary in his *Life*, i. p. 192.
[2] Letter of F. Monro, R.A., lent me by his representative. See *Fortnightly Review* for July 1912.

On the night of June 18th–19th the working party of the
6th Division succeeded in finishing the battery which was to
breach the main fort, and also commenced two smaller batteries,
to right and left, in places among the ruins, one by the College
of Cuenca, the other below San Bernardo[1]. On the morning of
the 19th the four 18-pounders and three howitzers opened,
and brought down the upper courses of the masonry of that
part of San Vincente on which they were trained. But they
could not move its lower part, or reach the counterscarp.
Wherefore two howitzers were put into the second battery,
near the College of Cuenca, which could command the counterscarp. The play of these guns proved insufficient, however, to
shake it, and the garrison concentrated such a fire upon them,
mainly from musketry at loopholes, that twenty gunners were
killed or hurt while working the two howitzers.

Next morning Dickson's six howitzers from Elvas came up,
and served to replace those borrowed from the field companies,
wherefore there was only an addition of three pieces net to the
battering-train. Two of the 18-pounders were moved round
to the battery (No. 2) which had been so hard hit on the preceding day : their fire proved much more effective than that of
the howitzers, and brought down an angle of the upper wall
of San Vincente and part of its roof, which fell on and crushed
many of the French.

But on the 21st it was impossible to continue the battering,
for the ignominious reason that there were hardly any more
shot left to fire. Only sixty balls remained in store for the
18-pounders, and a little over one hundred for the howitzers[2].
The calculations of the besiegers had been so erroneous that they
had used up their stock just as the critical moment had arrived.
On the previous day Wellington, seeing what was coming, had
sent a hurried message to Almeida for more shot and powder—
but the convoy, though urged on with all possible speed, did
not arrive at Salamanca till the 26th.

Meanwhile the general engagement for which Wellington

---

[1] Nos. 2 and 3 in the map respectively.

[2] Of course a few rounds more for the howitzers could have been borrowed from the field-batteries with the divisions. For the 18-pounders, the
really important guns, there was no such resource for borrowing.

had prepared himself seemed likely to come off. Marmont had all his army, save Bonnet alone, collected by the 19th, at Fuente Sauco. On the following day he came boldly forward and drove in the British cavalry vedettes. He showed three columns moving on a parallel front, which observers estimated at 18,000 foot and 2,000 horse—but there were more behind, still invisible. At four in the afternoon he was drawing so close that Wellington assumed his battle position. Five divisions and the two independent Portuguese brigades formed the fighting-line, from San Cristobal southward to Cabrerizos on the bank of the Tormes : the order was (from right to left) 1st–7th–4th–Light–3rd–Pack and Bradford. The reserve was composed of the 5th Division, of Hulse's brigade of the 6th (of which the remainder was left to blockade the Salamanca forts), and of Carlos de España's 3,000 Spaniards. Alten's cavalry covered the British right, Ponsonby's[1] the left, Bock's and Le Marchant's heavy squadrons were in reserve.

It looked at first as though Marmont intended to force on the battle that Wellington desired. Moving with great order and decision, his three columns deployed opposite the heights, and advanced to within a very moderate distance of them—not more than 800 yards at one point. They were extremely visible, as the whole country-side below the British position was a fine plain covered with ripening wheat. The only breaks in the surface were the infrequent villages—in this part of Spain they are all large and far apart—and a few dry water-courses, whose line could be detected winding amid the interminable cornfields. Warning to keep off the position was given to the French by long-range fire from several of the British batteries on salient points of the line. The enemy replied noisily and with many guns : Wellington's officers judged that he was doing his best to make his approach audible to the garrison of the besieged forts.

At dusk the French occupied the village of Castellanos de Morisco, in front of the right centre of the heights, and then advanced a regiment to attack Morisco, which was absolutely at the foot of them, and had been occupied by Wellington as an advanced post. It was held by the 68th regiment from the

---

[1] Acting vice G. Anson, absent.

7th Division, a battalion which had come out from England in the preceding autumn, but had, by chance, never been engaged before. It made a fine defence, and beat off three attacks upon the village: but after dark Wellington called it back uphill to the line of the position, abandoning Morisco [1]. Apparently he was glad to see the French pressing in close, and looked for an attack upon his position next morning. Standing on the sky-line above Castellanos at dusk, with a map in his hand, he demonstrated to all the assembled generals commanding divisions the exact part which they were to play, till several French round-shot compelled him to shift his position a little farther back [2]. The whole army slept that night in order of battle, with strong pickets pushed down to the foot of the slopes.

There was, however, no attack at dawn. Marmont's two rear divisions (those of Foy and Thomières) and a brigade of dragoons were not yet on the ground, and only got up in the course of the afternoon: hence he was naturally unwilling to move, as he had a certain knowledge that he was outnumbered. It would seem that Wellington had, that morning, an opportunity of crushing his enemy, which he must have regretted to have lost on many subsequent days of the campaign. Marmont's position was one of very great risk: he had pushed in so close to the British heights, that he might have been attacked and brought to action in half an hour, and could not have got away without fighting. His position was visible from end to end—it had no flank protection, and its only strong points were the two villages of Morisco and Castellanos de Morisco on its left centre. Behind was an undulating sea of cornfields extending to the horizon. Wellington (after deducting the two missing brigades of the 6th Division) could have come down in a general charge from his heights, with 37,000 Anglo-Portuguese infantry, and 3,500 horse—not to speak of Carlos de España's 3,000 Spaniards. Marmont had only five divisions of infantry (about 28,000 bayonets) on the ground at daybreak, and less than 2,000

---

[1] The 68th lost four officers and 46 men killed and wounded, and one officer taken prisoner. For a good account of the fight see the Memoirs of Green of the 68th, pp. 89–90.

[2] See Tomkinson's *Diary*, p. 165.

horse. He was in a thoroughly dominated position, and it is hard to see what he could have done, had Wellington strengthened his left wing with all his cavalry and delivered a vigorous downhill assault on the unprotected French right. The opportunity for an attack was so favourable that Wellington's staff discussed with curiosity the reasons that might be preventing it, and formed varying hypotheses to account for his holding back [1]. As a matter of fact, as his dispatch to Lord Liverpool explains [2], the British Commander-in-Chief was still hoping for a second Bussaco. He saw that Marmont was not going to attack till his rear had come up, but hoped that he might do so that afternoon or next morning, when he had all his men in hand. The daring way in which the Marshal continued to hold on to an untenable position, within cannon shot of his enemy's line, seemed to argue an ultimate intention to bring on an action.

Nor was Wellington very far out in his ideas : Marmont was in a state of indecision. When the missing 10,000 men came up he called a council of war—the regular resort of generals in a difficulty. We have concerning it only the evidence of Foy, who wrote as follows in his diary.

'At dusk on the 21st there was a grand discussion, on the problem as to whether we should or should not give battle to the English. The Marshal seemed to have a desire to do so, but a feeble and hesitating desire. Remembering Vimeiro, Corunna, and Bussaco, I thought that it would be difficult to beat the English, our superiors in number, on such a compact position as that which they were occupying. I had not the first word : I allowed Maucune, Ferey [3], and La Martinière to express their views, before I let them see what I thought. Then Clausel having protested strongly against fighting, I supported his opinion. Because we had left a small garrison in the Salamanca forts, we were not bound to lose 6,000 killed and wounded, and risk the honour of the army, in order to deliver them. The troops were in good spirits, and that is excellent for the first assault : but here we should have a long tough struggle :

---

[1] Tomkinson's *Diary*, p. 166.
[2] Wellington to Liverpool, Salamanca, June 25, in *Dispatches*, ix. p. 252.
[3] The first two were great fire-eaters, and always urged action.

I doubted whether we had breath enough to keep it up to the end. In short, I saw more chances of defeat than victory. I urged that we ought to keep close to the English, "contain" them, and wait for our reinforcements ; this could be done by manœuvring along the left bank of the Tormes above and below Salamanca. Clausel and I set forth this policy from every aspect. The Marshal was displeased : he fancied that his generals were plotting to wreck his plan : he wanted to redeem the blunder which he saw that he had made in leaving a garrison in Salamanca : he dreads the Emperor and the public opinion of the army. He would have liked a battle, but he had not determination enough to persist in forcing it on [1].'

It seems, therefore, certain that Wellington nearly obtained the defensive general action that he had desired and expected, and was only disappointed because Marmont was talked down by his two best divisional generals. If the Marshal had made his attack, it is clear that his disaster would have been on a far more complete and awful scale than the defeat which he was actually to endure on July 22. For he would have had behind him when repulsed (as he must have been) no friendly shelter of woods and hills, such as then saved the wrecks of his army, but a boundless rolling plain, in which routed troops would have been at the mercy of a cavalry which exceeded their own in the proportion of seven to five (or slightly more).

On the morning of the 22nd, the British general, who had now kept his army in position for thirty-six hours on end, began to guess that he was not to be attacked. Was it worth while to advance, since the enemy refused to do so? The conditions were by no means so favourable as at the dawn of the 21st, when Marmont had been short of 10,000 men. But the allied army still possessed a perceptible superiority in numbers, a stronger cavalry, and a dominating position, from which it would be easy to deliver a downhill attack under cover of their artillery.

Wellington, however, made no decisive movement : he threw up some *flèches* to cover the batteries in front of the 1st and 7th Divisions, of which the latter was pushed a little nearer to the Tormes. He brought up the six heavy howitzers which

[1] Foy's *Vie militaire*, ed. Girod de l'Ain, pp. 165–6.

had been used against the forts, and placed them on this
same right wing of his position.   Then he commenced a partial
offensive movement, which was apparently designed to draw
Marmont into a serious bickering, if he were ready to stand.
The 7th Division began to make an advance towards Morisco :
the skirmishers of the Light Brigade of the King's German
Legion moved down, and began to press in the pickets opposite
them, their battalions supporting. Soon after the 51st and 68th,
from the other brigade of the division, that of De Bernewitz,
were ordered to storm a knoll immediately above Morisco,
which formed the most advanced point of the enemy's line.
Wellington directed Graham to support them with the whole
1st and Light Divisions, if the enemy should bring up reinforcements and show fight. But nothing of the kind happened :
the two battalions carried the knoll with a single vigorous rush,
losing some 30 killed and wounded [1]. But the French made
no attempt to recapture it, drew back their skirmishing line,
and retired to the village, only 200 yards behind, where they
stood firm, evidently expecting a general attack. It was not
delivered : Wellington had been willing to draw Marmont into
a fight, but was not intending to order an advance of the whole
line, and to precipitate a general offensive battle.

There was no more fighting that day, and next morning the
whole French army had disappeared save some cavalry vedettes.
These being pressed in by Alten's hussars, it was discovered
that Marmont had gone back six miles, to a line of heights
behind the village of Aldea Rubia, and was there in a defensive
position, with his left wing nearly touching the Tormes near
the fords of Huerta. Wellington made no pursuit : only his
cavalry reconnoitred the new French position. He kept his
army on the San Cristobal heights, only moving down Anson's
brigade of the 4th Division to hold Castellanos, and Halkett's
of the 7th Division to hold Morisco. Hulse's brigade of the
6th Division was sent back to Salamanca, as were also Dickson's
six howitzers, and Clinton was directed to press the siege of

---

[1] The 51st lost 3 killed and an officer and 20 men wounded : the 68th
2 killed and 6 wounded, the K.G.L. Light Battalions 3 killed and 3 officers
and 17 men wounded. There are narratives of the combat in the Memoirs
of Green of the 68th, and Major Rice and Private Wheeler of the 51st.

the forts—notwithstanding the unhappy fact that there was
scarcely any ammunition left in the batteries.

Marmont had undoubtedly been let off easily by Wellington :
yet he hardly realized it, so filled was his mind with the idea
that his adversary would never take the offensive. His report
to King Joseph shows a sublime ignorance of his late danger.
As the document has never been published and is very short,
it may be worth quoting.

'Having concentrated the greater part of this army on the
evening of the 19th, I marched on Salamanca the same day.
I seized some outlying posts of the enemy, and my army
bivouacked within half cannon-shot of the English. Their army
was very well posted, and I did not think it right to attack
yesterday (June 21) without making a reconnaissance of it.
The result of my observations has convinced me that as long
as my own numbers are not *at least equal* to theirs, I must
temporize, and gain time for the arrival of the troops from the
Army of the North, which General Caffarelli has promised me.
If they arrive I shall be strong enough to take an enterprising
course. Till then I shall manœuvre round Salamanca, so as
to try to get the enemy to divide his army, or to move it out of
its position, which will be to my advantage. The Salamanca
forts are making an honourable defence. Since we came up
the enemy has ceased to attack them, so that I have gained
time, and can put off a general action for some days if I think
proper [1].'

Marmont's plan for 'manœuvring around Salamanca'
proved (as we shall see) quite ineffective, and ended within
a few days in a definite retreat, when he found that the succours
promised by Caffarelli were not about to appear.

Meanwhile the siege of the Salamanca forts had recommenced,
on the 23rd, under the depressing conditions that the artillery
had only 60 rounds (15 apiece !) for the four heavy 18-pounders,
which were their effective weapons, and 160 for the six howitzers,
which had hitherto proved almost useless. The two light field-
guns (6-pounders) were also replaced on the first floor of San
Bernardo to shell the enemy's loopholes—they were no good at all

---

[1] Marmont to Joseph, night of the 22nd June, from bivouac before
San Cristobal. Intercepted dispatch in the Scovell Papers.

for battering. This time the besiegers placed one of their heavy guns in the right flanking battery near San Bernardo, to get an oblique enfilading fire against the gorge of the San Cayetano fort. The new idea was to leave San Vincente alone, as too hard a nut to crack with the small supply of shot available, and to batter the lesser fort from flank and rear with the few rounds remaining. The entire stock, together with a hundred rounds of shell, was used up by the afternoon, when no practicable breach had been made, though the palisades of San Cayetano had been battered down, and its parapet much injured. Nevertheless Wellington ordered an attempt to storm (or rather to escalade) the minor fort at 10 p.m. on the same evening. It was to be carried out by the six light companies of Bowes's and Hulse's brigades of the 6th Division, a force of between 300 and 400 men. ' The undertaking was difficult, and the men seemed to feel it,' observes the official historian of the Peninsular sieges [1]. The major of one of the regiments engaged remarks, ' the result was precisely such as most of the officers anticipated —a failure attended with severe loss of life.' The storming-column, starting from the ruins near the left flanking battery, had to charge for the gorge of San Cayetano, not only under the fire of that work, but with musketry and artillery from San Vincente taking them in the rear. The casualties from the first moment were very heavy—many men never got near the objective, and only two ladders out of twenty were planted against the fort [2]. No one tried to ascend them—the project being obviously useless, and the stormers ran back under cover after having lost six officers and 120 men, just a third of their numbers [3]. Among the killed was General Bowes, commanding the second brigade of the division, who had insisted on going forward with his light companies—though this was evidently not brigadier's work. Apparently he thought that his personal influence might enable his men to accomplish the impossible. He was hit slightly as the column started, but bound up his

---

[1] Jones, i. p. 281.

[2] The regimental history of the 53rd says that the ladders were so badly made, of green wood, that many of them came to pieces in the hands of their carriers long before they got near the fort.

[3] The loss has got exaggerated in many reports, because the casualties in the 7th Division at Morisco on the preceding day are added to the total.

wound, and went forward a second time, only to be killed at the very foot of the ladders, just as his men broke and retired.

This, as all engaged in it agreed, was a very unjustifiable enterprise ; the escalade was impracticable so long as San Vincente was intact, and able to cover the gorge of San Cayetano with an effective fire from the rear. The siege now had a second period of lethargy, all the shot having been used up. It was only on the morning of the 26th, three days later, that the convoy from Almeida, ordered up on the 20th by Wellington, arrived with 1,000 rounds carried by mules, and enabled the battering to begin once more.

Meanwhile Marmont had been making persistent but ineffective diversions against Wellington. The advantage of the position to which he had withdrawn was that it commanded the great bend, or elbow, of the Tormes, where (at the ford of Huerta) that river turns its general course from northward to westward. Troops sent across the river here could threaten Salamanca from the south, and, if in sufficient strength, might force Wellington to evacuate part of the San Cristobal position, in order to provide a containing force to prevent them from communicating with and relieving the besieged forts. The Marshal's own statement of his intention [1] was that he hoped, by manœuvring, to get Wellington either to divide his army or to leave his strong ground, or both. He aimed, no doubt, at obtaining the opportunity for a successful action with some isolated part of Wellington's force, but was still too much convinced of the danger of fighting a general action to be ready to risk much. Moreover he was expecting, from day to day, the 8,000 men of the Army of the North whom Caffarelli had promised him : and it would be reckless to give battle before they arrived—if only they were really coming.

Wellington could see, by his own eyes no less than by the map, for he rode along Marmont's new front on the 23rd, that the French position gave good possibilities for a passage of the elbow of the Tormes at Huerta : wherefore he detached Bock's brigade of German Dragoons to the south of the river, with orders to watch the roads debouching from the fords, and to act as a detaining force if any hostile cavalry crossed them. He

[1] See above, p. 370.

also threw forward Alten's hussars to Aldea Lengua, a village and ford half-way between Cabrerizos and Aldea Rubia, with the object of keeping a similar close watch on any attempt of Marmont's to move north of the river. One brigade of the Light Division came forward to support Alten—the other was écheloned a little back, on hills above Aldea Lengua.

On the late evening of the 23rd Marmont sent a squadron or two across the Huerta fords, which turned back after running into Bock's vedettes. This was merely an exploring party to test the practicability of the passage ; but next morning, in a heavy fog, skirmishing fire and occasional reports of cannon told Wellington that some more important detachment was across the Tormes, and engaged with the Germans. The British head-quarters staff rode to the hill above Aldea Lengua, which commands a wide view over the south bank, and, when the morning vapours rolled up at 7 o'clock, saw Bock retiring across the rolling plain in very good order, pressed by a heavy force of all arms—two divisions of infantry headed by a light cavalry brigade with a horse artillery battery, which was doing some harm to the two dragoon regiments as they retired in alternate échelons across the slopes.

Fortunately there was excellent defensive fighting-ground south of the Tormes, in prolongation of the San Cristobal position north of it. The ravine and brook[1] called the Ribera de Pelagarcia with wooded heights above them, run in front of Santa Marta and its ford, for some miles southward from the Tormes. There was a similar line of high ground facing it, with the villages of Pelabravo and Calvarisa de Ariba on its top, which the French might occupy, but on passing down from them they would run against a formidable position. Along these hills, indeed, Wellington's first line of defence was to be formed a month later, on the day of the battle of Salamanca. On seeing Bock's careful retreat in progress, the Commander-in-Chief ordered Graham to cross the Tormes at Santa Marta with the 1st and 7th Divisions, and to occupy the ground in front of him. This was a short move, and easily accomplished while the French detachment was pushing the German dragoons slowly

---

[1] I find the name Ribera de Pelagarcia only in the more modern Spanish maps : contemporary plans do not give it.

backward. The 4th and 5th Divisions moved down to the
north bank of the Tormes, ready to follow if Marmont should
support his advanced guard, by sending more men over the
Huerta fords. Le Marchant's heavy brigade crossed the river
with a horse artillery battery, and went to reinforce Bock,
whom the French could now only push in by bringing forward
infantry. Their advance continued as far as the village of
Calvarisa de Abaxo, and a little beyond, where the whole 9,000
or 10,000 men deployed, as if intending to attack Graham.
But just as observers on the Aldea Lengua heights were beginning to think that serious fighting was probable [1], the whole
fell back into column of march, and, retiring to Huerta covered
by their *chasseurs*, recrossed the river.

The state of affairs at nightfall was just what it had been
at dawn. Graham and Le Marchant went back to their old
ground north of the river, and south of it cavalry alone was
left—this time Alten's brigade, for Bock's had had a heavy
day, and needed rest. So ended a spectacular but almost
bloodless manœuvre—the German dragoons lost three killed
and two wounded : the French light horse probably no more.

In a dispatch written the same night Marmont frankly owns
that he was foiled by Wellington's counter-move. This hitherto
unpublished document is worth quoting. It is addressed to
General Caffarelli, and runs as follows [2]. ' The movement
which I have made toward Salamanca has caused the enemy
to suspend his attack on the forts of that town. [An error,
as it was not the movement but the lack of ammunition which
stopped the bombardment.] This consideration, and the way
in which I found him posted to keep me off, and not least your
assurance that your powerful reinforcements would reach me
very soon, have determined me to suspend the attack which
I was about to deliver against him. I stop here with the object
of gaining time, and in the expectation of your arrival.' From
this it is clear that if Graham had not been found so well posted,

---

[1] Tomkinson, p. 170 : ' Just before they began to retire, I thought that
their advance looked serious. Our position was good, and if they had
fought with what had crossed, our force would have been the greater.'

[2] This is one of the many cipher dispatches in the Scovell Papers, which
I have found so illuminating in a period when Marmont's writings, printed
or in the French archives, are very few.

in a position where he could readily be reinforced from San
Cristobal, Marmont would have followed up his advanced
guard with the rest of his army, and have struck at Salamanca
from the South. But finding the ground on the left bank of
the river just as unfavourable to him as that on the north, he
gave up the game and retired. He risked a serious check, for
Wellington might have ordered Graham to follow and attack
the retreating divisions, who would have had great difficulty
in recrossing the Tormes without loss, if they had been pursued
and attacked while jammed at the fords. But Wellington was
still in his defensive mood, and took no risks, contented to
have foiled most effectively his enemy's manœuvre.

On the 25th Marmont remained stationary, waiting for
further advices from Caffarelli, which failed to come to hand.
Nor did Wellington make any move, save that of sending orders
that the siege of the forts was to be pressed as early and as
vigorously as possible. The guns were back in their batteries,
waiting for the ammunition which was yet to appear. All that
could be done without shot was to push forward a trench along
the bottom of the ravine between San Vincente and the other
two forts, to cut off communication between them. The French
fired fiercely at the workers, where they could look down into
the ravine, and killed some of them. But there was much
' dead ground ' which could not be reached from any point in
the forts, and by dawn on the 26th the trench was far advanced,
and a picket was lodged safely in it, close under the gorge of
San Cayetano.

On the morning of the 26th the convoy of powder and shot
from Almeida reached the front, and at three in the afternoon
the besiegers recommenced their fire. This time no guns were
placed in the original battery opposite the north front of San
Vincente ; the four 18-pounders all went into the right flank
attack, and were concentrated on the gorge of San Cayetano.
Four of the howitzers were placed in the left flank battery,
near the College of Cuenca, and directed to fire red-hot shot
into the roof and upper story of San Vincente. The field-guns
in San Bernardo, aided by one howitzer, took up their old work
of trying to keep down the fire of the forts.

The battering in of the gorge of San Cayetano made consider-

able progress, but the most effective work was that of the red-
hot shot, which before night had set the tower of San Vincente
and several points of its roof in flames. By heroic exertions the
garrison succeeded in extinguishing them, but the besiegers'
fire was kept up all night, and from time to time new conflagra-
tions burst out. The governor afterwards informed the British
engineers that eighteen separate outbreaks were kept down
within the twenty-four hours before his surrender[1]. The fort
was very inflammable, owing to the immense amount of timber
that had been used for casemating, traverses, barricades, and
parapets, inside its walls. Still it was holding out at daybreak, though the garrison was nearly exhausted : the governor
signalled to Marmont that he could not resist for more than
three days—a sad over-estimate of his power, as was to be
shown in a few hours. As a subsidiary aid to the work of the
guns two mines were commenced, one from the ravine, destined
to burrow under San Cayetano, the other from the cliff by the
river, intended to reach La Merced. But neither was fated to
be used, other means sufficing.

After four hours' pounding on the morning of the 27th, the
gorge of San Cayetano had been battered into a real and very
practicable breach, while a new fire had broken out in San
Vincente, larger than any one which had preceded it. It
reached the main store of gabions and planks within the
fort, and threatened the powder magazine. The garrison were
evidently flinching from their guns, as the counter-fire from
the place, hitherto very lively, began to flag, and the whole
building was wrapped in smoke.

Thereupon Wellington ordered San Cayetano to be stormed
for the second time. The column charged with the operation
crept forward along the trench at the bottom of the ravine,
fairly well covered till it had reached the spot immediately
below the gorge of the fort. Just as the forlorn hope was
about to start out of the trench, a white flag was shown from
the breach. The captain commanding in San Cayetano asked
for two hours' truce, to enable him to communicate with his
chief in San Vincente, promising to surrender at the end of that
time. Wellington offered him five minutes to march out, if he

[1] Jones, *Sieges of the Peninsula*, i. p. 285.

wished to preserve his garrison's lives and baggage. As the Frenchmen continued to haggle and argue, he was told to take down his white flag, as the assault was about to be delivered. When the stormers ran in, San Cayetano made practically no defence, though a few shots were fired, which caused six casualties in the assaulting column : the greater part of the garrison threw down their muskets and made no resistance.

At the same moment the white flag went up on San Vincente also : here the conflagration was now burning up so fiercely that the French had been able to spare no attention for the storming-party that captured San Cayetano. The governor, Duchemin, asked for three hours' suspension of arms, and made a proposal of terms of surrender. Wellington, here as at the smaller fort, refused to grant time, as he thought that the fire would be subdued and the defence prolonged, if he allowed hours to be wasted in negotiations. He sent in the same ultimatum as at San Cayetano—five minutes for the garrison to march out, and they should have all the ' honours of war ' and their baggage intact. Duchemin, like his subordinate, returned a dilatory message, but while his white flag was still flying, the 9th Caçadores pushed up out of the ravine and entered the battery on the east side of the work. They were not fired on, no one in San Vincente being prepared to continue the defence, and the French standard came down without further resistance.

Not quite 600 unwounded men of the garrison were captured. They had lost just 200 during the siege, including 14 officers [1]. The casualties among the British were, as might have been expected, much heavier, largely owing to the unjustifiable assault of June 23rd. They amounted to 5 officers and 94 men killed, and 29 officers and 302 men wounded. A considerable store of clothing, much powder, and 36 guns of all sorts were found in the three forts. The powder was made over to Carlos de España, one of whose officers, having moved it into the town on the 7th July, contrived to explode many barrels, which

---

[1] The total given by the governor to Warre of Beresford's staff (see his *Letters*, ed. Dr. Warre, p. 270) were 3 officers and 40 men killed, 11 officers and 140 men wounded. Martinien's lists show 12 officers hit, 5 in the 65th, 2 each in the 15th and 17th Léger, 1 each in 86th, artillery, and engineers. But these admirable lists are not quite complete.

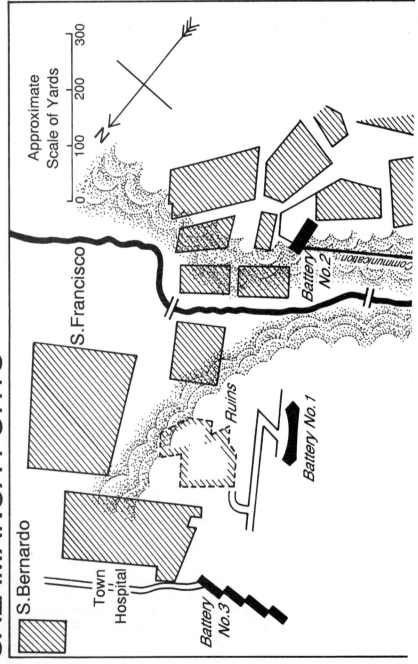

SALAMANCA FORTS

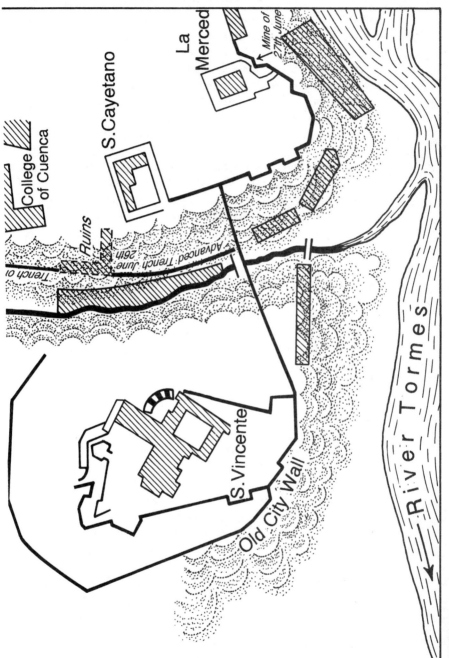

College of Cuenca

S. Cayetano

La Merced

Mine of 27th June

Ruins

Trench o...

Advanced Trench June 26th

S. Vincente

Old City Wall

River Tormes

B.V.Darbishire, Oxford, 1914

killed several soldiers and twenty citizens, besides wrecking some houses [1]. The three forts were destroyed with care, when they had been stripped of all their contents.

The fall of the Salamanca forts happened just in time to prevent Marmont from committing himself to a serious offensive operation for their succour. It will be remembered that, on June 24th, he had used the plea that Caffarelli's troops must be with him, ere many days had passed, as a justification for not pushing on to attack the British divisions in front of Santa Marta. And this expectation was reasonable, in view of that general's last dispatch from Vittoria of June 14th [2], which spoke of his appearance with 8,000 men as certain and imminent. On the 26th, however, the Marshal received another letter from the Army of the North, couched in a very different tone, which upset all his plans. Caffarelli, writing on the 20th, reported the sudden arrival on the Biscay coast of Sir Home Popham's fleet, whose strength he much exaggerated. In co-operation with the English, Longa, Renovales, and Porlier had all come down from their mountains, and Bilbao was in danger from their unexpected and simultaneous appearance. It would probably be necessary to march to drive off the ' 7th Army ' and the British expedition without delay. At any rate the transference of any infantry towards the Douro for the succour of the Army of Portugal had become impossible for the moment. The brigade of light cavalry and the guns might still be sent, but the infantry division had become indispensable elsewhere. ' I am sorry,' ended Caffarelli, ' but I could not have foreseen this development, and when I spoke of marching towards you I was far from suspecting that it could arise.'

This epistle changed the whole aspect of affairs : if the infantry division from Vittoria had been diverted into Biscay for an indefinite period, and if even the cavalry and guns (an insignificant force so far as numbers went, yet useful to an army short of horse) had not even started on June 20th, it was clear that not a single man would be available from the North for many days. Meanwhile the governor of the forts

---

[1] This is said to have been the result of the escort's smoking round the store !

[2] Printed in Marmont's *Mémoires*, iv. p. 410.

signalled at dawn on the 27th that seventy-two hours was the
limit of his power of resistance. Thereupon Marmont came to
the desperate resolve to attempt the relief of San Vincente with
no more than his own 40,000 men. He tells us that he intended
to move by the south side of the Tormes, crossing not at
Huerta (as on the 24th) but at Alba de Tormes, seven miles
higher up, where he had a small garrison in the old castle, which
protected the bridge. This move would have brought him
precisely on to the ground where he ultimately fought the
disastrous battle of July 22nd. He would have met Wellington
with 7,000 men less than he brought to the actual battle
that was yet to come, while the Anglo-Portuguese army was
practically the same in July as it was in June [1]. The result
could not have been doubtful—and Marmont knew that he was
taking a serious risk. But he did not fathom its full danger,
since he was filled with an unjustifiable confidence in his
adversary's aversion to battle, and thought that he might be
manœuvred and bullied out of his position, by a move against
his communications [2]. He would have found out his error in
front of the Arapiles on June 29th if he had persevered.

But he did not persevere : in the morning of June 27 the
firing at Salamanca ceased, and a few hours later it was known
that the forts had fallen. Having now no longer any reason
for taking risks, the Marshal changed his whole plan, and
resolved to remove himself in haste from Wellington's neighbourhood, and to take up a defensive position till he should
receive reinforcements. Two courses were open to him—the
first was to retire due eastward toward Arevalo, and put himself
in communication, by Avila and Segovia, with the Army of the
Centre and Madrid. The second was to retire north-eastward
toward Valladolid, and to go behind the strong defensive line
of the Douro. Taking this line the Marshal would sacrifice his
touch with Madrid and the South, but would be certain of
picking up the reinforcement under Bonnet which he was

---

[1] If Marmont had marched for Alba de Tormes on the 28th, as he
intended to do, Wellington would have had the 6th Division in hand, as
well as the rest of his troops, for a battle on the 29th : for the forts fell early
on the 27th June.

[2] See his explanation of his intentions in *Mémoires*, iv. pp. 219–20.

expecting from the Asturias, and would also be able to receive with security whatever succour Caffarelli might send—even if it turned out to be no more than cavalry and guns.

This alternative he chose, probably with wisdom, for in a position on the Douro he threatened Wellington's flank if he should advance farther eastward, and protected the central parts of the kingdom of Leon from being overrun by the Army of Galicia and Silveira's Portuguese, who would have had no containing force whatever in front of them if he had kept south of the Douro and linked himself with Madrid. His retreat, commenced before daybreak on the 28th, took him behind the Guarena river that night : on the 29th he crossed the Trabancos, and rested for a day after two forced marches. On the 30th he passed the Zapardiel, and reached Rueda, close to the Douro, on the following morning. From thence he wrote to King Joseph a dispatch which explains sufficiently well all his designs : it is all the more valuable because its details do not entirely bear out the version of his plans which he gives in his *Mémoires*.

' The Salamanca forts,' he said, ' having surrendered, there was no reason for lingering on the Tormes ; it was better to fall back on his reinforcements. If he had not done so, he would have been himself attacked, for Wellington was preparing to strike, and pursued promptly. He had detached one division [Foy] towards Toro and the Lower Douro to keep off Silveira, who had passed that river at Zamora. Moreover the Galicians had blockaded Astorga, and crossed the Orbigo. He felt that he could defend the line of the Douro with confidence, being aided by the line of fortified posts along it—Zamora, Toro, and Tordesillas. But to take the offensive against Wellington he must have 1,500 more cavalry and 7,000 more infantry than he actually had in hand—since the Anglo-Portuguese army was nearly 50,000 strong, and included 5,000 English horse.' This reinforcement was precisely what Caffarelli had promised, but by the 28th not one man of the Army of the North had reached Valladolid. ' If the general can trump up some valid excuse for not sending me the infantry, there is none for keeping back the cavalry—which is useless among his mountains—or the artillery, which lies idle at Burgos.' Would it

not be possible for the Army of the Centre to lend the Army of
Portugal Treillard's division of dragoons from the valley of the
Tagus, since Caffarelli sent nothing ? If only the necessary
reinforcements, 1,500 horse and 7,000 foot, came to hand, the
Army of Portugal could take the offensive with a certainty of
success [1] ; in eight days Wellington's designs could be foiled,
and Salamanca could be recovered. But without that succour
the Marshal must keep to the defensive behind the Douro—
' I can combat the course of events, but cannot master them [2].'

This interesting dispatch explains all that followed. Marmont was prepared to fight whenever he could show a rough
numerical equality with Wellington's army. He obtained it
a few days later, by the arrival of Bonnet with his 6,500 infantry,
and the increase of his cavalry by 800 or 900 sabres owing to
measures hereafter to be described. On July 15th he had got
together nearly 50,000 men of all arms, and at once took the
offensive, according to the programme which he had laid down.
It is, therefore, unfair to him to say that he declared himself
unable to fight till he should have got reinforcements either
from Caffarelli or from Madrid, and then (in despite of his
declaration) attacked Wellington without having received
them. He may have been presumptuous in acting as he did,
but at least he gave his Commander-in-Chief fair notice, a fortnight beforehand, as to his intentions. It was the misfortune
of the French that some of their dispatches miscarried, owing
to the activity of the guerrilleros, while others came to hand
very late. Marmont and King Joseph—as we shall see—were
very imperfectly and intermittently informed as to each other's
doings. But the Marshal cannot reasonably be accused of

---

[1] In this dispatch and that of July 6 following, Marmont seems to under-
state his own force at the moment, saying that he can dispose of only
30,000 infantry, and 2,000 cavalry or a trifle over. Allowing for the
artillery, engineers and sappers, gendarmerie and train, which the monthly
returns show, this would give an army of some 35,000 or 36,000 in all.
But the returns (see Appendix) indicate a higher figure for the infantry ;
after all deductions for detachments, garrisons, and sick have been made,
it looks as if there must have been 33,000 or even 34,000 available. Generals
with a ' point to prove ' are always a little easy with their figures.

[2] This is again one of the Scovell intercepted cipher-dispatches, captured
and brought to Wellington a day or two after it was written. It was
a duplicate, and presumably the other copy reached Madrid.

betraying or deluding the King out of jealousy or blind ambition. When he had collected a force very nearly equal to Wellington's in numbers, and far superior in national homogeneity, he cannot be blamed over-much for attacking a foe whose fighting spirit and initiative he much undervalued. That his conception of Wellington's character and capacity was hopelessly wrong cannot be denied : the estimate was to prove his ruin. But it had not been formed without much observation and experiment: after what he had seen on the Caya, and at Aldea da Ponte, and recently on the heights of San Cristobal, he thought he could take liberties with his opponent. He was to be undeceived in a very rude fashion before July was out.

SECTION XXXIII : CHAPTER V

MARMONT TAKES THE OFFENSIVE. JULY 1812

On July 2nd Wellington had arrived at the end of the first stage of his campaign. He had cleared the French out of the whole of southern Leon as far as the Douro, had taken the Salamanca forts, and had beaten off with ease Marmont's attempts to meddle with him. All this had been accomplished with the loss of less than 500 men. But the success, though marked, was not decisive, since the enemy's army had not been beaten in the open field, but only manœuvred out of the considerable region that it had evacuated. The most tangible advantage secured was that Marmont had been cut off from Madrid and the Army of the Centre : he could now communicate with King Joseph only by the circuitous line through Segovia. All the guerrilleros of Castile, especially the bands of Saornil and Principe, were thrown on the Segovia and Avila roads, where they served Wellington excellently, for they captured most of the dispatches which were passing between King Joseph and Marmont, who were really out of touch with each other after the Marshal's retreat from the Tormes on June 27th.

But till Marmont had been beaten in action nothing was settled, and Wellington had been disappointed of his hope that the Army of Portugal would attack him in position, and allow him to deal with it in the style of Bussaco. The Marshal had retired behind the Douro with his host intact : it was certain that he would be joined there by Bonnet's division from the Asturias, and very possible that he might also receive succour from the Army of the North. The junction of Bonnet would give him a practical equality in numbers with the British army : any considerable reinforcement from Caffarelli would make him superior in force. And there was still a chance that other French armies might intervene, though hitherto there were no signs of it. For it was only during the first fortnight of the campaign that Wellington could reckon on having to deal with his immediate adversary alone. He was bound to have that much start, owing to the wide dispersion of the French, and their difficulty in communicating with each other. But as the weeks wore on, and the enemy became more able to grasp the situation, there was a growing possibility that outlying forces might be brought up towards the Douro. If Marmont had only been defeated on June 21st this would have mattered little : and Wellington must have regretted more and more each day that he had not taken the obvious opportunity, and attacked the Army of Portugal when it placed itself, incomplete and in a poor position, beneath the heights of San Cristobal.

Now, however, since Marmont had got away intact, everything depended on the working of the various diversions which had been prepared to distract the other French armies. One of them, Sir Home Popham's, had succeeded to admiration, and had so scared Caffarelli that not a man of the Army of the North was yet in motion toward the Douro. And this fortunate expedition was to continue effective : for another three weeks Marmont got no succours from the army that was supposed to constitute his supporting force by the instructions of the Emperor and of King Joseph. But Wellington—not having the gift of prophecy, though he could see further into the fog of war than other men—was unable to rely with certainty on Caffarelli's continued abstinence from interference. As to Soult, there were as yet no signs of any trouble from Andalusia. The Duke of Dalmatia had somewhat reinforced D'Erlon's corps in Estremadura, but not to such an extent as threatened any real danger to Hill, who reported that he could keep D'Erlon in check on the Albuera position, and was not certain that he might not be able to attack him at advantage—a move for which he had his chief's permission [1]. If only Wellington had been fortunate enough to receive some of Soult's letters to King Joseph, written in the second half of June, he would have been much reassured : for the Marshal was (as we shall see) refusing in the most insubordinate style to carry out the

[1] See Wellington to Lord Liverpool, June 25. *Dispatches*, ix. pp. 253–4, and to Hill, ix. pp. 256–7, and again to Lord Liverpool, ix. pp. 261–2.

orders sent him to move troops northward. Two minor pieces
of intelligence from the South were of no primary importance—
though vexatious enough—one was that Ballasteros had
ventured on a battle at Bornos on June 1, and got well beaten :
but his army was not destroyed. The second was that General
Slade had suffered a discreditable check at Maguilla on June 11th
in a cavalry combat with Lallemand's dragoons. But neither
of these events had much influence on Soult's general conduct
at the time, as we shall show in the proper place.

There remained one quarter from which Wellington had
received information that was somewhat disturbing. An
intercepted letter from King Joseph to D'Erlon showed that
the latter had been directed to move towards the Tagus, and
that the King himself was evidently thinking of bringing
succour to Marmont, so far as his modest means allowed [1]. But
since this projected operation seemed to depend on assistance
being granted by Soult, and since it was doubtful in the highest
degree whether Soult would give it, Wellington was not without hopes that it might come to nothing. ' I have requested
the Empecinado,' he writes to Lord Liverpool, ' to alarm the
King for the safety of his situation about Madrid, and I hope
that Marshal Soult will find ample employment for his troops
in the blockade of Cadiz, the continued operations of General
Ballasteros, and those in Estremadura of Lieut.-General
Hill, whose attention I have called to the probable march of
this corps of the Army of the South through Estremadura.' As
a matter of fact Soult prevented D'Erlon from giving any help
to the King or Marmont ; but a contingency was to arise of
which Wellington, on July 1st, could have no expectation—viz.
that, though refused all help from the South, Joseph might
come to the desperate but most soldier-like determination to
march with his own little army alone to the Douro, in order to
bring to bear such influence as he possessed on what was
obviously a critical moment in the war. The King and Jourdan

---

[1] See Wellington to Lord Liverpool, June 18. *Dispatches*, ix. p. 241, and
June 25, p. 253. There was also in Wellington's hands an intercepted
letter of Joseph to Soult of May 26, distinctly saying that if Marmont is
attacked in June, D'Erlon must pass the Tagus and go to his help. This
is in the Scovell ciphers.

were the only men in Spain who showed a true appreciation of
the crisis : but they made their move too late : the fault was
undoubtedly Soult's alone. However, on July 1st, Wellington
was justified in doubting whether any danger would arise on
the side of Madrid. Joseph could not move the Army of the
Centre to the Douro, without risking his capital and abandoning
all New Castile. As late as July 11th Wellington suspected
that he would not make this extreme sacrifice, but would
rather push a demonstration down the Tagus to alarm central
Portugal, a hypothesis which did not much alarm him [1]. The
King and Jourdan knew better than to make this indecisive move, and marched where their 14,000 men might have
turned the whole course of the campaign—but marched too
late.

There was still a chance that Suchet might be helping the
King—this depended entirely on an unknown factor in the
game, the diversion which Lord William Bentinck had promised
to execute on the coast of Catalonia. If it had begun to work,
as it should have done, by the second half of June, there was
little chance that any troops from the eastern side of Spain
would interfere in the struggle on the Douro. But no information of recent date was yet forthcoming : it was not till July 14th
that the vexatious news arrived that Lord William was faltering
in his purpose, and thinking of plans for diverting his expeditionary force to Italy.

The situation, therefore, when Marmont went behind the
Douro on July 1st, had many uncertain points : there were
several dangerous possibilities, but nothing had yet happened
to make ultimate success improbable. On the whole the most
disappointing factor was the conduct of the Army of Galicia. It
will be remembered that Wellington had arranged for a double
diversion on Marmont's flank and rear. Silveira, with the
militia of the Tras-os-Montes and D'Urban's Portuguese cavalry
brigade, was to cross the Esla and besiege Zamora. Santocildes,
with the Army of Galicia, had been directed to attack Astorga
with part of his force, but to bring the main body forward to

---

[1] Wellington to Hill, July 11. *Dispatches*, ix. p. 281. The idea that
Joseph might operate on his own account begins to emerge in the correspondence on the 14th. *Dispatches*, ix. p. 283.

the Esla and overrun the plains of northern Leon. Silveira
had but a trifling force, and the task allotted to him was small :
but on July 1st he had not yet reached Zamora with his infantry,
and was only at Carvajales on the Esla [1]. On the other hand
D'Urban's cavalry had pushed boldly forward in front of him,
had swept the whole north bank of the Douro as far as Toro,
and reported that all the French garrisons save Astorga,
Zamora, and Toro had been drawn in—that Benavente, Leon,
and all the northern plain were unoccupied. On July 2 D'Urban
was at Castronuevo, north of Toro, right in the rear of Marmont's flank—a very useful position, since it enabled him to
keep up communication between Silveira and the Galicians, as
well as to report any movement of the French right. Moreover,
though his force was very small, only 800 sabres, it was enough
to prevent any foraging parties from Marmont's rear from
exploiting the resources of the north bank of the Douro. Some
such appeared, but were driven in at once, so that the Marshal
had to live on his magazines and the villages actually within
his lines : in the end these resources would be exhausted, and
the old choice—starvation or dispersion—would once more be
presented to the Army of Portugal [2].

But as a military body neither D'Urban's 800 horse nor
Silveira's 4,000 militia had any threatening power against
Marmont's rear. They might almost be neglected, while the
real pressure which Wellington had intended to apply in this
quarter was not forthcoming. He had hoped that, by the time
that he and Marmont were at close quarters, the Army of
Galicia would have been taking a useful part in the campaign.
It was not that he intended to use it as a fighting force : but if
it could have appeared in the French rear 15,000 strong, it would
have compelled Marmont to make such a large detachment

---

[1] By no fault of his own, according to D'Urban. The orders for him to
move were, by some delay at head-quarters, only forthcoming on June 8th.
Only two of the four Tras-os-Montes militia regiments were then mobilized,
and it took a long time to collect the rest and the transport needed for
moving across the frontier.

[2] D'Urban's manœuvres on both sides of the Douro are detailed at great
length in his very interesting diary, and his official correspondence, both
of which have been placed at my disposal. He worked on both sides of the
Douro, but went definitely north of it after July 1.

for the purpose of 'containing' it, that he would have been left in a marked numerical inferiority on the Douro.

Unfortunately the Galicians moved late, in small numbers, and with marked timidity. They exercised no influence whatever on the course of the campaign, either in June or in July. Yet after Bonnet evacuated the Asturias and went off eastward on June 15th, the Army of Galicia had no field-force of any kind in front of it. The only French left in its neighbourhood were the 1,500 men [1] who formed the garrison of Astorga. Castaños, who had moved up to Santiago in June, and assumed command, did not take the field himself, but handed over the charge of the troops at the front to Santocildes. The latter sat down in front of Astorga with his main body, and only pushed forward a weak division under Cabrera to Benavente, where it was still too remote from Marmont to cause him any disquiet. The siege of Astorga was only a blockade till July 2nd, as no battering-train was brought up till that date. First Abadia, and later Castaños had pleaded that they had no means for a regular siege, and it was not till Sir Howard Douglas pointed out a sufficient store of heavy guns in the arsenal of Corunna, that Castaños began to scrape together the battering-train that ultimately reached Astorga [2]. But this was not so much the weak point in the operations of the Galician army, as the fact that, of 15,000 men brought together on the Orbigo, only 3,800 were pushed forward to the Esla, while the unnecessarily large remainder conducted a leisurely siege of the small garrison of Astorga. Wellington had reckoned on having an appreciable force, 10,000 or 12,000 men, at the front, molesting Marmont's flank; this would have forced the Marshal to make a large detachment to keep it off. But not a man appeared on the east bank of the Esla, and the operations of D'Urban's small brigade were of far more service to the main army than that of the whole of the Galicians. Marmont ignored the presence of the few thousand men pushed forward to Benavente, and was justified in so doing. Meanwhile Santo-

---

[1] Two battalions of 23rd Léger and one of 1st Line from Thomières's division.

[2] For the curious story of their ignorance of their own resources see Sir Howard Douglas's *Life*, pp. 156–7.

cildes, with an optimism that proved wholly unjustifiable, sent
messages that Astorga would be taken within a few days, and that
he would then move forward with his main body.   As a matter
of fact the place held out till the 18th of August.

Wellington, therefore, was building on a false hypothesis when
he wrote to Lord Bathurst, on July 7, that he was surveying
all the fords of the Douro, and waiting till the river should
have fallen a little and made them more practicable. ' By that
time I hope that the Army of Galicia under General Santocildes
will have been able to advance, the siege of Astorga having
been brought to a conclusion [1].' Two days later he added, ' it
would not answer to cross the river at all in its present state,
unless we should be certain of having the co-operation of the
Galician troops [2].' His delay in making an attempt to force the
line of the Douro, therefore, may be attributed in the main
to the tiresome conduct of Santocildes, who played to him
much the same part that Caffarelli played to Marmont.

While remaining in this waiting posture, Wellington placed
his troops opposite the various passages of the Douro, on a line
of some fifteen miles.   His left, consisting of the 3rd Division,
Pack's and Bradford's Portuguese, and Carlos de España's
Spaniards, with Le Marchant's and Bock's heavy dragoons, lay
near the point where the Trabancos falls into the Douro, holding
the ford of Pollos, where the favourable configuration of the
ground enabled them to be sure of the passage, the enemy's line
being perforce drawn back to some distance on the north bank.
It was always open to Wellington to use this ford, when he
should determine on a general advance.   The Light, 4th, 5th,
and 6th Divisions, forming the right wing, lay opposite Tordesillas, with Rueda and La Seca behind them.   Their front was
covered by Alten's cavalry brigade, their right (or outer) flank
by Anson's.   The reserve was formed by the 1st and 7th
Divisions quartered at Medina del Campo, ten miles to the rear.
The whole could be assembled for an offensive or a defensive
move in a day's march.

Marmont was drawn up, to face the attack that he expected, in
an almost equally close and concentrated formation : his front,
extending from the junction of the Pisuerga with the Douro

---

[1] *Dispatches*, ix. p. 274.   [2] Ibid., ix. p. 276.

near Simancas on his left, to the ground opposite the ford of Pollos on his right, was very thickly held [1]; but on the 5th he rightly conceived doubts as to whether it would not be easy for Wellington to turn his western flank, by using the ford of Castro Nuño and other passages down-stream from Pollos. He then detached Foy's division to Toro and the neighbourhood, to guard against such a danger : but this was still an insufficient provision, since Toro is fifteen miles from Pollos, and a single division of 5,000 men would have to watch rather than defend such a length of river-line, if it were attacked in force. Therefore when Bonnet, so long expected in vain, arrived from the North on July 7th, Marmont placed him in this portion of his line, for the assistance of Foy. He still retained six divisions massed around Tordesillas, whose unbroken bridge gave him a secure access to the southern bank of the Douro. With this mass of 35,000 men in hand, he could meet Wellington with a solid body, if the latter crossed the Douro at or below Pollos. Or he might equally well take the more daring step of assuming a counter-offensive, and marching from Tordesillas on Salamanca against his adversary's communications, if the allies threatened his own by passing the river and moving on Valladolid.

A word to explain the tardiness of Bonnet's arrival in comparison with the earliness of his start is perhaps required. He had evacuated Oviedo and Gijon and his other posts in the Asturias as early as June 14th, the actual day on which Wellington commenced his offensive campaign. This he did not in consequence of Marmont's orders, which only reached him when he had begun to move, but on his own responsibility. He had received correct information as to the massing of the allied army round Ciudad Rodrigo, and of the forward movement of the Galicians towards Astorga. He knew of the dispersed state of Marmont's host, and saw the danger to himself. Should the Marshal concentrate about Salamanca, he could never join him, if the whole Army of Galicia threw itself between. Wherefore not only did he resolve to retreat at once, but he did

---

[1] An interesting dispatch from D'Urban to Beresford describes the information he had got on the 5th by a daring reconnaissance along Marmont's rear : there was not that morning any French force west of Monte de Cubillos, six miles down-stream from Pollos.

not move by the pass of Pajares and Leon—the obvious route
to rejoin the Army of Portugal. For fear that he might be
intercepted, he took the coast-road, picking up the small
garrisons that he had placed in one or two small ports. He
reached Santander on the 22nd, not molested so much as he
might have been by the bands of Porlier and Longa (whose
haunts he was passing), because the bulk of them had gone off
to help in Sir Home Popham's raid on Biscay. From Santander
he turned inland, passed Reynosa, in the heart of the Cantabrian
Sierras, on the 24th June, and arrived at Aguilar del Campo,
the first town in the province of Palencia, on the 29th. From
thence he had a long march of seven days in the plains, before
he reached Valladolid on the 6th, and reported himself at
Marmont's head-quarters on the 7th of July. He brought with
him a strong division of 6,500 infantry, a light field-battery, and
a single squadron of Chasseurs—even 100 sabres [1] were a welcome reinforcement to Marmont's under-horsed army. It was
an odd fact that Bonnet's division had never before met the
English in battle, though one of its regiments had seen them
during the last days of Sir John Moore's retreat in January
1809 [2]. For the three years since that date they had always
been employed in the Asturias.

The arrival of Bonnet brought up the total of Marmont's
infantry to 43,000 men, and his guns to 78. The cavalry still
remained the weak point : but by a high-handed and unpopular
measure the Marshal succeeded, during his stay on the Douro, in
procuring nearly 1,000 horses for the dismounted dragoons who
were encumbering his dépôt at Valladolid. In the French, as
in the British, Peninsular army it had become common for
many of the junior officers of the infantry to provide themselves
with a riding-horse ; most captains and many lieutenants had
them. And their seniors, *chefs de bataillon* and colonels,
habitually had several horses more than they were entitled to.
Marmont took the heroic measure of proclaiming that he should
enforce the regulations, and that all unauthorized horses were

---

[1] Ninety-four to be exact. See 28th Chasseurs in table of Marmont's
army in Appendix.

[2] The 122nd Line had been in Mermet's division, in January 1809, but
they had been in reserve at Corunna, and had not fired a shot in that battle.

confiscated. He paid, however, a valuation for each beast on a
moderate scale—otherwise the act would have been intolerable.
In this way, including some mounts requisitioned from doctors,
commissaries, and suttlers, about 1,000 horses in all were
procured. The number of cavalry fit for the field had gone up
by July 15th from about 2,200 to 3,200—a total which was only
300 less than Wellington's full strength of British sabres. It
occurs to the casual observer that the horses, having never been
trained to squadron drill or to act in mass, must have been
difficult to manage, even though the riders were competent
horsemen. This may have something to do with the very
ineffective part played by the French cavalry in the next fortnight's campaigning.

A quaint anecdote of the time shows us General Taupin, an
old Revolutionary veteran, with all the officers of his brigade
called together in a village church. ' He ascended the pulpit
and thundered against the abuse of horses in the infantry : he
would make an end of all baggage carried on mules or asses, but
most especially of the officers' riding-horses. " Gentlemen," he
cried, "in 1793 we were allowed a haversack as our only baggage,
a stone as our only pillow." Well—it was a long time since
1793 : we were in 1812, and the speaker, this old and gallant
soldier, had *six* baggage mules himself[1].'

During the first ten days after the deadlock on the Douro
began, the French were much puzzled by Wellington's refusal
to continue his advance. Foy, the ablest of them, noted in his
diary that he must conclude either that the enemy was not
numerous enough to take the offensive—his strength might
have been over-valued—or else that he was waiting for Hill to
bring up his corps from Estremadura. This last idea, indeed,
was running in the brains of many French strategists : it
obsessed Jourdan and King Joseph at Madrid, who were well
aware that Hill, marching by Alcantara and the passes of the
Sierra de Gata, could have got to the Douro in half the time
that it would have taken his opponent, D'Erlon, who would
have had to move by Toledo, Madrid, and Segovia. But the
simple explanation is to be found in Wellington's dispatch to
Lord Bathurst of July 13. ' It is obvious that we could not

[1] *Mémoires* of Lemonnier-Delafosse of the 31st Léger, pp. 177–8.

cross the Douro without sustaining great loss, and could not fight a general action under circumstances of greater disadvantage. . . . The enemy's numbers are equal, if not superior, to ours : they have in their position thrice the amount of artillery that we have, and we are superior in cavalry alone—which arm (it is probable) could not be used in the sort of attack we should have to make [1].' He then proceeds to demonstrate the absolute necessity of bringing forward the Army of Galicia against Marmont's rear. Its absence was the real cause of the deadlock in which he found himself involved. All offensive operations were postponed—meanwhile the enemy might receive reinforcements and attack, since he had not been attacked. ' But I still hope that I shall be able to retain, at the close of this campaign, those acquisitions which we made at its commencement.'

Meanwhile Marmont, having had a fortnight to take stock of his position, and having received reinforcements which very nearly reached the figure that he had named to King Joseph as the minimum which would enable him to take the offensive, was beginning to get restless. He had now realized that he would get no practical assistance from Caffarelli, who still kept sending him letters exaggerating the terrors of Sir Home Popham's raid on Biscay. They said that there were six ships of the line engaged in it, and that there was a landing-force of British regulars : Bonnet's evacuation of the Asturias had allowed all the bands of Cantabria to turn themselves loose on Biscay—Bilbao was being attacked—and so forth. This being so, it was only possible to send a brigade of cavalry and a horse artillery battery—anything more was useless to ask [2]. This was written on June 26th, but by July 11th not even the cavalry brigade had started from Vittoria, as was explained by a subsequent letter, which only reached Marmont after he had already started on an offensive campaign [3]. As a matter of fact, Caffarelli's meagre contribution of 750 sabres [4] and one

---

[1] Wellington to Bathurst. *Dispatches*, ix. p. 284.
[2] Caffarelli to Marmont, in the latter's *Mémoires*, iv. p. 417.
[3] Ibid., pp. 421–2.
[4] He sent finally only two regiments, not three as he had originally promised.

battery actually got off on July 16th [1]. Marmont may be pardoned for having believed that it would never start at all, when it is remembered that a month had elapsed since he first asked for aid, and that every two days he had been receiving dispatches of excuse, but no reinforcements. He had no adequate reason for thinking that even the trifling force which did in the end start out would ever arrive.

Nor, as he demonstrates clearly enough in his defence of his operations, had he any more ground for believing that Joseph and Jourdan would bring him help from Madrid. They resolved to do so in the end, and made a vigorous effort to collect as large a force as was possible. But the announcement of their intention was made too late to profit Marmont. The dispatch conveying it was sent off from Madrid only on July 9th [2], and never reached the Marshal at all, for the two copies of it, sent by separate messengers, were both captured by guerrilleros between Madrid and Valladolid, and came into Wellington's instead of into Marmont's hands. This was a consequence of the insecurity of the communication via Segovia, the only one route open when the Army of Portugal retired behind the Douro. On July 12th the last piece of intelligence from Madrid which Marmont had received was a dispatch from Jourdan dated June 30th—it had taken twelve days to get 150 miles, which shows the shifts to which its bearer had been exposed. This letter is so important, as showing what the King and Jourdan opined at the moment, that its gist is worth giving.

Jourdan begins by complaining that on June 30 the last dispatch from the Army of Portugal to hand was sixteen days old, of the date of June 14th. It is clear, then, that no copies of the reports sent by Marmont on June 22 and June 24 had got to Madrid—a circumstance to be explained by the fact that Wellington had them instead of their destined recipient [3]. Jourdan then proceeds to say that he is informed that Wellington has 50,000 men, but only 18,000 of them British. 'The King thinks that if this is so, you are strong enough to beat his

---

[1] Caffarelli to Marmont, in the latter's *Mémoires*, iv. p. 425, announcing their departure.

[2] Original is in the Scovell ciphers. It seems to be unpublished.

[3] They are both in the Scovell ciphers, and quoted above, p. 370.

army, and would like to know the motives which have prevented you from taking the offensive. He charges me to invite you to explain them by express messenger.' In the South it was known that Hill, with 18,000 men, was advancing on June 18th against D'Erlon. That officer was to be reinforced from Seville, and was probably at close quarters with Hill. The King had sent orders that D'Erlon was to move northward into the valley of the Tagus, if Hill marched up to join Wellington. But, it being probable that the order would not be very promptly executed, ' his Majesty would like you to take advantage of the moment, when Wellington has not all his forces in hand, to fight him. The King has asked for troops from Marshal Suchet, but they will never be sent. All that His Majesty can do at present is to reinforce the garrison of Segovia, and order its governor, General Espert, to help the garrison of Avila, if necessary, and to supply it with food.'

This letter, which clearly gives no hope of immediate help for the Army of Portugal from Madrid, and which might be taken as a direct incitement to bring Wellington to action at once, must be read in conjunction with the last epistle that Marmont had received from the same quarter. This was a letter of the King's dated June 18. The important paragraph of it runs as follows :—

' If General Hill has remained with his 18,000 men on the left (south) bank of the Tagus, you ought to be strong enough to beat the English army, more especially if you have received any reinforcements from the Army of the North. You must choose your battlefield, and make your best dispositions. But if Hill joins the main English army, I fancy they are too strong for you. In that case you must manœuvre to gain time. I should not hesitate to give you a positive order to defer fighting, if I were certain that Count D'Erlon and his 15,000 men, and a division from the Army of Aragon, were on their way to you : for on their arrival the English army would be seriously compromised. But being wholly uncertain about them, I must repeat to you that if General Hill is still on the south side of the Tagus, you should choose a good position and give battle with all your troops united : but if General Hill joins Lord Wellington, you must avoid an action as long as possible, in order to pick up the reinforcements which will certainly reach you in the end [1].'

I think that there can be no doubt in the mind of any honest critic that on the strength of these two dispatches from his Commander-in-Chief, Marmont was justified in taking the offensive against Wellington, without waiting for that help from Madrid which the King had not offered him. Hill being far away, and Wellington having no more than his own seven divisions of Anglo-Portuguese, Marmont is decidedly authorized to bring him to action. The sole factor which the second Madrid dispatch states wrongly, is the proportion of British troops in the allied army : Jourdan guesses that there are 50,000 men, but only 18,000 British. As a matter of fact there were 49,000 men at the moment [2], but about 30,000 were British. This made a difference, no doubt, and Marmont, if he had been determined to avoid a battle, might have pleaded it as his justification. But he was not set on any such timid policy : he had wellnigh attacked Wellington at San Cristobal on June 21st, when he had not yet received his own reinforcements. When Bonnet had come up, and the British had obtained no corresponding addition to their strength, he was eager to take the offensive, and Joseph's and Jourdan's dispatches distinctly authorized him to do so.

After the disaster of Salamanca, Napoleon drew up an indictment of Marmont, of which the three chief heads were :

(1) He took the offensive without waiting for reinforcements which were to join him.

(2) He delivered battle without the authorization of his Commander-in-Chief.

(3) He might, by waiting only two days longer, before he committed himself to a general action, have received at least the cavalry and guns which he knew that Caffarelli had sent him [3].

The very complete answer to these charges is that :

(1) When the Marshal took the offensive he had no reason

---

[1] Joseph to Marmont, June 18, in Ducasse's *Correspondance*, ix. pp. 28–39.

[2] Two battalions, the 1/38 and 1/5th, joined before the battle of the 22nd, bringing up the total force by 1,500 bayonets more.

[3] See the letter of Clarke to Marmont enclosing the Emperor's indictment, in Marmont's *Mémoires*, iv. pp. 453–4.

to suppose that any reinforcements were coming. Caffarelli had excused himself : the King had promised succour only if Hill joined Wellington, not otherwise. Hill had never appeared : therefore no help was likely to come from the southward.

(2) He had clear permission from Joseph to give battle, unless Hill should have joined Wellington.

(3) The succours from Caffarelli, a weak cavalry brigade and one battery, were so small that their arrival would have made no practical difference to the strength of the army. But to have waited two days for them, after the campaign had commenced, would have given Wellington the opportunity of concentrating, and taking up a good position. It was only after the manœuvring had begun [July 15th] that this little brigade started from Vittoria, on July 16th. The Army of Portugal had already committed itself to offensive operations, and could not halt for two days in the midst of them, without losing the initiative.

From his own point of view, then, Marmont was entirely justified in recrossing the Douro and assuming the offensive. He had got all the reinforcements that he could count upon: they made his army practically equal to Wellington's in numbers : in homogeneity it was far superior. If he had waited a little longer, he might have found 12,000 men of the Army of Galicia at his back, setting all Old Castile and Leon aflame. Moreover Astorga was only victualled up to August 1st, and might fall any day. He could not have foreseen King Joseph's unexpected march to his aid, which no dispatch received before July 12th rendered likely. His misfortune (or fault) was that he undervalued the capacity of Wellington to manœuvre, his readiness to force on an offensive battle, and (most of all) the fighting value of the Anglo-Portuguese army.

It cannot be denied that Marmont's method of taking the offensive against Wellington was neat and effective. It consisted in a feint against his adversary's left wing, followed by a sudden countermarch and a real attack upon his right wing.

On July 15th Foy and Bonnet, with the two divisions forming the French right, received orders to restore the bridge of Toro, to drive in Wellington's cavalry screen in front of it, and to cross to the south bank of the Douro. At the same time the divisions of the French centre, opposite the fords of Pollos, made an ostentatious move down-stream towards Toro, accompanied by the Marshal himself, and those on the left, near Tordesillas, shifted themselves towards Pollos. Almost the whole French army was clearly seen marching westward, and the two leading divisions were actually across the river next morning, and seemed to be heading straight for Salamanca by the Toro road.

Wellington was deceived, exactly as Marmont had intended. He drew the obvious conclusion that his adversary was about to turn his left flank, and to strike at Salamanca and his line of communications. It would have been in his power to make a corresponding move against Valladolid, Marmont's base. But his own line of communications meant much more to him than did Marmont's. There was a great difference between the position of an army living by transport and magazines, and that of an army living on the country by plunder, like that of the French marshal. Wellington had always been jealous of his left wing, and as early as July 12 had drawn up an elaborate order of march, providing for the contingency of the enemy crossing the Douro at Toro and the ford of Castro Nuño. If his entire force seemed on the move, the whole British army would make a corresponding shift westward—if only a division or two, the mass transferred would be less in similar proportion. He had no idea of defending the actual course of the river : in a letter written a few days later to Lord Bathurst, he remarked that ' it was totally out of my power to prevent the enemy from crossing the Douro at any point at which he might think it expedient, as he had in his possession all the bridges [Toro and Tordesillas] and many of the fords [1].' His plan was to concentrate against the crossing force, and fight a defensive action against it, wherever a good position might be available.

There were two reasons for which Wellington regarded a genuine offensive move of Marmont by Toro and Castro Nuño as probable. The first was that he had received King Joseph's dispatch of July 9th, captured by guerrilleros, which gave him the startling news that the King had resolved to evacuate all New Castile save Madrid and Toledo, and to march with his field-force of some 14,000 men to join the Army

[1] See *Supplementary Dispatches*, xiv. p. 68.

of Portugal [1]. Wellington wrote to Graham (who was now on his
way home) early on the 16th, that either the Galicians' approach
on his rear had induced Marmont to collect his troops near
Toro, or he had heard that Joseph was gathering the Army of
the Centre at Madrid, and was threatening the allied left ' in
order to prevent us from molesting the King.' It was clear that
if Wellington had to shift westward to protect his line of
communications, he could make no detachment to ' contain '
King Joseph, who would be approaching from the south-east.
Another letter, written an hour or so later, says, ' these movements of Marmont are certainly intended to divert our attention
from the Army of the Centre (which is collecting at Madrid), if
he knows of this circumstance, *which I doubt* [2].' The doubt was
well grounded.

That the whole movement on Toro was a feint did not occur
to Wellington, but his orders of the 16th, given in the evening,
after he had heard that two French divisions were actually
across the Douro on his left, provide for the possibility that
some serious force may still remain at Tordesillas and may
require observation.

The orders direct the transference of the great bulk of the
allied army to a position which will cover the road Toro–
Salamanca. They were issued in the evening to the following
effect. The reserve (1st and 7th Divisions) was to march from
Medina del Campo to Alaejos beyond the Trabancos river, and
subsequently to Canizal and Fuente la Peña behind the Guarena
river. The left wing, which was watching the fords of Pollos
(3rd Division, Bock's cavalry, Bradford's and Carlos de España's
infantry), to Castrillo on the Guarena. Of the right wing the
6th Division and two regiments of Le Marchant's horse were
to move on Fuente la Peña, the 5th Division on Canizal.
Alten's cavalry brigade was to follow the 1st Division. This
left the 4th and Light Divisions and Anson's cavalry still
unaccounted for. They were set aside to act as a sort of rearguard, being directed to move westward only as far as Castrejon
on the Trabancos river, ten miles short of the concentration-
point on the Toro road, to which the rest of the army was

---

[1] See *Dispatches*, ix. p. 294.
[2] Wellington to Clinton, July 16, 7 a.m. *Dispatches*, ix. p. 291.

ordered to proceed. It is clear (though Wellington does not say so) that they would serve as a containing force, if the enemy had left any troops at Tordesillas, and brought them over the Douro there, or at the fords of Pollos.

All these moves were duly executed, and on the morning of the 17th Wellington's army was getting into position to withstand the expected advance of the enemy on Salamanca by the Toro road. This attack, however, failed to make itself felt, and presently news came that the two divisions of Foy and Bonnet, which had crossed the Douro at Toro, had gone behind it again, and destroyed their bridge. What Marmont had done during the night of the 16th–17th was to reverse the marching order of his whole army, the rear suddenly becoming the head, and the head the rear. The divisions to the eastward, which had not yet got near Toro, countermarched on Tordesillas, and crossed its bridge, with the light cavalry at their head. Those which had reached Toro brought up the rear, and followed, with Foy and Bonnet, at the tail of the column. This was a most fatiguing march for all concerned, the distance from Toro to Tordesillas being about twenty miles, and the operation being carried out in the night hours. But it was completely successful—during the morning of the 17th the vanguard, consisting of Clausel's and Maucune's divisions and Curto's *chasseurs à cheval*, was pouring over the bridge of Tordesillas and occupying Rueda and La Seca, which the British had evacuated fifteen hours before. The rest followed, the two rear divisions cutting a corner, and saving a few miles, by crossing the ford of Pollos. This was a safe move, when the cavalry had discovered that there were none of Wellington's troops left east of the Trabancos river. By night on the 17th the bulk of the French army was concentrated at Nava del Rey, ten miles south-west of Tordesillas. In the afternoon Wellington's rearguard, the 4th and Light Divisions, and Anson's cavalry had been discovered in position at Castrejon, where their commander had halted them, when he discovered that he had been deceived as to his adversary's purpose. The rest of the British army had concentrated, according to orders, in the triangle Canizal–Castrillo–Fuente la Peña, behind the Guarena river and in front of the Toro–Salamanca road.

Wellington's first task was to drawback his rearguard to join his main body, without allowing it to become seriously engaged with the great mass of French in its front. This he undertook in person, marching at daylight with all his disposable cavalry, the brigades of Bock and Le Marchant, to join the force at Castrejon, while he threw out the 5th Division to Torrecilla de la Orden to act as a supporting échelon on the flank of the retiring detachment. The remaining divisions (1st, 3rd, 6th, 7th) took up a position in line of battle on the heights above the Guarena, ready to receive their comrades when they should appear.

The charge of the rearguard this day was in the hands of Stapleton Cotton, the senior cavalry officer with the army, who outranked Cole and Charles Alten, the commanders of the 4th and Light Divisions. He had received no orders during the night, and his last, those of the preceding afternoon, had directed him to halt, till his chief should have discovered the true position and aim of the French army. Wellington explained, in his next dispatch home, that the various details of intelligence, which enabled him to grasp Marmont's whole plan, did not reach him till so late on the 17th that it was useless to send Cotton orders to start. They could only be carried out at dawn, and he himself intended to be present with the rearguard before the sun was far above the horizon. He arrived at seven o'clock in the morning, in time to find his lieutenant already engaged with the French van, but not committed to any dangerous close fighting. Cotton had, very wisely, sent out patrols before daylight to discover exactly what was in front of him ; if it was only a trifling body he intended to drive it in, and advance towards La Nava and Rueda [1] ; if Marmont was in force he would take up a defensive position at Castrejon, and wait for further orders.

The patrols soon ran into French cavalry advancing in force, and were driven back upon Anson's brigade, which was drawn up on a long front in advance of the village of Castrejon. On seeing it, the enemy brought up two batteries of horse

---

[1] See report of one of the officers commanding patrols, Tomkinson of the 16th L.D. in the latter's *Memoirs*, p. 180.

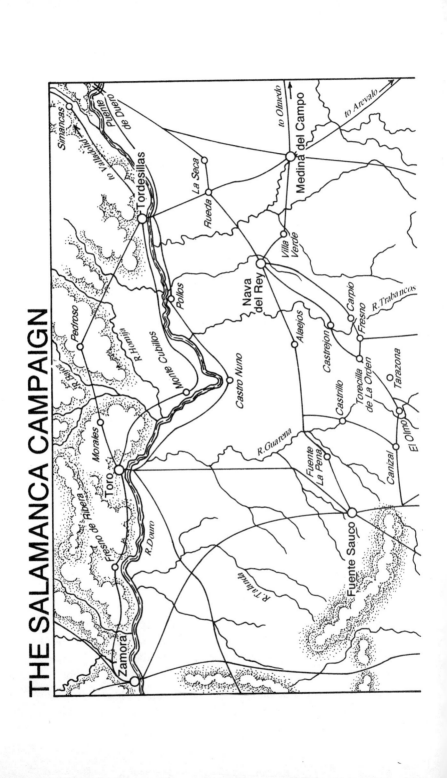

THE SALAMANCA CAMPAIGN

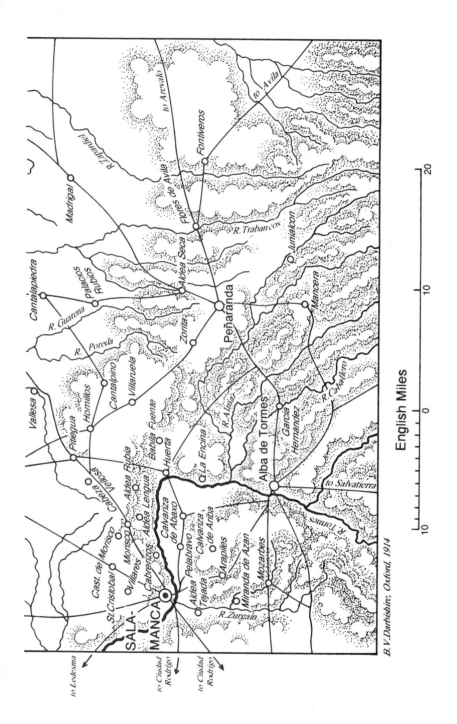

English Miles

B. V. Darbishire, Oxford, 1914

artillery, and began to play upon the scattered squadrons.
Bull's and Ross's troops [1] were ordered out to reply, and did
so with effect, but the total strength of the French cavalry was
too great, and Anson's regiments had presently to give way,
though not so much owing to the pressure on their front as
to the sight of a large column of French infantry turning the
left of their line, and marching on Alaejos, with the obvious
intention of getting round to their left rear and molesting their
retreat towards the Guarena, where the main body of the British
army was awaiting them.

Wellington was involved in person in the end of the cavalry
bickering, and in no very pleasant fashion. He and Beresford,
with their staffs, had arrived on the field about seven o'clock,
in advance of the two heavy cavalry brigades, who were coming
up to reinforce Cotton. He rode forward to the left of the
skirmishing line, where two squadrons, one of the 11th and one
of the 12th Light Dragoons, were supporting two guns of
Ross's troop, on high ground above the ravine of the Trabancos
river. Just as the Commander-in-Chief came on the scene,
a squadron of French cavalry, striking in from the flank, rode
at the guns, not apparently seeing the supporting troops.
They met and broke the squadron of the 12th Light Dragoons,
which came up the hill to intercept them. ' Some of Marshal
Beresford's staff, seeing this, and conceiving the guns to be in
danger, rode up to the retiring squadron calling "Threes
about [2]!"' This unfortunately was heard by the supporting
squadron of the 11th, who, imagining the order to be directed
to themselves, went about and retired, instead of advancing to
relieve their broken comrades above. Therefore the mass of
pursuers and pursued from the combat on the flank, came
hurtling down on the guns, and on the head-quarters staff just
behind them. Wellington and Beresford and their followers
were swept away in the rout, and had to draw their swords
to defend themselves. Fortunately the misdirected squadron
of the 11th soon saw their mistake ; they halted and turned,
and falling on the scattered and exhausted French dragoons
drove them back with great loss ; few, it is said, except their

[1] Belonging one to the cavalry, the other to the Light Division.
[2] Tomkinson, p. 188.

chef d'escadron, who showed uncommon gallantry, got away [1].
It was a dangerous moment for the allied army—a chance
thrust in the *mêlée* might have killed or disabled Wellington,
and have thrown the command into the hands of Beresford or
Stapleton Cotton.

Wellington had no sooner detected the flank movement of
Marmont's infantry towards Alaejos, than he ordered the 4th
and Light Divisions to retire towards the Guarena, covered
by G. Anson's brigade, while Bock's and Le Marchant's heavy
dragoons, farther to the left, drew up in front of the infantry
of the turning column, and detained it, retiring, when pressed,
by alternate brigades. Marmont's whole army was now visible,
moving on in two long columns, of which the more southern
followed the 4th and Light Divisions, in the direction of Torrecilla de la Orden, and tried to come up with their rear, while
the other, passing through Alaejos, made by the high-road for
Castrillo on the Guarena, where the British reserves were
posted.

There was a long bickering fight across the eight miles of
rolling ground between the Trabancos and the Guarena, not
without some exciting moments for Wellington's rearguard.
After passing Torrecilla de la Orden, and picking up there the
5th Division, which had been waiting as a supporting échelon
to cover their southern flank, all the British infantry had to
march very hard, for troops diverging from the northern
French column got close in upon their right, and, moving
parallel with them, bid fair to reach the Guarena first. In the
retreat the 4th Division moved on the right, and was therefore
most exposed, the Light Division next them, the 5th Division
farther south and more distant from the turning column of the
French. The cavalry pursuit in the rear of the retreating force
was never really dangerous : it was held off by Le Marchant's
Heavy and Anson's Light Dragoons without any great difficulty,
and the 5th and Light Divisions only suffered from some
distant shelling by the French horse artillery. But the 4th

---

[1] Compare Tomkinson's narrative of this incident (pp. 180–1) with
Napier's vivid and well-told tale (iv. pp. 254–5). Both agree that the
French were inferior in numbers to the two squadrons, and that there was
deplorable confusion.

Division, though covered from the pursuit in their direct rear by Bock's German squadrons, found a dangerous point about a mile on the near side of the Guarena, where two batteries from the French turning column had galloped forward to a knoll, commanding the ground over which they had to pass, and opened a teasing fire upon the flank of the brigades as they marched by. General Cole, however, threw out his divisional battery and all his light companies to form a screen against their attack, and moved on, protected by their fire, without turning from his route. The covering force fell in to the rear when the defiling was over, and the division suffered small loss from its uncomfortable march [1].

Wellington allowed all the three retreating divisions to halt for a moment on the farther side of the stream, at the bottom of the trough in which it runs. ' The halt near the water, short as it was, gave refreshment and rest to the troops, after a rapid march over an arid country in extremely hot weather [2].' But it could not be allowed to last for more than a very few minutes, for the pursuing enemy soon appeared in force at several points on the heights above the eastern bank of the Guarena, and many batteries opened successively on the three divisions, who were of necessity compelled to resume their march up the slope to the crest, on their own side of the water. Here they fell into position on Wellington's chosen defensive fighting-ground, the 4th Division forming the extreme northern section of the battle array, by the village of Castrillo, the Light and 5th Divisions falling in to the line of troops already drawn up in front of Canizal, while the 1st and 7th Divisions were extended to the south, to form the new right wing, and took their place on the heights of Vallesa, above the village and ford of El Olmo.

Some anxious hours had been spent while the retreat was in progress, but Wellington was now safe, with every man concen-

---

[1] See Vere's *Marches and Movements of the 4th Division*, p. 28. Napier's statement that the Light Division was more exposed than the 4th or 5th during the retreat, seems to be discounted by the fact that it had not one man killed or wounded—the 5th Division had only two (in the 3rd Royal Scots), the 4th Division over 200 ; and though most of them fell in the last charge, a good number were hit in the retreat.

[2] Vere's *Marches and Movements of the 4th Division*, p. 28.

trated on an excellent position, where he was prepared to accept the defensive battle for which he had been waiting for the last month. It seemed likely at first that his wish might be granted, for the French made a vigorous attack upon his left wing, almost before it had got settled down into its appointed ground. It would appear that General Clausel, who commanded the more northerly of the two great columns in which the French army was advancing (while Marmont himself was with the other), thought that he saw his chance of carrying the heights above Castrillo and turning the allied left, if he attacked at once, before the 4th Division had been granted time to array itself at leisure. Accordingly, without wasting time by sending to ask permission from his chief, he directed a brigade of dragoons to outflank Cole's left by crossing the Guarena down-stream, while Brennier's division passed it at Castrillo and assailed the front of the 4th Division. Clausel's own division advanced in support of Brennier's.

This move brought on very sharp fighting : the turning movement of the French dragoons was promptly met by Victor Alten's brigade [14th Light Dragoons, 1st Hussars K.G.L.], whose squadrons had been watching the lower fords of the Guarena all day. Alten allowed the hostile cavalry to cross the river and come up the slope, and then charged suddenly, in échelon of squadrons, the left squadron of the 1st Hussars K.G.L. leading [1]. The enemy had only begun to deploy when he was attacked, Alten's advance having been too rapid for him. The two French regiments (15th and 25th Dragoons) were, after a stiff fight, completely routed and driven downhill with great loss, till they finally found refuge behind a half-battery and an infantry battalion which formed their supports. General Carrié, commanding the two regiments, was taken prisoner by a German hussar, having got cut off from his men in the flight. The French lost in all 8 officers and more than 150 men, of whom 94 were prisoners—mostly wounded. How sharp the

---

[1] Brotherton of the 14th L.D. says with the *right* échelon advanced (Hamilton's *History of the 14th*, p. 107), but I fancy that the German Hussars' version that the *left* échelon led is correct, as the right squadron of their regiment would have been in the middle of the brigade, not on a flank. See narrative in Schwertfeger, i. pp. 368–9.

clash was may be seen from the fact that Alten's victorious brigade had not much fewer casualties—the 14th Light Dragoons lost 75 killed and wounded, the German hussars 60 [1]. But no doubt some of these losses were suffered not in the cavalry combat, but a little later in the day, when Alten charged the French infantry [2].

While this lively fight was in progress on the flank, Brennier's division had crossed the Guarena in a mass, and on a very short front, apparently in three columns of regiments, battalion behind battalion. They were ascending the lower slopes below Cole's position, when Wellington, who was present here in person, suddenly took the offensive against them, sending W. Anson's brigade (3/27th and 1/40th) against them in line, with Stubbs's Portuguese (11th and 23rd regiments) supporting, in columns of quarter distance. The French division halted, apparently with the intention of deploying—but there was no time for this. The line of Anson's brigade enveloped both the hostile flanks with its superior frontage, and opened fire : after a short resistance the French gave way in great disorder, and streamed down to the Guarena. As they fled Alten let loose part of his brigade against their flank : the horsemen rode in deep among the fugitives, and cut off 6 officers and 240 men as prisoners. Clausel had to bring up a regiment of his own division to cover the broken troops as they repassed the river ; it suffered severely from Cole's artillery, losing 6 officers killed and wounded, and many men [3].

The attempt to take liberties with Wellington's army, when it had assumed the defensive on favourable ground, had thus failed in the most lamentable style, and with very heavy loss— at least 700 men had been killed, wounded, or taken in Marmont's army that day, and all but a few scores belonged to the four infantry and two cavalry regiments which Clausel sent to

---

[1] These are the official returns. The regimental histories give only 45 and 56 respectively.

Martinien's lists show six casualties in officers in the two French regiments, and two more were taken prisoners, General Carrié and a lieutenant of the 25th Dragoons.

[2] Brotherton says that the first two squadrons which charged the French dragoons made no impression, and that it was the impact of the third, led by himself, which broke them.   [3] This was the 25th Léger.

attack the heights by Castrillo [1]. The corresponding British loss that day was 525, including about 50 stragglers taken prisoners during the retreat from the Trabancos to the Guarena, because they had fallen behind their regiments—foot-sore infantry, or troopers whose horses had been shot. The cavalry, which had so successfully covered the long march across the open, had a certain amount of casualties, but the only units that had suffered heavily were the four regiments—horse and foot—that dealt with Clausel's attack, who lost 276 men between them.

Wellington must have felt much disappointment at seeing Clausel's offensive move at Castrillo unsupported by the rest of the French divisions, who were lining the farther bank of the Guarena parallel with the whole of his front. But Marmont, unlike his venturesome subordinate, nourished no illusions about the advisability of attacking a British army in position. He made no move in the afternoon ; in his memoirs he points out that the infantry was absolutely exhausted, having been continuously on the march for three days and one night.

This day had been a disappointing one for the French marshal also. He had failed to cut off Wellington's two detached divisions, so that all the advantage which he had obtained by his marches and countermarches between Toro and Tordesillas was now exhausted. The allied army had succeeded in concentrating, and was now drawn up in his front, covering Salamanca and its own line of communications in a very tenable position. Napier truly remarks that, since the attempt to isolate and destroy Cotton's detachment had miscarried, Marmont had gained no more by his elaborate feint and forced marches than he would have obtained by continuing his original advance across Toro bridge on the 16th. He had got the whole Anglo-Portuguese army arrayed in a defensive position in front of him, on the line of the Guarena, instead of somewhere in the neighbourhood of Fuente Sauco, a few miles farther east.

---

[1] The exact figures, save for officers, are as usual missing. But Martinien's invaluable lists show that of 41 French officers killed, wounded, or taken that day, 35 belonged to the four infantry regiments (17th and 25th Léger, 22nd and 65th Line) and the two cavalry regiments (15th and 25th Dragoons) which fought at Castrillo.

On the morning of the 19th July it seemed as if a new deadlock was to bring the campaign to a standstill, for the two armies continued to face each other across the Guarena, Wellington hoping rather than expecting to be attacked, Marmont looking in vain for a weak point between Castrillo and Vallesa, where it would be worth while to try a forward thrust. While he was reconnoitring, his weary infantry got a much-needed rest. At about four o'clock in the afternoon, however, the whole French army was seen falling into column, and presently edged off southward till it lay between Tarazona and Cantalapiedra. Wellington thereupon made a corresponding movement, evacuating Castrillo to the north, and extending his line of battle beyond Vallesa to the south. There was a little distant cannonading across the valley of the Guarena, and some of the shells set fire to the vast fields of ripe wheat which covered the whole country-side in this region. The conflagration went rolling on for a long way across the plain, leaving a trail of smoke behind.

The situation on this evening had nothing decisive about it. It was clear that neither side intended to fight save at an advantage. Marmont had shown himself more cautious than had been expected. Wellington had at this moment every motive for risking nothing, unless the enemy proved more obliging than he had shown himself hitherto. He had reasons for self-restraint at this moment of which his adversary knew nothing. The first was that he was aware (from intercepted dispatches) of King Joseph's intention to march from Madrid to join the Army of Portugal : with a possible 15,000 men about to appear on his flank, he must look to the future with care. The second was that he had received a few days before the untoward news that Lord William Bentinck's long-promised expedition to Catalonia might not ever take place. The Commander-in-Chief in Sicily wrote that he had found new opportunities in Italy, which it might be his duty to seize. His troops had been embarked, but they were not to be expected for the present off the coast of Spain. This was a disheartening piece of intelligence : Wellington had been told to count upon this support both by Bentinck himself and by the Home Government. If it should fail, Marshal Suchet, left undisturbed by this diversion, might send considerable reinforcements to Madrid [1].

As a matter of fact he did not—being, like Soult, a general of much too self-centred a type of mind to help a neighbour if he could avoid it. Only one regiment of the Valencian army ever got to Madrid, and that came too late for King Joseph's purpose. But so far as Wellington could guess on July 19, it was quite possible that Suchet might find 10,000 men, to add to the disposable 15,000 of the Army of the Centre.

There was also the possibility that D'Erlon, obeying the orders which King Joseph kept sending to him, might make up his mind to cross the Guadiana and Tagus, and come north by Arzobispo and Madrid. If so, Hill was to make a parallel march by Alcantara, and would certainly arrive many days before D'Erlon. This was a mere possibility; there were good reasons for holding that Soult might forbid any such move; and till D'Erlon started northward, Hill must remain behind to contain him. The problem was not pressing: it could not develop for many days [2].

On the other hand there was news that the Galicians were at last on the move. Santocildes had been prevailed upon to leave a smaller force to besiege Astorga, and had come down with a second division to join Cabrera at Benavente. This force, advancing up the Douro valley, would find absolutely no enemy in front of it, and must obviously disturb Marmont's operations, since it might be at the gates of Valladolid, his base and storehouse, in a few days. He would then be forced to detach a division or so to save his dépôts, and he could not spare even a brigade if he wished to continue on the offensive. Certain intelligence that there was not a Frenchman left behind on the Douro, save the trifling garrisons of Toro, Zamora, and Tordesillas, had been brought in by General D'Urban. That officer, after conducting a very daring exploration round the rear of Marmont's army, almost to the gates of Valladolid, had recrossed the Douro by Wellington's orders at the ford of Fresno de

---

[1] For dismay expressed by Wellington at this news see dispatches to Henry Wellesley dated Rueda, July 15, and to Lord Bathurst (*Dispatches*, ix. pp. 285 and 287).

[2] See Wellington to Hill, *Dispatches*, ix. p. 290.

Ribera, and fell in upon the left flank of the allied army near
Fuente Sauco on, July 18th [1]. For the rest of the campaign
his 700 sabres were at Wellington's disposal [2]. His report
showed that Marmont's rear was absolutely undefended, and
that the Galicians could march up the Douro, if desired, without
finding any opponents : it would be perfectly possible for them
to cut all Marmont's communications with Valladolid and
Burgos, without being in any danger unless the Marshal
detached men against them.

The 20th of July proved to be a most interesting day of manœuvring, but still brought no decisive results. Early in the
morning the whole French army was seen in march, with its head
pointing southward, continuing the movement that it had begun
on the previous day. Marmont had made up his mind to proceed
with the hitherto unsuccessful scheme for turning his adversary's
right wing [3], in the hope of either cutting him off from his
communication with Salamanca, or of catching him with his
army strung out on too long a line from continuous and rapid
movement. The character of this day's march differed from
that of the 19th, because the single well-marked Guarena
valley ceased after a time to separate the two hostile armies.
That little river is formed by three tributaries which meet
at and above the village of El Olmo : each of them is a paltry
brook, and their courses lie along trifling irregularities of the
broad tableland from which they descend. It is only after their
junction that they flow in a deep well-marked valley, and
form a real military obstacle. Of the three brooks, that which
keeps the name of Guarena lies most to the east : up its right
bank and towards its source Marmont's march was directed.
Wellington's parallel movement southward, on the other hand,

[1] Not July 17th, as Napier says. D'Urban's diary proves that he
recrossed the Douro on the 18th.

[2] He left one squadron near Zamora, to serve as covering cavalry for
Silveira's militia, who remained waiting for Santocildes's advance, which
they were to observe and support. His force was therefore reduced to
700 men.

[3] He adds in his *Mémoires*, iv. pp. 251–2, that if he had not succeeded in
getting ahead of Wellington's van, he had a counter-project of trying to
get round his rear, but the British marched so exactly parallel with him
that he got no chance of this.

was directed along the left bank of the Poreda, the middle
brook of the three. Between them there was at first a narrow
triangular plateau, on which neither party trespassed save
with cavalry scouts.

After a few miles of marching Marmont ordered his advanced
guard to cross the Guarena, which they could do with ease, no
British being near, save a few cavalry vedettes. He then
turned the head of his column south-westward, instead of
keeping to his original direction due south. Having crossed the
Guarena he came in sight of the British column marching on
the other side of the Poreda brook from Vallesa. The movements of the two armies tended to converge, the point on which
both were moving being the village of Cantalpino. It seemed
likely that the heads of the marching columns must collide,
and that a combat, if not a general action, would ensue. Each
army was marching in an order that could be converted into
a battle line by simply facing the men to right or to left respectively. Wellington had his troops in three parallel columns, the
first one, that nearest to the French, being composed of the
1st, 4th, 5th, and Light Divisions, the second, which would
have formed the supporting line if the army had fronted and
gone into action, contained the 6th and 7th and Pack's and
Bradford's brigades : the 3rd Division and España's Spaniards
formed a reserve, moving farthest from the enemy. The light
cavalry were marching ahead of the column, the heavy cavalry
and D'Urban's Portuguese brought up their rear. Marmont
was clearly seen to be moving in a similar formation, of two
columns each composed of four infantry divisions, with Curto's
chasseurs ahead, and Boyer's dragoons at the tail of the line
of march [1].

The day was warm but clouded, so that the sun did not shine
with full July strength, or the long march which both armies
carried out would have been brought to an end by exhaustion
at a much earlier hour than was actually the case. As the
long morning wore on, the two hostile forces gradually grew
closer to each other, owing to the new westward turn which

[1] Marmont describes the formation (*Mémoires*, iv. p. 252) as ' gauche en
tête, par peloton, à distance entière : les deux lignes pouvaient être formées
en un instant par *à droite en bataille*.'

Marmont had given to his van. At last they were within long
artillery range ; but for some time no shot was fired, neither
party being willing to take the responsibility of attacking an
enemy in perfect order and well closed up for battle. Either
general could have brought on a fight, by simply fronting to
flank, in ten minutes ; but neither did so. Marmont remarks in
his *Mémoires* that in his long military service he never, before
or after, saw such a magnificent spectacle as this parallel march
of two bodies of over 40,000 men each, at such close quarters.
Both sides kept the most admirable order, no gaps occurred in
either line, nor was the country one that offered advantage
to either : it was very nearly flat, and the depression of the
Poreda brook became at last so slight and invisible that it was
crossed without being noticed. The ground, however, on which
the French were moving was a little higher than that on which
the allies marched [1].

The converging lines of advance at last almost touched each
other at the village of Cantalpino : the light cavalry and the
1st Division, at the head of Wellington's front (or eastern)
column of march had just passed through it, when Marmont
halted several batteries on a roll of the ground a few hundred
yards off, and began to shell the leading battalions of the
4th Division, which was following closely behind the 1st.
Wellington ordered Cole not to halt and reply, nor to attack,
but to avoid the village and the French fire by a slight westerly
turn, to which the other divisions conformed, both those in
the first and those in the second line [2]. This amounted to the
refusing of battle, and many officers wondered that the challenge
of Marmont had been refused : for the army was in perfect order
for fighting, and in excellent spirits. But Wellington was taking
no risks that day.

The slight swerve from the direct southerly direction at
Cantalpino made by the allied army, distinctly helped Marmont's
plan for turning its right, since by drawing back from its
original line of movement it allowed the enemy to push still

[1] There is an excellent description of the parallel march in Leith Hay,
ii. pp. 38–40, as well as in Napier.
[2] This swerve and its consequence are best stated in Vere's *Marches of the
4th Division*, p. 30.

farther westward than his original line of march had indicated. This meant that he was gradually getting south of Wellington's vanguard, and would, if not checked, ultimately arrive at the Tormes river, near the fords of Huerta, from which he would have been edged off, if both armies had continued in their original direction. During the early afternoon the parallel move continued, with a little skirmishing between cavalry vedettes, and an occasional outbreak of artillery fire, but no further developments. The baggage in the English rear began to trail behind somewhat, owing to the long continuance of the forced marching, and D'Urban's Portuguese, who shepherded the stragglers, had great difficulty in keeping them on the move. A few score sick and foot-sore men, and some exhausted sumpter-beasts, fell behind altogether, and were abandoned to the French [1].

Late in the afternoon the armies fell further apart, and all save the outlying vedettes lost sight of each other. This was due to the fact that Wellington had made up his mind to settle down for the night on the heights of Cabeza Vellosa and Aldea Rubia, where Marmont had taken up his position a month before, when he retired from before San Cristobal. This was good fighting-ground, on which it was improbable that the French would dare to deliver an attack. The 6th Division and Alten's cavalry brigade were detached to the rear, and occupied Aldea Lengua and its fords.

This had been a most fatiguing day—the British army had marched, practically in battle formation, not less than four Spanish leagues, the French, by an extraordinary effort, more than five. When the camp-fires were lighted up at night, it was seen that the leading divisions of the enemy were as far south as Babila Fuente, quite close to the Tormes and the fords of Huerta : the main body lay about Villaruela, opposite the British bivouacs at Aldea Rubia and Cabeza Vellosa. An untoward incident terminated an unsatisfactory day: D'Urban's Portuguese horse coming in very late from their duty of covering

---

[1] Marmont says that if he had possessed a superior cavalry he could have made great captures, but he dared attempt nothing for want of sufficient numbers : he alleges that he took 300 stragglers—certainly an exaggeration as the British returns show very few ' missing.' *Mémoires*, iv. p. 233.

the baggage-train, were mistaken for prowling French cavalry
by the 3rd Division, and shelled by its battery, with some little
loss of men and horses. The mistake was caused by a certain
similarity in their uniform to that of French dragoons—the tall
helmets with crests being worn by no other allied troops [1].

The net result of the long parallel march of July 20th was
that Marmont had practically turned Wellington's extreme
right, and was in a position to cross the Upper Tormes, if he
should choose, in prolongation of his previous movement. The
allied army was still covering Salamanca, and could do so for
one day more, if the marching continued : but after that limit
of time it would be forced either to fight or to abandon Salamanca, the main trophy of its earlier campaign. There remained
the chance of falling upon Marmont's rear, when his army should
be occupied in crossing the Tormes, and forcing him to fight
with his forces divided by the river. If this offensive move were
not taken, and the parallel march were allowed to continue, the
next day would see the armies both across the Tormes, in
the position where Graham and Marmont had demonstrated
against each other on June 24th. Wellington could not,
however, begin his southward move till he was certain that
the enemy was about to continue his manœuvre on the same
plan as that of the last two days. If he started too early,
Marmont might attack the San Cristobal position when it
was only held by a rearguard, and capture Salamanca. Till
an appreciable fraction of the French were seen passing the
Tormes it was necessary to wait.

It appeared to Wellington that his adversary's most probable
move would be the passage of the Tormes by the fords at and
just above Huerta. That he would abandon his previous tactics,
and attack the British army, was inconsistent with the caution
that he had hitherto displayed. That he would continue his
march southward, and cross the river higher up, was unlikely ;
for the obvious passage in this direction, by the bridge of Alba

[1] The heavy cavalry in the British army were still wearing the old
cocked hat, the new-pattern helmet with crest was not served out till 1813.
The light dragoons were still wearing the black-japanned leather head-
dress with the low fur crest : in 1813 they got shakos, much too like those
of French *chasseurs*.

de Tormes, was commanded by the castle of that town, which had been for some time occupied by a battalion detached from Carlos de España's division. Wellington looked upon this route as completely barred to the French : he was unaware that the Spanish general had withdrawn his detachment without orders on the preceding afternoon. This astonishing move of his subordinate was made all the worse by the fact that he never informed his chief that he had taken upon himself to remove the battalion. Indeed Wellington only heard of its disappearance on the 23rd, when it was too late to remedy the fault. He acted on the 21st and 22nd as if Alba de Tormes were securely held. It would appear that Carlos de España thought the castle too weak to be held by a small force, and moved his men, in order to secure them from being cut off from the main army, as they clearly might be when the French had reached Babila Fuente. But the importance of his misplaced act was not to emerge till after the battle of Salamanca had been fought.

At dawn on the 21st Wellington withdrew his whole army on to the San Cristobal position[1], and waited for further developments, having the fords of Aldea Lengua and Santa Marta conveniently close if Marmont should be seen crossing the Tormes. This indeed was the move to which the Marshal committed himself. Having discovered at an early hour that Alba de Tormes was empty, and that there was no allied force observing the river bank below it, he began to cross in two columns, one at the fords of Huerta, the other three miles higher up-stream at the ford of La Encina. Lest Wellington should sally out upon his rear, when the greater part of his army had got beyond the Tormes, he left a covering force of two divisions in position between Babila Fuente and Huerta. This, as the day wore on, he finally reduced to one division[2] and some artillery. As long as this detachment remained opposite him,

[1] Napier says that this move was made on the night of the 20th, under cover of the smoke of the already-lighted camp-fires of the army. This is contradicted by Vere's journal of march of the 4th Division, by Leith Hay's Journal ['at daylight we marched to the Heights of San Cristoval'], by Tomkinson's diary, and D'Urban, Geo. Simonds, and many others who speak of the move as being early on the 21st.

[2] This was the division of Sarrut.

Wellington could not be sure that the French might not attack him on both sides of the Tormes.

The defile of the French army across the fords naturally took a long time, and Wellington was able to allow his weary infantry some hours of much-needed rest in the morning. Only cavalry was sent forward at once, to form a screen in front of the hostile force that was gradually accumulating on the near side of the fords. In the afternoon, however, when the greater part of the French were over the water, nearly the whole allied army received orders to cross the Tormes, and occupy the heights to the south of it. It moved practically in battle order, in two lines, of which the front passed by the ford of Cabrerizos, the second by that of Santa Marta. Only a reserve, now consisting of the 3rd Division and D'Urban's Portuguese horse, remained on the north side of the river near Cabrerizos, to contain the French force which was still visible at dusk on the slopes by Babila Fuente. Till this detachment had disappeared, Wellington was obliged to leave a corresponding proportion of his men to contain it, lest the enemy might try a dash at Salamanca by the north bank. Marmont made no such attempt, and in the morning it was obvious that this rearguard was following the rest of his army across the Tormes.

During the night the French advanced cavalry were holding Calvarisa de Ariba on their left and Machacon on their right : the infantry were bivouacked in a concentrated position in the wooded country south of those villages. The British cavalry screen held Calvarisa de Abaxo [1], Pelabravo, and the height of Nuestra Señora de la Peña, close in to the corresponding front line of the enemy's vedettes. The infantry were encamped in two lines behind the Ribera de Pelagarcia, the ravine, which runs north from Nuestra Señora de la Peña to the Tormes, between Santa Marta and Cabrerizos. This was Graham's old position of June 24th, and excellent for defence. The right was

---

[1] That the British cavalry were still at dawn so far forward as Calvarisa de Abaxo is shown by Tomkinson's diary (p. 185), the best possible authority for light cavalry matters. The 4th Division camped in the wood just west of Nuestra Señora de la Peña (Vere, p. 31), the 5th on high ground in rear of Calvarisa de Ariba (Leith Hay, p. 45), the 7th a little farther south, also in woody ground (diary of Wheeler of the 51st).

on well-marked high ground, the centre was covered by woods. Only the left, near Santa Marta, was on lower slopes.

About an hour after nightfall the hills where French and English lay opposite each other were visited by an appalling tempest. ' The rain fell in torrents accompanied by vivid flashes of lightning, and succeeded by instantaneous peals of thunder : ' writes one annalist : ' a more violent crash of the elements has seldom been witnessed : its effects were soon apparent. Le Marchant's brigade of cavalry had halted to our left : the men, dismounted, were either seated or lying on the ground, holding their horses' bridles. Alarmed by the thunder, the beasts started with a sudden violence, and many of them breaking loose galloped across the country in all directions. The frightened horses, in a state of wildness, passing by without riders, added to the awful effect of the tempest[1].' The 5th Dragoon Guards suffered most by the stampede—eighteen men were hurt, and thirty-one horses were not to be found. Another diarist speaks of the splendid effect of the lightning reflected on the musket-barrels of belated infantry columns, which were just marching to their camping-ground. Before midnight the storm had passed over—the later hours of sleep were undisturbed, and next morning a brilliant sun rose into a cloudless sky[2]. The last day of manœuvring was begun, and the battle which both sides had so long avoided was at last to come.

[1] Leith Hay, ii. p. 46.   [2] Diary of Green of the 68th, p. 98.

SECTION XXXIII: CHAPTER VI

THE BATTLE OF SALAMANCA, JULY 22, 1812. THE EARLY STAGES

THE decisive moment of the campaign of 1812 had now been reached—though Marmont was wholly unaware of it, and was proposing merely to continue his manœuvring of the last five days, and though Wellington hardly expected that the 22nd of July would turn out more eventful than the 21st. Both of them have left record of their intentions on the fateful morning. The Duke of Ragusa wrote to Berthier as follows : ' My object was, in taking up this position, to prolong my movement to the left, in order to dislodge the enemy from the neighbourhood of Salamanca, and to fight him at a greater advantage. I calculated on taking up a good defensive position, against which the enemy could make no offensive move, and intended to press near enough to him to be able to profit from the first fault that he might make, and to attack him with vigour [1].' He adds in another document, ' I considered that our respective positions would bring on not a battle, but an advantageous rearguard action, in which, using my full force late in the day, with a part only of the British army left in front of me, I should probably score a point [2].' It is clear that he reckoned that his adversary would continue his policy of the last five days ; Wellington, if his flank were once more turned, would move on as before—always parrying the thrusts made at him, but not taking the offensive himself.

Nor was he altogether wrong in his expectation. Writing to Lord Bathurst on the evening of July 21st, the British Commander-in-Chief summed up his intentions in these words. ' I have determined to cross the Tormes, if the enemy should : to cover Salamanca as long as I can : and above all not to give up our communication with Ciudad Rodrigo : and not to fight

---

[1] Marmont to Berthier, July 31, printed in *Mémoires*, iv. p. 443.
[2] Marmont, *Mémoires*, iv. p. 237.

an action unless under very advantageous circumstances, or if it should become absolutely necessary [1].' This determination is re-stated in a dispatch which Wellington wrote three days later, in a very different frame of mind. ' I had determined that if circumstances should not permit me to attack him on the 22nd, I should move toward Ciudad Rodrigo without further loss of time [2].' Wellington was therefore, it is clear, intending simply to continue his retreat without delivering battle, unless Marmont should give him an opportunity of striking a heavy blow, by putting himself in some dangerous posture. He desired to fight, but only if he could fight at advantage. Had Marmont continued to turn his flank by cautious movements made at a discreet distance, and with an army always ready to form an orderly line of battle, Wellington would have sacrificed Salamanca, and moved back toward the Agueda. He was not prepared to waste men in indecisive combats, which would not put the enemy out of action even if they went off well. ' It is better that a battle should not be fought, unless under such favourable circumstances that there would be reason to hope that the allied army would be able to maintain the field, while that of the enemy would not [3].' For if the French were only checked, and not completely knocked to pieces, Wellington knew that they would be reinforced within a few days by the 14,000 men whom King Joseph (unknown to Marmont) was bringing up from Madrid. Retreat would then again become necessary, since the enemy would be superior in numbers to a hopeless extent. Wellington added that the 22nd was his best day of advantage, since within thirty-six hours Marmont would have been reinforced by the cavalry brigade under General Chauvel, which Caffarelli had at last sent forward from Burgos. It had reached the Douro at Valladolid on the 20th, and would be up at the front on the 23rd : this he well knew, and somewhat overrated its strength [4].

---

[1] *Dispatches*, ix. p. 299, July 21st.

[2] Wellington to Bathurst, July 24. *Dispatches*, ix. p. 300.

[3] Again from dispatch to Bathurst, July 21st. *Dispatches*, ix. p. 296.

[4] Supposing it, apparently, to be over 1,000 strong, while it was really not 800 sabres.

But though ready to take his advantage, if it were offered him, Wellington evidently leaned to the idea that it would not be given. He prepared for retreat, by sending off his whole baggage-train on the Ciudad Rodrigo road at dawn, escorted by one of D'Urban's three Portuguese cavalry regiments. This was a clear expression of his intention to move off. So is his letter of July 24 to Graham in which, writing in confidence to a trusted subordinate, he remarks, 'Marmont ought to have given me a *pont d'or*, and then he would have made a handsome operation of it.' Instead of furnishing the proverbial bridge of gold to the yielding adversary, the Marshal pressed in upon him in a threatening fashion, yet with his troops so scattered and strung out on a long front, that he was not ready for a decisive action when Wellington at last saw his opportunity and dashed in upon him.

At dawn on the 22nd each party had to discover the exact position of his adversary, for the country-side was both wooded and undulating. Wellington's army, on the line of heights reaching southward from Santa Marta, was almost entirely masked, partly by the woods in the centre of his position, but still more by his having placed all the divisions far back from the sky-line on the reverse slope of the plateau. The front was about three miles long, but little was visible upon it. Foy, whose division was ahead of the rest of the French army, describes what he saw as follows :—

'The position of San Cristobal had been almost stripped of troops : we could see one English division in a sparsely-planted wood within cannon-shot of Calvarisa de Ariba, on the Salamanca road : very far behind a thin column was ascending the heights of Tejares : nothing more could be made out of Wellington's army : all the rest was hidden from us by the chain of heights which runs from north to south, and ends in the high and precipitous knolls of the Arapiles. Wellington was on this chain, sufficiently near for us to recognize by means of the staff surrounding him [1].'

All, then, that Foy, and Marmont who was riding near him, actually saw, was the 7th Division in the wood opposite Nuestra Señora de la Peña, and the distant baggage-column already

[1] *Vie militaire*, edited by Girod de l'Ain, p. 173.

filing off on the Ciudad Rodrigo road, which ascends the heights
beyond Aldea Tejada four miles to the rear.

The French army was a little more visible to Wellington, who
could not only make out Foy's division behind Calvarisa de
Ariba, but several other masses farther south and east, in
front of the long belt of woods which extends on each side of
the village of Utrera for some two miles or more. It was
impossible to see how far the French left reached among the
dense trees : but the right was ' refused : ' no troops were
opposite Wellington's left or northern wing, and the villages of
Pelabravo and Calvarisa de Abaxo, far in advance of it, were
still held by British cavalry vedettes. In short, only the allied
right and centre had enemies in front of them. This indicated
what Wellington had expected—an attempt of Marmont to
continue his old policy of outflanking his adversary's extreme
right : clearly the British left was not in danger.

Marmont, as his exculpatory dispatch to Berthier acknowledges, was convinced that Wellington would retire once more
the moment that his flank was threatened. ' Everything led
me to believe,' he writes, ' that the enemy intended to occupy
the position of Tejares [across the Zurgain] which lay a league
behind him, while at present he was a league and a half in front
of Salamanca [1].' Foy's diary completely bears out this view
of Marmont's conception of the situation. ' The Marshal had
no definite plan : he thought that the English army was
already gone off, or at least that it was going off, to take
position on the heights of Tejares on the left [or farther] bank
of the river Zurgain. He was tempted to make an attack on the
one visible English division, with which a skirmishing fire had
already begun. He was fearing that this division might get out
of his reach ! How little did he foresee the hapless lot of his
own army that day ! The wily Wellington was ready to give
battle—the greater part of his host was collected, but masked
behind the line of heights : he was showing nothing on the
crest, lest his intention should be divined : he was waiting for
our movement [2].'

The skirmish to which Foy alludes was one begun by the

[1] Correspondence in *Mémoires*, iv. p. 254.
[2] Foy, p. 174.

voltigeurs of his own division, whom Marmont had ordered
forward, to push back the English pickets on the height of
Nuestra Señora de la Peña. These belonged to the 7th Division,
which was occupying the wood behind. Not wishing his
position to be too closely examined, Wellington sent out two
whole battalions, the 68th and the 2nd Caçadores, who formed
a very powerful screen of light troops, and pushed back the
French from the hill and the ruined chapel on top of it. Marmont then strengthened his firing line, and brought up a battery,
which checked the further advance of the allied skirmishers.
The two screens continued to exchange shots for several hours,
half a mile in front of Wellington's position. The *tiraillade* had
many episodes, in one of which General Victor Alten, leading
a squadron of his hussars to protect the flank of the British
skirmishers, received a ball in the knee, which put him out of
action, and threw the command of his brigade into the hands
of Arentschildt, colonel of the 1st Hussars K.G.L. After
much bickering, and when noon had long passed, the 68th
and Caçadores were relieved by some companies of the 95th
from the Light Division, as Wellington wished to employ the
7th Division elsewhere. He had at first thought it possible
that Marmont was about to make a serious attack on this part
of his front; but the notion died away when it was seen that the
Marshal did not send up any formed battalions to support his
voltigeurs, and allowed the light troops of the allies to cling
to the western half of the slopes of Nuestra Señora de la Peña.

It was soon evident that the French were—as so often before
during the last six days—about to extend their left wing. The
right or southern flank of Wellington's line rested on the rocky
knoll, 400 feet high, which is known as the 'Lesser Arapile.'
Six hundred yards from it, and outside the allied zone of
occupation, lay the 'Greater Arapile,' which is a few feet higher
and much longer than its fellow. These two curious hills,
sometimes called the 'Hermanitos' or 'little brothers,' are
the most striking natural feature in the country-side. They
rise a hundred and fifty feet above the valley which lies between
them, and a hundred feet above the heights on either side.
Their general appearance somewhat recalls that of Dartmoor
'Tors,' rough rock breaking out through the soil. But their

THE GREATER (OR FRENCH) ARAPILE SEEN FROM
THE FOOT OF THE LESSER ARAPILE

GENERAL VIEW OF THE BRITISH AND FRENCH
POSITIONS, TAKEN FROM THE REAR OF THE
FORMER, THE NEARER HILL WAS THE POSITION
OF THE 5TH DIVISION. THE VILLAGE OF ARAPILES
TO THE LEFT. THE DISTANT RIDGE, ALONG WHICH
SMOKE IS ROLLING, IS THE FRENCH POSITION.

(From photographs by Mr. C. Armstrong.   To face p. 422)

shapes differ : the Greater Arapile shows crags at each end, but has a comparatively smooth ascent to its centre on its northern front—so smooth that steep ploughed fields have been laid out upon it, and extend almost to the crest. The Lesser Arapile is precipitous on its southern front, where it faces its twin, but is joined at its back (or northern) side by a gentle slope to the main line of the heights where Wellington's army lay. It is in short an integral part of them, though it rises far above their level. The Greater Arapile, on the other hand, is an isolated height, not belonging to the system of much lower knolls which lies to its south. These, three-quarters of a mile away, are covered with wood, and form part of the long forest which reaches as far as the neighbourhood of Alba de Tormes.

Wellington had left the Greater Arapile outside his position, partly because it was completely separated from the other heights that he held, partly (it is said) because he had surveyed the ground in the dusk, and had judged the knoll farther from the Lesser Arapile than was actually the case ; they were within easy cannon-shot from each other [1]. At about eight o'clock, French skirmishers were observed breaking out from the woods to the south of the Arapile and pushing rapidly toward it. They were followed by supporting columns in strength—indeed Marmont had directed the whole of Bonnet's division to move, under cover of the trees, to the point where the woods approach nearest to the hill, and from thence to carry it if possible. Wellington, now judging that it was uncomfortably near to his right flank, ordered the 7th Caçadores —from the 4th Division, the unit that lay nearest—to race hard for the Greater Arapile and try to seize it before the French had arrived. They made good speed but failed : the enemy was on the crest first, and repulsed them with some loss. They had to fall back to behind the Lesser Arapile, which was held by the first British brigade of their division (W. Anson's).

Marmont had seized the Greater Arapile, as he tells us, to form a strong advanced post, behind which he could move his main body westward, in pursuance of his old design of turning Wellington's right. It was to be the ' pivot on which the flanking movement should be made,' the ' *point d'appui* of the

[1] So says Vere, in his *Marches of the 4th Division*, p. 31.

right of his army ' when it should reach its new position [1].
Bonnet's troops being firmly established on and behind it, he
began to move his divisions to their left.   On his original
ground, the plateau of Calvarisa de Ariba, he left Foy's division
in front line—still bickering with the skirmishing line of the
allies—Ferey's division in support, and Boyer's dragoons to
cover the flank against any possible attack from the British
cavalry, who were in force on Wellington's left, and still had
detachments out on the plateau by Pelabravo, beyond Foy's
extreme right.   Having made this provision against any
possible attempt to attack him in the rear while he was executing
his great manœuvre, Marmont marched his five remaining
divisions [2], under cover of Bonnet's advanced position, to the
edge of the wooded hills in rear of the Great Arapile, where
they remained for some time in a threatening mass, without
further movement.

Wellington, clearly discerning from the summit of the Lesser
Arapile this general shift of the enemy to the left, now made
great alterations in the arrangement of his troops, and adopted
what may be called his second battle-position.   The 4th
Division, about and around that height, was placed so as to
serve for the allied army the same purpose that Bonnet was
carrying out for the French on the other Hermanito.   Of Cole's
three brigades, that of Anson occupied the Arapile—the 3/27th
on the summit, the 1/40th in support on the rear slope.   Pack's
independent Portuguese brigade was placed beside Anson.   The
Fusilier brigade (under Ellis of the 1/23rd) and Stubbs's Portuguese, the remaining units of the 4th Division, were formed up
to the right of the hill, extending as far as the village which
takes its name of Arapiles from the two strange knolls.   Two
guns of Cole's divisional battery (that of Sympher [3]) were
hoisted up with some difficulty to the level of the 3/27th.   The
other four were left with the Fusiliers near the village [4].   Thus
the little Arapile became the obtuse angle of a formation

---

[1] Marmont, *Mémoires*, iv. p. 255.

[2] Clausel, Brennier, Maucune, Thomières, and Sarrut also, when the
latter arrived late from Babila Fuente, and joined the main body.

[3] A K.G.L. unit—the only German artillery present at Salamanca.

[4] All this from Vere's *Marches of the 4th Division*, p. 32.

' en potence,' with Pack and two brigades of the 4th Division on its right, and the 7th Division (still engaged at a distance with Foy) and the 1st and Light Divisions on its left. At the same time Wellington moved down the troops which had originally formed his left wing (5th and 6th Divisions, España's Spaniards, and Bradford's Portuguese) to a supporting position behind his centre, somewhere near the village of Las Torres, where they could reinforce either his right or his left, as might prove necessary in the end. As a further general reserve G. Anson's and Le Marchant's cavalry brigades, and the greater part of Victor Alten's, were brought away from the original left, and placed in reserve near the 6th Division ; but Bock and two of Victor Alten's squadrons [1] remained on the left, opposite Boyer's dragoons.

In connexion with this same general move, Wellington sent a most important order to the troops which he had left till this moment on the north bank of the Tormes, covering Salamanca, in the position by Cabrerizos. These consisted of the 3rd Division—which was under the temporary command of Edward Pakenham (Wellington's brother-in-law) during Picton's sickness—and the 500 sabres that remained of D'Urban's Portuguese horse, after one regiment had been sent off on escort-duty with the baggage-train. These corps were directed to march over the town-bridge of Salamanca, and take up a position between Aldea Tejada and La Penilla, to the east of the high-road to Ciudad Rodrigo. There placed, they were available either as a reserve to the newly-formed right wing, or as a supporting échelon, if the whole army should ultimately fall back for a retreat along the high-road, or as a detached force placed so far to the right that it could outflank or throw itself in front of any French troops which might continue Marmont's advance from the Arapiles westward. It is probable that Wellington, at the moment when he gave the orders, would have been quite unable to say which of these three duties would fall to Pakenham's share. The 3rd Division marched from Cabrerizos at noon, passing through the city, which was at this moment full of alarms and excursions. For the sight of Marmont close at hand, and of the British baggage-train

[1] From the 14th Light Dragoons.

moving off hastily toward Rodrigo, had filled the inhabitants with dismay. Some were hiding their more valuable property, others (who had compromised themselves by their friendly reception of the allied army) were preparing for hasty flight. Some used bitter language of complaint—the English were retreating without a battle after betraying their friends.

Pakenham and D'Urban reached their appointed station by two o'clock,[1] and halted in a dip in the ground, well screened by trees, between La Penilla and Aldea Tejada, where they could barely be seen from the highest slopes of Wellington's position, and not at all from any other point. For some time they were left undisturbed, listening to a growing noise of artillery fire to their left front, where matters were evidently coming to a head.

At about eleven o'clock Marmont had climbed to the summit of the French Arapile, from whence he obtained for the first time a partial view into the British position; for looking up the dip in the ground between the Lesser Arapile and the heights occupied by the Fusilier brigade of the 4th Division, he could catch a glimpse of some of the movements that were going on at the back of Wellington's first line. Apparently he saw the 1st and Light Divisions behind the crest of their destined fighting position, and the 5th and 6th and Bradford's Portuguese taking ground to their right. Pack's Portuguese on the flank and rear of the British Arapile must also have been visible at least in part. The conclusion to which he came was that his adversary was accumulating forces behind the Lesser Arapile with the object of sallying out against Bonnet, whose post was very far advanced in front of the rest of the French army, and against Foy and Ferey, who were left in a somewhat isolated position on the plateau by Calvarisa, when the main body of the army had moved so far to the west.

Some such intention seems for a moment to have been in Wellington's mind, though he says nothing of it in his dispatch. 'About twelve o'clock,' writes one of the most trustworthy British diarists, 'the troops were ordered to attack, and the 1st Division moved forward to gain the other Arapile, which the French had taken. . . . There was something singular, I think, in Lord Wellington's ordering the 1st and Light

---

[1] The hours are taken from D'Urban's diary.

Divisions to attack early in the day, and then counter-ordering them after they had begun to move. Marshal Beresford, no doubt, was the cause of the alteration, by what he urged. Yet at the same time Lord W. is so little influenced (or indeed allows any person to say a word) that his attending to the Marshal was considered singular. From all I could collect and observe " the Peer " was a little nervous: it was the first time he had ever attacked. When he *did* finally determine on the attack it was well done, in the most decided manner. There was possibly some little trouble in arriving at that decision [1].' Oddly enough this contemporary note is exactly borne out by Marmont's statement in his *Mémoires*, that meeting Wellington years after, he inquired about the point, and was frankly told that an attack had been projected at this moment, but that it had been put off in consequence of the representation of Beresford, who had counselled delay [2]. There was a heavy mass of troops available behind the Lesser Arapile and to both sides of it—the 4th Division, Pack's Portuguese, and the 1st, 7th, and Light Divisions, with the 5th and 6th and Bradford and the cavalry in reserve. The blow might have succeeded—but undoubtedly that delivered four hours later was much more effective.

The idea of an attack at noon having been finally rejected Wellington turned his mind to another possibility. If Marmont should commit no blunders, and should continue his turning movement at a safe distance, and with his whole army well concentrated, it was quite possible that a retreat might become necessary. The Commander-in-Chief called up Colonel Delancey, then acting as Adjutant-General [3], and directed him to draft a comprehensive scheme for the order in which the troops should be withdrawn, and the route which each division would take in the event of an evacuation of the position. The next stand was to be made, as Marmont had supposed, on the heights above Aldea Tejada, behind the river Zurgain [4]. Such a move

---

[1] Tomkinson's *Diary*, pp. 187–9.   [2] Marmont, *Mémoires*, iv. p. 256.

[3] Charles Stewart (Lord Londonderry), who had held the post for the last three years had just gone home, and his successor had not yet come out to Spain.

[4] The note concerning Delancey is from Vere's *Marches of the 4th Division*, p. 31.

would have involved the abandonment of the city of Salamanca to the French. The news spread from the staff round the commanding officers of divisions, and so downwards to the ranks, where it caused immense discontent. Every one was ' spoiling for a fight,' and the cautious tactics of the last six days had been causing murmurs, which were only kept from becoming acute by the long-tried confidence that the army felt in its chief.

At this very moment Marmont began to act in the fashion that Wellington most desired, by making an altogether dangerous extension of his left wing, and at the same time pressing in so close to his adversary that he could not avoid a battle if it were thrust upon him. His own explanation is that he took the putting off of Wellington's tentative movement against Bonnet as a sign that the allied army was actually commencing its retreat. ' Wellington renounced his intention of fighting, and from that moment he had to prepare to draw away, for if he had remained in his present position I should from the next day have threatened his communications, by marching on to my left. His withdrawal commenced at midday. . . . He had to retreat by his right, and consequently he had to begin by strengthening his right. He therefore weakened his left, and accumulated troops on his right. Then his more distant units and his reserves commenced to move, and in succession drew off towards Tejares [Aldea Tejada]. His intention was easy to discern. . . . The enemy having carried off the bulk of his force to his right, I had to reinforce my left, so as to be able to act with promptness and vigour, without having to make new arrangements, when the moment should arrive for falling upon the English rearguard [1].'

It is clear that the Duke of Ragusa had drawn his conclusion that Wellington was about to retreat at once, and had argued, from partly-seen motions in his adversary's rear, that the whole allied army was moving off. But this was not yet the case : Wellington was taking precautions, but he was still not without hope that the French would commit themselves to some unwise and premature movement. He had still every man in hand, and the supposed general retreat on Aldea Tejada, which

[1] *Mémoires*, iv. p. 257.

the Marshal thought that he saw, was in reality only the shifting of reserves more to the right.

Unwitting of this, Marmont, a little before two o'clock, began his extension to the left. To the westward of the woods on whose edge the five divisions composing his main body were massed, is a long plateau facing the village of Arapiles and the heights behind it. It is about three-quarters of a mile broad and three miles long, gently undulating and well suited for marching : in 1812 it seems to have been open waste : to-day it is mainly under the plough. Its front or northern side slopes gently down, toward the bottom in which lies the village of Arapiles : at its back, which is steeper, are woods, outlying parts of the great forest which extends to Alba de Tormes. It ends suddenly in a knoll with an outcrop of rock, called the Pico de Miranda, above the hamlet of Miranda de Azan, from which it draws its name. Along this plateau was the obvious and easy route for a force marching to turn Wellington's right. It was a very tempting piece of ground, with a glacis-like slope towards the English heights, which made it very defensible— a better artillery position against a force advancing from the village of Arapiles and the ridges behind it could not be conceived. The only danger connected with it seemed to be that it was over-long—it had more than two miles of front, and a very large force would be required to hold it securely from end to end. From the Pico de Miranda, if the French should extend so far, to Foy's right wing by Calvarisa de Ariba was a distance of six miles in all—far too much for an army of 48,000 men in the battle-array of the Napoleonic period.

Marmont says that his first intention was only to occupy the nearer end of the plateau, that part of it which faces the village of Arapiles. In his apologetic dispatch to Berthier, he declares that he wished to get a lodgement upon it, lest Wellington might seize it before him, and so block his way westward. ' It was indispensable to occupy it, seeing that the enemy had just strengthened his centre, from whence he could push out *en masse* on to this plateau, and commence an attack by taking possession of this important ground. Accordingly I ordered the 5th Division (Maucune) to move out and form up on the right end of the plateau, where his fire would link on perfectly with that from the [Great] Arapile : the 7th Division [Thomières] was to place itself in second line as a support, the 2nd Division (Clausel) to act as a reserve to the 7th. The 6th Division (Brennier) was to occupy the high ground in front of the wood, where a large number of my guns were still stationed. I ordered General Bonnet at the same time to occupy with the 122nd regiment a knoll intermediate between the plateau and the hill of the [Great] Arapile, which blocks the exit from the village of the same name. Finally, I directed General Boyer to leave only one regiment of his dragoons to watch Foy's right, and to come round with the other three to the front of the wood, beside the 2nd Division. The object of this was that, supposing the enemy should attack the plateau, Boyer could charge in on their right flank, while my light cavalry could charge in on their left flank [1].'

All this reads very plausibly and ingeniously, but unfortunately it squares in neither with the psychology of the moment, nor with the manœuvres which Maucune, Thomières, and Clausel executed, under the Marshal's eye and without his interference. He had forgotten when he dictated this paragraph —and not unnaturally, for he wrote sorely wounded, on his sick-bed, in pain, and with his head not too clear—that he had just before stated that Wellington was obviously retreating, and had begun to withdraw towards Aldea Tejada. If this was so, how could he possibly have conceived at the moment that his adversary, far from retreating, was preparing an offensive movement *en masse* against the left flank of the French position ? The two conceptions cannot be reconciled. The fact was, undoubtedly, that he thought that Wellington was moving off, and pushed forward Maucune, Thomières, and Clausel, with the object of molesting and detaining what he supposed to be the rearguard of his adversary. The real idea of the moment was the one which appears in the paragraph of his *Mémoires*, already quoted on an earlier page : ' I hoped that our respective positions would bring on not a battle but an advantageous rear-guard action, in which, using my full force late in the day, with a part only of the British army left in front of me, I should probably score a point.' Jourdan, a severe critic of his colleague, puts the matter with perfect frankness in his *Guerre d'Espagne.*

[1] Dispatch to Berthier, *Mémoires*, iv. pp. 445–6.

After quoting Marmont's insincere dispatch at length, he adds, ' it is evident that the Marshal, in order to menace the point of retreat of the allies, extended his left much too far [1].' Napoleon, after reading Marmont's dispatch in a Russian bivouac [2], pronounced that all his reasons and explanations for the position into which he got himself had ' as much complicated stuffing as the inside of a clock, and not a word of truth as to the real state of things.'

What happened under the eyes of Marmont, as he took a long-delayed lunch on the top of the Greater Arapile [3], was as follows. Maucune, with his strong division of nine battalions or 5,200 men, after breaking out from the position in front of the woods where the French main body was massed, marched across the open ground for about a mile or more, till he had got well on to the central part of the plateau which he was directed to occupy. He then drew up opposite the village of Arapiles, and sent out his voltigeur companies to work down the slope toward that place, which lay well in front of the British line. The position which he took up was on that part of the plateau which sweeps forward nearest to the opposite heights, and is little more than half a mile from them. A fierce artillery engagement then set in : Maucune's divisional battery began to shell the village of Arapiles. Sympher's battery, belonging to the 4th Division, replied from the slope behind the village and from two guns on the Lesser Arapile. The French pieces which had been dragged up on to the Greater Arapile then started shelling the Lesser, and silenced the two guns there, which were drawn off, and sent to rejoin the rest of the battery, on a less exposed position. The 3/27th on the hilltop had to take cover behind rocks as best it could. Soon after at least two more French batteries, from the artillery reserve, took ground to the right of Maucune, and joined in the shelling of the village of Arapiles. Wellington presently supported Sympher's battery with that of Lawson, belonging to the

[1] Jourdan's *Mémoire sur la Guerre d'Espagne*, p. 418.

[2] ' Il y a plus de fatras et de rouages que dans une horloge, et pas un mot qui fasse connaître l'état réel des choses.' For more hard words see Napoleon to Clarke, Ghiatz, September 2.

[3] See Memoirs of Parquin, who commanded his escort, p. 299. But he states the hour as 11 o'clock, much too early.

5th Division, which turned on to shell Maucune's supporting columns from ground on the lower slopes, not far to the right of Sympher's position. The effect was good, and the columns shifted sideways to get out of range. But one [or perhaps two] of the French batteries then shifted their position, and began to play upon Lawson diagonally from the left, so enfilading him that he was ordered to limber up and move higher on the hill behind the village, from whence he resumed his fire. Wellington also, a little later, brought up the horse-artillery troop belonging to the 7th Division ['E', Macdonald's troop] and placed it on the Lesser Arapile—two guns on the summit, four on the lower slopes near the 1/40th of W. Anson's brigade. The British fire all along the heights was effective and accurate, but quite unable to cope with that of the French, who had apparently six batteries in action against three. Marmont, indeed, had all along his line an immense superiority of guns, having 78 pieces with him against Wellington's 54. His artillery-reserve consisted of four batteries—that of his adversary of one only—Arriaga's Portuguese 24-pounder howitzers [1].

While Maucune and the French artillery were making a very noisy demonstration against the British line between the Lesser Arapile and the village of the same name, which looked like the preliminaries of a serious attack, more troops emerged from the woods of Marmont's centre, and began to file along the plateau, under cover of Maucune's deployed line. These were Thomières's division, succeeded after a long interval by that of Clausel. ' During the cannonade column followed column in quick and continued succession along the heights occupied by the enemy : Marmont was moving his army in battle-order along his position, and gaining ground rapidly to his left [2].' According to the Marshal's own account of his intentions, he had proposed to place Maucune on the (French) right end of the plateau, Thomières and Clausel in support of him. What happened, however, was that Maucune went well forward on to

---

[1] For this artillery business see especially the six narratives of artillery officers printed by Major Leslie in his *Dickson Papers*, ii. pp. 685–97. Also for doings of the 5th Division battery (Lawson's), Leith Hay, ii. pp. 47–8, and of the 4th Division battery (Sympher's), Vere's *Marches of the 4th Division*, pp. 33–4.

[2] Vere's *Marches of the 4th Division*, p. 33.

the right-centre of the plateau, and that Thomières marched along past Maucune's rear, and continued moving in a westerly direction along the summit of the plateau, though Clausel soon halted: before Thomières stopped he had gone nearly three miles. It is clear that if Marmont had chosen, he could have checked the manœuvres of his subordinates, the moment that they passed the limit which he alleges that he had set them. An aide-de-camp sent down from the back of the Greater Arapile could have told Maucune not to press forward toward the English position, or Thomières to stop his march, within a matter of twenty minutes or half an hour. No such counter-orders were sent—and the reason clearly was that Marmont was satisfied with the movements that he saw proceeding before him, until the moment when he suddenly realized with dismay that Wellington was about to deliver a counter-stroke in full force.

We must now turn to the movements of the allied army. The instant that Maucune deployed on the plateau in front of the village of Arapiles, and that the cannonade began, Wellington judged that he was about to be attacked—the thing that he most desired. A very few orders put his army in a defensive battle-position. The 5th Division was sent from the rear side of the heights to occupy the crest, continuing the line of the 4th Division. The 6th Division was brought up from the rear to a position behind the 4th. The 7th Division, abandoning the long bickering with Foy in which its light troops had been engaged, was drawn back from the left wing, and took post in second line parallel to the 6th and in rear of the 5th Division. The place of its skirmishers on the slopes in front of Nuestra Señora de la Peña was taken by some companies of the 95th, sent out from the Light Division. That unit and the 1st Division now formed the total of the allied left wing, with Bock's heavy dragoons covering their flank. They were ' containing ' an equivalent French force—Foy's and Ferey's infantry divisions, and the single regiment of Boyer's dragoons which Marmont had left in this quarter.

There still remained in reserve, near the village of Las Torres, Bradford's Portuguese and España's Spanish battalions, with the bulk of the allied cavalry—all Anson's and Le Marchant's

and the greater part of Arentschildt's squadrons, and in addition
Pakenham and D'Urban were available a little farther to the
right, near Aldea Tejada.   If the French were going to attack
the heights on each side of the village of Arapiles, as seemed
probable at the moment, all these remoter reserves could be
used as should seem most profitable.

But the battle did not go exactly as Wellington expected.
The cannonade continued, and Maucune's skirmishing line
pushed very boldly forward, and actually attacked the village
of Arapiles, which was defended by the light companies of the
Guards' brigade of the 1st Division and of the Fusilier brigade
of the 4th Division.   The *voltigeurs* twice seized the southern
outlying houses of the straggling village, and were twice driven
out.   But the battalions in support of them did not come
forward, nor did Bonnet attack on the right of them, nor
Thomières on the left.   The former remained stationary, on and
about the Great Arapile : the latter continued to march westward along the plateau : a perceptible gap began to appear
between him and Maucune.

Wellington at this moment was toward the right rear of his
own line—occupied according to some authorities in snatching
a late and hasty lunch [1] while matters were developing, but not
yet developed—according to others in giving orders concerning
the cavalry to Stapleton Cotton, near Las Torres—when he
received an urgent message from Leith.   It said that Maucune
had ceased to advance, but that the French extreme left was
still in march westward.   ' On being made acquainted with
the posture of affairs,' writes the officer who bore Leith's

---

[1] The traditional story may be found in Greville's *Memoirs*, ii. p. 39.
Wellington is said to have been in the courtyard of a farmhouse, where
some food had been laid out for him, ' stumping about and munching,' and
taking occasional peeps through his telescope.   Presently came the aide-de-
camp with Leith's message.   Wellington took another long look through
his glass, and cried, ' By God ! that will do !' his mouth still full.   He then
sprang on his horse and rode off, the staff following.   Another version may
be found in Grattan, pp. 239–40 : ' Lord W. had given his glass to an aide-
de-camp, while he himself sat down to eat a few mouthfuls of cold beef.
Presently the officer reported that the enemy were still extending to their
left.   " The devil they are !   give me the glass quickly," said his lordship—and then, after a long inspection, " This will do at last, I think—
ride off." '

report [1], ' Lord Wellington declared his intention of riding to
the spot and directed me to accompany him. When he arrived
at the ground of the 5th Division—now under arms and perfectly
prepared to receive the attack, his Lordship found the enemy
still in the same formation, but not displaying any intention
of trying his fortune, by crossing the valley at that point. He
soon became satisfied that no operation of consequence was
intended against this part of the line. He again galloped off
toward the right, which at this time became the most interesting
and important scene of action.'

The critical moment of the day was the short space of time
when Wellington was surveying the French army, from the
height where Leith's men were lying prostrate behind the
crest, above the village of Arapiles, under a distant but not
very effective artillery fire. The whole plateau opposite was
very visible : Maucune could be seen halted and in line, with
much artillery on his flank, but no infantry force near—there
was half a mile between him and Bonnet. Thomières was still
pushing away to his left, already separated by some distance
from Maucune. Clausel had apparently halted after the end
of his march out of the woods. Foy and Ferey were at least two
miles off to the French right. The enemy, in short, were in no
solid battle order, and were scattered on an immense arc, which
enveloped on both sides the obtuse angle *en potence* formed
by the main body of the allied army. From Foy's right to
Thomières's left there was length but no depth. The only
reserves were the troops imperfectly visible in the woods behind
the Great Arapile—where lay Brennier in first line, and Sarrut
who was now nearing Marmont's artillery-park and baggage.
Their strength might be guessed from the fact that Marmont
was known to have eight infantry divisions, and that six
were clearly visible elsewhere. Wellington's determination was
suddenly taken, to turn what had been intended for a defensive
into an offensive battle. Seeing the enemy so scattered, and so
entirely out of regular formation, he would attack him with the
whole force that he had in position west of the little Arapile, before
Marmont could get into order. Leith, Cole, and Pack in front

---

[1] His nephew, Leith Hay, whose memoir I have so often had to quote,
here ii. p. 49.

line, supported by the 6th and 7th Divisions in second line, and
with Bradford, España, and Stapleton Cotton's cavalry covering
their right flank in a protective échelon, should cross the valley
and fall upon Bonnet, Maucune, Clausel, and Thomières.
Meanwhile Pakenham and D'Urban, being in a hidden position
from which they could easily outflank Thomières, should
ascend the western end of the plateau, get across the head of
his marching column, and drive it in upon Maucune, whom
Leith would be assailing at the same moment. Pakenham's
turning movement was the most delicate part of the plan ;
wherefore Wellington resolved to start it himself. He rode
like the wind across the ground behind the heights, past Las
Torres and Penilla, and appeared all alone before D'Urban's
Portuguese squadrons. It was only some time later that first
Colonel Delancey and then others of his staff, quite outdistanced,
came dropping in with blown horses. The orders to D'Urban
were short and clear : Pakenham was about to attack the
western end of the plateau where Thomières was moving—near
the Pico de Miranda. It would be D'Urban's duty to cover
his right flank [1]. A minute later Wellington was before the 3rd
Division, which had just received orders to stand to its arms.

' The officers had not taken their places in the column, but
were in a group together, in front of it. As Lord Wellington
rode up to Pakenham every eye was turned towards him. He
looked paler than usual ; but, notwithstanding the sudden
change he had just made in the disposition of his army, he was
quite unruffled in his manner, as if the battle to be fought was
nothing but a field-day. His words were few and his orders
brief. Tapping Pakenham on the shoulder, he said, " Edward,
move on with the 3rd Division, take those heights in your
front—and drive everything before you." " I will, my lord,"
was the laconic reply of the gallant Sir Edward. A moment
after, Lord Wellington was galloping on to the next division,
to give (I suppose) orders to the same effect, and in less than
half an hour the battle had commenced [2].' The time was about
a quarter to four in the afternoon.

---

[1] D'Urban's unpublished diary gives the fact that he got his order from
Wellington personally before Pakenham was reached.

[2] Grattan's *With the Connaught Rangers*, pp. 241-2.

Having set Pakenham and D'Urban in motion, Wellington rode back to the ground of the 5th Division, sending on his way orders for Arentschildt to leave the cavalry reserve, and join D'Urban with the five squadrons that remained of Victor Alten's brigade [1]. Bradford, España, and Cotton at the same time were directed to come forward to Leith's right flank. On reaching the hilltop behind the village of Arapiles, the Commander-in-Chief gave his orders to Leith: the 5th Division was to advance downhill and attack Maucune across the valley, as soon as Bradford's Portuguese should be close up to support his right, and as Pakenham's distant movement should become visible. Wellington then rode on to give the corresponding orders to Cole, more to the left [2].

The 5th Division thereupon sent out its light companies in skirmishing line, and came up to the crest : the two neighbouring brigades of the 4th Division followed suit, and then Pack's Portuguese, opposite the Greater Arapile. Considerable loss was suffered in all these corps from the French artillery fire, when the battalions rose from their lying posture behind the crest and became visible. Some thirty or forty minutes elapsed between Wellington's arrival on the scene and the commencement of the advance : the delay was caused by the necessity for waiting for Bradford, who was coming up as fast as possible from Las Torres. The attack did not begin till about 4.40 p.m.

By the time that Leith and Cole came into action the French army had been deprived of its chief. Somewhere between three and four o'clock in the afternoon [3], and certainly nearer the latter than the former hour, Marmont had been severely wounded. According to his own narrative he had begun to be troubled by seeing Maucune pressing in too close to the village of Arapiles, and Thomières passing on too far to the left, and had been roused to considerable vexation by getting a message

---

[1] Two of 14th Light Dragoons, three of 1st Hussars K.G.L.

[2] All this from Leith Hay, ii. pp. 51–2.

[3] Marmont says that it was ' environ trois heures du soir.' But I think that about 3.45 should be given as the hour, since Maucune only left the woods at 2 o'clock, and had to march on to the plateau, to take up his position, to send out his *voltigeurs*, and to get them close in to Arapiles before he would have sent such a message to his chief. Foy says ' between 3 and 4 p.m.'

from the former that he observed that the troops in front of him were retiring, and therefore would ask leave to support his *voltigeurs* and attack the British position with his whole division. Marmont says that it was his wish to stop Maucune from closing that induced him to prepare to depart from his eyrie on the Great Arapile, and to descend to take charge of his left wing. Be this as it may, there is no doubt that he was starting to climb down and mount his horse, when a shell from one of Dyneley's two guns on the British Arapile burst near him, and flung him to the ground with a lacerated right arm, and a wound in his side which broke two ribs [1]. He himself says that there was nothing irremediable in the state of his army at the moment that he was disabled. His critic, Foy, held otherwise. ' The Duke of Ragusa,' he wrote, ' insinuated that the battle of the 22nd was lost because, after his own wounding, there was a gap in the command, anarchy, and disorder. But it was the Duke who forced on the battle, and that contrary to the advice of General Clausel. His left was already beaten when he was disabled : already it was impossible either to refuse a battle or to give it a good turn. It was only possible to attenuate the disaster—and that was what Clausel did [2].' Foy also insinuates that Maucune's advance, at least in its early stages, was consonant with Marmont's intentions. ' He had made his arrangements for a decisive blow : when the English were seen to take up their position, the heads of the columns were turned to the left, so as to occupy the elevations which dominate the plain, and swell up one after another. The occupation of one led to the temptation to seize the next, and so by advance after advance the village of Arapiles was at last reached. Maucune's division actually held it for some minutes. Nevertheless we had not yet made up our minds to deliver battle, and the necessary dispositions for one had not been made. My division was still occupying the plateau of Calvarisa, with the 3rd and 4th Divisions (Ferey and Sarrut) and the dragoons supporting

---

[1] Many years after, when Marmont, now a subject of Louis XVIII, was inspecting some British artillery, an officer had the maladroit idea of introducing to him the sergeant who had pointed the gun—the effect of the shot in the middle of the French staff had been noticed on the British Arapile.

[2] *Vie militaire de Foy*, p. 177.

me in the rear. Here, then, was a whole section of the army quite out of the fight : and the other divisions were not well linked together, and could be beaten one after the other.'

Foy is certainly correct in asserting that, at the moment of the Marshal's wound, he himself and Ferey were too far off to be brought up in time to save Maucune, and that Bonnet, Maucune, Clausel, and Thomières were in no solid connexion with each other. This indeed was what made Wellington deliver his attack. It is probable that the Marshal's wound occurred just about the moment (3.45) when Pakenham and D'Urban were being directed by Wellington to advance. Even if it fell a trifle earlier, the French left wing was already too dislocated to have time to get into a good position before it was attacked. Marmont, it must be confessed, rather gave away his case when, in his reply to Napoleon's angry query why he had fought a battle on the 22nd, he answered that he had not intended to deliver a general action at all—it had been forced on him by Wellington [1]. If so, he was responsible for being caught by his adversary with his army strung out in such a fashion that it had a very poor chance of avoiding disaster. If it be granted that the unlucky shell had never struck him, it would not have been in ' a quarter of an hour [2] ' (as he himself pretends), nor even in a whole hour, that he could have rearranged a line six miles long [3], though he might have stopped Maucune's attack and Thomières's flank march in a much shorter time.

---

[1] Marmont to Berthier, *Mémoires*, iv. p. 468.

[2] Ibid., ' la gauche eut été formée en moins d'un quart d'heure ' !

[3] The exact moment of Marmont's wound is very difficult to fix, as also that of Wellington's attack. The Marshal himself (as mentioned above, p. 438) says that he was hit 'environ les trois heures,' and that Leith and Cole advanced ' peu après, sur les quatre heures.' Foy places the wound merely ' between 3 and 4 p.m.' Parquin, who commanded Marmont's escort of *chasseurs*, says that the Marshal had been carried back to Alba de Tormes by 4 o'clock—impossibly early. On the other hand Napier gives too late an hour, when saying that Marmont was wounded only at the moment when Leith and Cole advanced, 4.45 or so, and was running down from the Arapile because of their movement. This is, I imagine, much too late. But it is supported by *Victoires et Conquêtes*, sometimes a well-documented work but often inaccurate, which places the unlucky shot at 4.30. Grattan places the order to the British infantry (Leith and Cole) to prepare to attack at 4.20—Leith Hay at ' at least an hour after 3 o'clock.' Gomm, on the other hand, makes Wellington move ' at 3 o'clock in the afternoon.'

On Marmont's fall, the command of the army of Portugal
fell to Bonnet, the senior general of division. He was within
a few yards of his wounded chief, since his division was holding
the Great Arapile, and took up the charge at once. But it was
an extraordinary piece of ill-luck for the French that Bonnet
also was wounded within an hour, so that the command passed
to Clausel before six o'clock. As Foy remarks, however, no
one could have saved the compromised left wing—Marmont
had let it get into a thoroughly vicious position before he was
disabled.

Since the main clash of the battle of Salamanca started at
the western end of the field, it will be best to begin the narrative
of the British advance with the doings of Pakenham and
D'Urban. These two officers had some two miles of rough ground
to cover between the point where Wellington had parted from
them, and the point which had now been reached by the head
of the French advance. They were ordered to move in four
' columns of lines,' with D'Urban's cavalry forming the two
outer or right-hand columns, the third composed of Wallace's
brigade (1/45th, 1/88th, 74th) and of Power's Portuguese
(9th and 21st Line and 12th Caçadores), while the fourth consisted of Campbell's brigade (1/5th, 2/5th, 94th, 2/83rd). The
object of this formation was that the division, when it came
into action, should be able to deploy into two lines, without
the delay that would have been caused if the third brigade
had followed in the wake of the other two [1].

The way in which the two sides came into collision was
rather peculiar. Thomières's column was accompanied by the
whole, or nearly the whole, of Curto's light cavalry division,
which, as one would have supposed, would naturally have
been keeping a squadron or so in advance to explore the way,

Tomkinson (usually very accurate) places Pakenham's and Leith's success
at ' about 5 p.m.' D'Urban thinks that he met Lord Wellington and
received his orders *after* 4 p.m.—probably he is half an hour too late in
his estimate.

[1] Wellington in his dispatch (ix. p. 302) speaks of the four columns,
D'Urban makes it clear that his own squadrons formed the outer two, but
the fact that Power's Portuguese followed Wallace in the 3rd column
only emerges in the Regimental History of the 45th (Dalbiac), p. 103.
This is quite consistent with the other information.

as well as others on the flanks to cover the infantry. But it appears that this simple precaution was not taken, for Pakenham and D'Urban met no French cavalry at all, till they had got well in touch with the hostile infantry. Curto, we must suppose, was marching parallel with the centre, not certainly with the head, of Thomières's division, without any vedettes or exploring parties in front. For D'Urban describes the first meeting as follows :—

' The enemy was marching by his left along the wooded heights, which form the southern boundary of the valley of the Arapiles, and the western extremity of which closes in a lower fall, which descends upon the little stream of the Azan, near the village of Miranda. As the head of our column approached this lower fall, or hill, skirting it near its base, and having it on our left, we became aware that we were close to the enemy, though we could not see them owing to the trees, the dust, and the peculiar configuration of the ground. Anxious, therefore, to ascertain their exact whereabouts I had ridden out a little in front, having with me, I think, only my brigade-major Flangini and Da Camara, when upon clearing the verge of a small clump of trees, a short way up the slope, I came suddenly upon the head of a French column of infantry, having about a company in front, and marching very fast by its left. It was at once obvious that, as the columns of the 3rd Division were marching on our left, the French must be already beyond their right, and consequently I ought to attack at once [1].'

This was apparently the leading battalion of the French 101st, marching with its front absolutely uncovered by either cavalry vedettes or any exploring parties of its own. D'Urban galloped back, unseen by the enemy, and wheeled his leading regiment, the 1st Portuguese dragoons—three weak squadrons of little over 200 sabres—into line, with orders to charge the French battalion, before it should take the alarm and form square. The 11th Portuguese, and two squadrons of the British 14th Light Dragoons, which had only just arrived on the ground, being the foremost part of Arentschildt's brigade, followed in support. The charge was successful—the French were so much taken by surprise that the only manœuvre they

---

[1] All this from D'Urban's unpublished narrative in the D'Urban papers.

were able to perform was to close their second company upon the first, so that their front was six deep. The two squadrons of the Portuguese which attacked frontally suffered severe loss, their colonel, Watson, falling severely wounded among the French bayonets. But the right-hand squadron, which over-lapped the French left, broke in almost unopposed on the unformed flank of the battalion, which then went to pieces, and was chased uphill by the whole of the Portuguese horse-men, losing many prisoners [1].

This sudden assault on his leading unit, which seems to have been acting as an advanced guard, and was considerably ahead of the next, must have been sufficiently startling to Thomières, who was taken wholly unawares. But the next moment brought worse trouble : the first brigade of the 3rd Division—Wallace's —emerged almost simultaneously with the cavalry charge from the scattered trees which had hitherto covered its advance, and was seen coming uphill in beautiful order against him. He was caught in a long column—battalion marching behind battalion, with considerable intervals between the regiments, of which there were three (101st, three battalions ; 62nd, two battalions ; 1st, three battalions) [2]. If he was able to see Pakenham's supporting lines, which is a little doubtful, Thomières must have known that he was considerably out-numbered : the British division had 5,800 men against his 4,500, while Curto's 1,800 light cavalry were not forthcoming at the critical moment to save the situation.

The space between the advancing line of Wallace's brigade and the head of the French column, when they came in sight of each other, was about 1,000 yards—the time that it took to bring them into collision just sufficed to enable Thomières to make some sort of hasty disposition of his battalions : those in the rear pushed out on to the flanks of the leading regiment,

---

[1] All this is from D'Urban's narrative, and letters from Colonel Watson to D'Urban. The colonel bitterly resented Napier's account of the charge (*Peninsular War*, iv. p. 268).

[2] The division was marching left in front, so that the senior regiment was in the rear. The fourth unit of the division (23rd Léger) was absent, garrisoning Astorga, as was also the 2nd battalion of the 1st, which was a very strong four-battalion corps. Hence there were only 8 battalions out of 11 present, or 4,300 men out of 6,200.

and made an irregular line of columns badly spaced. The
voltigeurs of each battalion had time to run to the front : ' their
light troops,' says a witness from the Connaught Rangers,
' hoping to take advantage of the time which our deploying
from column into line would take, ran down the face of the hill
in a state of great excitement.' Pakenham appears to have
sent out against them his three companies of the 5/60th and
the whole of the 12th Caçadores, a skirmishing line of superior
strength. Wallace's three battalions formed line from open
column without halting, when they had got to within 250 yards
of the enemy : ' the different companies, by throwing forward
their right shoulders, were in line without the slow manœuvre
of a deployment.' The French fire is said to have been rather
ineffective, because delivered downhill. The most serious loss
was that caused by Thomières's divisional battery, which got
up and into action very promptly. It was answered by Douglas's
battery, the divisional artillery of the 3rd Division, which
unlimbered on a knoll at the edge of the wood, and sent a raking
discharge uphill, against the right of the French division,
shelling it over the heads of the brigade advancing up the slope.
The two Portuguese line regiments, from the rear of Wallace's
brigade, formed in support of him : Campbell's brigade followed
as a third line.

The main body of the French [1] stood in a group, rather than
a line, of battalion columns near the brow of the hill, while
Wallace's brigade continued to press upwards with a front
which outflanked the enemy at both ends. ' Regardless of the
fire of the *tirailleurs*, and the shower of grape and canister, the
brigade continued to press onward. The centre (88th regiment)
suffered, but still advanced, the right and left (1/45th and 74th)
continued to go forward at a more rapid pace, and as the
wings inclined forward and outstripped the centre, the brigade
assumed the form of a crescent [2].' They were nearly at the
brow, when Thomières directed the French columns to charge
down in support of his *tirailleurs*. The mass, with drums
beating and loud shouts of *Vive l'Empereur*, ran forward, and

----

[1] It is not certain that the whole of the rear regiment (the 1st Line) was
in the group : possibly one or two of its battalions were not yet on the
ground.   [2] Grattan, p. 245.

the leading files delivered a heavy fire, which told severely on the
88th. But on coming under fire in return the French halted, and
then wavered : 'their second discharge was unlike the first—it
was irregular and ill-directed, the men acted without concert or
method : many fired in the air.' The three British battalions
then cheered and advanced, when the enemy, his columns
already in much confusion and mixed with the wrecks of his
tirailleurs, gave way completely, and went off in confusion
along the top of the plateau.

Just at this moment Curto's *chasseurs* at last appeared—where
they had been up to this moment does not appear, but certainly
not in their proper place. Now, however, six or seven squadrons
of them came trotting up on the outer flank of the broken
division, of whom some charged the two battalions which
formed the right of Pakenham's first and third lines—the 1/45th
and 1/5th respectively. The former, feebly attacked, threw
back some companies *en potence* and beat off their assailants
easily. The latter fell back some little way, and had many
men cut up, but finally rallied in a clump and were not broken [1].
Their assailants disappeared a moment after, being driven off
by Arentschildt, who had just come up on Pakenham's right
with the five squadrons of the 1st Hussars K.G.L. and 14th
Light Dragoons [2]. D'Urban's Portuguese were now a little to
the rear, rallying after their successful charge and collecting
prisoners : their commander says in his narrative of this part
of the battle that he never saw any French cavalry till later in

---

[1] The 1/5th lost 126 men, more than any other 3rd Division regiment
except the 88th. Sergeant Morley of the 5th, its only Salamanca diarist,
writes (p. 113) : 'There was a pause—a hesitation. Here I blush—but
I should blush more if I were guilty of a falsehood. We retired—slowly, in
good order, not far, not 100 paces. General Pakenham approached, and
very good-naturedly said " re-form," and after a moment "advance—there
they are, my lads—let them feel the temper of your bayonets." We
advanced—rather slowly at first, a regiment of dragoons which had retired
with us again accompanying . . . and took our retribution for our repulse.'
The dragoon regiment was presumably part of D'Urban's brigade.

[2] This comes from the report of Arentschildt on the doings of his brigade :
it is not mentioned by Napier, nor is there anything about it in Wellington's
dispatch. The time is fixed by Arentschildt speaking of it as ' during the
attack on the first hill.' He says that he closed with the main body of the
French horse and drove it off.

the day, but does not dispute that the 5th may have been attacked by them without his knowledge.

Curto's cavalry being driven off, the 3rd Division and its attendant squadrons pursued the broken French division of infantry along the top of the plateau, and very nearly annihilated it. Thomières was killed, his divisional battery was captured whole ; of his two leading regiments the 101st Line lost 1,031 men out of 1,449 present : its colonel and eagle were both taken with many hundred unwounded prisoners : the 62nd Line lost 868 men out of 1,123. The rear regiment, the 1st Line, got off with the comparatively trifling casualty-list of 231 out of 1,743 : it was possibly not up in time to take part in resisting Pakenham's first attack, and may perhaps have done no more than cover the retreat of the wrecks of the two leading regiments. The whole division was out of action as a fighting body fór the rest of the day, having lost 2,130 men out of a little over 4,500.[1] The victorious British 3rd Division, whose casualties had not amounted to more than 500 of all ranks, continued to press the fugitives before it, till it had gone a mile, and came in on the flank of Maucune's division, the next unit in the French line ; D'Urban's cavalry accompanied it close on its right flank, Arentschildt's squadrons lay farther out, watching Curto's defeated first brigade of *chasseurs*, which rallied upon a reserve, his second brigade, and made head once more against the pursuers, just about the same time that Pakenham's infantry began again to meet with resistance.

---

[1] The losses in officers of the three regiments were, taking killed and wounded only, not unwounded prisoners, 25 for the 101st, 15 for the 62nd, 5 for the 1st, by Martinien's lists. The British returns of prisoners sent to England, at the Record Office, show 6 officers from the 101st, 2 from the 62nd, and 1 from the 1st, received after the battle. I presume that nearly all the wounded, both officers and rank and file, count among the prisoners. The 1st entered in its regimental report 176 *tués ou pris*, 22 *blessés*, 29 *disparus* : here the only people who got away would be the 22 *blessés*. The regimental return of the 101st shows 31 officers wanting— which seems to correspond to the 25 killed and wounded plus the 6 prisoners sent to England.

SECTION XXXIII: CHAPTER VII

THE BATTLE OF SALAMANCA: THE MAIN ENGAGEMENT

WE must now turn from the exploits of Pakenham and the 3rd Division to deal with the great central attack of Wellington's frontal striking force, the 5th and 4th Divisions, under Leith and Cole, upon the French left centre. They had been told to move on when Bradford's Portuguese brigade should be sufficiently near to cover the right flank of the 5th Division, and the necessity of waiting for this support caused their attack to be delivered perceptibly later than that of Pakenham. Leith had drawn out his division in two lines, the first consisting of Greville's brigade (3/1st, 1/9th, and both battalions of the 38th) and the first battalion of the 4th, brought up from the rear brigade (Pringle's) to equalize the front of the two lines: the second consisted of the rest of that brigade (the second battalion of the 4th, the 2/30th, and 2/44th) and the Portuguese of Spry (3rd and 15th Line). There was a heavy skirmishing line in front, composed of all the British light companies and the 8th Caçadores [1]. Cole had a smaller force, as his left brigade (Anson's) had been told off to the defence of the British Arapile: the 3/27th was holding that rocky knoll, the 1/40th was at its foot in support. Only therefore the Fusilier brigade (under Ellis of the 23rd) and Stubbs's Portuguese formed the attacking force. They were in a single line of seven battalions, with a heavy skirmishing screen composed of four light companies and the whole of the 7th Caçadores [2]. The Fusilier brigade of the 4th Division went through the end of the village of Arapiles, which it did by files from the right of companies, the companies forming up again on the east side of the place, upon their

---

[1] All this from Leith Hay, ii. p. 53. The 1/38th had joined from Lisbon only twelve hours back.

[2] This is proved by the narrative of the Brunswick captain, Wachholz, who commanded the company of that corps attached to the Fusilier brigade.

sergeants regularly sent out as markers. This defile delayed
the advance of the division, which therefore attacked decidedly
later than Leith's men, the joint movement being in an échelon,
with the right leading and the left considerably refused. It was
obvious that when the 4th Division drew near to the French
line on the plateau, it would be exposing its left flank to the
hostile division (Bonnet's) which was massed on and near the
Greater Arapile. Wellington had noted this, and had given
special discretionary orders to Pack, directing him to use his
independent brigade for the sole purpose of protecting the near
flank of the 4th Division ; he might attack the Arapile, as the
best means of holding back Bonnet from descending against
Cole's line, or might manœuvre below the knoll for the same
purpose. When the dangerous moment came, Pack, as we
shall see, took the bull by the horns, and assailed the precipitous
height in front with his whole 2,000 men.

In the rear of the 4th Division the 6th was now coming up
the back slope of the hill behind the Arapile in second line :
similarly the 7th Division was following the 5th. To the right
of the 7th, Stapleton Cotton was moving up from Las Torres
with the cavalry reserve, now consisting only of the six regiments of Le Marchant and G. Anson. Bradford, more to the
right still, and not yet in line with Leith and Cole, moved with
España's small Spanish division behind him.

Of Wellington's front line Leith with the 5th Division had
Maucune in front of him : Cole would have to deal with Clausel,
who had arrived late on the ground, and was only just taking
up his position on the extreme right end of the French plateau.
Pack and W. Anson's detached brigade from the 4th Division,
with the Lesser Arapile in their power, looked across the valley
at Bonnet, massed around its greater twin-hill. The British
attacking line was amply provided with reserves : the defensive
line of the French was still very thin, though Brennier's division
was hurrying up from the head of the wood to support Maucune.
Sarrut's division was still invisible in the forest far to the rear :
Ferey's was better seen—it was hastening up across the open
ground on its way from the extreme French right, but must
obviously be too late to join in meeting Wellington's first
attack.

The roar of the cannon and musketry away in the direction of the Pico de Miranda had been announcing for some time that Pakenham was at close grips with Thomières, before Leith marched down from his heights to cross the valley that separated him from Maucune's position. Soon after five, however, the 5th Division was in close contact with the enemy, having suffered a considerable amount of casualties in reaching him, mainly from the very superior French artillery fire, which swept every yard of the glacis-like slope that ascends from the bottom of the Arapiles valley to the brow of the plateau that forms its southern limit.

' The ground,' writes Leith Hay, ' between the advancing force and that which it was to assail was crowded by the light troops of both sides in extended order, carrying on a very incessant *tiraillade*. The general desired me to ride forward, to make our light infantry press up the heights to cover his line of march, and to bid them, if practicable, make a rush at the enemy's guns. Our light troops soon drove in those opposed to them : the cannon were removed to the rear : every obstruction to the general advance of our line vanished. In front of the centre of that beautiful line rode General Leith, directing its movements. Occasionally every soldier was visible, the sun shining bright upon their arms, though at intervals all were enveloped in a dense cloud of dust, from whence at times issued the animating cheer of the British infantry.

' The French columns, retired from the crest of the heights, were formed in squares, about fifty yards behind the line at which, when arrived, the British regiments would become visible. Their artillery, although placed more to the rear, still poured its fire upon our advancing troops. We were now near the summit of the ridge. The men marched with the same orderly steadiness as at the first : no advance in line at a review was ever more correctly executed : the dressing was admirable, and the gaps caused by casualties were filled up with the most perfect regularity. General Leith and the officers of his staff, being on horseback, first perceived the enemy, and had time to observe his formation, before our infantry line became so visible as to induce him to commence firing. He was drawn up in contiguous squares, the front rank kneeling, and prepared to fire when the drum should beat. All was still and quiet in these squares : not a musket was discharged until the whole opened. Nearly at the same instant General Leith ordered our line to fire and charge. At this moment the last thing I saw through the smoke was the plunge of the horse of Colonel Greville, commanding the leading brigade, who, shot through the head, reared and fell back on his rider. In an instant every individual present was enveloped in smoke and obscurity. No serious struggle for ascendancy followed, for the French squares were penetrated, broken, and discomfited, and the victorious 5th Division pressed forward no longer against troops formed up, but against a mass of disorganized men flying in all directions . . . . When close to the enemy's squares Leith had been severely wounded and reluctantly forced to quit the field ; at the same moment I was hit myself, and my horse killed by a musket-ball : thus removed, I cannot detail the further movements of the division [1].'

In this clear and simple narrative the most remarkable point is Leith Hay's distinct statement that the French received the charge of the 5th Division in a line of squares, a most strange formation to adopt against infantry advancing deployed, even when it was supplemented by a strong screen of *tirailleurs*, and flanked by several batteries of artillery. It is possible that Maucune adopted it because, from his commanding position on the plateau, he could see a considerable body of cavalry coming up on Leith's right rear. This was composed of the brigades of Le Marchant and G. Anson, which Stapleton Cotton was bringing up to the front by Wellington's orders. While Leith was advancing they pressed forward, Le Marchant leading, and passed up the hill in the interval between the 5th Division and Pakenham's front—leaving behind them Bradford, who had crossed the valley parallel to, but much behind, the right of Leith. Bradford had no solid body of troops in front of him, being outside Maucune's extreme left, and suffered practically no loss—the total casualty list of his brigade that day was only seventeen men. This contrasts marvellously with the loss of Leith's front line, where Greville's brigade in their triumphant advance lost 350 men—mainly from the

[1] Leith Hay, ii. pp. 57–8.

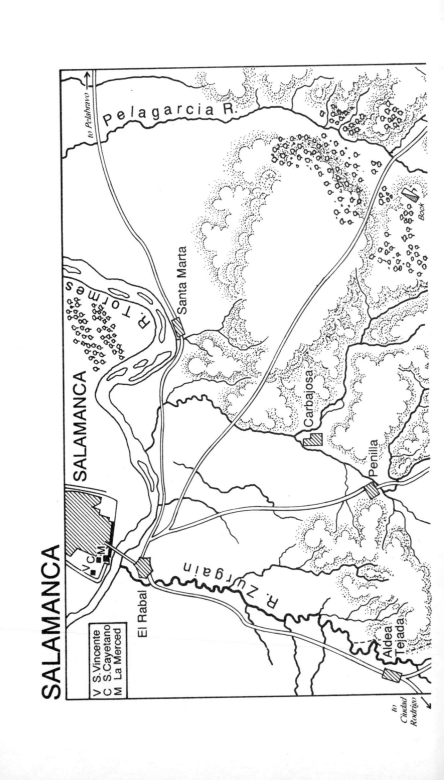

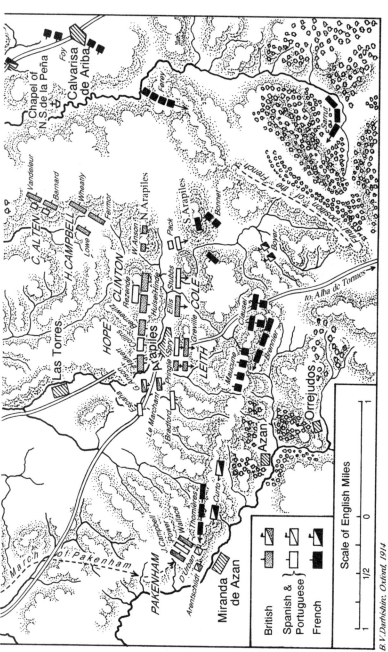

Chapel of
N.S. de la Peña

Calvarisa
de Ariba

Foy

Ferey

Sarrut

Vandeleur
C. ALTEN
Barnard
Wheatly
H. CAMPBELL
Lowe
Fermor
Anson
N. Arapiles
Pack
S. Arapiles
Bonnet

Las Torres
HOPE
CLINTON
Rezende
Hulse
Hinde
Stubbs
Ellis
Greville COLE
Spry
Arentschildt
Pringle
LEITH
Maucune
Clausel
Boyer
to; Alba de Tornes
Brennier

España
Le Marchant
Bradford
Arentschildt

Azan
Orrejudos

March of Pakenham
PAKENHAM
J. campbell power
Wallace
Thomières
Curto
D'Urban
Arentschildt
Miranda
de Azan

British
Spanish &
Portuguese }
French

Scale of English Miles

1   1/2   0   1

B.V.Darbishir; Oxford, 1914

artillery fire endured while the long slope of the French plateau was being mounted : for there were at least four batteries aligned on Maucune's right, and their guns had been worked till the last possible minute.

Whatever was the cause of the formation in square adopted by the French division, it would have been fortunate if only it could have preserved that formation a little longer ; for precisely when it had lost its order, and fallen back before Leith's shattering volleys of musketry, Le Marchant's heavy dragoons arrived upon the crest of the plateau. No better opportunity for the use of cavalry could have been conceived, than that which existed at this moment. Infantry already engaged with, and worsted by, other infantry is the destined prey of cavalry coming on the scene from the flank in unbroken order. Le Marchant had received his instructions directly from Wellington, who had told him to ' charge in at all hazards [1],' when he saw the French battalions on the plateau hotly engaged. He had formed his 1,000 sabres in two lines, the 5th Dragoon Guards and 4th Dragoons in front, the 3rd Dragoons in support, and had come over the sky-line and trotted down into the valley just as Leith's division got to close quarters with Maucune. Passing Bradford on his right, he came to the crest to find all confusion in front of him. The squares that Leith had just broken were rolling back in disorder : directly behind a new division (Brennier's), only just arriving upon the field, was beginning to form up, to cover and support the shaken battalions. Some distance to their left rear the remains of Thomières's division, in a disorderly crowd, were falling back in front of the triumphant advance of Pakenham.

Le Marchant charged in diagonally upon the flank of Maucune's left brigade, and caught the two battalions of the 66th regiment falling back from the crest. The Frenchmen were courageous enough to make a desperate attempt to club themselves together in a solid mass : their rear ranks faced about and opened a heavy fire upon the advancing squadrons. But it was given with uncertain aim and trifling effect, and before they could reload the dragoons were among them.

[1] See Le Marchant's *Life*, from notes supplied by his son, in Cole's *Peninsular Generals*, ii. p. 281.

A desperate minority attempted to resist with the bayonet, and were sabred : some hundreds cast down their muskets, raised their hands, and asked quarter. The rear ranks scattered and fled southward across the plateau. Leaving the gathering up of the prisoners to the infantry of Leith, Le Marchant led his brigade, so soon as some order could be restored, against the next regiment of Maucune's division, the 15th Line ; they were better prepared for resistance than the 66th, which had been caught quite unawares, they showed a regular front, and gave a more effective fire. Many of the dragoons fell ; but nevertheless their impetus carried them through the mass, which went to pieces and dispersed into a disorderly crowd : it fled in the same direction as the wrecks of the 66th.

Le Marchant's brigade had now lost its formation, ' the three regiments had become mixed together, the officers rode where they' could find places : but a good front, without intervals, was still maintained, and there was no confusion [1].' In front of them there was now a fresh enemy—the 22nd Line, the leading regiment of the division of Brennier, which had just arrived on the field, and was getting into order to save and support Maucune's routed battalions. It would seem that in the midst of the dust and smoke, and surrounded and interfered with by the fugitives of the broken regiments, the 22nd had either no time or no good opportunity for forming squares : they were found in *colonne serrée*, in good order, partly covered by a clump of trees, an outlying thicket from the great forest to their rear. They reserved their fire, with great composure, till the dragoons were within ten yards distance, and poured a volley so close and well aimed upon the leading squadron [5th Dragoon Guards] that nearly a fourth of them fell. Tremendous as was the effect of the discharge, the dragoons were not arrested : they broke in through the opposing bayonets, and plunged into the dense masses of the enemy. In the combat which ensued, broadsword and bayonet were used against each other with various results : the French, hewn down and trampled under the horses' feet, offered all the resistance that brave men could make. Le Marchant himself had some narrow escapes—he fought like a private, and had to cut down more

[1] *Life of Le Marchant,* p. 285.

G g 2

than one of the enemy. It was only after a fierce struggle that the French yielded, and he had the satisfaction of seeing them fly before him in helpless confusion. The brigade had now lost all order : the dragoons, excited by the struggle, vied with each other in the pursuit, and galloped recklessly into the crowd of fugitives, sabring those who came within their reach. To restrain them at such a moment was beyond the power of their officers [1].'

Le Marchant endeavoured to keep a few men in hand, in order to guard against any attempt of the French to rally, but he had only about half a squadron of the 4th Dragoons with him, when he came upon some companies which were beginning to re-form in the edge of the great wood. He led his party against them, and drove them back among the trees, where they dispersed. But at the moment of contact he was shot dead, by a ball which entered his groin and broke his spine. Thus fell an officer of whom great things had been expected by all who knew him, in the moment when he had just obtained and used to the full his first chance of leading his brigade in a general action. One of the few scientific soldiers in the cavalry arm whom the British army owned, Le Marchant had been mainly known as the founder and administrator of the Royal Military College at High Wycombe, which was already beginning to send to the front many young officers trained as their predecessors had never been. He was the author of many military pamphlets, and of a new system of sword exercise which had lately been adopted for the cavalry [2]. On his promotion to the rank of Major-General, in 1811, he had been unexpectedly sent to the Peninsula in command of the heavy brigade, which reinforced Wellington during that autumn. As an executive commander in the field he had given the first proofs of his ability at the combat of Villagarcia [3]—but this was a small affair—at Salamanca he proved himself a born commander of cavalry, and his services would have been invaluable to

[1] *Life of Le Marchant*, pp. 286–7.

[2] Le Marchant was also an admirable artist in water colours. I saw many of his pleasing sketches of Peninsular landscapes when his grandson, Sir Henry Le Marchant, allowed me to look through his correspondence and notes.

[3] See p. 277 above.

Wellington in later fields but for the disastrous shot that
ended his career. He was a man of a lofty and religious spirit,
ill to be spared by his country [1].

Le Marchant's charge made a complete wreck of the left
wing of the French army. The remnants of the eight battalions
which he had broken fled eastward in a confused mass, towards
the edge of the woods, becoming blended with the separate
stream of fugitives from Thomières's division. The 5th Division
swept in some 1,500 prisoners from them, as also the eagle of
the 22nd Line, which the heavy brigade had broken in their last
effort, while five guns were taken by the 4th Dragoons [2]. The
French, flying blindly from the pursuit, were so scattered
that some of them actually ran in headlong among D'Urban's
Portuguese horse, on the back side of the plateau. ' We were
so far in their rear,' writes that officer, ' that a mass of their
routed infantry (to our astonishment, since we did not know
the cause) in the wildness of their panic and confusion, and
throwing away their arms, actually ran against our horses,
where many of them fell down exhausted, and incapable of
further movement.' The same happened in the front of the
3rd Division, where, according to a narrator in the Connaught
Rangers, ' hundreds of men frightfully disfigured, black with
dust, worn out with fatigue, and covered with sabre-cuts and
blood, threw themselves among us for safety.'

---

[1] I have read with respect his admirable letters to his family. ' I never
go into battle,' he said, ' without subjecting myself to a strict self-examina-
tion : when, having (as I hope) humbly made my peace with God, I leave
the result in His hands, with perfect confidence that He will determine
what is best for me.'

[2] It is vexatious to find that neither the 22nd nor the 66th was among
the fourteen Salamanca regiments of which detailed casualty lists survive.
The 15th Line returned 15 officers and 359 men as their loss. Martinien's
tables show 21 officers lost in the 22nd, and 17 in the 66th. The deficits
of these two regiments as shown by the muster-rolls of August 1 were
respectively about 750 and 500, but these do not represent their total losses,
as all the regiments present at the battle had picked up many men at their
dépôts at Valladolid, and from the small evacuated posts, before August 1,
e.g. the 15th had 52 officers present on July 15, lost 15 at Salamanca, but
showed 46 present on August 1 ; 9 officers must have joined from somewhere
in the interim. So the 66th had 38 officers present on July 15, lost 17, but
showed 34 present on August 1. Thirteen more must have arrived, and
accompanied of course by the corresponding rank and file.

The 3rd Division had now, in its advance along the plateau, come in contact with the right flank of the fifth, and both of them fell into one line reaching across the whole breadth of the heights, while in front of them were recoiling the wrecks of Thomières, Maucune, and Brennier. The four French regiments which had not been caught in Le Marchant's charge were still keeping together, and making occasional attempts at a stand, but were always outflanked on their left by the 3rd Division and Arentschildt's and D'Urban's horse. Curto's French light cavalry had rallied, and picked up their second brigade, and were now doing their best to cover the southern flank of the retreating multitude [1]. An officer of one of their regiments speaks in his memoirs of having charged with advantage against red dragoons—these must apparently have been scattered parties of Le Marchant's brigade, pursuing far and furiously, since no other red-coated cavalry was in this part of the field [2]. But Curto's squadrons had mainly to do with Arentschildt and D'Urban, both of whom report sharp fighting with French horse at this moment. The 3rd French Hussars charged the 1st Hussars K.G.L., while the latter were employed in gleaning prisoners from the routed infantry, and were only driven off after a severe combat [3]. The pursuit then continued until the disordered French masses were driven off the plateau, and on to the wooded hills parallel with the Greater Arapile, where Marmont had massed his army before his fatal move to the left.

Meanwhile the 4th Division and Pack's Portuguese had fought, with much less fortunate results, against the French divisions of Clausel and Bonnet. There are good narratives

---

[1] The regiments of Maucune's brigade, which did not get caught in the cavalry charge (82nd and 86th), lost only 8 and 3 officers respectively, as against the 15 and 17 lost by the 66th and 15th. Of Brennier's division the 22nd Line had 21 casualties among officers, while the 65th and 17th Léger had only 3 and 9 respectively.

[2] So Parquin of the 13th Chasseurs in his *Mémoires*, p. 302. The only other red-coated dragoons in Wellington's army, Bock's brigade, were far away to the left.

[3] Arentschildt reports that his and D'Urban's men were all mixed and busy with the French infantry, when the French hussars charged in, and that he rallied, to beat them off, a body composed mostly of his own Germans, but with Portuguese and 14th Light Dragoons among them.

of their advance from three officers who took part in it, all so
full and clear that it is impossible to have any doubts about
its details. One comes from the Assistant Quarter-Master-
General of the 4th Division, Charles Vere : the second is from
the captain commanding one of the four light companies of the
Fusilier brigade, Ludwig von Wachholz of the Brunswick-Oels
Jägers : the third is the narrative of Pack's aide-de-camp,
Charles Synge, who was with the front line of the Portuguese
in their vigorous but unsuccessful attack on the Greater Arapile.
The three narratives have nothing contradictory in them.

The sequence of events was as follows. After deploying the
three battalions of the Fusilier brigade (1/7th, 1/23rd, 1/48th)
beyond the end of the village of Arapiles, and Stubbs's Portuguese brigade to their left, Cole started to cross the valley,
having a very strong skirmishing line, composed of the whole
of the 7th Caçadores and of the four light companies of the
British brigade. During the first stage of the advance, which
started at 5.45[1], a perceptible time after that of the 5th Division,
the two brigades suffered severely from French artillery fire,
but had no infantry opposed to them. Their objective was the
division of Clausel, which had by this time come into line on
the extreme eastern end of the plateau occupied by Maucune.
When the advancing line had reached the trough of the valley
which separated it from the French heights, Cole saw that his
left front was faced by a detached French force[2] on a low
rocky ridge half-way between the end of the plateau and the
Great Arapile, and also that behind the Arapile, and in a
position to support this detachment, were several other French
battalions. Pack was deploying to assault the Arapile, but
even if he won a first success there was visible a considerable
mass of troops behind it. After the valley was crossed Stubbs's
Portuguese brigade, coming first into action, with the caçadores
in front, attacked the French regiment on the knoll and drove
it back. It retired towards the Arapile and the bulk of Bonnet's

---

[1] The moment is fixed by Wachholz, who says that he looked at his
watch, to fix the hour.

[2] This was the 122nd (three battalions), of Bonnet's division, which
Marmont says (see above, p. 430) that he had placed as a connecting-link
between the Arapile and the troops on the plateau.

division, to which it belonged. Cole detached his caçador battalion to follow it, hoping that Pack might succeed in ' containing ' the rest of the French force in this direction. The remainder of his line pushed on, with the light companies of the Fusilier brigade acting as its screen, and attacked Clausel on the plateau. The advance was steady, but cost many lives, and the line was enfiladed by a tiresome flank fire from the French guns on the top of the Great Arapile. Nevertheless the crest was reached—on it lay the front line of the French division—five battalions—which engaged in a furious frontal combat of musketry with the Fusiliers and their Portuguese comrades, but was beaten in it, and fell back some 200 yards on to its reserves. The impetus of the attack was exhausted, Cole had just been wounded, so that there was a gap in the command, and the troops were re-forming and recovering their breath, when it was seen that things were going very badly behind and to the left. The attack on the Arapile had by this time been delivered, and had failed completely.

Pack had grasped the fact that when the 4th Division had crossed the valley, it would be much at the mercy of Bonnet's troops in the direction of the Arapile, which were now on its flank, and would presently be almost in its rear. He therefore resolved to use the option of attacking that Wellington had given him. He deployed the 4th Caçadores as a skirmishing line, gave them as an immediate support the four grenadier companies of his line regiments, and followed with the rest in two columns, the 1st Line on the right, the 16th on the left. The caçadores went up the comparatively level field which formed the central slope between the two rocky ends of the Arapile—it was sown with rye some three feet high that year. French skirmishers in small numbers gave way before them, but the main opposition of the enemy was from his battery placed on the summit. The skirmishing line got four-fifths of the way to the crest, and then found an obstacle before it, a bank of some four feet high, where the field ended. It was perpendicular, and men scrambling up it had to sling their muskets, or to lay them down, so as to be able to use both hands. The caçadores were just tackling the bank—a few of them were over it—when the French regiment on top, the 120th, which had been waiting till the Portuguese should reach the obstacle, delivered a shattering volley and charged. The caçadores were quite helpless, being more engaged in climbing than in using their arms [1]. They were swept off in a moment, and the French, jumping down into the field, pursued them vigorously, and overthrew first the supporting grenadier companies, and then the two regiments, which were caught half-way up the slope. As Napier truly observes, ' the Portuguese were scoffed at for their failure—but unjustly : no troops could have withstood that crash upon such steep ground, and the propriety of attacking the hill at all seems questionable.' Pack made the attempt purely because he thought that it was the only way of taking off the attention of the French from Cole's flank. The brigade suffered heavily, losing 386 men in ten minutes. It took refuge at the foot of the British Arapile, where it was covered by the 1/40th of Anson's brigade, which was standing there in reserve.

The French brigadier in command on the Greater Arapile wisely made little attempt to pursue Pack's fugitives, but having his front now clear of any danger, sallied out from behind his hill with three regiments, the 118th and 119th and the re-formed 122nd, against the flank and rear of the British 4th Division. There was nothing in front of him save the 7th Caçadores, which Cole had detached as a covering force, when he stormed the heights with the remainder of the brigades of Ellis and Stubbs. This isolated battalion behaved very well, it stood its ground in line, but was absolutely overwhelmed and broken up by the superior numbers converging on it [2].

Nearly at the same moment Clausel's whole force in column charged the two brigades of the 4th Division which had carried the heights. The French were in superior numbers—ten battalions to seven—and their two reserve regiments were fresh troops, acting against men who had just won a dearly-bought success by a great effort. The Anglo-Portuguese line gave way, from the left first, where the 23rd Portuguese began the movement. But it spread down the whole front, and the

---

[1] All this from the journal of Chas. Synge, Pack's aide-de-camp, who was with the caçadores, and was desperately wounded at the bank, in the first clash. It was printed in the *Nineteenth Century* for July 1912.

[2] See Vere's *Marches of the 4th Division*, p. 36.

Fusiliers, no less than Stubbs's brigade, recoiled to the very foot of the plateau [1].

This reverse gave Clausel, who was now in command since Bonnet's wound, an opportunity that looked unlikely a few minutes before. He could either withdraw the Army of Portugal in retreat, covering the three disorganized divisions with those which were still intact—his own, Bonnet's, and the two reserve divisions of Ferey and Sarrut, which had just come on the ground—Foy was far off and otherwise engaged—or he might adopt a bolder policy, and attempt to take advantage of the disaster to Pack and Cole, by bursting into the gap between Leith and the British Arapile, and trying to break Wellington's centre. Being an ambitious and resolute man he chose the latter alternative—though it was a dangerous one when Leith and Pakenham were bearing in hard upon his routed left wing. Accordingly he left Sarrut to rally and cover the three beaten divisions, and attacked with his right centre. His own division followed the retreating brigades of Ellis and Stubbs down the heights, while the three disposable regiments of Bonnet came into line to its right, and Boyer's three regiments of dragoons advanced down the depression between the Greater Arapile and the recovered plateau. Ferey was left in second line or reserve on the crest.

At first the advance had considerable success. Bonnet's regiments pushed forward on the right, driving in the 1/40th [2], which had come forward to cover Pack's routed battalions, and pressing quite close to the British Arapile, whose battery was turned upon them with much effect. Clausel's own division pushed the Fusiliers some way down the slope and right into the valley at its foot. The dragoons charged Stubbs's retreating Portuguese, and cut up many of them, though the 11th regiment finally succeeded in forming square with what remained solid of its companies, and beat off the main attack. Part of the French horsemen, however, pushed on, and reached the front of Wellington's reserve line, the 6th Division, which had now descended the heights to relieve the broken 4th. One battalion

[1] All this from Wachholz, who was now with the 7th Fusiliers.
[2] See Vere's *Marches of the 4th Division*, p. 36. The 3/27th on top of the hill was not brought forward, as some wrongly say.

of Hulse's brigade, the 2/53rd, was charged by several squadrons, but formed square in time and repulsed them. Some little way to the right the Fusiliers and the Portuguese 23rd formed a large parti-coloured square, expecting a similar attack, but it did not come their way [1].

Wellington, thanks to his own prescience, had ample reserves with which to parry Clausel's desperate stroke. Setting aside the Light Division, which now paired off against Foy on the extreme left of the field, there were the 1st, 6th, and 7th Divisions, not to speak of Bradford's Portuguese and España's Spaniards, all of them perfectly intact. And of these, such was his strength, only one fresh unit, Clinton's 6th Division, required to be brought up to turn the day. It was now coming over the valley where the 4th had preceded it, in a long majestic line, Hulse's brigade on the right, Hinde's on the left, the Portuguese of the Conde de Rezende in second line. The 1st Division, if it had been needed, could have supported Clinton, from its post just to the north of the Lesser Arapile, but had not yet got under way.

The repulse of the new French attack was carried out with no great difficulty, if not without serious fighting. The advance of Clausel's own division was checked by Marshal Beresford, who took Spry's Portuguese brigade out of the second line of the victorious 5th Division, and led it diagonally along the southern slope of the plateau to fall upon Clausel's flank. This it did effectively, for the French division could not dare to press on against the Fusiliers, and had to throw back its left, and form up opposite Spry, with whom it became engaged in a lively musketry fight. It could no longer move forward, and was immobilized, though it held its own : Beresford was wounded in the chest and taken to the rear, but Spry's five battalions had served the desired purpose, and stopped the French advance in this quarter.

But the decisive check to Clausel's offensive was given by Clinton and the 6th Division, who advancing straight before them—over the ground previously traversed by Cole—fell upon,

---

[1] This from Wachholz's narrative, very clearly explained. The Fusiliers were *not* relieved by the advance of the 1/40th and 3/27th, as some authorities state.

overlapped at both ends, and thoroughly discomfited in close musketry duel the nine battalions of Bonnet's division, which had pressed forward close to the Lesser Arapile, as if to insert a wedge in the British line. Unsupported by Boyer's dragoons, who had shot their bolt too early, and were now re-forming far to the rear, this French division was badly cut up. Each of the three regiments which had taken part in its advance lost more than 500 men in the struggle [1] : they fell back in disorder towards the hill behind them, and their rout compelled Clausel's division to give way also, since it exposed its flank to the oncoming line of Hulse's brigade on Clinton's right. Moreover the Great Arapile had to be evacuated, for while the routed troops passed away to its left rear, the 1st British Division was soon after seen steadily advancing towards its right. The regiment on the hill (the 120th) was exposed to be cut off and surrounded, and hastily ran down the back of the mount : while retreating it was much molested by the skirmishers of the German Legion Brigade of the 1st Division. It lost heavily, and the battery that had been on the summit was captured before it could get away.

Thus Clausel's brief half-hour of triumph ended in complete disaster, and the two divisions with which he had made his stroke were flung back against the slope in front of the woods in their rear, where they took refuge behind the intact division of Ferey, the sole available reserve in this part of the field. They were now as badly beaten as Thomières and Maucune had been earlier in the day [2].

While this lively action was in progress, the 5th and 3rd Divisions, supported by the 7th and by Bradford's Portuguese,

---

[1] The 122nd lost 21 officers and 508 men, the 118th and 119th probably as many or more—they had respectively 20 and 26 officers hit. The 120th, the regiment on the Great Arapile, lost only 8 officers—but 580 men, an almost inexplicable disproportion. The 118th claimed to have taken a flag—perhaps one of the 7th Portuguese Caçadores, who were badly cut up when Bonnet first advanced.

[2] The losses of three of Clausel's four regiments chance to have been preserved—the 25th Léger lost 16 officers and 322 men : the 27th Ligne 7 officers and 159 men : the 59th Ligne 17 officers and 253 men. The 50th, which had 26 officers hit, must have had more casualties than any of the other three, so the total divisional loss must have been well over 1,200. But Bonnet's division, much worse mauled, lost at least 2,200.

in second line, and assisted on their flanks by Arentschildt's, D'Urban's, and Anson's horse, had been driving in the wrecks of the French left wing towards the woods. There was much resistance : on Sarrut's intact battalions many of the broken regiments had rallied. ' These men, besmeared with blood, dust, and clay, half naked, and some carrying only broken weapons, fought with a fury not to be surpassed,' says a 3rd Division narrator of the battle. But the tide of battle was always moving backward, towards the woods from which the French had originally issued, and though it sometimes seemed about to stop for a minute or two, a new outflanking manœuvre by the troops of Pakenham, D'Urban, and Arentschildt, sufficed on each occasion to set it in motion again.

The last stage of the conflict had now been reached : the French centre was as thoroughly beaten as their left had been earlier in the day : many of the battalions had gone completely to pieces, and were pouring into the woods and making their way to the rear, with no thought except for their personal safety. Of intact troops there were only two divisions left, Ferey's in the centre, and Foy's on the extreme right near Calvarisa de Ariba. It was generally considered that Foy ought to have been overwhelmed by the much superior British force in front of him, for not only was he opposed by the Light Division, whose skirmishers had been bickering with him all the afternoon, but the 1st Division became available for use against him the moment that it was clear that the French offensive against the 4th Division had been shattered, by the advance of Clinton and Spry. Wellington, it is said [1], dispatched orders for the 1st Division to move forward and strike in between Foy and the Greater Arapile, at the moment that he saw that the 6th Division had broken Bonnet's troops. If so, the order was not executed, and General Campbell led out his three brigades much too late, and not in time either to cut off Foy or to encircle the right of the disordered mass of the enemy now retiring into the woods. He seems to have acted simply as a link between the 6th Division on his right, and the Light Division on his left, for the latter alone pressed Foy vigorously.

[1] This is stated by Napier, iv. p. 273, and seems reasonable. See also Tomkinson, p. 186.

The only part of Campbell's division which suffered any
appreciable loss at this time of the day were the light companies
of Löwe's brigade—that which was composed of the King's
German Legion : they fell on the flank of the French regiment
that was evacuating the Greater Arapile, and did it considerable
harm [1].

Meanwhile the last and not the least bloody fighting of the
day was beginning, on the hillside just outside the head of the
forest, where Marmont had deployed his main body at midday, and where Ferey's division was now standing in reserve,
while the broken troops both from its front and from its flank
were streaming by to the rear. Clausel had given Ferey orders
to cover the retreat at all costs, warning him that unless he could
hold back the advancing enemy for some time the disaster would
be complete. The general to whom this unenviable task was
assigned carried it out with splendid courage, and by his
constancy gave time for the escape of the whole of the confused
mass behind him. He drew out his nine battalions in a single
line, the centre a little advanced to suit the shape of the hillside, the flanks a little thrown back. The extreme battalions
at each end were in square, to guard against possible attacks
by cavalry, but the seven central units were deployed *en
bataille* in three-deep line, a formation which had not been seen
in the other episodes of the battle, and which made their fire
much more effective than that of regiments fighting in ' column
of divisions,' as most of their comrades had done [2].

Against the orderly front thus disposed Clinton came up with
the 6th Division, pursuing his victorious advance. He was
flanked on the left by the Fusilier brigade of the 4th Division,
which had long ago rallied and come up to the front since its
disaster of an hour back. On Clinton's right were the 5th and
3rd Divisions, but both were at the moment re-forming, after
their long struggle with Sarrut and the wrecks of the French
left wing. Anson's cavalry had at last got to the front in

---

[1] The losses in Campbell's Guards' brigade (62 men) were in the companies which defended the village of Arapiles earlier in the day—those in
his line brigade (Wheatley's) were trifling—16 wounded and no killed. The
K.G.L. brigade lost 60 or so, all in the light companies, during the advance.

[2] All this from Lemonnier-Delafosse of Ferey's division, pp. 158–9.

this direction, and replaced D'Urban and Arentschildt—whose squadrons were quite worn out—upon the extreme right of the allied line.

Clinton, it is said [1], refused to wait till the troops on his right were re-formed, and hurried on the attack : it was growing dark, and a few more minutes of delay would allow the French to make off under cover of the night. Therefore he advanced at once, and found himself engaged at once in a most desperate musketry contest, whose deadly results recalled Albuera, so heavy were the losses on both sides. But here the French had the advantage of being deployed, and not (as at Albuera) wedged in deep columns. The first fire of the French line, as Clinton's brigades closed in, was particularly murderous, and swept away whole sections of the attacking force. ' The ground over which we had to pass,' writes an officer in Hinde's brigade [2], ' was a remarkably clear slope, like the glacis of a fortress, most favourable for the defensive fire of the enemy, and disadvantageous for the assailant. The craggy ridge, on which the French were drawn up, rose so abruptly that the rear ranks could fire over the heads of the front. But we had approached within two hundred yards before the musketry began : it was far the heaviest fire that I have ever seen, and accompanied by constant discharges of grape. An uninterrupted blaze was thus maintained, so that the crest of the hill seemed one long streak of flame. Our men came down to the charging position, and commenced firing from that level, at the same time keeping touch to the right, so that the gaps opened by the enemy's fire were instantly filled up. At the first volley about eighty men of our right wing fell to the rear in one group. Our commanding officer rode up to know the cause, and found that they were every one wounded ! ' But heavy as was the loss of this regiment (137 out of 600 present), it was trifling compared to that of its neighbours to the right, in Hulse's brigade, where the right and centre regiments in the line, the 1/11th and 1/61st, lost respectively 340 men out of 516 and 366 out of 546— a proportion to which only Albuera could show a parallel. For

[1] But not on the best authority : regimental diaries are not always safe to follow on such points.

[2] Ross Lewin of the 32nd, ii. pp. 25–6.

many minutes—one observer calls it nearly an hour, but the
stress of the struggle multiplied time—the two hostile lines
continued blazing at each other in the growing dusk. ' The
glare of light caused by the artillery, the continued fire of
musketry, and by the dry grass which had caught fire, gave the
face of the hill a terrific appearance : it was one sheet of
flame, and Clinton's men seemed to be attacking a burning
mountain, whose crater was defended by a barrier of shining
steel [1].' The French, so far as losses went, probably suffered no
more, or perhaps less, than their assailants : but their casualties
were nevertheless appalling. And at last they gave way : ' the
cruel fire cost us many lives,' writes an officer of the 31st Léger,
' and at last, slowly, and after having given nearly an hour's
respite to the remainder of the army, Ferey gave back, still
protected by his flanking squares, to the very edge of the forest,
where he halted our half-destroyed division. Formed in line
it still presented a respectable front, and halted, despite of the
English batteries, which enfiladed us with a thundering fire.
Here Ferey met the form of death which the soldier prefers to
all others, he was slain outright by a round-shot [2].'

Clinton's English regiments were so disordered and reduced
by the awful fire through which they had passed in their
victorious march, that he put into front line for a final assault
on the enemy his Portuguese brigade, that of the Conde de
Rezende, which was still intact, as it had hitherto been in
reserve. Its five battalions deployed, and advanced against the
now much contracted line of Ferey's division : they were supported on the left by the Fusilier brigade of the 4th Division,
on the right by the 5th Division, which was now re-formed and
well to the front. Anson's cavalry was also in this direction.

The dying effort of Ferey's division was worthy of its previous
hard fighting. ' Formed right up against the trees,' writes the
French officer, whom we have already quoted, ' no longer with
any artillery to help, we saw the enemy marching up against us

---

[1] Grattan, p. 253.

[2] Lemonnier-Delafosse, p. 159. This note about Ferey's being slain
outright does not agree with the usual statement that he was mortally
wounded, and died two days later, given by several English diarists. But
Lemonnier-Delafosse is first-hand authority.

in two lines, the first of which was composed of Portuguese. Our position was critical, but we waited for the shock : the two lines moved up toward us ; their order was so regular that in the Portuguese regiment in front of us we could see the company intervals, and note the officers behind keeping the men in accurate line, by blows with the flat of their swords or their canes. We fired first, the moment that they got within range : and the volleys which we delivered from our two first ranks were so heavy and so continuous that, though they tried to give us back fire for fire, the whole melted away. The second line was coming up behind—this was English, we should have tried to receive it in the same way, still holding our ground though under a flank fire of artillery, when suddenly the left of our line ceased firing and fell back into the wood in complete disorder. The 70th Ligne had found itself turned by cavalry ; it broke ; the rout spread down the front to the 26th and 77th ; only our two battalions of the 31st Léger held firm, under the fire of the enemy, which continued so long as we showed outside the edge of the forest. We only gave back as the day ended, retiring some 250 yards from our original position, and keeping our *voltigeur* companies still in a skirmishing line in front [1].'

This vigorous account of the last stand of the French reserve is not far from being accurate. It is quite true that the Portuguese brigade of the 6th Division suffered terribly in its attack, and was completely checked. It lost 487 men during the fifteen minutes in which it was engaged—the heaviest casualty list in any of the brigades of its nation, even heavier than that of Stubbs's troops in the 4th Division. The only point that requires to be added is that it was not so much a panic caused by a partial cavalry charge which broke the 70th Ligne, and finally dispersed Ferey's regiments [2], as the pressure of the 5th Division upon the whole of the left of their line, which collapsed almost simultaneously. But they had done their work—before they dispersed, leaving only the 31st Léger to

[1] Lemonnier-Delafosse, pp. 161–2.

[2] Ferey's four regiments probably lost somewhat over 1,100 men—the 31st Léger had 380 casualties, the 47th Ligne (with 18 officers killed and wounded) something like 500 ; the 70th suffered least, it returned only 111 casualties ; the 26th slightly more, perhaps 150. The whole forms a moderate total, considering the work done.

act as a most inadequate rearguard, they had detained the allies for a half-hour or more, and night had set in. Wellington ordered the 6th Division to pursue, but it was so much cut up and fatigued that it only advanced a hundred yards into the forest, and then halted and settled down for the night. Why the intact 7th Division was not rather used for the pursuit it is hard to understand. Still more so is the fact that no cavalry was sent forward in this direction : the woods, no doubt, looked uninviting and dangerous, but the enemy was in a state of absolute panic, and ready to disperse at the least pressure. ' But,' says the most intelligent of the British diarists with the mounted arm, ' the cavalry during the assault on the last hill was ordered back to the point on the left where we assembled before the attack, leaving the infantry to pursue without us. Had this not been done (though it might not have been prudent to pursue with both in the night), yet by their being at hand there was a greater chance of accomplishing more. The order came from Sir Stapleton Cotton himself. The infantry moved in pursuit by moonlight. . . . I have heard from an officer in the 6th Division that although they had been marching all day, and were so tired, when ordered to halt for the night, that they could not possibly have marched much farther, yet they sat up through the night, talking over the action, each recalling to his comrade the events that happened [1].'

Some part of the slackness of the pursuit is to be explained by an unfortunate misconception by which Wellington (through no fault of his own) was obsessed that night. He was under the impression that the Castle of Alba de Tormes was still held by the Spanish garrison which he had left there, and that the bridge and the neighbouring ford were therefore unavailable for the retreat of the French, who (as he supposed) must be retiring by the fords of Huerta and Villa Gonzalo, which they had used to reach the field. Unhappily—as has been already mentioned—Carlos de España had withdrawn the battalion at Alba without making any mention of the fact to his Commander-in-Chief [2]. Wellington therefore put more thought to urging the

---

[1] Tomkinson (of Anson's brigade), p. 187.

[2] Tomkinson in his diary (p. 188) has a curious story to the effect that 'the Spanish general, before the action, asked if he should not take his

pursuit in the direction of the East than of the South, and it was not till late in the night, and when nothing but stragglers had been picked up on the Huerta road, that he discovered what had really occurred.

It remains to relate the unimportant happenings on this front during the evening. At the moment when the French attack on Wellington's centre failed, about 7 o'clock or soon after, Clausel sent to Foy, whose division still lay behind Calvarisa de Ariba, covering the way to the Huerta fords, the order to retire. His instructions were to cover the flank of the line of retreat of the broken army, and to take up successive detaining positions on its right, on the eastern side of the brook and ravine which lie between the two Arapiles and the village of Utrera. These orders Foy carried out skilfully and well. He fended off the Light Division, which had moved out in pursuit of him, with a heavy rearguard of light troops, always giving way when pressed. His concern was almost entirely with this British unit, for the 1st Division had started too late to get near him. The Light Division and its battery kept him on the run, but never came up with his main body. 'Night alone saved my division, and the troops that I was covering,' wrote Foy, ' without it I should probably have been crushed, and the enemy would have arrived at Alba de Tormes before the wrecks of our seven routed divisions got there. An hour after dark the English cavalry was still pushing charges home against my regiments, which I had placed in alternate chequers of line and column. I had the luck to keep the division in hand till the last, and to steer it in the right direction, though many routed battalions kept pressing in upon my left, and threatened to carry disorder into my ranks. The pursuit ceased near Santa Maria de Utrera[1].'

It is difficult to make out what became of the heavy dragoons of Bock during this long retrograde movement of Foy's division : they were certainly not the cavalry of which the French general speaks as charging him during his retreat, for they

troops out of Alba—after he had done it. Lord Wellington replied, " Certainly not," and the Don was afraid to tell what he had done. Lord W. therefore acted, of course, as if the place had been in our possession still.'   [1] Foy, *Vie militaire*, pp. 176–7.

returned no single man or horse killed or wounded that day [1]. Perhaps, far away to the left, they may have been driving in from position to position, the one regiment of Boyer's dragoons which had been left to cover Foy's extreme outer flank. More probably they may have been pushing their march towards the fords of Huerta, in the vain hope of finding masses of disbanded enemies on the way, and ultimately cutting them off from the river. This hypothesis is borne out by the fact that the bivouac of the heavy German brigade was that night in front of Pelabravo, much to the north-east of the resting-places of the rest of the army, and in the general direction of the fords [2].

That the pursuit was misdirected was a most lamentable chance for Wellington. If it had been urged in the right direction, the Army of Portugal would have been annihilated as a fighting-body, and would never have been able to make head again in the autumn. For the forest of Alba de Tormes was full of nothing but a disorderly crowd, making the best of its way towards the bridge, with no proper rearguard and no commander in charge of the retreat. Clausel, wounded in the foot, was being looked after by the surgeons in Alba, and was barely able to mount his horse next day. The rout was complete : ' a shapeless mass of soldiery was rolling down the road like a torrent—infantry, cavalry, artillery, wagons, carts, baggage-mules, the reserve park of the artillery drawn by oxen, were all mixed up. The men, shouting, swearing, running, were out of all order, each one looking after himself alone—a complete stampede. The panic was inexplicable to one who, coming from the extreme rear, knew that there was no pursuit by the enemy to justify the terror shown. I had to stand off far from the road, for if I had got near it, I should have been swept off by the torrent in spite of myself [3].' So writes the officer, already twice quoted for the narrative of the end of the battle, whose regiment, still hanging together in the most

---

[1] This cavalry *may* have been the two detached squadrons of the 14th Light Dragoons, which had not followed the rest of Arentschildt's brigade to the right.

[2] See Schwertfeger's *History of the German Legion*, i. p. 378.

[3] Lemonnier-Delafosse, p. 164.

creditable fashion, brought up the rear of the retreat. It is clear that any sort of a pursuit would have produced such a general block at the bridge-head that a disaster like that of Leipzig must have followed, and the whole of the rear of the Army of Portugal, brought up against the river Tormes, must have surrendered *en masse*.

From eight o'clock at night till three in the morning the routed army was streaming across the bridge and the ford. Once covered by the Tormes some regiments regained a certain order, but many thousands of fugitives, pressing on ahead in unthinking panic, were scattered all over the country-side, and did not come back to their colours for many days, or even weeks.

The actual loss of the Army of Portugal would appear to have been some 14,000 to 15,000 men, not including the ' missing,' who afterwards turned up and came back to the ranks. Marmont in his dispatch had the effrontery to write that he lost only 6,000 men [1], and 9 guns : a statement only equalled in mendacity by Soult's assertion that Albuera had cost him but 2,800 casualties [2]. No general list of losses by regiments was ever given to Napoleon, though he demanded it : but a return proposing to include the casualties not only of Salamanca but of the minor combats of Castrillo and Garcia Hernandez was drawn up, giving a total of 12,435 [3]. On the whole, however, it would be safe to allow for 14,000 men as the total loss, exclusive of stragglers. Among officers of rank the Commander-in-Chief was wounded : Ferey and Thomières were killed : the latter died inside the English lines after the battle. Clausel and Bonnet were both wounded, the former slightly, the latter severely, so that four of the eight divisional generals of infantry were hit. Of the brigadiers, Desgraviers (division Thomières) was mortally and Menne (division Foy) severely wounded. The trophies lost were

---

[1] Marmont to Berthier, Tudela, July 31, in his *Mémoires*, iv. p. 448.

[2] See vol. iv. p. 295.

[3] viz. killed or prisoners—officers 162, men 3,867 ; wounded—officers 232, men 7,529 ; *traînards*, 645 men ; 12 guns and 2 eagles missing. This return is in the Paris archives. It is certainly incomplete : 60 officers were killed, 137 prisoners, which makes 197 *tués ou pris* instead of 162. And 20 guns were lost.

2 eagles (those of the 22nd and 101st), 6 other colours [1], and
20 guns [2]. Of these last 12 represented the divisional batteries
of Thomières and Bonnet, which were taken whole, and the
other 8, as it would seem, pieces captured from the long line
of batteries on Maucune's flank, which was rolled up when
Le Marchant and Leith swept the plateau in their triumphant
advance. Of the eight French divisions those of Thomières and
Bonnet would appear to have lost about 2,200 men apiece,
Maucune nearly 2,000, Clausel, Brennier, and Ferey above
1,200 each, Sarrut perhaps 500 : Foy's very heavy losses
nearly all fell on the next day. The cavalry, with 43 officers
hit, must account for at least 500 more of the total [3], and the
artillery must have lost, along with their 20 guns, at least 300 or
400 gunners [4]. Of prisoners (wounded and unwounded), there
were according to Wellington's dispatch 137 officers [5] and nearly
7,000 men.

Wellington returned his loss in the British units as 3,129, in
the Portuguese as 2,038 : of España's Spaniards 2 were killed
and 4 wounded. This makes up the total of 5,173, sent off
immediately after the battle. The separate Portuguese return
forwarded by Beresford to Lisbon gives the loss of the troops
of that nation as somewhat less—1,637 instead of 2,078 :
the difference of 441 is partly to be accounted for by the

---

[1] A regiment whose 1st battalion was elsewhere carried not an eagle
but a simple standard per battalion instead. Of such regiments, wanting
their senior battalion and therefore their eagle, there were with Marmont
three. Two, the 66th and 82nd, were in Maucune's division, one, the 26th,
in Ferey's. The colours probably belonged to some of these, of which several
were much cut up, especially the 66th.

[2] The returns of the Army of Portugal show a deficiency of 20 guns
between July 15 and August 1, of which 12 represent the divisional batteries
of Thomières and Bonnet, which have completely disappeared. Wellington
says, ' official returns account for only 11 guns taken, but it is believed
that 20 have fallen into our hands.' This was correct.

[3] The deficiency in cavalry rank and file shown by the muster rolls
between July 15 and August 1 was 512.

[4] Perhaps more : for the Reserve Artillery and Park alone show 1,450
rank and file on July 15 and only 707 on August 1.

[5] Sixty-three officers arrived in England as the Salamanca batch of
prisoners ; of these some were wounded, for their names occur both in
Martinien's tables as *blessés*, and in the Transport Office returns at the
Record Office as prisoners shipped off. The remainder of the 137 were
badly wounded, and came later, or died in hospital.

reappearance of stragglers who were entered as ' missing ' in
the first casualty-sheet, but cannot entirely explain itself in
that fashion. Which of the returns is the more accurate it is
hard to be sure, but a prima facie preference would naturally
be given to the later and more carefully detailed document.
Taking British and Portuguese together, it is clear that the
6th Division, which lost 1,500 men, was far the hardest hit. The
3rd and 5th, which decided the day on the right, got off easily,
with a little more than 500 each : the 4th Division, owing to
the mishap to the Fusilier brigade and Stubbs's Portuguese,
had very nearly 1,000 casualties. Pack's five battalions lost 386
men in the one short episode of the battle in which they were
engaged, the unsuccessful attack on the Great Arapile, and
were lucky to fare no worse. The cavalry total of 173 killed
and wounded was also very moderate considering the good
work that the brigades of Le Marchant, D'Urban, and Arentschildt performed. In the 1st, 7th, and Light Divisions, the
trifling losses were all in the flank-companies sent out in skirmishing line : of the battalions none was engaged as a whole [1].
The artillery were overmatched by the French guns all through
the day, and it is surprising to find that they returned only
four men killed, and ten wounded. The casualty list of officers
of high rank was disproportionately large—not only was Le
Marchant killed, but Marshal Beresford, Stapleton Cotton,
commanding the cavalry [2], and Leith and Cole, each a divisional
general, were disabled. Of officers in the Portuguese service,
Collins, commanding a brigade of the 7th Division, was mortally hurt, and the Conde de Rezende, who led the Portuguese
of the 6th Division, was wounded.

The victory of Salamanca was certainly an astonishing feat
of rapid decision and instantaneous action. The epigrammatic
description of it as ' the beating of 40,000 men in forty minutes '
hardly over-states its triumphant celerity : before that time
had elapsed, from the moment when Pakenham and Leith

---

[1] The 7th Division would have had practically no loss but for the
skirmishing in the early morning near Nuestra Señora de la Peña, and the
heaviest item in the 1st Division casualties was the 62 men of the Guards'
flank-companies who were hit while defending the village of Arapiles.

[2] Cotton was shot after the battle was over by a caçador sentry, whose
challenge to halt he had disregarded while riding back from the pursuit.

struck the French left, the battle was undoubtedly in such a condition that the enemy had no chance left—he could only settle whether his retreat should be more or less prompt. Clausel chose to make a hopeless counter-offensive move, and so prolonged the fight till dark—he would probably have been wiser to break off at once, and to retreat at six o'clock, covering his routed left with his intact reserve divisions. He would certainly have lost several thousand men less if he had retired after repulsing Cole and Pack, and had made no attempt to press the advantage that he had gained over them. It may be argued in his defence that the last hour of battle, costly though it proved to him, prevented Wellington's pursuit from commencing in the daylight, an undoubted boon to the defeated army. But at the most the victor would have had only one hour at his disposition before dusk ; the French were taking refuge in a forest, where orderly pursuit would have been difficult ; and looking at Wellington's usual methods of utilizing a victory (e. g. Vittoria) we may feel doubtful whether the beaten enemy—if covered by Sarrut, Ferey, and Foy, as a regular rearguard, would have suffered more than he actually did. For Wellington's whole idea of pursuit turned on the false notion that the castle, bridge, and ford of Alba de Tormes were still blocked by the Spaniards whom he had left there. By the time that he had discovered that the enemy was not retreating towards Huerta and Villa Gonzalo, but escaping over the Tormes in some other way, the hour would have been late.

Undoubtedly the best summary and encomium of Wellington's tactics on this eventful day is that of an honest enemy, the very capable and clear-sighted Foy, who wrote in his diary six days after the fight [1] :

' The battle of Salamanca is the most masterly in its management, the most considerable in the number of troops engaged, and the most important in results of all the victories that the English have gained in these latter days. It raises Lord Wellington almost to the level of Marlborough. Hitherto we had been aware of his prudence, his eye for choosing a position, and his skill in utilizing it. At Salamanca he has shown himself a great and able master of manœuvres. He kept his dispo-

---

[1] Diary in *Vie militaire*, ed. Girod de l'Ain, p. 178.

sitions concealed for almost the whole day : he waited till we
were committed to our movement before he developed his own :
he played a safe game [1] : he fought in the oblique order—it
was a battle in the style of Frederic the Great. As for ourselves,
we had no definite intention of bringing on a battle, so that we
found ourselves let in for it without any preliminary arrangements having been made. The army was moving without
much impulse or supervision, and what little there was stopped
with the wounding of the Marshal.' In another note he adds :
' The Duke of Ragusa committed us to the action—he brought
it on contrary to Clausel's advice. The left was already checked
when he received his wound : after that moment it was impossible either to refuse to fight, or to give the fight a good direction :
all that could be done was to attenuate the sum of the disaster—
that Clausel did. There was no gap in the command—we
should have been no better off if the Marshal had never been
hurt. He is not quite honest on that point in his dispatch [2].'

With this criticism we may undoubtedly agree. Foy has
hit upon the main points in which Salamanca was a startling
revelation to the contemporary observer—no one on the French
side, and but few upon the British, had yet realized that Wellington on the offensive could be no less formidable and efficient
than Wellington on the defensive. After July 22, 1812, no
opponent could dare to take liberties with him, as Soult, Masséna,
and Marmont, each in his turn, had done up till that date.
The possible penalty was now seen to be too great. Moreover,
the prestige of the British general was so much enhanced that
he could safely count upon it as not the least of his military
assets—as we shall see him do in the Pyrenees, a little more
than a year after Salamanca had been won. To the other thesis
that Foy lays down—the statement that Marmont had, by
his initial movement, made disaster inevitable before he was
wounded—we may also give our assent. Jourdan came to the
same conclusion—the Emperor Napoleon also fixed the responsibility in the same way. The Marshal's ingenious special
pleading, to the effect that but for his personal misadventure

---

[1] *Il a joué serré.* This idiom is explained in the Dictionary of the Academy
as ' jouer sans rien hasarder.'

[2] Note in same volume, p. 177.

he would yet have won the day, will convince none but blind enemies of Wellington. Of some of the charges which Napoleon laid to his charge he must be acquitted : he did not know in the least that King Joseph was on his way to join him from Madrid with 15,000 men. The dispatches sent to warn him of this fact had all miscarried, and the last news from the Army of the Centre which had reached him had intimated that no immediate help was to be expected from that quarter. Nor was he wrong in not waiting for the succours from Caffarelli : these were so trifling—800 sabres and one horse battery—that their presence or absence could make little difference in the battle.

But the Marshal's flagrant and irreparable fault was that, having made up his mind that Wellington would not fight under any provocation—a conclusion for which the earlier episodes of the campaign gave him some justification—he got his army into a position in which he had battle suddenly forced upon him, at a moment when he was not in a position to accept it with advantage. The attempt to turn Wellington's right wing on the afternoon of July 22nd was an unpardonable liberty, only taken because the Marshal had come to despise his opponent. The liberty was resented in the most forcible way—and there was no means of avoiding disaster when Thomières and Maucune had once started out on their rash turning movement.

SECTION XXXIII : CHAPTER VIII

THE CONSEQUENCES OF SALAMANCA

THE dawn of July 23rd revealed to Wellington that the French army had passed the Tormes at the bridge and forts of Alba, and that nothing remained on the western bank of the river save small parties of fugitives and wounded, who had lost their way in the forest. Some of these were gleaned up by Anson's and Bock's brigades of cavalry, who were pushed forward to search the woods and seek for the enemy. Anson's patrols reached the bridge, and found a French rearguard watching it. This was composed of Foy's division, to whom Clausel had committed the covering of his retreat. It cleared off, after firing a few shots. Foy had been told to block the passage till 9 o'clock, but went off long before, when the disordered main body had got a good start. On the report that he was gone, Wellington sent Anson's squadrons across the bridge of Alba de Tormes, while Bock forded the river lower down at La Encina. The state of the roads, strewn with baggage and wounded men, showed that the French had used all the three roads leading east from Alba [1], and were on their way to Arevalo, not towards their base at Valladolid : to have marched in that direction would have brought them right across the front of the advancing British army. Wellington sent out detachments on all the roads which the enemy had taken, but urged the main pursuit by the central and most important road, that by Garcia Hernandez on Peñaranda. Contrary to his wont, he pushed on this day with great celerity, riding himself with the head of the column formed by the main body of Anson's light dragoons. This vanguard was followed, at some distance, by the

---

[1] See Tomkinson's *Diary*, p. 190. He gives the three roads used as (1) Alba, Mancera de Abaxo, Junialcon ; (2) Alba, Garcia Hernandez–Peñaranda ; (3) Encina, Zorita, Cebolla [names all badly spelled]. It is doubtful whether the troops on the last road were not disorderly masses of fugitives only. The bulk of the army certainly went by Peñaranda.

1st and Light Divisions. Those infantry units which had fought
hard on the previous day were allowed a rest. About seven
miles beyond Alba de Tormes Anson's patrols came upon
a regular rearguard of the enemy, behind the Caballero brook
(a tributary of the Almar), in and about the village of Garcia
Hernandez. This was, of course, Foy and the French
1st Division, the only troops in Clausel's army which had not
been seriously engaged in the battle. They were accompanied
by a battery and a brigade of Curto's *chasseurs*. Around and
about the formed troops scattered parties were visible—the village
was full of men drawing water from the wells. On the approach
of the British cavalry column—the infantry were still miles
behind—Foy prepared to resume his retreat, the cavalry drew
up on a rising ground, to the north of Garcia Hernandez, to
cover the movement : the leading regiments of the foot started
off at once along the high-road, the others halted for a space,
to the right of the *chasseurs*, out of sight of the British, whose
view of them was intercepted by the slope on which the French
cavalry were drawn up.

Wellington, as it seems, saw only the hostile squadrons, and
resolved to drive them off without delay, in order to be able to
press in upon the infantry columns which were retiring farther
away. He directed Anson to attack the *chasseurs* with so
much of his brigade as was up at the front : several squadrons
were absent, some guarding the prisoners of yesterday, others
exploring on distant roads. Two squadrons each of the 11th
and 16th Light Dragoons delivered the frontal attack on the
French brigade, while the leading squadrons of Bock's brigade,
which was coming up rapidly from the flank, and was not yet
formed in line, were to turn its right wing.

The French light cavalry, which had been much mauled on
the preceding day, and was evidently in no fighting mood,
gave way precipitately before the attack of the Light Dragoons,
and rode off in confusion to their own right rear. There was
no time for Bock's Germans to come up with them : but the
leading squadrons of the 1st Heavy Dragoons of the Legion,
pushing on in pursuit, received, to their surprise, a heavy volley
in their flank from a French battalion in square, which they
had not noticed in their advance.

There were, in fact, two regiments of infantry to the right of the routed *chasseurs*, and by the sudden flight of their comrades they found themselves suddenly uncovered and engaged. They were the 6th Léger and 76th Line, each two battalions strong, and counting together about 2,400 bayonets. Of these the unit nearest the cavalry was a battalion of the 76th in square : it was the fire of this body which had struck the leading German squadron in flank, and thrown it into disorder as it was charging the routed French horse. Farther to the east were the other battalion of the 76th and the two of the 6th Léger, on the slopes above the road, which here winds below the small eminence which the French cavalry had occupied and the hill of La Serna, a long and fairly steep height, which gives its name in many histories to the combat that ensued.

What followed on the unexpected discovery of the French infantry was the effect not of Wellington's direct orders, nor of the leading of the short-sighted Bock, who had hardly realized the situation when his subordinates were already making their decision. It was entirely the exploit of the gallant squadron-leaders of the two regiments of German dragoons. They were coming up in a sort of échelon of squadrons, the first regiment leading, so that when the fire of the French square struck and disordered the leading unit, the responsibility for action fell on the officers commanding the others. Captain von der Decken who led the 3rd squadron determined without hesitation to charge the French square—his men were already getting up speed, and the enemy was but a short distance from him. Shouting to the squadron to throw forward its right wing and ride home, he led it straight at the French. The first fire of the square, delivered at eighty yards, brought down several men and horses, and wounded (mortally as it proved in the end) von der Decken himself. He kept his saddle, however, and only fell when the second fire was given, at twenty yards range. This volley was destructive, but did not break the impetus of the squadron, which charged right home. In most cases where cavalry reached the bayonets of a square during the Peninsular War, it had proved unable to break in, and had recoiled with loss—like Craufurd's squadrons at the

combat of Barquilla [1], and Montbrun's at Fuentes de Oñoro.
Here, however, the rare feat of riding down well-formed
infantry was performed—it is said by several eye-witnesses
that the breach was originally made by a mortally-wounded
horse, which reared right on top of the kneeling front rank of
the French, and then rolled over kicking, and bore down six
or eight men at once. Several dragoons leapt the bank of
struggling and overthrown soldiers, and broke into the rear
ranks—thereupon the whole square fell to pieces in disorder.
Many of the Frenchmen were hewn down, but the majority
dropped their muskets and surrendered unhurt. The lists of
prisoners at the Record Office give the names of sixteen officers
of the 76th sent to England, of whom only two were wounded.
Of the rank and file not more than fifty, it is said, got
away [2]. Observers who came on the field later in the day
noted with curiosity the long lines of muskets laid down
in orderly rows. This was an astonishing achievement for a
single squadron of 120 men—they had captured or cut down
five times their own numbers of veteran troops of Ney's old
6th Corps.

Some way to the right of this unlucky battalion were two
more, forming the 6th Léger. Seeing the havoc made of his
comrades, and noting the remaining squadrons of the Germans
sweeping across the slope toward him, the colonel of this regiment ordered his men to retreat uphill and climb the steep
slope behind. He hoped to get upon ground where cavalry could
not easily follow. The two battalions, still in column, for they had
not (like the 76th) formed square, moved hastily upwards : the
voices of officers were heard shouting, '*allongez le pas, gagnons la*

[1] See vol. iii. p. 255.

[2] I took the trouble to work out the names from the immense list of
prisoners at the Record Office, in order to test the truth of the statement
that the whole battalion was captured. The following names appear from
the 76th—Bailly, Cavie, Catrin, Demarest, Denis, Duclos, Dupin, Dupont,
Dusan, Gautier, Guimblot, L'Huissier, Richard, Ravenal, besides two
wounded officers, Lambert and Martinot. In addition, one officer (Lebert)
was killed, and in Martinien's *Liste des officiers tués et blessés* we have
five more down as wounded, Dessessard, Lanzavecchia, Massibot, Norry,
Rossignol. These may have died of their wounds, and so never have reached
England ; or they may have escaped, though wounded. The twenty-two
names must represent practically the whole of the officers of the battalion.

hauteur [1].' The nearest enemy to them was the second squadron
of the 1st Dragoons K.G.L., led by Captain von Reizenstein,
who put on the pace when he saw the French scrambling higher,
and came up with the rearmost battalion before it was very far
from the road. The two rear companies faced about when the
dragoons drew near, and delivered a fire that was fairly effective,
when it is considered that the men had been going as hard as
they could trot, and were halted and put into action at a
second's notice. But it did not suffice to stop the dragoons,
who rode in, at the cost of many killed and wounded, and cut
up the companies that had stood to meet them : many men
were sabred, more taken prisoners. The rear of the column,
however, scrambled uphill in a mass, and there joined the
other battalion of the 6th Léger, which formed square on the
sky-line. They had on their flank a squadron or so of *chasseurs*,
apparently a fragment of the brigade that had given way so
easily before Anson's attack twenty minutes before.

Against this mass charged the leading squadrons of the 2nd
Heavy Dragoons K.G.L., which had at last come up to the
front, and some of the officers and men of the 1st, who had
already done such good work lower down the hill. The French
square was not perfect or regular—apparently it was disordered
by the fugitives from the broken battalion, who ran in for
shelter, and formed up as best they could. The charge of the
Germans was delivered with splendid impetus—though the
regiment had been galloping for 300 yards uphill—and was
completely successful. The French *chasseurs* rode off without
engaging : the ill-formed square crumpled up : many of the
men threw down their arms and surrendered, the rest dispersed
and ran in coveys along the slopes of the plateau, towards the
nearest friendly troops. These were the four battalions of the
39th and 69th Line, the surviving regiments of the division.
Foy himself was in one of the squares ; his surviving brigadier,
Chemineau, in the other.

Intoxicated with the glorious successes that they had gained,
a large but disordered mass of the victorious dragoons rode
after the fugitives, and charged the nearest of the French
squares—one of the 69th Line. The enemy held firm, their

---

[1] All this from Schwertfeger, i. p. 381.

fire was given with effect, and killed the officer who led this last effort (Captain von Uslar) and many of his men. The rest swerved back, and rode away under a pelting fire from the battalion that they had attacked and from the other three, which lay close on its flank.

So ended the charge of Garcia Hernandez, the most dashing and successful attack made by any of Wellington's cavalry during the whole war, as Foy—the best of witnesses—formally states in his history[1]. Though not more destructive in its results than Le Marchant's onslaught on Maucune at Salamanca, it was a far more difficult affair. For Le Marchant had charged troops not in square, and already shaken by conflict with Leith's division ; while the Germans attacked without any infantry support, and fell upon intact battalions, of which two at least had formed square. Moreover, the French were supported by artillery and cavalry, though the former cleared off promptly, and the latter allowed themselves to be routed very easily by Anson's squadrons. Altogether it was a glorious first experience of war for the Heavy Dragoons—neither of the regiments had ever charged before, and they had seen but a little skirmishing during the six months since their arrival at Lisbon. They were duly granted the battle-honour, ' Garcia Hernandez,' which they continued to bear on their guidons as long as Hanover was an independent state. Two Hanoverian cavalry regiments of to-day in the Prussian army continue to show it, as theoretical heirs of the old Heavy Dragoons. The most astonishing feature of the exploit was that it was the sole work of the squadron-leaders—Wellington had only given the general order to attack—Bock had been with the fraction of the 1st Dragoons which charged along with Anson, and was not directing the marvellous uphill ride. It was a regimental triumph, not an exhibition of cavalry tactics by the Commander-in-Chief or the brigadier[2].

[1] Foy, *Guerre de la Péninsule*, i. pp. 290–1.

[2] I have used for the narrative of this interesting fight not only the numerous and valuable K.G.L. sources printed or quoted by Beamish and Schwertfeger, but the letters of von Hodenberg, aide-de-camp to Bock, lent me by his representative, Major von Hodenberg, now resident in Hanover. For this officer's interesting career see *Blackwood* for May 1912, where I published large sections from these letters.

The losses of the victors were very heavy—the 1st Regiment had 2 officers and 28 men killed, 2 other officers wounded (one—von der Decken—mortally), and 37 men. The 2nd Regiment lost 1 officer (von Uslar) killed, with 21 men, and 1 officer and 29 men wounded. In this total the striking figure is the high proportion of killed to wounded—52 to 69—which bears witness to the murderous power of the old musket-ball when delivered point-blank, into the bodies of men who were pressing right up to the muzzles of the infantry in square. There were six men missing to be added to the total of losses—127 in all—whether these were individuals who were taken prisoners in the last attempt to break the square of the 69th, or whether they were mortally wounded men, whose horses carried them far from the scene of action and whose bodies were not found, it is impossible to say. The loss of 127 officers and men out of about 770 present was, however, by no means disproportionately heavy, when the results of the charge are considered.

Of the two French regiments engaged, a whole battalion of the 76th was captured or destroyed—of the 27 officers with it one was killed, 5 wounded, 16 taken prisoners : taking the same proportion of its rank and file, very few out of 650 can have escaped. The 6th Léger was less completely annihilated, but it had its colonel (Molard) and 6 other officers taken prisoners [1], and 8 more wounded, with about 500 rank and file taken or hurt. Allowing for some small losses to the *chasseurs*, the total casualties of the French must have been about 1,100.

When the last charge of the Heavy Dragoons was over, Foy led his surviving battalions off, followed at a distance by Anson's brigade, when it had re-formed. The Germans were too fatigued to do more : the leading British infantry, the Light Division, was only just coming in sight far to the rear. The pursuit, therefore, by the four British squadrons had no further results—if they had chanced to have a horse battery with them it might have been much more effective. Six miles from Garcia Hernandez, Foy was relieved to find, waiting for him by the roadside, the long-expected cavalry brigade from the Army of

---

[1] Their names were the colonel, Molard (who died, a prisoner, of his wounds, August 4), Baudart, Paulin, Piancet, Turpin, Paris, Bouteille ; they were verified in the prisoners-rolls at the Record Office by me.

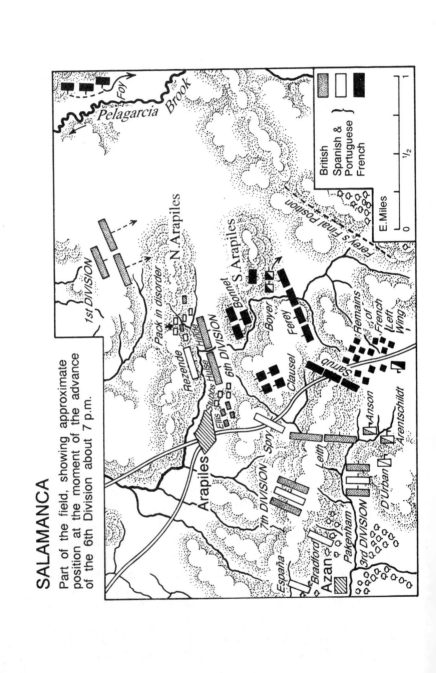

SALAMANCA

Part of the field, showing approximate position at the moment of the advance of the 6th Division about 7 p.m.

Combat of GARCIA HERNANDEZ (July 23 1812)

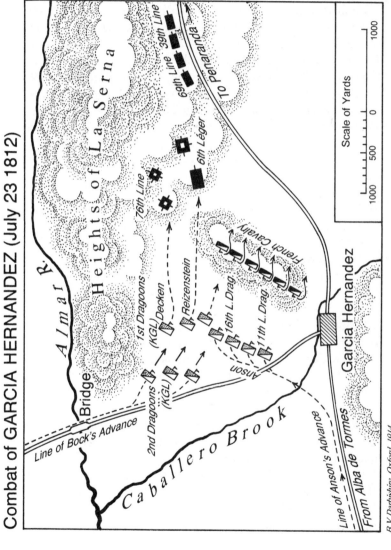

Almar R.

Bridge

Heights of La Serna

69th Line

39th Line

To Peñaranda

76th Line

6th Léger

1st Dragoons
(KGL) Decken

Reizenstein

French Cavalry

6th L.Drag.

11th L.Drag.

2nd Dragoons
(KGL)

Anson

Line of Bock's Advance

Caballero Brook

Garcia Hernandez

Line of Anson's Advance

From Alba de Tormes

Scale of Yards

1000   500   0   1000   1000

B.V.Darbishire, Oxford, 1914

the North—Chauvel's 1st Hussars and 31st Chasseurs : these fresh squadrons took up the rearguard duty for the rest of the day, and covered the march of the infantry to Peñaranda.

From this day onward Wellington's pursuit cannot be said to have been urged with any great vigour. On the morning of the 24th the vanguard entered Peñaranda, to find that the French had started off before dawn. G. Anson's brigade followed, accompanied this time by Bull's and Ross's horse artillery, which had come up from the rear. The tail of the enemy's column was found at Aldea Seca, a few miles beyond Peñaranda : he started off without firing a shot, and was out of sight before more than two guns had been brought to shell him. It seems that opportunities were lost this day—an intelligent observer remarks that ' if only the whole brigade and twelve guns had come up, we might have taken 500 of them—great part of the infantry were without arms [1].'

That night the British head-quarters and vanguard were at Flores de Avila, but the enemy were quite out of sight. ' How they get on their troops at such a rate I cannot conceive,' wrote Wellington, ' but they left this about two in the morning, and they will arrive in Valladolid to-morrow [2].' He gave up all attempt at close or rapid pursuit on the 25th, reporting to Lord Bathurst, ' I find the troops so much fatigued by the battle and their previous and subsequent marches, and the enemy have got so far before our infantry, that I halted this day, and have sent on only the light cavalry and guerrillas.' After this there was no prospect of doing any further harm to Clausel, or of scattering his demoralized army before it had time to recover its cohesion. ' This does not look like the quick advance following up a great victory,' wrote a critical dragoon [3], ' and I think they will be let off too easily. The peasants report them as in a dreadful state : all their cavalry, except a few for their rearguard, is employed in carrying their sick.' It may be taken for certain that a general of the Napoleonic school

[1] Tomkinson's *Diary*, p. 191.
[2] Wellington to Lord Bathurst, night of July 24. *Dispatches*, ix. p. 309.
[3] Tomkinson, p. 191.

would have urged on his cavalry at all costs—there was plenty of it, and none save Le Marchant's and Bock's brigades had suffered any serious loss. Nor can it be doubted that such a hunt would have been richly rewarded by captures. Clausel wrote on the 25th that he could only rally 22,000 men [1]; and as some 48,000 had fought at Salamanca, and the actual losses seem to have been about 14,000, it is clear that he must be allowing for over 12,000 stragglers and unarmed fugitives—whom an active pursuit might have swept up.

Wellington's defence for the slowness of his movement would undoubtedly have been that a headlong chase might have cost him over-much—he would have lost too many men, and—what was even more important—too many horses by forcing the pace. Clausel's army had been put out of action for some weeks by the battle of Salamanca—to smash it up still further would give him no such profit as would justify the expenditure of several thousands of his precious British troops. He was looking forward to the possibility of having to fight Soult and Suchet—not to speak of King Joseph—and wished to be as strong as possible for the present. It is probable that he made a mistake in holding back—Clausel, being left practically unmolested, was able to rally his army somewhat sooner than his adversary calculated. By August it was again able to give trouble : in October its strength was sufficient to wreck the Burgos campaign. If it had been well hunted in the last days of July, it would seem that no such reorganization would have been possible—only negligible fragments of it should have reached Valladolid or Burgos. Yet it must always be remembered that economy of men was the cardinal necessity for Wellington—his total British force was so small, the difficulty of getting up drafts and reinforcements was so enormous, the total number of the enemy's armies in the Peninsula was so overpowering, that he could not afford to thin down his regiments by the exhausting forced marches that were necessary in an active pursuit. It would have been little profit to him if he had exterminated the Army of Portugal, only to find himself left victorious, indeed, but with a force so weak and so tired out that further exertion was impossible. As it was, many

---

[1] Clausel to King Joseph from Arevalo. Joseph's *Correspondence*, ix. p. 54.

of his battalions in August showed only 300 bayonets in line [1], and only recovered their strength, by the reappearance of Badajoz and Salamanca convalescents, and the arrival of drafts, during the following winter.

It was at Flores de Avila on July 25th that Wellington received the news that a new factor had come into the game. King Joseph had left Madrid four days earlier with the Army of the Centre, and was marching northward by the Guadarrama Pass and Villa Castin, with the obvious intention of joining Marmont. This move would have been all-important if it had taken place ten days earlier : but when the Army of Portugal was in absolute rout, and flying by forced marches towards the Douro, the appearance of the King was too late to be dangerous. He could not strengthen the beaten army sufficiently to enable it to fight—and he would expose himself to some peril if he continued his forward march, and came any nearer to the British line of advance.

Joseph's long hesitation and tardy start require a word of explanation. It will be remembered [2] that his last communication which had got through to Marmont was a dispatch dated June 30, in which he had expressed his surprise that the Army of Portugal was refusing battle, and stated that he could offer no immediate help. If Hill, from Estremadura, should march to join Wellington, he had directed that D'Erlon should move up in a similar fashion northward, and he himself would come also, with all or part of the Army of the Centre. But supposing that Hill should remain in the far south, beyond the Guadiana, Joseph gave no promise of coming to Marmont's aid. Indeed he never mentioned this contingency at all, except to say that if Wellington had not been joined by his lieutenant, 'you should choose a good position and give battle with all your troops united.'

Since writing this epistle Joseph had experienced many searchings of heart. On the very day on which it was sent off he had received a dispatch from Soult, which filled him with dismay : the Duke of Dalmatia said that he had forbidden

---

[1] Already on the day of Salamanca there were eight battalions in the army with less than 400 men present. See the tables in Appendix.

[2] See chapter v above, pp. 394-5.

D'Erlon to cross to the north bank of the Tagus, even if it were
certain that Hill and his corps had gone to join Wellington.
Writing in high wrath, the King, on July 2nd, threatened to
remove Soult from his command in Andalusia. ' If you have
formally forbidden D'Erlon to pass the Tagus, in case the
English force in Estremadura goes off to join the enemy's
main body, you have given him orders contradictory to
those which I sent both to him and to you. You set your
authority above mine, you refuse to recognize me as Commander-in-Chief of the Armies of Spain. Consequently, placed
as I may be between the two alternatives—of either depriving
myself of the service of your talent and military experience, or
of allowing the powers confided to me by the Emperor to be
broken in my hand almost as soon as given—I can have no
hesitation. . . . Painful as it is to me, therefore, I accept the
offer which you formerly made me, to resign your command
if I do not revoke my original order ; for not only do I refuse
to revoke it, but I hereby repeat it again both to you and to
Comte d'Erlon. If you prefer to take this extreme step of
disobedience, resign your command to D'Erlon, as your senior
general of division, and he will take it up till the Emperor shall
nominate your successor [1].'

This angry dispatch was followed by another, written on
July 6th, which varied the original order to Soult in an important feature. For instead of speaking of a northern movement
of D'Erlon's troops as consequent on a similar transference of
Hill's corps to Castile, it makes no mention of Hill, but pre-
scribes a definite manœuvre without any reference to the
action of that British general. ' Send at once to Toledo a force
of 10,000 men : 8,000 infantry, 2,000 horse, with the men and
horses for 12 guns. By leaving the guns behind, the march of
the corps will be made more rapid, and the roads are good. . . .
I authorize you to evacuate any part of the occupied territory
that you may choose, in order to hasten the departure of these
10,000 men, whose arrival I await with great impatience [2].'

Clearly it would take many days for these orders to get to
Soult, who was at this time before Cadiz. As a matter of fact

---

[1] Joseph to Soult, Madrid, June 30. *Correspondence* of Joseph, ix. p. 42.
[2] *Correspondence* of Joseph, ix. pp. 44–5.

they only reached his hands on July 16th, and long before that date Joseph was becoming very anxious at the state of affairs on the Douro. He got news that Caffarelli, scared by Home Popham's diversion, had sent no succours to Marmont, and he received letters from Suchet, which showed him that he could not count on any reinforcement from Valencia [1]. It was certain that, even if Soult yielded to the peremptory orders sent on July 2 and July 6, the detachment under D'Erlon could not reach Toledo till somewhere about the 1st August. That it would start at all seemed doubtful, in face of a letter of July 3 from D'Erlon, stating that he was being ' contained ' by no less than 30,000 men under Hill—a scandalous perversion of fact, for Hill had not over two-thirds of that force [2].

The days were running on, Marmont was still unsuccoured : it seemed likely that neither from the North, from Valencia, nor from Andalusia, would any help come to hand. The King grew more and more anxious—all the more so because he had ceased to receive reports from Marmont, since the line of communication with him had been cut by the guerrilleros. Finally, on July 9th [3], he made up his mind that, since no other help could be got for the Army of Portugal, he would march himself with the Army of the Centre, even though to concentrate it he must evacuate all New Castile and La Mancha, and even imperil the safety of Madrid. On that day he issued orders to Treillard to evacuate the valley of the Tagus—all the Talavera and Almaraz region—and to the Rheinbund Germans to abandon La Mancha. All the small posts in the direction of the eastern mountains were also drawn in, even those watching the passes of the Somosierra and the Guadarrama. Only in Toledo, Guadalajara, and Segovia, were small garrisons left behind. By the morning of the 19th July [4] the most distant detachments had all come in, and the Army of the Centre was

---

[1] Joseph to Clarke, July 13, *Correspondence*, ix. p. 45.

[2] For d'Erlon's letter see Joseph to Clarke of July 17th ; *Correspondence*, ix. p. 48.

[3] This date is fixed by a letter of Joseph to Marmont, of that day, in the Scovell ciphers. It never got to Marmont.

[4] Jourdan in his *Mémoires* (p. 419) says that the concentration took place on the 17th, but Joseph's letter to Clarke of July 18 says that Treillard's dragoons would only reach Naval Carnero on the 19th, which is conclusive.

concentrated at Madrid, about 14,000 strong, and able to spare 10,000 for the field when the capital had been garrisoned. But the King resolved to wait two days longer before marching, because he had just received news of the approach of an unexpected but most welcome reinforcement. Early in the month he had heard that Palombini's Italian division of the Army of Aragon was hunting the Empecinado and Mina in the direction of Calatayud and Tudela. He had sent out a Spanish emissary with a letter to Palombini, bidding him to draw in towards Madrid, if he had not already marched to join Marmont, who had hoped to get his assistance. It does not seem that the King had built much upon the results of this letter : orders sent to Suchet's troops had generally been disregarded. But it chanced to reach the Italian general at Alfaro on the Ebro on July 12th, and Palombini, having no opportunity of referring the responsibility to his immediate commander, who was 200 miles away at Valencia, resolved to obey. He marched for Soria and Siguenza, brushing off guerrillero bands that strove to molest him, and sent to Joseph the news that he might be expected at Madrid on the 21st. These tidings came to hand on the 18th, and filled the King with such high satisfaction that he resolved to wait for the Italian division. It arrived on the appointed day, having made a most creditable forced march of 150 miles by mountain roads, through a burnt-up and desolate country. Without leaving it even one night's rest at Madrid, the King started it off in company with his own troops, which had been awaiting all day the signal for departure [1].

Joseph's expeditionary force, thus increased to 14,000 men, consisted of his Guards, horse and foot, one French brigade (28th and 75th Ligne), D'Armagnac's Germans (five battalions and one cavalry regiment), Treillard's strong division of dragoons, and part of Hugo's division of Spanish *Juramentados*, together with Palombini's detachment, which amounted to six battalions and a regiment of dragoons. The garrisons of Madrid, Toledo, Segovia, and Guadalajara were made up partly of *Juramentados*, and partly of the large body of drafts for the Army of Andalusia, which had accumulated at Madrid since

[1] All this from Vacani, vi. p. 110, where the movements of Palombini are very carefully detailed.

the posts in the Sierra Morena had been given up in April. The King had been in no hurry to send them on to Soult, and now found them very useful. The command of the garrison was left to General Lafon Blaniac, who was acting as governor of Madrid and Captain-General of New Castile. A few days after Joseph's departure a welcome addition turned up, in the shape of Suchet's garrison of Cuenca, under General Maupoint, consisting of two battalions of the 16th regiment and a squadron of *chasseurs*. On getting the King's order to evacuate Cuenca, this officer (like Palombini) had obeyed it, and, instead of retiring on Valencia, had come on to Madrid, with his 1,000 men and three millions of reals, representing the provincial treasury[1].

Having once collected his army, the King marched with great speed, passed the defiles of the Guadarrama on the 22nd, and reached Espinar, the great junction of roads in the province of Avila, next day. The cavalry that night were at Villa Castin, eight miles farther to the front, on the road to Arevalo and Valladolid. Here the news came to hand, not from any authorized source but from the rumours of the country-side, that Marmont had crossed the Douro on the 17th, and was closely engaged with Wellington somewhere in the direction of Salamanca. On receiving this information Joseph and Jourdan resolved not to continue their march towards Valladolid, but to swerve westward, with the intention of joining the Duke of Ragusa on the Tormes. Turning off from the main road, the cavalry reached Villanueva de Gomez on the night of the 24th; the King and the infantry got to Blasco Sancho. Orders were issued for the whole army to march on Peñaranda next morning. But during the hours of darkness rumours of the battle of Salamanca and its results came to hand, and on the following morning they were confirmed by the arrival of two Spanish emissaries, one bearing a letter from the wounded Marmont, the other a second from Clausel. The Marshal's letter was insincere and inconclusive—after giving a long account of the battle, which threw all the blame on Maucune, he said that

---

[1] Maupoint's letter to the King, announcing his arrival at Madrid on the 29th–30th July, was captured by guerrilleros, and is in the Scovell collection of ciphers.

he had lost 5,000 men, the enemy infinitely more (!), and that the army was falling back to take a position behind the Eresma river[1], or perhaps behind the Douro. Clausel's epistle was a far more honest document ; it said that he was in a state of incapacity to resist Wellington, that he could not put even 20,000 men in line for some days, that he must retreat as fast as possible on Valladolid, to pick up his dépôts and magazines, which he must send off without delay, and that he would then fall back on the Army of the North. He distinctly told the King that, even if the Army of the Centre joined him, they would be unable to resist Wellington for a moment. He recommended Joseph to call up succours from Soult and Suchet : if Wellington and the English main body marched on Madrid the Army of Portugal would remain on the Douro, but only in that case. If pursued by Wellington he must retire towards Burgos. He evidently regarded any junction between his troops and the King's as impracticable and useless[2].

Confronted by this new and unpromising situation, Joseph and Jourdan had to choose between two policies—they might retire towards Madrid and cover the capital, in the hope that Soult might conceivably have carried out the orders given him on July 6th, and have sent a detachment toward Toledo and Madrid. Or they might, despite of Clausel's advice and warning, move northward towards the Douro and try to get into communication with the Army of Portugal. If the direct road by Arevalo to Valladolid was too dangerous, there remained another and more circuitous route by Cuellar, which Wellington was too far off to reach.

The King and Jourdan chose the first alternative without a moment's hesitation[3] : if they joined the Army of Portugal, they had Clausel's assurance that they could effect nothing. They would be driven back on Burgos ; Madrid would be exposed to a raid by any small detachment that Wellington might send against it, and touch with Soult and Suchet would be lost. The King, therefore, marched back by the way that

---

[1] Which falls into the Adaja near Olmedo, twenty miles south of Valladolid.

[2] Clausel to Joseph, *Correspondance*, ix. pp. 54–5.

[3] ' Certainement, c'était le meilleur,' says Jourdan, commenting on the choice years after.

he had come, and had reached on the 26th the Venta de San Rafael, at the foot of the Guadarrama pass. He had got so rapidly out of Wellington's way that their armies did not touch —save indeed that a patrol of Arentschildt's brigade surprised and captured near Arevalo 2 officers and 25 men of the King's light cavalry [1]—Juramentado *chasseurs*.

When informed that the Army of the Centre had fallen back in haste toward Madrid, Wellington resolved that his duty was to continue pushing Clausel northward, and away from the King. The latter might be disregarded ; his strength was known, and it was almost certain that he would not be reinforced. For Hill had just sent in a report, which had come through in four days, that Drouet was showing no signs of moving toward Toledo ; and he enclosed an intercepted dispatch of Soult's, which proved that the latter had no intention whatever of carrying out the King's oft-repeated orders [2]. Accordingly the British head-quarters were moved on to Arevalo on the 27th of July, and to Olmedo on the 28th. Anson's and Arentschildt's light cavalry went on in front : they reported that the enemy was still in a complete state of disorganization. He was burning the villages as he went, and leaving many stragglers dead in the cornfields beside the road, for the wounded were sinking by the way, and any marauders who went far from the main column were being killed by the peasantry and the guerrilleros [3].

Clausel crossed the Douro by the two bridges of Tudela and Puente de Douro on the 27th–28th, leaving only some light troops to the south of the river, and entered Valladolid, where he set to work at once to evacuate all the more valuable stores, and so many of the sick and wounded as could find transport, along the high-road to Palencia and Burgos. The Anglo-Portuguese infantry was already approaching Medina del Campo and Olmedo, while Santocildes, with the section of the

---

[1] For this business see Hamilton's *History of the 14th Light Dragoons*, p. 109. The leader of the patrol, a Corporal Hanley of that regiment, had only eight men, but surprised the *chasseurs* in an inn, and bluffed them into surrender.

[2] See Wellington to Hill of July 26. *Dispatches*, ix. p. 314. The Soult letter is in the Scovell collection of ciphers.

[3] For details, see Tomkinson, p. 192.

Army of Galicia which was not employed on the siege of Astorga, was ordered to march past Toro and Tordesillas to threaten Valladolid from the north bank of the Douro, and Silveira was directed to resume the blockade of Zamora with his militia-division.

On the 29th the Light and 1st Divisions, Wellington's infantry vanguard, drove in the screen of light troops which Clausel had left in front of the Douro : the French retired and blew up the bridges. But this was of little avail, for the British cavalry forded the river at Boecillo and continued their advance. Thereupon the enemy evacuated the city of Valladolid, and withdrew along the direct road to Burgos, save one division (Foy's), which retreated excentrically, up the north bank of the river toward Aranda. In Valladolid were found 17 guns, 800 sick and wounded, whose condition had rendered it impossible for them to travel, and a large magazine filled with artillery material, besides other stores. The people received Wellington with every mark of enthusiasm, though they had the reputation of including a greater proportion of *Afrancesados* than any other city of northern Spain [1]. They treated him to illuminations, a ball, and copious harangues of congratulation. Meanwhile Anson's brigade swept the country to the east and north, and reported no enemy visible ; while the guerrillero Marquinez entered Palencia, and captured 300 stragglers from Clausel's rearguard. The French had gone back beyond the Arlanza river, and were lying at Lerma, Torquemada, and Santa Maria del Campo, ready to retreat to Burgos itself if any further pressure was applied. It was not forthcoming—much to Clausel's surprise—and he halted and began to reorganize his shattered army. What survived of his train and stores, his sick, and the *cadres* of several skeleton battalions were sent back to Burgos. The rest stood still, awaiting further developments.

Wellington, meanwhile, had brought none of his infantry north of the Douro, though all were now near at hand, and the Light Division had repaired the bridge of Tudela. He had resolved to turn his attention to King Joseph and Madrid. Only Santocildes and his two Galician divisions were ordered up to Valladolid (where they arrived on August 6th) to support

[1] See von Hodenberg's letter concerning this in *Blackwood* for June 1912.

Anson's cavalry, who took up cantonments at various villages in front and to the flank of the city.

The movements of the King and his army on July 27th–31st had been somewhat puzzling to the British general. On arriving at the foot of the Guadarrama pass, they had halted, and then (instead of pursuing the straight road to Madrid) had swerved off to Segovia, which lies on the northern slope of the mountains, as if they had abandoned their original intention of leaving the Army of Portugal to its own devices. This flank march was the result of the receipt of letters borne by Marmont's aide-de-camp, Fabvier, which said that Clausel was no longer being pursued with energy, and that it was possible that he might stop on the Adaja and cover Valladolid [1]. It was a momentary inspiration, with no reality behind it, for Clausel was in full retreat again before the King reached Segovia. But misled by its fallacious cheerfulness, Joseph had made a move which rendered it possible for him to join the Army of Portugal, if it had really halted. He was soon undeceived, and after remaining three days at Segovia in some peril, for Wellington had now turned against him, he evacuated that high-lying city on August 1st, and made his final retreat on Madrid by the Guadarrama pass.

Just after he had left Segovia [2] King Joseph received a dispatch from Soult, dated July 16. It was a reply to the peremptory orders sent him on July 6th, which had directed him to evacuate part of Andalusia and to send a large detachment to Toledo. This was a strange document, which amounted to an absolute refusal to obey instructions. After stating (quite falsely) that Hill was advancing with 30,000 men in Estremadura, and that in consequence he was himself about to repair thither, he announced that the evacuation of Andalusia would be ruinous to the French cause in Spain. 'We could not find means to subsist either on the Tagus or in Estremadura, and from one position to another we should retreat as far as the Ebro. There is a way to avoid this ; by taking the initiative we can save 6,000 sick and maimed men whom I should probably have to abandon, as well as 200,000 Spaniards (who have

[1] Printed in Joseph's *Correspondence*, ix. pp. 46–7.
[2] On the next day, August 2, the letter came to hand at Galapagar.

declared for your Majesty, and will be lost without hope), also 2,000 guns, and the only artillery arsenal now existing in Spain. A single order by your Majesty can effect this, and shorten the Spanish war by six campaigns. Let your Majesty come to Andalusia in person, with every man that can be collected : if the number is large we can increase the expeditionary force in Estremadura to 25,000 or 30,000 men, and transfer the seat of war to the left bank of the Tagus. The Army of Portugal, being relieved of pressure, will be able to come into line again. Whatever occurs, your Majesty will find yourself at the head of a splendid army, ready to deliver battle. If the worst came, and we were unlucky, there is always the resource of retiring on the Army of Aragon [in Valencia] and so keeping the field. . . . I have the honour to repeat to your Majesty that I cannot send any detachments beyond the Sierra Morena or the Guadiana, save by evacuating all Andalusia and marching with my whole army. I must have a positive order from your Majesty to that effect [1].'

This was an astonishing letter for a Commander-in-Chief to receive from a subordinate. Instead of obeying a very definite order to move a certain number of troops to a certain point, Soult replies by sending to the King an alternative plan of campaign. And this plan, it is not too much to say, was an absolutely perverse and insane one. It must be remembered that, when Soult was writing, the battle of Salamanca was still six days in the future, and the Army of Portugal was known to be at close quarters with Wellington and in urgent need of reinforcements. Soult urges his master to abandon Marmont to the enemy, to evacuate Madrid, to give up his communication with France, and to retire into Andalusia, where he would be cut off from all the other imperial armies, for it was not possible even to communicate with Suchet and Valencia, since the Spanish Army of Murcia blocked the way. The cardinal sin of this project was that if the French were to hold Spain at all, it was necessary for them to be strong in the North : Soult proposed to deliver over the North to Wellington, by leaving Marmont in the lurch. As Napoleon had observed, five months earlier, ' a check to the Army of Portugal would be a calamity

[1] Soult to Joseph, *Correspondance*, ix. pp. 45-7.

which would make itself felt all over Spain. A check to the
Army of the South might force it back on Madrid or Valencia,
but would be of a very different degree of importance [1].' He
had said much the same thing four years before, when first his
armies were invading Spain ; for he then expressed the opinion
that a disaster to Bessières in Castile would be the one ruinous
possibility: defeats in the South or East mattered comparatively
little. Soult, blinded by his own interest in the viceroyalty of
Andalusia, refused to see this obvious fact. Long after he had
received the news of Salamanca, he persisted in maintaining
that the true policy was to hold on to Seville, even when the
British army was at Madrid, and the wrecks of Marmont's
forces were retiring on Burgos. Of this we shall hear more
presently.

King Joseph on receiving Soult's letter returned answer :
' You will see by my letter of the 29th July the errors that you
have been labouring under as to Lord Wellington's real designs.
Hasten, therefore, to carry out the orders which I give you—viz.
to evacuate Andalusia and march with your whole army on
Toledo [2].' Even so the King did not obtain exact obedience
to his commands, but received a second series of counter-
projects : and in the end Soult marched not on Toledo but on
Valencia, and only many days after he had been instructed to
commence his movement.

Wellington was, of course, unaware of the exact motives
which had induced King Joseph to make his flank march to
Segovia, but he considered that it might mean that there was
some intention on the part of Clausel to bring the Army of
Portugal to join the Army of the Centre by way of the Upper
Douro [i.e. via Aranda]. He therefore resolved to make such
a conjunction impossible, by driving the King over the mountains and towards Madrid [3].

While Anson's and Arentschildt's cavalry continued the

[1] Berthier to Marmont—writing from the Emperor's personal direction—
of February 18th, 1812, printed in Marmont's *Correspondence*, iv. p. 332.

[2] Joseph to Soult of 29 July and August 2, *Correspondence*, ix. pp. 60–1.

[3] Wellington to Bathurst, Olmedo, July 28 : ' I think it probable that
they [the Army of Portugal] will endeavour to join the King on the Upper
Douro, if the King should continue on this side of the mountains, unless
I should previously have it in my power to strike a blow against his corps.'

pursuit of Clausel on the 29th–30th, and the 1st and Light Divisions were brought up to the neighbourhood of Tudela, opposite Valladolid, the rest of the army was turned against King Joseph. It was necessary to find out, as a preliminary, whether he was really making a stand at Segovia. To ascertain this point D'Urban's Portuguese horse pushed out from Olmedo on the 29th, and found the King's cavalry in Santa Maria de Nieva, ten miles in front of Segovia. Deserters from the Spanish Guards here came in to D'Urban, and gave him useful information as to the exact strength of the Army of the Centre. On the 30th Wellington placed at D'Urban's disposal the German Heavy Dragoons, a battalion of Halkett's brigade of the 7th Division, and a British battery, telling him to drive in the enemy's screen. The French gave way reluctantly, and on hearing of their attitude Wellington ordered the whole 7th Division to follow D'Urban's detachment, and other divisions to make ready to move in succession. But the report that Segovia was being firmly held, as the *point de rassemblement* [1] for Clausel, turned out to be false, for when the flying column approached that city it learnt that the main body of the enemy had left it in the morning for the Guadarrama pass. A considerable rearguard, under General Espert [2], however, was left to guard Segovia till the King should have got a fair start; and its mediaeval walls made it defensible for a short time against a force without heavy artillery. D'Urban could do nothing with his cavalry, but sent to Wellington a request that the 7th Division might move round to intercept Espert's retreat towards the Guadarrama by a forced march. His chief replied that he had no great faith in the success of any of these attempts to ' cut the French off,' and that it did not appear to him more practicable at Segovia than elsewhere. ' The result of such attempts would merely be to fatigue the troops in getting into Segovia, and it might as well be done without fatiguing them.' And so it was, for Espert decamped by night on August 3 unmolested, and D'Urban entered the

---

[1] This was the term that D'Urban used when describing, on July 30, the position of the French.

[2] Apparently two battalions of the Baden regiment, some *Juramentados*, and a regiment of dragoons, about 1,800 men.

place next morning, followed some time later by the infantry. He at once explored the mountain road toward the pass, and found that the French had completely disappeared : not even at the ' Puerto ' of the Guadarrama was a vedette to be seen.

Wellington had now to revise his whole plan of campaign, since it had become clear that the two armies opposed to him had retreated in different directions, and could not possibly combine. While it was still conceivable that Clausel might defend the line of the Douro, he had brought up the main body of his infantry to Olmedo. But after his entry into Valladolid on the 30th, and the precipitate retreat of the Army of Portugal toward Burgos, he had been for two days under the impression that King Joseph might stand at Segovia. Not only had he sent on the German dragoons and the 7th Division to follow D'Urban, but on July 31st he moved his own head-quarters and the 3rd Division to Cuellar, while the 4th, 5th, and 6th Divisions were at El Pino on the Cega river, a few miles behind. He wrote next morning (August 1st) that he was in such a position that Joseph and Clausel could not possibly join, and that if the King lingered any longer at Segovia, ' I can move upon him, and make him go quicker than he will like [1].' But he imagined that the Army of the Centre would fall back instantly on Madrid—as indeed it was doing at the very moment that he was writing his dispatch.

On receiving the information that Joseph had vanished, Wellington halted for three whole days [August 2nd, 3rd, 4th] with his head-quarters at Cuellar, and his infantry gathered round him in its neighbourhood. The 1st and Light Divisions, which had marched as far as the Douro, came southward to join the rest. But it was only on the 5th that orders were issued for the march of nearly the whole army on Segovia, by the road to Mozencillo. During these three days of halt Wellington had made up his mind as to his general policy. Clausel, whose army was harmless for the present, was to be ignored : only a small containing force was to be left in front of him,

---

[1] All these details are from dispatches of Wellington to D'Urban in the unpublished D'Urban papers, dated between July 30 and August 2, or from D'Urban's report to Wellington.

while the main body of the Anglo-Portuguese host marched on Madrid.

The strategical purpose that determined this decision was never set forth in full by Wellington. His contemporary dispatches to Lord Bathurst and to Hill are short, and lack explanatory detail—he states his decision, but says little of his reasons for making it. Nor did he, at the end of the campaign, write any long official narrative of his doings, as he had done in 1810 and 1811. The causes that governed his action have to be deduced from scattered opinions expressed in many different documents. We need hardly take seriously the common French dictum, found in many a book written by his exasperated opponents, that he ' wished to parade himself as conqueror and liberator in the Spanish capital.' That was not the sort of motive which any serious student of Wellington's character would dream of imputing to him. Nor, if we translate it into less offensive terms, would it be true to say that it was the political advantage of expelling the King from Madrid, and so demonstrating to all Europe the weakness of the French hold on the Peninsula, that was the determining cause of the march into New Castile and the abandonment of the campaign on the Douro. We must rather look for definite military reasons. And of these the predominant one was that he conceived that the most probable result of the battle of Salamanca would be to force the King to call up Soult and Suchet to Madrid, in order to check the Anglo-Portuguese army, even at the cost of abandoning great tracts of conquered land in Andalusia and Valencia. Such indeed, as we have already seen, was Joseph's purpose. The order to Soult to evacuate his viceroyalty and to march on Toledo with his whole army had been issued a day or two before Wellington had made up his mind to turn southward. Suchet had been directed at the same time to send all that he could spare toward Madrid. Though the pursuit of Clausel to the Ebro offered many advantages, it would be a ruinous move if the enemy should concentrate 70,000 men at Madrid, and then march on Valladolid, to take the allied army in the rear and cut it off from Portugal.

It was quite uncertain whether Soult or Suchet would make this move. But that it was the correct one is certain.

Wellington was aware that Soult had been summoned to send troops northward. Hitherto he had found excuses for refusing to obey, as his last intercepted dispatch of July 8th sufficiently showed. But the results of Salamanca might probably render further disobedience impossible : and the moment that Soult should hear of that tremendous event, it was reasonable to suppose that he would abandon his viceroyalty, and march to join the King with every available man. If he found Joseph and his army still in possession of Madrid, they would have a central base and magazines from which to operate, and a very favourable strategic position. It was true that Wellington could call up Hill's 18,000 men, but this was the only succour on which he could count : neither Ballasteros nor the numerous garrison of Cadiz would ever appear in New Castile, if old experience was to be trusted. If some Spaniards did arrive, they would be very uncertain aid. Granted, therefore, that Soult marched on Toledo and Madrid to join the King, Wellington must take almost every man of the Salamanca army to face them, even allowing for the certain junction of Hill. He could only afford to leave a small ' containing force ' to look after Clausel.

But there was another possibility which made the situation still more doubtful. Would Suchet also push up to join King Joseph with the Army of Valencia, or the greater part of it ? If he should do so, the odds would be too great, and a defensive campaign to cover Portugal, and so much as was possible of the newly regained Spanish provinces, would be the only resource. But Suchet's action depended upon a factor over which Wellington had some influence, though not a complete and dominating control. When he had started on the Salamanca campaign he had been relying on Lord William Bentinck's Sicilian expedition to keep the French in Valencia engaged : an attack on Catalonia would draw Suchet northward with all his reserves, and nothing would be left which O'Donnell and the Spanish army of Murcia could not ' contain.' It will be remembered that a few days before the battle of Salamanca [1] Wellington had received the disheartening news that Bentinck had countermanded his expedition, and was turning himself to some chimerical scheme

[1] See above, p. 408.

for invading Italy. This had left Suchet's attention free for the moment, and he might conceivably have sent troops to join the Army of the Centre. Fortunately he had not done so—only Palombini's division and the small garrison of Cuenca had been swept up by King Joseph, without the Marshal's consent and much to his disgust.

Now, however, the whole prospect in eastern Spain had been transformed by the cheering news, received on July 30th near Valladolid [1], that Bentinck had once more changed his mind, and that a considerable expeditionary force under General Maitland had been sent to Majorca, to pick up the Spaniards of Whittingham and Roche, and to execute, after all, the projected diversion. Maitland's own dispatch arrived four days later ; it had travelled with extraordinary celerity from Palma to Cuellar in fifteen days, and announced his arrival on the Spanish coast and his intention to operate at once. This being so, Suchet would be ' out of the game ' if all went well, and only the King and Soult need be taken into consideration for the next month. But it was all-important that the diversion on the East Coast should be executed with firmness and decision.

The best summary of Wellington's views at this moment is to be found in his letter to Lord William Bentinck [2], explaining the importance of Maitland's action in August.

' I have lately, on the 22nd, beaten Marshal Marmont in a general action near Salamanca, and I have pursued him beyond the Douro and entered Valladolid. The King is at Segovia with 12,000 or 15,000 men, and, having driven Marmont from the lower Douro, my next object is to prevent him and Marmont (if possible) from joining : this I am about to attempt. Either the French [i. e. King Joseph] must lose all communication with their troops in the north of Spain, or they must oblige me to withdraw towards the frontiers of Portugal. This they cannot effect without bringing against me either Suchet's army, or Soult's army, or both. I cannot but think, therefore, that it is very important that the attention of Suchet should be diverted from his possible operations against me by the Sicilian army, which will go to such important objects as Tarragona and Valencia. . . . If Suchet's attention cannot be

[1] See *Dispatches*, ix. p. 320.   [2] Ibid., p. 321.

diverted from me, and (notwithstanding Marmont's defeat)
the French become too strong for me, I shall at least have
the satisfaction of reflecting, while I am retiring, that General
Maitland's progress will be unopposed, and we shall take
Tarragona and Valencia.'

A few days later Wellington was pleased to find that Suchet
had been duly scared. An intercepted dispatch from him to
King Joseph showed that he was thinking of nothing but the
appearance of an English fleet off the Valencian coast, and that
it was most unlikely that he would send any serious succours
to the King [1]. There remained therefore only Soult to be
considered. The natural thing for him to do would be to
evacuate Andalusia : as Wellington wrote a fortnight later,
' any other but a modern French army would now leave that
province [2].' Hill was writing at the same time, ' Lord Wellington
continues advancing, and if he is able to keep his forward
position, Soult will be ordered to reinforce the King. Indeed
I think that he *must* quit this part of the country entirely, if
matters do not go better with them ' [the French] [3].

What neither Wellington nor Hill could foresee, in early
August, was that the Marshal would still hang on to Andalusia,
and renew, in a more pressing form, his proposal of July 16th
that Joseph and the Army of the Centre should take refuge with
him beyond the Sierra Morena. But whether King Joseph
received, or did not receive, succours from the South or East, it
was clearly good military policy to turn him out of Madrid,
while the Army of Portugal was still completely negligible as
a factor in the game. The loss of Madrid would be ruinous to
him if he was left without reinforcements : if he received them,
the enemy would find the problem of subsistence much more
difficult if he had not Madrid to rely upon as his central base
and magazine. Toledo would not serve him half so well. And
the political effects of the recovery of the Spanish capital, even
if only for a time, must be well worth gaining. It would shake
the confidence of the *Afrancesado* party all over the Peninsula,
and it would be noted all round Europe.

---

[1] Wellington to Maitland, Cuellar, August 3rd, *Dispatches*, ix. p. 327.
[2] Wellington to Bathurst, *Dispatches*, ix. p. 370.
[3] Letter in Sidney's *Life of Hill*, p. 211.

Accordingly Wellington resolved to leave only a small containing detachment on the Douro, to look after Clausel, whose recuperative power he somewhat underrated, and to march on Madrid with a force that would enable him, if joined by Hill, to fight Soult and King Joseph in combination. The containing body was put in charge of Clinton, who was almost the only divisional general of the old stock who still remained with the army. Graham and Picton were invalided, Leith and Lowry Cole had been wounded at Salamanca, along with Beresford and Stapleton Cotton. Nearly all the divisions were under interim commanders. Another reason for choosing Clinton for the detached duty was that his division, the 6th, had suffered more than any other unit at the recent battle. It was very low in numbers, only 3,700 men, including its Portuguese brigade, and needed to pick up convalescents and drafts before it could be considered effective for field service. Along with the 6th Division there were left the five battalions [1] that had recently joined the army from England or the Mediterranean stations : they were all Walcheren regiments, and still riddled with sickness ; and all had suffered from the forced marches which had brought them to the front just before. Wellington was discontented with their condition. ' The truth is, neither officers nor soldiers are accustomed to march. The men are very irregular, and owing to their irregularities not able to bear the labour of marching in the heat of the sun [2].' They were left to strengthen Clinton, and to acclimatize themselves to the Spanish summer : if taken on to Madrid they would have sown the roadside with broken-down stragglers.

The five newly-arrived battalions brought Clinton's strength up to 7,000 infantry. The whole of this force was cantoned in and about Cuellar, while the cavalry allotted to it, Anson's brigade, took a more advanced position, along and beyond the Douro, covering not only its own infantry but the two Spanish divisions of Santocildes, who had occupied Valladolid on

[1] viz. the 2/4th, 1/5th, 1/38th, 1/42nd, which had arrived in time for the battle of Salamanca, the 1/38th on the very battle morning, and the 1/82nd which came up after the battle. They were all Walcheren regiments : 1/82nd came from Gibraltar, 2/4th from Ceuta, the other three from England direct. The 1/5th and 2/82nd went on to Madrid in September.

[2] Wellington to Bathurst, Cuellar, August 4. *Dispatches*, ix. p. 339.

August 6th. The remainder of the Army of Galicia was still occupied in the interminable siege of Astorga, which to Wellington's disgust still lingered on. The heavy guns had at last come up from Corunna, but the bombardment seemed to have little effect. Silveira had resumed the blockade of Zamora, but having no siege artillery could only wait till starvation should compel its garrison of 700 men to submit. Toro and Tordesillas were the only other places where Marmont had left a detachment ; the latter surrendered to Santocildes on his march to Valladolid—about 300 French were taken there. The former was still holding out, observed by a small Spanish force. The task of keeping a close look-out upon Clausel was handed over to the guerrilleros—the Castilian chiefs Saornil, Marquinez, and Principe. An English officer, who spent some days with the two last at this juncture, describes them as ' bandits, but very troublesome ones for the French.' Deducting the Spaniards left before Astorga, and the Portuguese left before Zamora, there were some 18,000 men in all told off to ' contain ' Clausel. The orders left behind [1] were that they should remain in their cantonments unless the enemy should move—which Wellington did not think a likely contingency, ' as they have nothing but their cavalry in a state fit for service.' But if, rallying sooner than he expected, the French should march by Palencia to try to rescue the garrisons of Astorga and Zamora, Santocildes was to retire, and to endeavour to defend the line of the Esla, while Silveira was to raise the blockade of Zamora and fall back behind that same river. If, instead of making a raid westward to save the garrisons, Clausel should move against Valladolid and the line of the Douro, Anson's cavalry was to retire and join Clinton at Cuellar ; and if the enemy came on against them in full force, both were then to fall back on Segovia. Santocildes was then directed to endeavour to move round Clausel's rear, and to cut his communication with Burgos. Contrary to Wellington's expectation [2], as we shall presently

---

[1] Memorandum for General Clinton, to be communicated to General Santocildes. *Dispatches*, ix. pp. 344–6.

[2] It is curious to find that while in the ' Memorandum ' of August 4 Wellington states that it is ' not very probable ' that Clausel will move, in a letter to Santocildes sent off the very next day, he remarks that an

see, the French general made both the moves suggested—he
sent a column to relieve Astorga and Zamora, and marched
with his main body on Valladolid.   The consequences of his
advance will be related in their due place.

advance from Burgos into the kingdom of Leon, to relieve Astorga, is
' most likely.'   I fancy that the former was his real opinion, and that the
latter was spoken of with some stress in the directions to Santocildes,
mainly because Wellington wished to impress on the Spaniard the duty
of being cautious and retiring to the Esla without offering battle.

SECTION XXXIII: CHAPTER IX

THE PURSUIT OF KING JOSEPH. MAJALAHONDA.
WELLINGTON AT MADRID

HAVING thus made all his arrangements for 'containing' Clausel, and for dealing with what he considered the unlikely chance of an offensive move by the Army of Portugal, Wellington was at liberty to carry out his new strategical move. The mass of troops collected at Cuellar and its neighbourhood was at last set in motion, and, after his short halt and time of doubting, he himself marched against Madrid with the whole remaining force at his disposal—the 1st, 3rd, 4th, 5th, 7th, and Light Divisions, Arentschildt's, Bock's, and Ponsonby's [late Le Marchant's] cavalry brigades, the Portuguese infantry of Pack and Bradford, with D'Urban's horse of that same nation, as also Carlos de España's Spanish infantry and Julian Sanchez's lancers. The whole, allowing for Salamanca losses and the wear and tear of the high-roads, amounted to about 36,000 men [1]. It was ample for the hunting of King Joseph, and sufficient, if Hill were called up, to face the King and Soult in conjunction, supposing that the latter should at last evacuate Andalusia and march on Toledo. Santocildes and Clinton were informed that it was the intention of the Commander-in-Chief to return to Castile when affairs in the South had been settled in a satisfactory fashion. No date, of course, could be assigned: all would depend on Soult's next move.

On August 7th the vanguard, consisting of the force that had occupied Segovia—D'Urban's Portuguese squadrons, the heavy German dragoons, Macdonald's horse artillery troop, and one

[1] The 1st and 7th Divisions alone were up to their usual strength. The 4th and Light Divisions were still showing very weak battalions, owing to their dreadful Badajoz losses ; and the former had also suffered very severely (1,000 casualties) at Salamanca. The 5th and 3rd had comparatively moderate casualties at each of these fights, but the combination of the two successive sets of losses had reduced them very considerably.

light battalion of the German Legion—marched forward six
leagues, ' five of them against the collar,' remarks an artillery
officer. The steep route lay past the royal summer-palace of
San Ildefonso, ' a beautiful place, and most magnificently
fitted up : what is very singular, the French have not destroyed
a single stick of it : the rooms are hung as thick as can be with
paintings *of sorts* [1].' No hostile vedettes were discovered on the
Guadarrama, and a reconnoitring party pushed as far as the
Escurial, and reported that the enemy's most outlying picket
was at Galapagar, three or four miles to the south-east of that
melancholy pile. Meanwhile the main body, a march behind the
vanguard, started from Segovia on the 8th, Ponsonby's dragoons
and the 7th Division leading ; then came Alten's brigade, the
3rd, 4th, and 5th Divisions, and Pack. The rear was brought
up by the 1st and Light Divisions and Bradford, who only
started from the neighbourhood of Segovia on the 9th [2]. The
necessity for moving the whole army by a single mountain
road—though it was a well-engineered one—caused the column
to be of an immoderate length, and progress was slow. Head-
quarters were at San Ildefonso on the 8th and 9th August, at
Nava Cerrada (beyond the summit of the Guadarrama) on the
10th, at Torre Lodones near the Escurial on the 11th.

Meanwhile D'Urban, far ahead of the main body, occupied
the Escurial on the 9th, and pushed on cautiously to Galapagar,
from whence the enemy had vanished. His rearguard was
discovered at Las Rosas and Majalahonda, five miles nearer to
Madrid. Wellington's orders were that his vanguard was to
keep well closed up, the Germans close behind the Portuguese,
and that nothing was to be risked till support from the leading
divisions of the army was close at hand. Wherefore on the
10th D'Urban, finding the French in force at Las Rosas, only
advanced a few miles, and bivouacked on the Guadarrama river
at the bridge of Retamar. He received news from the peasantry
that King Joseph was preparing to evacuate Madrid, that
convoys had already started, and that the main body of the

---

[1] Dyneley's diary in *R. A. Journal*, vol. xxiii. p. 454.

[2] Many of the brigades did not march through Segovia, but by cross-
roads around it : steep gradients and fatigue were thereby avoided. One
route was by the deserted palace of Rio Frio, an old royal hunting-box.

Army of the Centre was to march by the road of Mostoles on
Toledo, where Soult was expected in a few days. The information—true as regards the evacuation, false as regards the
approach of Soult—was duly sent back to Wellington, who
lay that night at Nava Cerrada, fifteen miles to the rear, with
the 7th Division and Ponsonby's cavalry [1].

Madrid was at this moment a scene of tumult and despair.
The King had retired from Segovia still in a state of uncertainty
as to whether Wellington intended to turn against him, or
whether he would pursue Clausel. He quite recognized the
fact that, even if Soult obeyed the last dispatch sent to him on
August 2nd, it would be too late for him to arrive in time to
save Madrid. But there was a pause of some days, while
Wellington was making up his mind at Cuellar, and it was only
on the morning of the 8th that the news arrived that a strong
column (D'Urban and the advanced guard) had started from
Segovia on the preceding day, and that more troops were
following. The orders to make ready for departure were issued
at once, and a veritable panic set in among the French residents
and the *Afrancesados*. ' Every one,' wrote a keen observer
on the 9th August, ' is packing up his valuables and making
ready for a flitting. Not to speak of the many Spaniards
of birth and fortune who have committed themselves to the
King's cause, there is an infinite number of minor officials and
hangers-on of the palace, who by preference or by force of habit
stuck to their old places. All these poor wretches dare not stay
behind when the King goes—their lot would be undoubtedly
a dreadful one, they would fall victims to the ferocious patriotism
of their fellow-citizens, who have never forgiven their desertion.
Since the word for departure went round, every one has been
hunting for a vehicle or a saddle-beast, to get off at all costs. Add
to this crowd a swarm of valets, servants, and dependants of all
sorts. Most of the merchants and officials are, as is natural,
taking their families with them : the caravan will be interminable. All night the noise of carriages, carts, and wagons,
rolling by without a moment's cessation under my windows,
kept me from sleep.' On the next morning he adds, ' More

---

[1] All this from D'Urban's unpublished diary, as are also most of the
details about the movements of the troops.

than 2,000 vehicles of one sort and another, loaded with bundles and bales and furniture, with whole families squatting on top, have quitted Madrid. Adding those who follow on foot or on horseback, there must be easily 10,000 of them. They are mostly without arms, there are numbers of women, old people, and children : it is a lamentable sight : they take the Aranjuez road, guarded by a considerable escort [1].'

The King, after resigning himself to the retreat, and giving orders for the departure of the convoy and the greater part of his infantry, had still one troublesome point to settle. Should he, or should he not, leave a garrison behind, to defend the great fortified *enceinte* on the Retiro heights, outside the eastern gate of the city, which his brother had constructed, to serve as a citadel to hold down Madrid, and an arsenal to contain the assortment of stores of all kinds. Heavy material, especially in the way of artillery—had been accumulating there since the French occupation began. Here were parked all the guns captured at Ucles, Almonaçid, and Ocaña, and tens of thousands of muskets, the spoil of those same fields. There was a whole convoy of clothing destined for the Army of the South, and much more that Joseph had caused to be made for his skeleton army of *Juramentados*. There were 900 barrels of powder and some millions of rounds of infantry cartridges, not to speak of much arsenal plant of all kinds. All this would have either to be blown up or to be defended. The fortifications were good against guerrilleros or insurgents : there was a double *enceinte* and a star-fort in the interior. But against siege-guns the place could obviously hold out for not more than a limited number of days. After twenty-four hours of wavering, Joseph— contrary to Jourdan's advice—resolved to garrison the Retiro, on the chance that it might defend itself till Soult reached Toledo, and a counter-attack upon Madrid became possible. If Soult should not appear, the place was doomed clearly enough : and the previous behaviour of the Duke of Dalmatia made it by no means likely that he would present himself in time. However, the King directed Lafon Blaniac, the governor of the province of La Mancha, to shut himself in the works, with some 2,000 men, consisting mainly of the drafts belonging to the

---

[1] Reiset's *Souvenirs*, ii. pp. 358–60.

Army of Andalusia : he would not leave any of the Army of the Centre. Probably he considered that Soult would feel more interest in the fate of the Retiro if his own men formed its garrison. They were a haphazard assembly, belonging to some dozen different regiments [1], under-officered and mostly conscripts. But they were all French troops of the line ; no *Juramentados* were among them. To their charge were handed over some 500 non-transportable sick of the Army of the Centre, mostly men who had collapsed under the recent forced marches to and from Blasco Sancho. They were not in the Retiro, but at the military hospital in the Prado, outside the fortifications.

Having sent off towards Aranjuez his convoy and the larger part of his troops, the King was suddenly seized with a qualm that he might be flying from an imaginary danger. What if the column that had been heard of on the Guadarrama was simply a demonstration—perhaps half a dozen squadrons and a few battalions of infantry ? He would be shamed for ever if he evacuated his capital before a skeleton enemy. Obsessed by this idea, he ordered General Treillard to take the whole of his cavalry—over 2,000 sabres—and drive in Wellington's advanced guard at all costs: Palombini's Italian division marched out from Madrid to support the reconnaissance. Treillard was ordered to use every effort to take prisoners, from whom information could probably be extracted by judicious questioning.

On the morning of the 11th the French outpost-line outside of Madrid had been held only by Reiset's brigade of dragoons (13th and 18th regiments), about 700 sabres. It was these troops that D'Urban had discovered on the previous night at Las Rosas : at dawn he proceeded to drive them in, making sure that they would retire, as they had regularly done hitherto. His own force was much the same as that of the enemy, his three weak regiments (seven squadrons) amounting to a little over 700 men. But he had with him Macdonald's horse artillery, and the French were gunless. Demonstrating against Reiset's front with two regiments, D'Urban turned him with the third

---

[1] The surrender-rolls show that there were also some small leavings of Marmont's troops in the Retiro, notably from the 50th Line [of which there were no less than six officers]. Of the Army of the South the 12th and 27th Léger, and 45th and 51st Line were strongly represented.

and two guns. The flank movement had its due effect, and the
dragoons gave back, when shelled diagonally from a convenient
slope. They retired as far as the village of Las Rosas, and made
a stand there : but on the flanking movement being repeated,
they again drew back, and passing a second village—Majalahonda—went out of sight, taking cover in woods in the direction
of Mostoles and Boadilla. D'Urban was now within seven miles
of Madrid, and thought it well to write to Wellington to ask
whether he should endeavour to enter the city or not. The
reply sent to him was that he was to go no farther than Aravaca
—three miles outside the walls—till he should be supported ; the
head of the main column, headed by Ponsonby's heavy dragoons,
would be up by the evening.

Long before this answer reached him D'Urban was in terrible
trouble. The manœuvring of the morning had taken up
some four hours ; it was about 10 when the French disappeared. While waiting for orders, the brigadier directed
his regiments to quarter themselves in Majalahonda, water
their horses, and cook their midday meal. After the pickets
had been thrown out, all went quietly for five hours, and
most of the men were enjoying a siesta at 3.30. They had
now support close behind them, as the heavy German brigade,
and the 1st Light Battalion of the K.G.L. had come up as far as
Las Rosas, only three-quarters of a mile to their rear. The
advance was to be resumed when the worst heat of the day
should be over.

But a little before four o'clock masses of French cavalry were
seen debouching from the woods in front of Boadilla. This
was Treillard, who had come up from the rear with four fresh
regiments (19th and 22nd Dragoons, Palombini's Italian *Dragons
de Napoléon*, and the 1st Westphalian Lancers [1]), and had
picked up Reiset's brigade on the way. The whole force was
over 2,000 strong, and was advancing in three lines at a great
pace, evidently prepared to attack without hesitation. D'Urban
had barely time to form a line in front of Majalahonda, when
the enemy were upon him.

---

[1] Treillard calls them only *les lanciers* in his report. Dyneley in his
narrative calls them Polish lancers, but they were really the Westphalian
Chevaux-légers-lanciers of the Army of the Centre.

It is certain that the wise policy would have been to make a running fight of it, and to fall back at once on the Germans at Las Rosas, for the Portuguese were outnumbered three to one. But D'Urban was a daring leader, honourably ambitious of distinction, and the excellent behaviour of his brigade at Salamanca had inspired him with an exaggerated confidence in their steadiness. He sent back messengers to hurry up the German dragoons, and took position in front of Majalahonda, throwing out one squadron in skirmishing line [1], deploying five more in line of battle (1st and 12th regiments), and keeping one in reserve on his left flank to cover four horse artillery guns there placed. Here also were placed a party of forty of the German Dragoons, who had been sent out on exploring duty, and joined the Portuguese in time for the fight.

Treillard came on in three successive lines of brigades, each composed of six squadrons, Reiset's dragoons (13th and 18th) forming the front line, the other dragoon brigade (19th and 22nd) the second, and the two foreign regiments the reserve. The clash came very quickly, before the British guns had time to fire more than three or four rounds. The Portuguese rode forward briskly enough till they were within a few yards of the enemy, when they checked, wavered, and went about, leaving their brigadier and their colonels, who were riding well in front, actually in the French ranks. D'Urban cut his way out— the Visconde de Barbaçena and Colonel Lobo were both severely wounded and taken prisoners. The broken line shivered in all directions, and went to the rear pursued by the French : some of the fugitives rode into and carried away the reserve squadron, which abandoned the guns on the left as they were limbering up. There was a wild chase for the mile that intervened between the battle spot in front of Majalahonda and the village of Las Rosas. In it three of the four horse artillery guns were captured—one by a wheel breaking, the other two by their drivers being cut down by the pursuing dragoons. Captain Dyneley, commanding the left section of the battery, and fourteen of his men were taken prisoners— mostly wounded. The small party of German dragoons, under

---

[1] This was a squadron of the 11th, whose other squadron formed the reserve.

an officer named Kuhls, who chanced to be present, made a desperate attempt to save the guns. ' Oh, how those poor fellows behaved ! ' wrote Dyneley, 'they were not much more than twenty in number, but when they saw the scrape our guns were in, they formed up to support us, which they had no sooner done than down came at least 150 dragoons and lancers : the poor fellows fought like men, but of course they were soon overpowered, and every soul of them cut to pieces.'

The main body of the leading French brigade rode, without a check, up to the first houses of Las Rosas, where they found the German heavy brigade only just getting into order, so swift had the rout been. When D'Urban's first alarm came to hand, the horses were all unsaddled, the men, some asleep, some occupied in grooming their mounts or leading them to water. The trumpets blew, but the squadrons were only just assembling, when in a confused mass and a cloud of dust flying Portuguese and pursuing French hurtled in among them. That no irreparable disaster took place was due to two causes—two captains [1], who had got a few of these men already together, gallantly charged the head of the French to gain time, and some of the light infantry opened a spattering fire upon them from the houses. Reiset called back his regiments to re-form them, and meanwhile the Germans came pouring out of the village and got into line anyhow, ' some on barebacked horses, some with bare heads, others in forage-caps, many in their shirt-sleeves.' By the time that the French were advancing again, all the four squadrons of the heavies were more or less in line, and D'Urban had rallied the greater part of his Portuguese on their left. The fight in front of Las Rosas was very fierce, though the Portuguese soon had enough of it and retired. But the Germans made a splendid resistance, and ended by beating back the front line of the enemy. Treillard then put in his second line, and under the charge of these fresh squadrons the dragoons of the Legion, still fighting obstinately, were pressed back to the entrance of the village : Colonel Jonquières, commanding the brigade in Bock's absence, was taken prisoner with a few of his men. The salvation of the overmatched cavalry was that the light infantry battalion of the Legion

[1] Reizenstein and Marshalk.

had now lined the outskirts of the village, and opened such
a hot fire that the enemy had to draw back.

What Treillard would have done had he been left undisturbed
it is impossible to say, but just at this moment Ponsonby's
cavalry brigade and the head of the infantry column of the
7th Division came in sight from the rear, hurrying up to support
the vanguard. The French drew off, and retired in mass, with
such haste that they did not even bring off the captured guns,
which were found by the roadside not much damaged, though
an attempt had been made to destroy their carriages.

In this fierce fight, which was so honourable to the Germans
and so much the reverse to the Portuguese, the vanguard lost
nearly 200 men. The heavy brigade had 1 officer and 13 men
killed, 5 officers and 35 men wounded, 1 officer (Colonel
Jonquières) and 6 men prisoners. The Portuguese naturally
suffered much more—by their own fault, for it was in the
rout that they were cut up. They had 3 officers and 30 men
killed, 3 officers and 49 men wounded, and 1 officer [1] and
22 men missing. Macdonald's unfortunate battery lost 6 killed,
6 wounded, and its second captain (Dyneley) and 14 men
missing : most of the latter were more or less hurt. The K.G.L.
light battalion had 7 wounded. The total casualty list,
therefore, was 15 officers and 182 men. It is probable that the
French did not suffer much less, for they had as many as
17 officers disabled, including Reiset, the brigadier who led
the first line, and 11 more of the officers of his two regiments :
the supporting corps lost only 5 officers wounded among the
four of them [2]. But a loss of 17 officers must certainly imply
that of at least 150 men : the Germans had used their broad-
swords most effectively. Treillard sought to diminish the
effect of his loss by making the preposterous statement that he
had killed 150 of the allies, wounded 500, and carried off
60 prisoners ; he forgot also to mention that he left the three
captured guns behind him.

[1] Colonel Lobo : the other colonel (the Visconde de Barbaçena) who was
taken, had been so severely wounded that the French left him behind.

[2] Three in the 19th Dragoons, one in the 22nd, one in the Italian regiment. Oddly enough, of seventeen officers in the casualty list, only one
(a *chef d'escadron* of the 13th) was killed. The sabre disables, but does not
usually slay outright.

After this affair Wellington made the memorandum : 'the occurrences of the 22nd of July [Salamanca] had induced me to hope that the Portuguese dragoons would have conducted themselves better, or I should not have placed them at the outposts of the army. I shall not place them again in situations in which, by their misconduct, they can influence the safety of other troops [1].' It is fair to D'Urban's men, however, to remember that they were put into action against superior numbers, and with a knowledge that they themselves were unsupported, while the enemy had two lines of reserve behind him. To be broken under such circumstances was perhaps inevitable. But the second rout, in the vicinity of Las Rosas, was much more discreditable. Their brigadier, very reticent in his dispatch to Wellington, wrote in a private letter : ' The same men who at Salamanca followed me into the French ranks like British dragoons, on this 11th of August at the first charge went just far enough to leave me in the midst of the enemy's ranks. In the second, which, having got them rallied, I attempted, I could not get them within ten yards of the enemy—they left me alone, and vanished from before the helmets like leaves before the autumn wind [2].'

Treillard brought back to King Joseph the news that Wellington in person was certainly marching on Madrid with the greater part of his army. Indeed his prisoners had tried to scare him by saying that 8,000 horse were coming down on him, and otherwise exaggerating the numbers of the allies. The cavalry brigades fell back to form the rearguard of the King's army, which moved on Valdemoro and Aranjuez, not toward Toledo, for certain information had come that none of Soult's troops were anywhere near that ancient city. The convoy had been turned towards Ocaña, and the road to Valencia.

---

[1] *Dispatches*, ix. p. 354.

[2] There are very full narratives of Majalahonda to be got from D'Urban's correspondence, Reiset's memoirs, and the letters of Dyneley, who was lucky enough to escape a few days later and rejoin his troop. Schwertfeger's *History of the German Legion* gives the facts about the part taken by the K.G.L. Light Battalion, whose service Wellington ignored in his dispatch—wrongly stating that it was not engaged. Treillard's dispatch is a fine piece of exaggeration, but useful as giving the official French view of the affair.

Wellington entered Madrid unopposed next day—vexed that his arrival should have been marred by the untoward business at Majalahonda, ' a devil of an affair,' as he called it in a private letter to Stapleton Cotton [1]. But the inhabitants of the Spanish capital took little heed of the mishap—the departure of the French was the only thing that mattered. Their enthusiasm was unbounded.

' I never witnessed,' wrote an intelligent observer in the ranks [2], ' such a scene before. For a distance of five miles from the gates the road was crowded with the people who had come out to meet us, each bringing something— laurel boughs, flowers, bread, wine, grapes, lemonade, sweet-meats, &c. The road was like a moving forest from the multitude who carried palms, which they strewed in the way for us to march over. Young ladies presented us with laurel, and even fixed it in our caps : others handed us sweetmeats and fruit. Gentlemen had hired porters to bring out wine, which they handed to us as we passed by : every individual strove to outvie each other in good nature. On the other hand the feelings of each British soldier were wound up to the highest pitch—Wellington himself rode at the head of our regiment, we were flushed with victory, and a defeated enemy was flying in our front : proud of the honour paid us by the people, we entered Madrid, the air rent with cries of " Long live Wellington, Long live the English." The crowd and shouts and ringing of bells was beyond description. The men on the flanks were involuntarily dragged out of their subdivisions into houses, and treated with the best that could be found for them. It was with difficulty that Lord Wellington could keep his seat on horseback—every one was pressing round him.' They kissed his hands, his sword, even his horse and the ground he had passed over. It would have been a moment of intoxicating exultation to most men : but Wellington looked beyond the laurels and the shouting. ' It is impossible to describe the joy of the inhabitants on our arrival : ' he wrote, in his rather ponderous style, ' I hope that the prevalence of the same sentiment of detestation of the French yoke which first induced

[1] *Dispatches*, ix. p. 351.
[2] Journal of Wheeler of the 51st, p. 27.

them to set the example of resistance to the usurper, will
again induce them to make exertions in the cause of their
country, which, being more wisely directed, will be more
efficacious than those they formerly made [1].' But hope is not
the same as expectation.

That evening the whole city was illuminated, and the streets
were so full, till long after midnight, of crowds tumultuously
joyful, that some cautious officers feared that the French
garrison of the Retiro might sally out to make mischief in
the confusion. Lafon-Blaniac, however, kept quiet—he was
already quailing over two discoveries—the one that his water
supply was very short, the other that the inner *enceinte* of the
works was so full of miscellaneous combustible stuff, shot in
at the last moment, that nothing was more probable than
a general conflagration if he were to be bombarded. It had
also begun to strike him that his outer line of defences was
very weak, and his second one very constricted for the amount
of men and material that he had in charge. The larger *enceinte*,
indeed, only consisted, for the greater part of its extent, of the
loopholed wall of the Retiro Park, with some *flèches* placed in
good flanking positions. On the side facing the Prado were
buildings—the Retiro Palace and the Museum, which had been
barricaded and made tenable : they formed the strongest section
of the exterior line. The inner *enceinte* was a more formidable
affair—with ten bastioned fronts on the scale of a powerful
field-work. The star-fort, which constituted the final refuge
for the garrison, was built around the solid building that
had once been the royal porcelain manufactory (where the
celebrated Buen Retiro china was made) : it had a ditch
twelve feet deep and twenty-four wide, and was formidably
palisaded.

Wellington reconnoitred the works on the 13th, and directed
that the outer line should be stormed that night. Three
hundred men of the 3rd Division were told off to break into the
Park wall on the north, near the Bull-Ring : 300 more from
the 51st and 68th regiments of the 7th Division were to attack
the south-west angle of the *enceinte*, which was formed by the
wall of the Botanical Garden. Both assaults were completely

---

[1] To Lord Bathurst, August 13. *Dispatches*, ix. 355.

successful—the walls were so flimsy that they were easily hewn through with picks, or beaten in with beams used as battering-rams, and the 68th found and broke open a postern. The resistance was very weak—only ten of the storming-parties were killed or wounded, and the enemy retired almost at once into his second line, abandoning the Palace and other fortified buildings.

Lafon-Blaniac was now in a deplorable position, for there was only one well of moderate capacity within the second *enceinte* to serve the whole garrison. He had lost those in the Palace at the foot of the hill: and the old porcelain manufactory, within the star-fort, had been wont to be supplied by a little aqueduct, which had of course been cut by the British. It was clear that a lack of water would soon be a serious problem : but a superfluity of fire was a still more probable one—the garrison was crowded up among buildings and stores, and the large factory inside the star-fort was specially dangerous—a very few shells would suffice to kindle it and to smoke out or smother its defenders.

On the morning of the 14th Lafon-Blaniac sent out a flag of truce, ostensibly to deliver a threat to fire upon the town if he were pressed, really to see if he could get tolerable terms, before the British had begun to batter him, for he could note preparations to bring up heavy guns being made. Wellington saw the *parlementaire* in person, and a conclusion was arrived at in a very few minutes. Tolerable conditions of surrender were granted—the garrison to march out with honours of war, the officers to keep their swords, horses, and baggage, the men their knapsacks unsearched. All arms and stores were to be handed over intact. At four o'clock the French marched out, ' most of them drunk, and affecting a great rage against the governor for surrendering so tamely.' Yet it is clear that he could not have held out for more than a day or two, with great loss of life and no strategical profit, since there was absolutely no chance of the place being relieved. The prisoners were sent off under escort to Lisbon. On the way they were joined by the garrison of Guadalajara, which had surrendered with equal facility to the Empecinado—this was a force of *Juramentados* and foreigners—regiments Royal-Étranger and Royal-Irlandais, about 900 strong, under a General de Prieux, of the Spanish not the French service. They feared for their necks if they resisted the guerrilleros, and made practically no resistance.

The stores in the Retiro proved most useful—nearly every regiment at Madrid was supplied with new shoes from them : the stock of blue French regimental coats was issued to the artillery and light dragoons, to be cut up into jackets ; Joseph's *Juramentado* uniforms served to reclothe Carlos de España's and Julian Sanchez's men. The most unexpected find in the fort was the eagles of the 51st Line and 12th Léger, which had somehow got into the Retiro, though the bulk of those corps were with Soult's army, and only detachments of them were at Madrid. They were sent to the Prince Regent, and now hang in the chapel of Chelsea Hospital[1]. The garrison was found to consist of 4 *chefs de bataillon*, 22 captains, 42 other officers, and 1,982 men—the latter including some 200 non-military employés. In addition, 6 officers and 429 rank and file had been surrendered in the hospital, which was outside the Retiro, before the attack on the place began[2].

Here we must leave Wellington for a space, triumphant in the Spanish capital, and much worried by the polite and effusive attentions of the authorities and inhabitants, who lavished on him and his officers banquets, balls, and bull-fights for many days, in spite of the penury which had been prevailing for years in the half-ruined city. Never was an army better treated—wine could be had for the asking, and at last the men had to be confined to their quarters for many hours a day, lest they should be killed by kindness. The Constitution was proclaimed in state, a patriotic municipality elected, and Carlos de España was made governor. He signalized his appointment by arresting a good many *Afrancesados* and garotting with much ceremonial the priest Diego Lopez, who had been one of King Joseph's most noted spies.[3]

---

[1] The second eagle is in error described in Wellington's dispatch as that of the 13th—which was in Russia at the time.

[2] For the ' siege ' of the Retiro see (besides the official sources) Burgoyne's *Diary*, i. pp. 208–9, and the narratives of Green of the 68th and Wheeler of the 51st. For the use of the French uniforms see the *Dickson Papers*, ed. Major Leslie, ii. pp. 738–9.

[3] Grattan's *With the Connaught Rangers*, p. 275.

Note.—For the garrison of the Retiro I can find no regular details ; Wellington gives only totals of the surrendered force. But a paper of Jourdan's (at Paris), though dated so far back as July 17th, speaks of the Madrid garrison as containing 230 men of the 3/12th Léger, 250 of the 3/45th, and a whole *bataillon de marche* more of Soult's army, 750 strong, together with 200 *hommes isolés*, and a considerable number of dismounted cavalry. I suspect that these formed the Retiro garrison in August as well as in July. The other troops noted as left at Madrid on July 18th—a battalion of Nassau, the dépôts of the Royal Guard, 28th and 75th, and three Spanish battalions, were certainly *not* in the surrender, and had marched off on August 10th with the King. But a good many scores of the 50th, belonging to Marmont's army, were among the prisoners. I suspect that these were the garrison of Avila, which retired on Madrid on getting the news of the battle of Salamanca.

SECTION XXXIII: CHAPTER X

AFFAIRS IN THE SOUTH. JUNE–AUGUST 1812.
SOULT, HILL, AND BALLASTEROS

Two months elapsed between Wellington's passage of the Agueda on his offensive march into the kingdom of Leon, and his triumphal entry into Madrid. During this critical time there had been constant alarms and excursions in Andalusia and Estremadura, but nothing decisive had occurred. This was all that Wellington wanted : if employment were found for the French Army of the South, so that it got no chance of interfering with the campaign on the Douro, he was perfectly satisfied, and asked for nothing more.

It will be remembered that his instructions to Hill, before he started on the march to Salamanca, were that Soult must be diverted as far as possible from sending troops northward. The main scheme was that Ballasteros and Hill should, if possible, combine their operations so as to bring pressure upon the enemy alternately [1]. The Cadiz Regency had readily agreed to stir up the Spanish general to activity : if he would demonstrate once more (as in April) against Seville, so as to attract Soult's attention, and cause him to concentrate, Hill should press in upon Drouet and the French troops in Estremadura, so as to force the Marshal to draw off from the Spaniard. Similarly, if Soult should concentrate against Hill, Ballasteros was to strike again at Seville, or the rear of the Cadiz Lines, which would infallibly bring the Marshal southward again in haste [2].

---

[1] Wellington to Henry Wellesley at Cadiz, *Dispatches*, ix. p. 169, same to same of June 1, *Dispatches*, ix. p. 197, Wellington to Hill (June 6th), *Dispatches*, ix. p. 215, and more especially the last paragraph of Wellington to Henry Wellesley of June 7th, *Dispatches*, ix. p. 219, and same to same of June 10th, *Dispatches*, ix. p. 224.

[2] To quote Wellington's own rather heavy but quite explicit phrases : ' I am certain that the enemy will move into Estremadura upon Hill, as soon as it is known that *I* have moved : and I hope everything will then be done by Ballasteros, and the Army of Murcia, and the troops in Cadiz, to divert the enemy from their intentions upon Hill.' And, on the other hand, in a letter differing in date from that first cited by three days, ' The

When Wellington crossed the Agueda [June 13] Hill had his corps collected in central Estremadura—head-quarters at Almendralejo, the troops cantoned about Ribera, Villafranca, Fuente del Maestre, and Los Santos, with Penne Villemur's Spanish horse in front at Zafra. Hill had in hand his old force—the 2nd Division and Hamilton's Portuguese, with two (instead of the usual one) British and one Portuguese cavalry brigades. He could also call up, if needed, the three strong Portuguese infantry regiments (5th, 17th, 22nd) which were holding Badajoz till a sufficient native garrison should be provided for it. At present only a few hundred Spaniards [Tiradores de Doyle] had appeared. Far away, to the north of the Guadiana, observing the French posts on the Tagus, there was a detached Portuguese cavalry regiment at Plasencia. This outlying unit was also put under Hill's charge : its object was to give early notice of any possible stir by the French, in the direction of Almaraz or the recently restored bridge of Alcantara. Morillo's infantry division of Castaños's army was lying on the right of Hill, in south-western Estremadura : Wellington suggested that the Spanish general might be willing to throw it into Badajoz, and so liberate the Portuguese regiments lying there, if Soult should advance before the regular garrison intended for the great fortress should arrive from Cadiz. The whole force watching Soult amounted to nearly 19,000 men, not including the Spaniards. Of this total about 7,500 sabres and bayonets were British—something over 11,000 were Portuguese. In addition, Morillo and Penne Villemur had not quite 4,000 Spanish horse and foot. Supposing that a minimum garrison were thrown into Badajoz—Morillo's infantry for choice—Hill could dispose of 18,000 Anglo-Portuguese for field-operations, not including the Portuguese cavalry by the Tagus, who had the separate duty of watching the Army of the Centre.

The French in Estremadura still consisted of the old con-

Spanish government have desired that in case of a movement by Marshal Soult on General Ballasteros, General Hill should make a movement to divert his attention from Ballasteros. I have directed this movement, in the notion that the Conde de Villemur [the Spanish commander in Estremadura] will also co-operate in it.' The see-saw of alternate distractions is clearly laid down—but Ballasteros (as usual) proved a difficult factor to manage.

tingent which D'Erlon had been administering since the year began, viz. his own and Daricau's infantry divisions, with Lallemand's and Perreymond's cavalry—altogether not more than 12,000 men, for several of the infantry regiments had lost a battalion apiece when Badajoz fell. Since his excursion to Don Benito and Medellin at the time of Hill's raid on Almaraz, D'Erlon had drawn back, abandoning all southern and most of eastern Estremadura to the allies. He himself was lying at Azuaga and Fuente Ovejuna, on the slopes of the Sierra Morena, while Daricau was more to the north, about Zalamea, rather too far off to give his chief prompt support. Daricau's detachment in this direction seems to have been caused by a desire to make communication with the Army of Portugal easy, if the latter should ever come southward again from the Tagus, and push to Truxillo as in 1811. It was clear that unless Soult should reinforce his troops to the north of the mountains, Hill need fear nothing : indeed he had a distinct superiority over D'Erlon.

Early in June, however, there was no danger that any troops from Seville would come northward, for Ballasteros's diversion had taken place somewhat earlier than Wellington had wished, and the disposable reserve of the Army of Andalusia was far away in the extreme southern point of the province. After his success at Alhaurin in April, and his subsequent pursuit by Soult's flying columns, Ballasteros had taken refuge—as was his wont when hard pressed—under the guns of Gibraltar. The French retired when they had consumed their provisions, and fell back to their usual stations at Malaga and Ronda, and along the line of the Guadalete. When they were gone, the Spanish general emerged in May, and recommenced his wonted incursions, ranging over the whole of the mountains of the South. Having received the dispatches of the Regency, which directed him to execute a diversion in favour of the allied army in Estremadura, he obeyed with unexpected celerity, and took in hand a very bold enterprise. General Conroux, with the column whose task it was to cover the rear of the Cadiz Lines, was lying at Bornos, behind the Guadalete, in a slightly entrenched camp. He had with him about 4,500 men[1]. Ballasteros

[1] 9th Léger, 96th Ligne, a battalion of the 16th Léger, and the 5th Chasseurs.

resolved to attempt to surprise him, on the morning of June 1. Having got together all his disposable troops, 8,500 infantry and a few squadrons of horse [1], he made a forced march, and, favoured by a heavy mist at dawn, fell upon the enemy's cantonments and surprised them. He won a considerable success at first : but the French rallied, and after a hard fight broke his line by a general charge, and drove him back across the Guadalete. Conroux was too exhausted to pursue, and Ballasteros remained in position, apparently meditating a second attack, when on seeing some cavalry detachments coming up to join the enemy, he sullenly retired. He had lost 1,500 men and 4 guns, the French over 400 [2]. The first note of alarm from Bornos had caused Soult to send what reserves he could collect from the Cadiz Lines and Seville—six battalions and two cavalry regiments, and since Ballasteros had been beaten, but not routed, he thought it necessary to give prompt attention to him. Thereupon the Spaniard retreated first to Ubrique, and when threatened in that position, to his old refuge in the lines of San Roque before Gibraltar.

Soult would have liked to make an end of him, and would also have been glad to direct a new attack upon Tarifa, which served as a second base to the roving Spanish corps ; he mentions his wish to capture it in more than one of his dispatches of this summer. But his attention was drawn away from Ballasteros and the South by the prompt advance of Hill, who (as had been settled) pressed in upon Drouet at the right moment. On the 7th June he moved forward his head-quarters from Almendralejo to Fuente del Maestre, and two days later to Zafra. On the 11th, Penne Villemur's cavalry pushed out from Llerena towards Azuaga, while Slade's brigade, advancing parallel with the Spanish general, pressed forward from Llera on Maguilla, a village some fifteen miles in front of Drouet's head-quarters at Fuente Ovejuna. This reconnaissance in force brought on the most unlucky combat that was ever fought

---

[1] Figures in *Los Ejércitos españoles*, p. 128.

[2] Possibly more—the casualty list of officers in Martinien's admirable tables is very heavy—9 officers hit in the 9th Léger, 13 in the 96th Ligne, 3 in the 16th Léger, 5 in the 5th Chasseurs à cheval. Thirty officers hit might very probably (but not certainly) mean 600 casualties in all.

by the British cavalry during the Peninsular War, the skirmish of Maguilla.

Slade, an officer whose want of capacity we have before had occasion to notice [1], after some hours of march began to get in touch with French dragoon vedettes, and presently, after driving them in, found himself facing Lallemand's brigade. Their forces were nearly equal—each having two regiments, Slade the 1st Royals and 3rd Dragoon Guards, Lallemand the 17th and 27th Dragoons—they had about 700 sabres a side: if anything Slade was a little the stronger. The French general showed considerable caution and retired for some distance, till he had nearly reached Maguilla, where he turned to fight. Slade at once charged him, with the Royals in front line and the 3rd Dragoon Guards supporting. The first shock was completely successful, the French line being broken, and more than 100 men being taken. But Slade then followed the routed squadrons with headlong recklessness, 'each regiment,' as he wrote in his very foolish report of the proceedings, 'vying with the other which should most distinguish itself.' The pursuit was as reckless as that of the 13th Light Dragoons at Campo Mayor in the preceding year, and resolved itself into a disorderly gallop of several miles. After the French had passed a defile beyond Maguilla a sudden cry was heard, 'Look to your right' —a fresh squadron which Lallemand had left in reserve was seen bearing down on the flank of the disordered mass. Charged diagonally by a small force, but one in good order, the British dragoons gave way. Lallemand's main body turned upon them, and 'the whole brigade in the greatest disorder, and regardless of all the exertions and appeals of their general and their regimental officers, continued their disgraceful flight till victors and fugitives, equally overcome and exhausted by the overpowering heat and the clouds of thick dust, came to a standstill near Valencia de las Torres, some four miles from Maguilla, where at last Slade was able to collect his regiments, and to retire to the woods beyond Llera [2].'

In this discreditable affair Slade lost 22 killed, 26 wounded, and no less than 2 officers and 116 men taken prisoners—most

---

[1] See vol. iv. pp. 187 and 437.
[2] See Ainslie's *History of the 1st Royals*, p. 133.

of the latter wounded—a total casualty list of 166. Lallemand
acknowledges in his report a loss of 51 officers and men [1]. The
defeated general irritated Wellington by a very disingenuous
report, in which he merely wrote that ' I am sorry to say our loss
was severe, as the enemy brought up a support, and my troops
being too eager in pursuit, we were obliged to relinquish a good
number of prisoners that we had taken, and to fall back on
Llera.' He then added, in the most inappropriate phrases,
' nothing could exceed the gallantry displayed by both officers
and men on this occasion, in which Colonels Calcraft and
Clinton, commanding the two regiments, distinguished themselves, as well as all the other officers present [2].'

Wellington's scathing comment, in a letter to Hill, was :
' I have never been more annoyed than by Slade's affair, and
I entirely concur with you in the necessity of inquiring into it.
It is occasioned entirely by the trick our officers of cavalry
have acquired, of galloping at everything—and then galloping
back as fast as they galloped *on* the enemy. They never consider
their situation, never think of manœuvring before an enemy—
so little that one would think they cannot manœuvre except
on Wimbledon Common : and when they use their arm as it
ought to be used, viz. offensively, they never keep nor provide
for a reserve. . . . The Royals and 3rd Dragoon Guards were
the best cavalry regiments in this country, and it annoys me
particularly that the misfortune has happened to them. I do
not wonder at the French boasting of it : it is the greatest blow
they have struck [3].' It is curious to find that Slade retained
command of his brigade till May 1813. One would have
expected to find him relegated to Great Britain at a much
earlier date. But Wellington was not even yet in full control
of the removal or promotion of his senior officers. Other
generals with whom he was equally discontented, such as
Erskine and Long, were also left upon his hands after he had
set a black mark against their names.

[1] Including one officer killed and four wounded.
[2] See Slade's report in *Dispatches*, ix. pp. 242–3. Tomkinson (p. 174)
says that Slade's report to Cotton, commanding the cavalry, was ' the
best I ever saw. He made mention of his son having stained his maiden
sword ! '
[3] Wellington to Hill, *Dispatches*, ix. p. 238.

The combat of Maguilla, however unsatisfactory in itself, made no difference to the general strategy of the campaign. Drouet, having drawn back on Hill's advance, sent messages to Soult, to the effect that unless he were strongly reinforced he must retire from the Sierra Morena, and cover the roads to Cordova on the Andalusian side of the mountains. He reported that he had only 6,000 men in hand, and that Hill was coming against him with 30,000, including the Spaniards. Both these figures were fantastic—for reasons best known to himself D'Erlon did not include Daricau's division in his own total, while he credited Hill with 15,000 men in the 2nd British division alone [which was really 8,000 strong, including its Portuguese brigade], and reported with circumstantial detail that the 7th Division had come down from Portalegre and joined the 2nd [1].

Soult sent on D'Erlon's dispatch to Madrid, with the comment that Hill's advance showed that the main intention of Wellington was certainly to attack Andalusia, and not to fall upon Marmont. But that he did not consider such an attack very imminent is sufficiently shown by the fact that he detached to Drouet's aid only one division of infantry, that of Barrois— which composed his central reserve—and one of cavalry, that of Pierre Soult, or a total of 6,000 infantry and 2,200 cavalry : such a reinforcement would have been futile if he had really believed that Wellington was marching against Seville. His real view may be gathered from his estimate of Hill's force at 15,000 Anglo-Portuguese and 5,000 Spaniards—a total very remote from the alarmist reports of Drouet, and not far from the truth. The reinforcement sent under Barrois would give the Estremaduran detachment a practical equality in numbers with Hill, and a great superiority in quality. The orders sent to Drouet were that he was to advance against Hill, to strive to get him to an engagement, at any rate to 'contain' him, so that he should not detach troops north of the Guadiana to join Wellington or to demonstrate against Madrid. If things went well, Drouet was to invest Badajoz, and to occupy Merida, from whence he would try to get into communication via Truxillo with the troops of the Army of the Centre. The final paragraph

[1] Letters of D'Erlon to Jourdan on June 9th, and of Soult to King Joseph June 12, copies from the Paris archives—lent me by Mr. Fortescue.

of his directions stated that Drouet's main object must be to make such a formidable diversion that Wellington would have to reinforce Hill. ' When the Army of Portugal finds that it has less of the English army in front of it, we may perhaps persuade it [i.e. Marmont] that the enemy's plan is certainly to invade the provinces of the south of Spain before he acts directly against the North : then, no doubt, changed dispositions will be made.' Unfortunately for the strategical reputation of Soult, Wellington crossed the Agueda with seven of his eight divisions to attack Marmont, on the very day after this interesting dispatch was written.

D'Erlon had been promised that Barrois should march to his aid on the 14th, but it was not till the 16th that the column from Seville started to join him, and then it marched not by the route of Constantina and Guadalcanal, as D'Erlon had requested, but by the high-road from Andalusia to Badajoz, via Monasterio. If Hill had been pressing the troops in front of him with vigour, the French would have been in an awkward position, since they were on separate roads, and might have been driven apart, and kept from junction by a decisive movement from Llerena, where Hill's cavalry and advanced guard lay. But the British general had orders to attract the attention of Soult and to ' contain ' as many of the enemy as possible, rather than to risk anything. He resolved, when he heard of the approach of Barrois, to retire to the heights of Albuera, which Wellington had pointed out to him as the most suitable position for standing at bay, if he were pressed hard. Accordingly he drew back by slow stages from Zafra towards Badajoz, covering his rear by his cavalry, which suffered little molestation. Barrois joined Drouet at Bienvenida near Zafra on the 19th, and their united force, since Daricau had come in to join them from the direction of Zalamea, with the greater part of his division, must have amounted to over 18,000 men, though Drouet in a report to King Joseph states it at a decidedly lower figure [1]. They

[1] In this report (the copy of which I owe to Mr. Fortescue's kindness) Drouet says that Soult had told him to expect reinforcements to the total of some 15,000 men, but that Barrois brought him only 3,500 infantry and 1,500 horse, and Daricau 4,500 infantry and 1,000 horse, so that his reinforcements were only 10,500 men instead of 15,000. Drouet stated his own force, horse and foot (his own division and Lallemand's cavalry) in

advanced cautiously as far as Villafranca and Fuente del
Maestre, which their infantry occupied on June 21, while their
numerous cavalry lay a little way in front, at Villalba, Azeuchal,
and Almendralejo. On the same day Hill had taken up the
Albuera position, on which several points had been entrenched.

As Hill had just called out the three garrison regiments of
Portuguese from Badajoz, he had now between 18,000 and
19,000 of his own army in position, besides Villemur's Spanish
cavalry. This last, together with Long's and Slade's squadrons,
were thrown out in front of the Albuera river, with their
vedettes in Santa Marta, Almendral, and Corte de Peleas, only
a mile or two from the French advanced posts. They were
directed not to give way till they were severely pressed, as
Hill wished to avoid at all costs the kind of surprise that had
befallen Beresford in 1811, when Long had retired so precipitately before the French horse that he could give no account
of their strength, nor of the position of Soult's infantry. But
the expected advance of the enemy hung fire—from the 21st
onwards Hill was waiting to be attacked, and sending almost
daily accounts of the situation to Wellington : but the main
body of the French moved no farther forward. This was all the
more surprising to the English general because he had intercepted a letter written on May 31 from King Joseph to Drouet,
in which the latter was directed to ' passer sur le corps à Hill [1],'
and then to come up to the Tagus to join the Army of the Centre.
Not knowing how entirely Soult and D'Erlon were ignoring all
orders from Madrid, both Wellington and his trusty lieutenant
thought that such instructions must almost certainly bring
about an action. The former wrote to the latter on June 28th,
after receiving several statements of the situation : ' if you
should find that Drouet separates his troops, or if he pretends

a preceding letter of June 9th at 6,000 of all arms, so that the concentration
would only give 16,000 men. I fancy that he is deliberately understating
Barrois, for that general had 7,000 men in March, and 5,000 still in October
at the end of a long and fatiguing campaign, and Pierre Soult too. Drouet's
object in giving these figures to Joseph was to prove that he was so weak
that he could make no detachment towards the Tagus, as the King had
directed him to do. Was it for the same purpose that he always over-stated
Hill's army ? Or did he really believe that the latter had 30,000 men
arranged opposite him, as he repeatedly told Soult ?

[1] Cf. Wellington to Hill of July 11th. *Dispatches*, ix. p. 280.

to hold you in check with a smaller body of men than you think you can get the better of, fall upon him, but take care to keep a very large proportion of your troops in reserve. . . . I should prefer a partial affair to a general one, but risk a general affair—keeping always a large body of reserve, particularly of cavalry—rather than allow Drouet to remain in Estremadura and keep you in check.' But the enemy neither came on for a general action, nor scattered his troops so widely as to induce Hill to risk an attack on any point of his line. He remained with his infantry massed about Villafranca and Fuente del Maestre, and only demonstrated with his cavalry.

The cause of this inactivity on Drouet's part was partly, perhaps, his over-estimate of Hill's strength, but much more Soult's unwillingness to obey the orders sent him from Madrid. He was determined not to detach a third part of his army to the Tagus, to join the Army of the Centre. He was by this time fully embarked on his long course of insubordinate action, with which we have already dealt when writing of the King's desires and their frustration[1]. On the 26th May Joseph had sent him the dispatch which directed that D'Erlon must come up northward, if Wellington's main attack turned out to be directed against Marmont and the Army of Portugal : ' his corps is the pivot on which everything turns : he is the counter-poise which can be thrown into the balance in one scale or the other, according as our forces have to act on the one side or the other[2].' Drouet himself had at the same time received that order to the same effect, sent to him directly and not through his immediate superior, which so much scandalized Soult's sense of hierarchical subordination[3]. On getting the Madrid dispatch of May 26 upon June 8th, Soult had written to say that Wellington's real objective was Andalusia and not the North, that Marmont was utterly misled if he supposed that he was to be attacked by the main body of the allies, that Graham, with two British divisions, was still at Portalegre in support of Hill, and that Drouet had therefore been forbidden to lose touch with the Army of the South by passing towards the Tagus. If he

---

[1] See chapter i above, pp. 309–10.
[2] Joseph to Soult, May 26, intercep   dispatch in the Scovell ciphers.
[3] See above, p. 332.

departed, the whole fabric of French power in the South would go to pieces, ' I should have to pack up and evacuate Andalusia after the smallest check.' Drouet should ' contain ' Hill, but could do no more. In a supplementary dispatch of June 12, provoked by the receipt of Joseph's direct orders to Drouet, Soult went further, definitely stating that the troops in Estremadura should not go to the Tagus, ' where they would be lost to the Army of the South, but would never arrive in time to help the Army of Portugal.' If Drouet passed the Tagus, Hill would march on Seville, and on the sixth day would capture that insufficiently garrisoned capital, put himself in communication with Ballasteros, and raise the siege of Cadiz. ' I repeat that the Army of the South cannot carry out its orders, and send Count D'Erlon and 15,000 men to the valley of the Tagus, without being compelled to evacuate Andalusia within the fortnight. . . . If your Majesty insists, remove me from command, I do not wish to be responsible for the inevitable disaster that must follow [1].'

At the same time Drouet, much vexed at having personal responsibility thrown upon his shoulders, by the King's direct orders to him to march without consulting Soult, wrote to Madrid that he was very weak, that Hill was in front of him with a superior force, and that Barrois and Pierre Soult, who had just joined him, were under strict orders not to go beyond the Guadiana, so that if he himself marched towards the Tagus it would be with a very small force. But he dare not make that move : ' I am absolutely obliged to stop where I am [Villafranca] in presence of Hill, who still remains concentrated on the Albuera position, which he has entrenched, with at least 25,000 men.' Indeed an attack by Hill was expected day by day : ' at the moment of writing there is lively skirmishing going on at the outposts, and news has come in that the whole allied army is advancing [2].' Drouet, in short, was determined to evade responsibility, and summed up the situation by the conclusion that he was acting for the best in ' containing ' Hill

---

[1] Soult to Joseph, printed in Joseph's *Correspondence*, ix. pp. 31–3.

[2] Drouet to Joseph, Villafranca, July 3, Paris Archives [paper communicated to me by Mr. Fortescue]. Cf. Drouet to Jourdan to much the same general effect, of June 18, in King Joseph's *Correspondence*, ix. pp. 36–7.

ESTREMADURA

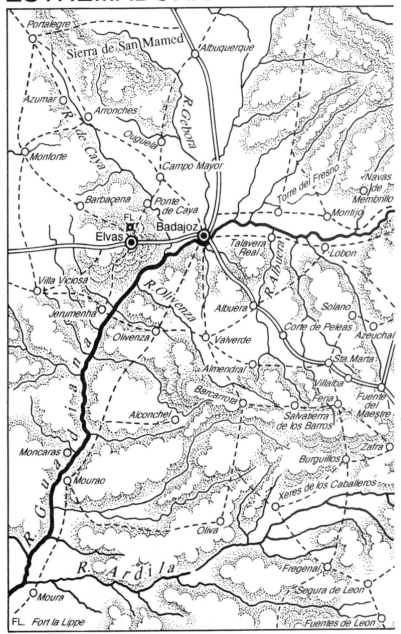

Portalegre
Sierra de San Mamed
Albuquerque
Azumar
R. de Caya
Arronches
Ouguela
R. Gebora
Monforte
Campo Mayor
Torre del Fresno
Navas de Membrillo
Barbaçena
Ponte de Caya
Montijo
FL.
Badajoz
Elvas
Talavera Real
R. Albuera
Lobon
Villa Viciosa
R. Olivenza
Albuera
Solano
Jerumenha
Olivenza
Valverde
Corte de Peleas
Azeuchal
Almendral
Sta. Marta
Barcarrota
Villalba
Feria
Fuente del Maestre
Alconchel
Salvatierra de los Barros
Moncaras
Zafra
Burguillos
Mourao
Xeres de los Caballeros
Oliva
R. Ardila
Fregenal
Moura
Segura de Leon
FL. Fort la Lippe
Fuentes de Leon

B.V. Darbishire, Oxford, 1914

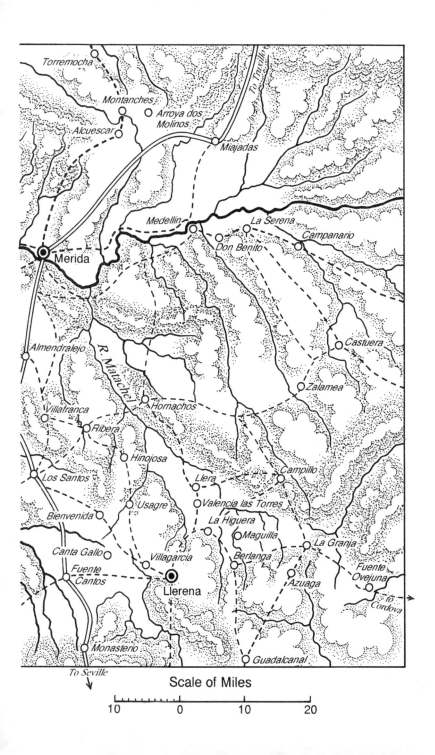

Torremocha

Montanches

Arroya dos
Molinos

Alcuescar

To Trujillo

Miajadas

Medellin

La Serena

Campanario

Don Benito

Merida

Almendralejo

R. Matachel

Castuera

Zalamea

Villafranca

Hornachos

Ribera

Hinojosa

Los Santos

Llera

Campillo

Usagre

Valencia las Torres

Bienvenida

La Higuera

Canta Gallo

Villagarcia

Maguilla

La Granja

Berlanga

Fuente
Cantos

Llerena

Azuaga

Fuente
Ovejuna

to
Cordova

Monasterio

Guadalcanal

To Seville

Scale of Miles

10   0   10   20

and his very large detachment, who could be of no use to Wellington in the campaign which the latter was now reported to have begun against Marmont in the North. He could do no more.

The deadlock in front of the Albuera position lasted for many days—from June 21st till July 2nd. This was a very trying time for Hill's corps—the weather was excessively hot, the ground was hideous with the insufficiently buried corpses of the battle of last year, and sickness was very prevalent in some regiments. For the first day or two after the arrival of the French at Villafranca and Almendralejo, an attack was expected each morning, but nothing in particular happened. Drouet kept quiet behind his cavalry screen, and did no more than send foraging parties out on his flanks, which ravaged the countryside as far as Merida and Feria. Over-valuing Hill's strength, he dreaded to commit himself to an attack on a superior force, covered by field-works and in a fine position. Nothing was seen of him for ten days, save that on the 26th he felt the posts of the allies at Corte de Peleas and Santa Marta, and retired after a little cavalry skirmishing. On July 1, however, he executed a more searching reconnaissance, with three brigades of cavalry under the direction of Pierre Soult, Vinot's in the centre, Sparre's on the right, Lallemand's on the left. Barrois's infantry division came up in support. Vinot drove in a Portuguese cavalry regiment of J. Campbell's brigade from Corte de Peleas [1], but retired when he found it supported by Long's light dragoons in front of the Albuera position. Lallemand found Santa Marta held by Penne Villemur's cavalry, and turned them out of it with considerable loss, for the Spanish general unwisely offered battle, and was routed after a very short contest. He retired into the wood of Albuera, whose edge was occupied by Slade's heavy dragoons, supported by the pickets of Byng's infantry brigade. A troop of the 3rd Dragoon Guards made a gallant charge to cover the retreat of the Spaniards, and suffered some loss in bringing them off. Lallemand at dusk pressed forward, and cut off a small party of the Buffs, who would have been taken prisoners if a troop of the 2nd Hussars

---

[1] Espinchal says that the 2nd Hussars captured a Portuguese gun : I have no corroboration for this.

K.G.L. had not rescued them by a sudden counter-attack. Sparre's brigade on the right did no more than skirmish with the allied outposts along the lower course of the river Albuera. At night all the French cavalry retired, and D'Erlon wrote to Soult that his reconnaissance had 'completely fulfilled its object,' by making him certain that Hill had 25,000 foot, 3,000 horse, and a very strong force of artillery in position, so that it would be insane to attack him [1].

On the next morning, July 2nd, Hill determined to make use of Wellington's permission to bring on an action, if he should judge that Drouet was not strong enough to face him. The weakness of the French demonstration had convinced him that the enemy was not ready to fight. Collecting the whole of his army, he advanced from the Albuera position towards Santa Marta, thus challenging Drouet to a fight. The enemy's vedettes made no stand and retired when pushed. On reaching Santa Marta Hill halted for the night in battle order, and on the morning of the 3rd resumed his movement, which was directed to cutting off Drouet from the great road to Seville. While Erskine with the light cavalry (Long, and J. Campbell's Portuguese) advanced down the high-road to Villalba, supported by one British and one Portuguese brigade of infantry, Hill himself, with the rest of his army, executed a flank march to Feria, and, having got behind the French left wing, turned inward and moved toward Los Santos. The enemy's main body, at Villafranca and Fuente del Maestre, were thus prevented from using the high-road to Seville, and placed in a position which compelled Drouet either to fight, or to retire south-eastward towards Usagre and Llerena.

Next morning (July 4) Hill expected a battle, for Barrois's division and all Pierre Soult's cavalry were found in a strong position at Fuente del Maestre, and the rest of the French were close behind at Almendralejo. But when he continued his movement toward the right, outflanking Barrois instead of attacking him, the enemy gave way and retired, protected by

---

[1] Details of all this in Soult's dispatch to Joseph of July 10, in Espinchal's *Mémoires* (he served in Vinot's brigade), and in the diaries of Swabey of the R.A. and of Stolzenberg of the 2nd Hussars K.G.L., printed in full in Schwertfeger's *History of the K. G. Legion*, ii. pp. 257–8.

his cavalry, retreating on Ribera, Hinojosa, and Usagre [1]. There was lively skirmishing between the squadrons of the British advanced guard, and those of the French rearguard, but no serious engagement.

The same general plan of action continued on the 5th. Hill, keeping his army well concentrated, moved in two columns on Usagre and Bienvenida, the bulk of his cavalry riding at the head of his left-hand column and pressing in the French horse. Drouet took up a position at Valencia de las Torres, where he had found strong ground, and thought on the 6th that he would risk a defensive action. But Hill, instead of marching in upon him, continued his flanking movement towards Llerena. Thereupon Drouet, finding that he would be cut off from Andalusia if he remained in his chosen position, evacuated it and fell back by Maguilla on Berlanga and Azuaga [July 7]. The two armies had thus got back into exactly the same positions in which they had lain on June 19th, before Hill's retreat to Albuera. The tale of their manœuvres bears a curious resemblance to the contemporary movements of Wellington and Marmont between Salamanca and Tordesillas. In each case one combatant, when pressed, retired, and took up a strong position (Marmont at Tordesillas–Pollos–Toro, Hill at Albuera). He then issued from it after some days, and by persistent flank movements dislodged his opponent, and drove him back to the same position from which he had started, so that the situation came back to that which it had been three weeks before. But here the parallel ended—Marmont pressed his advantage too far, and got entangled in the disastrous manœuvre of July 22, which brought on the battle of Salamanca and his own ruin. Hill, contented with what he had achieved, halted at Llerena, and did not push matters to a decisive action. He had done all that Wellington desired in keeping Soult's attention diverted from Marmont's peril, and in ' containing ' a hostile force as great as his own. Moreover he had driven it off the road to Seville, and if it retreated on Andalusia it would have to be on Cordova, by the road of Constantina, since no other remained available.

But a new development of this complicated and indecisive

[1] All this from Hill's dispatch to Wellington of July 4, from Los Santos.

campaign began on July 10th. Drouet, thinking apparently
that Hill's farther advance might be stopped as effectively by
assuming a position on his flank as by direct opposition in
front, shifted his right wing (Daricau's division and Sparre's and
Vinot's cavalry) back to Zalamea and its neighbourhood, where
Daricau had lain in May and June. He himself resumed his
old head-quarters at Fuente Ovejuna. Now just at this time
Hill received an intercepted letter of King Joseph to Drouet,
dated June 21st, which repeated in angry terms the long-
ignored orders that the Estremaduran detachment of the Army
of the South was to march on Toledo without delay. ' Vous
aurez sans doute reçu les renforts que j'ai donné l'ordre au duc
de Dalmatie de vous envoyer. Vous devez avoir quinze mille
hommes. Agissez avec ce corps, et tout ce qui est sous le
commandement du général Daricau. Rapprochez-vous de
moi : passez le Tage, et mettez-vous en état d'agir suivant les
événements ; n'attendez aucun ordre [1].'
The capture of this dispatch coincided with the news that
Drouet had pushed Daricau and a large body of cavalry
towards Zalamea. Hill drew the natural deduction that the
French opposite him were at last about to obey the King's
orders, and to march to the Tagus, via Zalamea, Medellin, and
Truxillo. ' The intelligence that I have of the enemy's movements ' (he wrote to Wellington) ' indicates his intention of
carrying Joseph's instructions into execution. . . . I have
received information [false as it chanced] that Drouet was
yesterday at Zalamea, with his main body, having sent troops
by Berlanga and Azuaga. I shall move immediately in the
direction of Zalamea.' That is to say that if Drouet was going
off northward towards the King, Hill was prepared to carry
out the original instructions which Wellington had left him,
and if he could not stop the enemy, would move parallel to
him, so as to join his chief before Drouet could transfer himself
to the northern sphere of operations. His route would be by
Badajoz or Merida and the newly-restored bridge of Alcantara
on Ciudad Rodrigo, a much shorter one than that of his

[1] See Wellington to Hill of July 11 (*Dispatches*, ix. p. 280) and Hill to
Wellington of July 9. The text of the order is in Joseph's *Correspondence*,
ix. p. 41.

opponent. He had just begun to move his left wing in the direction of Merida, when he received a letter from Wellington exactly conforming to his own ideas. If Drouet is making for the Tagus in full force, wrote Wellington, you must take all the cavalry except one English regiment and Campbell's Portuguese, along with Byng's and Howard's brigades of the 2nd Division, and Hamilton's division, and send orders to have all preparations made at Alcantara to lay down the bridge : your route across the mountains will be by the pass of Perales : you will find elaborate instructions for the further movement at Ciudad Rodrigo. If Drouet only takes a small force, more allied troops may be left in Estremadura ; Zafra had better be their head-quarters. Hill would conduct the marching column as far as Perales, and then return to take charge of whatever is left in the South to watch Soult [1].

A few days later it became evident that no general movement of the French towards the Tagus was in progress. Daricau's infantry and the attached cavalry settled down at and about Zalamea, and pushed nothing but reconnaissances in the direction of the Guadiana—parties of horse appeared about Don Benito and Medellin, but no solid columns in support [2]. Hill therefore halted, with his head-quarters at Zafra and his rear-guard (which had but a moment before been his advanced guard) at Llerena : only a few of J. Campbell's Portuguese squadrons moved to Merida, though some Spanish infantry came up to the same direction [3]. Things then remained very quiet till July 24th, when Drouet at last appeared to be on the move with some definite purpose. On that day Lallemand's dragoons appeared at Hinojosa, pressed in a Portuguese cavalry regiment, and seemed inclined to push towards Ribera, but retired when Long's brigade came up against them : the losses on both sides were trifling. Three days later (July 27) a brigade of Daricau's infantry advanced to Medellin and drove off the observing force of the Spanish infantry, while Vinot's

[1] Wellington to Hill, Rueda, July 11.

[2] There is plenty of detail about these quite unimportant movements in Espinchal, ii. pp. 26–33.

[3] Not, however, the bulk of Morillo's division, which was at Medina de las Torres near Zafra, as the general's correspondence of that date shows [Villa's *Life of Morillo*, ii. p. 224].

cavalry executed a raid on Merida, expelled the Portuguese
detachment there, and exacted a requisition of food from the
town. They then retired in haste ; but Hill thought it well
for the future to strengthen his left, and moved up Byng's
British and A. Campbell's Portuguese infantry brigades to
Merida. But Drouet was only feinting, and had no serious
intentions of drawing up to the Guadiana, or crossing that
river northward. His main purpose was simply the raising of
requisitions ; for his detachments in the mountains of the
Serena were living on the edge of famine, and could only feed
themselves by keeping constantly on the move. It is curious
to find from the dispatches of the two opposing generals at this
time that both were fairly satisfied with themselves : each
thought that he was ' containing ' a somewhat superior force
of the enemy, and was doing his duty by keeping it from
interfering in the more important theatre of war. Hill knew
that he was detaining Drouet, when he was much wanted at
Madrid : Drouet knew that he was preventing Hill from
joining Wellington on the Douro. But the real balance of
advantage was on the side of the allies : Hill, with only 8,000
British and 11,000 Portuguese was claiming the attention of
three veteran divisions of the infantry of the Army of the
South, and of the major part of Soult's cavalry. The French in
Andalusia were left so weak by the absence of 18,000 men
beyond the Sierra Morena, that they could neither molest
Cadiz nor the Army of Murcia. Indeed, Ballasteros, though
his forces were less than they had been at the time of his defeat
at Bornos, was able to provide employment for all the troops
that Soult could spare for operations in the open field.

Six weeks after his disaster of June 1st, that enterprising, if
irresponsible, general started out again from the lines of San
Roque with between 5,000 and 6,000 men. Keeping to mountain roads and concealing his march, he surprised, on July 14,
the great harbour-city of Malaga, though he failed to capture
its citadel, Gibalfaro, into which the wrecks of the garrison
escaped. Ballasteros got money, stores, and recruits from the
captured town, but knew that he dare not tarry there for long.
For Soult, naturally enraged at such a bold and successful
raid, turned troops toward him from all sides. Leval, the

governor of Granada, marched against him with every spare battalion that could be got together from the eastern side of Andalusia, some 5,000 bayonets. Villatte, in command before Cadiz, came from the other quarter with 6,000 men ; they had orders to catch Ballasteros between them, to intercept his retreat upon Gibraltar, and annihilate him.

In order to cut off the Spaniard from his usual place of refuge, Villatte took a turn to the south, appeared in sight of Gibraltar on July 20, and then, keeping himself between the British fortress and Ballasteros, advanced northward to wait for him. Leval was to have driven him into Villatte's arms, advancing from Antequera and pressing the hunt southward. But the raider, instead of retreating in the expected direction, slipped unseen across Villatte's front by Alora, and made off into the plains of central Andalusia. On the 25th at dawn he appeared, most unexpectedly, at Osuna and surprised the small French garrison there. The governor, Colonel Beauvais, cut his way through the streets to a fortified convent, where he held out. But Ballasteros, satisfied with having captured a quantity of stores, mules, and baggage, and a few prisoners, vanished. Leval was on his track, and he had to evade his pursuer by a flank march, first to Grazalema and then to Ubrique. This was bringing him dangerously near to Villatte's position. But that general had no accurate knowledge of what was going on to the north, and having waited for ten days in the mountains beyond Gibraltar for a prey that never appeared, found himself starved out. On the 30th he started on his enforced return towards the Cadiz Lines, and had reached Medina Sidonia when Ballasteros, who had quite outmarched Leval, came down in safety to Ximena on August 1, and placed himself in touch with Gibraltar once more. Thereupon Leval, seeing that it was no use to push the Spaniard (for about the tenth time) under the guns of the British fortress, and finding his column utterly worn out, went home to Granada [1].

Thus Ballasteros gave no small help to the allied cause by distracting some 11,000 or 12,000 French troops for a long fortnight, while Hill was detaining Drouet in Estremadura. By the time that the hunt after the evasive Spaniard had

---

[1] The best account of all this is in Schepeler, pp. 661–3.

come to an end, the battle of Salamanca had been fought, and the aspect of affairs in the Peninsula had been completely changed. Even Soult, who had so long shut his eyes to the obvious, had at last to acknowledge that a new situation had arisen.

The news of Salamanca had reached Hill on July 29th, and caused a general expectation that the French in Estremadura would retreat at once, and that Soult would be retiring from Andalusia also in a few days. No such results followed—the intelligence was late in penetrating to the French camps ; and Soult, still hoping to induce King Joseph to join him, lingered for many days in his old posture. On August 4 Hill wrote that the ' recent glorious event ' appeared to have had very little effect on his immediate opponent, who continued in a strong position in his front. ' Therefore for the present I shall remain where I am, and watch for a favourable opportunity of acting [1].' Soult at Seville had, as late as August 8, no official news of Marmont's defeat, and only knew of it by Spanish rumours, which he— of set purpose—discounted. ' Les relations qu'ils ont publiées exagèrent sans doute les avantages : mais il paraît que quelque grand événement s'est passé en Castille [2].' He continued to urge King Joseph to come to Seville, join him, and attack Hill with such superior forces that Wellington would be forced to fly to the aid of his subordinate. It was only on August 12th that certain information regarding the battle of July 22nd reached the head-quarters of the Duke of Dalmatia, in the form of Joseph's Segovia dispatch of July 29th, containing the orders for the complete evacuation of Andalusia, and the march of the whole Army of the South upon Toledo. Even then Soult did not think it too late to make a final appeal to the King: ' the loss of a battle by the Army of Portugal was nothing more than a great duel, which can be undone by another similar duel. But the loss of Andalusia and the raising of the siege of Cadiz would be events whose effects would be felt all round Europe and the New World. . . . What does it matter if the enemy is left in possession of the whole space between Burgos and the Sierra Morena, until the moment when

---

[1] Letter of August 4 in Sidney's *Life of Hill*, p. 210.

[2] Soult to Joseph, August 8, Paris Archives (lent me by Mr. Fortescue).

great reinforcements come from France, and the Emperor has
been able to make his arrangements ?   But this sacrifice of
Andalusia once made, there is no way of remedying it.   The
imperial armies in Spain will have to repass the Ebro—famine
perhaps will drive them still farther [1],' &c.

On reflection, however, Soult did not venture to disobey, and,
before his last appeal could possibly have reached the King's
hands, began to issue orders for evacuation.   But so great was
his rage that he wrote an extraordinary letter to Clarke, the
Minister of War at Paris, in which he made the preposterous
insinuation that Joseph was about to betray his brother the
Emperor, and to come to an agreement with the Cadiz Cortes.
The evidence which he cited for this strange charge was flimsy
in the extreme.   ' I have read in the Cadiz newspapers the
statement that His Majesty's Ambassador in Russia has joined
the Russian army : that the King has opened intrigues with
the Insurrectional Government [2].   Sweden has made peace
with England, and the Hereditary Prince (Bernadotte) has
begun to treat with the Regency at Cadiz [3]. . . . I draw no
deduction from all these facts, but I am all the more attentive
to them.   I have thought it necessary to lay my fears before
six generals of my army, after having made them take an oath
not to reveal what I told them save to the Emperor himself,
or to some one specially commissioned by him.   But it is my
duty to inform your Excellency that I have a fear that all the
bad arrangements made [by the King] and all the intrigues
that have been going on, have the object of forcing the imperial
armies to retreat to the Ebro, or farther, and then of representing this event as the " last possible resource " (an expression
used by the King himself in a letter of July 20), in the hope of
profiting by it to come to some compromise [4].'

This letter, as obscurely worded as it was malicious, was not

---

[1] Soult to Joseph, Seville, August 12, in Joseph's *Correspondence*,
ix. pp. 67–8.

[2] There *had* been such intrigues between the King and persons in Cadiz
(see above, p. 140), but they had been opened by Napoleon's own advice,
in order to sow seeds of dissension among the patriots.

[3] The point of this insinuation is that Bernadotte and Joseph were
brothers-in-law, having married the two sisters Clary.

[4] Printed in Joseph's *Correspondence*, ix. pp. 68–70.

sent to France by the usual channels, lest the King should get
wind of it, but consigned to the captain of a French privateer,
who was about to sail from Malaga to Marseilles. By an ill
chance for Soult, the vessel was chased by a British ship, and
compelled to run for shelter into the harbour of Valencia.
There the King had recently arrived, on his retreat from
Madrid. The privateer-captain, who did not know what he was
carrying, sent the letter in to the royal head-quarters. Hence
came an explosion of wrath, and a series of recriminations with
which we shall have to deal in their proper place.

The evacuation of Andalusia commenced from the western
end, because the retreat of the army was to be directed east-
wards. The evacuation of the Castle of Niebla on August 12th
was its first sign—the troops in the Condado had retired to
San Lucar near Seville by the 15th. A little later the garrisons
in the extreme south, at Ronda and Medina Sidonia, blew up
their fortifications and retired. These were small movements,
but the dismantling of the Cadiz Lines was a formidable business,
and took several days. Soult covered it by ordering a furious
bombardment of the city and the Puntales fort from his
batteries across the bay ; during each salvo of the heavy guns
one or two of them were disabled, others being fired at an angle
against their muzzles, so as to split them. More were burst
by intentional over-loading, others had their trunnions knocked
off, but a good many were only spiked or thrown into the water.
The ammunition remaining after two days of reckless bombardment was blown up ; the stores set on fire ; the flotilla of gunboats was sunk, but so carelessly that thirty of them were
afterwards raised with no difficulty and found still seaworthy.
This orgy of destruction continued for the whole of the 24th :
at night the sky was red all round the bay, from Rota to
Chiclana, with burning huts and magazines, and the explosions
were frequent.

This was the moment when the large allied force in Cadiz
might well have made a general sortie, for the purpose of
cutting up the enemy while he was engrossed in the work of
destruction. Wellington had written a week before, to General
Cooke, then in command of the British contingent in the Isla
de Leon, to bid him fall upon the enemy when opportunity

should offer, considering that the French troops in the Lines were reduced to a minimum by the detachment of the division that had gone out to hunt Ballasteros. He suggested that the allies should cross the Santi Petri river and attack Chiclana, taking care, however, not to be cut off from their retreat. Unfortunately this letter of August 16th came too late, for Cooke (after conferring with the Spanish authorities) had committed himself to another and a more circuitous expedition to molest the French. General Cruz Murgeon, with a Spanish division of 4,000 men (which had originally been intended for the reinforcing of Ballasteros) had landed at the port of Huelva, in the Condado de Niebla, on August 11th. Cooke reinforced him with the pick of the British contingent—six companies of Guards, half of the 2/87th [1], two companies of Rifles [2], part of the 20th Portuguese, and the squadron of the 2nd Hussars K.G.L., which was the only cavalry at his disposition. These, placed under the charge of Colonel Skerrett, made up 1,600 men in all [3]; they landed at Huelva, joined Cruz Murgeon, and advanced with him against Seville. On the 24th they discovered the French outposts at San Lucar la Mayor, and drove them out of that town. But they hesitated over the idea of attacking Seville, where French troops were collecting from all quarters, though the divisions of Conroux and Villatte from the Cadiz Lines had not yet come up.

On the night of August 26th–27th, however, Soult, apprised of the near approach of his column from the Lines, evacuated Seville with the main part of his force, escorting a vast horde of Spanish refugees, who feared to remain behind to face their countrymen, and a long train of wagons and carriages loaded with the accumulated spoils of three years of tyrannous misrule in Andalusia. He left a rearguard to occupy the outworks of the city, which was to be picked up and taken on by Villatte when he should appear on the next day.

On hearing of the departure of the Marshal, Cruz Murgeon

---

[1] Minus four companies left at Tarifa.

[2] Two from the 2/95th, those of Cadoux and Jenkins.

[3] Skerrett in his dispatch (Wellington, *Supplementary Dispatches*, xiv. p. 108), speaks of attacking San Lucar with 800 men : but this was not his whole force.

and Skerrett resolved to attack Seville, knowing that the troops
left behind to guard it were insufficient to man effectively all
its long line of defences. Being on the western side of the
Guadalquivir, they had first to win the large transpontine
suburb of Triana, the home of potters and gipsies, through
which alone access could be got to the city. It was attacked
at several points and stormed, but the enemy then held to the
great bridge over the river linking Triana and Seville, and made
a long resistance there. The bridge had been barricaded, part
of its planks had been pulled up, and artillery had been trained
on it from the farther side. Notwithstanding these obstacles
the Spaniards attacked it ; the well-known Irish adventurer
Colonel Downie charged three times at the head of his Estremaduran Legion. Repelled twice by the heavy fire, he reached
the barricade at the third assault, and leaped his horse over
the cut which the French had made in front of it, but found
himself alone within the work, and was bayoneted and made
prisoner [1]. But soon after the allies brought up guns through
the streets of Triana, and so battered the barricade that the
French were compelled to evacuate it. Skerrett sent the Guards
across : they passed by the beams which had been left unbroken,
and many Spanish troops followed. After a running fight in
the streets of the city, in which some of the inhabitants took
part, the garrison was completely driven out, and fled by the
Carmona Gate towards Alcala. The victors captured two field-
pieces, about 200 prisoners [2], and a rich convoy of plunder,
which was to have been escorted by the French rearguard [3].
Villatte's column, approaching the city in its march from the

---

[1] Toreno (iii. p. 151) and other historians tell the tale how Downie,
finding that none of his men had followed him, though they had reached
the other side of the cut, flung back to them his sword, which was the
rapier of the *Conquistador* Pizarro, presented to him by a descendant of
that great adventurer. It was caught and saved, and he recovered it, for
he was left behind by the French a few miles from Seville, because of his
wounds. They stripped him and left him by the wayside, where he was
found and cared for by the pursuing Spaniards.

[2] The defence of Seville seems mainly to have been by the French
63rd Ligne, which lost eight officers in the fight.

[3] For a curious story of the contents of a captured carriage, which turned
out to be stuffed with silver plate, see the Memoirs of Harley of the 47th,
ii. p. 24.

Cadiz Lines and Xeres, found it in the hands of the allies, so swerved off eastward and followed Soult, picking up the expelled garrison by the way.

Cruz Murgeon and Skerrett did not pursue, not thinking themselves strong enough to meddle with the French, but only sent their cavalry forward to watch their retreat. They stayed in Seville, where the Cadiz Constitution was proclaimed with great enthusiasm on August 29th. On the other flank of the French Ballasteros was trying at this moment to molest the column formed by the garrisons retiring from Ronda, Malaga, and Antequera on Granada. He followed them for ten days, and fought their rearguard at Antequera on September 3rd, and at Loja on September 5th ; but though he captured many stragglers and some baggage, as also three guns, he was unable to do any material harm to the main body, which General Sémélé brought in to join Leval at Granada on September 6th.

Soult, meanwhile, with the troops from Cadiz and Seville, had to halt at Cordova for some days, to allow of the junction of Drouet from Estremadura ; for that general had to collect his troops and to bring down detachments from places so far away as Don Benito and Zalamea, before he could concentrate and march across the Sierra Morena to join his chief. Drouet had kept up a bold countenance in front of Hill to the last moment, even after he had received orders from Soult to prepare for a sudden retreat. Indeed one of the most lively of the many cavalry affairs fought in Estremadura during the summer of 1812 took place in August. On the 1st of that month, when Hill was already expecting that the news of Salamanca would have driven his opponent away, Pierre Soult tried a raid upon Ribera, with two regiments of cavalry and two battalions, and drove in the 2nd Hussars of the Legion, who maintained a long and gallant skirmishing fight, till General Erskine came up with Long's brigade, when the French retreated. Erskine was thought to have missed a fine opportunity of cutting up the raiding detachment by his slow and tentative pursuit[1]. On

[1] 'Confound all spiritless and dilatory generals,' writes Swabey of the R.A. in his diary, ' . . . Sir W. E. actually halted while four squadrons and 400 infantry were doing what they liked in Ribera, though he had the Hussars, the 9th and 13th Light Dragoons, the 3rd Dragoon Guards and our guns, and he might have had the 71st regiment also, though it did not

the 18th Soult made another reconnaissance in force, with four regiments, in the same direction, on a false report that Hill had moved from Ribera and Almendralejo. This brought on another long day of bickering, with no definite result : it was mainly remembered afterwards for the courteous behaviour of Drouet in sending back unharmed Erskine's aide-de-camp Strenowitz, the most daring officer for raids and reconnaissance work in the German Legion. He had been captured while scouting, and a general fear prevailed that he would be shot, for he had served for a short time in the French army, and might have been treated as a deserter. Drouet most handsomely dispatched him to the British camp on parole, with a request that he might be exchanged for an officer of his own, who had been taken a few days before. ' A most courteous and liberal enemy ! ' wrote a diarist in Hill's camp, ' Strenowitz's exploits are well known : certainly in strict law he might have been hung[1].'

It was not till August 26th that all the French troops in front of Hill suddenly vanished, Drouet having had orders to keep his position till Seville was ready to be evacuated ; for Soult feared that if he withdrew his forces in Estremadura too early, in the direction of Cordova, the allied troops might make a forced march on Seville, and arrive there before the divisions from the Cadiz Lines had gone by. Wherefore Drouet was in evidence before Hill till the precise day when Soult left Seville. He then retired through the Sierra Morena, going by the remote mountain road by Belalcazar with such speed that he reached Cordova on the fourth day (August 30). He was not pursued by Hill, whose orders from Wellington were to come up to the Tagus and join the main army, and not to involve himself in operations in Andalusia. Only some of Penne Villemur's Spanish horse, under the German colonel Schepeler—one of the best historians of the war—followed on Drouet's track, and saw him join Soult at Cordova[2]. The

arrive till all was over. The transaction was calculated to dispirit the soldier, to discontent the officers, and to take away all confidence in the general.'

[1] Swabey's diary, p. 307. There is an interesting account of Strenowitz's capture and release in Espinchal's *Mémoires*, ii. pp. 36–40, as also of the long skirmish of this day.

[2] Schepeler says that he scared the French rearguard out of Cordova on

united French force then marched on Granada, where the
garrisons of eastern Andalusia, under Leval, had concentrated to
meet the Marshal. Up to this moment Soult had been uncertain
whether he should retreat by way of La Mancha, or across the
kingdom of Murcia. His decision was settled for him by news
brought by Drouet, who had heard in Estremadura of King
Joseph's evacuation of Madrid and Toledo. Since the Army
of the Centre was now known to be on the road for Valencia,
to join Suchet, it would be too dangerous to cross La Mancha
in search of it. Wellington might descend from Madrid in
force, upon an enemy who dared to march across his front.
Wherefore Soult resolved that his retreat must be made across
the kingdom of Murcia. It was true that O'Donnell's army was
in occupation of the inland in that direction, but it was weak
and disorganized. Moreover, Suchet had lately inflicted a
severe defeat upon it at Castalla (on July 21st), and O'Donnell
was practically a negligible quantity in the problem. A far
more important factor in determining Soult's exact route was
the news that the yellow fever had broken out at Cartagena
and was spreading inland : it had reached the city of Murcia.
Wherefore the French army avoided the coast, and took the
inferior roads across the northern part of the province.

Soult, when once he had concentrated 45,000 men at Granada,
had nothing to fear from any enemy. The gloomy picture of
'a retreat harrassed by 60,000 foes,' with which he had tried
to scare King Joseph a month before, turned out to be a work
of pure imagination. Hill had turned off towards the Tagus :
Cruz Murgeon and Skerrett remained at Seville, awaiting the
appearance of the 10,000 men left in Cadiz. But these were
slow to move, because they had been on garrison duty for long
years, and had to provide themselves with transport. Only
Ballasteros hung about Granada, bickering with the outposts
of the French army, and as he had no more than 5,000 or
6,000 men he was not dangerous, but only tiresome.

Soult therefore was able to spend many days at Granada,
making deliberate preparations for the toilsome march that
was before him. He only started out, after destroying the

September 3 by lighting fires along the mountain slopes, and giving out
that Hill was behind him with his army. See p. 666 of his history.

fortifications of the Alhambra and other posts, on September 16th. His route was by Baza, Huescar, Caravaca, and Hellin, through a mountainous and thinly-peopled country, where his troops suffered considerable privations. But these were nothing compared to the misery of the immense convoy of *Afrancesados* of all ages and both sexes, who had joined themselves to his train, and had to be brought through to a place of safety. Nor did the 6,000 sick and wounded whom he was dragging with him enjoy a pleasant journey. Yet it was only the September heat and the mountain roads that harassed the army and its train : Ballasteros did not pursue farther than the borders of Andalusia : the Murcians were cowed by the approach of a force which could have destroyed them with ease if it had lingered within their borders. Some of them shifted north toward Madrid, others south toward Alicante : none did anything to attract the notice of such a formidable enemy. Touch with Suchet's outposts was secured before September was quite ended, and by the appearance of the whole Army of Andalusia near Valencia, a new military situation was produced by October 1st. With this we shall have to deal in its proper place—the fortunes of Wellington and the main army of the allies have not been followed beyond the middle of August.

Summing up the events of June–July–August 1812 in southern Spain, it is impossible to avoid the conclusion that Soult's personal interests wrecked any chance that the French might have had of retaining their dominant position in the Peninsula, when once Wellington had committed himself to his offensive campaign upon the Tormes and the Douro. If the Duke of Dalmatia had obeyed in June King Joseph's peremptory orders to send Drouet to Toledo, he would have had, no doubt, to evacuate certain parts of Andalusia. But Joseph and Jourdan could have marched many weeks earlier, and with a doubled force, to interfere with Wellington's campaign against Marmont. It is true that Hill would have made a corresponding movement by Alcantara, and would have joined the main allied army under his chief many days before the King and Drouet would have been able to link up with Marmont. But Hill, on leaving Estremadura, would have removed the larger and more efficient part of his corps from Soult's vicinity, and the Marshal might easily have held Seville and the Cadiz Lines, when faced by no stronger enemies than Ballasteros and the garrison in the Isla. If Soult had made up his mind to sacrifice Andalusia, and had marched with his whole army on Toledo, in June or even early in July, Wellington's whole game would have been wrecked. It was, perhaps, too much to expect that the Marshal would consent to such a disinterested policy. But if, without making this sacrifice, he had merely obeyed King Joseph, and reinforced the Army of the Centre at an early date, he would have made the Salamanca campaign impossible. Wellington would probably have retired behind the Agueda and abandoned his conquests in Leon, without risking a battle, if the French forces in contact with him had been 25,000 men stronger than they actually were. The junction of Hill and some 12,000 men of the best of his Estremaduran detachment would have given him the power to fight out a defensive campaign on the Portuguese frontier, but hardly to deliver an offensive battle like Salamanca. The net results of all his manœuvres in June would then have been no more than an indirect success—the delivery of eastern Andalusia from Soult. Seville and the Cadiz Lines might still have remained occupied by the French.

It is scarcely necessary to repeat once more that Soult's counter-plan of inviting the King and the Army of the Centre to retire to Andalusia, throwing up all communication with France and the imperial armies beyond the Douro, was wrong-headed in the extreme, though Napier calls it 'grand and vigorous [1].' Joseph could have brought no more than the 15,000 men that he owned, and they, when added to the 50,000 men of the Army of the South, would not have provided a force large enough to make a decisive move. For, as we have already seen, half the French in Andalusia were necessarily pinned down to garrison duties, and the 'containing' of Ballasteros and other partisans. Soult could never bring more than 25,000 men of his own into Estremadura: if 15,000 more are added for King Joseph's troops [2], only 40,000 in all would have been

---

[1] Napier, iv. p. 371.

[2] Soult suggested that the less efficient of Joseph's troops should go on garrison duty, and set free a corresponding number of his own best battalions.

available for a demonstration (or a serious invasion) in the direction of Portugal. Such a force would have given Wellington no very great alarm. It would have had to begin by besieging Badajoz and Elvas, in face of the existing ' containing ' army under Hill, a delicate business, and one that would have taken time. Meanwhile Wellington could have come down, with reinforcements strong enough to make up a total sufficient to fight and beat 40,000 men, since he had the advantage of a central position and the shorter roads. At the worst he would have blocked the French advance by taking up an unassailable position, as he had before on the Caya in June 1811. But now he would have had a far superior game in his hands, since Badajoz was his and not his enemy's, and his total disposable force was considerably larger than it had been in 1811.

Thus, if Soult's plan had been carried out, all central Spain, including the capital, would have been lost just as much as it was by the actual campaign of July–August 1812, and the disorganized Army of Portugal could have done nothing. For Wellington could have left not Clinton's one division (as he actually did) but three at least to look after it—not to speak of the Galicians and the *partidas*. Isolated and cut off from all communication with other French armies, Soult and the King would have had to evacuate Andalusia in the end, if they did not suffer a worse fate—a crushing defeat in a position from which there would have been no retreat possible. Hypothetical reconstructions of campaigns which might have happened are proverbially futile—but it is hard to see how any final profit to the French could have come from Soult's extraordinary plan.

SECTION XXXIII: CHAPTER XI

THE TWO DIVERSIONS: (1) OPERATIONS IN THE NORTH:
SIR HOME POPHAM AND CAFFARELLI. (2) OPERATIONS
IN THE EAST: SUCHET, O'DONNELL, AND MAITLAND.
JUNE–AUGUST 1812

IT has already been made clear that the whole of Wellington's victorious advance, from Ciudad Rodrigo to Madrid, was rendered possible by the fact that he had only to deal with the Army of Portugal, succoured when it was too late by the Army of the Centre. If Caffarelli and his 35,000 men of the Army of the North had been able to spare any help for Marmont, beyond the single cavalry brigade of Chauvel, matters must have taken a very different turn from the first, and the Douro (if not the Tormes) must have been the limit of the activity of the Anglo-Portuguese army. How Caffarelli was to be detained, according to Wellington's plan, has been explained in an earlier chapter[1]. The working out of the scheme must now be described.

The essential duty of the French Army of the North was twofold, according to Napoleon's general conception of the Spanish war. It was Marmont's reserve, bound to assist him in time of trouble; but it was also the force of occupation for the Biscayan provinces, Navarre, Santander, and Burgos. Of its 35,000 men more than half were at all times immobilized in the innumerable garrisons which protected the high-road from Bayonne to Burgos, and the small harbours of the coast, from San Sebastian to Santoña. The system of posts was complicated and interdependent. Since the great guerrillero Mina started on his busy career in 1810, it had been necessary that there should be fortified places at short intervals, in which convoys moving to or from France (whether by Vittoria and San Sebastian, or by Pampeluna and Roncesvalles) could take

---

[1] See above, pp. 340–1.

refuge when attacked by the bands.   And since a convoy, when it had sought shelter in one of the minor garrisons, might be blockaded there indefinitely, unless the high-road were cleared betimes, large movable columns had to be ready in three or four of the larger places.   Their duty was to march out on the first alarm, and sweep the guerrilleros away from any post that they might have beset.   Such bodies were to be found at Bayonne, where the ' Reserve of the Army of Spain ' kept a brigade of 3,500 men under General D'Aussenac to watch for any exceptional outbreak of trouble in Guipuzcoa ; at Pampeluna, where General Abbé had the head-quarters of his division ; and at Vittoria, where the General-in-Chief, Caffarelli himself, normally lay with the brigade of Dumoustier—the last unit of the Imperial Guard still remaining in Spain—ready to keep the line of the Ebro under surveillance, and to communicate when necessary with the three large outlying garrisons of Santoña, Santander, and Burgos.   Each of these last consisted of some 1,300 or 1,500 men[1]; even so, they were only strong enough to provide for their own safety in normal times, and might require assistance from head-quarters in face of any specially large and threatening combination of the insurgents. But the larger half of Caffarelli's army was locked up in small towns, forts, and blockhouses, in bodies ranging down from a battalion to half a company.   Every one of the dozen little ports on the Biscay coast had to be held, in order to prevent the bands of the inland from communicating with the English cruisers, which occasionally appeared in the offing to throw weapons and ammunition ashore.   And similarly all the little towns along the Ebro had to be garrisoned, in order to keep touch with Reille at Saragossa ; wherever there was a gap Mina's Navarrese slipped in between.

Since the autumn of 1810, when Porlier and Renovales had made their vain attempt, with British naval aid, to break up the line of communication along the coast,[2] there had been no general attempt to shake the French occupation of Biscay

---

[1] In and about Santander, 2 battalions of the 130th, 2 squadrons of gendarmes, &c.   In Santona, 93 officers and 1,382 men of the 28th, 75th, and 34th.   In Burgos, 2 battalions of 34th Line.

[2] See vol. iii. pp. 486–7.

and Cantabria. The Spanish resources were at a low ebb whenever Bonnet held the Asturias, and (as we have seen) he was generally in possession of that province, or at least of its capital and its chief harbours, from 1810 down to the summer of 1812. The idea of attacking the harbour-fortresses of the northern coast with a considerable naval force, which should get into regular touch with the patriot forces of the inland, and establish posts to be held permanently on suitable points of the northern littoral, had been started by Sir Home Popham, approved by Sir Howard Douglas, the British Commissioner in Galicia, and warmly adopted by Wellington himself, who at once realized the pressure which such a policy would bring upon Caffarelli. He counted upon this diversion as one of his most valuable assets, when he drew up his scheme for the invasion of Leon in May 1812. It more than fulfilled his expectation.

On June 17th, four days after the Anglo-Portuguese army crossed the Agueda, Sir Home Popham sailed from Corunna with two line of battleships [1], five frigates [2], two sloops [3], and one or two smaller vessels, carrying two battalions of marines, and several thousand stand of small-arms for the insurgents. Popham had credentials from Castaños, as captain-general of Galicia, for Mendizabal, the officer who was supposed to exercise authority over all the bands of Cantabria and Biscay. These scattered forces consisted in the more or less organized brigades of Porlier in the Eastern Asturias, and Longa in Cantabria—both of which were reckoned part of the national army—and in addition of the guerrilleros of Jauregui [' El Pastor '] in Guipuzcoa, Renovales in Biscay, Marquinez, Saornil, the Curé Merino, and others in the mountains between the Douro and the sea. These were bands of varying strength, often scattered by the French, but always reassembled after a space, who roamed from region to region according as the enemy was stronger or weaker at one point or another. Occasionally Mendizabal was in touch with Mina and the Navarrese,

[1] The *Venerable* (his flag-ship) and the *Magnificent*. The *Magnificent* went home with prisoners some weeks later, and was replaced for a time by the *Abercrombie*, from the Brest blockading squadron.

[2] *Medusa, Isis, Diadem, Surveillante,* and *Rhin.* The *Belle Poule* looked in for a short time later in the season.

[3] *Sparrow* and *Lyra.*

but generally the French were in too great force about the
high-road from Burgos to Pampeluna to make co-operation
practicable.

At the moment of Popham's start matters were exceptionally
favourable along the Biscay coast, because Bonnet was just
evacuating the Asturias, in order to join his chief Marmont in
the plains of Leon.   His departure isolated Santoña and
Santander, which had been the links by which he was joined
to Caffarelli's army.   It also gave Porlier and Longa an open
communication with Galicia, from which they had hitherto
been cut off by Bonnet's presence in Asturias, and a safe retreat
thitherward if they should be pressed.   In addition Marmont
had called up all the small garrisons and detached columns
from his rear, for the main struggle with Wellington ; so that
the Upper Douro valley and the Soria country were much more
free from the French than they had been for a long time.   The
opportunity for molesting Caffarelli and his much-scattered
Army of the North was unique.

The idea which lay at the back of Popham's plan was that
a fleet furnished with the heaviest ship guns, and with a landing-
force of over 1,000 men, could operate at its choice against
any one of the long chain of posts which the French held,
calling in to its aid the local bands in each case.   The insurgents
had never been able to capture any of these places because they
lacked a battering-train.   The fleet supplied this want, and
with few exceptions the French strongholds were not suited
for resistance against heavy guns.   They were mediaeval castles,
fortified convents, or the patched-up walls of little towns, all
defensible against irregular bands without cannon, but most
vulnerable to 18- or 24-pounders.   The number of the French
garrisons gave ample liberty of choice between one and another :
individually they were generally weak—not over 300, 500, or
1,000 men.   There were succouring columns, no doubt, ready
to relieve them, at Bayonne and Vittoria and elsewhere.   But
the squadron had the power of misleading these forces to any
extent—of drawing them from one remote port to another by
false attacks and demonstrations, and then of attacking some
third point when the enemy had been lured as far as possible
from it.   Here lay the beauty of naval operations—the squadron

could appear to threaten any objective that it chose, could attract the enemy thither, and then could vanish, and be fifty miles away next day. The relieving column could only follow slowly over mountain roads, and would invariably be late in learning what new direction the squadron had taken. It was something like the advantage that the Danes had in their attacks on England in the ninth century : a defending army cannot guard all points of a coast-line at once against a movable landing force on shipboard. The weaker points of the scheme were, firstly, the dependence of all operations on fine weather— contrary winds could in those days delay a fleet for whole weeks on end ; secondly, the want of a base nearer than Corunna, till some good and defensible haven should have been captured ; and third and greatest of all, the difficulty of inducing the local chiefs to combine : they paid a very limited amount of obedience to their nominal chief, Mendizabal : they had private grievances and jealousies against each other : and each of them disliked moving far from the particular region where his men were raised, and where every inch of the mountain roads was known to him.

However, all these dangers were known and were chanced, and the game was well worth the risk. The operations began with the appearance of the squadron before Lequeitio on June 21st. Popham landed a heavy gun and some marines, and the band of El Pastor [' Don Gaspar ' as the English dispatches call him] appeared to co-operate from the inland. The defences consisted of a fort and a fortified convent : the 24-pounder breached the former, which was then stormed by the guerrilleros in a very handsome fashion [1] : its garrison was slain or captured. The gun was then brought up against the fortified convent, whose commander, the *chef de bataillon* Gillort, surrendered without further fighting ; the prisoners amounted to 290 men, a half-battalion of the 119th regiment (June 22). Popham then moved off to Bermeo and Plencia, both of which the French evacuated in haste, leaving guns unspiked and some useful stores of provisions. The British force had set the

---

[1] So says Popham in his dispatch at the Record Office : though Napier (iv. p. 246) says that the Spaniards attacked and were repulsed. But Popham must have known best ! Sir Howard Douglas corroborates him, *Life*, p. 168.

wildest rumours abroad, and Renovales, the Spanish commander in Biscay, appeared at Orduña with his bands and threatened Bilbao, the capital of the province. It was these reports which made Caffarelli suddenly break off his project for sending reinforcements to Marmont, and prepare rather to march northward when he was most wanted on the Douro [1].

Popham's next blow was at Guetaria, a most important post, owing to its nearness to the great *chaussée* leading to Bayonne, which passes quite close to it between Tolosa and Ernani. If it had fallen, the main road from France to Spain would have been blocked for all practical purposes. But being far to the East and near the French border, it was remote from the haunts of the guerrilleros : few of them turned up : after a few days Popham had to re-embark guns and men, and to take his departure, owing to the arrival in his neighbourhood of a strong French flying column. He then sailed off to Castro Urdiales, where he had much better luck : Longa had left the Upper Ebro with his brigade and joined him there on July 6th, by Mendizabal's orders. Their united force drove off on the 7th a small French column which came up from Laredo to raise the siege. The governor of Castro then surrendered with some 150 men, and 20 guns on his walls fell into Popham's hands (July 8). The place seemed so strong that the commodore resolved to keep it as a temporary base, and garrisoned it with some of his marines.

Three days later Popham appeared before Portugalete, the fortified village at the mouth of the Bilbao river, and bombarded it from the side of the sea, while Longa (who had marched parallel with the squadron along the shore), demonstrated against its rear. But a French flying column happened just to have arrived at Bilbao, and the force which marched out against the assailants was so powerful that they made off, each on his own element [July 11th.] Popham now turned his attention for a second time to the important strategical post of Guetaria ; he had enlisted the support of the Guipuzcoan bands under Jauregui, and the distant Mina had promised to send a battalion to his aid from Navarre. Popham got heavy guns on shore, and began to batter the place, while Jauregui

[1] See above, p. 378.

blockaded it on the land side. This move drew the attention of D'Aussenac, commanding the flying column which belonged to the Bayonne reserve : he marched with 3,000 men towards Guetaria, and drove off Jauregui, whereupon Popham had to re-embark in haste, and lost two guns which could not be got off in time and thirty men [July 19]. Mina's battalion came up a day too late to help the discomfited besiegers.

This petty disaster was in the end more favourable than harmful to Popham's general plan, for he had succeeded in drawing all the attention of the French to the eastern end of their chain of coast-fortresses, between Santoña and San Sebastian. But now he used his power of rapid movement to attack unexpectedly their most important western stronghold. On July 22nd he appeared in front of the harbour of Santander, while (by previous arrangement) Campillo—one of Porlier's lieutenants—invested it on the land side. Porlier himself, with his main body, was blockading at the moment the not very distant and still stronger Santoña.

There was very heavy fighting round Santander between the 22nd July and August 2. Popham landed guns on the water-girt rock of Mouro, and bombarded from it the castle at the mouth of the port : when its fire was subdued, he ran his squadron in battle order past it, and entered the harbour, receiving little damage from the other French works (July 24). The enemy then evacuated the castle, which the marines occupied : but an attempt to storm the town with the aid of Campillo's men failed, with a rather heavy casualty list of two British captains [1] and many marines and seamen disabled (July 27th). However, Popham and Campillo held on in front of Santander, and Mendizabal came up on August 2nd to join them, bringing a captured French dispatch, which proved that the enemy intended to evacuate the place, a strong relieving column under Caffarelli himself being at hand to bring off the garrison. And this indeed happened : the General-in-Chief of the Army of the North had marched with all the disposable troops at Vittoria to save his detachment. The governor Dubreton—the same man who afterwards defended Burgos so well—broke out of the place with his 1,600 men on the night

---

[1] One of them, Sir George Collier, commanding the *Medusa*.

of the 2nd–3rd and joined his chief in safety : he left eighteen guns spiked in his works. Caffarelli then drew off the garrison of the neighbouring small post of Torrelavega, but threw a convoy and some reinforcements into Santoña, which he had determined to hold as long as possible. He then hastened back to Vittoria, being under the impression at the moment that Wellington was in march against him from Valladolid, in pursuit of the routed host of Clausel. But the Anglo-Portuguese main army—as will be remembered—had really followed the retreating French no farther than Valladolid, and no longer than the 30th July. Instead of finding himself involved in the affairs of the Army of Portugal, Caffarelli had soon another problem in hand.

The capture of Santander by the allies was the most important event that had happened on the north coast of Spain since 1809, for it gave the squadron of Popham possession of the sole really good harbour—open to the largest ships, and safe at all times of the year—which lies between Ferrol and the French frontier. At last the Spanish ' Seventh Army ' had a base behind it, and a free communication with England for the stores and munitions that it so much needed. It might be developed into a formidable force if so strengthened, and it lay in a position most inconvenient for the French, directly in the rear of Clausel and Caffarelli. Popham saw what might be made of Santander, and drew up for Wellington's benefit a report on the possibilities of the harbour, in which he details, from the information given by Porlier and his staff, the state of the roads between it and Burgos, Valladolid, and other points. Six weeks before the siege of Burgos began, he wrote that by all accounts six or eight heavy guns would be required to take that fortress, and that he could manage that they should be got there—a distance of 115 miles—by ox-draught, if they were wanted[1]. But Wellington, at the moment that this

---

[1] Popham's prescience is shown by the fact that his papers relating to Burgos began to be drawn up as early as July 26. He cross-questioned not only Porlier but other Spanish officers. Their answers did not always tally with each other. See all Popham's dispatches of the time, in the Admiralty Section at the Record Office—under the general head ' Channel Fleet ! ' They have this misleading heading because Popham was under Lord Keith, then commanding that fleet.

useful information was being compiled, was turning away from
Valladolid and Burgos toward Madrid ; and when his attention
was once more drawn back to Burgos, he made no use of
Popham's offers till it was too late. Of this more in its proper
place.

Having brought all his squadron into Santander, and made
himself a fixed base in addition to his floating one, Popham
began to concert plans for further operations with Mendizabal,
whom he described as a man of ' vacillating councils,' and
hard to screw up to any fixed resolution. The scheme which the
commodore most recommended to the general was one for
a general concentration of all his scattered forces against Bilbao,
in which the squadron should give its best help. But he
suggested as an alternative the sending of Porlier to join
Longa, who had already gone south to the Upper Ebro after
the failure at Portugalete on July 11th. Porlier and Longa
would together be strong enough to cut the road between
Burgos and Vittoria, and so divide Clausel from Caffarelli. If
the two French generals combined against them, they could
always escape north-westward into their usual mountain
refuges.

According to Popham's notes Mendizabal first seemed to
incline to the second scheme, and then decided for the first. He
even in the end ordered up Longa—then very usefully employed
against Clausel's rear about Pancorbo and Cubo—to join in the
attack upon Bilbao. But Longa came late, being busy in
operations that he liked better than those which his chief
imposed on him. After waiting a few days for him in vain,
Mendizabal marched against Bilbao by land with two battalions
belonging to Porlier and one recently raised in Alava, while
Popham took three Biscayan battalions belonging to Renovales
on board his squadron and sailed for Lequeitio, where he put
them ashore. He himself then made for Portugalete, at the
mouth of the Bilbao river. The triple attack, though made
with no very great total force was successful. The officer
commanding in Bilbao, went out to meet Mendizabal, and in
order to collect as many men as possible, drew off the garrison
of Portugalete. The British squadron, arriving in front of the
port, found it undefended and threw the marines ashore.

Hearing of this descent in his rear the French general, then indecisively engaged with Mendizabal and Renovales, thought that he was in danger of being surrounded, and retired hastily toward Durango, abandoning Bilbao altogether [August 13].

Learning next day that they had overrated the enemy's force, the French returned and tried to reoccupy the Biscayan capital, but were met outside by all Mendizabal's troops, arrayed on the position of Ollorgan. An attack entirely failed to move them, and the French fell back to Durango. General Rouget, the commanding officer in the province, then drew in all his minor garrisons, and sent Caffarelli notice that all Biscay was lost, unless something could be done at once to check Mendizabal's progress [August 14]. Indeed the situation looked most threatening, for Longa had at last come up and joined his chief with 3,000 men, and the Biscayans were taking arms on every side. A general junta of the Basque provinces was summoned by Mendizabal to meet at Bilbao, and the French had for the moment no foothold left save in San Sebastian and Guetaria. Thereupon Caffarelli, collecting every man that he could at Vittoria, marched to join Rouget. Their united forces, making some 7,000 men, attacked Bilbao on August 27th–29th, and after much confused fighting drove Mendizabal and Longa out of the place, only a fortnight after it had come into Spanish hands. The defeated troops dispersed in all directions, each section seeking the region that it had come from—Porlier's men retired towards Cantabria, Longa's toward the Upper Ebro. Renovales and his Biscayan battalions were caught in their retreat, and badly cut up at Dima.

While this fighting was going on around Bilbao, Popham was trying a last attack on Guetaria, with his own resources only, as nearly all the Spaniards were engaged elsewhere. He had accomplished nothing decisive when he heard of Mendizabal's defeat, and had to reship his guns and take his departure before the victorious Caffarelli came up. He retired to Santander, and heard there that Wellington was leaving Madrid, and once more marching on Burgos. He determined to open up communications with the British army without delay, and on August 31 sent off Lieutenant Macfarlane to seek for the head of the approaching columns. That officer, skirting the flank of Clausel's retreating host, reached Valladolid betimes, and explained to Wellington that the Santander road would be open and available for the transport of ammunition, guns, and even food, so soon as he should have driven the French past Burgos. And—as will be seen—it was so used during the unlucky siege of that fortress again and again—but not (as Popham recommended) for the bringing up of the heavy artillery that Wellington so much lacked.

By September 1st Caffarelli had patched up matters for a time on the side of Biscay, but though he had recovered Bilbao and preserved Guetaria, all the other coast-towns were out of his power save Santoña, and that important place was cut off from the nearest French garrison by a gap of some sixty miles. Even now Popham's useful diversion had not ceased to have its effect. But its further working belongs to a later chapter.

So much for the annals of the war in northern Spain from June to August. The diversion which Wellington had planned had been brilliantly successful. A very different story must be told of the equally important scheme that he had concerted for keeping his enemies distracted on the eastern side of the Peninsula, by means of the Anglo-Sicilian expedition and the Spanish Army of Murcia.

Suchet, it will be remembered[1], had been stayed from further conquests after the fall of Valencia partly by the indirect results of Wellington's operations on the Portuguese frontier—starting with the fall of Ciudad Rodrigo—partly by Napoleon's action in drawing back to the Ebro the two divisions of Reille, and calling out of Spain the numerous Polish battalions serving in the Army of Aragon. But not the least of the hindering causes was a purely personal one—the long illness which kept Suchet confined to his bed for ten weeks in February, March, and April. By the time that he was in the saddle again a notable change had come over the aspect of the war all over the Peninsula. During his sickness his lieutenants, Habert and Harispe, maintained their position in front of the Xucar river, and observed the wrecks of the Valencian and Murcian divisions that had escaped from Blake's disaster in January. The whole

<hr>

[1] See above, p. 86.

force remaining under Suchet—excluding the troops left behind in Catalonia and Aragon—was not above 15,000 men, and of these nearly 4,000 were locked up in garrisons, at Valencia, Saguntum, Peniscola, Morella, and other places. It is not surprising, therefore, that no farther advance was made against the Spaniards. Joseph O'Donnell, the successor of the unlucky Mahy, was able during the spring to reorganize some 12,000 men on the *cadres* of his old battalions. In addition he had Roche's reserve at Alicante, 4,000 strong, which had now been profiting for many months by the British subsidy and training, and was reckoned a solid corps. He had also Bassecourt's few battalions in the inland—the troops that D'Armagnac had hunted in December and January in the district about Requeña [1]. Cartagena, the only fortress on the coast still in Spanish hands save Alicante, had been strengthened by the arrival of a British detachment [2]. Altogether there were some 20,000 enemies facing Suchet in April, and he regarded it as impossible to think of attacking Alicante, since he had not nearly enough men in hand to besiege a place of considerable size, and at the same time to provide a sufficient covering army against Joseph O'Donnell. So little was the Murcian army molested that General Freire, O'Donnell's second-in-command, ignoring Suchet altogether, took advantage of Soult's absence in Estremadura, at the time of the fall of Badajoz, to alarm eastern Andalusia. He occupied Baza on April 18th, and when driven away after a time by Leval, governor of Granada, turned instead against the coast-land of the South. On May 11th an expedition, aided by English war-ships from Alicante, landed near Almeria, and cleared out all the French garrisons from the small towns and shore batteries as far west as Almunecar. Already before this (on May 1–3) an English squadron had made a descent on Malaga, seized and destroyed the harbour-works, and carried off some privateers and merchant vessels from the port. But naught could be accomplished against the citadel of Gibalfaro. Soult did little or nothing to resent these insults, because he was at the time obsessed

----

[1] See above, p. 56.

[2] The 2/67th and a part of the foreign Regiment of de Watteville, also a British battery, from Cadiz.

with his ever-recurring idea that Wellington was about to invade Andalusia, and his attention was entirely taken up with the movements of Hill and Ballasteros in the West and North, so that the East was neglected. Leval at Granada had a troublesome time, but was in no real danger, since Freire's raids were executed with a trifling force.

Suchet was occupied at this time more with civil than with military affairs : for some time after his convalescence he was engaged in rearranging the administration of the kingdom of Valencia, and in raising the enormous war-contribution which Napoleon had directed him to exact—200,000,000 reals, or £2,800,000—in addition to the ordinary taxes. The Marshal in his *Mémoires* gives a most self-laudatory account of his rule ; according to his rose-coloured narrative [1], the imposts were raised with wisdom and benevolence, the population became contented and even loyal, the roads were safe, and material prosperity commenced at once to revive. Napier has reproduced most of Suchet's testimonials to his own wisdom and integrity, without any hint that the Spanish version of the story is different. The Marshal who drove the civil population of Lerida under the fire of the cannon [2], and who signalized his entry into Valencia by wholesale executions of combatants and non-combatants [3], was not the benevolent being of his own legend. Since that legend has been republished in many a later volume, it may be well to give as a fair balance the version of an enemy—not of a Spaniard, but of a Prussian, that Colonel Schepeler whose authority on the war of Valencia we have so often had occasion to quote.

' Napoleon Bonaparte looked upon Valencia as the prey of France, and Suchet did not fall behind in his oppressive high-handedness. The long-desired goal, the wealthy city, now lay open to their rapacity, and the riches that the clergy had denied to the needs of the nation went to fill the plunder-bag of the conqueror. The miraculous statue of Our Lady of Pity was stripped of her ancient jewelled robe : only a light mantle now draped her, and showed the cut of the nineteenth century. The silver apostles of the cathedral took their way to France

---

[1] See *Mémoires*, ii. pp. 283–99.   [2] See vol. iii. p. 307.

[3] See above, p. 75.

with many other objects of value, and the Chapter was forced to pay ransom for hidden treasures. The magnanimous marshal imposed on the new French province, as a sort of "benevolence," six million dollars (ten had been spoken of at first), with an additional million for the city of Valencia. The churches had to buy off their bells with another 60,000 dollars. Suchet, in his moderation, contented himself with exacting 500 dollars a day for his own table and household expenses.

'Political persecution began with a decree of March 11, which ordered the judges of the local *Audiencia* [Law Court] to meet as before, but to administer justice in the name of Napoleon *Empereur et Roi*. The patriots refused to serve and fled; whereupon their goods were confiscated, their families were harried, and when some of them were captured they were threatened with penal servitude or death. A decree drawn up in words of cold ferocity, declared every Spaniard who continued to oppose the French to be a rebel and a brigand, and therefore condemned to capital punishment. Several villages were punished with fire and sword, because they were too patriotic to arrest and deliver up insurgents. Contrary to the promise made at the capitulation in January [1], many patriots were arrested and executed, under the pretence that they had been concerned in the murder of Frenchmen in 1808, even though they might actually have saved the lives of certain of those unfortunates at that time.

'Valencia produces little wheat: there was much lack of it, and the French would not accept rice. Their requisitions were exacted with cruel disregard of consequences, even from the poorest, and quickly brought back to the patriotic side the mutable Valencian people, who had already been sufficiently embittered when they found that they were annexed to France. All over the province there began to appear slaughter, rebellion, and finally guerrillero bands [2].'

The point which Schepeler makes as to Valencia being practically annexed to France—as shown by the administration of justice in the name of Napoleon, not of King Joseph—should be noted. It illustrates Suchet's determination to consider himself as a French viceroy, rather than as the general of one

[1] See p. 73 above. [2] Schepeler, pp. 609–10.

of the armies recently placed by the Emperor under the King as Commander-in-Chief in the Peninsula. We have already noted the way in which he contrived to plead special orders from Paris, exempting him from the royal control, whenever Joseph tried to borrow some of his troops for use against Wellington[1]. At the same time it must be conceded that he had a much better excuse than Soult for his persistent disobedience to such orders—his whole available force was so small, that if he had sent 6,000 men to San Clemente or Ocaña, as Joseph directed, there would have been little or nothing left in Valencia save the garrisons, and the Spaniards from Alicante and Murcia could have taken their revenge for the disasters of the past winter[2]. He represented to the King that to draw off such a body of troops to La Mancha implied the abandonment of all his recent conquests, and that if something had to be evacuated, it was better that Soult should begin the process, since Andalusia was a more outlying possession than Valencia— 'les provinces du sud devaient être évacuées avant celles de l'est.' And here he was no doubt right : as we have been remarking again and again, the only solution for the situation created by Wellington's successes was to concentrate a great mass of troops at all costs, and the Army of the South could best provide that mass. It had 50,000 men under arms at the moment—Suchet had not in Valencia more than 15,000.

Hitherto we have spoken of those parts of the east coast of Spain which lie south of the Ebro. But if the situation in Valencia had not altered much between February and June, the same was also the case in Catalonia. Since Eroles's victory over Bourke at Roda in March[3] there had been much marching and counter-marching in that principality, but nothing decisive. Lacy, the unpopular captain-general, was at odds with the Junta, and especially with Eroles, the best of his divisional officers, who was the most influential man in Catalonia, owing to his local connexions and his untiring energy. Lacy was a stranger, an enemy of the 'Somaten' system, and a pronounced Liberal. The political tendencies of the Catalans were

[1] See above, pp. 304–5.

[2] This is Suchet's own view, see his *Mémoires*, ii. p. 251.

[3] See above, p. 98.

distinctly favourable to the other or 'Servile' party. The captain-general was also accused of nourishing jealousy against Sarsfield, his second-in-command : and it is certain that both that officer and Eroles believed him capable of any mean trick toward them. But though divided counsels and mutual suspicions often hindered the co-operation of the commanders and the people, all were equally bitter enemies of the invader, and none of them showed any signs of slackening in their grim resolve to hold out to the end. The Catalan army did not now count more than 8,000 men in the field, but its central position in the mountains of the interior, round which the French garrisons were dispersed in a long semicircle, gave it advantages that compensated to a certain extent for its lack of numbers. It could strike out at any isolated point on the circumference, and, whether its blow failed or succeeded, generally got off before the enemy had concentrated in sufficient numbers to do it much harm. On the other hand, Decaen, now commanding in Catalonia, and Maurice Mathieu, the governor of Barcelona, though they had some three times as many men under arms as Lacy, were reduced to a position that was little more than defensive. It is true that they occasionally collected a heavy column and struck into the inland : but the enemy avoided them, and replied by counter-attacks on depleted sections of the French circle of garrisons. On April 9th, for example, 4,800 men marched from Gerona against Olot : the local levies under Claros and Rovira skirmished with them, giving ground, and finally losing the town. But though they did not stop the advance of the enemy, Milans, with a larger force, moved on the important harbour of Mataro, and laid siege to the garrison there (April 22), a stroke which soon brought the bulk of French troops back from Olot to drive him off. At the same time Sarsfield's division pressed in upon the garrison of Tarragona, and cut off its communications with Barcelona.

This forced Decaen to march to open the road, with all the men that Maurice Mathieu could spare from Barcelona (April 28). Letting them go by, Lacy at once renewed the attack on Mataro, bringing up the forces of Sarsfield and Milans, and borrowing four ship-guns from Commodore Codrington to batter the fort, in which the French had taken refuge after evacuating

the town [May 3]. Decaen and Lamarque promptly turned
back, and on the third day of the siege came hastily to break
it up. The Spaniards dispersed in various directions, after
burying the guns, which (much to Codrington's regret) were
discovered and exhumed by the enemy. The net result of all
this marching and counter-marching was that much shoe-
leather had been worn out, and a few hundred men killed or
wounded on each side : but certainly no progress had been made
in the conquest of Catalonia. Indeed, Manso, at the end of the
campaign, established himself at Molins de Rey, quite close to
Barcelona, and Sarsfield occupied Montserrat, so that between
them they once more cut off the communications from Barcelona southward and westward. Both had to be driven off
in June, in order that the roads might again be opened.

Early in July Lacy devised a scheme which made him more
hated than ever in Catalonia. He concerted with some Spanish
employés in the French commissariat service a plan for blowing
up the powder magazine of the great fortress of Lerida, and
arranged to be outside its walls on the day fixed for the explosion,
and to storm it during the confusion that would follow. Eroles
and Sarsfield both protested, pointing out that a whole quarter
of the city must be destroyed, with great loss of life. Lacy
replied that the results would justify the sacrifice, persisted in
his scheme, and moved with every available man towards
Lerida to be ready on the appointed day. He miscalculated
his hours, however ; and, though he left hundreds of stragglers
behind from over-marching, his column arrived too late. The
explosion took place on the 16th, with dreadful success ; not
only did a hundred of the garrison perish, but a much larger
number of the citizens ; many houses and one of the bastions
fell. The governor Henriod, a very firm-handed man whose
record in Lerida was most tyrannical [1], had been entirely
unaware of the approach of the Spaniards, but proved equal
to the occasion. He put his garrison under arms, manned the
breach, and showed such a firm front, when Lacy appeared,
that the captain-general, having tired troops and no cannon,
refused to attempt the storm. He went off as quickly as he

---

[1] See notes in Vidal de la Blache's *L'Evacuation d'Espagne*, 1914, which
reaches me just as this goes to press, for anecdotes concerning his doings.

had come, having caused the death of several hundred of his countrymen with no profit whatever. If he was ready to adopt such terrible means, he should at least have had his plans correctly timed. The Catalans never forgave him the useless atrocity [1].

Operations in Catalonia and Valencia were thus dragging on with no great profit to one side or the other, when Wellington's great scheme for the Anglo-Sicilian diversion on the east coast began at last to work, and—as he had expected—set a new face to affairs. Unfortunately the expedition was conducted very differently from his desire. We have already shown how, by Lord William Bentinck's perversity, it started too late, and was far weaker than was originally intended [2]. But on July 15th General Maitland arrived at Port Mahon with a fleet carrying three English [3] and two German battalions, and parts of three foreign regiments, with a handful of cavalry, and two companies of artillery. He sent messengers across Spain to announce to Wellington his arrival, and his purpose of landing in Catalonia, as had been directed. At Majorca he picked up Whittingham's newly-organized Balearic division, and after some delay he set sail on July 28 for Palamos, a central point on the Catalan coast, off which he arrived on the morning of July 31st with over 10,000 men on board.

[1] About the same time a still more dreadful plot was said to have been formed in Barcelona, with the knowledge and approval of Lacy—arsenic was to be mixed with the flour of the garrison's rations by secret agents. [See Suchet's *Mémoires*, ii. p. 256, and Arteche, xii. p. 353.] How far the plan was a reality is difficult to decide. There is a large file of papers in the Paris War Office concerning experiments carried out by a commission of army-doctors, in consequence of a sudden outbreak of sickness among the troops in July. One or two soldiers died, a great number were seized with vomiting and stomach-cramps ; poison being suspected, the doctors took possession of the flour, attempted to analyse it, and tried its effects on a number of street dogs. A few of the animals died : most were violently sick, but got over the dose. Poison was not definitely proved, and dirty utensils and bad baking might conceivably have been the cause of the outbreak. Some Catalan writers say that there was a poisoning-plot, or I should have doubted the whole story. See the Appendix to Arteche, xii. p. 483.   [2] See above, p. 347.

[3] 1/10th, 1/81st, 1/58th, 4th and 6th Line battalions K.G.L., and parts of the foreign battalions of De Roll, Dillon, and the Calabrian Free Corps. See table in Appendix XIV. The total was 248 officers, and 6,643 rank and file.

Owing to Bentinck's unhappy hesitation in May and June, after the expedition had been announced and the troops ordered to prepare for embarkation, French spies in Sicily had found the time to send warning to Paris, and Suchet had been advised by the Minister of War that a fleet from Palermo might appear in his neighbourhood at any moment. He received his warning in the end of June, a month before Maitland's arrival [1], and this turned out in the end profitable to the allied cause ; for, though the fleet never appeared, he was always expecting it, and used the argument that he was about to be attacked by an English force as his most effective reply to King Joseph's constant demands for assistance in New Castile. The arrival at Alicante of transports intended to carry Roche's division to Catalonia, and of some vessels bearing the battering-train which Wellington had sent round for Bentinck's use, was duly reported to him : for some time he took this flotilla to be the Anglo-Sicilian squadron. Hence he was expecting all through June and July the attack which (through Bentinck's perversity) was never delivered. The threat proved as effective as the actual descent might have been, and Wellington would have been much relieved if only he could have seen a few of Suchet's many letters refusing to move a man to support the King [2].

Suchet's great trouble was that he could not tell in the least whether the Sicilian expedition would land in Catalonia or in Valencia. It might come ashore anywhere between Alicante and Rosas. He prepared a small movable central reserve, with which he could march northward if the blow should fall between Valencia and Tortosa, or southward—to reinforce Habert and Harispe—if it should be struck in the South. Decaen was warned to have a strong force concentrated in central Catalonia, in case the descent came in his direction, and Suchet promised him such assistance as he could spare. On a rumour that the Sicilian fleet had turned northward—as a matter of fact it was not yet in Spanish waters—the Marshal thought it worth while to make a rapid visit to Catalonia, to concert matters with Decaen. He marched by Tortosa with

---

[1] Clarke's dispatch with the information was dated June 9th.

[2] Two of them dated July 22 and August 12 did ultimately fall into his hands, but only after the victory of Salamanca. See below, pp. 617–18.

a flying column, and on July 10th met Decaen at Reus. Here
he learned that there were no signs of the enemy to be discovered, and after visiting Tarragona, inspecting its fortifications, and reinforcing its garrison, returned southward in a more
leisurely fashion than he had gone forth.

During Suchet's absence from his Valencian viceroyalty the
captain-general of Murcia took measures which brought about
one of the most needless and gratuitous disasters that ever
befell the ever-unlucky army of which he was in charge.
Joseph O'Donnell knew that the Sicilian expedition was due,
and he had been warned that Roche's division would be taken
off to join it; he was aware that Maitland's arrival would
modify all Suchet's arrangements, and would force him to draw
troops away from his own front. He had been requested by
Wellington to content himself with ' containing ' the French
force in his front, and to risk nothing. But on July 18th he
marched out from his positions in front of Alicante with the
design of surprising General Harispe. He knew that Suchet had
gone north, and was not aware of his return ; and he had been
informed, quite truly, that Harispe's cantonments were much
scattered. Unfortunately he was as incapable as he was
presumptuous, and he entirely lacked the fiery determination
of his brother Henry, the hero of La Bispal. According to
contemporary critics he was set, at this moment, on making
what he thought would be a brilliant descent on an unprepared
enemy, without any reference to his orders or to the general
state of the war [1]. And he wished to fight before Roche's troops
were taken from him, as they must soon be.

Harispe had only some 5,000 men—his own division, with
one stray battalion belonging to Habert [2], and Delort's cavalry
brigade [3]. He had one infantry regiment in reserve at Alcoy [4],
another at Ibi [5], the third [6]—with the bulk of Delort's horsemen
—in and about Castalla, the nearest point in the French cantonments to Alicante. O'Donnell's ambitious plan was to surround
the troops in Castalla and Ibi by a concentric movement of

[1] See Schepeler, pp. 617 and 623.   [2] Of the 44th Line.
[3] The 13th Cuirassiers and 24th Dragoons.
[4] The 116th Line, 2 battalions.   [5] The 1st Léger, 3 battalions.
[6] The 7th Line, 2 battalions.

several columns marching far apart, and to destroy them before
Harispe himself could come up with his reserve from the rear.
Bassecourt and his detachment from the northern hills was
ordered to fall in at the same time on Alcoy, so as to distract
Harispe and keep him engaged—a doubtful expedient since
he lay many marches away, and it was obvious that the timing
of his diversion would probably miscarry.

O'Donnell marched in three masses : on the right Roche's
division went by Xixona with the order to surprise the French
troops in Ibi. The main body, three weak infantry brigades
under Montijo, Mijares, and Michelena, with two squadrons of
cavalry and a battery, moved straight upon Castalla. The
main body of the horse, about 800 strong, under General Santesteban, went out on the left on the side of Villena, with orders to
outflank the enemy and try to cut in upon his rear. The whole
force made up 10,000 infantry and 1,000 cavalry, not taking
into account the possible (but unlikely) advent of Bassecourt,
so that Harispe was outnumbered by much more than two to
one. As an extra precaution all the transports ready in Alicante
were sent out—with only one battalion on board—along the
coast, to demonstrate opposite Denia and the mouth of the
Xucar, in order to call off the attention of Habert's division,
which lay in that direction.

Having marched all night on the 20th July, the Spanish
columns found themselves—in a very fatigued condition—in
front of the enemy at four o'clock on the morning of the 21st.
They were out of touch with each other, Roche being separated
from the centre by the mountain-spur called the Sierra de Cata,
and the cavalry having been sent very far out on the flank.
General Mesclop was opposed to Roche at Ibi, with four
battalions and a squadron of cuirassiers—General Delort, at
Castalla, had only one squadron of the cuirassiers, two battalions, and a battery, but was expecting the arrival of the
24th Dragoons from the neighbouring town of Biar, some way
to his right, and of the remaining two squadrons of the 13th
Cuirassiers from Onil on his left. Meanwhile he evacuated
Castalla, but took up a position on a hillside covered by a stream
and a ravine crossed by a narrow bridge, with his trifling force.
He had already sent orders to Mesclop at Ibi to come in to his

aid, leaving only a rearguard to hold off as long as possible the Spanish column in front of him. The latter did as he was bid; he threw into the Castle of Ibi a company of the 44th and two guns, and left the rest of that battalion and a troop of cuirassiers to support them. With the rest of his force, the three battalions of the 1st Léger and the remaining troop of cuirassiers, he set off in haste for Castalla.

O'Donnell assailed Delort in a very leisurely way after occupying the town of Castalla—his troops were tired, and four of his six guns had fallen behind. But Montijo's brigade and the two pieces which had kept up with it were developing an attack on the bridge, and Michelena and Mijares had passed the ravine higher up, when the French detached troops began to appear from all directions. The first to get up were the 400 men of the 24th Dragoons, who—screened by an olive wood—came in with a tremendous impact, and quite unforeseen, upon Mijares's flank, and completely broke up his three battalions. They then, after re-forming their ranks, formed in column and charged across the narrow bridge in front of O'Donnell's centre, though it was commanded by his two guns. An attack delivered across such a defile, passable by only two horses abreast, looked like madness—but was successful! The guns only fired one round each before they were ridden over, and the brigade supporting them broke up. Delort then attacked, with his two battalions and with the cuirassiers who had just come up from Onil. Montijo's brigade, the only intact Spanish unit left, was thus driven from the field and scattered. The 6,000 infantry of O'Donnell's centre became a mass of fugitives— only one regiment out of the whole[1] kept its ranks and went off in decent order. Of the rest nearly half were hunted down and captured in droves by the French cuirassiers and dragoons. Mesclop with the three battalions from Ibi arrived too late to take any part in the rout. Delort sent him back at once to relieve the detachment that he had left in front of Roche. The latter had driven it out of the village of Ibi after some skirmishing, when he saw approaching him not only Mesclop's column, but Harispe coming up from Alcoy with the 116th of the Line. He at once halted, turned to the rear, and retired

---

[1] Cuenca, of Montijo's brigade. Schepeler, p. 619.

in good order towards Xixona : the enemy's cavalry tried to break his rearguard but failed, and the whole division got back to Alicante without loss. The same chance happened to Santesteban's cavalry, which, marching from Villena at 7 o'clock, had reached Biar, in the enemy's rear, only when the fighting—which had begun at 4—was all over. O'Donnell tried to throw blame on this officer ; but the fact seems to be that his own calculation of time and distance was faulty : he had sent his cavalry on too wide a sweep, separated by hills from his main body, and had kept up no proper communication with it. Nor does it appear that if Santesteban had come up to Biar a little earlier he would have been able to accomplish anything very essential. Bassecourt's diversion, as might have been expected, did not work : before he got near Alcoy the main body had been cut to pieces : he retired in haste to Almanza on hearing the news.

O'Donnell's infantry was so shattered that his army was reduced to as bad a condition as it had shown in January, after Blake's original disaster at Valencia. He had lost over 3,000 men, of whom 2,135 were unwounded prisoners, three flags, and the only two guns that had got to the front. The survivors of the three broken brigades had dispersed all over the country-side, and took weeks to collect. It was fortunate that Roche's division had reached Alicante intact, or that city itself might have been in danger. The French had lost, according to their own account, no more than 200 men[1] : only the two cavalry regiments, two battalions of the 7th Line, and one of the 44th had been put into action. As Suchet truly remarks in his *Mémoires*[2] the total numbers engaged—3,000 men[3]—on his side were somewhat less than the casualty list of the enemy.

The rout of Castalla put the Murcian army out of action for months—a lucky thing for Suchet, since the force of the allies at Alicante was just about to be increased by the arrival there

---

[1] This is the figure given by Suchet in his contemporary dispatch to King Joseph, of which a copy lies in the Scovell papers. In some French accounts the number is cut down to 70.

[2] Vol. ii. p. 260.

[3] 7th Line, about 1,200; 13th Cuirassiers and 24th Dragoons, about 1,000; one battalion 44th, about 650 ; artillery, &c., about 150 = 3,000 in all. The 1st Léger and 116th Line were practically not engaged.

of Maitland's expedition, and if O'Donnell's army had been
still intact, a very formidable body of troops would have been
collected opposite him. It remains to explain the appearance of
the Anglo-Sicilians in this direction, contrary to the orders of
Wellington, who had expressed his wish that they should land in
Catalonia, join Lacy, and lay siege to Tarragona—an operation
which he thought would force Suchet to evacuate Valencia
altogether, in order to bring help to Decaen.

We left Maitland anchored in the Bay of Palamos on July 31.
The moment that he appeared Eroles went on board his ship,
to urge his immediate disembarkation, and to promise the
enthusiastic assistance of the Catalans. The energetic baron
gave a most optimistic picture of the state of affairs, he declared
that the whole country would rise at the sight of the red-coats,
that Tarragona was weakly held, and that the total force of
the French, including Suchet's column near Tortosa, was only
13,000 men. Lacy and Sarsfield appeared later, and gave much
less encouraging information : they rated the enemy at a far
higher figure than Eroles, and were right in so doing, for Decaen
had some 25,000 men, and could by an effort have concentrated
15,000, exclusive of succours from Suchet. The Spanish Army
of Catalonia could only furnish 7,000 foot and 300 horse, of
whom many were so far off at the moment that Lacy declared
that it would take six or eight days to bring them up. By the
time that they were all arrived, the French would have concentrated also, and would be equal in numbers to the whole force
that the allies could collect. Tarragona was reported to be in
a better state of defence than Eroles allowed, and the engineers
declared that it might take ten days to reduce it. But the
greatest problem of all was that of provisions : Lacy declared
that the country could furnish little or nothing : he could not
undertake to keep his own small army concentrated for more
than a week. The Anglo-Sicilians must be fed from the fleet,
and he could provide no transport. Evidently the expedition
would be tied down to the shore, and the siege of Tarragona
was the only possible operation. Since the Anglo-Sicilian army
could not manœuvre at large or retire into the inland, it would
have to fight Decaen, to cover the investment of Tarragona,
within a few days of its landing. On the other hand if, as

Eroles promised, the *somatenes* rose on every side at the news
of the disembarkation, the outlying French troops might not
be able to get up to join Decaen, the roads would be blocked,
the enemy might never be able to concentrate, and the force
about Barcelona, his only immediately available field army,
was not more than 8,000 strong, and might be beaten.

There were those who said that Lacy never wished to see
the expedition land, because he was jealous of Eroles, and
thought that a general rising which ended in success would
have meant the end of his own power and tenure of office [1]. It
is at least certain that the views which he expressed caused
Maitland much trouble, and made him to flinch from his original
idea of landing without delay and attacking Tarragona, according to Wellington's desire. The English general took refuge in
a council of war—the usual resource of commanders of a wavering purpose. His lieutenants all advised him to refuse to land,
on the ground that his forces were too small and heterogeneous,
that Lacy could give no prompt assistance, and that there was
no sign as yet of the general rising which Eroles promised.
Moreover, some of the naval officers told him that anchorage
off the Catalan coast was so dangerous, even in summer, that
they could not promise him that the army could be taken
safely on board in case of a defeat. To the intense disgust of
Eroles and the other Catalan leaders, but not at all to Lacy's
displeasure, Maitland accepted the advice of his council of war,
and resolved to make off, and to land farther south. The
original idea was to have come ashore somewhere in the midst
of the long coast-line south of the Ebro, between Tortosa and
Valencia, with the object of breaking Suchet's line in the middle.
But the news of Joseph O'Donnell's gratuitous disaster at
Castalla, which obviously enabled the Marshal to use his whole
army against a disembarking force, and the suggestion that
Alicante itself might be in danger, induced Maitland in the end
to order his whole armament to steer southward. He arrived
at Alicante on August 7th, and commenced to send his troops
ashore—both his own 6,000 men and Whittingham's 4,000
auxiliaries of the Balearic division. Since Roche was already

---

[1] This seems to have been Codrington's view, see his *Memoirs*, i. p. 278,
and he knew Lacy and the Catalans well.

there, with his troops in good order, there were 14,000 men
collected in Alicante, over and above the wrecks of O'Donnell's
force. If only the Murcians had been intact, the mass assembled
would have caused Suchet serious qualms, since it would have
outnumbered the French corps in Valencia very considerably,
and there was in it a nucleus of good troops in Maitland's
British and German battalions. The news of Salamanca had
also come to hand by this time, and had transformed the
general aspect of affairs in Suchet's eyes : King Joseph was
again demanding instant help from him, in the hope of retaining
Madrid, and had called in (without his knowledge or consent)
the division of Palombini from Aragon, and the garrison of
Cuenca [1]. If Wellington should advance—as he actually did—
against the King, and should drive him from his capital, it was
possible that the main theatre of the war might be transferred
to the borders of Valencia.

The Marshal therefore resolved to concentrate : he ordered
Habert and Harispe to fall back behind the Xucar with their
8,000 men, abandoning their advanced positions in front of
Alicante, and placed them at Jativa ; here he threw up some
field-works and armed a *tête-de-pont* on the Xucar at Alberique.
He ordered Paris's brigade to come down from northern Aragon
to Teruel, and he warned the generals in Catalonia that he
might ask for reinforcements from them.

Maitland therefore, after his landing, found that the French
had disappeared from his immediate front. He was joined by
Roche, and by the 67th regiment from Cartagena, and proposed
to drive Harispe from Castalla and Ibi. But he marched
against him on August 16th–18th, only to find that he had
already retired behind the Xucar. Farther than Monforte he
found himself unable to advance, for want of transport and
food. For the expedition from Sicily had not been fitted out
for an advance into the inland. It had been supposed by
Bentinck that the troops would be able to hire or requisition
in Spain the mules and carts that they would require for
a forward movement. But the country-side about Alicante
was already exhausted by the long stay of the Murcian army in
that region ; and O'Donnell—before Maitland had come to

[1] See above, pp. 487 and 488.

know the difficulties of his position, got from him a pledge that he would not take anything from it either by purchase or by requisition. The British general had hired mules to draw his guns, but found that he could not feed them on a forward march, because the resources of the district were denied him. He himself had to stop at Elda, Roche at Alcoy, because the problem of transport and food could not be solved. All that he could do was to feel the French line of outposts behind the Xucar with a flying column composed of his own handful of cavalry—200 sabres—and a detachment of Spanish horse lent him by Elio, the successor of O'Donnell [August 20th–21st].

But even the thought of farther advance had now to be given up, for the news arrived that King Joseph had evacuated Madrid on the 14th, and was marching on Valencia with the 15,000 men that he had collected. To have tried any further attack on Suchet, when such an army was coming in from the flank to join the Marshal, would have been insane. The French force in this region would be doubled in strength by the King's arrival. Wherefore Maitland drew back his own division to Alicante, and brought Roche back to Xixona, not far in front of that fortress, expecting that he might ere long be pushed back, and perhaps besieged there. Wellington in the end of the month, having the same idea, sent him elaborate directions for the defence of the place, bidding him to hold it as long as possible, but to keep his transports close at hand, and to re-embark if things came to the worst [1].

On the 25th King Joseph's army and its vast convoy of French and Spanish refugees, joined Suchet's outposts at Almanza, and the dangerous combination which Maitland and Wellington had foreseen came to pass. But what was still more threatening for the army at Alicante was the rumour that Soult was about to evacuate Andalusia, and to bring the whole of the Army of the South to Valencia. This would mean that nearly 80,000 French troops would ere long be collected within striking distance of the motley force over which Maitland and Elio now held command, and it seemed probable that Soult in his march might sweep over the whole country-side, disperse the Spanish forces on the Murcian border, and perhaps

[1] See Wellington to Maitland, *Dispatches*, ix. p. 386, dated Aug. 30.

besiege and take Cartagena and Alicante as a *parergon* on the way. We have seen in chapter X that nothing of this kind happened : Soult hung on to Andalusia for a month longer than Wellington or any one else deemed probable : he only left Granada on September 17th, and when he did move on Valencia he took the bad inland roads by Huescar, Calasparra, and Hellin, leaving Murcia and Cartagena and the whole sea-coast undisturbed. The reason, as has been already pointed out, was the outbreak of yellow fever at Cartagena, which caused the Duke of Dalmatia so much concern that he preferred to keep away from the infection, even at the cost of taking inferior and circuitous roads.

For the whole of September, therefore, Suchet on the one side and Maitland and the Spaniards on the other, were waiting on Soult : in the expectation of his early arrival both sides kept quiet. Thus tamely ended the first campaign of the Anglo-Sicilian army, on whose efforts Wellington had so much counted. And its later operations, as we shall presently see, were to be wholly in keeping with its unlucky start.

SECTION XXXIII : CHAPTER XII

WELLINGTON RETURNS TO THE DOURO.   FINIS

THE garrison of the Retiro had surrendered on August 14th :
Wellington remained for seventeen days longer in Madrid, and
did not leave it, to take the field again, until August 31st.
His stay in the Spanish capital was not due, in the first instance,
to the causes which might seem most plausible—a desire to give
his war-worn infantry a rest during the hottest weeks of the
year, or a determination to reorganize the military resources
of Madrid and New Castile for the profit of the allied
cause [1].   Both these ideas existed, and the latter in especial
absorbed much of his attention—he spent long hours in trying
to concert, with Carlos de España, measures for the utilization
of the captured munitions of the Retiro, and for the recruiting
of the regiments of the Spanish ' Fifth Army.'   In this he
accomplished less than he had hoped, partly because of the
dreadful exhaustion of the central provinces of Spain after the
famine of the preceding year, partly because of the inefficiency
of most of the Spanish officials with whom he had to deal.   He
was much discontented with the list of persons appointed by
the new Regency to take up authority in the reconquered
provinces ; and Castaños, whom he most trusted, and desired
to have with him, was lingering in Galicia [2].

But the main reason for the halt at Madrid was the uncertainty as to the movements of Soult. Was the Duke of Dalmatia
about, as would seem reasonable, to evacuate Andalusia ?
And if so, would he pick up King Joseph and the Army of the
Centre in La Mancha, and march on Madrid with the 65,000 men

---

[1] Wellington to Henry Wellesley, *Dispatches*, ix. p. 364.

[2] Same to same, *Dispatches*, ix. p. 373. He was particularly indignant
at the supersession of Mexia, Intendant of Castile, by Lozano de Torres,
with whom he had quarrelled in Estremadura in 1809, ' the most useless
and inefficient of all God's creatures, and an impediment to all business.'

whom they could collect ? Or would he retire on Valencia and
join Suchet ? Or again, would he persist in his intention,
expressed in dispatches to Joseph, which had fallen into
Wellington's hands, of holding on to Andalusia and making it
a separate base of French power, despite of the fact that he
had been cut off from communication with the imperial armies
of the East and North ?

' Any other but a modern French army would now leave the
province [of Andalusia],' wrote Wellington to Lord Bathurst
on July 18 [1], ' as they have now absolutely no communication
of any kind with France or with any other French army ; and
they are pressed on all sides by troops not to be despised, and
can evidently do nothing. Yet I suspect that Soult will not
stir till I force him out by a direct movement upon him : and
I think of making that movement as soon as I can take the
troops to the South without injuring their health.' All military
reasons were against the probability of Soult's holding on in
Andalusia, yet he had certainly expressed his intention of
doing so as late as the middle of July, and, what was more
important still in judging of his plans, he had not made a
sudden movement of retreat when the news of Salamanca
reached him. Hill writing on August 4th, six days after the
receipt of the tidings of Marmont's disaster, had to report [2] that
' the recent glorious event ' seemed to have had very little
effect on the enemy, who ' continued in a strong position in his
front.' And this was true, for Soult, after hearing the news
of Salamanca, had made his last frantic appeal to King Joseph
to fall back on Andalusia, and make his base at Seville if Madrid
were lost. Wellington was right in suspecting that, if the
Marshal had got his desire, the South would have been maintained against him, and he would have had to march thither
in person, to pick up Hill, and to bring matters to an issue by
another pitched battle. It was only on August 12th that
Soult reluctantly resolved to evacuate Andalusia : his first
precautionary movements for retreat were made on August 15th,
but it was not till the 24th that the Cadiz Lines were destroyed,
or till the 26th that all the French troops in front of Hill
suddenly vanished. Wellington was therefore kept for more

---

[1] *Dispatches*, ix. p. 370.   [2] See above, p. 537.

than a fortnight in a state of complete uncertainty as to whether he might not have to march southward in the end, to evict Soult from his viceroyalty. It was only on the 24th that he got information from Hill (written on the 17th) which gave the first premonitory warning that the French seemed to be on the move[1]. Next day confirming evidence began to come to hand : ' it is generally reported, and I have reason to believe, that the Army of the South is about to make a general movement . . . it is supposed in the direction of Granada and Valencia[2].' On August 30, ' though Sir Rowland Hill on the 17th instant had no intelligence that the march was commenced, there was every appearance of it.' The fact that seemed to make it incredible that Soult could be proposing to hold Andalusia any longer, was precise information that King Joseph and the Army of the Centre had marched upon Valencia to join Suchet, and had passed Chinchilla on August 24th, going eastward[3]. If the King had gone by the passes of the Sierra Morena southward, to join Soult, doubt might still have been possible : but since he had made Valencia his goal, and was crawling slowly along in that direction with his immense convoy of refugees and baggage, Soult—left entirely to his own resources—could not retain his present position. He must march on Valencia also, and it would be many weeks before he could place himself in touch with Suchet, and produce a threatening combination on the Mediterranean coast.

On August 31st, therefore, with no absolutely certain news yet to hand as to Soult's retreat, but with every military probability in favour of its having been begun, Wellington resolved to leave Madrid and to return to the valley of the Douro, where the movements of Clausel and the French Army of Portugal demanded his attention. He never thought for a moment of endeavouring to march through La Mancha to intercept or molest Soult's retreat. The distance was too great, the roads unknown, the problem of feeding the army in the

---

[1] *Dispatches*, ix. p. 377.

[2] Ibid., ix. pp. 380–1.

[3] News from Joseph O'Donnell commanding the Spanish army of Murcia. *Dispatches*, ix. p. 388.

desolate and thinly-peopled country about the Murcian and Andalusian borders too difficult. Wellington made up his mind that he had some time to spare : he would march against Clausel and then ' return to this part of the country [Madrid] as soon as I shall have settled matters to my satisfaction on the right of the Douro. And I hope I shall be here [Madrid] and shall be joined by the troops under Sir Rowland Hill, before Soult can have made much progress to form his junction with the King[1].' It is important, therefore, to realize that, in Wellington's original conception, the operations in Old Castile, which we may call the Burgos campaign, were to be but a side-issue, an intermediate and secondary matter. The real danger in Spain, as he considered, was the approaching, but not immediate, junction of Soult, Suchet, and King Joseph at Valencia. And the Commander-in-Chief evidently proposed to be at Madrid, to face this combination, by October 1st. How and why he failed to carry out this intention must be explained at length in the next volume.

Meanwhile, when he marched off to the Douro with part of his army, he had to make provisions for the conduct of affairs in the South during his absence. Hill, as has been shown in another chapter, had been told to march on Madrid, as soon as Soult's forces had made their definitive departure for the East. As Drouet only disappeared from Hill's front on August 26th, the northward march of the army from Estremadura began late : it had not commenced to cross the Guadiana on September 1 : its progress to and along the Tagus valley was slow, owing to the difficulty of procuring food, and its main body had not reached Almaraz and Talavera before the 20th September, and was only concentrated about and behind Toledo at the end of the month. But though Hill's movement was not rapid, it was made in sufficiently good time to face the danger that was brewing on the side of Valencia. And there can be no doubt that if he had received orders to hurry, he could have been in line some days before he actually appeared[2]. He brought up

---

[1] Wellington to Lord Bathurst, August 30, from Madrid. *Dispatches*, ix. p. 390.

[2] The cavalry at the head of the column were at Truxillo on the 15th September, Almaraz on the 19th, Talavera on the 21st. The infantry in the

all his force [1] except Buchan's Portuguese brigade [2], which was left at Truxillo and Merida, to keep up his communication with Elvas. Estremadura, so long the contending ground of armies, had now no solid body of troops left in it save the Spanish garrison of Badajoz. For Penne Villemur and Morillo, with the division which had so long operated in Hill's vicinity, moved with him into New Castile. They went by the rugged roads through the mountains of the province of Toledo [3], and took post at Herencia, on the high-road from Madrid to the Despeña-perros pass, in front of the British 2nd Division.

In the rear of Hill's column, and separated from it by many days' march, was another small British force toiling up to Madrid from a very distant point. This was the force under Colonel Skerrett, which had taken part in the fighting round Seville. It consisted of the battalion of the Guards from Cadiz, the 2/47th and 2/87th, two companies of the 2/95th, a squadron of the 2nd Hussars K.G.L., the 20th Portuguese Line, and a battery. By Wellington's orders no British troops were now left in Cadiz save the 2/59th, part of de Watteville's regiment, the 'battalion of foreign recruits,' soon to become the 8/60th, and a few artillery. Skerrett's column, some 4,000 strong, marched by Merida and Truxillo, and reached Toledo in time to join Hill for the autumn campaign in front of Madrid. Hill's corps, when joined by Skerrett, provided a force of over 20,000 men, about equally divided between British and Portuguese.

It would have been profitable to Wellington, as matters went in the end, if he had handed over the entire task of observing Soult's operations to Hill. But being under the impression that he would return ere long to Madrid, he left

rear of the division only crossed the Guadiana at Medellin on September 14th, was at Truxillo on the 17th, Almaraz on the 20th, Talavera on the 26th, Toledo on the 30th (Swabey's diary).

[1] Hill brought up the 2nd Division—British, 7,000 ; Portuguese, 2,900 ; Hamilton's Portuguese, 5,300 ; Long's and Slade's cavalry, about 1,900 ; artillery, about 400 = 17,500 of all ranks.

[2] Late Power's brigade : The 5th and 17th, the old garrison of Elvas, and the 22nd.

[3] They marched from Cabeza del Buey, on the borders of Andalusia and Estremadura, via Talarubia and Mazarambros to Herencia. ' Journal of Regiment of Leon,' in Clonard, vol. iv.

there and in the neighbourhood nearly half the force that he had brought from Salamanca. He only took with him to oppose Clausel the 1st, 5th, and 7th Divisions, with Pack's and Bradford's Portuguese, and Bock's and Ponsonby's (late Le Marchant's) brigades of heavy dragoons, a force of some 21,000 men [1]. He left the 3rd and Light Divisions at Madrid, the 4th Division at the Escurial, and Carlos de España's Spaniards at Segovia. The cavalry of Victor Alten and D'Urban were assigned to this force, and remained, the former at Madrid, the latter at the Palacio de Rio Frio, near Segovia. The British infantry divisions had all suffered heavily at Badajoz, and the 4th at Salamanca also—they were weak in numbers, but were expecting ere long to be joined by numerous convalescents. The total force left behind amounted to about 17,000 men, including the Spaniards [2]. Thus when Hill and Skerrett came up from the South, there was a mass of nearly 40,000 men accumulated round Madrid, while Wellington himself, after picking up Clinton and the 6th Division, and the other troops left on the Douro, had a little under 30,000. This proved in the autumn campaign an ideally bad partition of the army, for on each wing the Anglo-Portuguese force was decidedly less numerous than that which the French could bring against it. If Wellington had taken his full strength to the North, he could have defied Clausel and Caffarelli, and they could never have made head against him, or pressed him away from Burgos. Hill, on the other hand, in front of Madrid, would have been no more helpless with 22,000 men than he actually was with 38,000 men, when Soult and King Joseph brought 60,000 against him in October. In either case he could only retreat without offering battle. But Wellington, if the three additional divisions left in New Castile had been brought to the North, would have had such a superiority over the French in Old Castile that he could have dealt with them as he pleased. The only explanation

---

[1] There marched with Wellington—1st Division, 5,980 of all ranks; 5th Division, 4,726 ; 7th Division, 4,841 ; Pack and Bradford, 3,954 ; Bock and Ponsonby, 1,673 ; artillery, &c., about 500 = 21,674.

[2] There remained at Madrid, the Escurial, &c.—Arentschildt's cavalry, 515 ; D'Urban's Portuguese cavalry, 552 ; 3rd Division, 4,234 ; 4th Division, 4,548 ; Light Division, 3,462 ; artillery, about 350 ; Carlos de España's Spaniards, about 3,000 = 16,661.

of the unfortunate proportional division of his army, is that Wellington undervalued the task he had to execute beyond the Douro, thought that he could finish it more quickly than was to be the case, and calculated on being back at Madrid in October before Soult could give trouble.

Yet when he started he was not comfortable in his mind about the general situation. If the French drew together, their total strength in Spain was far too great for him. In a moody moment he wrote to his brother Henry: ' though I still hope to be able to maintain our position in Castile, and even to improve our advantages, I shudder when I reflect upon the enormity of the task which I have undertaken, with inadequate powers myself to do anything, and without assistance of any kind from the Spaniards. . . . I am apprehensive that all this may turn out ill for the Spanish cause. If by any cause I should be overwhelmed, or should be obliged to retire, what will the world say ? What will the people of England say ? What will those in Spain say ?[1] '

Wellington's forebodings were, only too soon, to be justified. But the tale of the campaign against Clausel and Caffarelli, of the advance to and retreat from Burgos, must be told in another volume.

[1] *Dispatches*, ix. p. 375.

APPENDICES

I

SUCHET'S ARMY IN VALENCIA. MORNING STATE OF OCT. 1, 1811

		Officers.	Men.	Total.
1st Division (Musnier):				
Robert's Brigade	114th Line (3 batts.)	58	1,579	1,637
	1st of the Vistula (2 batts.)	27	836	863
Ficatier's Brigade	121st Line (3 batts.)	44	1,156	1,200
	2nd of the Vistula (2 batts.)	26	1,103	1,129 = 4,829
2nd Division (Harispe):				
Paris's Brigade	7th Line (4 batts.)	55	1,584	1,639
	116th Line (3 batts.)	42	1,105	1,147
Chlopiski's Brigade	44th Line (2 batts.)	35	1,191	1,226
	3rd of the Vistula (2 batts.)	26	724	750 = 4,762
3rd Division (Habert):				
Montmarie's Brigade	5th Line (2 batts.)	31	771	802
	16th Line (3 batts.)	56	1,261	1,317
Bronikowski's Brigade, 117th Line (3 batts.)		49	1,291	1,340 = 3,459
Palombini's Italian Division:				
Saint Paul's Brigade	2nd Léger (3 batts.)	59	2,141	2,200
	4th Line (3 batts.)	57	1,603	1,660
Balathier's Brigade	5th Line (2 batts.)	37	893	930
	6th Line (3 batts.)	51	1,378	1,429 = 6,219
Compère's Neapolitan Division:				
1st Léger (1 batt.)		27	419	446
1st Line (1 batt.)		24	536	560
2nd Line (1 batt.)		27	358	385 = 1,391
Cavalry (General Boussard):				
4th Hussars (4 squadrons)		30	720	750
24th Dragoons (2 squadrons)		17	419	436
13th Cuirassiers (4 squadrons)		27	557	584
Italian 'Dragoons of Napoleon'		24	442	466
Neapolitan Chasseurs		13	156	169 = 2,405
Artillery (General Vallée)		48	1,757	1,805
Engineers (General Rogniat)		16	584	600
Équipages Militaires and Gendarmerie		10	653	663 = 3,068
		916	25,217	26,133 26,133

N.B.—Ficatier's Brigade, 3 battalions of Palombini's division, and two squadrons f 4th Hussars were not present at the battle of Saguntum, being on the line of communications, and blockading Peniscola and Oropesa.

This return, lent me by Mr. Fortescue who found it in the Paris Archives, differs by over 2,000 men from Suchet's figures given in his *Mémoires*, p. 436 of vol. ii. The Marshal has left out the 3 battalions and 2 squadrons on the line of communications, mentioned above.

II

STRENGTH OF BLAKE'S ARMY AT THE BATTLE OF SAGUNTUM

I. ' The Expeditionary Corps.'

	Officers.	Men.	Total.
Lardizabal's Division : Africa (2 batts.), Murcia (2 batts.), 2nd of Badajoz (2 batts.), Campo Mayor (1 batt.), Tiradores de Cuenca (1 batt.) .	149	2,823	2,972
Zayas's Division : 2nd Spanish Guards, 4th ditto, 1st Walloon Guards, Voluntarios de la Patria, Toledo, Ciudad Rodrigo, Legion Estrangera (1 batt. each), Companies of Cazadores . . .	177	2,373	2,550
Loy's Cavalry : Granaderos (2 squadrons), Rey (1 ditto), Husares de Castilla (1 ditto) . .	50	244	294
Horse Artillery : two batteries	11	214	225
Total of the ' Expeditionary Corps ' .	387	5,654	6,041

II. Valencian Troops (' Second Army ').

	Officers.	Men.	Total.
Miranda's Division : Valencia (3 batts.), Voluntarios de Castilla (2 batts.), 1st of Avila (1 batt.), 2nd Cazadores de Valencia (1 batt.) . . .	120	3,844	3,964
Obispo's Division : Cariñena (2 batts.) 2nd of Avila (1 batt.), 1st Voluntarios de Aragon (1 batt.), Daroca (1 batt.), Tiradores de Doyle (1 batt.) .	110	3,290	3,400
Villacampa's Division : Princesa (2 batts.), Soria (2 batts.), 2nd Voluntarios de Aragon (1 batt.), 1st Cazadores de Valencia (1 batt.), Molina (1 batt.)	162	3,190	3,352
Reserve (General Velasco) : 3rd Battalions of Voluntarios de Castilla, Don Carlos, Avila, Cazadores de Valencia, and Voluntarios de Orihuela	75	3,595	3,670
San Juan's Cavalry : Cuenca, Dragones del Rey, Reina, Numancia, Husares de Aragon, Cazadores de Valencia, Alcantara, Husares Españoles, Husares de Granada (none over two squadrons strong)	111	1,610	1,721
Artillery : 1 horse, 2 field batteries . . .	21	340	361
Total ' 2nd Army '	599	15,869	16,468

III. MURCIAN TROOPS ('3rd ARMY').

	Officers.	*Men.*	*Total.*
Creagh's Brigade : Corona, Alcazar, Tiradores de Cadiz (1 batt. each)	97	2,121	2,218
Montijo's Brigade : 1st of Badajoz, 1st of Cuenca, Voluntarios de Burgos, Sappers (1 batt. each) .	108	2,302	2,410
Cavalry : Reina (2 squadrons), Pavia (2 squadrons), Granada (2 squadrons), Madrid (1 squadron), Husares de Fernando 7me (1 squadron) . .	83	743	826
Horse Artillery : 1 battery	3	78	81
Total '3rd Army'	291	5,244	5,535

General Total of the Army : 1,277 officers, 26,767 men = Total, 28,044.

III

SUCHET'S ARMY AT THE
SIEGE OF VALENCIA. MORNING STATE OF DEC. 31

N.B.—The regiments of the Army of Aragon are the same
as in Appendix I.

I. ARMY OF ARAGON (officers and men).

Musnier's Division (10 battalions)	3,727
Harispe's Division (10 battalions)	4,828
Habert's Division (8 battalions)	3,150
Palombini's Division (10 battalions)	3,591
Compère's Division (3 battalions)	1,092
Boussard's Cavalry (13 squadrons)	1,839
Artillery	1,511
Engineers, &c.	857
Total Army of Aragon	20,595

II. REILLE'S CORPS (officers and men).

Pannetier's Brigade } 10th and 81st Line (7 battalions) . . .	2,834
Bourke's Brigade } 20th and 60th Line (7 battalions) . . .	3,961
Severoli's Italian Division { 1st Line (3 batts.), 7th Line (2 batts.) } 1st Léger (3 batts.) . . . }	4,370
Cavalry { 9th Hussars	543
{ 1st Italian Chasseurs.	262
Artillery	1,153
Total Reille's Corps	13,123

General Total of combined forces, 33,718.

IV

SURRENDER-ROLL OF BLAKE'S ARMY OF
VALENCIA, JAN. 9, 1812

	Officers.	Rank and file.
Zayas's Division	96	1,319
Lardizabal's Division	165	3,385
Miranda's Division	237	5,513
Division of Reserve, &c.	130	3,171
Cavalry	77	818
Artillery	73	1,581
Engineers and Sappers	38	383
Total	816	16,170

General total, 16,986 of all ranks, not including 62 officers in staff or administrative employments, 23 chaplains, and 19 surgeons.

Of the remainder of Blake's army there had rallied at Alicante by January 14 of infantry 361 officers and 5,125 men, of cavalry 164 officers and 671 men, of artillery 30 officers and 720 men—total of all arms, 7,071.

V

FRENCH TROOPS EMPLOYED AT THE SIEGE OF
TARIFA (DEC. 1811–JAN. 1812)

[From the table in Belmas, iv. pp. 40–2.]

	Of all ranks.
From Leval's Division, 43rd Line, 7th and 9th Poles (2 batts. each)	3,000
From Barrois's Division, 16th Léger (3 batts.), 51st Ligne (2 batts.), 54th Ligne (2 batts.)	4,200
From Villatte's Division, 27th Léger (1 batt.), 94th and 95th Ligne (1 batt. each)	1,800
Cavalry, 16th Dragoons, and one squadron 21st Dragoons . .	585
Artillery	469
Engineers, Sappers, Marines, &c.	385
Total	10,439

In addition three battalions of the 8th and 63rd line and two squadrons of the 2nd Dragoons were occupied on the lines of communications, between Vejer and Fascinas.

ANGLO-SPANISH GARRISON OF TARIFA

	Of all ranks.
British (Colonel Skerrett) :	
2/47th	570
2/87th	560
Battalion of Flank Companies	400
1 company 95th regiment	75
1 troop 2nd Hussars K.G.L.	70
Artillery (Hughes's Company R.A.)	83
Total	1,758
Spanish (General Copons) :	
Cantabria (1 batt.)	450
Irlanda (1 batt.)	357
Cazadores	333
Artillery	106
Sappers	83
Cavalry	17
Total	1,346

N.B.—Another return makes the total of the British part of the garrison 67 officers and 1,707 men, a total of 1,774.

VI

CIUDAD RODRIGO

A. THE FRENCH GARRISON

The garrison, according to Belmas, iv. pp. 282–3, stood on the day of the investment as follows :

34th Léger, one battalion . . .	975 officers and men effective.	
113th Ligne, one battalion . . .	577 ,,	,,
Artillery, 2 companies	168 ,,	,,
Engineers	15 ,,	,,
Non-combatants (Civil officers, &c.). .	36 ,,	,,
Sick in Hospital	163	
Staff	3	
Total	1,937	

B.

BRITISH LOSSES DURING THE SIEGE

The British losses between the investment and the storm were, according to the official returns at the Record Office, 1 officer and 69 men killed, 19 officers and 462 men wounded, 2 men (both Portuguese) missing, or a total of 553. These figures added to the 568 lost in the storm (for details see below), make altogether 1,121, which does not agree with the statement in Wellington *Dispatches*, viii. p. 557 ; this gives as the total for the siege 9 officers and 169 men killed, 70 officers and 748 men wounded, 7 men missing, or only 1,003, over a hundred less than the total from the return quoted above. Napier gives 1,290 as the casualties for the whole siege, which much exceeds the return in the Record Office ; he also makes the total for the storm 60 officers and 650 killed and wounded, while the official return here printed makes it only 59 officers and 509 men. Lord Londonderry and Sir John Jones also give figures agreeing with no others. I prefer to take the total of the official report, which is here appended.

C.

BRITISH LOSSES AT THE STORM OF CIUDAD RODRIGO.
JANUARY 19, 1812

	Killed.		Wounded.		
	Offi-cers.	Men.	Offi-cers.	Men.	Total.
Staff	1 [1]	—	2 [2]	—	3
Engineers	—	—	2	2	4
3rd Division :					
Mackinnon's Brigade ⎰ 1/45th	3	14	4	27	48
5/60th	—	1	1	3	5
74th	—	4	4	13	21
⎱ 1/88th	—	7	4	23	34
Campbell's Brigade ⎰ 2/5th	1	33	8	52	94
77th	—	14	5	31	50
2/83rd	—	1	—	4	5
⎱ 94th	2	13	6	48	69
Divisional Total . . .					326
Light Division :					
Vandeleur's Brigade ⎰ 1/52nd	1	2	2	23	28
2/52nd	—	1	1	7	9
⎱ 3/95th	—	—	—	9	9
Barnard's Brigade ⎰ 1/43rd	—	7	3	31	41
1/95th	—	1	3	16	20
⎱ 2/95th	—	—	2	4	6
Divisional Total . . .					113
Portuguese	—	19	4	91	114
Grand Total	8	117	51	384	560

Adding 5 British and 3 Portuguese missing, the total loss is 568 in the storm.

[1] General Mackinnon.   [2] Generals Craufurd and Vandeleur.

VII

NOTE ON SOME POINTS OF CONTROVERSY REGARDING THE STORM OF CIUDAD RODRIGO

Beside the controversy alluded to on page 183 about the exact amount of co-operation by the Light Division in helping the 3rd to clear the French from behind the Greater Breach, there are several other vexed points concerning the storm of Ciudad Rodrigo. The one on which most dispute arose was that concerning the capture of General Barrié. Gurwood of the 52nd claimed to have been the first officer to enter the Castle, and to receive the surrender of the governor and his staff. He is mentioned as doing so in Wellington's Rodrigo dispatch, and generally had the credit at the time. But Lieutenant Mackie of the 88th, who had led the forlorn hope of the 3rd Division, also put in a claim, and had many supporters. Many years after the war was over, Maxwell (the author of one of the several *Lives of the Duke of Wellington*, which came out in early Victorian times) championed Mackie's claim with such vehemence that Gurwood issued a pamphlet defending his own credit. Considerable controversy arose in the *United Service Journal* for 1843, and elsewhere. Mackie's story was that he, with some of the 88th, arrived first at the Castle, summoned the governor to surrender, and was received by several French officers, who handed him over a sword and announced that the general yielded. Some moments after, according to Mackie, Gurwood came up, spoke to the governor himself, and obtained his sword, which, when the prisoners were brought before Wellington, he presented to his commander, who gave it him back, telling him to retain it as a trophy, and entered Gurwood's name in his dispatch as the officer who had received the surrender. Gurwood's story, told with as much detail and circumstance as Mackie's, is that he, with two soldiers of the 52nd, arrived at the citadel, got the gate opened by threatening the officer in charge that no quarter would be given if resistance were made, and was received by Barrié, who in a great state of nervousness, threw his arms round his neck, kissed him, and said, '*je suis le Gouverneur de la place—je suis votre prisonnier*,' handing over his sword at the same time. He accompanied the captive staff-officers to Wellington's presence, and presented them to him. It is difficult to come to any certain conclusion in face of two such contradictory tales, but there is a bare possibility of reconciling them, by supposing that Mackie entered first, that the door was closed behind him and his party, and that Gurwood was let in a moment later, and spoke to the governor, while Mackie had been dealing only with his aide-de-camp, whose sword he had received. But if so, it is odd that Gurwood never saw Mackie : Mackie is quite positive that he saw Gurwood, and that he came in some minutes later than himself. The dispute tended to become a controversy between Light Division and 3rd Division veterans, each backing their own man. A synopsis of the papers may be found in the last two chapters of vol. i of Grattan's second series of *Adventures with the Connaught Rangers* (London, 1853). Napier, who was much interested in the discussion, put in his final definitive edition the non-committal statement that ' the garrison fled to the Castle, where Lieutenant Gurwood, who though severely wounded had entered among the foremost at the Lesser Breach, received the governor's sword' (iv. p. 90). Harry Smith says (i. p. 58): 'Gurwood got great credit here unfairly. Johnstone and poor Uniacke were the first on the ramparts, Gurwood having been knocked down in the breach, and momentarily stunned. However, Gurwood's a sharp fellow, and he cut off in search of the governor and brought his sword to the Duke. He made the *most* of it.'

Another controversy is as to which troops of the 3rd Division got first into the body of the town. The 88th claimed the priority, but also the 94th. The late Mr. Andrew Lang lent me a very interesting letter of his kinsman, William Lang of the 94th, very clearly stating that a solid body of 200 men of his regiment were the first troops that penetrated in force to the Plaza Mayor, and received the surrender of the garrison there.

Still another controversy, about which there is much in the Rice Jones papers, in the possession of Commander Hon. Henry Shore, R.N., is as to what engineer officers conducted the storming-columns. Apparently some credit has been misplaced among individuals here, but to decide upon the point would take more space than a book like this can afford.

VIII

ARMY OF THE SOUTH

REORGANIZED AFTER THE DEPARTURE OF THE POLES AND OTHER REGIMENTS

RETURN OF MARCH 1, 1812

[From the returns in the *Archives Nationales*. Lent me by Mr. Fortescue.]

	Officers.	Men.
1st Division : Conroux. Head-quarters : Villamartin (near Bornos).		
1st Brigade, Meunier ; 9th Léger (2 batts.) *, 24th Ligne (3 batts.).		
2nd Brigade, Mocquery ; 96th Ligne (3 batts.).		
Total, including artillery	182	5,263
2nd Division : Barrois. Head-quarters : Puerto Real (near Cadiz).		
1st Brigade, Cassagne : 16th Léger, 8th Ligne (3 batts. each).		
2nd Brigade, Avril : 51st Ligne, 54th Ligne (3 batts. each).		
Total, including artillery	225	7,551
3rd Division : Villatte. Head-quarters : Santa Maria (near Cadiz).		
1st Brigade, Pécheux : 27th Léger, 63rd Ligne (3 batts. each).		
2nd Brigade, Lefol : 94th Ligne, 95th Ligne (3 batts. each).		
Total, including artillery	244	7,115

	Officers.	*Men.*

4th Division : Leval. Head-quarters : Granada.
1st Brigade, Rey : 32nd Ligne, 43rd Ligne (4 batts. each).
2nd Brigade, Vichery : 55th Ligne (4 batts.), 58th Ligne * (3 batts.).

| Total, including artillery . . . . | 273 | 9,131 |

5th Division : Drouet D'Erlon. Head-quarters : Zafra (Estremadura).
1st Brigade, Dombrowski : 12th Léger, 45th Ligne (3 batts. each).
2nd Brigade, Reymond : 64th Ligne * (2⅔ batts.), 88th Ligne * (2 batts.)

| Total, including artillery . . . . | 192 | 5,927 |

6th Division : Daricau. Head-quarters : Zalamea (Estremadura).
1st Brigade, Quiot : 21st Léger, 100th Ligne (3 batts. each).
2nd Brigade, St. Pol : 28th Léger *, 103rd Ligne * (2 batts. each).

| Total, including artillery . . . . | 174 | 4,854 |

| Total of six divisions . . . . . | 1,290 | 39,841 |

The regiments marked * had each one battalion in garrison at Badajoz, except the 64th, which had two companies there only [9th Léger, 28th Léger, 58th, 88th, 103rd Ligne]. The total of these 5½ battalions was 2,951 officers and men. Adding these to the six divisions the total was 44,082 French infantry present under arms.

CAVALRY.

1st Division. Head-quarters : Ribera (Estremadura).
1st Brigade, Perreymond : 2nd Hussars, 21st Chasseurs, 26th Dragoons.
2nd Brigade, Bonnemain : 5th Chasseurs, 27th Chasseurs.

| Total . . . . | 116 | 1,840 |

2nd Division. Head-quarters : Cordova.
1st Brigade, Digeon : 2nd, 4th, 5th Dragoons.
2nd Brigade, Lallemand : 14th, 17th, 27th Dragoons.

| Total . . . . | 170 | 3,307 |

3rd Division, Pierre Soult. Head-quarters : Granada.
1st Brigade, Boille : 10th Chasseurs, 12th Dragoons.
2nd Brigade, Ormancey : 16th Dragoons, 21st Dragoons.

| Total . . . . | 135 | 2,203 |

| Total Cavalry . . . . . . | 421 | 7,350 |

N.B.—7th Lancers, a Polish regiment, is omitted here, but actually stayed with the Army of the South till the end of 1812.

Spanish Troops [by return of April 1] :	Officers.	Men.
Infantry	218	2,732
Cavalry	163	2,358
Total *Juramentados*	381	5,090
Artillery (deducting divisional batteries) . . .	100	2,800
Engineers and Sappers	20	900
Three naval battalions (43rd and 44th *équipages de flotte*, and a battalion of *ouvriers de marine*) . . .	60	1800
Gendarmerie, &c.	10	600
General Total of army	2,282	58,381

Or adding the garrison of Badajoz (2,951 infantry, 268 artillery, 265 sappers, 42 cavalry, of the Army of the South, *not* including 910 Hessians of the Army of the Centre), a total of 64,189, without sick, &c.

When Soult on April 1st, 1812 marched to attempt the relief of Badajoz, he drew up the following statistics as to the strength of his army, *omitting the naval troops, and the gunners of the Cadiz Lines* :

(1) Marched for Badajoz :	Officers.	Men.
Infantry	600	17,964
Cavalry	237	3,944
Artillery	26	613
Engineers	2	116
Total	865	22,637 = 23,502

(2) Left before Cadiz and in Granada, &c.:		
Infantry	611	18,312
Cavalry	152	2,555
Total	763	20,867 = 21,630

(3) Garrisons of the Provinces of Cordova, Jaen, Granada, and Seville :		
Infantry	90	2,547
Cavalry	57	1,654
Total	147	4,201 = 4,348

(4) Spanish troops :		
Infantry	218	2,732
Cavalry	163	2,358
Total	381	5,090 = 5,471

Adding up these four totals we get officers 2,156, rank and file 52,795 = 54,951. This total omits the artillery in the Cadiz Lines and other fortified places, and the three marine regiments, and such sappers, gendarmes, military train, &c., as did not form part of the expedition that marched with Soult to relieve Badajoz. Adding these, at their strength of March 1, we get a total of about 59,000 of all ranks, not including the garrison of Badajoz. This agrees well enough with the March total of 60,663, allowing for a month's wear and tear.

IX

THE SIEGE OF BADAJOZ, MARCH 15–APRIL 6, 1812

(A) STRENGTH OF THE FRENCH GARRISON ON MARCH 15

[See the Tables in Belmas, iv. pp. 364–5 and in Jones, i. p. 229.]

Staff		25
Infantry :		
3/9th Léger . . .	officers and men	580
1/28th Léger . .	,, ,,	597
1/58th Ligne . .	,, ,,	450
3/88th Ligne . .	,, ,,	600
3/103rd Ligne . .	,, ,,	540
64th Ligne (2 companies)	,, ,,	130
Hesse-Darmstadt (2 batts.)	,. ,,	910
Juramentados		54 = 3,861 infantry.
Cavalry		42
Artillery		261
Engineers and Sappers		260
Sick in Hospital		300
Civil Departments, non-combatants, &c. . .		254
		5,003

A report of the governor at noon on April 5, found among his papers after the storm, gave the following as surviving under arms (sick excluded)— infantry 3,403, artillery 282, engineers 217, cavalry 50, *Juramentados* 86. This report, printed in Jones, i. p. 230, implies a higher original total than Belmas allows—the artillery and *Juramentados* are actually more numerous on April 5 than on March 15 ! And the infantry are only 458 less, despite of losses of a considerably higher figure, for another paper of the commandant shows (Jones, i. p. 230)—Sortie of March 19 : killed 30, wounded 287 = 317 [1]. Storm of Picurina Fort : killed or prisoners, 8 officers, 278 men = 286. We have thus 603 casualties in these two affairs only, beside the ordinary wear and tear of the siege.

Noting the considerable number of ' round figures ' in Belmas's table, I am inclined to think that the total of the garrison must have been a few hundreds over what he allows.

[1] Phillipon's report to Clarke, drawn up on June 12, gives 273 instead of 317 for the loss in this sally (see Belmas, iv. p. 414).

(B) LOSSES AT STORM OF BADAJOZ, APRIL 6, 1811

[From the Returns at the Record Office.]

	Killed.		Wounded.		Missing.		
	Offi-cers.	Men.	Offi-cers.	Men.	Offi-cers.	Men.	Total.
General Staff	1	—	16	—	—	—	17
Royal Artillery	1	6	1	9	—	—	17
Royal Engineers . . .	2	—	3	5	—	—	10
Assistant Engineers . . .	—	—	3	—	—	—	3
THIRD DIVISON.							
Kempt's Brigade :							
1/45th Foot	6	19	8	64	—	—	97
3/60th Foot	1	4	4	26	—	—	35
74th Foot	—	12	7	33	—	2	54
1/88th Foot	3	28	7	106	—	—	144
J. Campbell's Brigade :							
2/5th Foot	1	11	3	28	—	—	43
77th Foot	—	—	3	11	—	—	14
2/83rd Foot	1	22	7	39	—	—	69
94th Foot	1	12	1	51	—	—	65
Total 3rd Division . .	13	108	40	358	—	2	521
FOURTH DIVISION.							
Kemmis's Brigade :							
3/27th Foot	4	37	12	132	—	—	185
1/40th Foot	2	51	13	170	—	—	236
Bowes's Brigade :							
1/7th Foot	5	44	12	119	—	—	180
1/23rd Foot	3	22	14	92	—	20	151
1/48th Foot	3	32	16	122	—	—	173
Total 4th Division . .	17	186	67	635	—	20	925
FIFTH DIVISION.							
Hay's Brigade :							
3/1st Foot	—	—	—	—	—	—	—
1/9th Foot	—	—	—	—	—	—	—
2/38th Foot	1	12	3	26	—	—	42
Walker's Brigade :							
1/4th Foot	2	40	15	173	—	—	230
2/30th Foot	—	38	6	86	—	—	130
2/44th Foot	2	37	7	88	—	—	134
Total 5th Division . .	5	127	31	373	—	—	536

LIGHT DIVISION :	Killed. Offi-cers.	Men.	Wounded. Offi-cers.	Men.	Missing. Offi-cers.	Men.	Total.
1/43rd Foot	3	74	15	249	—	—	341
1/52nd Foot	5	53	14	248	—	—	320
1/95th Foot	3	27	10	154	—	—	194
3/95th Foot	4	9	4	47	—	—	64
Total Light Division .	15	163	43	698	—	—	919
Brunswick Oels, dispersed in companies in 4th and 5th Divisions	—	7	2	26	—	—	35
Total British loss . .	54	597	206	2,104	—	22	2,983
PORTUGUESE	8	147	45	500	—	30	730
General Total . . .	62	744	251	2,604	—	52	3,713
Losses during previous operations	10	219	54	661	—	13	957

The total loss during the siege and storm would therefore appear to have been 4,670.

X

WELLINGTON'S ARMY AT SALAMANCA. STRENGTH AND LOSSES

N.B.—Strength by the morning state of July 15, 1812. Losses of the British by the return annexed to Wellington's dispatch : those of the Portuguese from the official returns at Lisbon. The fighting strength on July 22, owing to losses at Castrejon and Castrillo, and to weary men falling out during the retreat, may have been perhaps 1,000 less.

I. BRITISH TROOPS

CAVALRY (Stapleton Cotton) :	Strength. Offi-cers.	Men.	Total.	Killed. Offi-cers.	Men.	Losses. Wounded. Offi-cers.	Men.	Miss-ing. Men.	Total Loss.
Le Marchant's Brigade — 3rd Dragoons . .	17	322	339	1	6	—	11	2	20
4th Dragoons . .	22	336	358	—	7	1	21	—	29
5th Dragoon Guards	22	313	325	—	9	2	42	3	56
G. Anson's Brigade — 11th Light Dragoons	30	361	391	—	—	—	—	—	—
12th Light Dragoons	19	321	340	1	2	—	2	—	5
16th Light Dragoons	14	259	273	—	—	—	—	—	—
V. Alten's Brigade — 14th Light Dragoons	23	324	347	—	1	—	2	—	3
1st Hussars K.G.L. .	23	376	399	—	2	5	16	—	23
Bock's Brigade — 1st Dragoons K.G.L.	25	339	364	—	—	—	—	—	—
2nd Dragoons K.G.L.	23	384	407	—	—	—	—	—	—
Total British Cavalry . .	218	3,335	3,543	2	27	8	94	5	136

INFANTRY. 1st Division (H. Campbell) :	Officers.	Strength. Men.	Total.	Killed. Offi-cers.	Men.	Losses. Wounded. Offi-cers.	Men.	Miss-ing. Men.	Total Loss.
Fermor's Brigade { 1st Coldstream Guards	26	928	954	—	7	1	22	8	38
1st Third Guards	23	938	961	—	1	1	20	2	24
1 comp. 5/60th Foot	1	56	57	—	—	—	—	—	—
Wheatley's Brigade { 2/24th Foot	23	398	421	—	—	—	5	—	5
1/42nd Foot	40	1,039	1,079	—	—	—	3	—	3
2/58th Foot [1]	31	369	400	—	—	—	3	1	4
1/79th Foot	40	634	674	—	—	—	1	3	4
1 comp. 5/60th	1	53	54	—	—	—	—	—	—
Löwe's Brigade { 1st Line Battalion K.G.L.	26	615	641	—	1	—	8	—	9
2nd Line Battalion K.G.L.	26	601	627	—	1	2	40	4	47
5th Line Battalion K.G.L.	30	525	555	—	1	1	17	—	19
Total 1st Division	267	6,156	6,423	—	11	5	119	18	153
3rd Division (Pakenham) :									
Wallace's Brigade { 1/45th Foot	26	416	442	—	5	5	45	—	55
74th Foot	23	420	443	—	3	2	40	4	49
1/88th Foot	21	642	663	2	11	4	110	8	135
3 comps. 5/60th Foot	11	243	254	—	6	3	24	3	36
J. Campbell's Brigade { 1/5th Foot	32	870	902	—	10	6	110	—	126
2/5th Foot	19	289	308	—	1	2	21	—	24
2/83rd Foot	24	295	319	—	2	2	30	—	34
94th Foot	24	323	347	1	3	3	21	—	28
Total 3rd Division	180	3,498	3,678	3	41	27	401	15	487
4th Division (Lowry Cole) :									
W. Anson's Brigade { 3/27th Foot	19	614	633	—	—	1	7	—	8
1/40th Foot	24	558	582	—	12	5	115	—	132
1 comp. 5/60th	2	44	46	—	—	—	—	—	—
Ellis's Brigade { 1/7th Foot	24	471	495	1	19	10	165	—	195
1/23rd Foot	19	427	446	1	9	6	90	—	106
1/48th Foot	22	404	426	—	9	10	60	—	79
1 comp. Brunswick Oels [2]	1	53	54	—	—	—	—	—	—
Total 4th Division	111	2,571	2,682	2	49	32	437	—	520

[1] The 2/58th though properly belonging to the 5th Division, appears to have acted on this day with the 1st Division.

[2] The losses of the attached companies of Brunswick Oels are only to be found under its regimental total in 7th Division.

| | | Strength. | | Killed. | | Losses. Wounded. | | Miss- ing. | Total |
	Offi- cers.	Men.	Total.	Offi- cers.	Men.	Offi- cers.	Men.	Men.	Loss.
5th Division (Leith) :									
3/1st Foot	32	729	761	—	23	8	129	—	160
1/9th Foot	31	635	666	—	3	1	42	—	46
Greville's 1/38th Foot [1]	36	764	800	2	14	12	115	—	143
Brigade 2/38th Foot	20	281	301	—	9	2	40	1	52
1 comp. Brunswick Oels [2]	2	76	78	—	—	—	—	—	—
1/4th Foot	36	421	457	—	—	1	17	—	18
2/4th Foot	27	627	654	—	2	—	23	6	31
Pringle's 2/30th Foot	20	329	349	—	3	1	22	1	27
Brigade 2/44th Foot	20	231	251	2	4	—	23	—	29
1 comp. Brunswick Oels [2]	3	66	69	—	—	—	—	—	—
Total 5th Division	227	4,159	4,386	4	58	25	411	8	506
6th Division (Clinton) :									
1/11th Foot	31	485	516	1	44	14	281	—	340
Hulse's 2/53rd Foot	25	316	341	—	26	11	105	—	142
Brigade 1/61st Foot	29	517	546	5	39	19	303	—	366
1 comp. 5/60th	2	59	61	—	—	—	—	—	—
Hinde's 2nd Foot	27	381	408	1	13	6	77	12	109
Brigade 1/32nd Foot	33	576	609	2	15	9	111	—	137
1/36 Foot	29	400	429	4	16	5	74	—	99
Total 6th Division	176	2,734	2,910	13	153	64	951	12	1,193
7th Division (Hope) :									
1st Light Batt. K.G.L.	25	544	569	—	—	2	7	—	9
Halkett's 2nd Light Batt. K.G.L.	21	473	494	1	5	1	9	—	16
Brigade Brunswick Oels [2] (9 companies)	23	573	596	—	4	2	42	1	49
De Berne- 51st Foot	27	280	307	—	—	—	2	—	2
witz's 68th Foot	21	317	338	1	3	2	14	—	20
Brigade Chasseurs Britan- niques	27	686	713	—	5	—	10	14	29
Total 7th Division	144	2,873	3,017	2	17	7	84	15	125
Light Division (Chas. Alten) :									
Barnard's 1/43rd Foot	30	718	748	—	—	1	15		16
Brigade Detachments 2/95th and 3/95th Rifles	19	373	392	—	—	—	5	—	5
Vandeleur's 1/52nd Foot	28	771	799	—	—	—	2	—	2
Brigade 8 comps. 1/95th	27	515	542	—	—	—	2	2	4
Total Light Division	104	2,377	2,481	—	—	1	24	2	27

[1] This battalion only joined the division on the battle-morning.

[2] The losses of the attached companies of Brunswick Oels are only to be found under its regimental total in 7th Division.

	Offi-cers.	Strength. Men.	Total.	Killed. Offi-cers.	Men.	Losses. Wounded. Offi-cers.	Men.	Miss-ing. Men.	Total Loss.
Royal Horse Artillery (troops of Ross, Macdonald, and Bull, and drivers)	18	403	421	—	1	—	2	—	3
Field Artillery (companies of Law-son, Gardiner, Greene, Douglas, May, and drivers) . . .	35	650	685	—	1	—	4	—	5
King's German Legion Artillery (battery of Sympher) . .	5	75	80	—	2	—	4	—	6
Artillery Total . . .	58	1,128	1,186	—	4	—	10	—	14
ENGINEERS	12	9	21	—	—	—	—	—	—
STAFF CORPS	5	81	86	—	—	—	—	—	—
WAGON TRAIN	24	115	139	—	—	—	—	—	—

BRITISH TOTAL

	Offi-cers.	Strength. Men.	Total.	Killed. Offi-cers.	Men.	Losses. Wounded. Offi-cers.	Men.	Miss-ing. Men.	Total Loss.
Infantry	1,209	24,368	25,577	24	329	159	2,387	69	2,968
Cavalry	218	3,335	3,553	2	27	8	94	5	136
Artillery	58	1,128	1,186	—	4	—	10	—	14
Engineers	12	9	21	—	—	—	—	—	—
Staff Corps	5	81	86	—	—	—	—	—	—
Train	24	115	139	—	—	—	—	—	—
General Staff	?	?	?	2	—	9	—	—	11
Total	1,526	29,036	30,562	28	360	176	2,491	74	3,129

II. PORTUGUESE TROOPS

	Offi-cers.	Strength. Men.	Total.	Killed. Offi-cers.	Men.	Losses. Wounded. Offi-cers.	Men.	Miss-ing. Men.	Total Loss.
CAVALRY :									
D'Urban's Brigade : 1st and 11th Dragoons (12th Dragoons absent)[1]	32	450	482	2	5	2	18	10	37
INFANTRY :									
Power's Brigade, 3rd Division : 9th and 21st Line, 12th Caça-dores	90	2,107	2,197	1	29	9	23	14	76
Stubbs's Brigade, 4th Division : 11th and 23rd Line, 7th Caça-dores	137	2,417	2,554	3	177	18	267	11	476
Spry's Brigade, 5th Division : 3rd and 15th Line, 8th Caçadores .	156	2,149	2,305	3	45	4	64	7	123

[1] The 12th Dragoons were marching to the rear in charge of the baggage-train.

	Officers.	Strength. Men.	Total.	Killed. Officers.	Men.	Losses. Wounded. Officers.	Men.	Missing. Men.	Total Loss.
Rezende's Brigade, 6th Division : 8th and 12th Line, 9th Caçadores	134	2,497	2,631	8	113	10	336	20	487
Collins's Brigade, 7th Division: 7th and 19th Line, 2nd Caçadores .	132	2,036	2,168	—	5	1	10	1	17
Pack's Independent Brigade : 1st and 16th Line, 4th Caçadores .	85	2,520	2,605	5	97	15	242	17	376
Bradford's Independent Brigade : 13th and 14th Line, 5th Caçadores	112	1,782	1,894	—	8	—	3	6	17
Attached to Light Division : 1st and 3rd Caçadores . . .	30	1,037	1,067	—	5	—	12	—	17
ARTILLERY :									
Arriaga's battery . . .	4	110	114	—	—	—	1	—	1
Total	912	17,105	18,017	22	484	59	976	86	1,627

III. SPANISH TROOPS

	Officers.	Strength. Men.	Total.	Killed. Officers.	Men.	Losses. Wounded. Officers.	Men.	Missing. Men.	Total Loss.
Carlos de España's Division : 2nd of Princesa, Tiradores de Castilla, 2nd of Jaen, 3rd of 1st Seville, Caçadores de Castilla, Lanceros de Castilla . .	160	3,200	3,360	—	2	—	4	—	6

GENERAL TOTAL

	Officers.	Strength. Men.	Total.	Killed. Officers.	Men.	Losses. Wounded. Officers.	Men.	Missing. Men.	Total Loss.
BRITISH	1,526	29,036	30,562	28	360	176	2,491	74	3,129
PORTUGUESE	912	17,105	18,017	22	484	59	976	86	1,627
SPANISH	160	3,200	3,360	—	2	—	4	—	6
Total	2,598	49,341	51,939	50	846	235	3,471	160	4,762

XI

STRENGTH AND LOSSES OF MARMONT'S ARMY AT SALAMANCA

To fix the fighting strength of Marmont's army at Salamanca is comparatively easy. It consisted of the 49,636 officers and men accounted for by the return of July 15th printed on the next page, minus some 700 men lost at the combats of Castrillo and Castrejon [also called ' combat of the Guarena '] on July 18, and such few hundreds more as may have fallen behind from fatigue during the long marches of July 20-1. Roughly speaking, it must have counted some 48,500 men, as opposed to Wellington's 50,000. The French translators of Napier's *Peninsular War* (Mathieu Dumas and Foltz) only give a table of June 15, which is of course a month out of date for Salamanca, and append a note that ' deducting artillery, engineers, *équipages militaires*, officers, sergeants, and garrisons, as also losses between June 15 and July 15 they find the result of about 42,000 sabres and bayonets for the battle.' Why any sane person *should* deduct officers, sergeants, and artillerymen from a fighting total I am unable to conceive, though contemporary British writers, including Wellington himself, often did so. But the results of adding to their ' 42,000 sabres and bayonets ' the list of 1,925 officers, 3,244 artillerymen and artillery train (both in the divisions and in the reserve), 332 engineers, and 742 *équipages militaires*, is to give the figure 48,343, which practically agrees with the total that I state above ; if sergeants are added it would much exceed that total. We may take this, therefore, as fairly correct—bearing in mind that the 26 officers and 742 men of the *équipages militaires* cannot be counted as combatants.

These totals do not include the 23rd Léger (2 batts.) and the 2/1st Line, both from Thomières's division, which were garrisoning Astorga, about 1,500 strong. Nor do they include the minor garrisons left at Toro, Zamora, Olmedo, Valdestillas, Tordesillas, Simancas, Cabezon, Medina del Campo, Puente de Duero, Tudela de Douro, Amagro, &c., which appear to have been altogether about 4,184 strong, nor the dépôts at Valladolid, 3,307 strong on June 15, but probably much less on July 15, when Marmont had remounted nearly 1,000 dismounted dragoons and picked up all detachments and convalescents that he could gather. Nor do they include the sick, who had been 8,633 on June 15th, and 8,332 on May 15th— probably the total in hospital was a trifle more on July 15, owing to the fatigues of the campaigns round San Cristobal in the latter days of June.

Parallel with the return of July 15th, I have printed that of August 1. The difference between the two—211 officers and 10,124 men—might be supposed to represent the losses in the campaign between those dates. It does not, however, because the total of August 1 represents not only the survivors from the battle of Salamanca, but all the men from garrisons evacuated after it, and from the Valladolid dépôt, who joined the colours after the disaster of July 22, in consequence of the district in which they were lying having been evacuated by the army. The garrisons of Toro and Zamora held out till they were relieved, that of Tordesillas surrendered to the Galicians : but the men from the other smaller garrisons and from the dépôts fell in to their respective corps before August 1. I imagine that we may take these additions to be some 5,000 men at least, but cannot give the exact figures, through being unable to say what the Valladolid dépôts (3,307 strong on June 15) amounted to on July 15.

After comparing the totals of the brigades and regiments shown under July 15 and August 1, we must proceed to show the reasons why, in individual cases, the regimental differences between the two sets of figures cannot be taken to represent the sum of the losses in the Salamanca campaign. The proof is clear.

THE ARMY OF PORTUGAL BEFORE AND AFTER THE BATTLE OF SALAMANCA

From two returns of effectives in the Archives of the Ministry of War, Paris, dated July 15 and August 1, respectively.

			July 15. Offi-cers.	July 15. Men.	August 1. Offi-cers.	August 1. Men.
1st Division (Foy) :						
Brigade	6th Léger (2 batts.)	. .	46	1,055	41	684
Chemineau	69th Ligne (2 batts.)	. .	50	1,408	47	1,322
Brigade Desgraviers-Berthelot	39th Ligne (2 batts.)	. .	49	918	49	872
	76th Ligne (2 batts.)	. .	56	1,351	45	887
Artillery Train, &c.	. . . . .		7	207	7	207
Divisional Total	. . . . .		208	4,939	189	3,972
2nd Division (Clausel) :						
Brigade	25th Léger (3 batts.)	. .	54	1,485	43	1,222
Berlier	27th Ligne (2 batts.)	. .	40	1,637	31	1,248
Brigade	50th Ligne (3 batts.)	. .	52	1,490	46	1,177
Barbot	59th Ligne (2 batts.)	. .	47	1,531	38	1,278
Artillery Train, &c.	. . . . .		7	219	7	216
Divisional Total	. . . . .		200	6,362	165	5,141

		July 15.		August 1.	
		Officers.	*Men.*	*Officers.*	*Men.*
3rd DIVISION (Ferey) :					
Brigade	31st Léger (2 batts.) . .	46	1,359	45	1,325
Menne	26th Ligne (2 batts.) . .	44	1,145	43	1,116
?	47th Ligne (3 batts.) . .	67	1,558	62	1,650
	70th Ligne (2 batts.) . .	49	1,114	36	1,061
Artillery Train, &c.		5	302	3	193
Divisional Total		211	5,478	189	5,345
4th DIVISION (Sarrut) :					
Brigade	2nd Léger (3 batts.) . .	66	1,772	68	1,702
Fririon	36th Ligne (3 batts.) . .	69	1,570	71	1,514
Brigade	4th Léger (3 batts.) . .	63	1,219	63	989
?	130th Ligne (absent) . .	—	—	—	—
Artillery Train, &c.		5	238	5	214
Divisional Total		203	4,799	207	4,419
5th DIVISION (Maucune) :					
Brigade	15th Ligne (3 batts.) . .	52	1,615	46	1,229
Arnaud	66th Ligne (2 batts.) . .	38	1,131	34	661
Brigade	82nd Ligne (2 batts.) . .	41	966	39	729
Montfort	86th Ligne (2 batts.) . .	30	1,155	28	961
Artillery Train, &c.		4	212	4	212
Divisional Total		165	5,079	151	3,792
6th DIVISION (Brennier) :					
Brigade	17th Léger (2 batts.) . .	46	1,074	42	855
Taupin	65th Ligne (3 batts.) . .	59	1,527	52	1,302
?	22nd Ligne (3 batts.) . .	61	1,486	40	716
	Régiment de Prusse (remnant of)	9	79	9	79
Artillery Train, &c.		4	213	4	213
Divisional Total		179	4,379	147	3,165
7th DIVISION (Thomières) :					
Brigade	1st Line (3 batts.) [1] . .	80	1,683	79	1,454
Bonté	62nd Line (2 batts.) . .	47	1,076	45	1,048
?	23rd Léger (absent) [2] . .	—	—	—	—
	101st Line (3 batts.) . .	61	1,388	29	412
Artillery Train, &c.		5	203	nil	nil
Divisional Total		193	4,350	153	2,914

[1] Not including 2nd battalion, about 450 strong, at Astorga in garrison.
[2] In garrison at Astorga.

		July 15.		August 1.	
8th DIVISION (Bonnet) :		Offi-cers.	Men.	Offi-cers.	Men.
Brigade Gautier	{ 118th Line (3 batts.)	53	1,584	37	1,024
	{ 119th Line (3 batts.)	64	1,265	48	831
?	{ 120th Line (3 batts.)	63	1,745	66	1,152
	{ 122nd Line (3 batts.)	55	1,582	40	1,000
Artillery train, &c.		3	107	nil	nil
Divisional Total		238	6,283	191	4,007

		July 15.		August 1.	
LIGHT CAVALRY DIVISION (Curto) :					
?	3rd Hussars (3 squadrons)	17	231	14	165
	22nd Chasseurs (2 squadrons)	17	236	18	233
	26th Chasseurs (2 squadrons)	16	278	18	225
	28th Chasseurs (1 squadron)	7	87	3	39
?	13th Chasseurs (5 squadrons)	20	496	28	426
	14th Chasseurs (4 squadrons)	14	308	18	332
	Escadron de marche	11	141	9	52
Divisional Total		102	1,777	108	1,472

		July 15.		August 1.	
HEAVY CAVALRY DIVISION (Boyer) :					
?	{ 6th Dragoons (2 squadrons)	19	376	19	332
	{ 11th Dragoons (2 squadrons)	19	411	18	359
Brigade Carrié	{ 15th Dragoons (2 squadrons)	15	328	16	294
	{ 25th Dragoons (2 squadrons)	18	314	18	282
Artillery attached to cavalry		3	193	3	148
Divisional Total		74	1,622	74	1,415
Total Cavalry Divisions		176	3,399	182	2,887
Artillery Reserve, Park, &c.		50	1,450	22	707
Engineers and Sappers		17	332	16	345
Gendarmerie		6	129	6	186
Équipages militaires		26	742	22	707
État-Major Général		54	—	54	—
General Total { Infantry Divisions		1,597	41,669	1,392	32,755
{ Cavalry Divisions		176	3,399	182	2,887
{ Auxiliary Arms		153	2,653	120	1,945
		1,925	47,721	1,694	37,587

N.B.—Guns, July 15, 78 ; August 1, 58 ; lost 7 12-pounders, 3
8-pounders, 9 4-pounders, 1 3-pounder. Horses, July 15, 4,278 ; August 1,
3,231. Draught horses, July 15, 2,037 ; August 1, 1,847. Équipages
militaires, horses, July 15, 800 ; August 1, 331.

To these two tables we must append, as a side-light, the results of a compilation of the totals of officers killed and wounded at Salamanca, from Martinien's admirable *Liste des officiers tués et blessés pendant les guerres de l'Empire.* This of course does not include unwounded prisoners.

	Killed.	Wounded.
Foy's Division (including losses at Garcia Hernandez on July 23rd):		
6th Léger .	1	10 = 11
69th Line .	2	8 = 10
39th Line .	—	2 = 2
76th Line .	1	7 = 8
Total . . .		31
Clausel's Division :		
25th Léger	4	10 = 14[1]
27th Line .	2	5 = 7
50th Line .	9	17 = 26
59th Line .	4	15 = 19
Total . . .		66
Ferey's Division :		
31st Léger	1	6 = 7
26th Line .	—	6 = 6
47th Line .	5	13 = 18
70th Line .	2	3 = 5
Total . . .		36
Sarrut's Division :		
2nd Léger	—	3 = 3
36th Line .	—	3 = 3
4th Léger .	—	2 = 2
Total . . .		8
Maucune's Division :		
15th Line .	4	12 = 16
66th Line .	2	15 = 17
82nd Line	1	7 = 8
86th Line .	—	3 = 3
Total . . .		44

	Killed.	Wounded.
Brennier's Division :		
17th Léger .	1	3 = 4[2]
65th Line .	1	8 = 9[3]
22nd Line .	2	19 = 21[4]
Total . . .		34
Thomières's Division :		
1st Line .	—	4 = 4
62nd Line .	1	14 = 15
101st Line	6	19 = 25
Total . . .		44
Bonnet's Division :		
118th Line	2	18 = 20
119th Line	3	23 = 26
120th Line	—	8 = 8
122nd Line	3	13 = 16
Total . . .		70
Curto's Light Cavalry :		
3rd Hussars .	—	2[5]
13th Chasseurs .	—	7
14th Chasseurs .	—	5[6]
22nd Chasseurs .	—	5
26th Chasseurs .	—	4
28th Chasseurs .	—	2
Total . .		25
Boyer's Division of Dragoons :		
6th Dragoons .	—	9
11th Dragoons .	—	2[7]
15th Dragoons .	—	1[8]
25th Dragoons .	—	6[9]
Total . .		18

[1] Plus 1 killed and 5 wounded at the combat of the Guarena, July 18.

[2] Plus 2 killed 6 wounded at the Guarena.

[3] Plus 2 killed 1 wounded at the Guarena.

[4] Plus 5 wounded at the Guarena.

[5] Plus 1 killed 1 wounded at Castrejon.

[6] Plus 3 wounded at Castrejon.

[7] Plus 1 wounded on July 21, and 2 wounded at Garcia Hernandez, July 23.

[8] Plus 1 killed 1 wounded at the Guarena, July 18.

[9] Plus 4 wounded at the Guarena.

	Killed.	*Wounded.*		*Killed.*	*Wounded.*
Artillery, Horse	—	1	Staff . . 3		$17^1 = 20$
,, Field .	—	5	Miscellaneous offi-		
,, Train .	—	1	cers, whose regi-		
Total . . .		7	ments were not		
			present at Sala-		
Engineers . .	—	3 = 3	manca . . —		2 = 2

General total 60 officers killed, 347 wounded at Salamanca and Garcia Hernandez ; plus 7 officers killed and 27 wounded at the Guarena on July 18, and 2 wounded in minor engagements.

Loss in killed and wounded, not including unwounded prisoners, during the campaign, 67 killed, 376 wounded = 443 officers in all.

After arriving at this general loss in killed and wounded officers, so far as is possible from Martinien's tables, which are not quite complete for all corps, it only remains to estimate the unwounded prisoners. I searched the immense volumes of rolls of French officers in captivity at the Record Office, and found 63 names of prisoners taken at Salamanca, the Guarena, and Garcia Hernandez. A few of these duplicate the names of wounded officers to be found in Martinien's tables, the remainder must represent the unwounded prisoners. Wellington in his Salamanca dispatch wrote that he had 137 French officers prisoners—evidently the larger number of them must have been wounded, as only 63 were sent off to England that autumn. Probably many died in hospital. Prisoners are most numerous from the 101st, 22nd, and from Foy's two regiments cut up at Garcia Hernandez, the 76th and 6th Léger.

In the Library of the *Archives de la Guerre* at the Paris Ministry of War I went through the regimental histories of all the French infantry regiments present at Salamanca. Like our own similar compilations, they differ much in value—some are very full and with statistics carefully worked out from regimental reports and pay-books ; others are very thin and factless. Fourteen units give their losses, which I herewith annex :

Clausel's Division : 25th Léger, 336 ; 27th Line, 159 ; 59th Line, 350.

Ferey's Division : 70th Line, 111 ; 31st Léger, 340.

Sarrut's Division : 2nd Léger, 202.

Maucune's Division : 15th Line, 359.

Brennier's Division : 17th Léger, 264 ; 65th Line, 359.

Thomières's Division : 1st Line, 227 ; 62nd Line, 868 ; 101st Line, 1,000.

Bonnet's Division : 120th, 458 ; 122nd, 527.

The total of this makes 5,560 for these fourteen corps ; we leave fifteen others unaccounted for. As a rough calculation I suppose that we may hold that as these regiments lost, as we know from Martinien's lists [which are not *quite* complete], at least 152 officers out of 5,560 of all ranks, then the other fifteen regiments with 181 officers killed or wounded must have lost something like 6,000. The vagaries of the proportion between officers and men hit are extraordinary in individual units, but these

---

[1] Plus 1 general wounded July 16, died next day (Dembouski), and 1 general wounded and taken July 18 (at the Guarena), Carrié, and 1 officer wounded at Garcia Hernandez.

tend to rectify themselves on a large total consisting of many regiments. I therefore believe that 11,560 would be something very like the total loss *killed and wounded* in the French infantry. We have then to allow for some 40 unwounded officers taken prisoners, and corresponding to them perhaps 1,200 unwounded men. The total loss for the infantry would thus be 12,800. For cavalry and artillery, &c., 53 officers hit—as by Martinien's tables—must imply something over a thousand men lost. We should thus arrive at a total of 14,000 for the casualties—the sum which I suggest in my text (p. 469).

To show the worthlessness of any attempt to deduce the French losses by a mere comparison of the official ' morning states ' of July 15 and August 1, the following instances may suffice.

The 65th Line shows 59 officers and 1,527 men present on July 15, 52 officers and 1,302 men on August 1. The apparent loss is 7 officers and 225 men. But this unit's regimental report shows 3 officers killed, 5 officers wounded, 204 men killed or prisoners, 106 men wounded, 39 missing ; total, 8 officers and 349 men. Therefore, as is obvious, one officer and 124 men must have joined from somewhere (dépôt at Valladolid ?) between the two dates, or the deficiency would be 125 greater between the ' present under arms ' of the two dates than is shown.

A more striking case is the 62nd Line, of Thomières's Division. It shows present on July 15, 47 officers and 1,076 men, on August 1st 45 officers and 1,048 men—the apparent loss is only 2 officers and 28 men. But Martinien's lists show us that the regiment lost at least 15 officers, killed and wounded, and the regimental report gives 20 officers and 848 men killed, wounded, or missing! The real loss is 868 not 30 ! Therefore 18 officers and about 800 men, the equivalent of a strong battalion, must have joined between July 15 and August 1. This corresponds to the fact that the 62nd showed only 2 battalions[1] at Salamanca, while the ' morning state ' of June 15th showed it as having at the front three battalions and 1,900 rank and file. Clearly the third battalion rejoined the colours after the battle—having presumably been quartered in the small garrisons of Castile evacuated after the disaster of July 22. Many men must also have rejoined the other two battalions.

But the most absurd case of all is that of the 47th Line, whose total figures actually *go up* from 1,625 to 1,712 of all ranks between July 15th and August 1st—in despite of the fact that it lost (as Martinien's lists show), 18 officers and not less therefore than 360 rank and file (20 men per officer is a low allowance) at Salamanca. It must have picked up from Valladolid and the small garrisons 13 officers and 452 men at least[2].

Clausel, writing to King Joseph on July 25, said that of the whole Army of Portugal he could not yet show in the field on that day 20,000 men. This tallies well enough with the conclusion that we have already drawn, that the total loss from the army, which on July 15 had about 48,000 men, must have been some 14,000 killed, wounded, and prisoners, and over 10,000 men dispersed who were only just rallying.

---

[1] And one odd company of its 3rd battalion, 61 of all ranks, while in the return of August 1, the 3rd battalion has 13 officers and 480 men.

[2] The 2/47th shows on July 15, 310 of all ranks, on August 1, 513.

XII

BRITISH LOSSES AT THE COMBATS OF CASTREJON AND CASTRILLO[1], JULY 18, 1812

	Officers. Killed.	Officers. Wounded.	Men. Killed.	Men. Wounded.	Missing. Men.	Total.
G. Anson's Brigade :						
11th Lt. Dragoons	—	2	3	10	—	15
12th Lt. Dragoons	—	1	5	11	1	18
16th Lt. Dragoons	—	—	—	—	—	—
V. Alten's Brigade :						
1st Hussars K.G.L.	—	4	7	45	4	60
14th Lt. Dragoons	—	3	14	49	9	75
Bock's Brigade :						
1st Dragoons K.G.L.	—	—	—	1	—	1
2nd Dragoons K.G.L.	—	—	5	1	1	7
Le Marchant's Brigade :						
3rd Dragoons .	—	1	—	9	—	10
4th Division.						
W. Anson's Brigade :						
3/27th Foot . .	2	1	11	58	—	72
1/40th Foot . .	—	1	8	59	1	69
Ellis's Brigade :						
1/7th Foot . .	—	1	1	14	3	19
1/23rd Foot . .	—	—	—	2	2	4
1/48th Foot . .	—	—	—	5	1	6
5th Division.						
Greville's Brigade :						
3/1st . . .	—	—	—	2	—	2
Detached Companies of 5/60th . .	—	—	—	1	2	3
Horse Artillery .	—	1	2	2	—	5
German Artillery .	—	—	—	2	—	2
Portuguese . .	1	6	33	90	27	157
Total . .	3	21	89	361	51	525

[1] The fight at Castrillo is often called the ' Combat of the Guarena '.

XIII

SPANISH TROOPS ON THE EAST COAST OF SPAIN IN THE SPRING OF 1812

(A) REMAINS OF THE 2ND (VALENCIAN) AND 3RD (MURCIAN) ARMIES, MARCH 1

	Officers.	Men.
1st Division: Conde de Montijo, 1st of Badajoz (2 batts.), Cuenca (2 batts.), 2 squadrons cavalry . . .	110	2,049
2nd Division : General Luis Riquelme, 2nd Walloon Guards, Guadalajara (3 batts.), 1st of Burgos (3 batts.), Guadix (2 batts.), Bailen (1 batt.), Alpujarras (1 batt.), dismounted cavalry (1 batt.)	335	5,214
Reserve Division : General Philip Roche. Voluntarios de Aragon, Canarias, Alicante, 2nd of Murcia, Alcazar de San Juan, Chinchilla (1 batt. each), 2 squadrons of Husares de Fernando 7°	300	5,576
Cavalry : General A. Rich. Principe (2 squadrons), España (2 squadrons), Reina (2 squadrons), Carbineros Reales, Farnesio, Montesa, Dragones del Rey, Cazadores de Valencia, Pavia, Rey, Granaderos a caballo, Husares de Castilla (one squadron each), three provisional squadrons	321	1,565
Cadres of dispersed battalions, now reorganizing : Lorca, Velez Malaga, Almanza, America . . .	98	1,079
Artillery (Field)	38	651
Artillery (Garrison) in Alicante and Cartagena . .	17	582
Engineers	8	202
Total	1,227	16,918

(B) JOSEPH O'DONNELL'S ARMY, JULY 21, 1812, AND ITS LOSSES AT CASTALLA

[The figures of the former from *Los Ejércitos españoles*. The list of prisoners from Suchet's dispatch in the Paris *Archives de la Guerre*.]

		Strength. Officers.	Men.	Total.	Unwounded prisoners reported by Suchet.
Michelena's Brigade	Corona (1 batt.) . . .	24	630		255
	Velez Malaga (1 batt.) . .	36	834	2,035	—
	Guadix	24	487		337
Montijo's Brigade	2nd Walloon Guards (1 batt.) .	20	569		350
	Cuenca (2 batts.) . . .	33	890	2,152	112
	1st of Badajoz (1 batt.) . .	27	613		—

		Strength. Officers.	Men.	Total.	Unwounded prisoners reported by Suchet.
Mijares's Brigade	Bailen (1 batt.)	32	708		405
	Alcazar de San Juan (1 batt.) .	31	855	2,187	434
	Lorca (1 batt.)	25	536		242
Cavalry (Provisional Regiment, 2 squadrons) .		29	207		—
Engineers		26	325		—
Roche's Division :					
1st of Burgos (2 batts.)		27	786		—
Canarias (1 batt.)		34	818		—
Alicante (2 batts.)		35	1,110		—
Chinchilla (2 batts.)		26	918		—
Total		429	10,286		2,135

Suchet also reports 697 wounded prisoners, of whom 56 died of their wounds. No figures are given for the detached cavalry division of Santesteban, which was not in action at Castalla.

XIV

THE BRITISH FORCES ON THE EAST COAST OF SPAIN IN 1812

[A NOTE BY MR. C. T. ATKINSON]

I. MAITLAND'S FORCE, EMBARKATION RETURN, JUNE 25, 1812

(War Office : *Secretary of State's Original Correspondence*, Series I, vol. 311.)

	Officers.	N.C.O.'s and Men.
20th Light Dragoons	9	158
Foreign Troop of Hussars	3	68
R.A. (including drivers)	8	73
Marine Artillery	1	29
R.E.	5	42
Staff Corps	1	13
1/10th Foot	33	902
1/58th Foot	31	840
1/81st Foot	44	1,230
4th Line Battalion, K.G.L.	36	953
6th Line Battalion, K.G.L.	33	1,041
De Roll's Regiment (3 companies) . . .	11	320
Dillon's Regiment (5 companies) . . .	18	536
Calabrian Free Corps (1 division) [1] . . .	14	338
Total	247	6,543

[1] This corps was organized in five 'divisions,' each of three companies.

II. CAMPBELL'S CORPS, EMBARKATION RETURN, PALERMO, NOVEMBER 14, 1812

(Ibid., vol. 312.)

	Officers.	N.C.O.'s and Men.
20th Light Dragoons	—	13
Guides	—	14
R.A. (including drivers)	4	131
Grenadier Battalion [1]	35	924
Light Infantry Battalion [2]	21	582
1/27th Foot	25	828
2nd Battalion, Anglo-Italian Levy [3] . .	33	1,184
Sicilian Artillery	—	155
Sicilian Grenadiers [4]	—	605
Total	118	4,436 [5]

III. SUBSEQUENTLY EMBARKED, DECEMBER 25 [6]

	Officers.	N.C.O.'s and Men.
20th Light Dragoons	8	223
R.A.	—	60
2nd Anglo-Italians	2	176
Calabrian Free Corps (1 division) . . .	14	325
Sicilian Cavalry	22	204
Sicilian Infantry (the Estero Regiment) . .	77	1,185
Total	123	2,173

It may be well to give here the garrisons of Cadiz and Gibraltar in 1812, as both of them supplied troops to the field army during that year.

In Gibraltar, under General Campbell, there were the 2/9th, 2/11th, 37th, and the 4th and 7th Veteran Battalions throughout the year. The 1/82nd was there till the summer, when it was relieved by the 1/26th,

---

[1] From 2/10th, 1/21st, 1/31st, 1/62nd, 1/75th, 3rd, 7th, and 8th K.G.L.

[2] Schwertfeger, i. pp. 480–1, says it was composed of the light companies of De Roll's, Dillon's, De Watteville's (this is inaccurate, as De Watteville's regiment had moved to Cadiz before the end of 1811), and the 3rd, 7th, and 8th K.G.L.

[3] 150 men were left behind from lack of room but sent later.

[4] 140 men were left behind from lack of room but sent later.

[5] A ' division' of the Calabrian Free Corps, 300 strong, was left behind for want of room, as well as the Sicilian Regiment de Presidi, 1,200 strong.

[6] In a letter to Lord Bathurst of December 9 Bentinck announces his intention to add to this force 2/27th Foot and 1st Anglo-Italians, who had been 28 officers and 823 men and 40 officers and 1,153 men respectively in the ' state ' of October 25, but are not present in the ' state ' of December 10 (except for 288 men of 1st Anglo-Italians).

sent back from Portugal by Wellington. The 1/82nd sailed for Lisbon and marched up to the front, but arrived just too late for the battle of Salamanca.

At Cadiz General Cooke commanded, at the commencement of the year, the 3/1st Guards (which had arrived and relieved the ' composite battalion of Guards' before the end of 1811), also the 2/47th, 2/67th, 2/87th, two companies of the *Chasseurs Britanniques*, De Watteville's regiment (which arrived before the end of 1811), the strange corps sometimes called the ' battalion of Foreign Deserters,' sometimes the ' battalion of Foreign Recruits,' two companies of the 2/95th, and a squadron of the 2nd Hussars K.G.L., also the 20th Portuguese.

Early in the year the 2/67th and five companies of De Watteville's regiment were sent off to Cartagena.

In September the 3/1st Guards, 2/47th, 2/87th, two companies 95th, and 20th Portuguese marched to join Hill at Madrid, taking with them the German squadron and two field-batteries : they were just 4,000 strong.

The 2/59th came out from home about the same time, and was in October the only *British* battalion at Cadiz. With them remained the ' Foreign Deserters,' seven companies of De Watteville, and two companies of *Chasseurs Britanniques*, as also some artillerymen.

XV

THE SCOVELL CIPHERS

By the very great kindness of Mr. G. Scovell of Brighton, I have had placed at my disposition the papers of his great-uncle, General Sir George Scovell, G.C.B., who served during the Peninsular War in the Intelligence branch of the Quartermaster-General's department. In the beginning of 1812 the number of intercepted French dispatches in cipher which came into Wellington's hands, through the happy activity of Julian Sanchez and other guerrillero chiefs, began to be so considerable that the Commander-in-Chief thought it worth while to detail a member of his staff to deal with them. Captain Scovell was selected because of his ingenuity in this line, and became responsible for attempting to interpret all the captured documents. They were made over to him, and, having done what he could with them, he placed the fair-copy of the ' decoded ' result in Wellington's hands, but seems to have been allowed to keep the originals—which were, of course, unintelligible because of their form, and therefore useless to his chief. The file of documents which thus remained with him is most interesting : they range in size from formal dispatches of considerable bulk—eight or ten folio pages long—down to scraps of the smallest size written on thin paper, and folded up so as to go into some secret place of concealment on the bearer's person. Some of them look as if they had been sewed up in a button, or rolled under the leather of a whip handle, or pushed along the seam of a garment. I take it that these must all have been entrusted to emissaries sent in disguise, *Afrancesados* or peasants hired by a great bribe. Presumably each of these scraps cost the life of the bearer when it was discovered—for the guerrillero chiefs did not deal mildly with Spaniards caught carrying French secret orders. The large folio dispatches, on the other hand, must no doubt have been carried by French aides-de-camp or couriers, whose escorts were dispersed or captured by the *partidas* at some corner of the mountain roads between Madrid and the head-quarters of the Armies of Portugal and Andalusia.

The cipher letters are of two sorts—in the first (and more numerous) class only the names of persons and places, and the most important sentences are in cipher—invariably a numerical cipher of arbitrary figures. In the other class the whole dispatch is written in figures, not merely its more weighty clauses. The reason for adopting the former method was that it saved much time ; the transliterating of unimportant parts of the dispatch (such as compliments, and personal remarks of no strategical import) would have taken many extra hours, when it was necessary to get a letter sent off in a hurry. But, as we shall see later on, there was grave danger in using this system, because the context might sometimes allow the decipherer to make a good guess at the disguised words, after reading that part of the letter which was not so guarded.

Occasionally a French dispatch is ciphered after the same infantile system that readers of romances will remember in Poe's *Gold Bug* or Conan Doyle's *Sherlock Holmes,* where letters or numbers are merely substituted for each other—where, for example, 2 always means letter *e,* or 25 letter *r.* This sort of cipher is dangerously easy to an expert reader, especially if the words are separated from each other, so that the number of letters in each can be counted. Take, for example, a letter sent to Soult in 1813 by Cassan, the blockaded governor of Pampeluna [1]. Only one precaution had been taken in this cipher-epistle, viz. that elaborate care has been taken to defeat the attempt of the reader to arrive at results by counting what figures appear most frequently, and so deducing by their repetition that these must be *e* (the most frequently used letter in French, as in English), *s, i, a, t,* and other common letters. This is done by having six alternative numbers for *e,* four each for *a* and *i,* three for *t, s,* and *n.* Taking the simple phrase 47.50.40.41.14.26 58.24 3.51.10.36.44.23.17.24.10.50.53.27 47.46 11.18.39.17.46.21, which deciphers into ' depuis le commencement du blocus,' we see that *e* appears five times, but is represented by both 50, 24, and 44 ; *u* three times, but varied as 14 and 46 ; *m* thrice, varied as 10 and 36. This made the reader's work harder, but not nearly so difficult as that required for certain other ciphers : for the whole set of signs, being not much over 60 in number, there was a limited amount of possibilities for each figure-interpretation. And the words being separated by spaces, there was a certainty that some of the two-letter units must represent *et, de, ce, eu, du,* and similar common French two-letter words. As a matter of fact this particular dispatch was deciphered in a few hours owing to the lucky guess that its initial words 10.45.23.21.16.2.41.25 5.24 10.4.25.24.3.9.8.5 might be ' Monsieur le Maréchal,' the preliminary address to the intended recipient. This hypothesis was verified at once by finding that this rendering made good sense for the two-letter words 23.24=*ne,* and 10.2=*me,* lower down in the letter. After this all was plain sailing.

---

[1] This particular letter is *not* one of the Scovell file.

But the usual French cipher, the ' Great Paris Cipher ' as Scovell called it, was a very much more complicated and difficult affair, as the list of figures, instead of being only a few score, ran to many hundreds. And of these only some few represented individual letters, more were parts of a syllabary : *ma, me, mi, mo, mu,* for example, had each a figure representing them, and so had *ab- ac- ad- af- ag-* &c. Moreover, there was a multitude of arbitrary numbers, representing under a single figure words that must often be used in a dispatch, such as *hommes, armée, général, marche, ennemi, corps d'armée, canons.* In addition there was a code of proper names, e.g. 1216 meant the River Douro, 93 Portugal, 1279 Talavera, 585 King Joseph, 1391 General Dorsenne, 1327 the Army of the South, 1280 Soult, 1300 Wellington, 400 Ciudad Rodrigo, &c. If the King wished the Duke of Dalmatia to send 9,000 men of the Army of the South to Talavera, he had only to write ' 585 désire que 1280 dirige 1156 (neuf) 692 (mille) 1102 (hommes) de 1327 sur 1279.' He would then cut up *désire* and *dirige* into the syllables *de-si-re* and *di-ri-ge,* for each of which the syllabary had set figures ; there were also arbitrary numbers for *sur, de,* and *que.* So the whole sentence would take up only fourteen numbers when written out.

It would seem at first sight that to interpret such a dispatch would be a perfectly hopeless task, to any one who had not the key to the cipher before him. That the admirably patient and ingenious Scovell at last made out for himself a key from the laborious comparison of documents, was nevertheless the fact. He was started on the track by the fortunate circumstance that most of the intercepted dispatches were only *partly* in cipher. Marmont would write ' Avec les moyens que j'ai, et 798, 1118, 602, 131, 1112.663.1135.502 au delà de Sabugal,' or ' J'avais donné l'ordre que 1003, 497, 1115, 1383, 69,711, 772, 530, de descendre cette rivière et de se mettre en communication avec moi.' Clearly the cipher-figures in the first case have something to do with a march on Sabugal, in the second with orders to some general or body of troops (to be identified hereafter) to march down a river which the context shows must be the Tagus. This is not much help, and the task looked still very hopeless. But when intercepted dispatches accumulated in quantities, and the same cipher-figures kept occurring among sentences of which part was written out in full, it became evident that various cryptic figures must mean places and persons who could be guessed at, with practical certainty. Occasionally a French writer completely ' gives himself away ' by carelessness : e.g. Dorsenne wrote on April 16 to Jourdan, 'Vous voulez de renseignement sur la situation militaire et administrative de 1238 :' obviously the probable interpretation of this number is ' the Army of the North,' and this is rendered almost certain by passages lower down the same letter. Equally incautious is King Joseph when he writes to Marmont, ' J'ai donné l'ordre au général Treillard de 117.8.7 la vallée du 1383, afin de marcher à 498.' Considering the situation of the moment 117.8.7 must almost certainly mean *evacuate,* 1383 *Tagus,* and 498 some large town.[1] [The particular dispatch in which this occurs is on a most curious piece of paper, half an inch broad, a foot long, and excessively thin. It is bent into twelve folds,

[1] Wellington wrongly guessed Plasencia : it was Aranjuez.

and would fit into any small receptacle of one inch by half an inch. I fear the bearer who had it on his person must have come to a bad end.] Suchet also made Scovell the present of some useful words when he wrote on September 17 to Soult, 'Le Général Maitland commande l'expédition anglaise venue de 747 : O'Donnell peut réunir 786 692 1102 en y comprenant le corps de l'Anglais Roche. Le 19 août je n'avais que 135 692 1102 à lui opposer.' Here it is quite clear that ' 747 ' means *Sicily* ; that ' 692. 1102 ' in the two statements of forces means *thousand men*. A little guessing and comparison with other cryptic statements of forces would soon show that 135 meant 7 and 786 meant 12.

Notwithstanding much useful help it was still a marvellous feat of Scovell to work out by the end of 1812 no less than *nine hundred* separate cipher-numbers, ranging in complexity from the simple vowel *a* to the symbol that represented ' train des équipages militaires ' ! He must have had a most ingenious brain, and unlimited patience. Down to the end there remained numbers of unsolved riddles, figures that represented persons or places so unfrequently mentioned that there was no way of discovering, by comparison between several documents, what the number was likely to mean.

Sometimes very small fish came into the net of the guerrilleros, and were sent on to Wellington ; take, for example, the tiny scrap containing the pathetic letter of the young wife of General Merlin, of the cavalry of the Army of the Centre—I fear that the bearer must have fallen into the hands of Julian Sanchez or one of his lieutenants, and have had short shrift :—

' Mon cher Ami,—Depuis ton départ je n'ai reçu qu'un seul mot de toi— pendant qu'il arrive des courriers (c'est-à-dire des paysans) du quartier général. Mon oncle qui écrit régulièrement dit toujours qu'on se porte bien, mais tu peux te mettre à ma place ! Je crains que ta goutte ne soit revenue, je crains tant de choses, qui peut-être passent le sens commun, mais qui me tourmentent. Je ne dors plus, et n'ai d'autre plaisir que celui de regarder ma fille, qui se porte bien. Encore si elle pouvait m'entendre et me consoler ! Adieu ! Je suis d'une tristesse insupportable, parce que je t'aime plus que moi-même.—Mercédes.'

It may suffice to show the general character of a typical cipher-dispatch if we give a few lines of one, with the interpretation added below—the following comes from a dispatch of Marmont written on April 22, 1812, to Berthier, from Fuente Guinaldo :—

Le roi après m'avoir donné l'ordre   1060 462 810 195 1034 1282
     de faire par- tir deux divisions

971 216 13 192 614 20 90 92   1265 582 637 851 809 388 177
et plus de la moi- ti- é de la cavalerie dis- po- ni- ble, et avoir

669 112 923 2 786 692 1102 le nombre de troupes que j'ai disponible
ré- du- it à douze mille hommes

    13 1040 1003 370 860   400   817 69 862 718 1100
m'ordonne de chercher à pren-dre Ciudad Rodrigo lors que je ne ai

423 815 591 710 850
pas un canon de siège !

It will be noted that of all the words only *partir, moitié, disponible, réduit, prendre*, required to be spelled out in the syllabary : single fixed numbers existing for all the common words, and for the military terms *siège, cavalerie,* and *division.*

It was, of course, only by degrees that Scovell succeeded in making out the bulk of the French phrases. In Wellington's dispatches there is often, during the spring and summer of 1812, an allusion to information only partly comprehensible, obtained from captured letters. On June 18 (*Dispatches,* ix. p. 241) Wellington writes to Lord Liverpool that he ' is not able entirely to decipher ' the intercepted papers that have been passing between King Joseph and Soult and Marmont. On June 25th he sends to the same recipient the happy intelligence that he has now the key to King Joseph's cipher. Yet again, on July 16th (*Dispatches,* ix. p. 290)— with No. 36 of the file catalogued below before him—he says : ' I have this day got a letter from the King to Marmont of the 9th inst. in cipher, which I cannot entirely decipher : it appears, however, that he thinks Drouet will not cross the Tagus, and I suspect he orders General Treillard to collect some troops in the valley of the Tagus, and to move on Plasencia.' The interpretation was correct, save that Treillard was to move not on Plasencia but on Aranjuez. The code-numbers for the two places were neither of them known as yet. But by September all essential words were discovered, and Wellington could comprehend nearly everything, unless Joseph or Soult was writing of obscure places or distant generals.

A list of the whole of Scovell's file of 52 French dispatches may be useful : those whose number is marked with a star are wholly or partly in cipher, the remaining minority are in plain French without disguise. It is clear that Wellington had many more French papers not in cipher, which did not get into Scovell's portfolio.

Date.	Sender.	Recipient.	Contents.
1. Mar. 6, 1812	Col. Jardet	Marmont	Long interview with Berthier. He says you must ' contain ' Wellington in the North. All else in Spain matters comparatively little.
2*. April 11	,, Marmont	Brennier	See that Silveira does not molest my communications.
3*. April 14	,, Soult	Berthier	Marmont has betrayed me, and caused the loss of Badajoz. Synopsis of Andalusian affairs.
4*. April 16	,, Marmont	Berthier	As I prophesied, my raid into Portugal produces no effect : we begin to starve.
5*. April 16	,, Dorsenne	Jourdan	I refuse to acknowledge the king as controlling my army.
6*. April 17	,, Soult	Berthier	Details of the fall of Badajoz, ' événement funeste.'
7*. April 22	,, Marmont	Berthier	I have been starved out of Portugal. Have seen no British troops, save a few cavalry

Date.	Sender.	Recipient.	Contents.
8*. April 23, 1812	Foy	Jourdan	Send me food. My division is nearly starved.
9*. April 25 „	King Joseph	Dorsenne	I am your Commander-in-Chief. Send me a report of your army.
10. April 26 „	Gen. Lafon-Blaniac [1]	Gen. Treillard [2]	News from Andalusia at last: Soult has failed to save Badajoz.
11*. April 28 „	Marmont	Dorsenne	Send me 8,000 quintals of wheat at once.
12*. April 28 „	Marmont	Berthier	I have sent Bonnet, as ordered, to invade the Asturias.
13. April 28 „	Gen. Lamartinière [3]	Clarke	I send parole of Colquhoun Grant, a suspicious character. The police should look to him [4].
14*. April 29 „	Marmont	Jourdan	If I keep troops on the Tagus, I am too weak on the Douro and Tormes. I must draw my divisions northward.
15*. April 29 „	Marmont	Berthier	I find that five British divisions were chasing me last week. Wellington is very strong in the North.
16*. April 30 „	Marmont	Berthier	Send me a siege-train, I am helpless without one: also plenty of money.
17. April 30 „	Marmont	Gen. Tirlet [5]	Come up at once to join my army.
18*. May 1 „	Jourdan	Marmont	We will keep unhorsed guns for you at Talavera, so when moving South bring gunners and horses only.
19*. May 1 „	King Joseph	Dorsenne	You are placed under my command. Obey my orders.
20*. May 1 „	Jourdan	Dorsenne	Send a division to Valladolid, to support Marmont.
21*. May 1 „	Jourdan	Marmont	You must send more troops to the Tagus: Drouet is hard pressed in Estremadura.
22*. May 1 „	Jourdan	Berthier	Wellington is advancing in Estremadura. Marmont must send troops southward.

[1] Governor of La Mancha.
[2] Commanding cavalry on the Tagus.
[3] Marmont's Chief-of-the-Staff.   [4] See above, p. 293.
[5] Commanding artillery of the Army of Portugal, on leave.

Date.	Sender.	Recipient.	Contents.
23*. May 1, 1812	King Joseph	Berthier	Observations on the military situation.
24. May 1	,, Col. Bousseroque	Gen. Dogue-rau [1]	Technical artillery matters.
25. May 20	,, Proclamation by Suchet		The King is appointed Commander-in-Chief in Spain.
26*. May 26	,, King Joseph	Soult	Hill has stormed Almaraz. Why was not Drouet near enough to save it ?
27*. May 26	,, Jourdan	Soult	Hill has stormed Almaraz. Try to re-open communications with Foy.
28*. June 1	,, Marmont	Jourdan	The fall of Almaraz means that Wellington will attack me next. He is not threatening Soult, but me.
29*. June 22	,, Marmont	King Joseph	I stop in front of Salamanca manœuvring. I dare not attack Wellington till Caffarelli's reinforcements arrive.
30*. June 24	,, Marmont	Caffarelli	I am manœuvring opposite Wellington. Your reinforcements are required at once.
31*. July 1	,, Marmont	King Joseph	When the Salamanca forts fell, I retreated to the Douro. I cannot fight Wellington till I get 1,500 more horse and 7,000 more infantry.
32. July 1	,, Suchet	King Joseph	Narrative of guerrilla war in Aragon.
33. July 1	,, Suchet	King Joseph	Favour shall be shown to Afrancesados.
34*. July 6	,, Marmont	Jourdan	I had to retreat to the Douro because Caffarelli sent no help. Can you lend me Treillard's cavalry division ?
35*. July 7	,, King Joseph	Soult	Send 10,000 men to Toledo at once.
36*. July 9	,, King Joseph	Marmont	I shall march to your aid in a few days, when my troops are collected.
37*. July 22	,, Suchet	King Joseph	I am much worried by Maitland's approach. Have beaten Joseph O'Donnell at Castalla.
38. July 29	,, Gen. Lafon-Blaniac [2]	King Joseph	Madrid remains tranquil.

[1] Commanding artillery of the Army of the Centre.
[2] Now governor of Madrid.

Date.	Sender.	Recipient.	Contents.
41*. July 30, 1812	Marmont	King Joseph	We can never hope to unite. My army retires via Lerma on Burgos.
42. Aug. 2 ,,	Gen. Espert [1]	King Joseph	Wellington is marching on Segovia.
43*. Aug. 7 ,,	King Joseph	Marmont	Communicate with me by the Somosierra Pass.
44*. Aug. 12 ,,	Suchet	King Joseph	I am much alarmed at the possible results of Maitland's landing.
45*. Aug. 12 ,,	Soult	Clarke	The King is betraying the Emperor and negotiating with the Cadiz Cortes [2].
46*. Sept. 17 ,,	Suchet	Soult	Explains situation in Valencia.
47*. Dec. 9 ,,	King Joseph	Napoleon	Plans for reorganizing the armies.
48*. Dec. 22 ,,	King Joseph	Napoleon	Plans for next year. Should I make Burgos my capital, and hold Madrid only as an outpost ?
49*. Jan. 8, 1813	King Joseph	Napoleon	Soult is intolerable. Let D'Erlon replace him. Send us money.
50*. Jan. 28 ,,	King Joseph	Napoleon	Your decision about Soult shocks me. I shall send him away on my own authority.
51*. Mar. 14 ,,	King Joseph	Gen. Reille	D'Erlon shall look after Salamanca. Send two divisions to hunt the guerrilleros.
52. Mar. 16 ,,	Col. Lucotte	King Joseph	Discouraging news from Paris. No men or money for Spain !

In addition to the ciphers, the Scovell papers consist of short diaries of Major Scovell for the Corunna Campaign, and for 1809–10–11–12–13, as also a large bundle of reports and maps of roads and passes in Portugal, all the papers concerning the raising of the Corps of Guides, a number of notes and reports on suggested travelling forges for the artillery and engineers, and some whole or mutilated contemporary Spanish newspapers. There is some curious and interesting information scattered through all of them.

[1] Governor of Segovia.
[2] For the story of this letter see above, pp. 538–9.

XVI

BRITISH AND PORTUGUESE ARTILLERY IN THE CAMPAIGNS OF 1812

[DETAILS COLLECTED BY MAJOR J. H. LESLIE, R.A.]

I. ROYAL HORSE ARTILLERY

The following troops were serving in the Peninsula in 1812 :—

Troop.	Under Command of	Arrived in Peninsula.	Designation in 1914.
A	Brevet Major H. D. Ross	July 1809	' A ' Battery, R.H.A.
D	Captain G. Lefebure [1] [Later 2nd Captain E. C. Whinyates]	March 1810	' V ' Battery, R.H.A.
E	Captain R. Macdonald	August 1811	' E ' Battery, R.H.A.
I	Brevet Major R. Bull	August 1809	' I ' Battery, R.H.A.

A, E, and I were serving with Wellington's main army in 1812, attached respectively to the Light Division, the 7th Division, and the 1st Division of Cavalry (Stapleton Cotton). All three were present at Salamanca, but A was left at Madrid in August with the Light Division, and did not take part in the Burgos Campaign. D was attached to Erskine's ' 2nd Cavalry Division,' and served under Hill in Estremadura from the beginning of the year till Hill marched up to Madrid in October.

II. ROYAL (FOOT) ARTILLERY

A.

The seven companies shown in the following tables were serving in the Peninsula in 1812 with the field army.

NOTE.—In 1812 there were ten battalions of Royal (Foot) Artillery, the companies of which were always designated by the name of the commanding officer, whether he was actually present with his company or no.

Battalion.	Under Command of	Arrived in Peninsula.	Designation in 1914.
1st	Captain J. May [2]	March 1809	2nd Battery, R.F.A.
4th	Captain S. Maxwell	October 1810	72 Company, R.G.A.
5th	Captain F. Glubb [3]	March 1809	48 Company, R.G.A.

[1] Lefebure died of sickness in October, and the battery was commanded till next spring by Whinyates.
[2] Actually under command of 2nd Captain H. Baynes.
[3] Actually under command of 2nd Captain W. G. Power.

Battalion.	Under Command of	Arrived in Peninsula.	Designation in 1914.
8th	Brevet Major R. W. Gardiner	April 1811	78 Company, R.G.A.
8th	Captain R. Lawson	August 1808	87th Battery, R.F.A.
8th	Captain J. P. Eligé [1] [Later, Captain T. A. Brandreth]	October 1810	Reduced in 1819.
9th	Captain R. Douglas	March 1812	45th Battery, R.F.A.

Of these, Gardiner's company was attached to the 1st Division, Maxwell's to the 2nd, Douglas's to the 3rd, Lawson's to the 5th, Eligé's to the 6th. May's company accompanied the main army without guns, in charge of the Reserve ammunition train.

Glubb's company was attached to the heavy 18-pounders and 24-pounder howitzers of the Reserve Artillery.

Gardiner's, Douglas's, Lawson's, and Eligé's [now temporarily under 2nd Captain W. Greene, Eligé having been killed at the Salamanca forts] companies were present at Salamanca, as was also the Reserve Artillery, but the last-named was not engaged.

Maxwell's company was with Hill in Estremadura from January till the march to Madrid in September–October. Part of it was present at the capture of Almaraz on 19 May.

B.

The following additional companies were in Portugal in 1812, but did not join the field army :—

Battalion.	Under Command of	Arrived in Peninsula.	Designation in 1914.
6th	Brevet Major H. F. Holcombe	April 1811	102 Company, R.G.A.
1st	Captain A. Bredin	September 1808	37th Battery, R.F.A.
6th	Captain G. Thompson	March 1809	18th Battery, R.F.A.
5th	Captain H. Stone	March 1812	92 Company, R.G.A.
6th	Captain W. Morrison	October 1812	51 Company, R.G.A.

Of these Holcombe's company was employed at the sieges of Ciudad Rodrigo and Badajoz. The other companies present at these leaguers were Glubb's and Lawson's at Rodrigo, and Glubb's and Gardiner's at Badajoz.

In June Holcombe's and Thompson's companies were sent round by sea to the east coast of Spain, and there joined the Anglo-Sicilian expedition of General Maitland, with which they continued to serve.

[1] Eligé was shot through the heart on the second day of the siege of the Salamanca forts. 2nd Captain W. Greene commanded the company at the battle of Salamanca.

C.

At the beginning of 1812, there were present at Cadiz, Cartagena, and Tarifa, doing garrison duty, the following companies under Lieut.-Col. A. Duncan :—

Battalion.	Under Command of	Arrived in Peninsula.	Designation in 1914.
2nd	Captain P. Campbell [1]	March 1810 [2]	62 Company, R.G.A.
5th	Captain H. Owen	January 1810	60 Company, R.G.A.
9th	Captain P. J. Hughes	January 1810	Reduced in 1819.
10th	Captain W. Roberts	March 1810	63 Company, R.G.A.
10th	Major A. Dickson	April 1810	21 Company, R.G.A.
10th	Captain W. Shenley	April 1810	11 Company, R.G.A.

Of these Hughes's company was detached to Tarifa, and took a brilliant part in its defence in Dec. 1811–Jan. 1812. The rest were in Cadiz and the Isle of Leon. Owen's and Dickson's companies (the latter until July 1812 being commanded by Captain R. H. Birch, whose own company of the 10th battalion was at Gibraltar, as Dickson, with the rank of Major, was serving with the Portuguese Army) marched from Cadiz to Madrid with Skerrett's column at the end of September 1812, and in October joined Wellington's main field army. Hughes's, Roberts's, and Shenley's companies remained in garrison at Cadiz, and Campbell's was divided between Cartagena and Tarifa.

D.

At Alicante, under General Maitland, there were present during the later months of the year not only Holcombe's and Thompson's companies, which had come round from Lisbon, but also the two following British companies from Sicily :—

Battalion.	Under Command of	Arrived in Peninsula.	Designation in 1914.
8th	Captain J. S. Williamson	August 1812	40th Battery, R.F.A.
4th	Captain R. G. Lacy	December 1812	25 Company, R.G.A.

III. KING'S GERMAN LEGION ARTILLERY

Of the three companies of the Legionary Artillery in the Peninsula only one (No. 4) was with the field army, that of Captain F. Sympher, attached to the 4th Division. This unit was present at the siege of Ciudad Rodrigo, and also at the battle of Salamanca.

Captain K. Rettberg's (No. 1) and Captain A. Cleeves's (No. 2) companies were doing garrison duty in the Lisbon forts ; but Rettberg himself, with a detachment of two officers and thirty men of his company, came up to the siege of Badajoz in March–April.

[1] This company went to Cartagena from Cadiz at the end of January 1812, where it remained until the end of the war. Campbell was not with it, having command of an infantry regiment in the Spanish Army.

[2] From Gibraltar.

IV. PORTUGUESE ARTILLERY

[The details are taken from Major Teixeira Botelho's *Subsidios*.]

Only three field batteries accompanied the allied field army during the campaign of 1812, though seven had been at the front in 1811. These batteries were :—

Captain J. da Cunha Preto's 6-pounder [from the 1st regiment] and Captain W. Braun's 9-pounder [from the 2nd regiment] batteries, both attached to General Hamilton's Portuguese division, which always acted with Hill in Estremadura, and Major S. J. de Arriaga's 24-pounder howitzer battery, which formed part of the Artillery Reserve, and accompanied Wellington's own army to Badajoz, Salamanca, and Burgos. This company came from the 1st (Lisbon) regiment.

But in addition the 2nd or Algarve regiment supplied one company, under Captain J. C. Pereira do Amaral for the siege of Badajoz.

The 4th or Oporto regiment gave two companies (200 men) under Captain J. V. Miron for the siege of Ciudad Rodrigo, and one (70 men) under Captain William Cox for the siege of Badajoz. Cox's company was sent round to Alicante in June, along with the British companies of Holcombe and Thompson, and joined Maitland's Anglo-Sicilian corps for the rest of the war.

Another company of the 4th regiment under Captain D. G. Ferreri formed the divisional artillery of Silveira's Militia corps, and was present at the blockade of Zamora in June–July 1812.

The 1st or Lisbon regiment sent a company under Captain M. A. Penedo to Alicante, along with the company of Cox mentioned above from the 4th regiment. It also supplied one company under Lieutenant A. da Costa e Silva for the siege of Ciudad Rodrigo.

The 3rd or Elvas regiment supplied three companies, under the command of Major A. Tulloh [1], for the siege of Badajoz—they were those of Captains A. V. Barreiros, J. Elizeu, and J. M. Delgado.

[1] Captain R.A., but now serving in the Portuguese Artillery, with the rank of Major.

INDEX

Abadia, Francisco Xavier, general, orders for, 220 ; tiresome conduct of, 337.

Abbé, general, governor of Navarre, his proclamation against guerrilleros, 102 ; defeated by Mina, 198.

Alba de Tormes, Carlos de España fails to hold castle of, 415, 466.

Albuera, Hill in position at, 269 ; combats in front of, 527–30.

Alcantara, bridge of, restored by Wellington, 333.

Aldaya, combat of, 64.

Alicante, occupied by Mahy, repulses Montbrun, 78, 79 ; Maitland lands at, 573.

Almaraz, forts of, stormed by Hill, 322–30.

Almeida, re-fortified by Wellington, 160 ; repulses the attack of Clausel, 281.

Almendralejo, seized by Hill, 132.

Altafulla, combat of, 96.

Alten, Victor, general, fails to assist Carlos de España at Rodrigo, 280 ; retreats to Villa Velha, 284 ; results of his action, 290 ; with Wellington's advance into Spain, 352 ; at Salamanca, 365, 369, 372–3 ; at Pollos, 389, 399, 401 ; his successful charge at Castrillo, 405–6 ; wounded at Salamanca, 422.

America, Spanish colonies in, troubles of, 136–8, 337.

Andalusia, position of Soult in, 80, 108, 109, 110, 274, 305 ; evacuation of, proposed by Jourdan, 307, 308 ; resisted by Soult, 309–10 ; operations in, during June–August, 521, 522, 535, 536 ; evacuation of, by Soult, 539–43.

Andriani, Luis, colonel, defends Saguntum, 13, 17–30 ; surrenders, 45–6.

Anson, George, major-general, operations of his cavalry, 401, 402 ; at Salamanca, 449, 461 ; at Garcia Hernandez, 501.

Anson, William, major-general, his brigade at Castrillo, 406 ; at Salamanca, 457, 458.

Aragon, French army of, 5 ; Suchet's garrisons in, 6 ; operations of Duran and the guerrilleros in, 21–3 ; French reinforcements for, 51–2 ; Palombini's and Severoli's campaigns in, 98–101.

Arentschildt, Friedrich, colonel, takes command of a brigade at Salamanca, 442–5, 454, 461, 494 ; marches on Madrid, 504.

Artificers, Royal Military, at siege of Badajoz, 225, 255–6 ; converted into Royal Sappers and Miners, 256.

Artillery, the allied, table of the, in 1812, Appendix, pp. 619–22.

Astorga, siege of, 337–8, 388, 502.

Asturias, the, evacuated by Bonnet, 196–8 ; reconquered by him, 338 ; evacuated again, 390, 391.

Aubert, colonel, governor of Almaraz, slain there, 324–6.

Ayerbe, skirmish at, 22.

Baccelar, Manuel, general, commands Portuguese of the North, 219–21 ; concentrates to keep off Marmont, 282–3 ; dissuades Trant from attacking Marmont, 285.

Badajoz, siege of, 217–56 ; disgraceful sack of, 256–64.

Ballasteros, Francisco, general, harasses Soult in south Andalusia, 111 ; harasses the besiegers of Tarifa, 116–17 ; unwilling to receive orders from British, 230 ; threatens Seville, 274 ; retires prematurely, 275 ; his ineffective raids on Zahara and Osuna, 275 ; routs Rey at Alhaurin, 276 ; checked at battle of Bornos, 336, 348,

419 ; relieves Santander, 554 ; retakes Bilbao from Mendizabal, 556, 557.

Calatayud, captured by Duran, 21, 22 ; attacked by Montijo, 51–2 ; captured by Gayan, 101.

Campbell, Colin, general, governor of Gibraltar, garrisons Tarifa, 112; forbids abandonment of the town, 123.

Campbell, John, colonel, commands brigade of Portuguese horse in Estremadura, 219, 530, 531, 534.

Caro, José, general, at battle of Saguntum, 33, 41, 42.

Caroline, queen of the Two Sicilies, her intrigues against the British, 346, 347.

Carrera, La, Martin, brigadier, encompasses Boussard's cavalry at Aldaya, 64 ; his gallant raid on Murcia, 81 ; death, 81.

Carrié, general, beaten and captured at Castrillo, 405.

Castalla, battle of, 567–70.

Castaños, Francis Xavier, general, in command in Galicia, 197, 219, 337, 388.

Castello Branco, sacked by Clausel, 284.

Castlereagh, Lord, succeeds Canning at the Foreign Office, 155, 349.

Castrejon, combat of, 401, 402.

Castrillo, combat of, 405, 406.

Castro Urdiales, taken by Popham, 553.

Catalonia, French army of, 4, 5 ; operations of Lacy, Eroles, and Decaen in, 90–9; formally annexed by Napoleon, 97 ; projected British landing in, 344 ; Lacy's summer campaign in, 562–4; Maitland refuses to land in, 571.

Ceccopieri, colonel, slain near Ayerbe, 22.

Cerdagne, ravaged by Eroles, 93 ; by Sarsfield, 99.

Chauvel, general, arrives after Salamanca, and covers retreat of French army, 482.

Chlopiski, general, commands flankguard at Saguntum, 35 ; his victorious charge, 37.

Chowne, Christopher Tilson, general, makes false attack on castle of Miravete, 324–8.

Ciudad Real, seized by Morillo, 134.

Clausel, Bertrand, general, fails to attack Almeida, 281 ; occupies Castello Branco, 284 ; dissuades Marmont from attacking at Salamanca, 367, 368 ; his unsuccessful attack at Castrillo, 405, 406 ; at battle of Salamanca, 430, 435 ; assumes command after Marmont and Bonnet are disabled, 440 ; advances on Wellington's centre, 458 ; repulsed, 460 ; wounded, 469 ; his dispatch to Joseph, 489 ; continues to retreat north, 491.

Clinton, Henry, general, his victorious advance at Salamanca, 459–60 ; left to contain Clausel, 501.

Codrington, Edward, captain R.N., operations of, on the coast of Catalonia, 92, 563, 564 ; his views on Lacy and Eroles, 572.

Colborne, John, colonel, leads storming-party at Ciudad Rodrigo, 167 ; wounded, 182, 184.

Cole, Hon. Lowry, general, his operations on June 10, 403–6 ; his advance at Salamanca, 455 ; wounded, 456.

Conroux, Nicolas, general, surprised by Ballasteros, 522.

Constitution, the Spanish, drawn up by the Cortes, 140, 144.

Copons, Francisco, general, at the siege of Tarifa, 112, 118 ; opposes evacuation of the town, 123, 125.

Cortes, the, at Cadiz, Constitution drawn up by, 140.

Cotton, Stapleton, general, routs Drouet's rearguard at Villagarcia, 278 ; commands rearguard on retreat to Salamanca, 401 ; in the battle, 434–47, 449 ; wounded there, 471.

Craufurd, Robert, general, observing Ciudad Rodrigo, 159 ; mortally wounded in storm of Ciudad Rodrigo, 182 ; Charles Stewart's high estimate of him, 186.

Creagh, Juan, general, at Valencia, 60, 65.

Cruz Murgeon, Juan, general, storms Seville, 540, 541.

Cuenca, occupied by Mahy, 24 ; taken by D'Armagnac, 56 ; evacuated by Maupoint, 488.

Rodrigo, 170 ; at Badajoz, 228,
237 ; wounded, 238 ; again on
duty, 243.
Fortescue, Hon. John, his estimate
of the British Ministers and their
dealings with Wellington, 152.
Foy, Maximilien, general, moves
with Montbrun against Valencia,
52–78 ; attempts to divert British
from Badajoz, 233, 266 ; fails to
help Almaraz, 329 ; his description of Marmont's plans at
San Cristobal, 367 ; at Toro, 390 ;
makes feigned advance against
Wellington, 397 ; describes opening of battle of Salamanca, 420,
421, 424, 433 ; criticism of Marmont, 438, 461 ; successfully
covers French retreat, 467 ; his
account of battle of Salamanca,
472–3 ; defeated at Garcia Hernandez, 475–8.
Freire, Manuel, general, prevented
from joining Blake at Valencia,
57 ; with Mahy's force, 77, 78 ;
his raid on eastern Andalusia, 559.
Frère, general, protects Suchet's
rear in Catalonia, 6, 92.

Galicia, state of, in 1812, 220, 337, 338.
Garcia Hernandez, combat of,
467–8.
Gaspard-Thierry, colonel, governor
of Picurina fort at Badajoz,
taken prisoner, 240.
Gayan, guerrillero chief, seizes
Calatayud, 101.
Gijon, occupied by the French, 338.
Gough, Hugh, colonel, takes part
in defence of Tarifa, 118 ; opposes
its evacuation, 122–7.
Graham, Thomas, general, overruns
Estremadura, 228 ; fails to catch
Reymond, 230–2 ; falls back on
Albuera, 268 ; obliged to throw
up his command, 352–3 ; before
Salamanca, 359, 369, 373–5.
Granada, evacuated by Soult, 544,
545.
Grant, Colquhoun, major, captured
at Idanha Nova, 292, 318.
Guarda, Trant's disaster at, 285–6.
Guarena, combat of the, 404–5.
Gudin, colonel, at the storming of
Saguntum, 17, 18.
Guetaria, attacked by Home Pop-
ham, 553, 557.

Gurwood, lieutenant, J., leads forlorn hope at storm of Ciudad
Rodrigo, 181 ; controversy concerning, 589.

Habert, general, at storming of
Saguntum, 17, 28, 33, 39 ; at
capture of Valencia, 58–63 ; joins
Harispe, 67 ; at Gandia, 85.
Hamilton, general A., commands
a Portuguese division under Hill,
130, 520.
Harispe, general, in invasion o
Valencia, 14 ; at battle of Saguntum, 34, 40 ; at capture of Valencia,
58, 61–4 ; moves toward Alicante,
85 ; defeats O'Donnell at Castalla,
567–70 ; retires behind the Xucar,
573.
Hay, Andrew Leith, captain, his
account of the storming of Badajoz,
255 ; of the battle of Salamanca,
448–9.
Henriod, governor of Lerida, repulses Lacy, 564.
Hill, Rowland, General, his advance
into Estremadura, 86 : retires into
Portugal, 106 ; seizes Merida,
130–2 ; forms covering force for
siege of Badajoz, 218, 228, 233 ;
joins Graham at Albuera, 268 ;
contains Drouet in Estremadura,
291 ; his raid on Almaraz, 311–29,
348 ; Wellington's instructions to
him to harass Drouet, 519 ; advances to Zafra, 522 ; awaits
Drouet's attack, 527 ; his manœuvres against Drouet, 531–5 ;
does not pursue when Drouet joins
Soult, 543 ; warns Wellington of
Soult's evacuation of Andalusia,
578 ; marches on Madrid, 579.
Hodenberg, Karl, captain in the
K.G.L., his account of the sack
of Badajoz, 262 ; of Garcia
Hernandez, 480.

Infantado, J. de Silva, Duke of,
created a member of the Regency
144, 145.

Jones, John, colonel R.E., his
remarks on the siege of Ciudad
Rodrigo, 173 ; on the storming of
Badajoz, 247 ; on the siege of the
Salamanca forts, 371.
Joseph Bonaparte, King of Spain,